Chronicle
of the OLYMPICS
1896–1996

Olga Korbut
Munich, 1972

Matti Nykänen
Calgary, 1988

Florence Griffith-Joyner
Seoul, 1988

Ed Moses
Los Angeles, 1984

Jayne Torvill and
Christopher Dean
Sarajevo, 1984

Linford Christie
Barcelona, 1992

Alberto Tomba
Albertville, 1992

Vitali Sherbo
Barcelona, 1992

Chronicle
of the OLYMPICS
1896–1996

Chris Boardman
Barcelona, 1992

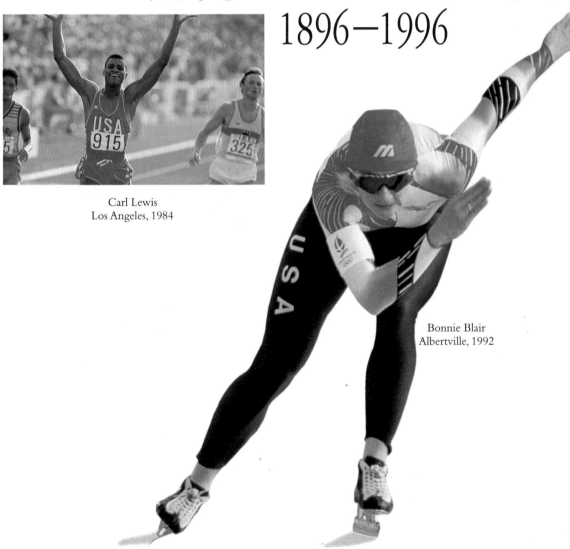

Carl Lewis
Los Angeles, 1984

Bonnie Blair
Albertville, 1992

DORLING KINDERSLEY
London • New York • Stuttgart • Moscow

A DORLING KINDERSLEY BOOK

First published in Great Britain in 1996
by Dorling Kindersley Limited,
9 Henrietta Street, London WC2E 8PS

English adaptation by Brown Packaging
255-257 Liverpool Road, London N1 1LX

© Chronik Verlag
im Bertelsmann Lexikon Verlag, Gütersloh/München 1995

This edition copyright © 1996 Dorling Kindersley Limited, London

Dorling Kindersley
Managing Editor Jane Laing
Senior Editor Sue Leonard
Editor Christina Bankes
Production Manager Ian Paton

A CIP catalogue record for this book is available from the British Library.

ISBN 0 7513 3013 2

Reproduced by D&L Reichenberg, Bocholt
Printed and bound in Belgium by Brepols

Foreword

The Olympic Games will always have a special place in my heart. Ever since I was young, I dreamt of representing my country, and the Seoul Olympics in 1988 was when the dream became reality.

I went to Seoul with no expectation of winning the gold or even taking any medal. But that did not matter because the Olympic Games, unlike any other major sporting spectacle, has room for both the elite athlete for whom winning is everything and my own wide-eyed naïvety, whose sole objective was to enjoy the magic of the Olympic Games.

There can surely be little dispute that the Games are the greatest sporting festival that the modern world knows. The best footballers may not be there; the best tennis players and basketball players have not always been there – but in as much as no other event has the ability to capture the imagination of the entire world, the Games are without equal. One can envisage even the most ardent sports-hater tuning in to view those "never to forget moments" that the Olympic Games inevitably throw up.

Those moments will of course be different for all of us. For some, it will be the grace and artistry of Torvill and Dean; for others, the dominance of Mark Spitz's seven gold medals; for still others, the beautiful, flowing running of Carl Lewis – the list goes on and on. These moments stick in the memory not simply for the performances themselves, but also for the occasion that brought them to us – the Olympic Games.

My most vivid recollection of the Olympics would have to be the clashes of Sebastian Coe and Steve Ovett in Moscow in 1980. Coe was the ultimate professional; Ovett, the master tactician. The anticipation heightened to an almost unbearable pitch as the two religiously avoided each other until the Games themselves. It was more than sport, and perhaps therein lies the unique appeal of the Olympics.

This book traces the Olympic story, from the first Games of the modern era in 1896 right up to a preview of the forthcoming Games in Atlanta. There are many excellent photographs that bring back to life the triumphs, disasters, and human interest stories that litter Olympic history. It also contains comprehensive lists of medal winners and results and fascinating background information. In short, it has something for everyone, whether your desire is to have a pictorial reminder of the moments that made Olympic history or to know who won the bronze medal in the 1956 flyweight boxing competition!

And what of the future? Atlanta 96 beckons. Who will be the stars? What will be the big stories? There are many fascinating scenarios waiting to unfold. Will Linford Christie really not defend his 100 metres title? Can Michael Johnson of America achieve double gold in the 200 and 400 metres events, perhaps with world records in both? Beyond athletics, we in Britain will look forward to Steven Redgrave continuing his incredibly successful career and perhaps hope for Nick Gillingham to follow David Wilkie and Duncan Goodhew to Olympic gold.

As I look forward to the Games, I am filled with a sense of great anticipation, mixed with not a little trepidation. I experienced the devastation of failing at the Olympics in 1992 and those kinds of disasters are an ever present reality in the life of every sportsman. Nevertheless, making the world record and gaining the world championship gold in 1995 – both of which achievements still leave me bereft of words – fill me with hope that perhaps the title of which all sportsmen and women dream could be mine.

And what of the Olympic movement itself? A tide of professionalism is sweeping through sport at present and the Olympics has felt its force and will continue to do so. Whatever the future holds, though, let us hope there will always be room for those to whom winning is not everything.

JONATHAN EDWARDS MBE
Triple jump world champion, world record holder, and BBC Sports Personality of the Year, 1995

Contents

Carl Lewis
Barcelona, 1992

Kitty McKane
Antwerp, 1920

Katarina Witt
Calgary, 1988

Olga Korbut
Munich, 1972

Matti
Nykänen
Sarajevo, 1984

Said Aouita
Los Angeles, 1984

The Olympic Games: *From ancient times to the 21st century*

Since their renaissance 100 years ago in 1896, the Olympic Games have become the greatest sports event in the world. No matter how many world or continental championship wins an athlete may gain, to compete in the Olympic Games will remain his or her supreme ambition.

SINCE THEY BEGAN IN 1896, THE modern Olympic Games have faced many political crises and their demise has been often predicted. However, the Olympic movement has survived two world wars as well as periods of upheaval, coups d'etat, and revolutions – though in most cases there have been changed external circumstances and political considerations to be taken into account.

The origin of the Olympic Games lies in the ancient world in which they were treated as a ritual festival. The idea of winning was of far more significance in these Games than in the Olympic philosophy established by Pierre de Coubertin more than 2500 years later. In fact, victory was of paramount importance, with defeat bringing disgrace for the whole *polis* (city-state). Because no measurements or times were kept, few records of performances have been handed down through the ages. However, it is known that the victors were awarded an olive wreath.

Although we have details of the winners only from 776 BC onwards, archaeologists have demonstrated that the Olympics can be traced far back into the second millennium before Christ. The five-day-long games included running, wrestling, the pentathlon, horse riding, and chariot races, as well as competitions to determine the best trumpeters and heralds. The ceremonies to honour the victors were all held on the last day of the Olympic Games. A temporary end to the Olympic movement came in AD 391, when a decree issued by the Roman emperor Theodosius I prohibited all pagan worship, which included the Olympic Games.

During the Middle Ages, athletic activities had little significance and were slow to gain any importance afterwards. By the 19th century, the

The Wrestlers
The decoration on this ancient vase depicts a wrestling bout. In these times, there were no weight categories and there was also no time limit inside which a fight had to be finished. Wrestling first became an "Olympic" sport in 708 BC.

Greek ideal of developing one's body and mind in harmony, one with the other, was rediscovered. Sports such as boxing, golf, and cricket had become popular, and football, tennis, and gymnastics increased in importance from the late 1800s onwards. More and more people gathered in order to play and exercise together, founding sports clubs and associations. Scientists discussed the role of sport in society, for adolescents in particular. At this time, however, the new sports were played predominantly by the upper classes and the aristocracy.

In the 1880s, Pierre de Coubertin (born on 1 January 1863 in Paris), who belonged to a long-established French family of noble descent, made a study of the impact of sport on society. In his youth, he had been greatly taken with the ancient Olympic Games and was very interested in archaeological excavations in Greece. Even though it was as early as in 1766 that the British scientist Richard Chandler discovered the area of the ancient Olympia, it took more than 100 years before the mud-covered re-

mains were laid open in 1875-81 by Ernst Curtius, a German archaeologist from Berlin.

In his studies of physical exercise, de Coubertin was influenced by the ancient concept of the human being on the one hand and by the views held by the British educationalist Thomas Arnold on the other. He became convinced that exercise had to be the basis of sensible education. The fact that France had had great difficulty in getting over its defeat by Germany in the war of 1870/71 plus the desire of his homeland to regain national pride and strength formed the background to de Coubertin's theories. However, the new social order was not to be based on the development of new animosities. Rather, it was to be expressed by means of fair competition between nations. De Coubertin was convinced that equal opportunities for all participants were a prerequisite for these competitions. Besides physical education as practised in Britain, it was again the ancient Greek concept which served as de Coubertin's ideal since in those days all athletes had trained together for competition. The amateur ideal was to be the indispensable prerequisite for de Coubertin in order to underline the "noble and chivalrous character" of physical exercise. Rewards had to come from the sporting activities themselves. No material gifts, no desire for profit, and no business interest in sport were to be allowed to prejudice in any way the coming together of athletes.

To start with, the impact of these theories was limited to the aristocracy, who could afford to pursue sporting activities in this way. Difficulties soon arose, however, as the lower social classes refused to be excluded. Eventually, in the late 1920s, after many years of negotiations, the IOC gave its permission for loss-of-income compensation to be paid to athletes.

Despite his initial difficulties in recruiting followers for his "religion of sport", de Coubertin continued to look for a way of spreading his ideas of an Olympic renaissance. He first mentioned the idea of reviving the Olympic Games during a lecture in 1892, when it was met with little comprehension. Undeterred, he invited interested persons from all over the world to participate in a sports congress in Paris in June 1894. The congress, which was held at the Sorbonne, part of the University of Paris, closed with unanimous support for a resolution to revive the Olympic Games in 1896. The plan was that after the first celebration in Athens, the competitions would be hosted in turns by all capitals at four-year intervals.

The new Olympic movement was to be co-ordinated and led by a panel entitled the International Olympic Committee (IOC). Besides de Coubertin himself, its members included Lord Arthur O. Ampthill (Great Britain), Viktor Balck

1 **Attic chalice:** This chalice dates from around 510-500 BC. Prior to the ancient Olympic Games, the athletes were made ready for competition with massage and oil. However, the actual period of preparation started weeks earlier. All athletes gathered at a special training camp for at least the last 30 days before the beginning of the Games. Here they were all fed the same diet and lived in the same kind of accommodation. Besides being coached in their sports, the athletes were given lectures about the importance of participating in the Olympic Games. Additionally, the athletes were briefed on how they were

expected to comport themselves during the competitions.

2 **Inside of a drinking bowl (c. 500 BC):** In classical times, competitors in the jumping events were required to carry extra weights in their hands. The ancient Olympic pentathlon consisted of long jump, discus, javelin, running, and wrestling events. According to Greek mythology, the hero Jason was responsible for creating the pentathlon.

3 **Renaissance of the Olympic Games accomplished:** The delegates to the International Congress of Paris, which was held at

the Sorbonne, part of Paris University, in 1894, gave their approval to Pierre de Coubertin's proposal to revive the Olympic Games. At the conclusion of the congress an international committee was set up to implement this resolution. Here International Olympic Committee (IOC) members pose for the camera on the occasion of the first modern Olympic Games in Athens. They are (from left to right): Willibald Gebhardt (Germany), Pierre de Coubertin (France), Jiri Guth (Bohemia), Dimitrios Vikelas (Greece, president), Ferenc Kemeny (Hungary), Aleksei Butovsky (Russia), and Viktor Balck (Sweden).

(Sweden), Dimitrios Vikelas (Greece), Aleksei Butovsky (Russia), Ernest Callot (France), Leonard A. Cuff (New Zealand), Jiri Guth (Bohemia), Charles Herbert (Great Britain), Ferenc Kemeny (Hungary), Ferdinando Lucchesi-Palli (Italy), William M. Sloane (USA), and José B. Zubiaur (Argentina). Pierre de Coubertin, who initially acted as the committee's secretary general, went on to hold the IOC's presidency from 1896 until 1925.

After a promising start with the Athens Games of 1896, the Olympic movement stuttered a little, with the Games of 1900 and 1904 being somewhat of a disappointment. Held as part of the World Exhibitions of those years, they were hardly taken notice of. Matters took a turn for the better with the 1906 "Intermediate" celebration. Though these rescued a staggering Olympic movement and helped establish the Olympic Games as a sporting event, the 1906 Games were not originally considered an official Olympic celebration in the eyes of the IOC.

Political developments began to affect events in the stadium from an early stage. World War I resulted in the cancellation of the VI Olympic Games, which were scheduled to take place in Berlin in 1916. Nevertheless, the Olympic movement was still in existence when hostilities came to an end, and the first post-war celebration was awarded to Antwerp in Belgium, a country that had been ravaged by the conflict. Even though the Berlin Games had not taken place, their designation as the VI Olympiad was not carried over and the Antwerp Games became the VII Olympics. The Belgians excelled themselves in organizing the Games at such short notice and in such circumstances. Twenty-nine nations were represented. Among those missing were Germany, Austria, Hungary, and Bulgaria, excluded from the IOC as a result of the war.

Besides the inclusion of figure skating in the programme for the London Games of 1908 and of ice hockey and figure skating in the schedule for Antwerp, winter sports in general remained outside the scope of the Olympic movement. Winter sports lovers had long been campaigning for their introduction, and by the early 1920s this lobby had gained so much recognition that in 1924, despite initial resistance, the IOC allowed an "International Winter Sports Week" to be staged at Chamonix in France. It was highly successful, and a year later the IOC agreed to stage the Winter Olympic Games. They were to be held in the same year as the Summer Games but would be organized as separate celebrations. The Scandinavian nations, which had believed that winter sports competitions already established in their countries would be in danger were Winter Olympics to take place, dropped their objections. In 1925, the Belgian Henri de Baillet-Latour took over from Pierre de Coubertin as IOC president. He continued the work started by the Frenchman until 1942.

Like his predecessor, de Baillet-Latour attempted to prevent the increasing participation of women in the Olympics, but momentum was gathering. In the ancient Olympic Games, women were strictly forbidden to take part (in fact, they were allegedly put to death if they were caught so much as watching), and in the early years of the modern Olympics, the IOC also frowned on the idea of women competing in the Games. Though there were female competitors as early as 1900, the IOC did not regard their presence as official until 1912, when women's swimming events were sanctioned. The number of women participants grew with each Games, but it was not until 1928 that the IOC finally

Dimitrios Vikelas
(Born 15 February 1835, Syros; died 20 July 1908, Athens) Dimitrios Vikelas was one of the original founder members of the International Olympic Committee and acted as its first president from 1894-96.

Pierre de Coubertin
(Born 1 January 1863, Paris; died 2 September 1937, Geneva) De Coubertin was IOC secretary general and then president from 1896-1925. His dream was of the "youth of the world" meeting in peaceful competition.

Henri de Baillet-Latour
(Born 1 March 1876, Brussels; died 6 January 1942, Brussels) The Belgian was IOC president from 1925-42. He gained much experience as head of the organizing committee of the 1920 Antwerp Games.

Johannes Sigfrid Edström
(Born 21 November 1870, Gothenburg; died 18 March 1964, Stockholm) Edström was vice president of the IOC from 1937-42, acting president from 1942, and elected president from 1946 to 1952.

Avery Brundage
(Born 26 September 1887, Detroit; died 8 May 1975, Garmisch-Partenkirchen) He was a US Olympic athlete in 1912. As IOC president (1952-72), he was considered a supporter of the idea of amateurism.

Michael Morris Killanin
(Born 30 July 1914, London) An Irishman, Killanin was IOC president from 1972-80. After his retirement, the Committee appointed the journalist, writer, and film producer its honorary chairman for life.

Juan Antonio Samaranch – IOC president since 1980
(Born 17 July 1920, Barcelona) Samaranch supports commercialization of the Games. He is pictured (second from left) talking to US NOC president Leroy Walker (second from right) and Deedee Corradini (right), mayor of Salt Lake City, at the ceremony to award the 2002 Winter Games to Salt Lake City.

allowed women to take part in track-and-field competitions for the first time. Nevertheless, after the 1928 Games, which were held in Amsterdam, the IOC barred women from running distances of more than 200 metres – a decision that lasted until 1960.

The last Games before World War II took place in 1936 in Berlin, and the Nazis turned them into a unique propaganda event, with the public being presented with a picture of a peace-loving German Reich. War then intervened. In 1938, the XII Summer Games, scheduled to take place in Japan in 1940, were transferred to Helsinki, Finland, due to the outbreak of the Sino-Japanese war in 1937. The Winter Games, also awarded originally to Japan, were moved first to St. Moritz and then to Garmisch-Partenkirchen. However, the Soviet invasion of Finland in 1939 and the outbreak of World War II the same year prevented either Games from taking place. The 1944 Games, scheduled for Cortina d'Ampezzo and London, were likewise cancelled, and few IOC members were able to attend the ceremony marking the 50th anniversary of the renaissance of the Olympic ideal, which was held in Lausanne in 1944.

In 1948, in the presence of the Swede Sigfrid Edström, elected IOC president in 1946, the Olympic Games resumed, with London as the venue. However, as the post-war era progressed, first-class sporting performances could not disguise the fact that these peaceful meetings of the "youth of the world" were developing into a struggle for prestige. The Cold War between the East and the West extended into the stadiums, while the idea of international understanding was abandoned as a result of ideological incompatibilities and the prohibition of contact between athletes. With the suppression of the uprising in Hungary, the British-French intervention in the Suez crisis, the practice of apartheid in South Africa and Rhodesia, as well as the Soviet invasion of Afghanistan, boycotts and exclusions overshadowed the Olympic Games from 1956 onwards.

In 1952, the IOC had appointed the American Avery Brundage its new president, and he served until 1972. He was regarded as a vigorous supporter of amateurism and penalized breaches by immediately banning the offender, as in the case of the Austrian alpine skier Karl Schranz in 1972. The last days of Brundage's term were overshadowed by the attack on Israel's team in the Munich Olympic village in 1972, which, he believed, confirmed his fear that the bigger and more important the Olympic Games became, the more they would suffer from economic, political, and, from that point on, criminal pressure as well.

In the boycotts of 1980 and 1984, the political pressures reached a temporary peak. Whereas the Games in Moscow were boycotted by the USA and numerous allied countries because of the Soviet invasion of Afghanistan, the USSR and allies reacted with a counter-boycott of the Los Angeles Games, citing worries over local security arrangements as the reason.

The Summer Games of 1984 revealed for the first time that the Olympic Games was no longer affordable without marketing, sponsorship, and revenue from television rights. Television companies had to pay hundreds of millions of dollars in order to obtain these rights. The fact that the most popular disciplines were scheduled for times with the highest advertising appeal constituted a sacrifice to increasing commercialism. The pressure on athletes intensified as well, as the public were only interested in champions.

Furthermore, the business world would only take on champions to advertise their products.

Under the presidency of Spain's Juan Antonio Samaranch, who took over in 1980, the IOC has made the Games partly accessible to professional athletes, bringing an end to the controversial clause 26. The regulation regarding the exclusive admission of amateur athletes disappeared from the IOC statutes in 1981.

A considerable problem has been posed, and will continue to be posed, by drugs. Even though the IOC set a warning example in 1988 by disqualifying the Canadian sprinter Ben Johnson – he was stripped of his gold medal and his world record disallowed – it has so far not succeeded in implementing effective drug tests that can be carried out any time and in all countries, in particular during training. Critical voices have remarked that athletes are compelled to take performance-enhancing drugs in order to convert their efforts into money through victories and subsequent advertising contracts. Furthermore, television companies and the public continue to demand better and better performances from the athletes.

Samaranch is regarded as a supporter of increasing commercialization of the Olympic Games. In his eyes, it is only through commercialism that the Olympic movement – 100 years after its revival – will remain fit enough to survive into the 21st century.

1 **Symbolic emblem:** The Olympic flag, which was designed and presented to the IOC by Pierre de Coubertin, has flown above Olympic Games since the 1920 celebration at Antwerp. The five coloured rings intertwined symbolize the five continents whose athletes meet for fair competition. When the symbol was devised, the flags of all the nations of the world could be made up from the five colours and white background.

2 **Olympic flame:** Since 1928, the lighting of the Olympic flame has been traditional. Since 1936, torchbearers have been carrying the flame from Greece to the host venue in commemoration of the ancient games.

3 **Farewell for four years:** At the closing ceremony of each Games, the host of the next Games is ceremonially presented with the Olympic flag.

4 **Sydney celebrates:** On 23 September 1993 in Monaco, the IOC announced that the venue for the Olympic Games in the year 2000 would be Sydney, Australia.

100 Years
of the
Olympic Games
1896–1996

Athens

On 6 April 1896 at Athens, King George I of Greece opened the I Olympic Games of modern times. An audience of over 60,000 had gathered in the city's newly refurbished stadium to witness the event.

INITIALLY, PIERRE DE COUBERTIN had intended to stage the first Games in Paris in 1900 in association with the World Exhibition. However, it was eventually decided that the first Olympiad should take place in 1896, with the Greek capital Athens as host city. Consequently, Dimitrios Vikelas, Greek delegate to the 1894 International Congress of Paris that had revived the Games, was appointed president of the newly formed International Olympic Committee – the IOC.

Greece ran into financial difficulties as it prepared for the Games, and Budapest repeatedly offered itself as an alternative venue, since Hungary was getting ready for its millennium celebrations. In the end, though, thanks to the efforts of Crown Prince Constantine of Greece, who set up and presided over an organizing committee, donations started to roll in. One gift of over 900,000 drachmas by Greek businessman Georgios Averoff went towards the reconstruction of the city's stadium. In addition, the first sports postage stamps were launched and a lottery organized to raise further funds. The Olympic Games were able to go ahead in Athens as planned.

The opening ceremony coincided with the 75th anniversary of the start of the Greek independence movement. At the beginning of the Games, therefore, the hosts' national enthusiasm was at a peak. Men from 14 countries competed in nine events. The majority of the 200 or so participants were Greeks.

Many of the other competitors had made their way to Athens under their own steam. The Irishman John Pius Boland, for example, who competed for Britain, spent four weeks in Athens ahead of the Games in order to prepare himself. It paid off; Boland went on to win the individual tennis event and also the doubles competition, in which he was partnered by Fritz Traun, a German who also took part in the 800 metres.

Classical Theme
The cover of the report on the 1896 Games evoked the Olympics' classical ancestry. At Athens, as in early times, only men took part.

Besides tennis and athletics, fencing, weightlifting, cycling, wrestling, shooting, swimming, and gymnastics also featured. Rowing and sailing competitions were also due to be contested, but were cancelled because of poor weather. The cricket and football tournaments were also called off – in their case because of a lack of participating teams.

Event winners were presented with an olive branch, a certificate, and a silver medal. The runners-up received a laurel sprig and a copper medal. The first man to win an Olympic competition was the American track-and-field athlete James Brendan Connolly, who took the triple jump, clearing 13.71 metres.

The hosts had to wait until the final event to record their first Olympic win. A French archaeologist had suggested a race from Marathon to Athens be included in the schedule in commemoration of the legendary run by a herald after the Battle of Marathon in 490 BC. The organizers concurred and the 40-kilometre race was commandingly won by the Greek runner Spyridon Louis, who was immediately hailed as a national hero.

Local Hero
On the last day of the Games, the Greek athlete Spyridon Louis (in traditional dress) is honoured for his win in the marathon.

Long Jump King
The American Ellery Clark won the long jump with a leap of 6.35 metres.

US All-rounder
James B. Connolly (USA) was victorious in the triple jump and came away from Athens with one second and one third place into the bargain.

Double Victor
Robert Garrett (USA) outperformed Connolly: he was a double champion as well as picking up two second places.

German Wins Four
Having already lifted three gymnastics titles, Carl Schuhmann of Germany added a fourth win, to take the wrestling championship.

1 **Olympic enthusiasm:** The Greek spectators followed the 1896 Athens Games with great interest. On the first day, thousands packed the stadium, hearing a speech by the president of the organizing committee, Crown Prince Constantine, before the Games were declared open by King George I. The picture shows the Athens stadium during the 1906 Games, held to celebrate the tenth anniversary of the inaugural competition.

2 **US athletes dominate:** The Americans were by far the most successful team at Athens. Herbert Jamison (second from left) took second place in the 400 metres behind Thomas Burke, with third place being taken by the German Fritz Hofmann. Robert Garrett (second from right) became discus champion ahead of the Greeks Panagiotis Paraskevopoulos and Sotirios Versis. Garrett secured his second title in the shot event, once again consigning Greek competitors, this time Militadis Gouskos and Georgios Papasideris, to second and third places. In the long jump, Garrett had to settle for second place behind his team mate Ellery Clark. Third place went to another American, James B. Connolly. In the high jump, meanwhile, Garrett came equal second with Connolly, behind Clark. Albert Tyler (right) was second in the pole vault, which was won by his team mate William Hoyt who cleared 3.30 metres. Francis Lane (left) had to be content with fourth place in the 100 metres final.

3 **Souvenir photographs:** Athletes and officials had numerous group pictures taken of themselves in the Greek capital. Souvenir photographs like this were so popular, it seems, because many participants, notably those from the United States, wanted to be able to prove on their return home that they had taken part in an historic event – the first Olympic Games of modern times.

4 **Starting in style:** Using various techniques, the athletes take their marks for the start of the second heat of the 100 metres. While Thomas Curtis (USA, second from left) prefers to start from a crouching position, the Dane Eugen Schmidt (centre) leans on two short sticks. The remainder opt for the traditional starting position. The eventual champion was Thomas Burke (USA), who won the final in 12.0 seconds.

5 **Six cycling events:** The Frenchman Paul Masson was the most successful cyclist of the Games: he won the sprint (333.33 metres) ahead of the Greek Stamatios Nikolopoulos and the Austrian Adolf Schmal. In the 2000 metres sprint, Masson again defeated Nikolopoulos, with Frenchman Léon Flameng coming home third. Masson secured his third title by winning the 10 kilometres track race ahead of Flameng and Schmal. Flameng it was, though, who took the 10,000 metres track title, while Schmal also scored a success in the 12-hour race. In the meantime, the 87 kilometres road race was won by the Greek Aristidis Konstantinidis ahead of German rider August Goedrich.

6 British strongman: In 1896, the weightlifting competition was not divided into categories as it is today, but consisted of a one-armed lifting event and a two-armed event. Britain's Launceston Elliott came first in the one-armed, lifting 71 kilograms. He was followed by Viggo Jensen of Denmark and Alexandros Nikolopulos of Greece, who both lifted 57.2 kilograms. In the two-armed event, both Elliott and Jensen lifted 111.5 kilograms, but the Dane was named the winner because Elliott had moved one of his feet. Third place went to the Greek lifter Sotirios Versis.

7 Unbeatable Greeks and French: The fencing was dominated by athletes from two nations. In the individual foil event, Emile Gravellote (FRA) won ahead of his compatriot Henri Callot and Greek swordsman Perikles Pierrakos-Mavromichalis. The foil for masters event was claimed by Leon Pyrgos (GRE), and the sabre competition by Jean Georgiadis (GRE) ahead of team mate Telemachos Karakalos.

8 Greeks on high: The home crowd saw the Greek athletes

Nicolaos Andriakopoulos and Thomas Xenakis come first and second in the rope climbing. Fritz Hofmann (GER) was third.

9 Royal congratulations: Athletes and officials assemble for a medal ceremony in the Olympic Stadium. King George I was keen on conducting the ceremonies himself. At the Athens Olympics, there were no gold medals, a silver medal being the winner's prize.

10 Team gymnastics in the open air: In front of the judges

and audience in the centre of the Olympic Stadium, gymnasts put themselves through their paces in the team events. Having won the parallel bars ahead of both Greek teams, the German team moved on to claim the Olympic title in the horizontal bar competition.

11 Versatility: The German Carl Schuhmann added the Olympic wrestling title to his successes in gymnastics, beating the Greeks Georgios Tsitas and Stephanos Christopoulos. The picture shows a wrestling match from the Athens Games of 1906.

Paris

The sporting events that accompanied the World Exhibition were regarded by the IOC and international media as the II Olympic Games. However, public interest in these Games was relatively subdued.

Ace Alvin
Alvin Kraenzlein (USA) won four athletics titles to become the Games' most successful competitor.

THERE HAD BEEN some controversy before these Games, as Greece had laid claim to the right to stage all future Olympiads. However, the Cretan revolt and the subsequent Greek-Turkish war effectively put Greece out of the running for 1900. Consequently, the Olympic Committee fell back on its resolution of 1894 to bring the Olympic Games to Paris. However, because of a lack of organization and information, the public took hardly any notice of the Games. Another reason for people's indifference was that the competitions took place throughout the complete five-month duration of the World Exhibition. And the Games could hardly be called a meeting of athletes when the track-and-field competitions were held in July in the Bois de Boulogne, while the swimming events took place during August in a pool on the River Seine. Also, athletes' complaints about the sometimes miserable state of facilities went unheeded. Competitions in the Bois de Vincennes, for example, were reputedly disrupted by odours drifting across from the agricultural show nearby.

Paris 1900
The Eiffel Tower, erected for the World Exhibition in 1889, and a huge globe were the symbols of the 1900 World Exhibition.

Sailing was among the sports featured for the first time. Also for the first time, women took part in the Olympic Games, though they competed in only a limited number of events, among them golf and tennis. America's Margaret Abbott won the golf tournament, while Great Britain's Charlotte Cooper was victorious in the tennis, taking both the singles and mixed doubles titles. She was partnered in the latter by fellow Briton Reggie Doherty, who won the men's doubles with his brother Laurie, the men's singles champion.

The long jump final ended in bizarre fashion by today's standards. Since in 1900 the results from the qualifying rounds were taken into account in the final result, America's Myer Prinstein finished second in the competition without having made a single jump in

Rendezvous in Paris
The Games lasted from May to October. A range of trophies were awarded, since the modern medal system was not yet in place.

the final. Prinstein was absent from the final because it took place on Sunday, and his Methodist college would not allow him to compete on that day.

By winning three titles (standing high jump, standing long jump, and standing triple jump), the American track-and-field athlete Ray Ewry embarked upon a glittering Olympic career. He competed until 1908 and won no less than ten titles, making him, in terms of first places, the most successful Olympic competitor of all time. The most successful competitor of the 1900 Games, however, was Alvin Kraenzlein. The son of German emigrants to America, he won the 60 metres, both the 110 metres and 200 metres hurdles, as well as the long jump.

The hosts dominated the fencing, taking five of the seven titles contested. With one win each, only the Cuban Ramón Fonst and the Italian Antonio Conte were able to break the French monopoly. In rowing, the Netherlands celebrated their first Olympic title win, François Brandt and Roelof Klein triumphing in the coxed pairs final.

Australia Advances
The Australian swimmer Frederick Lane won two events at Paris.

Mighty Magyar
Rudolf Bauer of Hungary out-threw all rivals to become discus champion.

Frenchman Foils All
The Frenchman Albert Ayat won two fencing events – the épée for masters and the épée for amateurs and masters.

1 Little Olympic interest: The Olympic Games formed part of the World Exhibition in Paris, and it was often rather by chance that passers-by came across the sporting events that were taking place at various places across the city. Even the athletes themselves seem to have had little chance to savour the Olympic spirit that should have pervaded the meeting of the "youth of the world". The majority of participants went straight home to their respective countries once the competitions had been decided.

2 Discontinued events: The American Charles Sands (pictured here) won the golf tournament ahead of the Britons Walter Rutherford and Dave Robertson. In the women's event, Margaret Abbott was victorious leaving second and third places to her fellow Americans Pauline Whittier and Daria Pratt. By the 1908 Games, however, golf had ceased to be an Olympic sport. A number of other sports have fallen by the wayside over the years, including cricket. The only Olympic cricket tournament took place in 1900 and the winners were Great Britain. Rugby is another discontinued Olympic sport that was first contested in 1900. On that occasion France ran out winners, but had to settle for second place behind the USA when rugby made its final Olympic appearance in 1924.

3 Bows and arrows: The French and Belgians dominated in archery. Among the Olympic champions of 1900 were the Frenchmen Henri Herouin (in the *Au cordon doré* 50 metres event), Eugène Mougin (*Au chapelet* 50 metres), Emmanuel Foulon (*Sur la perche à la herse*) and Emile Grumiaux (*Sur la perche à la pyramide*). In the *Au cordon doré* 33 metres and *Au chapelet* 33 metres events, the Belgian Hubert van Innis was the victor. Archery continued as an Olympic competition until 1908. It reappeared in 1920 before vanishing once again. In 1972, it was reinstated for the Munich Games and has been an Olympic sport ever since, though the number of events is much reduced compared with the early days.

4 Professional touch: As well as the amateur sportsmen who flocked to Paris in 1900, professional athletes were invited to the World Exhibition to take part in a number of events, some of which were seen as world championships. The professional high jump was won by the much-fancied world record holder Michael Sweeney from the USA, whereas the amateur event was taken by the American Irving Baxter ahead of the Irishman Patrick Leahy, who was competing in the British team. Third place went to the Hungarian Lajos Gönczy. In the amateur standing high jump, Ray Ewry (USA) outjumped fellow countrymen Irving Baxter and Lewis P. Sheldon. Ewry added two other Olympic titles to his collection by winning the standing long jump, once again ahead of Baxter, with Emile Torcheboeuf of France in third place, and the standing triple jump, defeating Baxter yet again, along with Robert Garrett, a double champion at Athens. The triple jump was won by America's Myer Prinstein, while his rival Alvin Kraenzlein took the long jump. Kraenzlein had a wonderful Games, winning the 60 metres sprint and the 110 metres and 200 metres hurdles titles as well.

5 Different high jumping techniques: In the high jump events, the athletes used a wide variety of techniques in order to get themselves over the bar. Here the American Alvin Schoenfield "rolls" himself over. A professional athlete, Schoenfield was taking part in the world championships held at the 1900 World Exhibition at the same time as the Olympic Games.

6 Authority on the move: IOC president Pierre de Coubertin was eager to attend as many sporting events as possible and pedalled all over the city on his tricycle on his way to and from the various venues. It was not long before the father of the modern Olympics came to realize that it did not make much sense to link the Olympic Games to a World Exhibition. De Coubertin regretted the fact that under these circumstances the intrinsic value of the Olympic Games could not really be appreciated. However, besides the 1906 "intermediate" Games, it was a further eight years before the Games gained the status of independent event.

7 Consolation for Norway in athletics: In the pole vault, the Norwegian Carl-Albert Andersen (pictured here) came third with a jump of 3.20 metres. This was just five centimetres short of American Meredith Colkett's second-placed effort. Colkett in turn was only five centimetres adrift of his compatriot Irving Baxter. The Scandinavian countries had a disappointing time in the track-and-field competitions. Indeed, apart from Andersen, the Scandinavians managed only three top three track-and-field finishes – Ernst Schulz (DEN), third in the 400 metres, Ernst Fast (SWE), third in the marathon and the joint Swedish and Danish team, which came first in the tug-of-war event.

8 Long wait for his win: With a jump of 3.30 metres, America's Irving Baxter was a worthy victor in the pole vault. However, he had to wait for his title win to be confirmed. Originally, the pole vault had been scheduled to take place on a Sunday. It was then rescheduled and then moved back to Sunday once again. Many competitors, in particular a number of Americans, failed to turn up on Sunday because their colleges were religious institutions. Following a protest, a second competition was organized for a later date. Even though some athletes managed to clear heights that would have won them the title, Daniel Horton, for example, jumped 3.45 metres, their efforts amounted to little more than statistics.

9 First and second for the USA: With a throw of 12.85 metres, the American shot putter Josiah McCracken (shown here) secured second place behind his compatriot Richard Sheldon (14.10 metres). Both Sheldon, who added a third place in the discus to his shot title, and McCracken no doubt benefited from the absence of world record holder Dennis Horgan.

10 Unsuccessful defence: Robert Garrett, who had won the shot (and the discus) at the Athens Olympic Games, had to settle for third place in Paris. The American also finished third in the standing triple jump.

11 First champion in new event: The Irish-born American John Flanagan became the first Olympic champion in the hammer. Second and third places were taken by Flanagan's fellow Americans Truxton Hare and Josiah McCracken.

12 Swimming marked by great variety: In 1900, the swimming competition was held in the River Seine. Among the events contested were two that have long since vanished from the Olympic programme – the 200 metres obstacle race and the underwater swimming event. In the former, the competitors had to climb over a bar and a chain of boats as well as dive under another chain of boats. In the end, it was the Australian Frederick Lane who took the title. He added another win in the 200 metres freestyle ahead of the Hungarian Zoltàn Halmay

and the Austrian Karl Ruberl. Britain's John Jarvis also secured two title wins. In the 1000 metres freestyle, he beat the Austrian Otto Wahle and Halmay, and in the 4000 metres freestyle, he defeated Halmay once again and France's Louis Martin in fine style. In the 200 metres backstroke, it was Germany's turn to triumph with Ernst Hoppenberg coming in ahead of Austria's Ruberl and Johannes Drost of Holland. Charles de Veudeville of France won the underwater swimming event ahead of his compatriot P. Alexandre Six and the Dane Peder Lykkeberg. The Germans won the 5 x 200 metres team event convincingly, leaving two French teams trailing in their wake, while in the water polo tournament, Great Britain ran out winners ahead of Belgium and France.

13 Scandinavians pull out the stops: Since Sweden and Denmark were unable to come up with the required six athletes each for the tug-of-war, the two countries joined forces to form a combined team, which went on to win the competition ahead of the USA and France. Some authorities believe that the USA's participation may have been limited to an exhibition pull, and that they were not in the competition proper. Tug-of-war featured in every Games from 1900 until 1920. It was then dropped as an Olympic sport. Great Britain was the most successful tug-of-war country, with two first places, two second places, and a third.

St. Louis

In St. Louis as in Paris, the Olympics took place as part of a World Exhibition. As a result, the inscription on the winners' medals read "Universal Exhibition" on the front and "Olympiad" on the reverse.

Ewry Again
Ray Ewry (USA) successfully defended his Olympic titles in the standing high jump, long jump, and triple jump.

Help for Hicks
As he approached the finish in the marathon, Thomas Hicks (USA) was grateful for every kind of support.

ONCE AGAIN THE SPORTS EVENTS failed to stand out from the rest of the World Exhibition's schedule. And once again, the public took hardly any notice of the Games as an independent entity. The general lack of interest was further increased by the long duration of the Games, as had also been the case in Paris, and the high number of competitions. The organizers wanted to avoid an overlap, and from July until November nearly 400 competitions were held. However, not all of them could call themselves "Olympic events", since some were for professionals or students. As far as the Olympics were concerned, the organizers announced competitions in 16 sports with 104 titles to be won. For the first time, boxing was included in the Olympic programme.

IOC president Pierre de Coubertin could not attend the Games and was disappointed that the Olympic spirit had not been sufficiently stressed. He also criticized the so-called "anthropological" days, on which contests, such as stone-throwing and steeplechase running, were organized for ethnic minorities by the World Exhibition's ethnological department. De Coubertin considered these "competitions" discriminatory.

The enormous cost of travel resulted in the number of participating athletes decreasing by almost half compared with 1900. Approximately 680 competitors took part, with more than 500 of them coming from the USA and 50 from Canada. American domination in track-and-field was broken by the Irishman Thomas Kiely, who won the combined events (it was not yet the decathlon). The programme for this was punishing: all ten events – 100 and 1500 metres, 110 metres hurdles, walking, high jump, long jump, pole vault, shot, hammer, and weight throwing – had to be completed in a day.

The American marathon runner Fred Lorz triggered a scandal when it was

Meet Me in St. Louis
The programme of the St. Louis World Exhibition, during which the 1904 Olympic Games took place.

discovered that he allowed an escort to give him a lift and drop him off a short distance away from the finish. Lorz received a lifetime ban, but this was lifted a short time later.

In 1906, a second celebration of the Olympic Games was held in Athens. Against de Coubertin's will, the IOC had decided in 1901 to stage Olympiads at two-year intervals, with Athens and other international cities taking turns as host.

In the event, the 1906 Games turned out to be decisive for the Olympic movement. After the difficulties encountered in Paris and St. Louis, these Games were just as successful as those held in the Greek capital a decade earlier. For the first time, the teams paraded for the opening ceremony, while gold, silver, and bronze medals were awarded in most events. Despite their providing a much needed boost to the ailing Olympic movement, the 1906 Games were later downgraded, becoming known as the Intermediate, or Intercalated, Games.

Ireland's Finest
Thomas Kiely of Ireland (left) won the combined events, the forerunner of the decathlon. With Kiely is his fellow Irishman J.J. Holloway.

Rausch Wins Twice
The German swimmer Emil Rausch won two titles in St. Louis and added a third place in the 200 metres freestyle.

All-purpose Daniels
In the swimming, Charles Daniels (USA) secured three title wins, one second place, and a third.

Flanagan's Reprise
John Flanagan (USA) repeated his Olympic title win of 1900 by taking the hammer event. In the weight throwing, he could manage only second.

1 On his way to victory: The American sprinter Archie Hahn scorched home in the 60 metres, defeating his fellow Americans William Hogenson and Fay Moulton. Hahn also triumphed in the finals of the 100 and 200 metres. In both races he left Nathaniel Cartmell and Hogenson to fight it out for second and third.

2 Tough fight: Out of 32 entrants in the marathon, only 14 made it to the finishing line. America's Thomas Hicks came first, Albert Coray of France second, and Arthur Newton (USA) third.

3 Favourite in the jump events remains unbeaten: The great Ray Ewry (USA) entered three events and was a three-time winner, thus repeating his performance in Paris in 1900. In the standing high jump, he cleared 1.50 metres, putting five centimetres between himself and James F. Stadler and Lawson Robertson, both also representing the USA. In the standing triple jump, Ewry took the title with a leap of 10.55 metres, almost 40 centimetres ahead of Charles King (USA), with Stadler in third place. Ewry's third title win was in the standing long jump. He became champion with a world record jump of 3.476 metres. Charles King was once again runner-up with 3.276 metres, and John Biller, another American, came third with 3.263 metres.

4 Dramatic decider settles discus title: At the end of the competition, Martin Sheridan (pictured here) and Ralph Rose (both USA) jointly led the discus event with 39.28 metres. In the subsequent "throw-off" Sheridan outdistanced Rose by 1.52 metres to take the title. Rose, who won the shot competition and came third in the hammer, had to settle for second place ahead of the Greek Nicolaos Georgantas.

5 Triple victory: James Lightbody (USA) is rewarded for one of his many victories at the 1904 Olympics. Over 800 metres, Lightbody beat his compatriots Howard Valentine and Emil Breitkreuz to the tape, while in the 1500 metres he pushed W. Frank Verner and Lacey Hearn (both also USA) into second and third spots. Lightbody's third win came in the 3000 metres steeplechase ahead of the Irishman John Daly, who was competing for the British team. Third place in the steeplechase was taken by Arthur Newton of the USA. Lightbody added a second place in the four-mile team event.

6 Strychnine sulphate to enhance performance: By the day after the marathon, the winner Thomas Hicks (USA, shown here) had recovered from his physical exhaustion and was able to pose for photographers in front of his trophies. His coach explained how Hicks had managed to finish the race. He stated that he had noticed that Hicks was in distress some ten miles from the finishing line. In order to rally his man, the coach had felt compelled to give him a small amount of strychnine sulphate dissolved in egg white. After this ministration, Hicks was able to continue, but the last mile was an ordeal. The athlete was barely able to lift his feet and, though conscious, was suffering from hallucinations. Eventually, completely drained, Thomas Hicks staggered to the finishing line, supported by stewards.

7 Gold in the pole vault: The American Charles Dvorak cleared a height of 3.505 metres, which was enough to secure him the Olympic title ahead of fellow countrymen LeRoy Samse and Louis Wilkins.

8 Starting from the landing stage: The 400 metres freestyle was won by Charles Daniels (USA), who secured victory over 200 metres as well. He added a third victory as a member of the winning American 4 x 50 metres relay team.

9 German gymnasts: A photograph of the gymnasts that represented Germany at St. Louis. Team captain F. Hofmann is seated in front with his team behind (from right): A. Weber, E. Mohr, O. Wiegand, W. Lemke, H. Peitsch, C. Busch, W. Weber, and A. Spinnler (a member of the Swiss team).

10 Little interest in the sporting competitions: James E. Sullivan (second from right), chairman of the organizing committee, could do nothing to prevent the Games being simply a part of the World Exhibition.

London

The IV Olympiad in London opened a new chapter in Olympic history. As at Athens in 1906, the Games were not merely a part of a World Exhibition, but were staged as an event in their own right.

THESE GAMES WERE ORIGINALLY to be held in Rome, but the Italians withdrew their capital's candidacy after the 1906 eruption of Mount Vesuvius – the money that would have been spent on the Olympics was now badly needed elsewhere. In the event, Britain declared itself willing, at short notice, to organise and hold the 1908 Games in London.

The London Games were held in the Shepherd's Bush district of west London, in the White City stadium constructed for the Franco-British Exhibition that took place earlier in the year. The stadium was equipped with a running track and a velodrome, as well as a large swimming pool, which featured an adjustable diving board, in front of the stand. A crowd of almost 100,000 watched the proceedings. For the first time, stands supported by simple steel tubes were erected, helping to reduce costs.

As they had done at the opening ceremony of the second Athens Games in 1906, the participating athletes paraded behind their respective national flags on their entry into the stadium. However, they were not dressed in uniform.

The first medals had been awarded even before the opening ceremony took place. The indoor tennis and real tennis (*jeu de paume*) tournaments had been held in the spring. The Games proper got underway in July, with the track-and-field events including tug-of-war and the first Olympic 1600 metre relay, which consisted of two 200 metre legs, one over 400 metres, and one over 800 metres. Motorboating, polo, wrestling, and rowing were also part of the programme. In the autumn, figure skating became the first winter sports discipline. There were also football, hockey, and lacrosse tournaments. Once again, women took part in only a limited number of sports: archery, figure skating, yachting, and tennis.

Welcome to London
The official programme featured a high jumper in action at the White City.

Controversy arose between the American delegation and the British. The US team management accused the host nation's judges of partiality. As a result, the IOC announced its intention to use judges from various nations on future occasions.

The most successful competitors at the London Games, with three gold medals each, were the British swimmer Henry Taylor (400 metres and 1500 metres freestyle and 4 x 200 metres freestyle) and the American athlete Melvin Sheppard (800 metres, 1500 metres, and relay).

In the 110 metres hurdles, the 27-year-old US athlete Forrest Smithson (USA) showed his class. In the final, he took the gold medal with a time of 15.0 seconds ahead of fellow Americans John Garrels and Arthur Shaw. Meanwhile, the great Ray Ewry, in his last Olympics before retirement, successfully defended his Olympic titles in the standing high jump and standing long jump. These successes raised his first-place tally to ten, if his wins in 1906 are taken into account.

Marathon Success
After the disqualification of Italy's Dorando Pietri, the 22-year-old American John Joseph Hayes was declared Olympic marathon champion.

Triple Winner
With three gold medals, the middle distance runner Melvin Sheppard (USA) shared the honour of being the most successful competitor of the Games with British swimmer Henry Taylor.

Determined Douglas
Britain's Johnny Douglas won the middleweight boxing title. An all-round sportsman, he won an England amateur football cap and captained Essex and his country at cricket.

Discus Double
America's Martin Sheridan claimed two discus golds, winning both the Greek-style and modern-style competitions.

1 **Olympic Games open at the White City:** After the teams had paraded into the brand new White City stadium, the national flags were lowered to greet the Royal Family. In the foreground is the 100-metre open-air pool where the swimming events were held.

2 **Successful title defence:** The American Ralph Rose repeated his shot put success of the 1904 Games.

3 **Three silver medal winners:** Harry Porter (USA, pictured) won the high jump, clearing 1.905 metres. Three competitors went clear at 1.88 metres to share the silver medal: Georges André (FRA), Con Leahy (GBR/ IRL), and István Somody (HUN).

4 **Swan song for a great champion:** With a gold medal in the standing high jump, the legendary American athlete Ray Ewry continued his winning run in the Olympics, uninterrupted since 1900. The silver medal was jointly won by Greece's Konstantin Tsiklitiras and the American John Biller. In the standing long jump, Ewry was victorious for the fourth time in a row, with the silver medal going to Tsiklitiras ahead of Martin Sheridan (USA). No one has yet beaten Ewry's incredible haul of ten first places from 1900 to 1908,

which included two at Athens in 1906. After the London Games, 34-year-old Ewry retired from competitive sport.

5 **Hat-trick for Sheridan:** Following his victories in St. Louis in 1904 and Athens in 1906, American discus maestro Martin Sheridan triumphed once again. He won the modern-style event with a throw of 40.89 metres, ahead of his compatriots Merritt Giffin and Marquis Horr. He also won the Greek-style event. At the London Games, discus Greek-style had the athletes ascend a small podium and hurl the discus from it. However, it seems that this was an incorrect interpretation of the ancient technique.

6 **Exciting finish:** Canadian Robert Kerr (second from left) becomes Olympic champion over

200 metres. Robert Cloughen (USA, left) takes the silver ahead of Nathaniel Cartmell (USA, second from right). George Hawkins (GBR, right) is fourth.

7 **Wyndham's walkover:** Britain's Wyndham Halswelle on his way to qualifying for the 400 metres final, which he won on a walkover.

8 **One and two for US hurdlers:** Charles Bacon (right) won the 400 metres hurdles final ahead of Harry Hillman. Britain's Leonard Tremeer picked up the bronze medal.

9 **Smithson protests:** The US hurdles star Forrest Smithson appears to be in action clutching a Bible. In fact, Smithson posed for this shot in protest at having to compete on a Sunday.

10 Britain pulls ahead: In the tug-of-war event, the gold, silver, and bronze medals all went to British teams.

11 – 13 Marathon drama: (Picture 11) Inside the stadium and on his last lap, the marathon race leader, Dorando Pietri of Italy, collapsed four times from exhaustion. Each time, he struggled back to his feet and staggered on towards the line. For the final few yards to the finish, the nearly unconscious Italian was supported by, among others, the stadium announcer (picture 12, second from left) and a second official, thought by some to be Arthur Conan Doyle (right). The spectators celebrated what they believed to be Pietri's Olympic title win. However, the Italian was disqualified for having "used external support". The gold medal was awarded to John Joseph Hayes (USA), who finished in a time of 2:55:18.4, ahead of South Africa's Charles Hefferon and Joseph Forshaw (USA). Pietri later vigorously denied having asked for help. However, things took a turn for the better when on the following day he received from Queen Alexandra a golden trophy donated by herself in acknowledgement of his heroic performance (picture 13).

Stockholm

The Swedish hosts ensured that the V Olympic Games ran smoothly. For the first time, there were athletes representing all the continents of the world.

THE ORGANIZATION AND SPORTS facilities in Stockholm were both impeccable, making the V Games a model for future Olympiads. The diplomatic controversies of the time were almost forgotten in the general atmosphere of harmony. That said, the opening parade, in which teams marched behind signs bearing the name of their country, threatened to lead to serious ructions. The Austrians criticized the participation in the Games of a separate team representing Bohemia, since it was part of the Austro-Hungarian Empire, and Russia objected to a team being fielded by the Grand Duchy of Finland, which then belonged to the Russian Empire. In the end, for the parade, the Bohemians and Finns were asked to march directly behind the Austrian and Russian teams respectively, to use smaller print on the signs bearing their country names, and to enter the stadium without their national flags. However, during medal ceremonies small pennants bearing the countries' national colours were hoisted together with the flags of the respective empires.

In total, around 2540 athletes from 28 countries took part in the Games. The Japanese made their Olympic debut, and women increased the range of sports in which they took part by participating in the swimming events.

Trailblazing technological innovations at the Stockholm Games included the photo-finish for athletics events and the electronic timer to back up the conventional stopwatch.

For the second time, equestrianism featured in the Olympic programme and has been included ever since. Equestrian events were first contested at the Paris Games, but were discontinued. They had been scheduled for London in 1908, but the organizers had been unable to cope with the vast number of entries.

The Swedish "sports philosophy", which demanded that people exercise

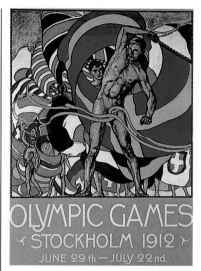

It's Official
Elements of athletics, art, and several national flags intermingle to form the first official Olympic Games poster.

their bodies in a balanced fashion, had a major impact upon the timetable. The shot, javelin, and discus events each had two competitions scheduled. In the one, the athletes threw using their strong arm; in the other, they were to use both arms alternately – and the result was an aggregate of both throws. A further addition to the Olympic programme was the modern pentathlon. Designed by de Coubertin, it consisted of horse riding, fencing, swimming, shooting, and cross-country running.

The American athlete Jim Thorpe was outstanding in Stockholm. He won the track-and-field pentathlon and the decathlon. The following year, however, it was revealed that, in his youth, Thorpe had received payment for playing baseball. As a result of rigid interpretation of the IOC's rules on amateurism, he became the first athlete to be disqualified as a "professional". He was stripped of his medals. Only in 1982 was Jim Thorpe rehabilitated and his medals restored. They were presented in 1983 to his family, since, sadly, the great man himself had died in 1953.

Double Act
The Finn Armas Taipale took the gold medals in the one-handed and two-handed discus events.

Rose Returns
Ralph Rose (USA) picked up the gold medal in the two-handed shot and silver in the one-handed event.

Dazzling Duke
Duke Paoa Kahanamoku (USA), of Hawaiian royal descent, won the 100 metres freestyle and was a silver medallist in the 4 x 200 metres freestyle relay.

First Flying Finn
Finland's Hannes Kolehmainen (right) was victorious in the 5000 metres, the 10,000 metres, and the individual cross-country event and won a silver in the team cross-country event.

1 Athletes from all around the globe: The opening parade at the V Olympic Games in Stockholm was the first at which nations from all five continents were represented. The organizers were much praised for all their work ahead of the Games, and this Olympiad may be regarded as being the real forerunner of today's Olympic celebrations. The Swedish monarch, King Gustav V, seemingly fell victim to "Olympic fever" when he offered some of his private land to accommodate the Olympic stadium. The stadium, which was designed by the Swedish architect Torben Grut, provided 30,000 covered seats for the Games' international visitors.

2 Wrestlers fight to the point of exhaustion: The Greco-Roman wrestling bout between Russia's Martin Klein (left) and the Finn Alfred Asikainen lasted for more than 11 hours before Klein clinched victory. Completely exhausted by their exertions, both wrestlers had to pull out of their scheduled fights against Claes Johansson of Sweden. Thus, the Swede was declared Greco-Roman middle-weight champion, with Klein second and Asikainen third. At light-heavyweight, the fight between the Swede Anders Ahlgren and the Finn Ivar Böhling was abandoned after nine hours. Both wrestlers received a silver medal with no gold medal being awarded. The bronze medal was taken by the Hungarian Béla Varga.

3 Women make their debut at swimming: Setting a world record time of 5:52.8 minutes, the Great Britain team, comprising Bella Moore, Jennie Fletcher, Annie Speirs, and Irene Steer, shown here with their chaperone Clara Jarvis, won the 4 x 100 metres freestyle relay ahead of the German four of Margarete Rosenberg, Wally Dressel, Luise Otto, and Hermine Stindt. In third place came the Austrian quartet, made up of Margarete Adler, Klara Milch, Josefine Sticker, and Berta Zahourek. In the women's individual 100 metres freestyle, the Australian Fanny Durack became Olympic champion in a time of 1:22.2 minutes ahead of her fellow Australian Wilhelmina Wylie and Britain's Jennie Fletcher. In the women's highboard diving event "Greta" Johansson of Sweden defeated her team mate Lisa Regnell and Isabelle White (GBR).

4 Enormous variety in gymnastics: The team event in the so-called "Swedish system" was won by the hosts ahead of Denmark and Norway, while the gold medal in the "free system" team event went to Norway ahead of Finland and Denmark. These two gymnastic events were introduced in 1912, contested once more in 1920, and then discontinued. In the individual combined exercises, Italy's Alberto Braglia took the gold. Silver went the Frenchman Louis Ségura ahead of Adolfo Tunisi of Italy. In the team event, Italy finished top above Hungary and Great Britain.

5 Gold medal in the high jump: America's Alma Richards clears at 1.93 metres to win the high jump gold medal ahead of the German Hans Liesche and George Horine (USA). The remaining jump events were dominated by the Americans and the Swedes. The long jump was taken by Albert Gutterson (USA) ahead of Calvin Bricker (CAN) and Georg Aberg (SWE). The host nation completed a clean sweep in the triple jump, while in the pole vault, Harry Babcock of the USA, with a vault of 3.95 metres, beat Frank Nelson and Marcus Wright (both USA) into joint second place.

6 A premature celebration: Anchorman Richard Rau (left) is jubilant about what he believes is a German 4 x 100 metres win. The German team, though, was disqualified for an incorrect changeover, a ruling that was hotly disputed. As a result, Britain (anchorman William Applegarth pictured right) took the gold.

7 **Results in horse riding:** In the team three-day event, the Germans (pictured here) picked up the silver medal behind the Swedish hosts, with the bronze being taken by the USA. In the individual three-day event, Axel Nordlander of Sweden became champion ahead of Friedrich von Rochow (GER) and Jean Cariou (FRA). In the dressage competition, Sweden won all three medals, with the gold going to Carl Bonde ahead of Gustav-Adolf Boltenstern and Hans von Blixen-Finecke. The hosts added another gold medal in the team show jumping, which they won ahead of France and Germany. The individual show jumping event was won by France's Jean Cariou ahead of Rabod Wilhelm von Kröcher of Germany and Emanuel de Blommaert de Soye of Belgium.

8 **New technology:** The Stockholm Olympics were the first at which the photo-finish was available to verify judges' decisions. In the 1500 metres a photo managed to separate silver medallist Abel Kiviat (USA) from bronze medallist Norman Taber (also USA).

9 **Wins in rowing:** In the coxed fours event, the German team of Albert Arnheiter, Otto Fickeisen, Rudolf Fickeisen, Hermann Wilker, and coxswain Otto Maier (centre) took the gold medal ahead of Great Britain, with Denmark and Norway sharing bronze-medal position. In the coxed eights event, Great Britain took first and second places ahead of Germany, while in the single sculls, there was success for Britain again as William Kinnear

secured gold ahead of Polydore Veirman of Belgium, with Everard Butler of Canada and Russia's Mikhail Kusik coming joint third.

10 **The Americans fete their winners:** On their return from the Stockholm Olympics, the US winners were welcomed with a festive parade. Here mayor of New York William J. Gaynor (left) congratulates Jim Thorpe, champion in the pentathlon and decathlon. There is a wonderful story concerning this remarkable athlete from Prague, Oklahoma, and King Gustav V of Sweden. It is said that when Thorpe was presented to the king to receive his medals, the Swedish monarch told him, "Sir, you are the greatest athlete in the world". Thorpe is reputed to have replied simply – "Thanks, King".

Antwerp

There had been no more "intermediate" celebrations after Athens, and war stopped the 1916 Games from taking place. It was 1920 before the Olympics were staged again – in the Belgian city of Antwerp.

IN THE RUN-UP TO THE EVENT, THE public passionately debated whether or not athletes should be admitted from those countries that were held responsible for the outbreak of the Great War. For its part, the IOC excluded the delegates from the Central Powers (Austria, Bulgaria, Germany, Hungary, and Turkey). In so doing, it prevented those countries from being invited to the Games, since it was customary to invite only nations represented on the IOC.

Whereas during the previous Games, there had been hardly any ceremonial or symbolic acts, at Antwerp, doves of peace were released at the opening ceremony, a repeat of events at Athens in 1896. The Belgian fencer and water polo player Victor Boin took the first Olympic oath, which is still taken on behalf of all competitors by a representative of the host nation, who pledges that the athletes will take part in the Games, "in the true spirit of sportsmanship".

Throughout the Games, the Olympic flag flew above and within all sports facilities. Bearing five coloured rings interwoven to symbolize the unity of the five continents, the flag had been presented to the Olympic movement on its 20th anniversary by Pierre de Coubertin. Now, for the first time, it became the official symbol of the Games.

Spectators at Antwerp witnessed the last Olympic tug-of-war contest. Tug-of-war had first appeared in 1900 when the event was won by a joint Swedish and Danish team. This time, on a specially designed strip in the stadium, the British team outclassed all comers. A number of other events were also discontinued after 1920. Weight throwing vanished, as did the 3000 metres walk, the 400 metres breaststroke, and several sailing events. Ice hockey, on the other hand, made its debut – a sure indication of the increasing importance of winter sports.

Assembly at Antwerp
The official poster for the first Games after World War I showed a classical discus thrower alongside flags of the participating nations.

In the track-and-field events, only a handful of countries were represented. The number of actual participants was less than expected as a number of athletes had been killed in the war. Of the four athletics world records set at Antwerp, two were in the hurdles: Earl Thompson (CAN) ran 14.8 seconds at 110 metres, while Frank Loomis (USA) recorded 54.0 seconds over 400 metres.

The throwing events were dominated by the Finns, who took first and second in both shot and discus and picked up all three medals in the javelin. The 1920 Games were also significant for the emergence of another major Finnish distance running talent: Paavo Nurmi.

However, the most important conclusion to be drawn from the Antwerp Games was that the Olympic movement had survived the turmoil of the Great War. That this was the case can be attributed to Pierre de Coubertin and to the chairman of the Belgian organizing committee, Henri de Baillet-Latour.

America First
Charles Paddock (USA, right) secures the 100 metres title. He added a second gold medal in the 4 x 100 metres relay, but had to be content with silver in the 200 metres.

Stylish Suzanne
In tennis, France's Suzanne Lenglen won two gold medals and a bronze.

Nurmi Arrives
Finland's Paavo Nurmi attracted a lot of attention at Antwerp with his three gold medals and one silver.

Youngest Champ
American Aileen Riggin became the youngest Olympic champion up to that time when she won the springboard diving gold medal at 14 years old.

Gold for Sweden
The long jump was won by Sweden's William Pettersson.

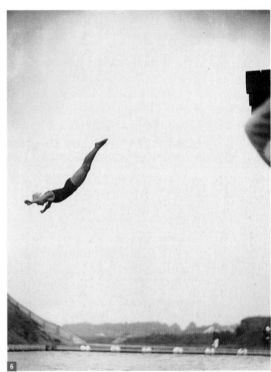

1 **The Olympic flag:** At Antwerp, the flag bearing five interwoven rings fluttered over an Olympic celebration for the first time. The coloured rings symbolize the five continents.

2 **General air of jubilation:** Following his win at 10,000 metres, the Finn Paavo Nurmi (right) is the centre of attention. However, the Italian Augusto Maccario (left), fourth in the race behind Joseph Guillemot (FRA) and James Wilson (GBR), is also paraded by his fans. Nurmi added two more gold medals to his collection by winning the individual cross-country event and being in the winning Finnish cross-country team. In the 5000 metres, Nurmi had to settle for second place behind Guillemot.

3 **Commanding victory:** Percy Hodge (GBR, left) gets within reach of the Olympic 3000 metres steeplechase title. The American Patrick Flynn (second left) was second, ahead of Ernesto Ambrosini of Italy.

4 Collecting tennis medals: Suzanne Lenglen (FRA) secured her first gold medal by defeating Dorothy Holman (GBR) in the singles final. In the mixed doubles, she and her compatriot Max Décugis beat the British pairing of Kitty McKane and Max Woosnam. Together with French partner Elisabeth d'Ayen, Lenglen also won a bronze medal in the women's doubles.

5 Figure skating brought forward: In April, before the Games proper got underway, the Finnish couple Ludovika and Walter Jakobsson won the pairs figure skating event. They are shown here on the left of the picture, next to fellow Finn Sakari Ilmanen, fifth-placed in the men's event. Gillis Grafström and Magda Julin (both SWE) won the individual competitions.

6 Triple victory for the USA: The springboard diving event from the one-metre and three-metre boards was won by the American Aileen Riggin ahead of her US team mates Helen Wainwright and Thelma Payne. In the highboard diving event, she took fifth place. The medallists were Stefani Clausen of Denmark, Eileen Armstrong (GBR), and Eva Ollivier (SWE).

7 Medals for Kitty: Kitty McKane (later Godfree) won gold in the women's doubles (with Winifred McNair), silver in the mixed, and a singles bronze. She later won Wimbledon twice.

8 Royal congratulations: Albert I of Belgium presenting medals. Here he is congratulating Warren Paoa Kealoha (USA) on his victory in the 100 metres backstroke. Kealoha won the final in 1:15.2 minutes ahead of Raymond Kegeris (USA) and the Belgian Gérard Blitz.

9 Further congratulations: The youngest Olympic gold medal winner so far (in 1920), 14-year-old diver Aileen Riggin (USA), stands atop the winners' podium to receive her prize.

10 Prize for success: Triple Olympic champion Ethelda Bleibtrey (USA), winner of the 100 metres freestyle, the 300 metres freestyle, and in the 4 x 100 metres freestyle relay, is delighted to accept this trophy from the Belgian king.

11 Unusual finish: In the 100 metres final, Olympic champion Charles Paddock's leap across the finish line caused a sensation. Clocking the same time, Morris M. Kirksey (also USA, right) was left with the silver medal ahead of Harry Edward (GBR, left).

Chamonix

Since the IOC did not sanction Winter Games until 1925, the Chamonix meet was staged as "International Winter Sports Week". Nevertheless, it is now recognized as the first Winter Olympics.

Repeat Performance
Sweden's Gillis Grafström won the men's figure skating competition, as he had at the 1920 Antwerp Olympics.

WITH FIGURE SKATING HAVING been included as part of the Olympic programme for the London Games of 1908, the Italian Eugène Brunetta d'Usseaux suggested, in 1911, that separate Winter Games be held. His idea met with resistance from the Scandinavian countries, who believed that such a move might jeopardize the Nordic games, which had been regularly staged in Sweden since 1901. Contrary to these protests, medals were awarded for figure skating and ice hockey at the Antwerp Games of 1920.

Then, in 1922, a meeting of the French Olympic Committee decided to organize an "International Winter Sports Week" in Chamonix in 1924. Sixteen nations were represented by a total of some 258 athletes, including 13 women. The preparations included the construction of a new ice stadium, which covered an area of 27,000 square metres and was equipped with two adjacent ice hockey pitches and a 400-metre-long ice track. Sadly, the well-organized competitions were beset by poor weather conditions, which brought Chamonix alternate drops in temperature and thaws.

The Scandinavians demonstrated their dominance in all five disciplines – bobsled, ice hockey, figure skating, speed skating, and Nordic competitions. Norway topped the medals table with four gold medals, seven silver medals, and six bronze medals. Finland came next with four gold medals, three silver medals, and three bronze medals.

Finland boasted the outstanding athlete of the meeting, too – speed skater Clas Thunberg. Thunberg won three gold medals, one silver medal, and one bronze medal to earn himself the nickname "Nurmi on ice" – a reference to the great Finnish distance runner and multiple-medallist Paavo Nurmi. Meanwhile, Norway's Thorleif Haug was being celebrated as the "king on skis" after his

Celebration in Chamonix
The official poster for "International Winter Sports Week" does not identify the event as a separate Winter Olympic Games, but does make a connection with the VIII Olympic Games being held in Paris later in the year.

victories in the 18 and 50 kilometres cross-country skiing and the Nordic combined event, consisting of cross-country skiing and ski jumping. Gillis Grafström of Sweden won the figure skating title, adding to his success at Antwerp in 1920.

Britain picked up a handful of medals at this first winter celebration. There was a silver in the four-man bob, and bronze medals for the British ice hockey team and for figure skater Ethel Muckelt. At the closing ceremony, Pierre de Coubertin awarded a prize for "Merit for Alpinism" to Charles Granville Bruce. Bruce, a British general, had been leader of the 1922 expedition that attempted to climb Mount Everest.

Spurred on by the huge success of "International Winter Sports Week", the IOC resolved the following year to begin staging Winter Games at four-year intervals. These meetings were to be separate from the summer celebrations.

1 **"International Winter Sports Week":** The Nordic combined event, consisting of an 18-kilometre cross-country ski race and a ski jump competition, was won by the Norwegian Thorleif Haug ahead of his compatriots Thoralf Strömstad and Johan Gröttumsbraaten. The Olympic rings at the top of the hill indicate IOC patronage for the meeting, held in early 1924, even though it was granted the title of I Winter Olympic Games only retrospectively. Among the demonstration sports (as opposed to official medal sports) on view at Chamonix were military patrol and curling. Curling has appeared on a number of occasions since and is set to become a full medal sport at Nagano, Japan, in 1998.

2 **Eight teams contest ice hockey:** Members of the Belgian ice hockey squad pose for the camera on their arrival at Chamonix. Following defeats against the USA (0-19), Great Britain (3-19), and France (5-7), the Belgians finished second

from bottom. Canada won the eight-team tournament ahead of the USA and Great Britain. During the tournament the Canadians scored no less than 110 goals, conceding only three. Having also won the ice hockey at Antwerp, Canada dominated Olympic ice hockey for many years, winning in 1924, 1928, and 1932, before taking the silver behind Great Britain in 1936.

3 **Speedster on ice:** Charles Jewtraw won the 500 metres speed skating gold medal, finishing in a time of 44.0 seconds, registering the United States' only gold of the Games. The remaining speed skating events were won by Finns, with Clas Thunberg taking the 1500, 5000, and the all-round event. The 10,000 metres was won by Julius Skutnabb, with Thunberg second. Thunberg also picked up a bronze in the 500 metres.

4 **The finishing line:** The finish for the cross-country skiing events was right next to the ice rink. Cheered on by the

spectators, the triple Olympic champion Thorleif Haug of Norway comes in ahead of his team mates Thoralf Strömstad and Johan Gröttumsbraaten in the 50 kilometres event. On the ice rink, the Swede Gillis Grafström took the figure skating title ahead of Austrian Willy Böckl and Georges Gautschi of Switzerland. The women's event was won by world champion Herma Planck-Szabo (AUT). The silver medal was claimed by the American Beatrix Loughran and the bronze medal went to Britain's Ethel Muckelt. However, the favourite with the crowd was 11-year-old Norwegian Sonja Henie, who won hearts even though she finished without a medal. Little could the spectators have known that the girl who came last at Chamonix would become the finest woman figure skater of all time. Her Olympic reign was still four years away.

5 **Germany still barred:** German ski jumpers pictured at the national championships in the Harz Mountains. In the meantime, top international performers competed in Chamonix. The first Olympic ski jump event was won by the Norwegian Jacob Tullin Thams ahead of his compatriot Narve Bonna and the Norwegian-born American jumper Anders Haugen. Olympic ski jumping took place only on the small hill until 1964.

6 **Risky discipline:** This picture shows a bobsled competition from the early 1920s. At that time, runs had few safety features, making the sport extremely perilous. At Chamonix, Switzerland II won ahead of Great Britain II and Belgium I. The two-man bob was not introduced until 1932.

7 **Participation is all:** The Italians took 23 competitors to Chamonix, including the ski jumping team shown here. In the end, there were no Italian medallists, but it is taking part, rather than winning, that lies at the heart of the Olympic idea.

Paris

For the second time in the young history of the modern Olympic Games, athletes from all over the world – approximately 3000 competitors from 44 countries – met to do battle in Paris.

AFTER THE ORGANIZATIONAL blunders made during the competitions in 1900, the 1924 Paris Games saw the French work particularly hard to ensure that the event ran smoothly. For the first time since 1906, a so-called "Olympic village" was erected to accommodate the athletes, and a new athletics stadium near Colombes, equipped with a 500-metre track, was finished just in time for the beginning of the Games. It was also the first time in the history of the Olympic Games that events could be followed by means of live radio transmissions. Another innovation was to be found at the newly built, 10,000-seat swimming arena at Tourelles; competitors' lanes were now separated by ropes supported by cork floats.

Technical problems had prevented construction of a regatta course for the rowing competitions. Even though the bend in the River Seine near Argenteuil seemed an ideal location for the rowing tournaments, medal chances were considerably affected by the drawing of lanes; certain areas of the bend put crews at a disadvantage and strong currents offered further handicaps.

Despite the efforts of IOC president Pierre de Coubertin to have the Germans reinstated, they were banned from these Games as they had been four years previously. The crowds celebrated Paavo Nurmi as their star of the Games. The Finnish runner won five gold medals, two of which were secured in the space of one hour.

Other athletics competitions ended rather bizarrely. One example was in the men's 400 metres, where the world record was improved three times. Having set a new world record of 48.0 seconds in the preliminary heat, the Swiss competitor Joseph Imbach fell in the final. In the intermediate heat, this record

French Pride
The 1924 Olympic poster was dominated by a picture of athletes and the French tricolour.

time was further improved on by the silver medal winner Horatio Fitch (USA, 47.8 seconds). The gold medal was eventually taken by Britain's Eric Liddell, who clocked a further record-breaking time of 47.6 seconds. However, the long track meant that competitors in the 400 metres had to run round only one bend and this meant that Liddell's performance was not officially recognized as a world record time until 1936.

The 1924 Paris Games was the last time tennis was seen as a full medal sport until it was reintroduced over 60 years later in Seoul. The reasoning behind this was that the IOC had doubts about the top players' amateur status, amateurism being a prerequisite of Olympic participation. Three competitors, all of whom were American, won two golds each in Paris: Vincent Richards in the men's singles and doubles, Helen Wills in the women's singles and doubles, and Hazel Wightman in the women's doubles and the mixed doubles.

Star Finn
Winning five gold medals, the Finnish athlete Paavo Nurmi became the undisputed star of the Summer Games in Paris.

Go Johnny Go
The American swimmer Johnny Weissmuller remained unbeaten in the 100 metres and 400 metres freestyle events as well as in the 4 x 200 metres freestyle relay. He also collected a bronze medal with the water polo team.

Flying Scotsman
Britain's Eric Liddell, a Scottish rugby union international, won the 400 metres and picked up a bronze in the 200 metres.

Chariot of Fire
The Briton Harold Abrahams won the gold medal over 100 metres and took a silver medal in the 4 x 100 metres relay.

Double Gold
Harold Osborn (USA) was a double Olympic champion, winning the high jump and the decathlon.

1 **Olympic oath:** Surrounded by the standard bearers of the participating nations, the French athlete Georges André takes the Olympic oath during the opening ceremony and sets the VIII Olympic Games in motion.

2 **Abrahams strikes:** Britain's Harold Abrahams (No. 419) dips to win the 100 metres in 10.6 seconds ahead of America's Jackson Scholz (No. 274, 10.7).

3 **Experienced champion:** Albin Stenroos (FIN) won the marathon by a margin of almost six minutes, beating the Italian Romeo Bertini and the American Clarence DeMar.

4 **British success:** In the 800 metres event, Britain's Douglas Lowe beat the Swiss Paul Martin

by a fifth of a second to secure one of the three British track victories. Bronze went to the American Schuyler Enck.

5 **"Rolling" towards gold:** The high jump competition was taken by Harold Osborn (USA). His successful attempt at 1.98 metres, using the rolling technique with crossed legs, secured his win over fellow American Leroy Brown and the Frenchman Pierre Lewden.

6 **Scandinavian domination:** The 5000 metres field is led by the Swede Edvin Wide (right). The eventual winner was the Finn Paavo Nurmi (left), who set an Olympic record only an hour after his triumph in the 1500 metres. The 27-year-old athlete defeated his compatriot Ville

Ritola (centre), with Wide taking bronze. In the cross-country event, Ritola and Earl Johnson (USA) did not stand a chance against Nurmi. The cross-country team event was taken by Finland, as was the 3000 metres team race. These provided Nurmi's fourth and fifth golds and confirmed his status as a quite exceptional athlete.

7 **Champion in the shadow:** Although Fred Tootell (USA) won the hammer, his compatriot Matthew McGrath became the hero of this event, winning the silver at the age of 45. McGrath had already collected a silver medal during the Games in London in 1908 and a gold medal in Stockholm in 1912. In Antwerp in 1920, he had finished in fifth position. Third in the

hammer in Paris was Britain's Malcolm Nokes.

8 **Three gold medals:** Johnny Weissmuller (USA) was the first Olympic swimmer to record a sub-one-minute (59.0 seconds) time in the 100 metres freestyle event. In the 400 metres freestyle, he defeated the Swede Arne Borg. He collected another gold medal when the United States won the 4 x 200 metres freestyle relay event; Australia and Sweden took second and third places.

9 **World record bronze:** With a distance of 7.76 metres, the American Robert LeGendre improved the long jump world record by seven centimetres. However, this achievement did not secure him a gold medal since the jump was part of the

pentathlon competition. In the final standings of that event, he took third place behind the Finn Eero Lehtonen (who successfully defended the title he won in Antwerp) and the Hungarian Elemér Somfay. In the long jump event, a distance of 7.445 metres secured William DeHart Hubbard his gold medal.

10 **Triumphs for the USA:** In the springboard diving event, Elizabeth Becker relegated the Olympic champion of 1920, Aileen Riggin, to second place. The bronze medal was taken by Caroline Fletcher. In the highboard diving, Caroline Smith picked up the gold medal ahead of Becker. The competitor who prevented a clean sweep by the Americans was the Swede Hjördis Töpel, who finished third.

St. Moritz

The IOC awarded the II Winter Olympic Games to Switzerland. Even though early February usually brings snow to the Engadin region, unseasonably mild weather conditions disrupted many events.

T St. Moritz, the organizers were fortunate enough to be able to exploit existing sports facilities at what was already a well-established ski resort. Athletes from 25 nations were full of praise for the organization and proposed timetable of events for these Winter Olympics and, for the first time since World War I, German athletes were admitted to Olympic competition.

However, weather conditions caused some concern: a thaw resulted in the 10,000 metres speed skating competition being cancelled and only two of the usual four bobsled runs went ahead. Nordic skiing was affected too as the outcome of the 50 kilometres cross-country skiing event very much depended on the right choice of ski wax since the athletes began the competition in the morning with temperatures around freezing and finished at midday with temperatures above 20°C.

Skeleton sledding made its debut as an Olympic discipline and proved popular with spectators. With athletes lying head first on a heavy sled and hurtling down St. Moritz's famous Cresta Run, this exhilarating yet dangerous competition was won by the American brothers Jennison Heaton with his brother John coming second. However, due to the high risk of injuries, the IOC dropped this discipline after 1948. As in 1924, bobsled teams were left the choice of whether to compete with four or five athletes; all teams decided to enter the competitions with five-man crews.

Even though the International Ski Federation (*Fédération Internationale de Ski* – FIS) had been founded in 1924, alpine skiing did not form part of the St. Moritz Games. The first international competitions featuring alpine events took place in March 1928; until 1936, the Winter Olympics remained the exclusive domain of the Nordic disciplines.

Young Winner
The figure skating gold medal won by Norway's Sonja Henie was the first of many Olympic accolades.

Swiss Hospitality
The peaks of the Engadin mountains dominate an Olympic poster that also featured the Swiss and IOC flags.

As happened four years before in Chamonix, Norway were the most successful team, winning six gold medals. Second place went to the USA, with two gold, two silver, and two bronze medals, ahead of Sweden and Finland. The two most successful competitors each claimed two titles. The Norwegian Johan Gröttumsbraaten won the Nordic combined and the 18 kilometres cross-country skiing, while Clas Thunberg of Finland was victorious in the 500 metres and 1500 metres speed skating events. As expected, the title holders Canada won the ice hockey tournament. With no US team, there was no stopping the Canadians, who scored 38 goals and conceded none.

Norway's Sonja Henie was the star of the Games. At 15 years of age, she became the youngest person to win the figure skating title, with the first of three consecutive Olympic golds in the event.

Ice Success
The Norwegian speed skater Ivar Ballangrud won a gold medal over 5000 metres in impressive style and added a bronze over 1500 metres.

Third Gold
The Swede Gillis Grafström skated superbly to secure his third Olympic figure skating title at the age of 30.

Norway's Hero
At St. Moritz, cross-country skier Johan Gröttumsbraaten from Norway became a double Olympic champion.

Personal Best
The Swede Per Erik Hedlund won the 50 kilometres cross-country skiing event, with fellow countrymen taking the other two places.

1 Swiss hosts: The opening ceremony of the II Winter Olympic Games in St. Moritz takes place in the midst of a snow-covered landscape that would soon melt. Surrounded by standard-bearers of all the teams, the skier Hans Eidenbenz (centre of picture with Swiss flag) takes the Olympic oath.

2 Triumph for Norway: The Scandinavians celebrated three medals in the 18 kilometres cross-country skiing event. Here Johan Gröttumsbraaten is on his way to his first gold medal, ahead of fellow Norwegians Ole Hegge and Reidar Ödegaard.

3 Group photograph: Female athletes from eight nations took part in the women's figure skating event and pose for the cameras before the start of the competition. World and European champion Sonja Henie won convincingly ahead of the Austrian Fritzi Burger and the American Beatrix Loughran.

4 Royal observer: Numerous guests of honour travelled to St. Moritz to attend the opening ceremony and the competitions that followed. A seat in the Royal Box is occupied by Prince Henry (front left), husband of Queen Wilhelmina of the Netherlands. With Amsterdam due to host the IX Summer Olympic Games later that year, his presence is not surprising.

5 The crowds' favourite: The Olympic figure skating champion Sonja Henie (NOR) is pictured acting as a "judge" for her colleagues. Even though this was only her second Olympics, the 15-year-old was already a popular star with the crowd and competitors alike.

6 Gold for France: Andrée Joly and Pierre Brunet won the pairs figure skating competition. Initially, the event had to be postponed because of a thaw. Behind the French couple, who were bronze medallists at Chamonix in 1924, Lilly Scholz and Otto Kaiser (AUT) secured the silver medal ahead of their compatriots Melitta Brunner and Ludwig Wrede. The victors would retain their title four years later at Lake Placid.

7 Best American skater: Beatrix Loughran (USA) delivers an expressive performance on the ice rink. She was the best-placed non-European figure skater, finishing the competition in bronze medal position. The figure skating competition consisted of two sections: a compulsory section containing 13 mandatory elements and a four-minute-long free programme.

8 Three Swedish medals: The start and finish line of the 50 kilometres cross-country skiing competition, an event that was affected by a daily temperature swing of over 20°C. The Swedish skiers coped best with the difficult conditions, with Per Erik Hedlund winning gold ahead of his team mates Gustav Jonsson and Volger Andersson. His winning margin of over 13 minutes is unmatched in Olympic history.

9 Repeat victory: The Finnish speed skater Clas Thunberg became joint Olympic champion in the 500 metres event. Four years earlier he had finished joint third and now secured first place alongside the Norwegian Bernt Evensen. Both finished in the Olympic record time of 43.4 seconds. Roald Larsen (NOR), John Farrell (USA), and Jaakko Friman (FIN) took joint third place, all recording 43.6 seconds. In the 1500 metres, which he won in 1924, Thunberg struck gold again. The silver medal in this event went to Evensen ahead of Ivar Ballangrud (NOR). The 5000 metres went to Ballangrud ahead of Julius Skutnabb (FIN) and Evensen. A continuing thaw forced the 10,000 metres competition to be abandoned.

10 Comprehensive coverage: The German media followed the Games closely, primarily because this was the first time that a German team had been allowed to participate in the winter meeting of the "youth of the world". Newspapers and magazines – including *Die Woche*, printed in Berlin – regularly reported training sessions, results, and other happenings at the Olympic Winter Games at St. Moritz.

11 Five in the four-man bob: The participating nations utilized the opportunity to compete using five men in the bobsled, even though the heavy thaw that affected the Games meant that only two (and not the usual four) runs were possible. Germany II, with pilot Hanns Kilian, Valentin Krempl, Hans Hess, Sebastian Huber, and Hans Nägle (from front) secured the bronze medal behind the two American teams. It was Germany's only medal at these Winter Olympics.

Amsterdam

The Olympic Stadium in Amsterdam was the outstanding arena of the IX Summer Olympic Games. Its Dutch architect, Jan Wils, won a gold medal for the stadium's design at the Olympic arts competition.

Titled Hurdler
The British athlete Lord David Burghley became Olympic champion in the 400 metres hurdles.

THERE WAS A CONTROVERSIAL start to the IX Summer Olympics when the organizers decided to grant exclusive photographic rights to one company and prohibited all private photography in the stadiums. In order to prevent spectators from smuggling cameras into the stadiums, checks were carried out at the entrances, resulting in long delays and numerous protests. These measures were eventually abandoned, and the attempt at imposing a photographic monopoly failed.

Around 3000 athletes (including about 290 women) from 46 nations competed in these "universal" Games. The German team, readmitted to the Summer Olympics after 16 years of Olympic exile, had a victorious return. Their ten golds secured them the runners-up position in the medals table, though still some way behind the USA's 22 victories. The swimmer Johnny Weissmuller (USA) and the Finnish runner Paavo Nurmi, who at his third Games picked up his tenth, eleventh, and twelfth Olympic medals, were the most successful athletes of the competition.

The spectators in the Olympic Stadium greeted Henri de Baillet-Latour as the new IOC president as he had succeeded Pierre de Coubertin in September 1925. Illness prevented the 65-year-old de Coubertin from attending the Games, the first that he had missed since 1908. However, the creator of the modern Olympic movement was able to listen to news of the events on the radio.

The Amsterdam Olympics saw new procedures introduced that are still in use today. For the first time, a flame was ignited on the marathon tower in front of the newly built Olympic Stadium, thereby introducing the Olympic flame to the Olympic Games. Greece, founders of the original Olympic competition, led the parade of the nations' teams. The admission of women to track-and-field events at Amsterdam was a new

Win Again
Johnny Weissmuller (USA) repeated his Paris feats with wins in the 100 metres freestyle and the 4 x 200 metres freestyle relay.

Amsterdam Hosts
A runner dominates the official poster of the Summer Games in Amsterdam. The Olympic flag is in the background.

Good Sign
The javelin competition was won by Erik Lundkvist, a sign painter from Sweden. He set a new world record two weeks later.

development that was to have far-reaching consequences. De Coubertin had always spoken out against women's participation and, until 1928, women had been ineligible for Olympic track-and-field athletics. However, a world women's organization, which had organized its own games for women, forced the IOC to compromise. Excellent performances by female competitors in Amsterdam only served to justify their right to compete in Olympic competition.

The German Lina Radke-Batschauer accomplished what had previously been achieved only by the tug-of-war team back in 1906: a German gold medal in an athletics event. In the 800 metres competition, she crossed the finishing line in a world record time of 2:16.8 minutes. Behind her, many women runners completed the race in an "exhausted" state, a fact that influenced the IOC's decision not to allow women to compete in middle distance running events again until the 1960 Rome Games.

Breaststroke Win
Hilde Schrader (GER) won the 200 metres breaststroke event, equalling the world record set in her semi-final.

Momentous Gold
Lina Radke-Batschauer's victory over 800 metres was Germany's first ever individual athletics gold medal.

1 Big interest: A view of the award-winning stadium in Amsterdam, full to capacity for the opening ceremony of the Summer Games.

2 Gold for Japan: Mikio Oda won the triple jump ahead of Levi Casey (USA) and Vilho Tuulos (FIN).

3 Narrow victory: In the 100 metres, Percy Williams (CAN, second from left) secures gold ahead of Jack London (GBR, left) and Georg Lammers (GER, second from right). He also won the 200 metres.

4 The favourites beaten: Britain's David Burghley (second from right) defeats the fancied American runners Frank Cuhel and Morgan Taylor in the 400 metres hurdles.

5 Golden quartet: Florence Bell, Myrtle Cook, Fanny Rosenfeld, and Ethel Smith of Canada won the 4 x 100 metres relay in the world record time of 48.4 seconds.

6 Scandinavian victories: In the 10,000 metres, Paavo Nurmi (FIN, centre) won ahead of Ville Ritola (FIN, left) and Edvin Wide (SWE, right). In the 5000 metres and 3000 metres steeplechase, Nurmi collected silver medals.

7 World record victory: A throw of 15.87 metres meant victory for the American John Kuck in the shot put.

8 Strongest athlete: Weightlifter Josef Strassberger (GER) won the gold medal in the heavyweight category

9 Victory for the USA: Pete Desjardins became Olympic highboard diving champion. He won the springboard diving event as well, having come second in Paris.

10 Favourites ahead: In the eights rowing event, the US crew (nearer camera) won ahead of Great Britain and Canada.

11 German medals: In the 200 metres breaststroke, Hilde Schrader (GER, lane 6) won, with Mietje Baron (HOL, lane 2) coming second and Lotte Mühe (GER, lane 5) third.

12 Extra time decision: The German water polo team beat Hungary 5-2 in the final, netting three goals in extra time. The score was 2-2 after normal time.

13 Hockey winners: A strong Indian team (nearest the camera) won the tournament ahead of the Netherlands (left) and Germany (dark bands on shirts).

14 Fencing medal: Queen Wilhelmina of the Netherlands presents the gold medal to Helene Mayer (GER) for her win in the individual foil.

Lake Placid

Despite the worldwide Depression, the III Winter Olympic Games went ahead. Unfortunately, they turned out to be a financial disaster for the organizers, who made a huge loss.

HARDLY ANY COUNTRY IN THE world had sufficient financial means to be able to send a well-prepared and well-equipped team to these Olympic Games. As a result, only 252 athletes from 17 nations competed for medals in the Adirondack Mountains in the US state of New York. The credibility of the competitions was further undermined by the fact that over half of these athletes were from the USA or from Canada.

For all this, the hosts had not spared any expense in creating a setting worthy of exciting competition. The Olympic Stadium had been newly built, as was the bobsled run on Mount Hoevenberg – notorious for being one of the fastest and most dangerous runs in the world. Only the weather foiled the organizers' plans: warm weather continually turned ice and snow into slush. As a result, competitions had to be rescheduled and postponed, and the Games actually finished two days late, with the four-man bobsled event being the final competition to take place.

In Lake Placid, three disciplines were presented for demonstration purposes only: the women's speed skating (officially admitted as an Olympic discipline in 1960), dog sled racing, and curling. This last discipline, which is due to be included as an official Olympic sport at the 1998 Winter Olympics at Nagano, Japan, was dominated by the Canadians. Their teams from Manitoba, Ontario, and Quebec took the first three places. Medals in the Nordic skiing events were monopolized by the Scandinavians, among them the Norwegians Johan Gröttumsbraaten (Nordic combined) and Birger Ruud (ski jumping). The cross-country competitions were also beset by adverse weather conditions, and an added organizational oversight hampered participants in the 50 kilometres event: the course wound through a solitary stretch of wood where there were no stewards to show

Retains Gold
The Norwegian skier Johan Gröttumsbraaten became Olympic champion in the Nordic combined and successfully defended the title he won at St. Moritz in 1928.

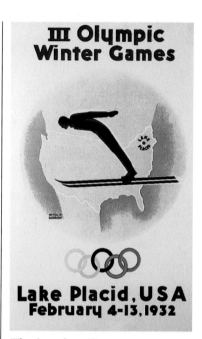

The American Games
A ski jumper as well as a map of the USA showing Lake Placid are featured on the poster advertising the Olympic Games.

competitors the way nor any spectators to cheer them on.

The remaining competitions were dominated by the Americans and Canadians. Two of Lake Placid's celebrated stars were the American speed skaters John Shea (gold medal winner over 500 and 1500 metres) and Irving Jaffee (gold medallist over 5000 and 10,000 metres).

After three Olympic wins in 1920, 1924, and 1928, the Swedish figure skater Gillis Gräfström could manage only second place and retired from international competition. Here he had to yield the ice to the Austrian Karl Schäfer, who had swum for his country in the Amsterdam Summer Games four years before. Sonja Henie from Norway repeated her victory of 1928 in the figure skating competition. Still only 19 years old, she won standing ovations from the crowds for the sensational interpretations of popular shows that she included in her free programme.

Repeat Victory
In Lake Placid, the ever popular Norwegian figure skater Sonja Henie repeated her Olympic title win of 1928.

King of the Ice
In front of his home crowd, the American Irving Jaffee won two long distance speed skating gold medals and was part of a clean sweep for the Americans in the speed skating events.

Figure Skating Win
By winning the gold medal, the Austrian Karl Schäfer ended the remarkable winning run of the triple Olympic champion Gillis Gräfström (SWE), who had to settle for second place.

Sven's Gold
Sweden's Sven Utterström took the 18 kilometres cross-country skiing gold medal with two minutes to spare over fellow Swede Axel Wikström.

1 Standard-bearers: At the opening ceremony, the US ice sprinter John Shea – who went on to win two golds – takes the Olympic oath, which is received by Admiral Byrd, the aviator who flew to the South Pole.

2 The crowds' favourite: Sonja Henie (NOR) secured her second Olympic win. The Norwegian figure skater's free programme included extracts from popular stage shows and enthralled the judges just as much as it did the audience. The Austrian Fritzi Burger and Maribel Vinson from the United States took silver and bronze medals respectively.

3 Most successful winner: Winning two gold medals each, John Shea (USA, front) and his team mate Irving Jaffee were the most successful competitors of the Winter Games in Lake Placid. In the 500 metres speed skating event, John Shea beat the Norwegian Bernt Evensen and the Canadian Alexander Hurd. In the 1500 metres competition, Shea stopped an overwhelming triumph by the Canadians who took places two to four; the silver medal was won by Hurd ahead of William Logan and Frank Stack.

4 Lack of snow: The shortage of snow that disrupted the Games can be best seen from the ski jump hill. As four years before, the Nordic combined, consisting of an 18 kilometres cross-country race and a ski jump competition, was won by the Norwegian competitor Johan Gröttumsbraaten ahead of his compatriots Ole Stenen and Hans Vinjarengen. The ski jump competition finished with another three medals for the Norwegians: Birger Ruud won the gold medal ahead of Hans Beck and Kaare Wahlberg. Ruud went on to successfully defend his title four years later at Garmisch-Partenkirchen.

5 Preliminary decision: The start to one of the two qualifying heats in the 10,000 metres speed skating event. The first four in each of the two heats reached the final. The final was won by the American Irving Jaffee ahead of world record holder Ivar Ballangrud of Norway and the Canadian Frank Stack. Jaffee also became

Olympic champion over 5000 metres, with the silver medal won by his team mate Edward Murphy and the bronze going to the Canadian William Logan.

6 A limited competition: The four teams in the ice hockey competition played each other twice. The title was decided by the first of two matches between Canada (white jerseys) and the host nation, USA. A 2-1 win by the Canadians in the first leg, followed by a 2-2 draw in the second leg, were enough to win them the gold medal. Germany took the bronze medal, with Poland clearly defeated back in fourth place.

7 The strongest survive: American rules dictated that instead of the usual procedure whereby skaters went out in pairs, the speed skating events had to have mass starts and this was highly controversial among the European skaters. Pushing and pulling often resulted in the judges having to remind competitors to compete fairly. The unpopular starting method was reason enough for the multiple world record holder and combined world champion Clas Thunberg (NOR) not to enter the competition.

8 Dangerous course: Bobsled USA I, with pilot William Fiske, Edward Eagan, Clifford Gray, and Jay O'Brien, won the four-man bobsled competition on the natural ice channel at Mount Hoevenberg. Not only was the course notorious for its bends, it was also 2366 metres long instead of the usual 1600 metres. The silver medal was won by USA II ahead of Germany I. This was Edward Eagan's second gold medal. He had won his first as a light-heavyweight boxer at the 1920 Summer Games in Antwerp. He remains the only Olympian to have won gold medals at both Winter and Summer Games.

9 New two-man bob: The two-man bobsled competition was held here for the first time and consisted of four runs. American brothers Hubert and Curtis Stevens (USA I) won the gold medal, ahead of Reto Capadrutt/Oscar Geier (SU II) and John Heaton/Robert Minton (USA II).

Los Angeles

Around 3500 musicians created a festive atmosphere at the opening of the X Olympic Games. In the midst of the Depression, the American "dream factory" captivated spectators and athletes alike.

Olympic Record

The Japanese swimmer Yasuji Miyazaki shaved 0.8 seconds off Johnny Weissmuller's 100 metres freestyle record in the semi-final, touching in 58.0 seconds. In the final, a time of 58.2 was enough for victory.

A CROWD MORE THAN 100,000 strong gathered in the Coliseum to watch the opening ceremony. As a result of the worldwide depression, only about 1400 athletes from 37 nations were able to travel to the USA. Male competitors lived in a specially built Olympic village as they had at the 1906 Olympic Games in Athens and again in Paris in 1924. However, female participants stayed in hotels. Once again, the number of athletes that each nation could enter in each competition was limited, with a maximum of three entries per country per event being permitted.

Even before the Games commenced, they were rocked by scandal: the IOC banned Paavo Nurmi for contravention of amateur regulations. On a number of occasions, the Finnish runner had claimed travel expenses in order to fund his journeys to meetings. Thus, the 35-year-old Nurmi was denied the chance to compete for the marathon gold medal with which he had hoped to mark the end of his career. It had been a glittering affair, during which this athletics legend set 22 official world records and won nine Olympic gold medals plus three silvers. At home in Finland, Nurmi was not banned and continued to race for another couple of years. His portrait featured on the official poster for the Helsinki Games, which took place in 1952. It irritated the IOC when in Helsinki, Nurmi, a "professional" athlete banned for life by the committee, was given the honour of carrying the Olympic torch into the stadium.

Scandal aside, the Los Angeles Games had many points of interest. Innovations included the use of a three-level podium for the medal ceremonies, and automatic timing for track events. For the first and only time since 1900, football was missing as a sport. In show jumping, meanwhile, no medals were awarded in the team event, since no team could get the

Tolan Triumphs

At 1.65 metres tall, Eddie Tolan (right, with Ralph Metcalfe) was thought too short to be a sprinter. He proved his doubters wrong by winning both the 100 and 200 metres.

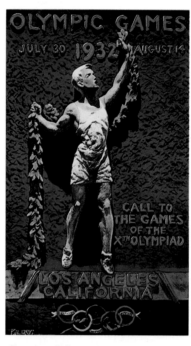

Come to LA

The official poster calls on the "youth of the world" to come together at Los Angeles for the Olympic Games.

necessary three riders around the difficult circuit successfully.

There were bizarre happenings in the 3000 metres steeplechase. A mistake by the lap counter caused the athletes to run an extra lap. Whilst this was of no consequence for the Finn Volmari Iso-Hollo, who was well in the lead, the American Joseph McCluskey was overtaken during this unscheduled lap. Nevertheless, he lodged no protest and settled for bronze behind Britain's Thomas Evenson.

The 1932 Games were a showcase for Mildred "Babe" Didrikson, who turned in a fine all-round performance. A superb sportswoman, on giving up athletics, she turned to golf, becoming perhaps the greatest woman player to date.

Once again a gold medal was awarded in the Merit for Alpinism category, the Germans Toni and Franz Schmid being rewarded for making the first ascent of the North Face of the Matterhorn.

Hampson for Britain

Britain's Thomas Hampson comes home to win the 800 metres gold medal ahead of Alexander Wilson of Canada. Wilson's fellow Canadian Phil Edwards was third.

Polish Express

The Pole Stanislawa Walasiewicz won the women's 100 metres. She had been living in the USA since 1913 and in 1947 became a US citizen.

Rowing Repeat

After a dramatic race against William Miller (USA), the Australian rower Henry Pearce retained the Olympic single sculls title he won in 1928.

1 **Solemn oath:** After the Games have been opened by US vice president Charles Curtis, the American fencer George Calnan, épée bronze medallist in 1928, takes the Olympic oath on behalf of all participants. Because of the global economic crisis, the turn-out at Los Angeles was only half that of the 1928 Games.

2 **India's superiority:** Only three teams competed in the hockey tournament. The Indians (pictured here during their match against Japan) were unbeaten, scoring 35 goals and conceding two. Japan took the silver medal, and the USA, beaten 24-1 by the victorious Indians, were third. India had also won in 1928 and remained invincible until 1960.

3 **Photo-finish:** Only the camera could decide who had won the final of the men's 100 metres at the Los Angeles Games. Although the electronic timer showed the same time (a world record 10.38 seconds) for first and second, Eddie Tolan (USA, right) was declared the winner ahead of Ralph Metcalfe (also USA, second from right). The bronze medal went to the German sprinter Arthur Jonath (third from right), who recorded 10.50 seconds.

4 **New procedure for medal ceremonies:** Since 1932, medal ceremonies have taken place on a special three-step podium. This picture shows the winner of the women's 100 metres freestyle, Helene Madison (USA, centre), flanked by Holland's Willemijntje den Ouden (left) and Eleanor Garatti-Saville (USA, right).

5 **Green walks to victory:** Britain's Thomas Green (No. 98) on his way to winning the 50 kilometres road walk, a new Olympic event at Los Angeles, in 4:50:10 hours. Second was the Latvian athlete Janis Dalinsh in 4:57:20 and the bronze was won by Italy's Ugo Frigerio, who finished in 4:59:06.

6 **A record performance:** With a throw of 40.58 metres, the American discus thrower Lillian Copeland set a new Olympic record and picked up the gold medal ahead of her team mate Ruth Osborn (40.12 metres) and the Polish world record holder Jadwiga Wajsowna (38.74 metres).

7 **Results of the water polo:** This match between eventual silver medallists Germany and the USA, who finished in third place, ended in a 4-4 draw. The gold medal was taken by the Hungarian team, who dominated the event, handing out heavy defeats to Germany (6-2), Japan (17-0), and the USA (7-0). Hungary went on to repeat their success at the 1936 Berlin Games.

8 The versatile "Babe": By winning gold medals in the 80 metres hurdles and javelin and a silver medal in the high jump, America's Mildred Didrikson (right) became the most successful track-and-field athlete of the Games.

9 Successful gymnast: In addition to two gold medals in the floor and pommel horse competitions, István Pelle (HUN) won silver medals in the combined exercises and parallel bars.

The Winter Games at the Bavarian resort of Garmisch-Partenkirchen were the first of two Olympic celebrations to take place on German soil in 1936. They were opened by Adolf Hitler.

WORRIED ABOUT NEWS OF discrimination against Jews in Germany, the IOC repeatedly demanded that Olympic rules be respected and Jewish athletes be added to the German team. However, an attempt by German emigrants living in the USA to prompt a boycott of the Games by all democratic countries failed. The Nazi regime, for its part, used the Games as an opportunity to present itself as peace-loving in front of more than half a million spectators from around the world. The newly built sports facilities, such as the Olympic ski jump hill, the ice rink, and the bobsled run near the Riessersee were opened amid much pomp and ceremony.

Right from the start, negative press coverage of the Games was suppressed. Only German photographers were admitted to the venues by the authorities, and only after extensive censorship by the propaganda ministry were "suitable" pictures released for publication in international newspapers and magazines.

As for the Games themselves, 28 nations attended, among which Australia, Bulgaria, Greece, Liechtenstein, Spain, and Turkey were being represented for the first time at an Olympic Winter Games. The increasing popularity of alpine skiing was reflected in the IOC's introduction of an alpine combined competition, consisting of downhill and slalom events. However, by classing Austrian and Swiss hotel skiing instructors as professionals and banning them from taking part, the IOC sparked a controversy. The men's gold medal in the new event was taken by German skier Franz Pfnür, with fellow countryman "Guzzi" Lantschner second, and France's Emile Allais third. Germany also struck gold and silver in the women's alpine combined, with Christl Cranz winning ahead of Käthe Grasegger.

Class Act
Ace Norwegian speed skater Ivar Ballangrud was the star of the Garmisch-Partenkirchen Games, winning three gold medals and a silver.

German Winter Games
The poster for the 1936 Winter Games suggests an athlete giving the Nazi salute.

Another newly introduced discipline was the Nordic 4 x 10 kilometres relay event, which was won by the Finnish team. In the meantime, the British ice hockey team registered the upset of the Games. They defeated the much-fancied Canadian side and went on to win the gold medal. It emerged that eight of the players in the British team lived and played their ice hockey in Canada. Nevertheless, they were eligible to represent Britain by virtue of having been born there.

The most successful individual at Garmisch was 31-year-old Norwegian speed skater Ivar Ballangrud. Taking part in his third Olympics, he added three gold medals and a silver medal to his collection and then retired from competitive sport. His team mate Sonja Henie said goodbye to amateur sport and turned professional after lifting her third consecutive Olympic figure skating title. Britain's Cecilia Colledge took silver.

8

9

10

11

12

1 The Games draw to a close: The closing ceremony at Garmisch featured a firework display by torchlight.

2 Hat-trick: With her third title in a row, Sonja Henie of Norway became (and still is) the most successful individual woman figure skater in Olympic history. The silver medal at Garmisch was won by Britain's Cecilia Colledge.

3 Successful start: A good performance in the compulsory section set world champion Karl Schäfer (AUT, right) on the way to the men's Olympic figure skating title ahead of Ernst Baier (GER) and Felix Kaspar (AUT).

4 Finnish relay: First skier Sulo Nurmela (FIN, left) hands over to Klaes Karppinen during the 4 x 10 kilometres cross-country, which Finland won ahead of Norway and Sweden. The 4 x 10 kilometres was a new event at Garmisch.

5 Swedish expertise: The first four places in the 50 kilometres skiing competition were taken by Swedes. The gold was won by Elis Viklund ahead of (from left) Axel Wikström, Nils-Joel Englund, and Hjalmar Bergström.

6 Curling demonstration: Curling featured at Garmisch as a demonstration sport as it had

at Chamonix and Lake Placid. Austria won the team event, and Georg Edenhauser (AUT) came out on top in the individual competition.

7 Italy on patrol: The military patrol event, another demonstration sport, was won by the Italian team.

8 Bob win: Switzerland II with (from right to left) pilot Pierre Musy, Arnold Gartmann, Charles Bouvier, and Joseph Beerli won the four-man bob ahead of Switzerland I and Great Britain I.

9 Change of fortune: Having led after the downhill, Laila Schou Nielsen (NOR) could not find the same form in the slalom and finished third overall in the alpine combined.

10 Medals for the USA: Ivan Brown (left) partnered by Alan Washbond in USA I took the gold medal in the two-man bob. Switzerland II was second and USA II third.

11 Scandinavians fly to victory: The ski jump was won by Birger Ruud ahead of the Swede Sven Eriksson. Third was Ruud's fellow Norwegian, Reidar Andersen.

12 Norway again: In the Nordic combined competition, Norway's Oddbjörn Hagen claimed the gold.

Berlin

The first Summer Olympic Games to be held in Germany were used by the Nazi Party as a gigantic propaganda exercise. Almost as a direct consequence, these would be the last Olympics until 1948.

Flying Finn
The European champion Ilmari Salminen of Finland took the 10,000 metres, in an event where Finland secured all three medals.

DESPITE IOC CONCERNS ABOUT the Nazis' rise to power in Germany, the committee were unable to move the 1936 Games away from Berlin. The German IOC members and the German Reich had repeatedly given assurances that they would abide by the rules of Olympic competition. Before the event, the chairman of the US National Olympic Committee and future IOC president, Avery Brundage, had rejected calls by Jewish emigrants for a boycott and warned that politics should not interfere with sport. In addition, the world had seen how smoothly the Germans had run the Winter Games at Garmisch-Partenkirchen earlier that year and there is no doubt that this helped to dispel much of the scepticism that had prevailed before the Games.

Jesse's Games
Winning four gold medals (100 metres, 200 metres, long jump, 4 x 100 metres relay), the American athlete Jesse Owens was the Games' undisputed star.

As suggested by Carl Diem, the head of the German organizing committee, this was the first time that the Olympic flame was ignited by the sun in Olympia, Greece. It was then relayed to the impressive new 100,000-seat stadium in the German capital by no less than 3075 torchbearers, each running one kilometre of the journey.

By employing the Third Reich's efficient propaganda machine, Adolf Hitler was able to use these Olympics as a platform from which to promote the host nation to a worldwide audience. This was typified by *Olympische Spiele*, Leni Riefenstahl's epic documentary on the Berlin Games, which although undoubtedly propaganda is also a respected cinematic work.

To deflect criticism of Germany's race legislation, the German team manager named two "half Jews" in the squad. Furthermore, the ice hockey player Rudi Ball and the 1928 Olympic fencing champion Helene Mayer were included without having to go through the usual qualification process. However, one of

Berlin in the Limelight
An oversized athlete and the quadriga of the Brandenburg Gate dominate the official poster of the Berlin Games.

the world's most accomplished high jumpers, the Jewish athlete Gretel Bergmann, was not chosen.

The ruling powers had supported the German athletes' preparations in every conceivable way since the athletes were supposed to prove the superiority of the "Aryan race" in contrast to athletes from other parts of the world. This was much undermined by the success of American black athletes. Nevertheless, Germany's 33 golds meant that they finished as overall medal winners in the competition, ahead of the United States' 24 golds and Hungary's ten.

Outdoor 11-a-side handball was introduced to the tournament for the first and last time, with Germany beating Austria in the final. Other new disciplines were canoeing and basketball. The Americans triumphed in the latter, embarking on a winning run which was interrupted only by the USSR in 1972.

Title Retained
The Finn Volmari Iso-Hollo successfully defended his Olympic title in the 3000 metres steeplechase and was bronze medallist over 10,000 metres.

Double Gold
The Frenchman Robert Charpentier was victorious in the 100 kilometres individual road race and picked up his second gold medal in the 4000 metres team pursuit event.

Four Medals
With three gold medals and one silver, the swimmer Hendrika "Ria" Mastenbroek (HOL) was the most successful female competitor in Berlin.

1 **Big interest:** Tens of thousands of spectators followed the competitions each day: this is a view of the swimming stadium and the Olympic Stadium, both seemingly filled to capacity.

2 **The oath is taken:** Following the parade of nations, the German weightlifter Rudolf Ismayr (who was Olympic champion in Los Angeles back in 1932) takes the Olympic oath. He was not, however, able to retain his title in Berlin.

3 **Italian in front:** Trebisonda Valla (third from left) won the 80 metres hurdles ahead of the German Anni Steuer and the Canadian Elizabeth Taylor. It took a photograph at the finish to decide the positions of the first four athletes.

4 **"King of the athletes":** The US decathletes turned out to be invincible. Glenn Morris (centre) picked up the gold medal ahead of Robert Clark (left) and Jack Parker (right).

5 **Third victory for India:** The seemingly invincible Indian hockey team became Olympic champions for the third time in a row. In the final, they beat the Germans 8-1. The Netherlands secured the bronze medal.

6 **German riding success:** The three-day event was won by Ludwig Stubbendorff (pictured here) on Nurmi, ahead of the American Earl Thomson and Hans Mathiesen-Lunding of Denmark. Stubbendorff picked

up his second gold medal in the team event with Rudolf Lippert and Konrad von Wangenheim, outclassing Poland and Great Britain. The German riders emphasized their superiority by winning gold (Heinz Pollay) and silver (Friedrich Gerhard) medals in the individual dressage event, a gold medal in the team event, dressage and through victories in the individual (Kurt Hasse) and team show jumping events. Hazardous conditions saw three horses killed in the competition.

7 **German foil:** The Jewish fencer Helene Mayer (right) was included in the German team to dispel growing international concern about Germany's blatantly racist anti-Semitism laws. At the medals ceremony for the foil competition (shown here), she received the silver behind the Hungarian Ilona Elek (centre) and ahead of bronze medallist, Ellen Preis of Austria.

8 **US pool win:** The 400 metres freestyle swimming event is decided when America's Jack Medica (lane 2) beats his Japanese rivals Shumpei Uto (nearer the camera) and Shozo Makino. The men's swimming medals were generally contested by just two nations. Apart from the gold in the 100 metres freestyle event (won by Ferenc Csik of Hungary) and the silver in the 200 metres breaststroke (Erwin Sietas of Germany), all the individual men's medals went to swimmers from either Japan or the United States.

9 **Three gymnastics golds:** Konrad Frey (GER) won gold medals in the pommel horse and parallel bars competitions, a silver in the horizontal bar event and bronze medals in the floor and combined exercises. Frey secured his third gold in the team event, thus becoming Germany's most successful competitor in Berlin.

10 **Japanese record:** Japan won the final of the 4 x 200 metres freestyle relay in a new world record time of 8:51.5

minutes. The USA finished over ten seconds behind in second position, with Hungary securing the bronze medal.

11 **British rowing gold:** In the double sculls, Jack Beresford (rear) and Leslie Southwood are ahead of Germany and Poland and went on to take the title. The British pair had been beaten by the Germans in the heats

12 **Canoeing debut:** Gregor Hradetzky (AUT) won the

single-seat kayak event over 1000 metres and also took the 10,000 metres folding kayak event.

13 **Estonian strength:** Wrestler Kristjan Palusalu (top, against the German Kurt Hornfischer) took the freestyle and Greco-Roman heavyweight wrestling events.

14 **Diving medals:** The American Marshall Wayne won the highboard diving competition ahead of his compatriot

Elbert Root and Hermann Stork of Germany. Wayne also took the silver medal in the springboard diving event. American success in the springboard was completed by Richard Degener's gold medal and Albert Greene's bronze medal.

15 **Tandem gold:** The German duo Ernst Ihbe (left) and Carl Lorenz won the 2000 metres tandem competition ahead of teams from the Netherlands and France.

St. Moritz

For the first time since Garmisch-Partenkirchen in 1936, athletes from all over the world met for Winter Olympic competition. The Olympic spirit had once again survived the horrors of a world war.

WHEN THE 1940 SUMMER Olympic Games were due to be staged in Tokyo, the Japanese organizers proposed Sapporo as the venue for the Winter Games. However, as a result of the outbreak of war between Japan and China, Japan withdrew and it was suggested that the Winter Games might instead be held in St. Moritz. Organizational disagreements ensued and the event was eventually handed to Garmisch-Partenkirchen. The outbreak of World War II saw the whole planning process grind to a halt.

Over the war years, the IOC had a change of leadership. After Henri de Baillet-Latour's death in 1942, vice president Sigfrid Edström duly took over as acting president, becoming elected president in 1946. Also in 1946, a newly expanded IOC decided to award the next Winter Games to Switzerland, which had remained neutral during the war; St. Moritz was again selected as the venue. The town had gained Olympic experience as hosts of the 1928 Winter Games, and its facilities, which had remained undamaged during hostilities, had only to be modernized.

However, these first post-war Games were still very much in the shadow of World War II. For a start, most athletes had only improvised equipment. In addition, a shortage of hard currency combined with restrictions on foreign travel for citizens in countries such as Great Britain meant that many visitors stayed away. Local hotel owners suffered as a consequence.

At St. Moritz, slalom and downhill skiing events for men and women were included for the first time as Olympic disciplines. This raised alpine skiing up to the same level as Nordic skiing. The surprise alpine skiing sensation turned out to be the 28 year-old American skier Gretchen Fraser, who started the competition as a compete outsider and went on to take the gold medal in the women's slalom event.

New Entries
Out of the 28 nations competing at St. Moritz, Chile, Denmark, Iceland, Korea, and the Lebanon were present for the first time.

Contrary to the IOC's emphatic plea for it not to go ahead, the military patrol competition was held, but for demonstration purposes only. The winter pentathlon – consisting of cross-country skiing, shooting, downhill skiing, fencing, and horse riding – was also a demonstration event, but it did not turn out to be very successful.

The newspaper headlines were dominated by a scandal concerning the ice hockey competition. The United States had sent two teams to Switzerland, each claiming to represent their country; one was nominated by the US National Olympic Committee and another nominated by the Amateur Hockey Association of the United States (AHAUS). The International Olympic Committee vice president Avery Brundage accused the AHAUS team of violating amateur rules, but was not able to prevent them from participating. The AHAUS team went on to finish fourth in the tournament. A year later, though, they were retrospectively disqualified.

Nils Wins
At the first post-war Winter Olympics, the four-times winner of the Wasa cross-country event, Nils Karlsson of Sweden, became Olympic champion in the 50 kilometres Nordic competition.

Final Victory
The United States took their first Olympic skiing medal when Gretchen Fraser won the women's slalom event. She retired straight after the Games.

Alpine King
The Frenchman Henri Oreiller won gold in the downhill and combined skiing events. With bronze in the slalom, he became the most successful athlete at St. Moritz.

Best Yet to Come
Britain's Jeannette Altwegg took the figure skating bronze behind Canada's Barbara Ann Scott and Austria's Eva Pawlik. Four years later, though, Altwegg was to be Olympic champion.

Crammond Third
Britain's John Crammond picked up the bronze medal in the skeleton sled tobogganing event. The event, now discontinued, was won by the Italian Nino Bibbia, with John Heaton of the United States in second place.

1 Alpine first: With the introduction of the downhill and slalom events as Olympic disciplines, alpine competitions finally won full recognition after the combined event had been included at the 1936 Olympic Winter Games in Garmisch-Partenkirchen. At St. Moritz, the downhill was taken by the Frenchman Henri Oreiller, ahead of the Austrian Franz Gabl. Oreiller picked up his second gold medal in the combined event, with Karl Molitor (SUI) second and James Couttet (FRA) third. Oreiller also took a bronze medal in the slalom event behind Edy Reinalter (SUI) and Couttet.

2 Momentous gold: Richard "Dick" Button was the first American to become Olympic figure skating champion. His athletic presentation secured him the gold medal ahead of Hans Gerschwiler of Switzerland and the Austrian Edi Rada. The pairs event was taken by the much-fancied world and European champions from Belgium, Micheline Lannoy and Pierre Baugniet.

3 Favourite's victory: The women's figure skating competition was won by the Canadian Barbara Ann Scott. The Austrian skater Eva Pawlik took the silver medal ahead of Jeanette Altwegg of Great Britain .

4 Joint silver: IOC president Sigfrid Edström (second from left) presents medals to the winners in the 500 metres speed skating. The Norwegian Finn Helgesen (fourth from left) took the gold. His compatriot Thomas Byberg (third from left) shared silver with Americans Robert Fitzgerald (second from right) and Kenneth Bartholomew (right) .

5 Speed skating results: The Swede Ake Seyffarth won the 10,000 metres event. The Norwegians took all remaining speed skating golds. Seyffarth added to his gold medal by winning the silver medal behind Sverre Farstad of Norway in the 1500 metres event.

6 **Surprise winner:** With an advantage of half a second, the American Gretchen Fraser relegates the Swiss skier Antoinette Meyer and Austria's Erika Mahringer to second and third positions in the women's slalom. Fraser added a silver medal to her tally when she secured second place in the alpine combined competition.

7 **Double Swiss victory:** Felix Endrich (in the cockpit) and Friedrich Waller won the two-man bobsled gold medal ahead of Fritz Feierabend and Paul Eberhard in the other Swiss bob. Feierabend's innovative bobsled design, in which the runners were individually suspended beneath the new aerodynamic cover, attracted a lot of attention during the competition.

8 **Medals for Austria:** Trude Beiser of Austria won the alpine combined event, which consisted of a downhill competition and a slalom. Another Austrian, Erika Mahringer, came third behind America's Gretchen Fraser. The silver medal in the women's downhill event was taken by Beiser behind the surprise winner, the Swiss skier Hedy Schlunegger. Beiser's fellow Austrian Resi Hammerer secured the bronze medal.

9 **Finns in front:** The Finn Heikki Hasu took the gold medal in the Nordic combined event ahead of his compatriot Martti Huhtala and the Swede Sven Israelsson. The Nordic combined is made up of an 18-kilometre cross-country skiing section and three attempts from the Olympic ski jump hill, of which the best two jumps are then taken into account.

10 **Ruud end:** With his Olympic title in the ski jumping competition, Petter Hugsted (NOR) took over from his compatriot and mentor Birger Ruud, who had collected gold in both 1932 and 1936. Ruud had to be content with the silver, ahead of another Norwegian, Thorleif Schjeldrup.

London

After a break of 12 years, the Olympic Summer Games were to be staged once again. For the second time since 1908, the IOC selected London – earmarked for the 1944 Games – as the venue.

LONDON WAS A LIKELY OPTION FOR the first post-war Summer Olympics because its existing facilities had remained largely intact through the war. In front of King George VI, the Swedish IOC president Sigfrid Edström, and more than 80,000 spectators, the XIV Olympic Summer Games were opened at the Empire Stadium, Wembley. Despite some concerns, the IOC continued the tradition of relaying the Olympic torch from Athens, but decided to re-route the runners. On their way from Olympia to London, the torchbearers were diverted via Pierre de Coubertin's tomb in Lausanne and thereby avoided having to run through Germany.

Not surprisingly, the Games took place without teams from Germany and Japan. Both countries were considered the aggressors of World War II and as a result were excluded from participating. Athletes from the Soviet Union did not take part either, the USSR not being affiliated to the IOC. Before the Games, the organizers dropped the idea of building an Olympic village because of anticipated high costs; Britain was, after all, almost bankrupt in the years following World War II. Instead, the athletes stayed in military barracks and colleges around the capital; rationing meant that many teams had to bring their own food along with them.

In the competitions, polo and outdoor handball were no longer included, while the Olympic arts competitions were held for the last time, thus ending Pierre de Coubertin's original idea of combining art with sport.

The women's competitions were expanded by the addition of the 200 metres, long jump, and shot events. Fanny Blankers-Koen of the Netherlands became the star of the Games, making history as the "flying housewife". A mother of two children, she won gold medals over 100 metres, 200 metres, in

Dutch Joy
With four gold medals, the Dutch athlete Fanny Blankers-Koen was the most successful female competitor of the Games.

London Statistics
Fifty-nine countries sent a total of 4099 athletes to the 1948 Summer Olympics.

the 4 x 100 metres relay, and in the 80 metres hurdles, where a photo-finish confirmed her win over Britain's Maureen Gardner. Even though the 30-year-old Blankers-Koen was already past her sporting best, a more favourable timetable might have seen her take further medals.

However, with three gold medals (combined, team, and pommel horse events), one silver (parallel bars), and a bronze (horizontal bar), the Finnish gymnast Veikko Huhtanen managed to surpass the Dutch athlete's medal tally. The Hungarian fencer Ilona Elek won a much celebrated gold medal and retained her 1936 Olympic title. Her compatriot Aladàr Gerevich won two golds in London. He competed in Olympic Games from 1932 right up until 1960, winning seven gold, one silver, and two bronze medals in various fencing events. In winning 38 events, the USA became the most successful team of the Games, ahead of Sweden with 16 golds and France with ten Olympic titles.

Swedish Double
The Swede John Mikaelsson won the 10 kilometres walking event, with compatriot John Ljunggren taking the 50 kilometres title.

Good Start
A gold medal over 10,000 metres and a silver medal over 5000 metres for the Czechoslovakian Emil Zatopek were the first medals of a highly successful Olympic career.

Javelin Gold
With his win in the javelin event, Tapio Rautavaara continued traditional Finnish success in this discipline. Four years later, however, the Finns would be beaten in front of their home crowd by the American Cyrus Young.

Olga's First
The Hungarian Olga Gyarmati won the first Olympic women's long jump competition. The world record holder was Fanny Blankers-Koen, who still won four gold medals in London, despite not entering this particular event.

1 Flame burns once more: Spectators watched events at Wembley Stadium, built for the 1924 British Empire Exhibition.

2 Swedish victory: Henry Eriksson is surrounded by well-wishers after his victory in the 1500 metres.

3 800 metres injury: The Dane Hans Christensen has to retire with a fractured leg.

4 US triple: William Porter (centre) won the 110 metres hurdles ahead of Clyde Scott (left) and Craig Dixon (right).

5 Narrow decision: In the 5000 metres, Emil Zátopek (TCH, left) is defeated by the Belgian Gaston Reiff (right).

6 Star of the Games: Fanny Blankers-Koen (HOL, centre) wins the 100 metres ahead of Dorothy Manley (GBR) and Shirley Strickland (AUS).

7 Sprint final: Harrison Dillard (USA, left) wins the 100 metres ahead of "Barney" Ewell (USA, second right) and Lloyd La Beach (PAN, third right).

8 French golds: Micheline Ostermeyer took gold medals in the discus and shot competitions and secured an additional bronze in the high jump.

9 Australian win: John Winter won the high jump with a jump of 1.98 metres.

10 Golden discus: Adolfo Consolini (ITA) defeated his compatriot Giuseppe Tosi and Fortune Gordien (USA).

11 Two wins: Hungarian fencer Aladár Gerevich (right) won golds in the individual and team sabre events.

12 Pool drama: The 100 metres freestyle winner, Greta Andersen (DEN), has to be rescued after fainting during the 400 metres freestyle.

13 Swedish success: The pentathlon was won by William Grut (right), while Gösta Gärdin (left) took the bronze.

14 Swedish canoeing gold: Hans Berglund and Lennart Klingström won the 1000 metres kayak pairs event.

15 Double diving winners: Double gold medal winner Victoria Draves (USA) congratulates Samuel Lee (USA) on his gold in the highboard and bronze in the springboard.

Oslo

For the first time, the Winter Olympics were held in a Scandinavian country. The event was received with great enthusiasm by the Norwegians, and a record number of spectators attended the Games.

BEFORE THESE GAMES BEGAN, THE organizers were concerned about Oslo's ability to stage the event; the city did not really have sporting facilities that met Olympic standards. However, this was remedied by refurbishing existing facilities and building new ones, which were ready well before the opening ceremony. In the end, any worries proved unfounded because these, as well as the courses for the newly introduced (men's and women's) giant slalom and (women's) 10 kilometres cross-country skiing, met the high expectations of athletes and officials alike.

Ahead of the Games, the Norwegians had picked up Carl Diem's idea and decided to relay the Olympic torch to the Winter Games in the same way as it was to the Summer Games. There had previously been plans for a "torch relay of friendship" from the venue of the first Winter Games (Chamonix) to Garmisch-Partenkirchen in 1940, but World War II scuppered the Games. The Norwegians started their relay run in the south Norwegian town of Morgedal, situated in the province of Telemark. Morgedal was the birthplace of the peasant Sondre Nordheim who, in 1868, had invented the first operational ski binding, making him one of the founders of modern skiing. As an added historical touch, the anchor runner carrying the torch into the Bislett Stadium was 19-year-old Egil Nansen, grandson of the polar explorer Fridtjof Nansen. He too was regarded as an early skiing pioneer.

For the first time since the end of World War II, German and Japanese teams were allowed to compete at the Olympics The organizing committee had made certificates of de-nazification mandatory for entry into Norway but any fears that the Norwegians might have been hostile to athletes of the former occupying power turned out to be unsubstantiated. The atmosphere was instead marked by the spectators'

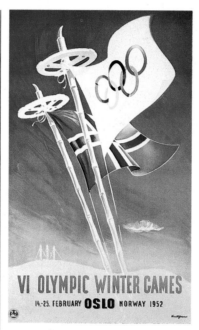

Norwegian Hosts
Tied to ski poles, the national flag of host nation Norway and the Olympic flag wave side by side on the official poster of the VIth Olympic Winter Games.

enthusiasm and impartiality. Attracting 150,000 spectators, the ski jump event at Mount Holmenkollen set a record in terms of crowd numbers that remains unbeaten today. And on the cross-country skiing slopes, it was difficult to distinguish between spectators and athletes as the majority of spectators had made their way there on skis. The American figure skater Richard "Dick" Button dominated the headlines when, during the successful defence of his 1948 figure skating title, he became the first skater to perform a triple jump and a toe-loop, as well as a double axle.

Victory by the 31-year-old Finn Lydia Wideman, turned out to be one of the highlights of the Games. Despite being the oldest competitor in the field, she won the 10 kilometres cross-country skiing event, and became the first athlete to win a women's Olympic Nordic skiing event. Finnish athletes also took the silver and bronze medal positions.

Home Win
Hjalmar "Hjallis" Andersen (right) after his race against the Japanese Sugawara. Winning three gold medals (1500 metres, 5000 metres, and 10,000 metres), the Norwegian skater was the most successful athlete in Oslo.

Ice Victor
The American Richard "Dick" Button proudly displays his figure skating gold medal. His triple loop was the first ever by a figure skater.

Slalom Queen
Andrea Mead (USA) won two gold medals in the slalom and giant slalom alpine skiing events. She was the first American to secure two golds in a Winter Olympics.

Norway's Star
The Norwegian skier Stein Eriksen put on an impressive display in front of his home crowd by becoming Olympic champion in the giant slalom and taking the silver medal in the slalom.

German Gold
Andreas Ostler led the German four-man bobsled team to victory by a margin of over two seconds over the four runs.

1 **Expressive Briton:** The 21-year-old British athlete Jeanette Altwegg, born in India and daughter of a Swiss father, won the figure skating gold medal ahead of the American Tenley Albright and Jacqueline du Bief of France.

2 **Olympic title retained:** Following his win at the 1948 Winter Games in St. Moritz, Richard "Dick" Button again took the figure skating gold medal, well ahead of the Austrian Helmut Seibt and James Grogan of the United States. After his retirement from an outstanding career as a competitive figure skater, he went on to achieve further success as a television sports commentator.

3 **Norway celebrates:** In front of more than 30,000 spectators, the VI Olympic Winter Games were officially opened in the Norwegian capital, Oslo. The newly readmitted German team are led by standard-bearer Hermann Böck and find themselves warmly welcomed. Thirty countries participated, a record for a Winter Olympics.

4 **US speed skating success:** Olympic champion Kenneth Henry (right), silver medallist Donald McDermott (left), and their coach (centre) celebrate a US 1–2 in the 500 metres speed skating event. The bronze medal position was shared by two athletes: the Norwegian Arne Johansen and Gordon Audley of Canada, who clocked exactly the same time. Henry had finished fifth in this event in St. Moritz in 1948.

5 **Harmony on ice:** The reigning world and European figure skating champions of the time, Ria and Paul Falk (GER) continued their winning run in the Oslo Olympics. The married couple took the gold medal ahead of the American brother and sister Karol and Michael Kennedy. The bronze medal was secured by Marianna and László Nagy of Hungary. Following their Olympic win, the Germans successfully defended their world championship title and moved on to pursue professional careers.

6 **Experienced winner:** The men's downhill event was won by the Italian woodcutter Zeno Coló. The icy slope made great demands on the athletes' technical skills. Coló, who was also world champion, relegated the Austrians Othmar Schneider and Christian Pravda to positions two and three respectively. The Italian almost collected another two medals but instead had to be content with fourth place in both the slalom and giant slalom.

7 **Austrian's silver and gold:** After coming a disappointing second in the men's downhill competition, the Austrian Othmar Schneider took the slalom gold, defeating the Norwegians Stein Eriksen and Guttorm Berge in the process.

8 **Fastest time:** Andreas "Anderl" Ostler, Friedrich

Kuhn, Lorenz Nieberl, and Franz Kemser (GER) took the gold medal in the four-man bobsled competition. The line-up was put together from the two existing German teams before the event after the other nations' bobsled, manned by considerably heavier athletes, had achieved much faster times in training. During the competition, the four German athletes, weighing a combined total of more than 500 kilograms, turned in the fastest time four runs in a row and finished well ahead of the USA I and Switzerland I teams. It was Germany's first ever gold medal

in this event. German success continued in the two-man bobsled, which was won by Ostler and Nieberl ahead of USA I and Switzerland I. Ostler became the first pilot to win both bobsled competitions at an Olympics. After the Oslo Games, the International Bobsled Association imposed overall weight limits.

9 Hosts celebrate victories: By pushing the Austrians Christian Pravda and Toni Spiss into second and third places, the Norwegian Stein Eriksen (pictured) secured the men's giant slalom gold medal. He

won the silver medal in the slalom event. In the downhill, Eriksen had to settle for sixth position. These two turned out to be the only Olympic medals he would ever win.

10 The favourite in front: The 1950 world champion Trude Jochum-Beiser (centre, gold) of Austria, the German Annemarie "Mirl" Buchner (left, silver), who was also a double bronze medal winner in the slalom and giant slalom, and the Italian Giuliana Minuzzo (bronze) show their delight during the medal ceremony for the women's downhill.

Helsinki

There was a wonderful atmosphere at the XV Olympics, which were held in the Finnish capital, Helsinki. To the delight of the crowd, the final torchbearers were their heroes, the great distance runners Paavo Nurmi and Hannes Kolehmainen.

FOR THE FIRST TIME SINCE 1912, athletes from Russia took part in an Olympic Games. In 1912, they had participated representing the Tsarist empire; now they were representing a communist Soviet Union. However, problems arose before the Games when the Soviet team refused to be accommodated alongside athletes from capitalist countries in the Olympic village at Kapyla. Following a declaration of solidarity from the other Eastern Bloc countries attending the Games, teams and officials were put up in alternative accommodation in students' quarters.

Having participated as part of a "united" Korea in 1948, South Korea now made its Olympic debut as a country in its own right. It had been the focal point of the Cold War that had developed between the United States and the Soviet Union, both of whom were involved in the conflict between North and South Korea. Unfortunately, the Helsinki Games were overshadowed by the polarization of the two systems; team officials considered every win achieved by "their" athletes as proof of the superiority of their own social system.

This was also the first time since World War II that a German team participated in a Summer Olympic Games. However, a united German team could not be assembled. Before the event, the Federal Republic of Germany and the German Democratic Republic could not agree on the selection criteria, resulting in the East German athletes remaining at home. One interesting addition was Saarland; as an independent German region with its own National Olympic Committee, it was allowed to send its own team to the Games.

The finest sporting achievements were those of Emil Zátopek. The army officer they called the "Czech Express"

Czech This
Emil Zátopek on his way to victory in the marathon. The Czechoslovakian also took the 5000 and 10,000 metres events.

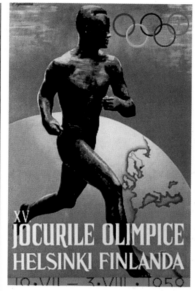

Pride in Paavo
As well as featuring a globe that highlighted the venue of the Summer Games, the official poster also illustrated the legendary Finnish long-distance runner Paavo Nurmi.

secured victories over 5000 metres, 10,000 metres, and in the marathon, enthralling spectators all the way. A further milestone was set by the American Bob Mathias, who became the first decathlete to successfully defend an Olympic title. However, the greatest personal success was achieved by the Danish rider Lis Hartel on her dressage horse, Jubilee. She won a silver medal in the event and thereby triumphed over the poliomyelitis (inflammation of the spinal cord) which required that she be lifted on and off her horse at the Games.

The Dutch athlete Fanny Blankers-Koen, the undisputed star of the last Games in London in 1948, had a disappointing end to her international career in Helsinki. In the 80 metres hurdles final – won by the Australian Shirley Strickland – the 34-year-old struck a hurdle and fell; she left the arena in tears and did not compete again.

Sprint Queen
The Australian track-and-field athlete Marjorie Jackson was victorious in the 100 and 200 metres finals. Her time of 11.5 seconds in the 100 metres was a new world record.

Soviet Strength
In Helsinki, the Soviet gymnast Viktor Chukarin took four gold and two silver medals. In 1956, he went on to add another three golds, one silver, and one bronze to his medal collection.

Hungary to Win
The Hungarian swimmer Váleria Gyenge was victorious in the 400 metres freestyle event in what was a successful Olympics in the pool for the Hungarians.

Bob's Back
Bob Mathias (USA) repeated his 1948 Olympic decathlon win, securing victory by the largest margin in Olympic history. It was also a world record points score.

1 **Legend lights the flame:** Inside the stadium, Paavo Nurmi handed the torch to fellow Finnish running legend Hannes Kolehmainen, who ignited the Olympic flame.

2 **Gold medal for Brazil:** Adhemar Ferreira da Silva took the triple jump gold medal ahead of Leonid Shcherbakov (URS) and Arnoldo Devonish (VEN).

3 **On her way to gold:** The South African Esther Brand won the high jump ahead of Britain's Sheila Lerwill and Aleksandra Chudina (URS).

4 **US quartet in front:** The Americans won the men's 4 x 100 metres relay ahead of the Soviet Union and Hungary.

5 **Star performer:** In a final sprint, Emil Zátopek (TCH, right) won the 5000 metres. Alain Mimoun (FRA, second right) took silver ahead of Herbert Schade (GER, second left). Britain's Chris Chataway (left) falls, before finishing fifth.

6 **Flush of victory:** In the 4 x 400 metres event, Jamaica's relay team beat the Americans (left) by only a tenth of a second and also set a new world record. Germany (right) took the bronze.

7 **Running in the family:** Like her husband Emil Zátopek, Dana Zátopková (TCH) was victorious. On the same day as Emil's 5000 metres win, she won gold in the javelin, ahead of

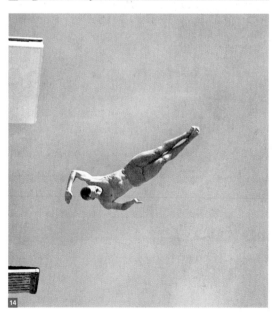

Aleksandra Chudina and Yelena Gorchakova of the USSR.

8 **Photo-finish:** Lindy Remigino (USA, third right) wins the 100 metres in front of Herb McKenley (JAM, second right) and Emmanuel McDonald Bailey (GBR, second left).

9 **Swimming gold:** In the 100 metres freestyle, Katalin Szöke (HUN) defeated Johanna Termeulen (HOL) and her fellow Hungarian Judit Temes.

10 **Surprise winner:** In the 400 metres freestyle final, the Frenchman Jean Boiteux beat

Ford Konno (USA) and Per-Olof Östrand (SWE).

11 **Fastest walker:** The Swede John Mikaelsson (right) won the 10 kilometres walking event in just over 45 minutes.

12 **Multiple champion:**

Viktor Chukarin (URS) won gold in the combined exercises, the pommel horse, the horse vault, and the team event and also secured silver in the rings and parallel bars.

13 **Swiss Gold:** The parallel bars final was won by Hans

Eugster, thus denying Viktor Chukarin a further gold medal.

14 **US clean sweep:** The American David Browning won the springboard with compatriots Miller Anderson and Robert Clotworthy second and third respectively.

Cortina d'Ampezzo

Cortina d'Ampezzo in the Italian Dolomites had bid three times to host the Winter Olympics, but it was not until 1956 that this resort had the opportunity to welcome the world's best athletes.

THE NORTHERN ITALIAN TOWN OF Cortina d'Ampezzo had been earmarked for the 1944 Winter Games but World War II forced this plan to be abandoned. Eight years later and more disappointment – Oslo was given preference over Cortina's renewed attempt to stage a Winter Olympic Games. In 1956, however, all the persistence paid off.

To finance the necessary construction projects, the organizers were able to rely on the support of Italian industrial groups and the event itself was also supported by a number of Italian companies. Even so, compared with the levels of sponsorship offered to later Olympic organizers, the amount of financial backing involved was very small indeed: Fiat and Olivetti provided a couple of cars and typewriters respectively.

Before the Games had even begun, a lack of snow cast a shadow over the competition timetable. Adverse weather conditions meant that athletes had insufficient opportunity to train and this resulted in numerous complaints. Such was the concern that a few days before the start, snow had to be transported down to the valley from higher snow fields. Ironically, heavy snow fell on the day of the opening ceremony and much of the imported snow had to be removed.

These Games saw the Olympic debut of a pan-German team of 75 athletes. As recently as 1955, the East German National Olympic Committee had provisionally been recognized by the IOC. Winning 16 medals and becoming the most successful nation, the Soviet team also made their debut at a Winter Olympics. Entries of 820 athletes from 32 countries set a record for participation in a Winter Olympic Games. Giuliana Chenal-Minuzzi, who was third in the downhill in Oslo in 1952, was the first woman athlete to take the Olympic oath at the opening ceremony.

In 1954, the Italian television station

Cortina's Finest Hour
The VII Winter Olympic Games in Cortina d'Ampezzo were as colourful as the poster that advertised them.

RAI had launched regular programmes and now offered live coverage from Cortina – a first in the history of the Winter Games. Thanks to "Eurovision", television audiences in Central Europe could now follow the competitions.

They witnessed the triumphs of the Austrian Anton "Toni" Sailer. The 20-year-old outclassed his rivals in all three alpine skiing events. These wins also counted as world championship titles, and secured him an additional world championship classification in the new combined event. Sailer was the most successful athlete in Cortina, ahead of the Soviet speed skater Yevgeny Grichin who won gold over 500 and 1500 metres.

The ice hockey tournament saw an end to Canada's dominance in this event. Apart from Great Britain's gold medal in 1936, the Canadians had taken all Olympic ice hockey titles since 1920. The victorious Soviet team that beat them included Vsevolod Bobrov, who had been a member of his country's football team during the 1952 Summer Olympics in Helsinki.

King Toni
In a reference to his home town of Kitzbühel, the triple gold medal winner Toni Sailer (AUT) was known to his fans as the "Blitz from Kitz".

Tenley Wins
The American Tenley Albright, world figure skating champion in 1953 and 1955, added an Olympic gold to the silver she collected in 1952.

Medals Galore
Veikko Hakulinen (FIN) was gold medallist in the 30 kilometres Nordic skiing competition and collected silver in the 50 kilometres and 4 x 10 kilometres relay cross-country events.

Swiss Success
Renée Colliard from Switzerland secured the gold medal in the women's slalom. The women's downhill was won by her team mate Madeleine Berthod.

Soviet Tie
The Soviet speed skater Yevgeny Grichin was Olympic champion over 500 metres and, in a dead heat with compatriot Yuri Michailov, became joint 1500 metres title holder.

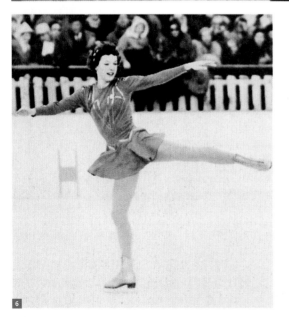

1 Natural ice rink: The 400-metre-long ice rink on Lake Misurina could accommodate 8500 spectators.

2 Opening ceremony: Moments before the Olympic flame is lit, the speed skater Guido Caroli stumbles over a cable on the ice rink. The torch had originally been lit on the Capitoline Hill in Rome.

3 Soviet debut: Winning all seven games in the ice hockey tournament, the Soviet Union (dark jerseys) concluded their Olympic debut in impressive style. In the final play-offs (pictured here), the Soviet team beat the eventual bronze medal winners Canada 2-0. The silver medal went to the United States. The USSR won a total of seven gold, three silver, and six bronze medals and thus became the most successful nation at the Winter Games in Cortina d'Ampezzo.

4 Figure skating pairs: The Austrian pair Elisabeth Schwarz and Kurt Oppelt defeated the Canadian world champions Frances Dafoe and Norris Bowden by a tiny margin, with Marianne and László Nagy from Hungary in third position.

5 Triple US triumph: The men's figure skating competition was won by an American for the third consecutive time as Hayes Alan Jenkins beat team mate Ronald Robertson and his own younger brother David.

6 Figure skating win: Despite a badly injured foot, the American Tenley Albright took the figure skating event ahead of her compatriot Carol Heiss and the Austrian Ingrid Wendl. Later in the year, Heiss beat Albright in the world championships.

7 Swiss gold medal: Renée Colliard was a surprise winner in the women's slalom. The silver medal was taken by the Austrian Regina Schöpf ahead of Jevgenja Sidorova of the Soviet Union.

8 Successful bobsleds: Pilot Franz Kapus with Gottfried Diener, Robert Alt, and Heinrich Angst took the gold medal for Switzerland I. The silver went to Italy II ahead of USA I. In the two-man bob, it was Italy first and second with the Swiss team third.

9 Happy winner: The slalom silver medallist at Oslo in 1952, Ossi Reichert (FRG), and her coach are jubilant about her win in the giant slalom. The silver and bronze medals were taken by the Austrians Frandl and Hochleitner.

10 Wonderful present: On her 25th birthday, the Swiss Madeleine Berthod became Olympic downhill champion. The silver medal was won by her team mate Frieda Dänzer while the bronze went to Lucile Wheeler of Canada.

11 Nordic skiing victories: At his third Olympic Games, the Finn Veikko Hakulinen won the newly introduced 30 kilometres cross-country event ahead of the Swede Sixten Jernberg and Pavel Kolshin of the USSR. Hakulinen added another two silver medals to his collection in the 50 kilometres event (in which he won gold in 1952) and the 4 x 10 kilometres relay. He secured seven medals in his Olympic career.

Melbourne

The XVI Olympic Games were opened in Melbourne by the Duke of Edinburgh in late November 1956. As the northern hemisphere moved into winter, Australia was just getting ready for summer.

THE FIRST OLYMPIC GAMES to be held south of the equator posed a particular set of problems for athletes from Europe and America. For a start, many athletes did not have sufficient funds to spend a period of time acclimatizing before the Games. In addition, the late timing of the competition within the athletics season meant that athletes had to retain their peak fitness over a longer period than usual. Contrary to the regulations laid down in the Olympic Charter, one discipline had to be separated from the rest of the programme. As the Australian government were unwilling to shorten the usual six-month quarantine period for horses entering the country, the horse riding events were forced to take place in June in the Swedish capital, Stockholm.

Fraser First
Australian swimming phenomenon Dawn Fraser (left) is congratulated after winning her heat of the 100 metres freestyle. Fraser went on to win the gold in a new world record time.

OLYMPIC GAMES

MELBOURNE
22 NOV – 8 DEC
1956

Australian Hosts
A kangaroo is featured on the Olympic poster for the XVI Olympic Games in the Australian city of Melbourne.

As a result of the high cost of travelling to Australia, fewer athletes participated in these Games than, for example, in Berlin 20 years previously. The already relatively low number of competitors (approximately 3200) further decreased when China pulled out (because of Taiwan's participation) and then Egypt and Lebanon decided not to attend (because of the Suez crisis). Liechtenstein, the Netherlands, Spain, and Switzerland also withdrew, in protest at the Soviet invasion of Hungary.

The competitions themselves also suffered from the effects of political crises. One water polo match in the final round between Hungary and the USSR had to be abandoned because of the misconduct of some of the players. However, by beating Yugoslavia in the final, Hungary successfully defended their 1952 title.

Outstanding athletes in Melbourne included the Soviet gymnast Larissa Latynina, who won four gold medals (in the team, the combined exercises, the horse vault, and the floor competitions), a silver medal (in the asymmetrical bars event), and a bronze medal (in the

portable apparatus). Betty Cuthbert turned on the style in front of her home crowd with three track-and-field wins: the 100 and 200 metres and the 4 x 100 metres relay. In the 5000 and 10,000 metres events, the Soviet Vladimir Kuts took the titles held by Emil Zátopek; the Czech himself retired from international competition after finishing sixth in the marathon. After winning two golds over 80 metres hurdles and in the 4 x 100 metres relay, the Australian Shirley de la Hunty (née Strickland) also retired. Between 1948 and 1956, she collected three gold, one silver, and three bronze medals.

The Australian swimmer Dawn Fraser marked the beginning of her Olympic career by taking two gold medals (100 metres and 4 x 100 metres freestyle) and one silver (400 metres freestyle). Her compatriot Murray Rose became the first male swimmer to win two individual freestyle events (400 metres and 1500 metres) since Johnny Weissmuller's achievements of 1924.

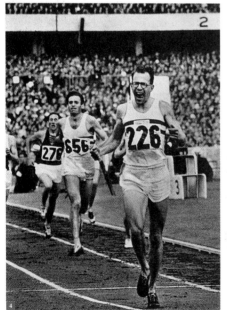

1 United Germany: A German team that included athletes from the Federal Republic of Germany and the German Democratic Republic enters the stadium.

2 Three home golds: The 18-year-old Australian Betty Cuthbert (No. 468) takes her first gold medal in the women's 100 metres. Two days later, she secured her second gold in the 200 metres and went on to win her third with the 4 x 100 metres relay team.

3 Duel decided: Vladimir Kuts of the Soviet Union (left) won this duel against Britain's Gordon Pirie (right) in the 5000 metres event. In the 10,000 metres, he crossed the finishing line ahead of the Hungarian József Kovács. Allan Lawrence gained a notable bronze for the host nation.

4 Bravo Brasher!: Britain's Chris Brasher heads for victory in the 3000 metres steeplechase. Brasher had been a pacemaker in Roger Bannister's four-minute mile and went on to found the London Marathon.

5 Exciting final: Bobby Joe Morrow (USA, right) wins the 100

metres. He secured victory over 200 metres three days later and with the 4 x 100 metres relay team added another gold to his medal collection.

6 Efforts rewarded: Alain Mimoun of France is the first athlete to enter the Olympic stadium in marathon competition.

7 Favourites win rowing gold: The American eight secured a narrow victory over the Canadian and Australian crews.

8 Diving accolades: America's Pat McCormick won the springboard and highboard diving competitions in convincing style. She had also won both titles at Helsinki in 1952.

9 Hat-trick in the boxing: At his third Olympics, and at the age of 30, the Hungarian boxer László Papp (right) became the first boxer to win three Olympic titles.

10 Swimming gold and record: European champion Ursula Happe (GER) after the medal ceremony for her victory in the 200 metres breaststroke, where she set a new Olympic record of 2:53.1 minutes.

11 A win despite injury: Having sustained an injury in the first round, the German show jumper Hans Günter Winkler was in severe pain, but still managed to guide his horse Halla over the course without any mistakes to win gold medals in the individual and team events. In an Olympic career that lasted until 1976, Winkler won five gold medals.

12 Six medals: The Hungarian gymnast Agnes Keleti won golds in the floor, the beam, the asymmetrical bars, and the team portable apparatus event and silvers in the combined exercises and the team event.

13 Soviet wins: Boris Shakhlin became the Olympic pommel horse champion. The Soviet team's success was wrapped up by Viktor Chukarin, with wins in the parallel bars and combined exercises, a silver in the floor event, and a bronze in the pommel horse. Valentin Muratov also won two golds in the floor and horse vault competitions and a silver in the rings. Further Soviet medals were Albert Azaryan's gold in the rings and Yuri Titov's silver in the horizontal bar and bronze in the combined exercises and the vault.

Squaw Valley

The organizers were unable to fully allay the scepticism that greeted the award of the VIII Winter Games to Squaw Valley in the Sierra Nevada. Nevertheless the celebration passed off smoothly.

Home Win

America's Carol Heiss, who had taken the Olympic oath during the opening ceremony, won the women's figure skating gold medal.

WHEN THE DECISION WAS MADE in 1955 on the venue for the 1960 Games, the area around Lake Tahoe was completely undeveloped as a winter sports centre. However, within four years, Squaw Valley, approximately 1900 metres above sea level, was ready, with sports facilities and accommodation for participants, as well as infrastructure for more than two million visitors. This came about thanks to the hard-working organizing committee, financial backing from the states of California and Nevada, together with subsidies from Washington.

Nevertheless, preparing the slopes for the alpine skiing competitions was fiercely expensive, since they had to have man-made obstacles incorporated in order to meet the high standard required for the Olympic Games. And despite the subsidies, the organizers delayed construction of a bobsled run for too long, with the result that the IOC had to call off both bob competitions (as usual two-man and four-man events had been scheduled).

For these VIII Winter Olympic Games, the flame had once again been lit in the Norwegian town of Morgedal. During the opening ceremony, which was stage-managed by Walt Disney, a pan-German team paraded into the stadium beneath a flag bearing the national colours of Germany (black, red, and yellow) and the five Olympic rings. This compromise had been worked out by officials after the East German delegation had initially insisted on marching behind the East German flag. South Africa was represented for the first time at a Winter Games, but because of the country's policy of apartheid, this first appearance was also its last until 1994.

Spectators at Squaw Valley were the first to watch the biathlon as an Olympic discipline. A combined event, consisting of cross-country skiing and shooting, the biathlon had been a recognized sport in

Monopoly Broken
Georg Thoma (GER) became the first non-Scandinavian to win a Nordic skiing event, taking the Nordic combined title.

Californian Connection
The five rings take pride of place on the official poster of the 1960 Winter Olympic Games, held in Squaw Valley, California.

Ski and Shoot

The first Olympic biathlon competition was held over a 20-kilometre course and was won by Sweden's Klas Lestander.

the Scandinavian countries for many years. It is perhaps unsurprising then that the first Olympic champion was a Swede – Klas Lestander.

Another newcomer to the Winter Olympic programme was women's speed skating. There were four events – the 500 metres, in which the gold medal was won by the German Helga Haase; the 1000 metres, won by Klara Guseva (URS); and the 1500 and 3000 metres, both of which were won by Lidia Skoblikova of the Soviet Union.

The figure skating turned out to be an all-American "family affair". The men's event was taken by David Jenkins, the brother of Hayes Alan Jenkins, the Olympic champion of 1956. The women's title was taken by David Jenkins' future sister-in-law, Carol Heiss.

The Germans Georg Thoma and Helmut Recknagel made headlines when they became the first non-Scandinavians to win the Nordic combined competition (Thoma) and the ski jump (Recknagel).

Teenage Triumph

The 19-year-old Heidi Biebl (GER) became the Olympic women's downhill champion.

Flying Flag-bearer

Helmut Recknagel (GER), the pan-German team's standard-bearer at the opening ceremony, secured the gold medal in the ski jump.

1 **Lighting the Olympic flame:** During the opening ceremony, the Olympic flame was lit by the 1952 500 metres speed skating champion, the American Kenneth Henry

2 **Hockey gold for the hosts:** In the semi-final of the ice hockey tournament, the eventual champions USA (dark jerseys) caused an upset by defeating the USSR 3-2. The Soviet team were much fancied. They had taken the gold at Cortina and indeed had not been beaten in internationals since 1956. The US team had qualified for the semi-finals by beating Czechoslovakia 7-5 and Australia 12-1 during their group matches. In the second qualifying group, Canada, six-times Olympic champions (1920-1932 and 1948-1952), had initially lived up to expectations by beating Sweden 5-2 and Japan 19-1. However, in the end they had to settle for second place, with the Soviet side taking the bronze medal.

3 **Tight finish:** With only 0.8 seconds in it, Veikko Hakulinen (right), anchor-man of the Finnish 4 x 10 kilometres relay team, secured his country the Olympic gold medal. Haakon Brusveen (left) is on the Finn's shoulder to earn

Norway the silver medal. The bronze was picked up by the Soviet team.

4 **Skiing "marathon":** In the 50 kilometres cross-country skiing race, Kalevi Hämäläinen (FIN) beat his fellow countryman Veikko Hakulinen and the Swede Rolf Rämgard. Earlier on, the 30 kilometres event had been won by Sixten Jernberg (SWE) ahead of Rämgard and Nikolai Anikin (URS). The 15 kilometres event was won by Haakon Brusveen (NOR) from Jernberg and Hakulinen.

5 **Two titles:** The speed skater Yevgeniy Grischin (URS) made the headlines by becoming a double Olympic champion. Over 500 metres, he defeated the Americans William Disney and Rafael Gratsch, while in the 1500 metres, he shared the title with the Norwegian Roald Aas, with the bronze medal going to Boris Stenin from the USSR. The Soviets took another speed skating gold with Viktor Kositschkin winning the 5000 metres ahead of the Norwegian Knut Johannesen and Holland's Jan Pesman. Over 10,000 metres, Johannesen took his revenge on Kositschkin, beating him into second place with Kjell Bäckman of Sweden coming in third.

6 Women make their debut: Helga Haase (GER) became the first woman to win an Olympic speed skating event. In the 500 metres, she clocked 45.9 seconds, 0.1 seconds better than Natalia Dontchenko (URS). America's Jeanne Ashworth was third. In the 1000 metres, Haase picked up a silver medal, being beaten to the gold by Klara Guseva (URS). The bronze medal in this event went to Tamara Rylova (also URS). In the two remaining women's speed skating competitions, Lidia Skoblikova of the USSR displayed the talent that was to make her a major force in the discipline for many years to come. Skoblikova had just missed out on a medal in the 1000 metres, but she made no mistake in the 1500 metres, pushing Poles Elvira Seroczynska and Helena Pilejczyk into second and third spots respectively. Over 3000 metres, Skoblikova picked up another gold medal ahead of her team mate Valentina Stenina and Eevi Huttunen of Finland.

7 Gold and bronze medals for France: Jean Vuarnet won the downhill skiing by 0.5 seconds ahead of Hans-Peter Lanig (GER). Vuarnet's fellow Frenchman Guy Perillat took the bronze.

8 Medal ceremony: The Canadian pair Barbara Wagner and Robert Paul (centre) clutch their figure skating gold medals won ahead of Germany's Marika Kilius and Hans-Jürgen Bäumler (left) and America's Nancy and Ronald Ludington (right).

9 Gold medal for Switzerland: In the giant slalom, Swiss alpine skier Roger Staub commandingly beat his Austrian rivals Josef Stiegler and Ernst Hinterseer. However, Hinterseer collected a gold medal in the slalom event ahead of his compatriot Matthias Leitner and Charles Bozon of France.

10 Concentrating on victory: The women's downhill competition was won by Germany's Heidi Biebl. The American Penny Pitou, a second adrift of the Olympic champion, picked up the silver medal, while Traudl Hecher of Austria took third place.

11 Favourite wins: Carol Heiss (USA) won the figure skating, with Sjoukje Dijkstra (HOL) and Barbara Roles (USA) coming second and third. In this Olympic year, Heiss also won the world championship for the fifth time in a row.

Rome

Pierre de Coubertin had wanted to stage the 1908 Olympics in Rome, but the eruption of Vesuvius in southern Italy had intervened. In 1960, 52 years on, the Games finally arrived in the Italian capital.

A COMBINATION OF NEW SPORTS facilities and historic buildings provided the backdrop to the XVII Olympics, held in Rome. The organizers successfully mixed traditional values with the demands of modern sport. For example, the gymnastics events were held in the Baths of Caracalla, while the wrestlers fought in the Basilica of Maxentius. The start and finish of the marathon were, untypically, sited outside the Olympic Stadium. The runners started on their 26-mile journey on the Capitoline Hill and finished at the Arch of Constantine. The indoor arena, the *Palazzetto dello Sport*, designed by Pier Luigi Nervi, fitted perfectly into its surroundings and was considered an outstanding example of modern architecture. Nevertheless, Nervi was accused of having taken his inspiration for the building from the Fascists' *Foro Italico*.

The opening ceremony, featuring the now-traditional parade by the participating nations, took place in front of more than 100.000 spectators in the Olympic Stadium. All but the Soviet athletes had received the blessing by Pope John XXIII in St. Peter's Square.

The Rome Games were broadcast by television to all European countries and were watched by millions. Sadly the events themselves were overshadowed by the rivalry between the USA and the USSR. In the final medal table, the Soviet Union, with 42 gold medals, finished ahead of the USA with 34.

The American sprinter Wilma Rudolph captured the public's imagination. The 20-year-old, known as the "Black Gazelle" because of her elegant running style, had suffered from polio during childhood. In Rome, she was a triple gold medallist, winning the 100 metres, 200 metres, and running in the USA's winning 4 x 100 metres relay team. In the men's 100 metres, the German Armin Hary's victory broke a US monopoly in the event, which had lasted since the Los Angeles Games of 1932.

In the City of Romulus and Remus
The official Olympic poster featured the Roman legend of the twins Romulus and Remus, who were suckled by a she-wolf.

Another sensation in Rome was the Ethiopian runner Abebe Bikila, who won the marathon barefoot. His performance suggested that the sports equipment industry might be wrong in its claims that success depended completely on continual improvements in equipment.

Besides the medals won, there were remarkable personal milestones reached at the Rome Games. At the age of 50, the Hungarian sabre maestro Aladár Gerevich rounded off his extraordinary career by winning his seventh gold medal to add to a silver and two bronzes. Gerevich had competed in no less than six Games (1932-1960). Another veteran fencer also called it a day. With a record tally for fencing of 13 medals (six golds, five silvers, and two bronzes), including a last victory in the team épée event, the Italian Edoardo Mangiarotti retired after having taken part in five Olympic Games (1936-1960).

In gymnastics, meanwhile, Larissa Latynina was still in the middle of a career that would eventually yield 18 medals. In Rome, she added three golds (including the team combined), two silvers, and a bronze to her collection.

Black Gazelle
America's Wilma Rudolph won two individual sprint gold medals and a relay gold in Rome.

Breaking the Run
The German sprinter Armin Hary won the men's 100 metres, breaking America's domination. He won a second gold medal as a member of the victorious German 4 x 100 metres relay team.

Veteran Bows Out
The Hungarian fencer Aladár Gerevich crowned a six-Games career with victory in the team sabre.

Number One
With three gold medals, two silvers, and one bronze, Soviet gymnast Larissa Latynina was the most successful female competitor of the Games.

First Ethiopian
In winning the marathon, Abebe Bikila became the first Ethiopian athlete to win a gold medal.

1 Let the Games begin: The "youth of the world" gather once more under the Olympic flag. At the opening ceremony, athletes from 83 nations paraded, and doves of peace were released. Adolfo Consolini, the 1948 discus champion, took the oath.

2 Thompson marches on: Don Thompson of Britain strides out on his way to triumph in the 50 kilometres walk. Thompson set a new Olympic record for the event of 4:25:30 hours. Second was John Ljunggren of Sweden with Italy's Abdon Pamich third.

3 Favourite first: A leap of 8.12 metres was enough to secure Ralph Boston, the world record holder, the Olympic long jump title in Rome. Boston beat his fellow American Irvin Robertson (8.11 metres) and the Soviet athlete Igor Ter-Ovanesian (8.04 metres).

4 All three for the USA: The great Al Oerter successfully defended his discus title, with a winning throw of 59.18 metres. Silver and bronze were picked up by Richard Babka and Richard Cochran (both also USA).

5 Sensational final: The world 100 metres record holder, Armin Hary (GER, second from right), defeats the American David Sime (right) and Britain's Peter Radford (second from left). Hary was the first German to win an Olympic gold medal in a running event.

6 Three gold medals for track-and-field star: American women athletes in high spirits. Wilma Rudolph (standing, right) had plenty to be cheerful about. In the 100 metres final, she beat Britain's Dorothy Hyman and the Italian Giuseppina Leone. Over 200 metres, she again showed her superiority, this time over Jutta Heine (GER) and Hyman. Rudolph added a third gold medal running the anchor leg for the US 4 x 100 metres relay team that won ahead of Germany and Poland.

7 Romanian win: Yolanda Balas (ROM) won the women's high jump, going clear at 1.85 metres. Silver was shared by Poland's Jaroslawa Jozwiakowska and Britain's Dorothy Shirley who both cleared 1.71 metres.

8 Results in the diving: In the diving competitions, Ingrid Krämer of Germany reigned supreme. In the springboard event, she won the gold ahead of Paula Myers-Pope from the USA and Britain's Elizabeth Ferris. In the highboard event, Krämer again showed her class to defeat Myers-Pope and the Soviet diver Ninel Krutova.

9 US victories in the pool: The American swimmer Lynn Burke won the 100 metres backstroke. Second and third places went to Britain's Natalie Steward and Satoko Tanaka of Japan respectively. Burke was also a member of America's 4 x 100 metres medley team that won from Australia and Germany.

10 Swim win for Britain: Britain's Anita Lonsbrough (centre) wears the gold medal for the 200 metres breaststroke, having set a new world record time of 2:49.5 minutes in the final. Wiltrud Urselmann (GER, right) and Barbara Göbel (GER, left) were second and third.

11 Narrow decision: Otis Davis of America became the Olympic champion over 400 metres, clocking a new world record of 44.9 seconds. However, it needed a photograph to separate him from Carl Kaufmann of Germany, who had to settle for the silver medal having recorded the same time. The bronze medal was taken by the South African Malcolm Spence (45.5 seconds).

12 Joy and anguish for the US relay teams: The American 4 x 100 metres relay team was disqualified as a result of an illegal changeover involving Ray Norton (left) and Frank Budd, which took place outside the zone. The gold medal was won by the German team (Bernd Cullmann, Armin Hary, Martin Lauer, and Walter Mahlendorf) ahead of the USSR and Great Britain. The Americans were more successful in the 4 x 400 metres, winning the gold medal in 3:02.2 minutes ahead of Germany and the Antilles and cutting 1.7 seconds off the world record held by Jamaica.

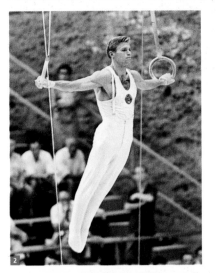

1 Double win for Italy: The brothers Raimondo (right) and Piero d'Inzeo (left) won gold and silver respectively in the show jumping. Britain's David Broome took the bronze. In the team event, the Italians finished third behind the Germans and the USA. The d'Inzeos appeared at eight Games.

2 Success of the Games: By winning four gold medals, two silver medals, and one bronze medal, the Soviet gymnast Boris Shakhlin became the Games' most successful competitor. He won the combined exercises from Takashi Ono (JPN) and Yuri Titov (URS), and picked up his second gold in the parallel bars ahead of Giovanni Carminucci (ITA) and Ono once again. In the horse vault, he shared the title with Ono and also split the pommel horse title, this time with Eugen Ekman of Finland. He won a silver medal as a member of the Soviet team that finished second behind Japan, a second silver in the rings behind team mate Albert Azaryan, and a bronze in the horizontal bar.

3 US dominates basketball: The picture shows the US basketball team beating Italy 112-81 on their way to winning the gold medal. The Americans, possibly the best ever amateur Olympic side, met the USSR in the final, winning 73-59. Brazil collected the bronze medal.

4 Successful heavyweight: Wilfried Dietrich of Germany (right), shown here with the Swede Stan Svenson, won the heavyweight (unlimited weight) freestyle wrestling title ahead of Turkey's Hamit Kaplan and Savkus Dsarassov of the Soviet Union. Dietrich also won a silver medal at heavyweight (unlimited weight) in the Greco-Roman style, as he had four years earlier. In Rome he was defeated by Ivan Bogdan of the Soviet Union, while the bronze was won by the Czechoslovak Bohumil Kubát.

5 Gold medal for US boat: Arthur Aryault, Ted Nash, John

Sayre, and Richard Wailes receive their gold medals for the coxless fours. Italy and the USSR were second and third. The USA also picked up a bronze in the coxed pairs with Richard Draeger, Conn Findlay and Henry Mitchell (cox). The event was won by Germany with the Soviet Union second.

6 **Celebration for shooting star:** Peter Kohnke (GER) is delighted at winning gold in the small-bore rifle (prone position). He is held aloft by Georg von Opel, president of the German shooting association. James Hill (USA) was second.

7 **"The Greatest" wins:** An Olympic title win in the light-heavyweight category proved a stepping stone to greater things for 18-year-old Cassius Clay (right).

8 **Rowing success:** The Germans won the gold in the coxed eights ahead of Canada and Czechoslovakia.

Innsbruck

With the IX Winter Games due to start, the Innsbruck area found itself with a shortage of snow. However, the Austrian army came to the rescue, shipping in thousands of tons of snow from elsewhere.

Lap of Honour
Before the closing ceremony at the ice rink, the Soviet Olympic figure skating champions Ludmilla Belosova and Oleg Protopopov were asked to present their free programme again.

ALTHOUGH THE ORGANIZERS of the IX Winter Olympic Games had made all the preparations they could for the competitions, the weather turned out to be beyond their sphere of influence. Innsbruck's mildest February for 58 years meant that Austrian troops had to transport more than 25,000 tons of snow from higher snowfields to the River Inn valley so that the slopes would be ready for the alpine skiing competitions. The cross-country skiers, meanwhile, competing in the town of Seefeld further up the Inn valley, found conditions to be ideal.

For the first time at a Winter Olympics, the number of competitors exceeded the 1000 mark, with around 900 male and 200 female athletes participating at Innsbruck. The schedule comprised a record 34 events, and luge tobogganing made its Olympic debut. In lugeing, competitors descend an ice run lying face upwards on the toboggan. (In 1928 and 1948, there had been skeleton sledding competitions, in which the athletes lay face down.) At Innsbruck there were three luge events – the singles and two-man for male competitors and the singles for women.

The bobsled competitions returned after their enforced break in Squaw Valley (1960) when the organizers had failed to build a bobsled run. Meanwhile in the the ski jump competition new rules were implemented, replacing those that had been in effect since 1930. Two separate events were now held: one on the small hill and one on the big hill. The athletes were granted three attempts, of which the shortest jump was ruled out by the judges. The winner on the small hill at Innsbruck was Veikko Kankkonen of Finland, while the large hill victor was Toralf Engan of Norway. However, the complicated judging procedure made the ski jump competitions rather confusing

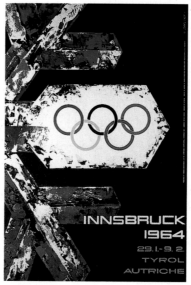

Crystal Promise
Only the official Olympic poster of the Winter Games in Innsbruck is dominated by snow crystals; the Games themselves are disrupted by a serious lack of snow.

and as a result, the rules were simplified for the 1968 Games in Grenoble.

The figure skating event held a surprise. After losing nine times in the European and world championships at the hands of their old rivals Marika Kilius and Hans-Jürgen Bäumler, the Soviet couple Ludmilla Belosova and Oleg Protopopov took the Olympic title. Their adversaries finished second but were disqualified for having taken part in a professional ice show before the Games, though they were later reinstated.

The Soviet speed skater Lidia Skoblikova was the most successful competitor of the Winter Games, winning all four speed skating competitions. The Swede Sixten Jernberg crowned his career by taking the 50 kilometres cross-country skiing gold. At three Winter Games, Jernberg collected four gold, three silver, and two bronze medals, giving him a long-standing record in the Nordic disciplines.

Queen of the Ice
The Soviet speed skater Lidia Skoblikova won all four gold medals in her discipline during the Innsbruck Winter Games and set three Olympic records in the process.

Dutch Title
The gold medal in the women's figure skating event was taken by Sjoukje Dijkstra from the Netherlands, giving her country its first Olympic gold since London 1948.

Manfred's Win
The former German roller skating champion Manfred Schnelldorfer (GER) is proud of his gold medal won in the men's figure skating competition.

Pepi Pips it
The Austrian Josef "Pepi" Stiegler won the Olympic slalom event by just 14 hundredths of a second and also took third place in the giant slalom.

1 Opening ceremony: Josef Rieder lights the Olympic flame in the Bergisel Stadium. For the first time the Winter torch had been lit in Olympia, Greece, and was relayed across to Innsbruck.

2 Jubilant sisters: In the slalom event, the French girl Marielle Goitschel (pictured) was defeated by her younger sister Christine. Positions were reversed in the giant slalom, where Marielle took gold.

3 Female figure skaters: World champion Sjoukje Dijkstra (HOL) took the gold medal ahead of Regine Heitzer (AUT) and Petra Burka (CAN).

4 Successful season: Manfred Schnelldorfer (GER) won the figure skating event ahead of Alain Calmat (FRA) and Scott Allen (USA). A few weeks later, he also claimed the world championship title.

5 Norwegian treble: Knut Johannesen (NOR) won the 500 metres speed skating event ahead of his team mates Per Ivar Moe and Fred Anton Maier. Over 10,000 metres, Johannesen was defeated by the Swede Jonny Nilsson and by Maier, but still collected his fifth medal.

6 Speed skating star: Over 5000 metres, Lidia Skoblikova (URS) beat her compatriots Irina Yegorova and Tatyana Sidorova. She was again victorious in the 1000 metres event, defeating Yegorova and the Finn Kaija Mustonen. Her third gold medal was won over the 1500 metres distance ahead of Mustonen and Berta Kolokoltseva (URS). She completed her amazing gold medal collection by winning over 3000 metres.

7 Two medals: The ski jump event from the small hill was won by Veikko Kankonnen (FIN) ahead of the Norwegians Toralf Engan and Torgeir Brandtzæg. On the big hill, he added another silver medal when beaten by Engan.

8 Ice hockey jubilation: The Soviet team celebrate their second Olympic title since 1956. The silver was taken by Sweden ahead of Czechoslovakia.

9 French family win: In the giant slalom, Marielle (pictured, gold medal) and Christine Goitschel (silver) swapped their first and second places from the earlier slalom event. Christine shared the silver medal with Jean Saubert (USA).

10 Gold medal for Austria: In the slalom, Pepi Stiegler defeated the Americans William Kidd and James Heuga. In the giant slalom, he took bronze behind French Olympic champion François Bonlieu and Karl Schranz of Austria.

11 Female tobogganing champion: Ortrun Enderlein of Germany won the first women's single-seater luge event. She defeated her team mate Ilse Geisler and Helene Thurrier of Austria.

12 British bobsled win: Tony Nash (pilot) and Robin Dixon in Great Britain I hurtle to victory in the two-man bob to become Britain's first gold medallists at a Winter Olympics for 12 years. In second place were Italy II, with Italy I taking the bronze medal.

13 Three skiing golds: Klaudia Boyarskikh (URS) won golds in the the 5 kilometres Nordic skiing event ahead of Mirja Lehtonen (FIN) and Alevtina Koltchina (URS), the 10 kilometres competition ahead of her team mates Yevdokia Mekshilo and Maria Gusakova, and with the Soviet 3 x 5 kilometres relay team.

14 Finn's Nordic win: Eero Mäntyranta won the 15 and 30 kilometres distances. He added another silver medal with the 4 x 10 kilometres relay team.

15 "King" of Nordic skiing: Sixten Jernberg (SWE) won golds in the 50 kilometres event and with the relay team. He had to settle for bronze over 15 kilometres, behind Eero Mäntyranta (FIN) and Harald Grönningen (NOR).

Tokyo

For the first time, the Olympic Games came to Asia. Tokyo's appointment as host city of the XVIII Olympiad confirmed Japan's readmission to the international community after World War II.

TOKYO HAD BEEN PENCILLED-IN to host the 1940 Olympic Games, but the outbreak of the Sino-Japanese war in 1937 saw its bid fall through. Twenty-six years later, the Japanese organizing committee set new standards in preparing for the Games. The hosts invested heavily in the latest in sports facilities as well as in improving the infrastructure of a city containing ten million inhabitants. The extraordinary architectural design of the swimming stadium led Avery Brundage to call it a "cathedral of sports". Other outstanding new buildings included the judo hall, which was modelled on the style of traditional Japanese temples.

The opening ceremony offered a convincing combination of established and contemporary elements. The first record was broken right away when, watched by the Imperial Japanese family, teams from 93 nations (ten more than in Rome in 1960) paraded into the Meiji stadium. It was to be the last time until 1992 that a combined German team would participate at an Olympic Games. With 377 competitors, the united German squad represented the largest team at the Tokyo Games.

Two events were newly introduced as Olympic disciplines: volleyball (wins for the Soviet men's team and for the Japanese women's team), and the traditional Japanese discipline of judo, where the hosts intended to demonstrate their superiority. However, they had to concede defeat in the most prestigious of the judo events (the open category) to the Dutchman Antonius Geesink.

In the swimming pool, the American Don Schollander won four gold medals and was celebrated as Tokyo's most successful participant. The Soviet gymnast Larissa Latynina crowned her final appearance before retiring with two gold, two silver, and two bronze medals. At three Olympic Games (1956-1964), she was on the podium no less than 18 times. In Tokyo, the Czechoslovakian Vera Cáslavská (three gold medals) became Latynina's successor.

The crowds reacted with great enthusiasm as many new world records were set. The Ethiopian distance runner Abebe Bikila, for example, received a hero's welcome when he successfully defended, in world record time, the Olympic marathon title he had won in Rome four years before. However, the high standards set by athletes at the Tokyo Games led some critics to warn about exaggerated expectations for the future development of all Olympic disciplines.

The Soviet rower Vyacheslav Ivanov won his third consecutive Olympic gold in the single sculls event; a similar feat was achieved by the Australian swimmer Dawn Fraser in the 100 metres freestyle, in which she set a new Olympic record.

Land of the Rising Sun
The symbol of Japan's national flag dominated the poster of the Olympic Games in Tokyo.

Tired Victor
The German athlete Willi Holdorf has to be supported by fellow athletes after the final decathlon event, the 1500 metres. He was rewarded with the gold medal, ahead of Rein Aun (USA) and Hans-Joachim Walde (GER).

King Don
The American swimmer Don Schollander picked up gold medals in two individual and two relay events, the first swimmer to achieve this feat.

Double Victor
In Tokyo, the Soviet track-and-field athlete Tamara Press successfully defended her Olympic shot put title and added the discus gold for good measure.

Lynn's Leap
Britain's Lynn Davies won the long jump gold ahead of reigning champion Ralph Boston. His winning leap was 8.07 metres, just four centimetres further than Boston's best.

Dutch Upset
The Dutch judo star Antonius Geesink was lauded after his Olympic title win in the open category which was expected to be won by one of the Japanese competitors.

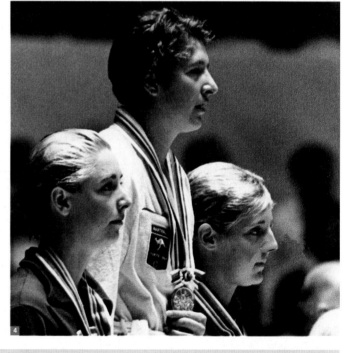

1 Symbol of peace: Yoshinoi Sakai lights the Olympic flame. The student was born near Hiroshima on 6 August 1945, the day when this Japanese city was razed to the ground by an atomic bomb.

2 Freestyle specialist: Over the 100 metres distance, Don Schollander of the United States beat Britain's Bobby McGregor and Hans-Joachim Klein from Germany. In the 400 metres event, he showed his superiority over Frank Wiegand (GER) and Allan Wood (GBR). He added two more gold medals as a member of the 4 x 100 metres and 4 x 200 metres relay teams.

3 Solemn ceremony: During the opening ceremony, hundreds of doves of peace are released in the national stadium.

4 Australian pool gold: In the 100 metres freestyle event, Dawn Fraser (centre) beat Sharon Stouder (USA, left) and Kathleen Ellis (USA, right). As part of the 4 x 100 metres freestyle relay, Fraser won an additional silver medal.

5 Clear victory: Irina Press (URS, seen here during the 80 metres hurdles event) took the pentathlon with a new world record score of 5246 points, ahead of Mary Rand (GBR, 5035 points) and Galina Bystrova (URS, 4956 points)

6 Winner's joy: Following her victory in the women's 800 metres event, Britain's Ann Packer is congratulated by her boyfriend Robbie Brightwell, who was himself a silver medallist with the British 4 x 400 metres relay team.

7 Fourth gold medal: A triple gold medallist in the Melbourne Games back in 1956, Australia's Betty Cuthbert defeated Britain's Ann Packer and fellow Australian Judith Amoore in the first women's 400 metres event.

8 Pole vault "marathon": After seven hours of competition, the pole vault tournament ended with a victory for Fred Hansen (USA). Silver and bronze medals went to the Germans Wolfgang Reinhardt and Klaus Lehnertz.

9 Successful title defence: Peter Snell (NZL, right) successfully defended his Olympic 800 metres title, ahead of Bill Crothers (USA, second from left) and the Kenyan Wilson Kiprugut (third from left).

10 Versatile athlete: Britain's Mary Rand took the long jump with a new world record performance of 6.76 metres. She took the silver medal in the pentathlon, and was a bronze medallist with the British 4 x 100 metres relay team, behind Poland and the USA.

1 **The way to the top:** Joe Frazier (USA) shows off his gold medal after winning the heavyweight boxing competition at Tokyo. He defeated West Germany's Hans Huber in the final. Frazier went on to fight as a professional in an era that boasted Muhammad Ali (who as Cassius Clay won the 1960 light-heavyweight gold) and George Foreman, who was Olympic heavyweight boxing champion at Mexico City in 1968. Nevertheless "Smokin' Joe" Frazier stood out as a great boxer even in this company and had a stint as undisputed world heavyweight champion from 1970, when he beat Jimmy Ellis, to 1973, when he was defeated by George Foreman. Frazier fought three epic duels with Muhammad Ali, including the "Thriller in Manila" in September 1975, which Ali won to retain his title. Several Olympic champions have gone on to win world titles, including Floyd Patterson (USA, middleweight gold, 1952), Sugar Ray Leonard (USA, light-welterweight gold, 1976), Michael Spinks (USA, middleweight gold, 1976), Leon Spinks (USA, light-heavyweight gold, 1976), and Lennox Lewis (CAN, super-heavyweight gold, 1988).

2 **Repeating his Olympic title win:** Twelve years after his victory in Helsinki, the Frenchman Pierre Jonquères d'Oriola took the show jumping title again. On this occasion, it was the turn of Hermann Schridde (GER) and Britain's Peter Robeson to be defeated by the Frenchman. The team event was won by the Germans ahead of France and Italy.

3 **Successful German dressage:** Harry Boldt, Reiner Klimke, and Josef Neckermann (GER, centre) won the dressage gold medal ahead of Switzerland (left) and the Soviet Union (right). The individual event was won by the Swiss rider Henri Chammartin ahead of Boldt and Sergey Filatov of the Soviet Union. The Italian Mauro Checcoli won the three-day event, with Carlos Moratorio (ARG) taking silver and Fritz Ligges (GER) taking the bronze. The Italians had further success in the team event, where they took the gold medal ahead of the US and German teams.

4 **Olympic judo debut:** The first Olympic judo competition saw world champion Antonius Geesink (HOL, left) take the open category by beating his world championship final opponent, Akio Kaminaga of Japan. The bronze medal was jointly secured by the Australian Theodore Boronovskis and Klaus Glahn (GER).

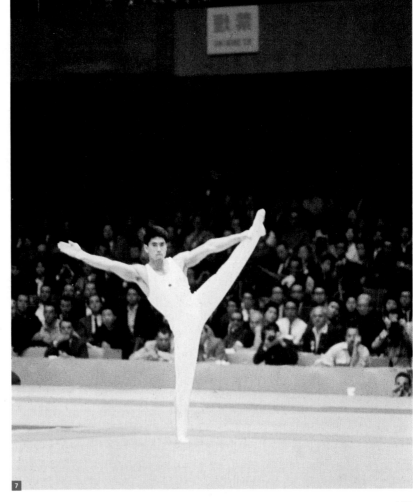

5 Cáslavská takes over: With three gold medals and one silver, the Czechoslovakian Vera Cáslavská was seen as the successor to gymnastics star Larissa Latynina (URS). Cáslavská won the combined exercises ahead of Latynina and Polina Astakova (URS). In the horse vault, she took the gold ahead of Latynina and Birgit Rodochla (GER), who shared silver with identical points. Cáslavská secured her third gold medal in the balance beam event, defeating Soviet team mates Tamara Manina and Latynina. A silver medal was added in the team competition behind the Soviets and ahead of the Japanese. After her four golds in 1968, she controversially spoke out against the events surrounding the quelling of the Prague uprising. In 1990, she became chairwoman of the Czech NOC and in 1995 became an IOC member.

6 Last Olympic Games: At her third Olympic Games, Larissa Latynina (URS, centre) won her third successive gold medal in the floor event, shrugging off opposition from the silver and bronze medallists Polina Astakova (URS) and Anikó Jánosi (HUN). Apart from her second gold medal in the team competition, Latynina also added two silvers in the individual combined exercises and in the horse vault as well as two bronze medals in the balance beam and asymmetrical bars events. With a tally of 18 Olympic medals (nine golds), Latynina is the most successful Olympic athlete ever.

7 Triumph for the hosts: In front of his home crowd, the Japanese Yukio Endo was the most successful male gymnast in Tokyo. In the individual combined exercises, he won ahead of the joint silver medallists Shuji Tsurumi (JPN), Boris Shakhlin (URS), and Viktor Lisitsky (URS). In the bars event, Endo was again victorious, this time beating his compatriot Tsurumi and Franco Menichelli of Italy. Endo secured his third gold medal with the Japanese team who won ahead of the USSR and Germany in the team event. In the floor event, Endo shared the silver medal with Lisitsky behind Menichelli.

Grenoble

Hosting the X Winter Olympics provided Grenoble with an economic boost. However, the long distances between the different venues created problems for athletes and spectators alike.

BEFORE THE INDUSTRIAL CITY OF Grenoble was able to become a suitable venue for the X Winter Games, large amounts of money needed to be invested in the construction of new sports facilities and an improved infrastructure. Even though this money was spent, Grenoble itself still did not have sufficient sports facilities, so competitions took place in the whole of the surrounding region, and athletes were accommodated in seven different Olympic villages. Although some critics complained that this meant the Games could not be considered as a true meeting of the "youth of the world", and that many spectators had to travel a long way for particular competitions, the Games were a triumph for the French.

The opening ceremony, conducted by the French president Charles de Gaulle, was held in a stadium whose improvised stands stood on steel girders. This was the first time at a Winter Games that two separate German teams paraded into the stadium. They were united only by their black, red, and yellow flag bearing the five Olympic rings, and a joint anthem (Beethoven's "Song of Joy"). During the competition, relationships between the two teams were decidedly frosty.

For the first time, the IOC ordered drug tests to be carried out after each competition, as well as introducing gender testing for women.

Twelve years after the triple win in alpine skiing competitions by the Austrian Toni Sailer, the Frenchman Jean-Claude Killy equalled this achievement and the Games were often referred to as the "Killympics". However, the 24-year-old earned his slalom win through the disqualification, for missing gates, of the Austrian Karl Schranz and the Norwegian Haakon Mjoen who had been ahead of him. Schranz was granted a re-run when it was shown he had been

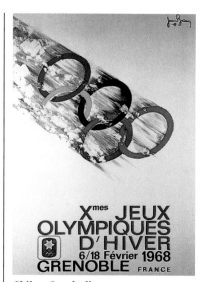

Skiing Symbolism
The five Olympic rings featured on the official poster of the X Winter Games in Grenoble were shown as though in a fast downhill skiing competition.

interfered with during his run. But his faster time was still not allowed as the interference was found to have taken place after he had missed the gates. Killy retired after the Games. His contribution to the organization of the 1992 Winter Games in Albertville earned him the highest Olympic distinction, and in 1995 he became a member of the International Olympic Committee.

In the luge, the female East German competitors reigning champion Ortrun Enderlein, Angela Knösel, and Anna-Maria Müller were disqualified for warming up the runners on their sledges before the race to achieve faster times.

The speed skating was once more dominated by the Dutch: Cornelis Verkerk won gold over 1500 metres and silver over 5000 metres; Carolina Geijssen took gold over 1000 metres and a silver medal over 1500 metres; Johanna Schut secured her win in the 3000 metres event. In the bobsled, Italy's Eugenio Monti won two golds at the age of 40.

French Home Win
In front of her home crowd Marielle Goitschel won the women's slalom. She had been runner-up to her sister Christine four years before.

Czech Mate
Jiri Raska won the gold medal in the small hill ski jump event. A week later, the Czech finished second on the big hill.

Keller Ahead
The surprise winner of the Nordic combined competition was Franz Keller of West Germany. Alois Kälin of Switzerland was second, and Andreas Kunz of East Germany third.

Swedish Honours
Toini Gustafsson of Sweden (pictured on the left with her team mate Barbro Martinsson) won the 5 and 10 kilometers Nordic skiing events and added a silver in the 3 and 5 kilometres cross-country relay.

1. Italian gold: Eugenio Monti and Luciano de Paolis secured their gold medal in the two-man bob ahead of West Germany I and Romania I. Having clocked an identical overall time to that of the West Germans after the four runs, the fastest time set by the Italians in the last run secured their win. Five days later, Monti and de Paolis claimed their second title, this time together with Mario Armano and Roberto Zandonella in the four-man bob, ahead of Austria I and Switzerland I. After his silver medal win in the two-man in Cortina d'Ampezzo in 1956 and his two bronze medals in Innsbruck in 1964, these two Olympic titles constituted the crowning achievement of 40-year-old Monti's Olympic bobsled career.

2. Favourite takes gold: The world record holder Erhard Keller (FRG) won the 500 metres speed skating sprint in 40.3 seconds. Magne Thomassen of Norway and Richard McDermott (USA) shared the silver, finishing 0.2 seconds adrift of Keller.

3. Two medals for Canada: In the giant slalom, Nancy Greene of Canada defeated the French skier Annie Famose and the Swiss Fernande Bochatay. The defending champion, Marielle Goitschel of France, could manage only seventh place. Two days earlier, Greene had won the slalom silver

behind Goitschel and ahead of Famose. In the downhill, Famose missed out on the chance of a medal when she finished fifth behind Olga Pall of Austria, Isabelle Mir (FRA), Christl Haas, and Brigitte Seiwald (both AUT).

4. Successful title defence: Despite this 4-5 defeat at the hands of the eventual silver medallists Czechoslovakia, the Soviet ice hockey team went on to successfully defend their Olympic title. The Czech team missed out on a possible gold medal win when they were held to a 2-2 draw by Sweden and then beaten 2-3 by the bronze medal winners, Canada. The Soviet team, for their part, completely outclassed the Canadians, handing out a 5-0 thrashing.

5. Flying to gold: The gold medal winner in the ski jump from the small hill was Jiri Raska (TCH). Silver and bronze medals were taken by the Austrians Reinhold Bachler and Baldur Preiml respectively. Raska added a silver medal in the big hill event.

6. Surprise winner: Experts were taken by surprise and the form-book was totally upset when Vladimir Belusov (pictured) won the ski jump from the big hill in front of 58,000 spectators. He defeated the Czech Jiri Raska and Lars Grini of Norway. This title win in Grenoble was to remain the

Soviet ski jumper's sole international success.

7 Swiss athlete defeated: The Nordic combined athlete Alois Kälin of Switzerland had to settle for a silver medal behind his West German rival Franz Keller. His clear win in the 15 kilometres event proved to be too little too late to catch up with the German, who had established a commanding lead after the ski jump event. In the end, Keller had a 1.05-point lead over his rival.

8 Scandinavians broken: The Italian Francesco Nones won the 30 kilometres cross-country skiing title ahead of Odd Martinsen of Norway and the Finn Eero Mäntyranta. Nones was the first athlete not from Scandinavia or the USSR to win a gold medal in a cross-country skiing event.

9 German Nordic win: Franz Keller (FRG) became Olympic champion in the Nordic combined competition. With a narrow lead, he left second and third places to Alois Kälin of Switzerland and Andreas Kunz of East Germany respectively.

10 Killy cleans up: Jean-Claude Killy (centre) was the first alpine skier to repeat the Austrian Toni Sailer's 1956 feat of winning all three alpine skiing events. The Frenchman took the downhill title ahead of his compatriot Guy Périllat and the Swiss skier Jean-Daniel Dätwyler. He had failed to

finish in the same event at Innsbruck four years earlier. In a slalom event shrouded by dense fog, he defeated the two Austrians Herbert Huber and Alfred Matt. Killy was happy to secure a third gold in the giant slalom competition, which he won ahead of Willy Favre of Switzerland (left) and Heinrich Messner of Austria (right).

11 Twilight gold medals: Following their 1964 title win, the gold medallists in the pairs figure skating event were once again the Soviet married couple, Ludmilla Belousova and Oleg Protopopov. Their team mates Tatyana Shuk and Aleksander Gorelik took the silver medal ahead of the West German couple Margot Glockshuber and Wolfgang Danne. During 1968, the Soviet Olympic champions also took their fourth European and world championship titles in a row. Belousova and Protopopov defected to Switzerland and turned professional. The pair's comeback attempt in 1971 was unsuccessful.

12 Austrian success: Following his Olympic figure skating title, Wolfgang Schwarz was another skater who moved on to pursue a professional career in a figure skating show. The silver medal was taken by the American Timothy Woods ahead of Patrick Péra of France. The women's event was won by the American Peggy Fleming ahead of the East German skater Gaby Seyfert and Hana Maskovà of Czechoslovakia.

Mexico City

Mexico City's high altitude made life difficult for distance runners, but in the "explosive" events, the XIX Olympiad was a festival of record breaking, with 34 world and 38 Olympic records being set.

THE INCREASING INFLUENCE OF politics on society, which had been evident in many countries during the late 1960s, played its part in the run-up to the 1968 Summer Olympic Games. Before the opening of the Games, complaints by ordinary Mexicans that the exorbitant amounts of money being invested in facilities could not be justified when placed alongside Mexico's own social problems culminated in violent riots. Police and army units were forced to quell protests led by Mexican students.

Arguments also resulted from the question of South Africa's participation at these Games; the majority of black African countries threatened a boycott if South Africa participated. The IOC eventually gave in to the pressure and withdrew its invitation to South Africa's athletes. As a result of IOC resolutions, two separate German teams paraded into the stadium beneath one flag for the first time at a Summer Olympics. And the Mexican hurdler Norma Enriqueta Basilio de Sotela became the first woman to light the Olympic flame.

Controversy would also continue once the competitions had begun. The medal ceremony for the winners of the men's 200 metres, for example, turned into a political demonstration. During the playing of the American national anthem, the US sprinters Tommie Smith and John Carlos raised their black-gloved fists, a symbol of the radical Black Power movement which had been fighting for the equal rights of black citizens in the USA. The team's management banned the two athletes from the national team and sent them home.

The avalanche of first-class performances during the Games was mainly a result of Mexico City's high altitude (almost 2240 metres). The altitude issue had dominated much of the pre-Games discussion, the consensus being that athletes from lowland

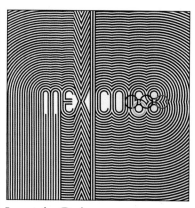

Innovative Design
The specially commissioned poster for the XIX Summer Games in Mexico City.

countries would be at a disadvantage in Mexico City. However, several weeks of high altitude training for many of these athletes led to an increased oxygen supply to the muscles and enhanced performances as a result.

In the sprint events, American athletes were dominant. Olympic champion Jim Hines set a new world record of 9.9 seconds for the 100 metres. This was later officially recognized as an inaugural electronic timing record of 9.95 seconds. In the running events from 1500 metres up to the marathon, African athletes established themselves as world beaters. However, the most outstanding track-and-field performance was achieved by the American Bob Beamon. He improved the world long jump record by a staggering 55 centimetres to 8.90 metres. It was not until 23 years later that his compatriot Mike Powell (at 8.95 metres) managed to improve on Beamon's "leap into the 21st century".

It was not so much Dick Fosbury's (USA) winning high jump of 2.24 metres itself that caused a sensation in Mexico City, but his innovative technique. The so-called "Fosbury Flop" – with the high jumper attempting to clear the bar shoulders first – revolutionized high jumping and replaced the conventional straddle technique.

Legendary Leap
With a jump of 8.90 metres, the American long jumper Bob Beamon set an historic world record which remained unbeaten until 1991.

Record Success
Al Oerter of the United States won his fourth Olympic discus title and became the first Olympic athlete to win four consecutive titles in the same event.

Prolific Medallist
The Czech gymnast Vera Cáslavská won four gold and two silver medals and became the "queen" of the Games. She added these to the three gold medals and one silver secured in Tokyo four years earlier.

Triple Champion
In the pool, the 16-year-old American Debbie Meyer secured three gold medals in the freestyle events and became the first swimmer to take three golds in individual events.

Sprint Nation
Jim Hines (USA) won the 100 metres final and picked up a second gold medal with the 4 x 100 metres relay team to reinforce American dominance in the sprints.

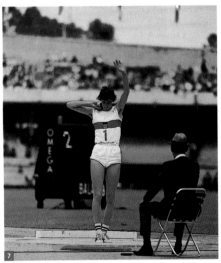

1 **Colourful opening:** At the opening ceremony, hundreds of balloons are released into the sky.

2 **Hemery victorious:** Britain's David Hemery comes home to win the 400 metres hurdles gold in a new world record time of 48.12 seconds. Fellow Briton John Sherwood was third.

3 **Black demonstration:** During the medal ceremony for the 200 metres, Olympic champion Tommie Smith (centre) and the third-placed

John Carlos (right, both USA) raise their black-gloved fists. The US team management did not tolerate this demonstration for black rights and sent both sprinters back to the USA. On the left is the silver medallist Peter Norman (AUS).

4 **Africans win:** The field of 5000 metres athletes is led by Ron Clarke (AUS), who eventually finished in fifth place. In the closing stages, the Tunisian Mohamed Gammoudi (second from right) sprinted past the Kenyan Kipchoge Keino (third from right) to take the gold.

5 **Lillian Board:** The hugely talented Lillian Board (left) won 400 metres silver behind Colette Besson (FRA, centre). Tragically, the "golden girl" of British athletics died of cancer in 1970.

6 **Smiling winner:** The gold medallist over 1500 metres, Kipchoge Keino (KEN, right), and the runner-up Jim Ryun (USA) at the medal ceremony. The bronze medal went to Bodo Tümmler (FRG).

7 **Pentathlon excitement:** Ingrid Becker (FRG, seen here in the shot event) secured her

pentathlon gold medal only in the final 200 metres event when she pushed the leading Austrian Liese Prokop and Annamária Tóth of Hungary into second and third positions respectively.

8 **Winning flop technique:** Richard "Dick" Fosbury (USA) invented the "Fosbury Flop" and used it to become Olympic high jump champion. The silver medal was taken by Edward Caruthers (USA) ahead of Valentin Gavrilov (URS).

9 **Two East German golds:** Start of the 100 metres

backstroke final, which was won by Roland Matthes ahead of the Americans Charles Hickcox and Ron Mills. Matthes secured his second gold medal in the 200 metres backstroke. He completed his medal collection with a silver in the 4 x 100 metres medley relay.

10 **USA victorious:** In the 4 x 200 metres freestyle relay, the USA proved to be invincible. The silver medal went to Australia ahead of the Soviet quartet.

11 **Double champion:** Don McKenzie (USA, bottom) wins

the 100 metres breaststroke. McKenzie took his second gold with the American 4 x 100 metres medley relay team.

12 **Freestyle specialist:** Debbie Meyer (USA) won three gold medals in the 200, 400, and 800 metres freestyle events.

13 **Highboard diving medals:** Klaus Dibiasi (ITA, second left) picks up the gold medal ahead of Alvaro Gaxiola (MEX, left) and Edwin Young (USA, second right). In the springboard event, the Italian took silver behind Bernie Wrightson (USA).

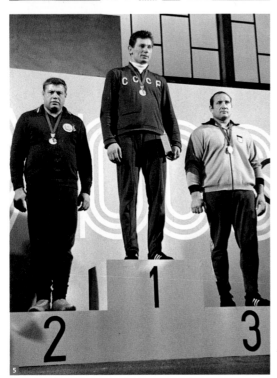

1 Finnegan's gold: Chris Finnegan, Britain's Olympic middleweight champion, sports his gold medal as he arrives at Heathrow airport. He later turned professional and won the British and European titles.

2 German riding success: Josef Neckermann, Liselott Linsenhoff, and Reiner Klimke (FRG, centre) seen during the medal ceremony for the dressage team event, having beaten the Soviet Union (left) and Switzerland (right). Neckermann and Klimke added further medals for West Germany.

3 Last win as an amateur: Following his victory over Ionas Tschepulis (URS) in the heavyweight division, George Foreman pursued a successful career as a professional boxer.

4 Gold medal disallowed: The gold medals are presented to the victorious Danish cycling pursuit team. West Germany's initial win in the 4000 metres team pursuit was disallowed and they were subsequently demoted to the silver medal position. Third place was taken by the Italian team.

5 Strongmen: In the freestyle wrestling, heavyweight Alexander Medved (URS, centre) took gold ahead of Osman Duraliev (BUL, left) and Wilfried Dietrich (FRG, right).

6 Four gymnastics golds: Vera Cáslavská (TCH) won the gold medal in the horse vault, with Erika Zuchold (GDR) second and Zinaida Voronina (URS) third. In the asymmetrical bars event, she beat Karin Janz (GDR) and Voronina. In the floor event, Cáslavská shared her title with Larissa Petrik (URS). Her fourth gold came in the combined exercises, defeating Voronina and Natalya Kuchinskaya (URS).

7 Football champions: Hungary (red jerseys) took the gold by beating Bulgaria 4–1.

8 Japanese triumph: In the rings event, Mikhail Voronin (URS) and the Japanese Sawao Kato had to surrender to Akinori Nakayama's (JPN, pictured) superiority; he also took gold in the parallel bars, the horizontal bar, and the team events. He added a silver medal in the floor event and a bronze in the combined exercises.

9 Dutch winner: Olympic single sculls champion Henri Jan Wienese (right) is congratulated by the runner-up, Jochen Meissner (FRG, left).

10 Jubilation in Mexico: The 17-year-old Mexican Felipe Muñoz secured a popular win in front of his home crowd in the 200 metres breaststroke final, ahead of Vladimir Kossinsky (URS) and Brian Job (USA). It was the hosts' first gold medal.

11 German eight-man win: The West German rowing eight picked up the gold medal ahead of Australia and the USSR.

Sapporo

The award of the XI Winter Games meant success at the third time of asking for Sapporo. The city had previously bid for the 1940 Games, which did not take place, and for the 1968 celebration.

THE JAPANESE GOVERNMENT regarded the XI Winter Games in Sapporo as a prestige event and invested enormous sums of money in the construction of new sports facilities. As a result, these Games turned out to be the most extravagant and expensive so far, but this was offset by selling the rights for television coverage; this constituted the main source of income for the organizers. While 2.6 million US dollars had been sufficient for purchasing the television transmission rights at the last Winter Games in Grenoble, this amount went up by more than 300 per cent to 8.47 million. Two thirds of this money was netted by the organizers.

The day before the opening ceremony, the "Schranz case" hit the headlines. The Austrian alpine skier Karl Schranz had to leave the Olympic village for breaking amateur regulations. At a time when many top skiers were making money from the sport – such as through sponsorships – Schranz was singled out for punishment. The ban was meant to be a warning against the increasing commercialism of sports, as outlined by the IOC president Avery Brundage in the year when his term was coming to an end. His demand to ban some 40 other alleged "professional" athletes from competing was rejected by a majority of IOC members.

The issue of amateur status also cast a shadow over the ice hockey tournament. The Canadians had intended to include several players in their team who were employed in the North American professional ice hockey league, as East European countries were also sending so-called state-sponsored amateurs to the Games, and the Canadians regarded them as *de facto* professionals. After the International Ice Hockey Federation and the IOC had vigorously turned down Canada's request, the Canadian ice hockey team made the decision to pull out of the event.

Island Games
The official poster of the XI Winter Olympic Games, which took place from 3 to 13 February in Sapporo, the capital of the Japanese island of Hokkaido. The resort was renowned for its winter sports facilities.

The Games themselves offered some sporting surprises. For the first time in the history of the Winter Games, all three medal positions in one discipline were taken by athletes from a non-European country: Yukio Kasaya, Akitsugu Konno, and Seiji Aochi won the small hill ski jump for Japan. Poland earned its first ever gold medal, with Wojciech Fortuna winning the ski jump from the big hill, as did Spain, through Francisco Fernandez Ochoa's victory in the slalom.

Winning three gold medals each, the Soviet cross-country skier Galina Kulakova and the Dutch speed skater Ard Schenk were the Games' most successful competitors. Schenk missed out on a fourth gold when he fell at the start of the 500 metres event. For the last time, figure skaters with a good compulsory programme benefited from the 50-50 judging system. Thus, the Austrian Beatrix Schuba won the gold medal even though she had been in only ninth position after the free programme.

Ard Luck
With three gold medals over 1500 metres, 5000 metres, and 10,000 metres under his belt, the Dutch speed skater Ard Schenk became the most successful male athlete of the Winter Games in Sapporo.

Gustavo's Gold
Gustavo Thöni picked up Italy's first gold medal in alpine skiing for 20 years by winning the giant slalom; he also collected a silver medal in the slalom.

Swiss Double
Marie-Theres Nadig (SUI) was a jubilant gold medal winner in the giant slalom event; she had already won the downhill event three days earlier.

X-Country Golds
Winning three gold medals in the 5 kilometres, 10 kilometres, and 3 x 5 kilometres cross-country skiing events, Galina Kulakova (URS) was the most successful female athlete in Sapporo.

Keller Again
Erhard Keller of West Germany successfully defended his 1968 Olympic 500 metres speed skating title and set a new Olympic record for good measure.

1 **Opening ceremony:** In Sapporo's Makomanai ice stadium, the Japanese emperor Hirohito declares the XIth Winter Games open.

2 **Closing ceremony:** The Olympic flag is folded together, symbolizing the end of the Winter Games. It was due to be handed over to Denver, the host of the next Games in 1976; however, it was kept in Sapporo for another four years until just before the next Olympiad.

3 **Favourite wins:** Ondrej Nepela (TCH) became figure skating champion ahead of Sergey Tchetveroukhin (URS) and the Frenchman Patrick Péra. During the Olympic season, Nepela added to his world (1971–73) and European (1969–73) championship titles.

4 **Austrian skating gold:** The European and world champion, Beatrix Schuba, took the women's figure skating title ahead of the Canadian Karen Magnussen. The bronze medal was won by Janet Lynn (USA).

5 **Champions victorious:** The figure skating pair of Irina Rodnina and Aleksey Ulanov (URS), who were undefeated in all world and European championships since 1969, beat compatriots Ludmilla Smirnova and Andrey Suraikin, with Manuela Gross and Uwe Kagelmann (GDR) third.

6 **New record and gold:** The speed skater Monika Pflug (FRG) set a new Olympic record over 1000 metres with a time of 1:31.40 minutes, winning by 0.21 seconds from

Atje Keulen-Deelstra (HOL) who was only 0.01 seconds ahead of the American Anne Henning. Pflug was a competitor in five Olympic Games and finished her Olympic career in Calgary in 1988, where she took seventh place in the 500 metres event.

7 **Fastest speed skater:** Ahead of the Olympic Games, the speed skater Erhard Keller (FRG) had lost his world record over 500 metres (38.3 seconds) to the Finn Leo Linkovesi (38.0 seconds). However, in Sapporo, the West German regained the initiative and successfully defended his 1968 Olympic title by defeating the Swede Hasse Börjes, and Valeri Muratov of the Soviet Union. Linkovesi was able to finish in only sixth position.

8 **First gold for Spain:** The first gold medal for Spain at a Winter Olympic Games was won by Francisco Fernandez Ochoa in the slalom competition. He defeated the Italian cousins Gustavo (silver medal) and Rolando Thöni (bronze medal). This was also the first time since 1948 that Austria did not take a medal in the slalom. The women's slalom was taken by the American Barbara Ann Cochran.

9 **Successful alpine skier:** The Italian Gustavo Thöni on his way to victory in the giant slalom, beating the Swiss skiers Edmund Bruggmann and Werner Mattle. Thöni also won the silver medal in the slalom and was to return to the limelight 16 years later as coach of the double Olympic champion, the great Alberto Tomba (ITA).

10 **Swiss gold and silver:** Bernhard Russi clocked the best time in the downhill to become the first Swiss skier to win this event. His compatriot Roland Collombin took the silver ahead of Heinrich Messner (AUT).

11 **Third Soviet gold medal:** The Soviet ice hockey team receive their medals after winning the Olympic title for the third time in a row. The silver medal went to the Americans, with the Czechs, whose 14-1 victory over Poland was the most emphatic win of the tournament, taking bronze.

12 **Double victory:** The two-man bobsled event was taken by the West German duo Wolfgang Zimmerer and Peter Utzschneider ahead of their compatriots Horst Floth and Pepi Bader. The bronze medal was taken by Switzerland I, driven by Jean Wicki and Edy Hubacher. In the four-man event, West Germany I, comprising team members Stefan Gaisreiter, Walter Steinbauer, Utzschneider, and pilot Zimmerer, took the bronze medal after being beaten by Switzerland I and Italy I.

13 **X-country skiing wins:** Galina Kulakova (URS) outclassed her rivals in the 5 kilometres and 10 kilometres events. Together with her Soviet team mates Lyubov Mukhatshova and Alevtina Olyunina, she also secured a commanding relay win ahead of Finland and Norway.

Munich

The XX Summer Olympic Games were intended as a cheerful, peaceful occasion. Instead, a terrorist attack by Palestinian guerrillas on Israel's team in the Olympic village brought shock and outrage.

ELEVEN ATHLETES, FIVE TERRORISTS, and one policeman were killed during the kidnapping of Israeli athletes at Munich and the subsequent attempt to rescue them. Even though numerous competitors and officials had advocated abandoning the Games after the tragedy, the IOC decided to continue the competitions, thus conforming to the wishes of the Israeli government and team who refused to give in to any Palestinian pressure. Avery Brundage demanded: "The Games must go on." The IOC president, who was due to retire after these Games and hand over the presidency to Lord Killanin, would not allow the peaceful spirit of the Olympic movement to be ruined by "a handful of terrorists". Despite his appeals, however, several athletes left Munich, concerned about inadequate security. The day after the memorial service, competitions were continued, with the Olympic flag at half-mast. All supporting events were called off.

But controversy did not stop there. Following the banning of South Africa and a threat of boycott by 27 African nations, the IOC were now forced to expel Rhodesia – admitted into the Olympic fold a year earlier and having already sent a team of 30 athletes to Munich – for its apartheid politics.

In Munich, indoor handball had its debut and became one of 195 Olympic disciplines. After its 1964 premiere, judo also established itself as a permanent sport while archery again returned to the Olympic schedule, having enjoyed a short Olympic spell between 1900 and 1908, and a brief reappearance in 1920.

With 20 gold medals, the East Germans confirmed their claim to be the third sports nation in the world behind the USSR (50 gold medals) and the USA (33 wins). In subsequent years, East Germany would go on to improve its

The £300 Million Olympiad
The sensational tent construction covering the Olympic park and the Olympic tower in Munich are the themes illustrated on the official poster for the XX Olympic Games.

world standing even further. West Germany won 40 medals (13 gold, 11 silver, and 16 bronze) and finished in fourth position in the medals table.

The sporting highlight of the Games was the performance of the American swimmer Mark Spitz. He won four gold medals in world record times in the 100 and 200 metres freestyle and in the 100 and 200 metres butterfly. He also took golds in the 4 x 100 and 4 x 200 metres freestyle relays, and in the 4 x 100 metres medley relay, thus becoming the most successful swimmer of all time. The female swimming star was the Australian Shane Gould, who picked up three gold medals as well as one silver and a bronze.

The Soviet gymnast Olga Korbut quickly became the crowds' favourite. The diminutive Korbut thrilled audiences with victories in the floor and balance beam events and took a silver medal in the asymmetrical bars event. She added a third gold in the combined exercises team event.

Star Spitz
The winner of seven gold medals in the swimming pool, Mark Spitz (USA) is hoisted aloft by his team mates.

Star Performer
The 17-year-old Soviet gymnast Olga Korbut hit the headlines by winning three gold medals and establishing Soviet dominance in the female gymnastics events.

Gould's Golds
By securing three gold medals, one silver, and a bronze, Australia's Shane Gould became the most successful female swimmer at the Munich Games.

European Judo Win
Wim Ruska of Holland won two judo victories at Munich – in the heavyweight and open categories.

Track Success
Anchor runner Heide Rosendahl (right) and her team mate Ingrid Mickler are elated about the gold medal won by West Germany in the 4 x 100 metres relay event.

1 **Stunning arenas:** The Olympic Stadium and the adjacent park with general sports and swimming halls set new architectural standards for Olympic arenas.

2 **In Nurmi's footsteps:** The Finnish policeman Lasse Viren (front) won the 5000 metres (in a new Olympic best time) and the 10,000 metres in a world record time. In doing so, he followed in the footsteps of his compatriot Paavo Nurmi, who won nine gold medals between 1920 and 1928.

3 **Narrow victory:** The new Olympic champion in the javelin was Klaus Wolfermann (FRG). With a distance of 90.48 metres, he took first place ahead of Janis Lusis from the USSR (90.46 metres) and Bill Schmidt (84.42 metres) of the USA.

4 **Marathon win:** Frank Shorter (USA) wins the marathon. Clocking a time of 2:12:19.8 hours, he won by over two minutes from the Belgian

Karel Lismont (2:14:31.8). Third place went to "Mamo" Wolde of Ethiopia.

5 **Fastest walker:** Bernd Kannenberg of West Germany was the winner in the 50 kilometres walk. He defeated the Soviet athlete Venyamin Soldatenko and the American Larry Young.

6 **Winning 16-year-old:** Experts regarded the Olympic high jump title win by the German Ulrike Meyfarth ahead of the Bulgarian Yordanka Blagoyeva and the Austrian Ilona Gusenbauer as a sensation. At the time, Meyfarth was the youngest gold medallist in an individual track-and-field event, and her winning height of 1.92 metres equalled Gusenbauer's world record.

7 **Kenya first and second:** Kipchoge Keino won the 3000 metres steeplechase in an Olympic record time ahead of his compatriot Benjamin Jipcho and Tapio Kantanen (FIN).

8 **Three medals:** Heide Rosendahl proved her versatility by winning golds in the long jump and with the West German 4 x 100 metres relay team. She also took a silver medal in the pentathlon behind Mary Peters (GBR).

9 **Favourite wins:** The European champion Valeri Borsov (URS) secured gold in the 100 metres ahead of Robert Taylor (USA) and Lennox Miller (JAM). Three days later, Borsov also won the 200 metres, with Larry Black (USA) and Pietro Mennea (ITA) behind.

10 **Two gold medals:** By beating Raelene Boyle (AUS) and Silvia Chivas (CUB), Renate Stecher (GDR) proved invincible over 100 metres. Five days later, she added a second gold medal in the 200 metres ahead of Boyle and the Olympic champion of 1968, Irena Szewinska (POL). She also took a silver medal with the East German 4 x 100 metres relay team, behind West Germany.

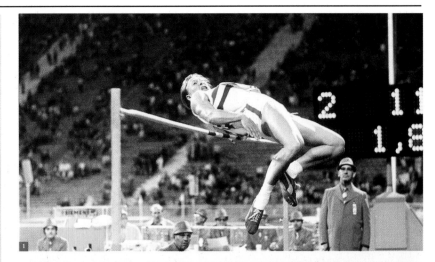

1 Mary rises to the occasion: Mary Peters on her way to becoming Britain's first pentathlon winner. Heide Rosendahl (FRG) and Burglinde Pollak (GDR) were second and third.

2 First round secures gold: In his first attempt in the shot put, the Pole Wladyslaw Komar achieved a distance of 21.18 metres, enough to secure him the gold medal ahead of the American George Woods and Hartmut Briesenick (GDR).

3 Hero of the Games: Winning seven gold medals, Mark Spitz was the most successful competitor of the Games. In the 100 metres freestyle, he beat his compatriot Jerry Heidenreich and Vladimir Bure of the Soviet Union. In the 200 metres freestyle final, he reduced Steven Genter (USA) and Werner Lampe (FRG) to second and third places. His third gold medal in an individual event followed in the 100 metres butterfly, where he beat Bruce Robertson (CAN) and Heidenreich. Over the longer distance of 200 metres in the butterfly, he won again by defeating team mates Gary Hall and Robin Backhaus. His collection of four individual gold medals was complemented by three golds in relay events as a member of what was an all-conquering American squad: they won the 4 x 100 metres freestyle, the 4 x 200 metres freestyle, and the 4 x 100 metres medley relay.

4 Australian star: With a new world record time of 2:03.56 minutes, the Australian Shane Gould won the 200 metres freestyle ahead of the Americans Shirley Babashoff (2:04.33 minutes) and Keena Rothhammer (with a time of 2:04.92 minutes). In the 400 metres freestyle, she could not be contained by the second-placed Italian Novella Calligaris or the bronze medallist Gudrun Wegner (GDR). Gould picked up her third gold medal in the 200 metres medley, where she defeated the favourites Kornelia Ender (GDR) and Lynn Vidali (USA). She also took silver in the 800 metres freestyle and bronze in the 100 metres freestyle behind Sandra Neilson and Babashoff (both USA).

5 Canoeing first: For the first and last time until 1992, slalom canoeing competitions (also known as white-water canoeing) took place. Siegbert Horn from East Germany won the K1 by beating the Austrian Norbert Sattler and his fellow East German team mate Harald Gimpel. The women's event produced more East German success when Angelika Bahmann took the gold medal ahead of Gisela Grothaus and Magdalena Wunderlich from West Germany.

6 Kato's three golds: Sawao Kato (JPN) won the parallel bars event for the first time. In the combined exercise individual and team events he successfully defended the titles he won in 1968. His medal collection was completed by two silvers in the pommel horse event (gold went to Viktor Klimenko, URS) and in the horizontal bar event, where he had to yield to his compatriot Mitsuo Tsukahara.

7 Five gymnastics medals: Karin Janz (GDR) took two golds in the asymmetrical bars and horse vault. Two silver medals followed in the combined exercises individual and team events. In the balance beam event, she had to settle for bronze when she was defeated by Olga Korbut and Tamara Lazakovitsch (both URS).

8 Fight for gold medal: In the light flyweight (Greco-Roman style) final, the Romanian wrestler Gheorghe Berceanu (blue jersey) defeated the Iranian Rahim Ahabadi.

9 Darling Olga: Olga Korbut of the Soviet Union won two gold medals in the floor event and in the balance beam event. In the latter she beat Tamara Lazakovitsch (URS) and Karin Janz (GDR). She picked up her third gold in the combined exercises team event. In the asymmetrical bars, Korbut shared second place with Erika Zuchold (GDR), behind gold medallist Janz.

10 Dutch victory: Judo star Wim Ruska (HOL) celebrates gold medals in the heavyweight (above 93 kilograms) and open categories. He was the only athlete to win two judo golds.

1 Wins for British riders: Richard Meade (centre on Laurieston) won the gold medal in the individual three-day event ahead of Italy's Alessandro Argenton (left, on Woodland) and Sweden's Jan Jonsson (right, on Sarajevo). Great Britain also won the team event ahead of the USA and West Germany. The British team consisted of Richard Meade (on Laurieston), Mary Gordon-Watson (on Cornishman), Bridget Parker (on Cornish Gold), and Lieutenant Mark Phillips (on Great Ovation).

2 Narrow decision: The water polo final between the USSR (white caps) and the eventual silver medallists Hungary ended in a 3-3 draw. In the final placings, the Soviet Union were established as Olympic champions on the grounds of their better goal difference. The bronze medal was taken by the United States.

3 First hockey gold: For the first time in the history of the Olympic Games, West Germany (white jerseys) won the hockey tournament. In the final, they dethroned title holders Pakistan by beating them 1-0.

4 Favourites beaten: The football tournament ended with the Polish team (red jerseys) taking the gold medal when they beat the three-times Olympic champions (1952, 1964, and 1968) Hungary 2-1 in the final. The bronze medal was shared by the Soviet Union and East Germany after they drew their third place play-off.

5 Gold medal for quartet: The West German quartet of (from left) Jürgen Colombo, Günter Haritz, Udo Hempel, and Günter Schumacher won the 4000 metres team pursuit ahead of teams from East Germany and Great Britain.

6 USSR victorious: In the volleyball final, the women's team from Japan (blue jerseys) suffered a 2-3 defeat at the hands of the Soviets. The bronze medal was taken by North Korea. The Japanese men's team were more successful when they beat East Germany 3-1 in the final. Third place was taken by the Soviets.

7 Games are continued: After the memorial service for

the victims of the attack on the Israeli team, the Olympic and national flags flew at half-mast up until the end of the tournament. Although criticized in some quarters for the insensitivity of some of his remarks, IOC president Avery Brundage was successful in advocating that the Games should continue. In addition, the German president Gustav Heinemann appealed to all nations of the world "to overcome hatred" and "to pave the way for reconciliation".

8 Athletes taken hostage: An armed policeman readies his weapon in the Olympic village where Arab terrorists went into hiding with their Israeli hostages. Germany's interior minister Hans-Dietrich Genscher twice negotiated an extension of the time limit set by the terrorists for the fulfilment of their conditions. The terrorists demanded that the Israeli government release 200 Arabs held in Israeli prisons. The kidnappers also demanded a flight for themselves and their hostages from Munich to Egypt. Under the watchful eye of special police units, the kidnappers and their hostages left the Olympic

village and boarded two helicopters that were provided for them on the evening of 5 September 1972.

9 Violent end: The rescue operation carried out by the German police ended in a bloodbath. The helicopters had brought the terrorists and their hostages to Munich's military airbase at Fürstenfeldbruck, where the group intended to board an aircraft. After a shoot-out with police marksmen, three of the guerrillas were killed; the remaining terrorists blew up the helicopters and shot the athletes. In total, the terrorist attack claimed the lives of 11 Israeli athletes, one policeman, and five of the eight terrorists.

10 Munich's mourning: Athletes and officials of the Israeli delegation are overcome with grief during the remembrance service at the Olympic Stadium in honour of their dead compatriots. In his address to the watching world, the Israeli ambassador to Bonn, Eliashiv Ben-Horin, made a plea for people to oppose the politics of killing, kidnapping, and terror. They were troubled times indeed.

Innsbruck

For the second time in 12 years, Innsbruck hosted the Winter Olympic Games. Two Olympic flames were lit in the Bergisel Stadium – one to symbolize the present Games, the other to commemorate 1964.

DENVER WAS THE INITIAL CHOICE to host the XII Winter Olympic Games because the 100th anniversary of the state of Colorado coincided with celebrations for the 200th anniversary of the birth of the United States in 1976. However, a 300 per cent increase in costs, as well as the anticipated environmental damage of winter tourism and the construction of new sports facilities, led to a referendum in which the majority of people voted against the event being hosted in Denver.

It was instead Innsbruck that had the privilege of staging its second Winter Games only 12 years after hosting its first successful games in 1964. The organizers were able to use existing sports facilities, with only minor refurbishments and modernization work needed to upgrade the resort. Projects such as the construction of a motorway through the River Inn valley and the building of publicly funded residential blocks (accommodation for more than 1250 athletes) were brought forward. Funding was partially raised through donations, and Austrian army troops helped out with the construction work.

One idea that was not very well received was that of conducting the medal ceremonies in the ice rink each evening after the day's competitions. The spectators would have preferred to see the medal ceremonies held on the spot.

The first competition of the Games, the blue riband downhill skiing event, was won by the Austrian Franz Klammer. While the hosts had to wait until the last day for another gold medallist (ski jumper Karl Schnabl), German fans were gripped by "Rosi fever". Twenty-five-year-old Rosi Mittermaier, who during her ten-year career had never been able to win a World Cup downhill race, won the downhill and slalom events and took a silver medal in the giant slalom.

In 1975, the International Figure Skating Federation had introduced a

Hosts Once More
The official Olympic poster shows a ski jump hill in front of Tyrolean mountains.

reorganized competition, consisting of a short compulsory programme and a long freestyle programme. Thus, the share of the obligatory section in the overall mark, which was unpopular with most athletes, fell from 50 per cent to 30 per cent. Ice dancing also made its debut as an Olympic discipline; its first gold medal went to the Soviet pair, Ludmilla Pakhomova and Aleksander Gorshkov.

The Dutch continued their long-standing success in the speed skating events. In the men's competitions over distances in excess of 1000 metres, Piet Kleine (gold medal over 10,000 metres and silver medal over 5000 metres) and Hans van Helden (bronze medals over 1500, 5000, and 10,000 metres) took five of the nine medals that were on offer.

The ice hockey tournament had begun before the official opening with a series of preliminary qualifying matches. The Soviet Union, the title holders, benefited when the Czechoslovakian team (who went on to win silver) were deducted one point after their captain, Frantisek Pospisil, was found guilty of taking a banned substance.

Flying Franz
The favourite Franz Klammer withstood intense mental pressure to win the downhill event in front of an expectant home crowd.

Record Breaker
Clocking a new Olympic record time of 14:50.59 minutes over 10,000 metres (ten seconds better than the previous record), the Dutch speed skater Piet Kleine secured gold in style.

Debut Winner
At her first Olympic Games, Raisa Smetanina (URS) won two gold medals in the 10 kilometres and 4 x 5 kilometres cross-country skiing events. She added a silver medal in the 5 kilometres event.

British Victor
Third at the world championships in 1975 and European champion in 1976, the British skater John Curry crowned his amateur career with a gold medal in the men's figure skating competition.

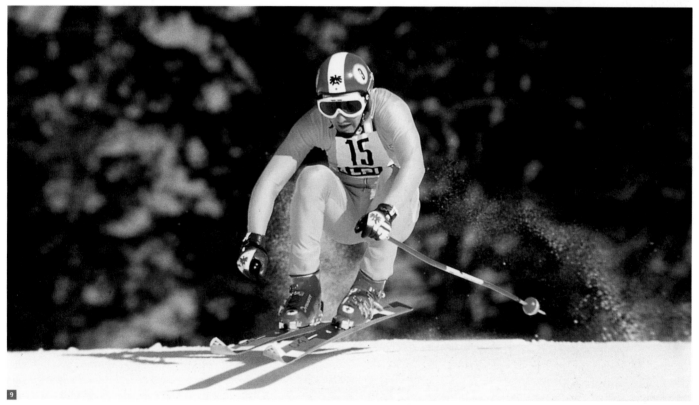

1 Double symbolism: During these Winter Games, two flames were visible above the Bergisel Stadium; one for the current Olympics, the other for Innsbruck's first Games back in 1964.

2 New skating rules: In 1976, the US figure skater Dorothy Hamill won the Olympic title to add to her world championship title, becoming the first Olympic champion under the new figure skating scoring system, which allotted only 30 per cent of marks to the compulsory programme. She

was coached by Carlo Fassi, who also helped Britain's John Curry to Olympic gold in Innsbruck.

3 Skating without jumps: Athletes competed in the ice dance event for the first time in Innsbruck. The discipline had staged its own world championships since 1952. Here the title was won by the Soviet favourites, Ludmilla Pakhomova and Aleksander Gorshkov. They remained unbeaten at the European and world championships later that year.

4 Career change: Speed skater Sheila Young (USA) won a gold medal over 500 metres, a silver medal over 1500 metres, and a bronze over 1000 metres. She retired from speed skating after the Games, but continued to be in the sporting limelight by pursuing a career as a sprint cyclist.

5 East Germans clean up: The luge titles were all taken by athletes from East Germany and competitors from other nations had to be content with silver or bronze medals. The singles were

won by Margit Schumann (pictured) and Detlef Günther; the two-man title went to Hans Rinn and Norbert Hahn.

6 Lucky number 1: In the women's giant slalom, the Canadian Kathy Kreiner clocked a time of 1:29.13 minutes, which meant that she took the title by just 0.12 seconds.

7 Nordic "marathon" win: The Norwegian Ivar Formo dominated the 50 kilometres cross-country skiing and won from

Gert-Dietmar Klause (GDR). However, this gold medal was to be his only international success.

8 Home ski jump victory: On the closing day of the Games, Karl Schnabl thrilled the home crowd when he won a gold medal in the ski jump from the big hill.

9 Austria's great start: On the opening day of the Games, the Austrian downhiller Franz Klammer won the most demanding and prestigious of all alpine disciplines.

After being beset by all manner of problems, including a major boycott, ahead of the event, the XXI Olympic Games, held in the Canadian city of Montreal, were characterized by perfect organization and strict security.

The American Edwin Moses won the Olympic title over 400 metres hurdles with a new world record time of 47.64 seconds. It was the third consecutive time at an Olympics that this record had been broken.

BUILDING CRANES DOMINATED the skyline during the opening ceremony for the XXI Olympiad, with speeches held in both languages of the host nation, English and French. Industrial disputes, an unusually long winter, and a severe lack of funds had made it impossible to finish work on the Olympic facilities in time. As a result, the opening ceremony took place under improvised conditions. To this day the city of Montreal is still repaying debts accrued during these Olympics.

With memories of the terrorist attack in Munich still very fresh in people's minds, the Montreal Olympics were marked by rigid security measures. Commemorating their murdered team mates of four years before, each member of the Israeli delegation paraded into the stadium at the opening ceremony wearing a black armband.

Once again, politics played a major role in these Olympic Games, with 24 of the 116 registered teams boycotting the competition. The explanation given by Guyana and the 22 black African countries who refused to take part was that they objected to New Zealand's participation on the grounds that their rugby team had toured apartheid South Africa. The Taiwanese team withdrew after a disagreement with the Canadians. Also, as in 1971, the IOC reiterated its banning of Rhodesia from the Games due to its own system of apartheid. Overall this meant that the number of athletes participating in Montreal was just over 6000 – 1000 less than had competed at the Munich Games in 1972.

Because the media were mainly interested in the winners of each event, many surprising results were given scant coverage; the silver medals won by the Belgian Ivo van Damme over 800 metres and 1500 metres were just one example.

A New Star
The 14-year-old Romanian gymnast Nadia Comaneci was the crowds' favourite in Montreal. She won three gold medals, a silver, and a bronze.

Montréal 1976

Summer in Canada
The official poster of the Montreal Summer Games featured a design based around the five intertwined Olympic rings.

The fifth place in the marathon taken by the Finn Lasse Viren was another momentous run considering that he had already successfully defended his 5000 and 10,000 metres titles. In doing so, he had earned himself a place in the history books. Although numerous experts expressed their doubts about the value of the running competitions in the absence of the strong African nations, new world and Olympic records on the track showed that standards remained high.

In the swimming competitions, the USA, with 13 gold medals, and East Germany, with 11 wins, dominated. Britain's David Wilkie and the Soviet Marina Kosheveya (both winning their respective 200 metres breaststroke finals) were the only swimmers to upset the US-German monopoly, both swimmers setting new world records for good measure. Women's rowing was admitted for the first time, with East Germany taking four of the six gold medals at stake. Basketball and handball were also new disciplines for women.

British swimming ace David Wilkie powers to victory in the final of the 200 metres breaststroke. Wilkie's time of 2:15.11 minutes was a new world record.

At her fourth Olympic Games, Irena Szewinska (POL) crowned her career with an Olympic title and world record in the 400 metres. She had won the 200 metres event in Mexico eight years before and another gold in the 1964 4 x 100 metres relay.

Lasse Viren (FIN) became the first athlete to successfully defend his Olympic 5000 and 10,000 metres titles. He finished the 5000 metres 30 metres in front of his nearest rival.

1 Second Olympic flame: As had been customary since 1936, the Olympic flame was lit at all Olympic venues, including Kingston on Lake Ontario, where the yachting events took place. These included the Finn-class (gold for Jochen Schürmann of East Germany), the Soling (Denmark), the Tornado (Great Britain), and the Flying Dutchman (West Germany).

2 Triple Soviet medals: In the hammer, Yuriy Sedykh won the gold medal with a distance of 77.52 metres, beating compatriots Alexey Spiridonov (76.08 metres) and Anatoliy Bondarchuk (75.45 metres).

3 World record win: The American Bruce Jenner won the decathlon. The silver medal was picked up by Guido Kratschmer (FRG) ahead of the 1972 gold medal winner, Nikolai Avilov

(URS). In eight of the events, Jenner improved on his own personal best performances. Up until the penultimate event, the three leading competitors were separated by only 76 points. Jenner subsequently increased his lead and improved his own world record by 80 points to 8617 points.

4 Favourite wins: The Olympic high jump champion was world record holder Rosemarie Ackermann (GDR), clearing a height of 1.93 metres. Second and third places were taken by Sara Simeoni (ITA) and Yordanka Blagoyeva (BUL).

5 Years of success: By winning the 400 metres title in 49.29 seconds, the Polish track-and-field athlete Irena Szewinska (No. 277) set a new world record. The East Germans Christina Brehmer (50.51

seconds) and Ellen Streidt (50.55 seconds) had to settle for silver and bronze respectively. During an Olympic career that spanned 16 years (1964–80), Szewinska (née Kirszenstein) amassed a collection of three gold, two silver, and two bronze medals.

6 First-time double: The Cuban Alberto Juantorena (No. 217) celebrates his Olympic 800 metres win. He had only ever run four 800 metres races before the Games, and all of these in 1976. Improving the three-year-old world record held by the Italian Marcello Fiasconaro by 0.2 seconds to 1:43.50 minutes, he defeated Ivo van Damme (BEL) and Richard Wohlhuter (USA). Juantorena completed an outstanding double by winning the 400 metres, beating the Americans Fred Newhouse and Herman Frazier.

7 Sprint record: The finish line of the 100 metres is crossed by Annegret Richter (FRG, lane 7) ahead of the East German title holder Renate Stecher (lane 4) and Richter's team mate Inge Helten (lane 1). Richter had set a new world record time of 11.01 seconds in an earlier heat. Over 200 metres, she added a silver medal when defeated by Bärbel Eckert (GDR); Stecher picked up bronze. Richter's third medal came in the 4 x 100 metres relay event, where the West German team took the silver medal behind the East German runners and ahead of the Soviet quartet.

8 Favourite beaten: The Finnish rower Pertti Karppinen (left) was the surprise Olympic winner in the single sculls. Over the last couple of yards, he overtook the world and European champion Peter-

Michael Kolbe (FRG, nearest the camera). The bronze medal was taken by Joachim Dreifke (GDR). Winning the coxed and coxless pairs, the quadruple sculls, the coxless fours, as well as the eights, East Germany were by far the most successful nation in the men's rowing events. The East German women also achieved success, in the single sculls (Christine Scheiblich), the quadruple sculls, the coxed fours, and the eights.

9 Swimming success: The American John Naber was the first backstroke swimmer to clock a sub-two-minute time over 200 metres when he won in 1:59.19 minutes and beat his compatriots Peter Rocca and Dan Harrigan. He took a further backstroke gold over 100 metres, with Rocca second and Roland Matthes of East Germany third. Two more gold

medals followed when the US 4 x 200 metres freestyle relay team beat the USSR and Great Britain and the 4 x 100 metres medley relay team beat Canada and West Germany. His medal collection was completed by a silver medal in the 200 metres freestyle event, losing out to compatriot Bruce Furniss.

10 Queen of the pool: Kornelia Ender (GDR, top) is overjoyed about her victory in the 100 metres freestyle final, beating Petra Priemer (GDR) and Enith Brigitha (HOL). Ender finished the Games with four gold medals plus a silver medal picked up with the East German freestyle relay team.

11 Kim's golds: Nelli Kim (URS) won golds in the floor, horse vault, and combined exercise team events and a silver in the individual combined.

1   Fencing victories: Alexander Pusch (FRG, right) took the gold medal in the individual épée event. Second and third places were taken by Pusch's team mate Jürgen Hehn (left) and the Hungarian Gyözö Kulcsár. In the team épée event, the West German team were not able to contain the Swedes, who took the gold medal.

2   Team cycling gold: In the 4000 metres team pursuit, the West Germans (from left) Peter Vonhof, Hans Lutz, Günter Schumacher, and Gregor Braun beat the USSR and Great Britain. Braun picked up a second gold medal in the 4000 metres individual pursuit event, with the Dutchman Herman Ponsteen second and Thomas Huschke (GDR) third.

3   Yachting medals: Jörg and Eckart Diesch (FRG) celebrate their gold medal in the Flying Dutchman category ahead of Rodney Pattisson and Julian Brooke Houghton (GBR, left). The Brazilians Reynaldo Conrad and Peter Ficker took third place.

4   Surprise win: Harro Bode and Frank Hübner (FRG) took an unexpected gold in the 470 yachting category.

5   Basketball's debut: In the first women's Olympic basketball tournament, the Soviet team (white jerseys, seen during their 112-77 win over silver medallists, USA) took the gold medal. The bronze medal was claimed by Bulgaria.

6   Equestrian medals: Alwin Schockemöhle (FRG) won the individual show jumping event ahead of Michel Vaillancourt (CAN) and François Mathy (BEL). The successful West Germans also took a silver medal in the show jumping team event, silver and bronze medals for Harry Boldt and Reiner Klimke respectively in the individual dressage, a bronze medal for Karl Schultz in the individual three-day event, a gold medal in the dressage team event, and a silver medal in the team three-day event.

7   USSR victorious: The men's handball final was won by the Soviet team (red jerseys), who defeated Romania 19-15. The Polish team finished in third place. The Soviet women's team also took gold.

8   Polish delight: In the men's volleyball final, Poland (white jerseys) beat the USSR 3-2; Cuba took the bronze. The women's tournament was won by the Japanese, who defeated the Soviets 3-0, with South Korea taking the bronze medal.

9   Weightlifting supremo: Vasiliy Alexeyev (URS) successfully defended his 1972 super-heavyweight Olympic title. Silver and bronze medals went to the East Germans Gerd Bonk and Helmut Losch.

Lake Placid

In 1980, the Winter Olympic Games came to the American resort of Lake Placid for the second time. Insufficient natural snow forced the organizers to use artificial snow, which made its Olympic debut.

King Eric
The American speed skater Eric Heiden, who had taken the Olympic oath at the opening ceremony, won five gold medals over 500, 1000, 1500, 5000, and 10,000 metres.

IN 1974, THE IOC AWARDED THE XIII Winter Games to Lake Placid, a resort in New York State's Adirondack Mountains. Lake Placid's first encounter with the Winter Olympic Games had been in 1932, and in 1980, as had happened 48 years before, the organizers had to cope with a snow shortage and with moving enormous crowds to and from a small town of 3000 inhabitants. Tens of thousands of people were sometimes forced to wait hours for the shuttle buses that served the venues. And many journalists were critical of the one-hour walk to the press centre. Many athletes also considered the Olympic village too confined; after the Games it would actually be used as a prison for young offenders. The sports facilities themselves, on the other hand, received high praise, even though they were some distance apart from each other.

At Lake Placid, artificial snow was used for the first time in Olympic competition, at a cost of five million dollars. However, the fake snow was extremely demanding on the athletes, especially when mixed with newly fallen snow – the two types formed a cocktail that produced somewhat unpredictable characteristics. Nevertheless, the snow shortage problem had been resolved.

Despite international political unrest, most spectators were impartial when it came to acknowledging sporting performance and achievement. Although the reception for the Soviet delegation was rather subdued during the opening ceremony, the display turned on by the figure skater Irina Rodnina, with her partner Alexander Saizev, earned standing ovations. One year after having given birth to a son, she won her third successive Olympic title. In a glorious career, Rodnina also took ten world championship titles, making her the most successful female figure skater of all time.

The battle for prestige between the two superpowers was evident in the ice

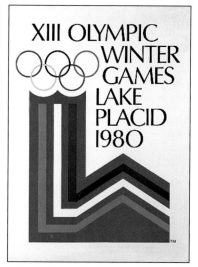

Return to Lake Placid
The official poster of the XIII Winter Olympic Games shows a ski jump hill beneath the five Olympic rings.

hockey tournament. The Soviets had been gold medallists in the sport at each Winter Olympics since their shock defeat at the hands of the Americans at Squaw Valley in 1960. They were hot favourites to continue the run, especially since they had thrashed the American team 10-3 only a week before the start of the Games. Once again, though, playing in front of a home crowd seemed to bring out the best in the Americans. They met the Soviets in the semi-finals and beat them 4-3, before going on to defeat Finland in the final. Carried away by this success, the media rather ignored the achievements of the American speed skater Eric Heiden, who won five gold medals, set a world record over 10,000 metres, and four other Olympic records.

For 12 days, sporting events dominated. However, late in 1979, the Soviet Union had invaded Afghanistan, and before the start of the Lake Placid celebration, President Jimmy Carter had threatened a US boycott of the Summer Olympics due to be held in Moscow later that year. The spectre of international politics lurked close by.

Downhill Gold
The Austrian Annemarie Pröll crowned her career by winning the women's downhill ahead of Liechtenstein's Hanni Wenzel and the Swiss skier Marie-Theres Nadig.

Final Glory
Ulrich Wehling (GDR) was the first winter sports athlete to win three successive gold medals in the Nordic combined event. Following his win in Lake Placid, he retired from competitive sports.

Third Gold
Irina Rodnina (URS) ended her career after winning her third consecutive Olympic pairs figure skating title. In 1972 she had won with Alexey Ulanov, and in 1976 and 1980 with Alexander Saizev.

Successful Recovery
The Swede Ingemar Stenmark took two gold medals – in the slalom and giant slalom events – and confirmed a return to form after a bad fall had put him out of action five months before the Games.

1 Opening of the Games: The nations parade as the Olympic flame is carried into the stadium.

2 Hockey sensation: The USA won the ice hockey tournament, with the Soviets, who had won gold at every Games since 1964, taking silver.

3 Three medals: Hanni Wenzel, born in Bavaria but skiing for Liechtenstein, took gold in the slalom and giant slalom, and a downhill silver.

4 East German luge win: Hans Rinn and Norbert Hahn defeated Peter Gschnitzer and Karl Brunner (ITA) and Georg Fluckinger and Karl Schrott (AUT), in the two-man event.

5 Surprise winner: The men's downhill was won by the outsider Leonhard Stock (AUT).

6 Double gold: Ingemar Stenmark (SWE) won the slalom ahead of Andreas Wenzel (LIE) and Hans Enn (AUT). He also won the giant slalom.

7 Final skating gold: Anett Pötzsch (GDR) retired after taking gold in Lake Placid.

8 Springboard to success: After the Games, figure skating champion Robin Cousins (GBR) turned professional.

9 In a spin: Figure skater Denise Biellmann (SUI) had to settle for fourth place in the women's event. However, the audience were spellbound by her free programme.

10 Figure skating win: Irina Rodnina and Alexander Saizev (URS) won the pairs title ahead of compatriots Marina Cherkassova/Sergey Shakhray.

11 X-country victory: Over 10 kilometres, Barbara Petzold (GDR) beat the the Finns into second and third.

12 Nikolai's title: In the 50 kilometres Nordic skiing event, Nikolai Simyatov (URS) outclassed Juha Mieto (FIN) and Alexander Savyalov (URS).

13 Consecutive wins: Ulrich Wehling (GDR) took his third Nordic combined title.

Moscow

The XXII Olympiad was the first to be staged in a country with a communist regime. However, it was overshadowed by a large-scale boycott in protest at the 1979 Soviet invasion of Afghanistan.

Multi-medallist
The Soviet gymnast Alexander Ditiatin picked up three gold medals, four silvers, and a bronze. He became the first gymnast to score a perfect 10 from the judges, in the horse vault event.

ONLY 80 COUNTRIES WERE represented at the Moscow Games, a third less than had participated in Munich eight years before. Notable absentees included Japan, West Germany, and the large team from the United States. After the terrible events at Munich and the African boycott in Montreal, the Moscow controversy was the last thing the Olympic movement needed. A question mark hung over the future of the Olympic idea and it was impossible to predict whether the nations of the world would ever again assemble for sporting competition. Three days before the 1980 Games opened, Juan Antonio Samaranch was elected IOC president to succeed Lord Killanin. He inherited a very difficult task.

The Games were opened on 19 July by the Soviet president, Leonid Brezhnev. The opening ceremony was perfectly staged, with groups dressed in colourful traditional costumes from all the Soviet republics. Gestures of protest, such as the entry of some delegations under the Olympic flag rather than their national flags, were largely ignored by television cameras.

Western countries have frequently referred to the Moscow Games as being of a low standard, and time and time again raised doubts about the sporting value of the results and medals. Experts seem in little doubt that Ed Moses would have won the 400 metres hurdles as he did in Montreal in 1976 and went on to do once again in Los Angeles in 1984. Some other results might also have been different had certain athletes not been absent. Nevertheless, although not of the highest calibre, the Moscow Games were hardly sub-standard; 36 world records, 39 European records, and 73 Olympic records were testimony to the high level of talent and competition on display. Vladimir Salnikov (URS), for example, became the first swimmer to break the magic 15-minute barrier in the 1500

Home Victor
During the Summer Games in Moscow, the Soviet swimmer Vladimir Salnikov won three gold medals in front of his home crowd.

OLYMPIAD 80
MOSCOU MOSCOW MOCKBA

Poor Turnout
The official poster of the 1980 Moscow Olympics, from which teams from the USA and other Western countries were absent.

Champion Jumper
The new Olympic champion in the women's high jump was the Italian world record holder, Sara Simeoni. She had secured a silver medal in the event four years earlier.

metres freestyle when he clocked a time of 14:58.27 minutes. In the women's pentathlon, the Soviet Nadyezda Tkatchenko scored 5083 points to become the first athlete to exceed 5000 points in the event at an Olympic Games. In the long distance events, the Ethiopian Miruts Yifter enthused the crowds with his blistering sprint finishes. At Moscow, "Yifter the Shifter", as he was dubbed, became only the sixth runner to do the long distance double of 5000 and 10,000 metres. He won the latter with a scorching final lap of 54.0 seconds.

Perhaps the most eagerly awaited contest was between the two British middle distance running stars, Steve Ovett and Sebastian Coe, in the 800 and 1500 metres. At the end of 1979, Coe held the world records for both events (as well as for the mile), but in the run-up to the Games, Ovett equalled Coe's 1500 metres record and bettered his time over the mile. The stage was set for a showdown in Moscow and, in an interesting final twist, Ovett won over Coe's preferred distance of 800 metres, while Coe triumphed in the 1500 metres.

Triple Gold
Rica Reinisch (GDR) won three swimming gold medals, in the 100 and 200 metres backstroke, and with the 4 x 100 metres medley relay team.

King Daley
In winning the decathlon, Britain's Daley Thompson became "king of the athletes" and disappointed the home crowd by pushing the Soviet athlete Yuriy Kutsenko into second position.

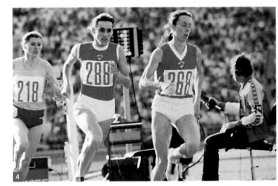

1   **Colourful opening:** During the opening ceremony, a section of the 102,000 crowd transformed the stands of the Lenin Stadium into alternating pictures by using colourful scarves. This type of visual display was customary during mass rallies in countries with communist regimes.

2   **Italian win:** Italy's Pietro Mennea (third from left), who had secured a bronze medal in this event at the Munich Games eight years before, wins the men's 200 metres in a time of 20.19 seconds. Britain's Allan Wells (fourth from left) took the silver medal, ahead of Don Quarrie of Jamaica (second from right). By taking bronze, Quarrie added another Olympic 200 metres medal to the gold that he won in Montreal four years before.

3   **Gold at 100 metres:** Britain's Allan Wells leads Don Quarrie of Jamaica, the Montreal silver medallist, in the first heat of the 100 metres. Wells went on to win the final in 10.25 seconds in a photo-finish ahead of Silvio Leonard (CUB) to become the first Briton to win the 100 metres since Harold Abrahams did so in Paris in 1924. Petar Petrov of Bulgaria took the bronze medal.

4   **Soviet superiority:** In the women's 1500 metres final, Tatyana Kasankina (URS, right) won gold as she had in Montreal. Christiane Wartenberg (GDR) and Nadyezda Olizarenko of the Soviet Union came second and third respectively. Olizarenko made no mistake in the 800 metres event, where she underlined her Olympic title

win by setting a new world record of 1:53.43 minutes.

5   **British battle:** Sebastian Coe (GBR, right) becomes the new Olympic champion over 1500 metres. He beat second-placed Jürgen Straub (GDR, centre) and Steve Ovett (GBR, left), joint world record holder (with Coe) over this distance.

6   **Ovett overtakes:** Though beaten in the 1500 metres, Steve Ovett (GBR, third right) made no mistake over 800 metres, taking the gold. Fellow Briton Sebastian Coe, world record holder over 800 metres and clear favourite for this event, took the silver medal, ahead of Nikolai Kirov (URS).

7   **High jump gold:** In Moscow, the silver medallist in

Montreal four years previously, the Italian Sara Simeoni, took the gold medal ahead of Urszula Kielan of Poland and Jutta Kirst of East Germany.

8   **World record gold:** The Pole Wladyslaw Kosakiewicz took the gold medal in the pole vault event and set a new world record (for the first time during Olympic competition since 1920) of 5.78 metres. His compatriot Tadeusz Slusarski and Konstantin Volkov (URS) shared the silver medal after they both cleared a height of 5.65 metres.

9   **Long distance star:** The Ethiopian Miruts Yifter (left) defeated Suleiman Nyambui of Tanzania (right) and the Finn Kaarlo Maaninka in the men's 5000 metres. Yifter won his second gold medal in the 10,000

metres event when he beat Maaninka and his Ethiopian compatriot Mohammed Kedir. Yifter's unconventional running style, where a steady pace was interrupted with numerous unexpected sprinting bursts, kept his rivals guessing.

10   **Duncan does it:** Duncan Goodhew won a swimming gold for Britain by taking the 100 metres breaststroke in 1:03.34 minutes ahead of Arsen Miskarov (URS) and Australia's Peter Evans. He could manage only sixth in the 200 metres, which was won by Robertas Schulpa (URS), with second and third going to Alban Vermes (HUN) and Miskarov of the Soviet Union. Goodhew was, however, part of the British medley relay team that came third behind Australia and the Soviet Union.

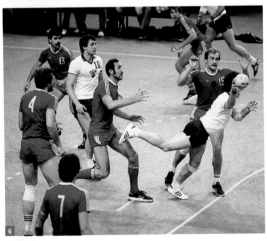

1 East Germans dominate: Bernd and Jörg Landvoigt celebrate their win in the coxless pairs event.

2 Soviet winners: Vladimir Parfenovitch and Sergey Chukhray (front) take gold in the 1000 metres K2.

3 Fencing medals: France won the final of the épée team competition when they beat Poland 8-4 (photograph shows the contest between Andrzej Lis and Hubert Gardas). France were also victorious in both the men's and women's foil team events. In addition, Pascale Trinquet secured another gold medal for France by winning the individual foil tournament.

4 Home gold: In the individual cycling road race, Sergey Sukhoruchenkov (URS) defeated Czeslaw Lang (POL) by a huge margin of nearly three minutes. Yuriy Barinov (URS) took bronze. The Soviets also won the 100 kilometres team time trial.

5 Winner's joy: Players and officials celebrate the Soviet water polo team's victory.

6 Narrow decision: The East German handball team (white jerseys) won the tournament by defeating the USSR 23-22 in the final. The women's tournament was won by the Soviet Union.

7 Swiss judo win: In the middleweight division, Jörg Röthlisberger beat the Cuban fighter Isaac Azcuy (standing) to secure a momentous victory.

8 Most successful athlete: Alexander Ditiatin (URS) took three gold medals, in the individual and team combined exercise competitions and in the rings event. He added four silvers to his medal collection and completed his tally with a bronze medal in the floor event.

9 Strongest lifter: With an overall lift of 440.5 kilograms in the combined competition, the 30-year-old Soviet weightlifter Sultan Rakhmanov (URS) took gold in the super-heavyweight category ahead of Jürgen Heuser (GDR, 410 kilograms).

10 Wrestling medals: The freestyle super-heavyweight champion was Soslan Andiev (URS, blue jersey). Silver went to József Balla (HUN), with Adam Sandurski (POL, red jersey) taking bronze.

11 Shooting for gold: In the prone small-bore rifle event, Karoly Varga (HUN) won the gold medal ahead of Hellfried Heilfort (GDR) and Petar Zapianov (BUL).

12 Two home golds: The modern pentathlon title was taken by Anatoliy Starostin (URS), who picked up a second gold medal as part of the USSR's team event victory.

Sarajevo

When Sarajevo polled more votes than Sapporo and Gothenburg, even the host's organizing committee was surprised. Nevertheless, 1984 saw the Winter Games held in the Balkans for the first time.

WHEN THESE GAMES WERE awarded to Sarajevo in 1978, the organizers knew they had six years to prepare. Funding was raised from the sale of television rights, sponsorships, and advertising contracts, as well as through the efforts of the people of Sarajevo themselves.

The organizers demonstrated their improvisational skills on a number of occasions. For example, they equipped the downhill slope with an elevated starting area in order to comply with regulations that insisted on a start-finish altitude difference of 800 metres. The Yugoslavs also coped well with the numerous schedule changes resulting from the adverse weather conditions. For the first time, the IOC agreed to pay the expenses of one male and one female member of each team. The number of participating nations was up from 37 at Lake Placid to 49, although Egypt, the Virgin Islands, Mexico, Monaco, Puerto Rico, and Senegal were represented by only one competitor each.

The most successful teams in Sarajevo were the East Germans with nine golds, the USSR with six golds, and the Americans with four golds. The most successful participant was the Finnish cross-country skier Marja-Liisa Hämäläinen, who won the 5, 10, and 20 kilometres individual events, and claimed a bronze medal as a member of the Finnish 4 x 5 kilometres relay team.

The Americans had considerable success on the ski slopes, with Bill Johnson winning the men's downhill, Phil Mahre winning the slalom, and Debbie Armstrong taking the gold medal in the women's giant slalom event. In the individual figure skating events, America's Scott Hamilton took the men's gold, while the women's event was won by East Germany's Katarina Witt.

Dream Team
The British ice dancers Jayne Torvill and Christopher Dean were the undisputed stars in Sarajevo. They crowned their amateur career with an Olympic title win and their fourth world championship title in 1984.

Balkan Glory
A snowflake is the main image on the official poster of the XIV Winter Olympic Games, held in the Bosnian capital Sarajevo.

However, the stars of the Sarajevo Games were the British ice dance pair Jayne Torvill and Christopher Dean, whose performances marked the dawn of a new era in this discipline. Their interpretation of Ravel's "Bolero" was one of the truly great moments in sport, for which they achieved a perfect score for artistic presentation – all nine judges awarded them the maximum six points. In the competition overall, they gained 12 out of a possible 18 sixes.

Tragically, Sarajevo and its sports facilities were reduced to rubble in the fighting that later engulfed the former Yugoslavia. During the Lillehammer Winter Olympics of 1994, IOC president Juan Antonio Samaranch flew to the Bosnian capital and appealed to the warring sides to impose a temporary ceasefire for the duration of the Games.

X-country Queen
Winning three gold medals and one bronze, Marja-Liisa Hämäläinen of Finland was the most successful athlete at the Winter Games in Sarajevo.

Twins Peak
The twin brothers Phil (right) and Steve Mahre of the USA took first and second positions respectively in the men's slalom. It was the first ever gold for the United States in this discipline.

Katarina's Grace
East Germany's Katarina Witt, won her first Olympic figure skating gold medal; she would successfully defend her title four years later in Calgary.

German Success
East Germany I, with the legendary Wolfgang Höppe in the team, won the four-man bobsled competition ahead of East Germany II. Höppe also took gold with Dietmar Schauerhammer in the winning East German two-man bob.

1 The Olympic flame is lit: After the Olympic torch had been carried through Yugoslavia by 1600 relay runners, the Olympic flame was lit by the figure skater Sandra Dubravcic in Sarajevo's Olympic Stadium. The site was badly damaged in the Balkan conflict a few years later.

2 Facelift for Olympic city: A view of Sarajevo, where sports facilities and the city's infrastructure were modernized with the help of investment of tens of millions of pounds. During the 13 days of competition, posters bearing the Olympic symbol made Sarajevo's streets beautifully colourful.

3 Successful flight: The Finn Matti Nykänen jumps from the big (90-metre) hill. He finished the competition as Olympic champion, beating his rival Jens Weissflog (GDR) with an Olympic record 116-metre jump. Weissflog had beaten Nykänen in the small (70-metre) hill contest a few days before.

4 Double medals for USA: After the two runs in the women's giant slalom, the American Debbie Armstrong became the new Olympic champion, ahead of her compatriot Christin Cooper and Perrine Pelen of France.

5 Swedish "king of skiing": In the 50 kilometres cross-country skiing competition, Thomas Wassberg was invincible. He secured a second gold medal as part of the Swedish 4 x 10 kilometres relay team.

6 Biathlete's three medals: The West German biathlete Peter Angerer recorded his greatest personal success by winning a gold medal over 20 kilometres, a silver over 10 kilometres, and a bronze with the 4 x 7.5 kilometres relay team.

7 Giant gold: Clocking a time of 2:41.18 minutes, Max Julen (SUI) won the giant slalom ahead of Juriy Franko (YUG) and Andreas Wenzel (LIE). There was further success for Switzerland when Peter Müller took second position in the blue riband men's downhill event.

8 Favourite wins: After his Olympic figure skating win, Scott Hamilton (USA), who had been world champion from 1981–84, turned professional.

9 USSR too strong: The ice hockey world champions from the Soviet Union commandingly took the Olympic title, with the Czechoslovakian and Swedish teams taking silver and bronze. The Soviets conceded only five goals in their seven games. Here at the medal ceremony, goal-keeper Vladislav Tretyak (centre) cannot hide his elation – this is his third gold medal in four Olympic Games. In 1980, he had to be content with a silver medal.

10 Fastest speed skater: Karin Enke (GDR) won two gold medals over 1000 and 1500 metres, as well as two silver medals over 500 and 3000 metres. The stunning success of the East German women speed skaters was completed by Christa Rothenburger's gold medal over 500 metres, Andrea Schöne's gold over 3000 and silver in both the 1000 and 1500 metres, and finally Gabi Schönbrunn's bronze over 3000 metres.

11 East German bobs win: Wolfgang Höppe was successful in the two-man and four-man bob events. In the two-man bob, he was victorious with Dietmar Schauerhammer ahead of his compatriots Bernhard Lehmann and Bogdan Musiol. In the four-man bob, he and his team mates Schauerhammer, Andreas Kirchner, and Roland Wetzig clinched the Olympic title ahead of East Germany II, represented by Lehmann, Musiol, Ingo Voge, and Eberhard Weise, and Switzerland I (Rico Freiermuth, Silvio Giobellina, Urs Salzmann, and Heinz Stettler).

Los Angeles

In 1984, Olympic athletes met in Los Angeles for the second time, having first gathered there in 1932. The Games were remarkable for being the first privately funded tournament in Olympic history.

THE DRIVING FORCE BEHIND Los Angeles' successful bid was the city's mayor, Tom Bradley, while entrepreneur Peter Ueberroth dedicated his time to bringing the project to fruition once the Games had been awarded. Ueberroth was able to attract more than 30 sponsors, who between them contributed more than 500 million dollars. Other companies funded the building of new sports facilities, in a deal which allowed them to advertise on the admission tickets. The television company ABC paid 225 million dollars for the exclusive television transmission rights, thereby ensuring that most events started in the evenings during prime television time. With all this money involved, many critics held the view that what had once been a festival of amateur sport had been converted into a purely commercial spectacle.

The Games were overshadowed by a boycott imposed by the Soviet Union and many of its allies, who explained their absence by alleging that they were not satisfied with security arrangements. However, their non-participation was generally seen as retaliation for the US-instigated boycott of the Moscow Olympics four years earlier.

The star of the Los Angeles Games was undoubtedly the American track-and-field athlete Carl Lewis, who followed in Jesse Owens' footsteps by taking four Olympic titles. Forty-eight years after Owens' triumphs in Berlin, Lewis emulated his achievements exactly, taking golds in the 100 and 200 metres, the 4 x 100 metres relay, and the long jump. Only the 17-year-old Romanian gymnast Ecaterina Szabó won more medals, claiming four golds and a silver.

Britain's Daley Thompson successfully defended his decathlon title, becoming only the second man (after Bob Mathias) to do so. Meanwhile, team mate Sebastian Coe recovered from serious illness to successfully defend the Olympic 1500

Star Games
The official Olympic poster shows different facets of life in the USA.

metres title for the first time since Jim Lightbody in 1906. As in Moscow, Coe also picked up a silver medal in the 800 metres, this time losing out to Brazil's Joaquim Cruz; the Brazilian set a new Olympic record in the process.

In the women's 400 metres hurdles, Nawal El Moutawakel, competing in her first Games, became the first Moroccan sportswoman to win an Olympic gold medal. Other surprise winners included Holland's Ria Stalman, who won the discus, West Germany's Ulrike Meyfarth, who repeated her 1972 high jump success, and the little-known Australian Glynis Nunn, who took gold in the first Olympic heptathlon. However, it seems likely that some of the medal winners at Los Angeles might have struggled to reach the finals had the East European teams been participating.

Among the new disciplines at Los Angeles were women's synchronized swimming, in which the solo event was won by Tracie Ruiz from the USA, and windsurfing, won by Holland's Stephan van den Berg. During the Olympic Congress of 1981, the term "Olympic amateur" had been removed from the Olympic Charter. This gave individual sports associations the power to decide on eligibility for the Olympics. As a result, professional footballers were eligible for the Olympics, though European and South American countries considered only players that had not appeared in the World Cup.

Daley Retains
Briton Daley Thompson celebrates a successful attempt in the discus, which put him on the road to victory in the decathlon. His winning points tally equalled the world record.

Double Diving Gold
The American diver Greg Louganis remained unbeaten from the three-metre springboard as well as from the ten-metre highboard and wowed the crowd with his precision.

Pool Giant
Michael Gross (FRG), whose nickname was "Albatross" because of the span of his outstretched arms, set a new world record when winning the 200 metres freestyle event.

Gymnast's Accolades
Winning four gold medals and a silver, the Romanian gymnast Ecaterina Szabó was the most successful competitor in Los Angeles. The judges awarded her a perfect 10 in one round of the floor exercises event.

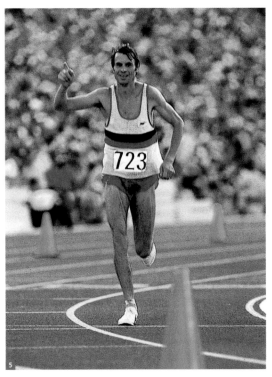

1 Spectacular opening: During the parade of nations, the home spectators give the American team an enthusiastic reception. One of the many attractions at the opening ceremony in the Coliseum was a jet-propelled "rocket man", who flew through the air, then landed in the stadium. A crowd of more than 90,000 in the stadium as well as a worldwide television audience in the hundreds of millions followed the four-and-a-half-hour-long spectacle, executed by more than 10,000 performers. The Olympics had come to the United States.

2 New 100 metres record: In the absence of her East German rivals, the American Evelyn Ashford (right) set a new Olympic record of 10.97 seconds in the women's 100 metres sprint. The silver medal

was picked up by Alice Brown (USA, 11.13 seconds) ahead of the Jamaican Merlene Ottey (11.16 seconds). Ashford secured a second gold medal as part of the United States' 4 x 100 metres relay team (along with Brown, Jeanette Bolden, and Chandra Cheeseborough). Canada were second and Great Britain third.

3 Olympic debut: Los Angeles witnessed the debut of the women's 400 metres hurdles competition, with Nawal El Moutawakel becoming the first Moroccan sportswoman to win a gold medal in Olympic competition. Clocking a time of 54.61 seconds, she defeated the American Judi Brown and Cristina Cojocaru of Romania. After her surprise victory, the winner is proud to wave her country's national flag and soak up the applause from the crowd.

4 Second gold medal: The American 400 metres hurdles world record holder, Edwin Moses, took the Olympic oath on behalf of all athletes during the opening ceremony. Following his victory in 1976, the world champion of 1983 and 1987 secured his second Olympic title. Silver and bronze medals went to compatriot Danny Harris and the European champion Harald Schmid (FRG) respectively.

5 Battling with the heat: At their debut Olympic marathon, the women athletes were caught by the midday heat, which led to many athletes suffering from exhaustion. Unlike the women, the men were allowed to start their event late in the afternoon. In addition, the rules were changed at short notice, to allow the athletes to be provided with water at an increased number of refreshment stands. This put the 37-year-old Portuguese Carlos Lopes in a position to set a new Olympic record of 2:09:21 hours. Second and third places were taken by the Irishman John Treacy (2:09:56 hours) and Britain's Charlie Spedding (2:09:58 hours) respectively. The women's event was won by the American Joan Benoit in 2:24:52 hours. The exhausted Swiss athlete Gaby Andersen-Schiess caused some concern when she was seen to visibly waver over the track during the final lap in the stadium, but she finished the race.

5 Glory for Tessa: Britain's Tessa Sanderson shows off her Olympic javelin gold medal. She threw 69.56 metres to beat Tiina Lillak (69.00 metres) of Finland into second place. Sanderson's British rival Fatima Whitbread

(67.14 metres), who was to be world champion in 1987, took the bronze medal. Tessa Sanderson is the only British athlete to have taken part in five Olympic Games (1976-1992).

7 Star of the Games: After the medal ceremony for the victorious American 4 x 100 metres relay team, Carl Lewis is carried around by his team-mates on a lap of honour. On the final day of the Games, Ron Brown, Sam Graddy, Lewis, and Calvin Smith set a new world record in the event of 37.83 seconds, defeating Jamaica (38.62 seconds), and Canada (38.70 seconds). It was Lewis' fourth gold meal of the Games after his 100 metres win over Graddy and Ben Johnson (CAN) and his success in the 200 metres final, in which he beat his compatriots Kirk Baptiste and Thomas

Jefferson in a time of 19.80 seconds. Lewis also won the long jump, with a winning leap of 8.54 metres which pushed the Australian Gary Honey and the Italian Giovanni Evangelisti (both 8.24 metres) into second and third places.

8 "King" once again: Britain's Daley Thompson (seen during the decisive pole vault event) successfully defended the Olympic decathlon title he won in Moscow four years before. Setting a new Olympic record of 8797 points that equalled Jürgen Hingsen's (FRG) world record, Thompson relegated Hingsen (8678 points) to the silver medal position. The West German team still had plenty to be proud of as Siegfried Wentz (8412 points) and Guido Kratschmer (8326 points) took positions three and four respectively. At the

European championships in Stuttgart two years later, Thompson again defeated Hingsen to take the title. However, following a disappointing ninth place at the world championships in Rome in 1987, the then 30-year-old Thompson came back to Olympic competition at the 1988 Games in Seoul. Despite carrying an injury, he came a respectable fourth and ended a marvellous career with dignity.

9 Surprise winner: Not even experts had expected the West German discus thrower Rolf Danneberg to be a serious medal contender. At his fourth attempt, the 1.98-metre-tall athlete (achieved a distance of 66.60 metres. Second place went to the American Mac Wilkins (66.30 metres), who had been champion at Montreal, ahead of his

compatriot John Powell (65.46 metres).

10 First heptathlon gold: The Olympic debut of the heptathlon (which replaced the pentathlon) at Los Angeles saw the relatively unknown Australian athlete, Glynis Nunn (centre, at the medal ceremony) win the event. The two-day-long competition consisted of 100 metres hurdles, high jump, shot, 200 metres sprint, long jump, javelin, and 800 metres run. The Australian (6390 points) finished only a whisker ahead of the much-fancied American Jackie Joyner (6385 points) and the West German Sabine Everts (6363 points). This was one event where the absence of Soviet athletes may have lowered standards; Soviet athletes had taken all the medals in the pentathlon at Moscow four years before.

1 Double diving victory: The American diver Greg Louganis won the highboard event with 710.91 points, ahead of his compatriot Bruce Kimball and the Chinese diver, Li Kongzhen. Never before had a diver achieved over 700 points in this event. Four days earlier, he had secured the springboard title with the largest ever margin of victory ahead of Tan Liangde (CHN) and Ronald Merriott (USA). This double Olympic diving victory had previously been accomplished only twice

before – by the Americans Albert White (in Paris in 1924) and Pete Desjardins (in Amsterdam in 1928).

2 Favourite takes first title: In Los Angeles, world champion Tracie Ruiz (USA, front) became the first Olympic synchronized swimming champion. The silver medal went to the Canadian Carolyn Waldo, with Miwako Motoyoshi of Japan third. In the duet, Ruiz and her partner, Candy Costy, were again in a class of their own when they beat

Sharon Hambrook and Kelly Kryczka (CAN) and Motoyoshi and Saeko Kimura (JPN).

3 Double victory for Gross: In the 100 metres butterfly, Michael Gross (FRG) set a new world record time of 53.08 seconds, which secured him the gold medal ahead of Pablo Morales (USA) and Glenn Buchanan (AUS). In the 200 metres freestyle event, he set another world record (1:47.44 minutes) and demonstrated his superiority over Michael Heath

(USA) and fellow West German Thomas Fahrner. He finished second in the 200 metres butterfly, beaten by Jon Sieben (USA). The 20 year-old German picked up another silver as part of the 4 x 200 metres freestyle relay team, with the USA winning, and Britain third.

4 Pool world records: The Canadian Alex Baumann won the 200 metres medley in a new world record time of 2:01.42 minutes. He secured another victory and another world record

in the 400 metres medley, with a time of 4:17.41 minutes.

5 Three gold medals: Mary T. Meagher (USA) won three gold medals, in the 100 and 200 metres butterfly events, and with the American 4 x 100 metres medley relay team.

6 Gymnast's five medals: The crowds' favourite, Mary Lou Retton (USA, seen during her floor performance which won her a bronze medal) won the individual combined exercises competition, picked up two silvers in the horse vault and the team event, and took a bronze in the asymmetrical bars event.

7 Prolific winner: The Romanian gymnast Ecaterina Szabó won the floor, balance beam (jointly), and horse vault events and contributed to her country's gold medal in the team combined exercises competition. In the individual combined exercises, she had to settle for a silver medal behind Mary Lou Retton (USA).

8 Olympic wins for China: The gymnast Li Ning won three gold medals in the floor, rings, and pommel horse (picture) events, two silvers in the horse vault and in the team combined exercises competition, as well as a bronze in the individual combined exercises. Chinese success was completed by Yun Lou, who secured gold in the horse vault and silver in the floor event.

9 Fencing success: The West German fencers celebrate their

success in the women's team foil event ahead of Romania and France. Cornelia Hanisch (second left) added a silver medal in the individual foil competition.

10 Italian swordsmen: The Italian Mauro Numa (left) took the gold medal in the men's individual foil ahead of West Germany's Matthias Behr (right). Numa secured a second gold as part of the Italian foil team. West Germany and France were second and third.

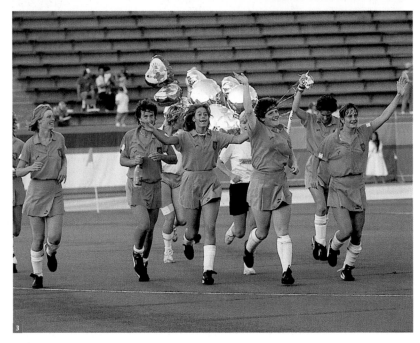

1 **Chinese win:** In the women's volleyball tournament the American team (left) were no match for the gold medallists China, at whose hands they suffered a straight sets defeat. The USA had to settle for silver ahead of the Japanese team. The men's tournament was won by the USA after they managed a 3-0 victory over silver medallists Brazil. Italy finished in bronze medal position.

2 **Yugoslavia win:** The final of the men's handball tournament between Yugoslavia (blue jerseys) and West Germany was decided by the narrow margin of 18-17, in favour of the team from the Balkans. The Romanian team won the bronze medal thanks to a 23-19 victory over Denmark. The women's tournament also saw Yugoslavia (silver medallists in Moscow) take the gold, in this case ahead of the Koreans and China.

3 **Dutch hockey gold:** The Dutch women hockey players celebrate their Olympic title. This second Olympic hockey tournament for women saw only six teams take part. West Germany picked up the silver medal, with the USA taking

bronze. The men's hockey tournament was won by Pakistan for the third time, having also been gold medallists in 1960 and 1968. The West Germans again took second place, this time ahead of bronze medallists Great Britain.

4 **Invincible USA:** In the basketball competition, none of the teams were able to prevent the favourites, the hosts, from taking their ninth Olympic title. In the final, the USA comprehensively beat Spain 96-65. The picture shows Pat Ewing (right) and the Spaniard Fernando Romay. The US team also starred Michael Jordan.

5 **US basketball gold:** Six teams competed in the women's basketball tournament. In the final, the US, which remained undefeated in the competition, beat South Korea 85-55. The picture shows Cheryl Miller targeting the basket, with the Korean Kyung Ya-Moon (left) too late to take any defensive action. The bronze medal was picked up by the Chinese, who beat Canada 63-57.

6 **Greco-Roman Wrestling success:** In the bantamweight division (up to 57 kilograms body weight), the West German

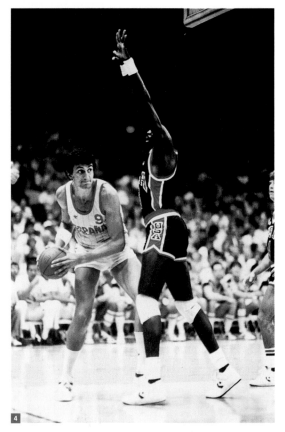

wrestler Pasquale Passarelli (blue jersey) took the gold medal thanks to a win over Japan's Masaki Eto (red jersey). The Greek wrestler Haralambos Holidis finished in third position. West Germany won another silver medal when the light-flyweight (up to 48 kilograms) Markus Scherer lost out to the impressive Olympic champion, Vincenzo Maenza of Italy in the final.

7 Strong men: Rolf Milser (FRG, pictured) dominated the 100 kilograms weightlifting category. Silver went to the Romanian Vasile Gropa and the bronze to the Finn Pekka Niemi. Earlier on, Karl-Heinz Radschinsky had won the gold medal in the middleweight category ahead of Jacques Demers (CAN) and Dragomir Cioroslan (ROM). West Germany's success was completed by the bronze medal secured in the over-110 kilograms category by Manfred Nerlinger, who had to concede to the superiority of Olympic champion "Dinko" Lukin (AUS) and Mario Martinez (USA).

8 Rowing hat-trick: The Finnish rower Pertti Karppinen won his third consecutive Olympic title in the single sculls

event by a margin of under two seconds from his greatest rival, and world champion, Peter-Michael Kolbe (FRG). He had to settle for a silver medal, with Canadian Robert Mills taking bronze. Canada took gold in the eights competition.

9 US cycling double: Americans Connie Carpenter (gold medal, centre) and Rebecca Twigg (silver medal, left) show their delight at the medal ceremony for the women's individual road race over 79.2 kilometres. The bronze medal went to Sandra Schumacher (FRG, right).

10 Financial expert: Los Angeles mayor Tom Bradley (left) had suggested that Peter Ueberroth (right) be chairman of the organizing committee for the first privately funded Games. Following the success of the event, Ueberroth was praised for his achievements.

11 Favourite wins: The world champion Reiner Klimke (FRG) rode Ahlerich to a commanding win in the dressage competition. The West German trio of Herbert Krug, Uwe Sauer, and Klimke won the gold medal in the dressage team event.

Calgary

In 1981, 24 years after it first formed its bidding committee, the Canadian city of Calgary, at the foot of the Rocky Mountains, was finally awarded the Winter Olympic Games by the IOC.

FUNDS FOR THE CALGARY GAMES originated from three sources. Half of the budget was put up by the Canadian government; sponsors, official suppliers, and licensees contributed another 90 million dollars; and the US television company ABC paid 309 million dollars for the broadcasting rights. ABC benefited from a decision made by the IOC in 1984 to extend the Games from 12 to 16 days. The consequence for the competitors was that start times for many events were chosen not for sporting reasons, but to meet the demands of television advertisers in the United States

The Olympic programme was again extended to include new disciplines. In Nordic skiing, team competitions in the combined and in the ski jump events made their Olympic debut. Further developments in Nordic skiing came as a result of the "skating technique" used by the Finnish Nordic skiier Siitonen in Sarajevo in 1984. Modified regulations for the cross-country events were introduced: while the shorter distances – the men's 15 and 30 kilometres and the women's 5 and 10 kilometres – were to be covered using the classic style, the freestyle (skating technique) could now be used in the men's 50 and the women's 20 kilometres competitions and also in the relay events. In alpine skiing, meanwhile, the super giant slalom ("Super G") made its first appearance, and for the first time since 1948, there was an alpine combined competition. Another first was that the speed skating events were held indoors, and the 5000 metres event was added to the women's speed skating programme.

Although the spectators enjoyed the Calgary Games, many saw them more as a well-rehearsed show than a series of competitive sporting competitions. Among the winners they cheered on were the Finnish ski jumper Matti Nykänen and the Dutch speed skater

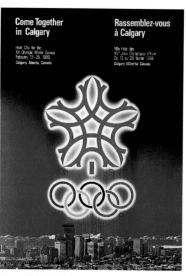

Canadian Welcome
The official poster of these Winter Olympic Games features a bilingual appeal for the youth of the world to come together.

Yvonne van Gennip, who each won three gold medals. The real favourites, though, were the Italian Alberto Tomba, who managed to attract considerable attention both through his gold medals in the slalom and giant slalom and his well-publicized laid-back lifestyle, and Katarina Witt, who was dubbed "Carmen on ice". The East German became the first female figure skater since Sonja Henie (1928–1936) to successfully defend her individual Olympic title.

For the first time since 1968, the Winter Games included demonstration sports. At Calgary, curling, short track speed skating, and freestyle skiing were all exhibited, with an encouraging response from the watching crowds. As a mark of the IOC's recognition of their sporting achievements, disabled athletes were given their own timetable of competitions. This had actually been introduced four years before at the Sarajevo Games, but was now a more comprehensive programme. However, officials turned down suggestions to integrate the competitions for disabled athletes into the official programme.

Italian Hero
The Italian Alberto Tomba won two gold medals in the slalom and giant slalom to become the most successful alpine competitor of the Games.

Close Result
America's Brian Boitano took the men's figure skating gold, just ahead of Canada's Brian Orser.

Triple Jump Wins
With Olympic titles in the small hill, big hill, and team ski-jumping events, the 24-year-old Finn Matti Nykänen was the most successful male competitor at these Winter Games.

Gennip's Golds
The Dutch speed skater Yvonne van Gennip demonstrated her superiority in this discipline by winning over the 1500, 3000, and 5000 metres.

Ski Champ
In Calgary, the 1985 world combined and downhill champion and the 1987 Super G world champion, Pirmin Zurbriggen (SUI), took a gold medal in the downhill and a bronze medal in the giant slalom.

1 Cheerful mascots: The official mascots for the Calgary Games, two polar bears called Hidy and Howdy, were conceived by the Canadian designer Sheila Scott. Marketed in many different ways, they were a prominent sight at the venues and on television screens.

2 Successful alpine skier: The Frenchman Franck Piccard won the first Olympic super giant slalom event ahead of the Austrian Helmut Mayer and Lars-Börje Eriksson of Sweden. Piccard picked up bronze medal in the downhill behind the two Swiss skiers Pirmin Zurbriggen and Peter Müller (who also came second in this event in 1984).

3 West Germans win: Adverse weather conditions forced the women's downhill race to be postponed by one day. Marina Kiehl coped best with the demanding course and exceptionally strong winds to take gold. The West German skier defeated Brigitte Oertli of Switzerland and the Canadian Karen Percy and was the only German alpine skiing gold medallist.

4 First giant slalom wins: In the women's Super G, Sigrid Wolf (centre) clocked a time of 1:19:03 minutes, which secured her the gold medal ahead of the Swiss skier Michela Figini (left, 1:20:03 minutes) and the Canadian Karen Percy (right, 1:20:29 minutes) who was also bronze medallist in the downhill.

5 Vreni's double: Switzerland's Vreni Schneider lived up to expectations when she took two gold medals in the skiing competitions. In the slalom, she beat the Yugoslav Mateja Svet and the West German Christa Kinshofer-Güthlein. In the giant slalom event, the 23-year-old Schneider defeated Kinshofer-Güthlein and Maria Walliser of Switzerland, silver medallist in the 1984 slalom.

6 Title and award to Witt: In the summer of 1988, the East German figure skater Katarina Witt (seen here during her interpretation of "Carmen" in the free programme) received an Olympic award from the IOC president Juan Antonio Samaranch. She was the first female figure skater since Sonja Henie (1928-36) to defend her Olympic title.

7 Unbeaten favourites: In the ice dancing competition, the Soviet pair of Natalia Bestemianova and Andrey Bukin lived up to their billing to win the gold medal ahead of their compatriots Marina

Klimova and Sergey Ponomarenko. The Canadians Tracy Wilson and Robert McCall took the bronze medal. The champions were invincible throughout the Olympic year in which they won their fourth successive world championship title.

8 Racing to gold: Tomas Gustafson (SWE) won the gold medal in the 5000 metres speed skating event (and successfully defended his 1984 Olympic title) when he defeated Leo Visser and Gerard Kemkers (both HOL). Four days later, he took the 10,000 metres event and improved the world record held by the Norwegian Geir Karlstad by 0.31 seconds to 13:48.20 minutes. Second and third places were taken by the Austrian Michael Hadschieff and Visser respectively.

9 Medals for Switzerland: Hippolyt Kempf (SUI) (seen here during the cross-country skiing) had been a world class Nordic combined athlete for a year by the time he competed at Calgary. He was part of the successsful Swiss team that took silver in the team event, beaten only by West Germany.

10 Double victory: At his second Olympic Games, Frank-Peter Roetsch (GDR), the silver medallist over 20 kilometres in Sarajevo, picked up two gold medals in the 10 kilometres and 20 kilometres biathlon events at Calgary.

11 Swiss on a roll: In the four-man bobsled event, the Switzerland I team of Ekkehard Fasser, Marcel Fässler, Kurt Meier, and Werner Stocker took the gold medal ahead of East Germany I and USSR II.

Happily, the large-scale boycotts of Moscow and Los Angeles did not recur at Seoul. For the first time in 12 years, all leading sporting nations, bar Cuba and Ethiopia, took part in the Olympic Games.

TWENTY-FOUR YEARS AFTER THE Tokyo Games of 1964, the Summer Olympics returned to Asia. However, the warm welcome given by the hosts could not cover up the tense political relations between the pro-Western South Korean government and the communist rulers of North Korea, who decided not to send a team. During the 16 days of the Games, athletes from 159 nations participated, and 27 new world records were set.

Sadly, though, the results on the track were overshadowed by the most spectacular drugs case in Olympic history. Three days after Ben Johnson had won the men's 100 metres gold in a new world best time of 9.79 seconds, official drug testers announced that the 26-year-old Canadian had tested positive for performance-enhancing drugs. Johnson was stripped of both his world record and gold medal and banned from ever representing Canada again. The ban was later reduced to two years.

Once again, the Soviet Union (55 gold medals) and East Germany (37) demonstrated their superiority over the Western nations by finishing first and second in the medals table. The East German swimmer Kristin Otto won six golds, coming close to equalling the phenomenal performance of America's Mark Spitz, who won seven gold medals in 1972. The US swimmer Matt Biondi won five gold medals as well as a silver and a bronze. In the 100 metres butterfly, he had no answer to Anthony Nesty, the only swimmer representing Surinam. In the women's sprints, America's Florence Griffith-Joyner was outstanding. Having for some time been a respected but not brilliant sprinter on the international circuit, "Flo-Jo" suddenly blossomed in 1988, winning golds in the 100 metres, 200 metres, and 4 x 100 metres relay, and taking a silver as a member of the 4 x 400

Seoul Man
The dramatic official poster for the Games shows a torch bearer carrying the Olympic flame to Seoul beneath the five intertwined Olympic rings.

metres team that finished second behind the USSR. She set a new world record of 21.34 seconds in the 200 metres final and also ran the fastest Olympic time ever over 100 metres (10.54 seconds). Unfortunately, that run was considered wind-assisted and did not count as a record.

The men's middle distance events were both won by Kenyans, with Paul Ereng taking the 800 metres and Peter Rono the 1500 metres. A Kenyan, John Ngugi, also won the 5000 metres, while the 10,000 metres gold went to Brahim Boutayeb of Morocco. The Africans had to settle for silver and bronze in the marathon, though, when Italy's Gelindo Bordin picked up the gold.

After 64 years, tennis regained its status as a full Olympic sport. The singles competitions were won by West Germany's Steffi Graf and Miloslav Mecir of Czechoslovakia The newly introduced sport of table tennis was almost completely dominated by the Chinese and Korean competitors.

Colourful Flo
The sprinter Florence Griffith-Joyner (USA) won three gold medals and a silver. She captured the public's attention not only through her sporting performances, but also by her outgoing personality.

Cooper Collects
Britain's Malcolm Cooper retained his Olympic title in the small-bore rifle (three positions) event. Alister Allan (also GBR) took the silver medal, having taken bronze at Los Angeles in 1984.

Multi-medallist
The Romanian Daniela Silivas picked up gold medals in the floor, balance beam, and asymmetrical bars events, and added two silver medals in the individual and team combined exercises events. She also took the bronze medal in the horse vault.

Six Golds
The East German swimmer Kristin Otto won six gold medals and set or helped set a number of new Olympic records to become the most successful competitor in Seoul.

Legendary Bubka
Sergei Bubka (URS) won the pole vault with his one and only valid attempt. He set a new Olympic record in an event where the Russians secured the first three places.

1 Colourful spectacle: During the athletes' parade at the opening ceremony in Seoul, some of the competitors appeared wearing their national costumes.

2 Short-lived victory: Three days after what Ben Johnson (CAN, right) believed to be his personal triumph in the 100 metres came by sobering news. He was disqualified for drug taking and Carl Lewis (USA, left) was declared Olympic champion.

3 Heptathlon: Scoring 7291 points, Jackie Joyner-Kersee (USA, right) improved her own world record by 79 points. She defeated Sabine John and Anke Behmer (both GDR). In the women's long jump, Joyner-Kersee leapt 7.40 metres to become the first American to win this event. Heike Drechsler (GDR, 7.22 metres) and Galina Chistyakova (URS, 7.11 metres) took second and third positions respectively.

4 African victories: Once again, Kenyans demonstrated their talent for middle-distance running. Here, Paul Ereng (left) wins the 800 metres ahead of Joaquim Cruz of Brazil (right) and Said Aouita (MAR, centre). In the 1500 metres, Ereng's compatriot Peter Rono became the first Kenyan since the legendary Kip Keino (in Mexico City, 1968) to win this event. Britain's Peter Elliott was second.

5 More African success:
Over 5000 metres, John Ngugi (KEN) ran a very controlled race. His finishing sprint secured him an advantage of 3.82 seconds over second-placed Dieter Baumann (FRG), with third place going to Hansjörg Kunze (GDR). In the 10,000 metres, gold went to Brahim Boutayeb (MAR) ahead of Salvatore Antibo (ITA).

6 Led from the start:
The women's marathon was dominated by Rosa Mota (POR). Silver went to Lisa Martin (AUS), the bronze to Katrin Dörre (GDR).

7 East German double:
Christian Schenk was the first East German to win the decathlon, ahead of his compatriot Torsten Voss.

8 Fashion-conscious:
Triple Olympic champion Florence Griffith-Joyner in one of the 100 metres heats.

9 One vault victory: On his third attempt at 5.90 metres, Sergei Bubka (URS) maintained his composure to win the pole vault over teammates Rodion Gataullin (5.85 metres) and Grigori Yegorov (5.80 metres).

10 Win over arch rival:
With a distance of 74.68 metres, Petra Felke (GDR) won the javelin competition ahead of her arch rival, the British world and European champion, Fatima Whitbread. The bronze medal went to Beate Koch (GDR).

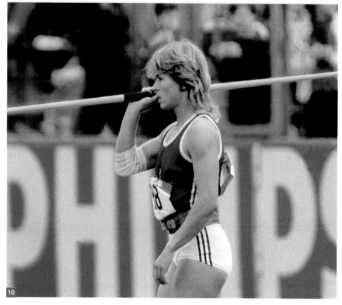

1 **Six wins in six starts:** Winning six gold medals, Kristin Otto (GDR) was without doubt the outstanding athlete of the Summer Games in Seoul. She won the first Olympic 50 metres freestyle event for women. In the 100 metres freestyle, she beat Yong Zhuang (CHN) and Cathérine Plewinski (FRA). In the 100 metres backstroke, 23-year-old Otto defeated the Hungarian Krisztina Egerszegy and fellow East German Cornelia Sirch. She proved her versatility by winning the 100 metres butterfly final, beating Birte Weigang (GDR) and the Chinese swimmer Hong Quian. Her gold medal collection was completed by her two relay wins with the 4 x 100 metres freestyle and 4 x 100 metres medley teams.

2 **Wins for Matt Biondi:** The star of the men's swimming competitions was the American Matt Biondi (nearest the camera). He took five gold medals, one silver, and a bronze. He won the 50 metres freestyle ahead of his team mate Thomas Jager and Gennadi Prigoda of the USSR. (This was the first short freestyle event for men since the 50 yards in 1904.) In the 100 metres freestyle, he outclassed his compatriot Christopher Jacobs and the Frenchman Stephan Caron to set a new Olympic record. He took silver in the 100 metres butterfly, and finished third behind Duncan Armstrong (AUS) and the Anders Holmertz (SWE) in the 200 metres freestyle. His other three golds were as a member of teams in the 4 x 100 metres and 4 x 200 metres freestyle and the 4 x 100 metres medley relays.

3 **Maestro Moorhouse:** Britain's Adrian Moorhouse (right) clinched the 100 metres breaststroke gold in a time of 1:02.04 minutes ahead of Károly Guttler (HUN, 1:02.05) and Dimitri Volkov (URS, 1:02.20). Moorhouse won European titles at this distance in 1985, 1987, and 1989 (the last in a world record time of 1:01.49), and in the 200 metres breaststroke in 1983.

4 **Victorious eights:** Twenty years after their win in Mexico City, West Germany reclaimed the Olympic eights title. In the final, Manfred Klein, Thomas Möllenkamp, Matthias Mellinghaus, Ansgar Wessling, Eckhardt Schultz, Armin Eichholz, Thomas Domian, Wolfgang Maennig, and Bahne Rabe (from right to left) beat the crews from the USSR and USA by just one length. Further successes for the West German rowers came courtesy of Peter-Michael Kolbe who won the silver medal behind Thomas Lange (GDR) in the single sculls, and the coxless fours (Norbert Kesslau, Jörg Puttlitz, and Volker and Guido Grabow) who took the bronze medal behind East Germany and the USA. The most successful rowing nation were East Germany, with five gold medals in the women's competitions and three golds in the men's events.

5 **Favourite wins:** The world champion in the springboard, the American Greg Louganis, dominated the three-metre competition and successfully defended his Olympic title. In the highboard diving, Louganis (world champion in this event also) repeated his winning performance to leave second and third places to Ni Xiong (CHN) and Jesus Mena (MEX). In the women's competitions, the Chinese divers Min Gao (three-metre) and Yanmei Xu (ten-metre) were in a class of their own.

6 **Dutch rowing gold:** The double sculls event produced a surprise win for the Dutchmen Roland Florijn (left) and Nicolaas Rienks. They defeated Switzerland (Schwerzmann and Bodenmann) by 1.46 seconds. The Soviet Union (Marchenko and Yakusha) took the bronze. Florijn and Rienks were Holland's only medallists in the rowing competitions at Seoul.

7 **Italian boat wins:** In the coxed pairs, the Italians Carmine (left) and Giuseppe Abbagnale (centre) successfully defended their 1984 Olympic title. On the right is cox Giuseppe di Capua. The silver medal was taken by the East Germans, with the bronze going to the British team. The two brothers were also part of the winning fours sculls team.

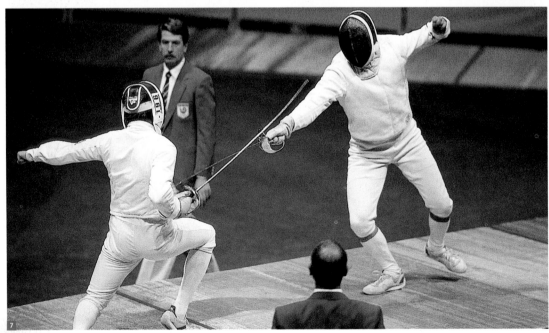

1 **Perfect presentation:** In the rhythmic gymnastics event, Marina Lobach (URS) gave an immaculate display. In the all-round competition, she won the gold medal ahead of Adriana Dunavska (BUL) and her Soviet team mate Alexandra Timoshenko.

2 **Soviet superiority:** With five medals under his belt, Vladimir Artemov was the Games' most successful gymnast. He won golds in the parallel and horizontal bars and the individual and team combined exercises events; and a silver in the floor event.

3 **Dressage win:** Nicole Uphoff (FRG) picked up the gold medal ahead of Margitt Otto-Crepin (FRA) and Christine Stückelberger (SUI). Uphoff also won a gold in the team event.

4 **On his way to gold:** The New Zealander Mark Todd, on Charisma, coped best with the demanding circuit to successfully defend his 1984 Olympic three-day event title, beating the Britons Ian Stark and Virginia Leng.

5 **Chinese triumph:** All medals in the women's table tennis singles went to China: Jing Chen (pictured) took gold, Huifeng Li the silver, and Zhimin Jiao the bronze.

6 **Korean 1-2:** The men's table tennis singles title went to Yoo Nam Kyu ahead of team mate Kim Ki Taik.

7 **Men's épée final:** This was won by Jean-François

Lamour (FRA, right) over Janusz Olech (POL, left).

8 Flood of medals: Svetlana Boginskaya (URS) won the horse vault and was in the winning Soviet combined exercise team. She also won a silver and a bronze.

9 The favourite wins: Silivas became a triple Olympic champion at Seoul. Daniela Silivas (ROM) won the balance beam event ahead of Elena Shushunova (URS).

10 Doubling up: The Olympic 1000 metres speed skating champion at the Calgary Winter Games, Christa Luding-Rothenburger (GDR, right), won a silver medal in the sprint cycling event, defeated only by Elena Salumä (URS, left).

11 Dutch gold medal: Eventual winner Meinque Knol (HOL, No. 32) leads the pack in the women's road race.

12 Tennis back: The first Olympic men's full medal tournament for 64 years was won by Miloslav Mecir (TCH).

13 Steffi's gold: The West German tennis ace Steffi Graf won the women's singles beating Gabriela Sabatini (ARG).

14 West German success: Sabine Bau (left, silver), Anja Fichtel (centre, gold), and Zita Funkenhauser (right, bronze) celebrate their medals in the individual foil event – and gold in the team event.

1 USSR leading nation: In the Greco-Roman wrestling, Aleksander Karelin (URS) took the super-heavyweight gold medal ahead of Rangel Guerovski (BUL) and Tomas Johansson (SWE). The USSR clinched four gold medals, one silver medal, and a bronze in the Greco-Roman competitions as well as four golds, three silvers, and two bronze medals in the freestyle events, thus becoming the most successful nation in the wrestling competitions.

2 Norwegian win: Jon Rönningen (blue jersey) won the flyweight (Greco-Roman style) final against Atsuji Miyahara of Japan.

3 Maske is champion: Henry Maske (GDR, right) beat Egerton Marcus (CAN, left) to win the middleweight boxing gold. Following German reunification, Maske pursued a professional career and became world light-heavyweight champion in 1993.

4 Turkish delight: With a lift of 342.5 kilograms, the weightlifter Nahim Süleymanogü (TUR) secured gold in the featherweight contest ahead of Stefan Topourov (BUL, 312.5 kilograms) and Huanming Ye (CHN, 287.5 kilograms).

5 Lewis leads: Lennox Lewis won the super-heavyweight boxing gold for Canada, to which he emigrated as a child. Lewis later became the first British-born world heavyweight champion this century.

6 First win for 68 years: For the first time since 1920, Great Britain took the gold medal in the men's hockey tournament, beating West Germany 3-1 in the final. Holland took the bronze medal. The women's tournament was won by Australia.

7 Soviet champions: In the final of the soccer tournament (picture here) a winning goal in extra time gave the USSR victory over Brazil. This was the Soviets' first football gold medal since 1956. In the third-place play-off for the bronze medal, West Germany defeated Italy 3-0.

8 Scintillating volleyball: The USSR lost the final in four sets (15-13, 10-15, 4-15, 8-15) to the United States. In the women's tournament, the Soviet team eventually beat the Peruvians to win 10-15, 12-15, 15-13, 15-7, 17-15.

9 Medal ceremony: The Olympic small-bore rifle (prone) champion at Seoul was Miroslav Varga (TCH, middle). The Korean Yuong Chul Cha (right) took silver and Attila Zahonyi (HUN) secured bronze.

10 Shooting star: Silvia Sperber (FRG) defeated Vessela Lecheva (BUL) and Valentina Cherkassova (URS) in the small-bore rifle (three positions) event. She also took a silver medal behind Irina Chilova (URS) in the air rifle competition.

Albertville

With the award of the XVI Winter Games, France joined the USA in the exclusive club of three-time hosts: in 1924, it had been Chamonix; in 1968, Grenoble; in 1992, it was to be Albertville.

ALBERTVILLE'S SUCCESSFUL BID TO stage the Winter Olympics had been inspired by the French triple Olympic skiing champion of 1968, Jean-Claude Killy. He was chairman of the organizing committee, which also included the politician Michele Barnier. With support from the French government, Killy wanted to stimulate the economic development of the Savoy region, an area whose winter sports and tourism potential had been largely untapped. The "Olympic venture" was paid for through sponsoring contracts, the sale of exclusive television broadcasting rights to a US television company, as well as through licence agreements that declared certain companies to be "official suppliers".

During the preparatory stage, there was increasing criticism about the decision to spread the competitions over 12 different venues. Additionally, extra construction work led to protests from environmentalists. As a result, the IOC president announced the Committee's future intention to allow certain competitions within a Games to take place in different regions or countries if it meant that such a move would decrease the chances of damage to the environment.

The main venue at Albertville saw all the athletes from the 64 participating nations convene only for the opening and closing ceremonies. The results of the political changes in Central and Eastern Europe were clearly noticeable during the nations' parade at the opening ceremony. Lithuania competed under its own flag for the first time since 1928; likewise Estonia and Latvia for the first time since 1936. In addition, competitors from other parts of the former Soviet Union formed a team that went under the name of the Unified Team (EUN). For the first time in 28 years, athletes from all over Germany were reunited in one team for the Winter Olympics.

A French Celebration
The official logo of the XVI Winter Olympics held in Albertville features the colours of the French national flag beneath a stylized Olympic flame.

For Albertville the Winter Olympic programme was augmented by short track speed skating and freestyle skiing on the moguls slope. With her three gold and two silver medals, the Nordic skier Lyubov Yegorova (EUN) was the most successful female athlete of the Games. Her team mate Raisa Smetanina crowned her career with a gold medal as part of the relay team. The 39-year-old athlete had picked up ten medals in a total of five Olympic Games, stretching back to 1976.

After having won the bronze medal in 1984 and the silver medal in 1988, the Russian ice dancing pair of Marina Klimova and Sergey Ponomarenko clinched their first Olympic title with a dazzling display on the ice. With Bart Veldkamp's success over 10,000 metres, the Netherlands celebrated their first men's Olympic speed skating title since Piet Kleine's Olympic-record-breaking triumph at Innsbruck in 1976.

Björn Again and Again
The Nordic skiing specialist Björn Daehlie of Norway took gold medals in the new combined styles event (10 kilometres classical and 15 kilometre freestyle), in the 50 kilometres cross-country freestyle, and with the 4 x 10 kilometres relay team. He also took a silver medal in the 30 kilometres classical.

Norwegian Treble
The Norwegian Vegard Ulvang won three gold medals in Nordic skiing events over 10 kilometres (classical), 30 kilometres (classical), and with the Norwegian 4 x 10 kilometres relay team.

Success on the Piste
There was double success for Petra Kronberger. The Austrian won both the slalom and the alpine combined, the latter ahead of her compatriot Anita Wachter (seen left).

Finn Wins
Ski jumper Toni Nieminen of Finland won two gold medals in the big hill (90-metre) and team events. He added a bronze medal in the small hill (70-metre) event.

Full Marks
Double Olympic biathlon champion Mark Kirchner (GER) won the 10 kilometres and added a second gold medal as part of the German 4 x 7.5 kilometres relay team. Over 20 kilometres, he took second place behind Yevgeni Redkin (EUN).

1 Opening ceremony: 2500 performers present a stunning "festival for the senses".

2 Next Games in Norway: During the closing ceremony, Viking ships prepare for Lillehammer 1994.

3 16-year-old wins: Using the V-style technique, Toni Nieminen (FIN) won the big hill event ahead of Martin Höllwarth and Heinz Kullin (both AUT).

4 Double win for Austria: On the small hill, Ernst Vettori beat his Austrian compatriot Martin Höllwarth.

5 Norwegian success: Vegard Ulvang on his way to gold in the 30 kilometres cross-country event.

6 French domination: In the Nordic combined competition, Fabrice Guy (FRA, left) picked up the gold medal.

7 Gold medal for Italy: Stefania Belmondo (ITA) won the 30 kilometres Nordic event ahead of Lyubov Yegorova and Yelena Wälbe (both EUN).

8 Japanese favourites: Japan's victory over Norway and Austria in the Nordic combined team event came as no surprise to the pundits. The picture shows anchor man Kenji Ogiwara.

9 Alpine surprise: Never having won a world cup event before, the Austrian Patrick Ortlieb picked up a surprise gold in the downhill at Albertville.

10 Most successful biathlete: Mark Kirchner of Germany won two gold medals and a silver to become the most successful biathlete at Albertville.

11 Tomba's triumph: Alberto Tomba successfully defended his Olympic title in the giant slalom.

12 Austria celebrates: With two gold medals under her belt, the Austrian Petra Kronberger became the most successful alpine skier at the Games. She took the slalom and combined events.

13 Outsider wins: Finn Christian Jagge (NOR) won a surprise gold medal in the men's slalom.

14 Norway's medals: Kjeti Andre Aamodt demonstrated his skill be taking the gold medal in the Super G and the bronze medal in the giant slalom.

15 Winning trio: Deborah Compagnoni (centre) celebrates after taking the gold medal in the Super G ahead of Carole Merle (FRA, right) and Katja Seizinger (GER, left).

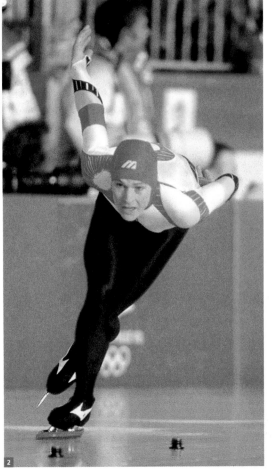

1 **Ice dance win:** After their bronze medal in Sarajevo in 1984 and silver medal in Calgary in 1988, it was third time lucky for the favourites Marina Klimova and Sergey Ponomarenko of St. Petersburg. They took the ice dance gold medal in Albertville. Isabelle and Paul Duchesnay (FRA) took second place.

2 **Germans on ice:** Gunda Niemann, Germany's most successful speed skater, won two gold medals (3000 and 5000 metres) and a silver (1500 metres). Further German successes were Jacquelin Börner's gold over 1500 metres, Heicke Warnicke's silvers over 3000 and 5000 metres, and the bronzes won by Christa Luding, Monique Garbrecht, and Claudia Pechstein over 500, 1000, and 5000 metres respectively.

3 **Favourite clinches title:** The women's world figure skating champion Kristi Yamaguchi (USA) beat Midori Ito (JPN) and Nancy Kerrigan (USA) to win the gold. The

European champion, Surya Bonaly (FRA), had to settle for fifth position.

4 **Win on old sledge:** On the luge track at La Plagne, the men had to cope with a 1250 metres long run with a gradient of 8.8 per cent and a difference in altitude of 110 metres. After having difficulties with a new type of sledge during preliminary training sessions, the German Georg Hackl (pictured) started the luge competition with an old sledge. His ability shone through as he won the competition and pushed the Austrian duo of Markus Prock and Markus Schmidt into silver and bronze medal positions. In the women's event, sisters Doris (gold) and Angelika Neuner (silver) secured a double win for Austria. Susi Erdmann (GER) finished in third position.

5 **Defeated favourites:** Stefan Krausse and Jan Behrendt (GER) on their way to the gold medal in the two-seater luge. Favourites Hansjörg Raffl and Norbert Huber (ITA) had to settle for a bronze medal behind

silver medallists Yves Mankel and Thomas Rudolph (GER).

6 **Swiss duo's success:** The Olympic champions in the two-man bob were Gustav Weder and Donat Acklin. They picked up a bronze medal with Lorenz Schindelholz and Curdin Morell in the four-man bob, beaten by the Austrian and German teams.

7 **Ice hockey enthusiasm:** Despite the collapse of the Soviet Union, coach Viktor Tikhonov ensured that the new-look EUN team were a gold medal-winning unit. In the final, they beat Canada 3-1 and gave a Russian-based team their sixth ice hockey gold out of the last seven Olympics. Next came the Canadian team, who clinched their first Olympic ice hockey medal since 1968. The Czechs took the bronze medal.

8 **Exciting jumps:** The exhibition sport of freestyle skiing (moguls) was introduced for the first time, and enthralled the spectators. Curling was once again a demonstration sport.

Barcelona

A crowd of 100,000 spectators in Barcelona's stadium plus a television audience of two billion watched one of the most spectacular Olympic opening ceremonies of all time.

Dream Team
In basketball no team stood a chance against the United States. Earvin "Magic" Johnson was the star player at Barcelona.

THESE TURNED OUT TO BE THE Olympic Games of the Spanish IOC president, Juan Antonio Samaranch, who had managed to bring the 1992 Games to his home region of Catalonia. Being an advocate of the commercialization of sport, he expressed his gratitude to the Games' sponsors at the end of the Barcelona celebration. The IOC registered millions of dollars in revenue from these Olympics, partly through the sale of television broadcasting rights. However, the IOC president's stance was not greeted with universal approval. Many athletes complained that the start times of several events were arranged to suit the TV and advertising industries.

Christie Wins for Britain
After taking silver in Seoul in 1988, British sprinter Linford Christie achieved his greatest triumph in winning the 100 metres final. In 1986 and again in 1990 he had been European champion over this distance.

Besides the wonderful cultural activities that accompanied the Games, the modernization and construction work carried out on sports facilities and in other key areas of the city attracted praise. The neo-classical Olympic Stadium on Montjuic and the velodrome were refurbished, while the 1700-seater Sant Jordi Sports Palace (named for the Catalonian patron saint) was built from scratch.

The 1992 Games were significant in that they marked the emergence, or re-emergence, of a number of teams onto the world sporting stage, following the recent waves of political change in Europe and elsewhere. The first appearance since 1964 of a pan-German team was greeted with pleasure. A similarly warm reception was extended to South Africa, which was welcomed back to the Olympic Games having last competed in 1960, in response to the government's reform programme. Despite the far-reaching upheaval in the former Soviet Union, a Unified Team (EUN) was again field by the Commonwealth of Independent States. In the Balkans, meanwhile, the bloody fight for Tito's legacy dragged on, and Yugoslavia, Bosnia-Herzegovina,

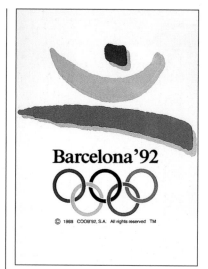

Spanish Summer
The official poster of the XXV Summer Olympics echoes the style of the Spanish painter Joán Miro.

Slovenia, and Croatia each sent its own team to Barcelona.

As for the sports, there were major upsets in some of the individual events. In the women's 100 metres hurdles, for example, Paraskevi Patoulidou became the first Greek sportswoman to claim an Olympic gold, and in the 800 metres, Holland's Ellen van Langen could hardly believe that she had won. There were also triumphs over adversity. Gail Devers (USA) overcame serious illness to win the 100 metres. Only a year earlier she had been suffering from Graves' disease, and there had been fears that she might have to have a leg amputated.

The single most successful participant at the Barcelona Olympics was the gymnast Vitali Sherbo (EUN), with six gold medals. He was followed in the medal list by swimmers Yevgeni Sadovi (EUN) and Krisztina Egerszegy (HUN) with three golds each. The subject of drugs was again on the agenda, and both China and Cuba were much criticized for having refused to take part in international drugs testing prior to the Games.

Sherbo's Song
During the five individual medal ceremonies for Vitali Sherbo, even though he was a member of the Unified Team, the flag of Belarus was raised and the national anthem of the republic played for the first time ever at the Olympic Games.

Drechsler Delighted
Heike Drechsler of Germany, one of the most successful track-and-field athletes of the early 1990s, emerged as the winner in the long jump.

Triple Gold
Krisztina Egerszegy of Hungary, world champion and world record holder in the 100 and 200 metres backstroke and reigning European champion for the 400 metres freestyle, confirmed her status as a favourite in Barcelona with three gold medals.

1 Mystical narratives: Among the extravagant tableaux that characterized the Barcelona Games' opening ceremony was the battle between humans and an ocean full of monsters (shown here). Other highlights were performances by Spanish opera stars Teresa Berganza, Montserrat Caballé, José Carreras, and Placido Domingo. A further treat for the audience was the appearance of the queen of Flamenco, Christina Hoyos, on horseback.

2 Linford is the fastest: Britain's Linford Christie won the men's 100 metres final ahead of Namibia's Frankie Fredericks (who also picked up the silver medal in the 200 metres) and the American Dennis Mitchell. The oldest man by four years to win this sprint title, Christie added the

world championship to his collection the following year.

3 Gail's force: Gail Devers (US, right) wins the women's 100 metres, beating Jamaica's Juliet Cuthbert (second from the right) and Irina Privalova (EUN, left) by one hundredth of a second. Gwen Torrence (USA) and Jamaica's Merlene Ottey (second and third from the left) are left empty-handed. Devers' hopes of a second title were dashed when she fell in the 100 metres hurdles, leaving Paraskevi Patoulidou to claim the first gold medal ever for a Greek woman athlete.

4 Golden Sally: In a time of 53.23 seconds, Britain's Sally Gunnell (right) wins the 400 metres hurdles. In 1993, Gunnell won the 400 metres world title and in 1994 she took the European and Commonwealth titles as well.

5 Long-distance scandal: In an extraordinary finish to the 10,000 metres, the Kenyan athlete Richard Chelimo (left) was obstructed by Morocco's Hammou Boutayeb, who had already been lapped. Khalid Skah (also Morocco, right), who was lying in second place, went on to cross the finishing line first. Skah was initially disqualified, but later declared Olympic champion. The silver went to Chelimo, who was, however, celebrated as the moral victor.

6 New record in hurdles: American Kevin Young won the 400 metres hurdles in 46.78 seconds, breaking the nine-year-old world record set by Ed Moses and becoming the first athlete to break 47 seconds for the event. Young was followed in by Winthrop Graham of Jamaica and Britain's Kriss Akabusi.

7 **Queen of track and field:** America's Jackie Joyner-Kersee was unbeatable in the heptathlon. With 7044 points, the 30-year-old decisively relegated Irina Belova (EUN, 6845 points) and Germany's Sabine Braun (6649 points) to second and third place. Jackie is the sister of the 1984 triple-jump champion, Al Joyner.

8 **Czech cashes in:** Czech athlete Robert Zmelik secured the decathlon gold medal at the end of two days of battle in the heat, amassing 8611 points. US champion Dave Johnson was involved in an incident during this event. Although he overstepped the base line when putting the shot, Johnson was not disqualified but was given a fourth attempt. He went on to win bronze with 8309 points. In the meantime, Spain's Antonio Penalver gave the home crowd plenty to cheer about, taking the silver with 8412 points.

9 **Lithuania's first gold:** Lithuania had not been represented at the Summer Olympics since 1928 and had never won a medal. Discus thrower Romas Ubartas – who had won the 1986 European title and the 1988 Olympic silver medal on behalf of the USSR – changed all that, bringing home gold from Barcelona.

10 **First jump wins:** No other athlete could match the 8.67 metres that Carl Lewis (USA, left) achieved in his very first jump during the long jump finals. Thus Lewis got his own back for his defeat by fellow American Mike Powell (right) at the 1991 world championships in Tokyo. In that competition, Powell had beaten Bob Beamon's 1968 world record of 8.90 metres by five centimetres. In Barcelona, Powell jumped into second place, with Joe Greene coming third to ensure a US clean sweep in the event. Gold in the long jump was at least some consolation for the legendary Lewis, who had failed to gain an individual sprint place with the US Olympic team.

11 **High jump nail-biter:** Heike Henkel (GER) was faced with an early departure from the high jump after twice failing to clear 1.97 metres. But unlike her great rival, the Bulgarian Stefka Kostadinova (a former world champion and the 1988 Olympic silver medallist), Henkel succeeded in her final attempt. She went on to jump 2.02 metres to win the event Second was Romania's Galina Astafel (2.00 metres), while the Cuban Joanet Quintero (1.97 metres) took bronze.

1 Team spirit: The EUN swimming team won the 4 x 200 metres freestyle relay ahead of Sweden and the USA.

2 Star swimmer: With three golds in the 100 and 200 metres backstroke and the 400 metres individual medley, Krisztina Egerszegy was the Games' most successful female swimmer.

3 Three gold medals: Yevgeniy Sadovyi (EUN) won the 200 and 400 metres freestyle and picked up a third gold in the 4 x 200 metres freestyle relay.

4 Medley specialist: Tamas Darnyi (HUN) retained his Olympic titles in the 200 and 400 metres medley events.

5 Surprise win: Dagmar Hase was the only German swimmer to win a gold medal. In the 400 metres freestyle, she defeated the title holder Janet Evans (USA). She added two silver medals – in the 200 metres backstroke and the 4 x 100 metres medley relay.

6 Winning twins: The synchronized swimming duet event was won by Karen and Sarah Josephson (USA). Penny and Vicky Vilagos (CAN) were second, and Fumiko Kuno and Aki Takayama (JPN) third.

7 Scintillating final: The Italian water polo team proudly present their gold medals. The longest final in the history of the Olympics, against the host nation Spain, was decided by a goal shortly before the end of the sixth period of extra time that gave Italy a 9-8 victory.

8 Wildwater renaissance: For the first time since its Olympic debut in Munich, slalom canoeing was in the Olympic programme. In the Canadian pairs, the Americans Scott Strausbaugh (pictured front) and Joe Jacobi won ahead of Miroslav Simek and Jiri Rohan (TCH) and the French pair of Franck Adisson and Wilfrid Forgues.

9 Title for Great Britain: The British rowers Steven Redgrave (left) and Matthew Pinsent are exhausted but happy, having won the Olympic coxless pairs title.

10 And another British rowing victory: Cox Garry Herbert (right) and oarsmen Jonathan and Greg Searle celebrate their victory in the coxed pairs.

11 Chinese domination: After Min Gao and Mingxia Fu had captured the women's springboard and highboard diving titles respectively, Shuwei Sun (pictured here) claimed a third gold for China with his win in the men's highboard event. In the men's springboard, Liangde Tan had to settle for silver.

12 French sailing gold: Yves Loday and Nicolas Henard demonstrated their invincibility in the Tornado class. Randy Smyth and Keith Notary (USA) and Mitch Booth and John Forbes (AUS) took second and third places respectively.

13 Fastest surfer: Windsurfing was enjoying its third Olympic appearance at the Barcelona Games. In the Lechner A-390 class, Franck David of France (pictured here) defeated the American Mike Gebhardt and Lars Kleppich of Australia.

1 Perfect programme: The Chinese gymnast Lu Li won the asymmetrical bars with a mark of 10 and was also second in the balance beam event.

2 Reward for perfection: Alexandra Timoshenko of the Unified Team presented a demanding programme in the rhythmic gymnastics to earn herself the gold medal.

3 Sole medal: Trent Dimas's win in the horizontal bars ahead of Grigoriy Misyutin (EUN) and Andreas Wecker (GER) gave the US men's gymnastics team its only medal.

4 Celebrated gymnast: Vitali Sherbo (EUN) underlined his superiority by winning gold medals in the rings, pommel horse, horse vault, and parallel bars as well as in the individual and team combined exercises .

5 More Unified success: Tatyana Lyssenko picked up gold medals in the balance beam and team events plus a bronze in the horse vault.

6 Floor triumph: Lavinia Milosovici (ROM) was the deserved gold medal winner in the floor exercises event.

7 Gold medal for Estonia: In the 1000 metres sprint, Erika Salumäe (EST) defeated Annett Neumann (GER) and Ingrid Haringa (HOL).

8 Boardman first: Britain's Chris Boardman won the 4000 metres individual pursuit ahead of Jens Lehmann (GER) and Gary Anderson (NZL).

9 Home win: José Moreno Perinan (ESP) won the 1000 metres time trial with Shane Kelly (AUS) and Erin Hartwell (USA) coming second and third respectively.

10 Fencing win: France's Philippe Omnes celebrates his individual foil gold medal win.

11 Italian title: The world champion in the foil, Giovanna Trillini, also clinched the Olympic title. She won a second gold as part of the victorious Italian foil team.

12 Shooting star: Michael Jakosits (GER) claimed the gold medal in the running game target event ahead of Anatoliy Asrabayev (EUN) and Lubos Racansky (TCH).

13 Chinese accuracy: In the skeet shooting competition, Shan Zhang (CHN) defeated all comers. The second-placed Juan Jorge Giha (PER, left) and the bronze medallist Bruno Rossetti of Italy (right) congratulate her.

14 Joint win: The archery title was won jointly by Sebastien Flute (FRA) and Jae-Hun Chung (KOR). Britain's Simon Terry took the bronze medal.

1 Strongest athlete: In the super-heavyweight weightlifting category, Alexander Kurlovich (EUN) won the gold medal with 450.0 kilograms ahead of his team mate Leonid Taranenko (425.0 kilograms) and the German Manfred Nerlinger (412.5 kilograms).

2 Jubilation in front of home crowd: Spain's Miriam Blasco can hardly believe that she is the new Olympic judo champion in the lightweight category (up to 56 kilograms).

3 Cubans dominate: Cuban boxers clinched Olympic titles in seven out of twelve weight categories. At middleweight, Ariel Hernandez (right) won the gold, with America's Chris Byrd (left) taking silver.

4 Featherweight gold: In the final, Andreas Tews (GER, right) was too good for Faustino Reyes (ESP, left).

5 Favourite wins: Hakki Busar (TUR, red jersey) could not prevent the world champion of 1989-91, Maik Bullmann (GER, blue jersey), from claiming the Olympic title in the light-heavyweight category (Greco-Roman style).

6 Light-heavyweight judo: Antal Kovacs (HUN, left) beat Britain's Raymond Stevens (right) to win the gold medal.

7 Wasted home advantage: In the women's doubles final, Arantxa Sanchez-Vicario and Conchita Martinez (ESP) were defeated by the Americans Gigi (left) and Mary Jo Fernandez (right) 7-5, 2-6, 6-2.

8 Tennis pros at Olympics: The Germans Michael Stich (right) and Boris Becker (left) made early departures from the singles. In the doubles, however, they won the gold, beating

Wayne Ferreira and Piet Norval (RSA) 7-6, 4-6, 7-6, 6-3.

9 USA defeated: America's most popular sport, baseball, was introduced to the 1992 Olympic schedule as a gesture towards Atlanta 1996. However, the USA was represented by a second-choice team and finished fourth behind Cuba, Chinese Taipei, and Japan.

10 Basketball dream: No other team stood a chance against the USA's "Dream Team" of National Basketball Association all-stars. In the final, the Croatians were

defeated 117-85.

11 Badminton's debut: Indonesian players won both singles in the inaugural badminton tournament. Alan Kusuma (pictured here) won the men's, whilst Susi Susanti took the women's gold medal.

12 Dressage gold medal for Germany: The German team of (from left) Klaus Balkenhol, Nicole Uphoff, Monica Theodorescu and Isabelle Werth claimed the gold medal in dressage. Second and third places went to the Netherlands and the USA respectively.

Lillehammer

Following Oslo's 1952 example, the Norwegian town of Lillehammer set about organizing a Winter Olympics "for everyone". The 16-day celebration took place in a festive atmosphere.

IN 1986, THE OLYMPIC CHARTER, which stipulated that Winter and Summer Games be held in the same year, was changed by the IOC. The Winter and Summer Olympics would now be held alternately every two years. In introducing the two-year interval, officials had envisaged better marketing prospects, partly because television companies had reached their limit under the previous arrangement. They could not attract the amount of advertising they needed in order to pay for Olympic television broadcasting rights twice a year – an outlay of millions of dollars. However, from now on, the Winter Games would fall in the same year as football's World Cup finals.

On its appointment as the site of the XVII Winter Games, Lillehammer was a town of 21,000 inhabitants, little known outside Norway. Inside four years, though, the organizers had turned it into a first-rate Olympic venue. They modernized existing sports facilities, built new ones from scratch where necessary, and generated the infrastructure required to stage a modern Olympic Games. The Norwegians were particularly concerned about environmental aspects. Future usage was a major consideration in the siting of buildings and in their architecture. Excessive tree-felling was avoided.

The political changes in South Africa and its readmission to the IOC allowed South African competitors to participate in a Winter Olympics for the first time in 34 years. Meanwhile, the Unified Team that had taken part at Albertville and Barcelona was no more. Instead, teams from Georgia, Russia, the Ukraine, and other newly independent former Soviet republics arrived in Norway to compete. Among the 67 teams taking part at Lillehammer was a small one from Bosnia-Herzegovina, whose homeland was in the grip of a bloody civil war.

Medals Galore
With a total of six gold and three silver medals from her two Olympics, the Russian skier Lyubov Yegorova became one of the most successful female Winter Olympics competitors of all time.

Logo for Lillehammer
The logo for the XVII Winter Games held in Lillehammer, Norway, was designed by the artist Sarah Rosenbaum.

New competitions included further short track skating events and the freestyle skiing aerials. The women's figure skating attracted most of the media's attention. Before the Games, the favourite Nancy Kerrigan of the USA, had been assaulted by persons believed to be connected with her rival Tonya Harding. Harding, the 1994 US champion, was nevertheless allowed to take part at Lillehammer, though she was not placed. The Ukraine's Oksana Bayul eventually won, with Kerrigan finishing second.

The 1000 metres short track skating event finished in unique fashion. After numerous falls and disqualifications, only the gold (Ki-Hoon Kim, KOR) and silver medals (Ji-Hoon Chae, KOR) were awarded in the usual manner. The bronze went to the winner of the "B" final, Marc Gagnon (CAN), who had in fact clocked a faster time than the two Koreans. Italian skier Alberto Tomba augmented his medal collection by winning another slalom silver, bringing his overall tally to five.

Winning Streak
At her second Olympic Games, the Russian Lyubov Yegorova won three golds (5 kilometres, combined pursuit event, and 4 x 5 kilometres relay) and one silver medal (15 kilometres).

High Point
Having won the giant slalom world title in 1985, Markus Wasmeier (GER) crowned his career in Lillehammer with gold medals in the giant slalom and the Super G.

Koss Cruises to Gold
In front of his home crowd, the speed skater Johann Olav Koss won three gold medals – over 1500, 5000, and 10,000 metres. In each event, Koss improved on the world record.

Nordic Master
With two gold and two silver medals, Norway's Björn Daehlie emphasized his standing as one of the finest cross-country skiers in the world.

1 **Festival of winter sports:** The opening ceremony of the Lillehammer Games was conducted by King Harald V of Norway. The pageant included local people in national costume driving traditional sleds pulled by reindeer.

2 **Joy of victory:** Markus Wasmeier (GER) celebrates his win in the giant slalom ahead of Urs Kälin (SUI) and Christian Mayer (AUT). The German picked up his second gold medal in the Super G.

3 **"Grande dame" of skiing:** With her slalom win, the Swiss skier Vreni Schneider became the only female alpine skier to have claimed three Olympic gold medals, having won the slalom and giant slalom in Calgary. At Lillehammer, she added a silver medal in the combined event and a bronze medal in the giant slalom.

4 **Comeback to gold:** Having suffered from countless injuries, Diann Roffe (USA) staged a brilliant comeback. She took the super giant slalom (Super G) ahead of the Russian Svetlana Gladisheva and Isolde Kostner of Italy.

5 **Three medals for Kazakhstan:** Vladimir Smirnov of the former Soviet republic of Kazakhstan won the gold medal in the 50 kilometres cross-country skiing (classical) and silver medals in the 10 kilometres (classical) and the combined pursuit event.

6 **Most successful male competitor:** By increasing his tally of gold medals to five, the Norwegian skier Björn Daehlie became the most successful male competitor in the history of the Winter Olympics in terms of gold medals. He has also won three silvers.

7 **Alaskan picks up gold medal:** The American Tommy Moe, who lives near Anchorage, Alaska, won the men's downhill ahead of Kjetil Andre Aamodt of Norway and Canada's Edward Podivinsky.

8 **Five celebrations:** The Italian skier Manuela di Centa (left, with team mate Stefania Belmondo) secured the gold medal in the 30 kilometres. She also won the gold in the 15 kilometres, silver medals in the 5 kilometres and the combined pursuit, and a bronze in the 4 x 5 kilometres relay.

9 **Double victory for Norway:** Espen Bredesen on his way to the gold medal in the small hill ski jump. The silver medal was clinched by team mate Lasse Ottesen ahead of Dieter Thoma (GER).

10 **Bédard dominates the biathlon:** In the 7.5 kilometres event, Canada's Myriam Bédard defeated Svetlana Paramygina (BLR) and Valentina Tserbe (UKR). Bédard also won the 15 kilometres biathlon ahead of Anne Briand (FRA) and Uschi Disl (GER).

11 **Happy biathletes:** The German 4 x 7.5 kilometres biathlon relay team of Ricco Gro, Frank Luck, Mark Kirchner, and Sven Fischer celebrate their Olympic victory over Russia and France.

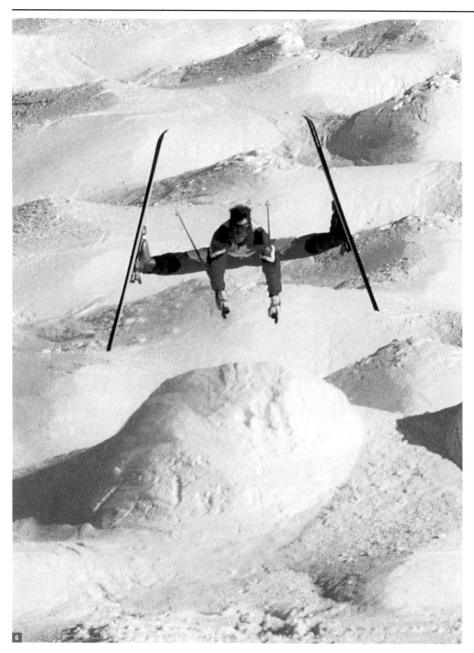

1 Favourite wins: Russia's Alexey Urmanov claimed the Olympic figure skating title ahead of Elvis Stojko (CAN) and Philippe Candeloro (FRA).

2 Gold medal for the Ukraine: Oksana Bayul secured the Olympic women's figure skating title. America's Nancy Kerrigan and the Chinese skater Lu Chen were placed second and third respectively.

3 Russians take ice dance gold: Oksana Grichuk and Yevgeniy Platov (RUS, centre) were the ice dance gold medallists. Jayne Torville and Christopher Dean (right) took the bronze medal behind the second-placed Russian pair, the world title holders Maya Usova

and Alexander Shulin (left). The British pair, who had won the Olympic title in Sarajevo in 1984, staged a marvellous comeback after ten years away from competition to become European champions earlier in the year. The favourites with the crowd, they were disappointed not to have won at Lillehammer.

4 Most successful female US athlete: At her fourth Olympics, the speed skater Bonnie Blair won the 500 metres and 1000 metres to bring her gold medal tally to five and make her the most successful female US Winter Olympic athlete. In the 500 metres sprint, she defeated Susan Auch (CAN) and Franziska Schenk (GER), while Anke Baier (GER) and the

Chinese skater Quiaobo Ye had to concede Blair's superiority over 1000 metres.

5 Gold medal for Sweden: The Swedish ice hockey team are clearly elated about winning the Olympic tournament. In the final, the Swedes defeated the Canadians 3–2 to record their first Olympic ice hockey title win. Finland took the bronze.

6 Spectacular performer: The Canadian trick skier Jean-Luc Brassard became the new Olympic moguls champion ahead of the Russian Sergei Shupletsov and Edgar Grospiron of France.

7 Italian double victory: Kurt Brugger and Wilfried

Huber (ITA) claimed the gold medal in the two-man luge. The event took place on the Hunderfossen ice track, which has an average gradient of 8.5 per cent. Their fellow Italians Hansjörg Raffl and Norbert Huber won the silver medal ahead of the German team of Stefan Krausse and Jan Behrendt.

8 Commanding win: The Italian luge tobogganist Gerda Weissensteiner turned out to be unbeatable. Her 3:15.517 minutes put her clear of Germany's Susi Erdmann (3:16.276) and Andrea Tagwerker of Austria (3:16.652).

9 Swiss bob team win: The Switzerland I team of Gustav Weder (right) and Donat Acklin

(left) on their way to the two-man bob gold medal. The silver was picked up by Switzerland II (Reto Götschi/Guido Acklin) ahead of Italy I (Günther Huber/Stefano Ticci).

10 Medals in short track: Britain's Nicholas Gooch (leading) won a bronze medal in the 500 metres short track speed skating behind Ji-Hoon Chae of Korea and Mirko Vuillermin of Italy. The Koreans dominated the short track, winning gold in four of the six events. In addition to Ji-Hoon Chae's success, Ki-Hoon Kim won the men's 1000 metres, Lee-Kyung Chun the women's 1000 metres, and the Koreans also won the women's 3000 metres relay. Korea also picked up a silver and a bronze.

Atlanta 1996

Atlanta

The Games to celebrate the centenary of the renaissance of the Olympic ideal will take place not in Athens, the venue of the first Games of modern times, but in the American city of Atlanta, Georgia, home of the soft drinks manufacturer and Olympic sponsor Coca-Cola.

AT THE INTERNATIONAL OLYMPIC COMMITTEE'S 96th plenary assembly, which took place in the Japanese capital of Tokyo on 18 September 1990, the agenda included the ballot to decide the venue for the XXVI Summer Olympics. The vote was held in the utmost secrecy. In previous years the choice had often been almost a foregone conclusion. This time, though, there was not so much as a hint of a favourite candidate.

For decades, the procedure for deciding on a host city has followed similar lines. Each IOC member writes the host city of his or her choice on a ballot paper, and the candidate that gains an absolute majority of the votes cast wins. If there is no outright winner, the candidate with the lowest number of votes is eliminated. In the event of the bottom two contestants in the ballot gaining an equal number of votes, a separate vote is taken to decide which of the two is to drop out of the race. Another full ballot is then held, and the same procedure followed until the required absolute majority has been gained.

At the Tokyo assembly, Belgrade, Manchester, Mel-

bourne, and Toronto were eliminated before the delegates finally opted for Atlanta over Athens in the decisive ballot by 51 votes to 35. IOC president Juan Antonio Samaranch abstained in the traditional manner. When the decision was announced, the elation of the American delegates and the Greeks' dejection was witnessed live by television viewers all over the world. As the USA was awarded a fourth Summer Olympics (after St. Louis in 1904 and Los Angeles in 1932 and 1984), Atlanta's mayor Maynard Jackson commented that from now on anything was possible, that the people of Atlanta were idealists and dedicated workers who had worked hard for their Olympic dream to come true.

Well-known supporters of Athens' candidacy expressed their regret over the result. The former Greek prime minister Andreas Papandreou said that they had been very confident about their candidacy and not only for historical reasons. The actress and former arts minister Melina Mercouri expressed her suspicion about the Games becoming "Coca-Colarized" because of the strong financial support provided by the Atlanta-based company. Officials

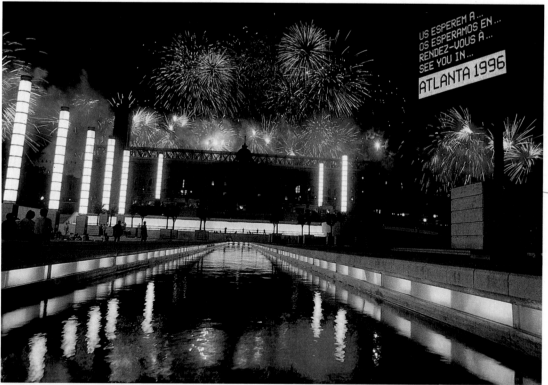

The Games Close
Even far outside Barcelona, the colourful fireworks marking the close of the 1992 Summer Games could be admired. Those who were not able to get a seat in the Olympic Stadium made their way to viewing points in the city in order to watch the pyrotechnics. As the Olympic flame was extinguished in the stadium at 11.02 p.m., the scoreboard display announced the Games that will commemorate the 100th anniversary of the Olympic movement. The multilingual display appealed to athletes to gather in Atlanta in 1996.

vigorously rejected rumours suggesting that Greece's NOC was contemplating its resignation from the IOC as a result of the ballot defeat. The Greek IOC member Nikos Filaretos demonstrated his faith in the democratic process when he commented that all Greeks found the result of the vote difficult to understand but were trying to accept it.

Atlanta is situated roughly 280 miles north of the Gulf of Mexico and has a population of approximately 435,000. In 1864, during the American Civil War, the city was completely destroyed. Since the turn of the twentieth century, however, it has developed into a major business centre of the southern United States.

The city gained worldwide publicity when Atlanta was the backdrop for the filming of the epic movie *Gone with the Wind* (which was set in the Civil War) during the late 1930s. Atlanta's most famous citizen was the black civil rights campaigner and Nobel Peace Prize winner Martin Luther King Jr, who was murdered in Memphis, Tennessee, in April 1968.

Atlanta's Olympic bid cost approximately seven million dollars and was spearheaded by the simple but effective slogan: "We want the Games". The campaign envisaged the creation of an "Olympic Ring" to include several sports facilities serving as venues for most of the competitions. The intention is that only the football, canoeing, rhythmic gymnastics, rowing, sailing, and softball competitions will have to be held at more distant venues. The "Ring" is centred on the Georgia World Congress Center and contains the indoor arena known as the "Georgia Dome" as well as new Olympic and swimming stadiums and a velodrome. The total cost has been calculated at 1.5 billion dollars.

Strong financial backing from two Atlanta-based companies contributed greatly to the city's successful bid. The corporations concerned were the television company CNN, owned by the media mogul Ted Turner, and the soft drink manufacturer Coca-Cola, which is the world's biggest sports sponsor and a commercial supporter of the Olympic Games. Additional advantages enjoyed by Atlanta are an excellent infrastructure and a state-of-the-art airport. Hotel capacity is intended to reach 70,000 in the run-up to the Games. By the time the Games open, the city of Atlanta will be geared up to cope with an influx of around two million visitors. Newly designed pictographs along with the Olympic mascot "Whatizit" will be there to give directions to tourists.

The 1996 Olympics will take place from 19 July until 4 August. The number of participating nations will be boosted by the republics that have emerged from the former Soviet Union. Most countries will organize qualifying competitions,

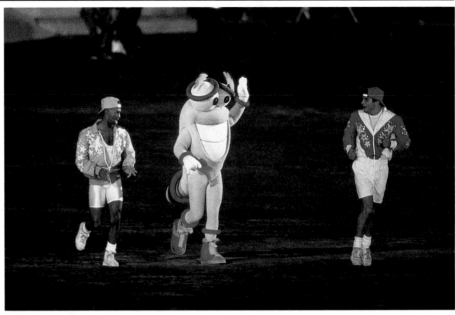

Atlanta's Mascot
At the closing ceremony of the 1992 Summer Olympics in Barcelona, the mascot of the 1996 Games in Atlanta, Georgia, a character called "Whatizit", makes its first appearance.

since the total number of athletes competing in Atlanta is not supposed to substantially exceed 10,000. Whereas some National Olympic Committees (for example, the German NOC) grant their athletes several opportunities to meet the required standards to qualify for the Olympics, other countries hold only one qualifier. (Track-and-field athletes in the USA, for instance, have just once chance to reach the mark.) Under this latter system, only those athletes delivering top performances on the day are assured of a place in their national squads. The IOC also admits athletes from countries where sporting standards are comparatively lower in order to allow all member countries to participate in the Games.

Compared with Barcelona 1992, there will be an extra 14 disciplines in the programme, bringing the total number of events to 271. Mountain biking, beach volleyball, and softball will be introduced as new sports, while additional events in established sports will include the individual road time trial (cycling) and double trap (shooting), in which there will be both men's and women's competitions. In track-and-field athletics, women will compete over 5000 metres for the first time and will have

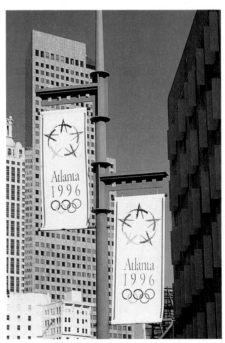

The Games Are Coming
Posters and flags in Atlanta, Georgia, announce the forthcoming big event. By the middle of 1995, Olympic building projects were well underway.

The Real Thing
One of the city's main attractions is the World of Coca-Cola, which covers the popular culture of the USA and the history of the local soft drink giant.

their own triple jump; in fencing, they will compete in the épée; in swimming they will contest a 4 x 200 metres freestyle relay; and there will be a women's football tournament. Furthermore, the 1996 Games will see some new team events, such as the badminton mixed doubles.

The 1995 world athletics championships gave some indications of whom to watch out for at Atlanta. Indeed, among the US gold medallists were two inhabitants of 1996's Olympic city – Derrick Adkins triumphed in the men's 400 metres hurdles, while Gwen Torrence, already Olympic champion at 200 metres, won the 100 metres. Other notable performances were American sprinter Michael Johnson's 200 and 400 metres double and Irish runner Sonia O'Sullivan's success in the women's 5000 metres.

A number of new world records were set at Gothenburg. America's Kim Batten broke Sally Gunnell's 400 metres hurdles mark and the Ukraine's Inessa Kravets smashed the women's triple jump record. But surely the athlete the world will be watching out for in 1996 is Britain's Jonathan Edwards, who became the first man to pass 18 metres (without wind assistance) in the triple jump. Before the championships, the record stood at 17.98 metres, Edwards having beaten Willie Banks's ten-year-old best of 17.97 metres just a month earlier. Then in the final, Edwards leaped 18.19 metres with his first jump and then extended the record to 18.29 metres (more than 60 feet).

Even before the 1996 Summer Games have taken place, preparations are already underway elsewhere in the world for the 2000 Olympics. The IOC always decides on the next Olympic venue seven years in advance. The site for the

"We Got the Games"
Citizens celebrate after Atlanta is awarded the 1996 Games on 18 September 1990. Some restaurant and cafe owners instantly renamed their businesses to advertise the forthcoming big event.

1998 Olympic Winter Games was decided upon at the IOC's 97th assembly in Birmingham in 1991. They will take place in the Japanese city of Nagano. Likewise, in 1995, the venue for the Winter Games of 2002 was selected. These Games will be staged at Salt Lake City in Utah, one of the cities that lost out to Nagano in the bid for the Games of 1998. Before the bandwagon arrives in Utah, however, the first Olympic Games of the new millennium will have taken place – in Sydney, Australia.

Rough and Tumble
New Olympic sports for the Atlanta Games include mountain biking, which is particularly popular with younger people.

Beach Ball
Another new Olympic discipline is beach volleyball, featuring only two players per team. This version of the game now seems to be more popular than the traditional one.

Women's Football
This is another new Olympic discipline. There have been world championships in women's football since 1991. The picture shows the match between Germany and Brazil during the 1995 finals, held in Sweden.

On Guard!
As of 1996, women will also have individual and team épée competitions at the Olympics. The picture shows Marina Varkonyi (HUN) and Katja Nass (GER) during the 1993 world championship in Essen, Germany.

A Man to Watch Britain's Jonathan Edwards heads past 18 metres to set a triple jump record of 18.29 metres.

1 **Atlanta by night:** During the hours of darkness, Atlanta is a dazzling sight. The cultural hub of the southeastern USA, its theatres include the Fox and the Alliance, which is situated in the Woodruff Arts Center, also the home of the Atlanta Symphony Orchestra. The city has plenty in store for "nightowls" as well. The wide variety of entertainment on offer includes shows in bars and restaurants, especially in the Buckhead district. However, in 1996 visitors will only be able to get to the city centre by public transport. Cars will have to be left in car parks on the outskirts. Many streets will be closed permanently or placed off limits to traffic between 7.30 a.m. and midnight.

2 **A view of Atlanta:** The 1996 Olympic city has come a long way since the 1830s when what is now Atlanta was known as "Terminus", because it fulfilled that function for the Western and Atlantic Railroad. In 1843, Terminus was renamed Marthasville, and two years later the name was changed once again to Atlanta.

Besides its varied cultural and night life and a remarkable history, Atlanta has a rich sporting heritage. It is home to an NFL football team, the Atlanta Falcons, a baseball team, the Braves, a basketball team, the Hawks, and an ice hockey team, the Knights.

Atlanta, capital of the state of Georgia, is preparing itself with meticulous attention to detail for the 1996 Olympic Games. Refurbishment and building works got underway soon after president of the IOC Juan Antonio Samaranch announced the result of the vote in September 1990. Even so, some projects will not be finished until the middle of 1996. The press regularly reports on how the preparations are progressing.

The organizers are advising the approximately two million visitors expected to flood into Atlanta in July 1996 to book their hotels early and are trying to dissuade them from making last-minute trips to the city during the summer months. In some participating countries, National Olympic Committees (NOCs) have made arrangements with tour organizers, who hold the exclusive rights for selling tickets as well as for making hotel bookings. A mass event like an Olympics will bring disadvantages as well as benefits to the people of Atlanta. For example, there have been complaints that rents in the city have rocketed, in some cases between 10 and 15 per cent since early 1995, in particular in the areas around the Olympic facilities. The tax authorities anticipate a total increase in income and sales taxes, as well as in excise, of several hundred million dollars.

In the meantime, the ACOG (Atlanta Committee for the Olympic Games) are doing their best to raise the estimated 1.6 billion dollars (mid-1995 figure) needed to cover the cost of the Games. The main source of money will be from the sale of television broadcasting rights, which will generate more than 500 million dollars alone. This will be topped up by the income received from the sale of about 11 million tickets, which will be priced at an average of 40 dollars each. In fact, they will range in price from 11 dollars for a first-round women's hockey match to 636 dollars to see the opening and closing ceremonies. In addition, it is expected that sponsorship and licence contracts will bring in nine-figure returns.

Atlanta's preparations for the Games also include the drafting of a crisis management plan for handling emergencies. Measures to be taken in case of disasters, such as storms and tornados, panic among spectators, serious traffic accidents, or setbacks such as power failures, are set out in minute detail.

3–**6** **Layout ensures short travelling times:** Most of the sports venues are close to each other, so that they can be easily reached on foot or by public transport. The new facilities cost around one billion dollars and include the Superdome (picture 3), the Omnidome, (picture 4), and the Georgia Dome (picture 6), home of the Atlanta Falcons. Atlanta's old stadium was demolished and replaced by the Atlanta-Fulton County Stadium (picture 5), which is where the Atlanta Braves play their home games.

Country Abbreviations

AFG	Afghanistan		JAM	Jamaica
AHO	Netherlands Antilles		JOR	Jordan
ALB	Albania		JPN	Japan
ANG	Angola		KAZ	Kazakhstan
ANT	Antigua and Barbuda		KEN	Kenya
ARG	Argentina		KOR	South Korea
AUS	Australia		LAT	Latvia (to 1939; from 1992)
AUT	Austria		LIB	Lebanon
BAH	Bahamas		LIE	Liechtenstein
BEL	Belgium		LIT	Lithuania (to 1939; from 1992)
BLR	Belarus		LUX	Luxemburg
BOH	Bohemia (to 1918)		MAR	Morocco
BOL	Bolivia		MDV	Maldives
BRA	Brazil		MON	Monaco
BSH	Bosnia-Herzegovina (from 1992)		MVR	Mongolia
BUL	Bulgaria		NGR	Nigeria
CAN	Canada		NIG	Niger
CHI	Chile		NOR	Norway
CHN	China		NZL	New Zealand
CIV	Ivory Coast		PAK	Pakistan
CMR	Cameroon		PER	Peru
COL	Colombia		PHI	Philippines
CRO	Croatia (from 1992)		POL	Poland
CUB	Cuba		POR	Portugal
CZE	Czech Republic (from 1994)		PRK	North Korea
DEN	Denmark		PUR	Puerto Rico
DOM	Dominican Republic		ROM	Romania
ECU	Ecuador		RSA	South Africa
EGY	Egypt		RUS	Russia (to 1919; from 1994)
ESP	Spain		SEN	Senegal
EST	Estonia (to 1939; from 1992)		SER	Serbia (from 1992)
ETH	Ethiopia		SLO	Slovenia (from 1992)
EUN	Unified Team (Commonwealth of Independent States, 1992)		SUI	Switzerland
FIN	Finland		SUR	Surinam
FRA	France		SVK	Slovakia (from 1994)
FRG	West Germany (1949–1990, then GER)		SWE	Sweden
GBR	Great Britain		SYR	Syria
GDR	East Germany (1949–1990, then GER)		TCH	Czechoslovakia (to 1992, then CZE; SVK)
GER	Germany (to 1949; from 1990)		THA	Thailand
GER★	pan-German team 1956–1964		TPE	Chinese Taipei
GHA	Ghana		TRI	Trinidad and Tobago
GRE	Greece		TUN	Tunisia
HOL	Netherlands		TUR	Turkey
HUN	Hungary		UAE	United Arab Emirates
INA	Indonesia		UGA	Uganda
IND	India		UKR	Ukraine
IOP	Independent Olympic Participant		URS	Soviet Union (to 1992, then EUN; BLR; KAZ; RUS; UKR)
IRL	Ireland		URU	Uruguay
IRN	Iran		USA	United States of America
IRQ	Iraq		VEN	Venezuela
ISL	Iceland		YUG	Yugoslavia (to 1992, then IOP; SER; CRO; BSH; SLO)
ISR	Israel			
ISV	Virgin Islands			
ITA	Italy			

Athens 1896

Participants: ca. 200 / Men: 200, Women: 0, Countries: 14,
Sports: 9, Events: 43

Medals Table

PLACE	COUNTRY	GOLD	SILVER	BRONZE
1	USA	11	6	2
2	Greece	10	19	18
3	Germany	7	5	3
4	France	5	4	2
5	Great Britain	3	3	1

Outstanding Athletes

PLACE	NAME (NATIONALITY)	DISCIPLINE	G	S	B
1	Carl Schuhmann (GER)	Gym/Wrestling	4	–	–
2	Hermann Weingärtner (GER)	Gymnastics	3	2	1
3	Alfred Flatow (GER)	Gymnastics	3	1	–
4	Paul Masson (FRA)	Cycling	3	–	–
5	Fritz Hofmann (GER)	Athletics/Gym	2	1	2

EVENT	GOLD		SILVER		BRONZE	
Athletics						
100 m	Thomas Burke (USA)	12.0	Fritz Hofmann (GER)	12.2	Alajos Szokolyi (HUN)	12.6
400 m	Thomas Burke (USA)	54.2	Herbert Jamison (USA)	55.2	Fritz Hofmann (GER)	55.6
800 m	Edwin Flack (AUS)	2:11.0	Nandor Dani (HUN)	2:11.8	Dimitrios Golemis (GRE)	2:28.0
1500 m	Edwin Flack (AUS)	4:33.2	Arthur Blake (USA)	4:34.0	Albin Lermusiaux (FRA)	4:36.0
Marathon (40 km)	Spyridon Louis (GRE)	2:58:50	Charilaos Vasilakos (GRE)	3:06:03	Gyula Kellner (HUN)	3:09:35
110 m Hurdles	Thomas Curtis (USA)	17.6	Grantley Goulding (GBR)	18.0		
High Jump	Ellery Clark (USA)	1.81	James B. Connolly (USA)	1.65		
			Robert Garrett (USA)	1.65		
Long Jump	Ellery Clark (USA)	6.35	Robert Garrett (USA)	6.18	James B. Connolly (USA)	6.11
Pole Vault	William Hoyt (USA)	3.30	Albert Tyler (USA)	3.25	Evangelos Damaskos (GRE)	2.85
Triple Jump	James B. Connolly (USA)	13.71	Alexandre Tuffère (FRA)	12.70	Ioannis Persakis (GRE)	12.52
Shot	Robert Garrett (USA)	11.22	Militadis Gouskos (GRE)	11.20	Georgios Papasideris (GRE)	10.36
Discus	Robert Garrett (USA)	29.15	Panagiotis Paraskevopoulos (GRE)	28.95	Sotirios Versis (GRE)	28.78
Weight Lifting						
One-arm Lifts	Launceston Elliott (GBR)	71.0	Viggo Jensen (DEN)	57.2	Alexandros Nikolopulos (GRE)	57.2
Two-arm Lifts	Viggo Jensen (DEN)	111.5	Launceston Elliott (GBR)	111.5	Sotirios Versis (GRE)	100.0
Wrestling						
	Carl Schuhmann (GER)		Georgios Tsitas (GRE)		Stephanos Christopoulos (GRE)	
Fencing						
Individual Foil	Emile Gravelotte (FRA)	4	Henri Callot (FRA)	3	Perikles Pierrakos-Mavromichalis (GRE)	2
Foil for Fencing Masters	Leon Pyrgos (GRE)	1	M. Perronet (FRA)	0		
Individual Sabre	Jean Georgiadis (GRE)	4	Telemachos Karakalos (GRE)	3	Holger Nielsen (DEN)	2
Shooting						
Free Rifle (200 m)	Pantelis Karasevdas (GRE)	2320	P. Pavlidis (GRE)	1978	Nicolaos Trikupis (GRE)	1718
Free Rifle (300 m)	Georgios Orphanidis (GRE)	1583	Jean Phrangoudis (GRE)	1312	Viggo Jensen (DEN)	1305
Rapid-Fire Pistol (25 m)	Jean Phrangoudis (GRE)	344	Georgios Orphanidis (GRE)	249	Holger Nielsen (DEN)	
Military Revolver (25 m)	John Paine (USA)	442	Sumner Paine (USA)	380	N. Morakis (GRE)	205
Free Pistol (50 m)	Sumner Paine (USA)	442	Viggo Jensen (DEN)	285	Holger Nielsen (DEN)	
Cycling						
Sprint	Paul Masson (FRA)	24.0	Stamatios Nikolopoulos (GRE)	25.4	Adolf Schmal (AUT)	26.6
2000 m	Paul Masson (FRA)	4:56.0	Stamatios Nikolopoulos (GRE)	5:00.2	Léon Flameng (FRA)	
10,000 m	Paul Masson (FRA)	17:54.2	Léon Flameng (FRA)	17:54.2	Adolf Schmal (AUT)	
100 km	Léon Flameng (FRA)	3:08:19.2	G. Kolettis (GRE)			
12 Hours Track	Adolf Schmal (AUT)	314.997	F. Keeping (GBR)	314.664	Georgios Paraskevopoulos (GRE)	313.330
Marathon (87 km)	Aristidis Konstantinidis (GRE)	3:22:31	August Goedrich (GER)	3:42:18	F. Battel (GBR)	
Gymnastics						
Parallel Bars - Individual	Alfred Flatow (GER)		Jules Zutter (SUI)		Hermann Weingärtner (GER)	
Parallel Bars - Team	Germany		Greece		Greece	
Horse Vault	Carl Schuhmann (GER)		Jules Zutter (SUI)			
Horizontal Bar - Individual	Hermann Weingärtner (GER)		Alfred Flatow (GER)		Pet Messas (GRE)	
Horizontal Bar - Team	Germany					
Rings	Ioannis Mitropoulos (GRE)		Hermann Weingärtner (GER)		Petros Persakis (GRE)	
Pommel Horse	Jules Zutter (SUI)		Hermann Weingärtner (GER)		Gyula Kakas (HUN)	
Rope Climbing	Nicolaos Andriakopoulos (GRE)		Thomas Xenakis (GRE)		Fritz Hofmann (GER)	

EVENT	GOLD		SILVER		BRONZE	
Swimming						
100 m Freestyle	Alfred Hajós (HUN)	1:22.2	Efstathios Chorophas (GRE)	1:23.0	Otto Herschmann (AUT)	
500 m Freestyle	Paul Neumann (AUT)	8:12.6	Antonios Pepanos (GRE)		Efstathios Chorophas (GRE)	
1200 m Freestyle	Alfred Hajós (HUN)	18:22.2	Jean Andreou (GRE)	21:03.4	Efstathios Chorophas (GRE)	
100 m Freestyle (Sailors)	Ioannis Malokinis (GRE)	2:20.4	S. Chasapis (GRE)		Dimitrios Drivas (GRE)	
Tennis						
Singles	John Pius Boland (GBR)		Dennis Kasdaglis (GRE)			
Doubles	John Pius Boland (GBR)/		Demis Kasdaglis (GRE)/			
	Fritz Traun (GER)		Demetrios Petrokokkinos (GRE)			

Paris 1900

14 May – 28 October

Participants: 1225 / Men: 1206, Women: 19, Countries: 26,
Sports: 24, Events: 166

Medals Table

Outstanding Athletes

PLACE	COUNTRY	GOLD	SILVER	BRONZE
1	France	29	41	32
2	USA	20	14	9
3	Great Britain	17	8	10
4	Belgium	8	7	5
5	Switzerland	6	2	1

PLACE	NAME (NATIONALITY)	DISCIPLINE	G	S	B
1	Alvin Kraenzlein (USA)	Athletics	4	-	-
2	Konrad Stäheli (SUI)	Shooting	3	-	1
3	Ray Ewry (USA)	Athletics	3	-	-
4	Irving Baxter (USA)	Athletics	2	3	-
5	Walter Tewksbury (USA)	Athletics	2	2	1

EVENT	GOLD		SILVER		BRONZE	
Athletics						
60 m	Alvin Kraenzlein (USA)	7.0	Walter Tewksbury (USA)	7.1	Stanley Rowley (AUS)	7.2
100 m	Francis Jarvis (USA)	11.0	Walter Tewksbury (USA)	11.1	Stanley Rowley (AUS)	11.2
200 m	Walter Tewksbury (USA)	22.2	Norman Pritchard (IND)	22.8	Stanley Rowley (AUS)	22.9
400 m	Maxwell Long (USA)	49.4	William Holland (USA)	49.6	Ernst Schultz (DEN)	
800 m	Alfred Tysoe (GBR)	2:01.2	John Cregan (USA)	2:03.0	David Hall (USA)	
1500 m	Charles Bennett (GBR)	4:06.2	Henri Deloge (FRA)	4:06.6	John Bray (USA)	4:07.2
5000 m Team Event	Great Britain	26	France	29		
Marathon (40,260 km)	Michel Theato (FRA)	2:59:45	Emile Champion (FRA)	3:04:17	Ernst Fast (SWE)	3:37:14
110 m Hurdles	Alvin Kraenzlein (USA)	15.4	John McLean (USA)	15.5	Fred Moloney (USA)	15.6
200 m Hurdles	Alvin Kraenzlein (USA)	25.4	Norman Pritchard (IND)	26.6	Walter Tewksbury (USA)	
400 m Hurdles	Walter Tewksbury (USA)	57.6	Henri Tauzin (FRA)	58.3	George Orton (CAN)	
2500 m Steeplechase	George Orton (CAN)	7:34.4	Sidney Robinson (GBR)	7:38.0	Jacques Chastanié (FRA)	
4000 m Steeplechase	John Rimmer (GBR)	12:58.4	Charles Bennett (GBR)	12:58.6	Sidney Robinson (GBR)	12:58.8
High jump	Irving Baxter (USA)	1.90	Patrick Leahy (GBR/IRL)	1.78	Lajos Gönczy (HUN)	1.75
Standing High Jump	Ray Ewry (USA)	1.65	Irving Baxter (USA)	1.52	Lewis Sheldon (USA)	1.50
Pole Vault	Irving Baxter (USA)	3.30	Meredith Colkett (USA)	3.25	Carl-Albert Andersen (NOR)	3.20
Long Jump	Alvin Kraenzlein (USA)	7.18	Myer Prinstein (USA)	7.17	Patrick Leahy (GBR/IRL)	6.95
Standing Long Jump	Ray Ewry (USA)	3.21	Irving Baxter (USA)	3.13	Emile Torcheboeuf (FRA)	3.03
Triple Jump	Myer Prinstein (USA)	14.47	James Connolly (USA)	13.97	Lewis Sheldon (USA)	13.64
Standing Triple Jump	Ray Ewry (USA)	10.58	Irving Baxter (USA)	9.95	Robert Garrett (USA)	9.50
Shot	Richard Sheldon (USA)	14.10	Josiah McCracken (USA)	12.85	Robert Garrett (USA)	12.37
Discus	Rudolf Bauer (HUN)	36.04	Frantisek Janda-Suk (BOH)	35.25	Richard Sheldon (USA)	34.60
Hammer	John Flanagan (USA)	49.73	Truxton Hare (USA)	49.13	Josiah McCracken (USA)	42.46
Tug-of-War	Sweden/Denmark		USA		France	
Swimming						
200 m Freestyle	Frederick Lane (AUS)	2:25.2	Zoltán Halmay (HUN)	2:31.4	Karl Ruberl (AUT)	2:32.0
1000 m Freestyle	John Jarvis (GBR)	13:40.2	Otto Wahle (AUT)	14:53.6	Zoltán Halmay (HUN)	15:16.4
4000 m Freestyle	John Jarvis (GBR)	58:24.0	Zoltán Halmay (HUN)	1:08:55.4	Louis Martin (FRA)	1:13:08.4
200 m Backstroke	Ernst Hoppenberg (GER)	2:47.0	Karl Ruberl (AUT)	2:56.0	Johannes Drost (HOL)	3:01.0
200 m Team Swimming	Germany	32	France	51	France	61
200 m Obstacle Event	Frederick Lane (AUS)	2:38.4	Otto Wahle (AUT)	2:40.0	Peter Kemp (GBR)	2:47.4
Underwater Swimming	Charles de Vendeville (FRA)	188.4	P. Alexandre Six (FRA)	185.4	Peder Lykkeberg (DEN)	147.0
Water Polo	Great Britain		Belgium		France	

EVENT	GOLD		SILVER		BRONZE	
Fencing						
Individual Foil	Emile Coste (FRA)		Henri Masson (FRA)		Jacques Boulenger (FRA)	
Foil for Fencing Masters	Lucien Mérignac (FRA)		Alphonse Kirchhoffer (FRA)		Jean-Baptiste Mimiague (FRA)	
Individual Épée	Ramón Fonst (CUB)		Louis Perrée (FRA)		Léon Sée (FRA)	
Épée for Fencing Masters	Albert Ayat (FRA)		Emile Bougnol (FRA)		Henri Laurent (FRA)	
Épée for Amateurs and Fencing Masters	Albert Ayat (FRA)		Ramón Fonst (CUB)		Léon Sée (FRA)	
Individual Sabre	Georges de la Falaise (FRA)		Léon Thiébaut (FRA)		Siegfried Flesch (AUT)	
Sabre for Fencing Masters	Antonio Conte (ITA)		Italo Santelli (ITA)		Milan Neralic (AUT)	
Rowing						
Single Sculls	Henri Barrelet (FRA)	7:35.6	André Gaudin (FRA)	7:41.6	St. George Ashe (GBR)	8:15.6
Coxed Pairs	Netherlands	7:34.2	France I	7:34.4	France II	7:57.2
Coxless Fours	Belgium	7:16.8	France I	7:23.8	France II	7:47.2
Coxed Fours	France	7:11.0	France I	7:18.0	Germany	7:18.2
2nd Final*	Germany	5:59.0	Netherlands	6:33.0	Germany	6:35.0
Coxed Eights	USA	6:09.8	Belgium	6:13.8	Netherlands	6:23.0
Yachting						
Open Class	Great Britain		Germany		France	
0.5 Ton Class	France		France		France	
0 5-1.0 Ton Class	Great Britain		France		France	
1-2 Ton Class	Germany		Switzerland		France	
2-3 Ton Class	Great Britain		France		France	
3-10 Ton Class	France		Netherlands		France/Great Britain	
10-20 Ton Class	France		France		Great Britain	
Cycling						
2000 m Sprint	Georges Taillandier (FRA)		Fernand Sanz (FRA)		John Lake (USA)	
Equestrianism						
Grand Prix (Jumping)	Aimé Haegeman (BEL)	2:16.0	Georges van de Poele (BEL)	2:17.6	Pierre de Champsavin (FRA)	2:26.0
Equestrian High Jump	Dominique M. Gardères (FRA)	1.85	Giangiorgio Trissino (ITA)†	1.85	André Moreau (FRA)	1.70
Equestrian Long Jump	C. van Langhendonck (BEL)	6.10	Giangiorgio Trissino (ITA)	5.70	Henri de Prunelle (FRA)	5.30
† Equal first.						
Shooting						
Rapid-Fire Pistol	Maurice Larrouy (FRA)	58	Léon Moreaux (FRA)	57	Eugène Balme (FRA)	57
Free Pistol (50 m)	Karl Röderer (SUI)	503	Achille Paroche (FRA)	466	Konrad Stäheli (SUI)	453
Olympic Trap Shooting	Roger de Barbarin (FRA)	17	René Guyot (FRA)	17	Justinien de Clary (FRA)	17
Running Game Target	Louis Debray (FRA)	20	Pierre Nivet (FRA)	20	Comte de Lambert (FRA)	19
Live Pigeon Shooting	Léon de Lunden (BEL)	21	Maurice Faure (FRA)	20	Donald Macintosh (AUS)	18
					Crittenden Robinson (GBR)	18
Military Rifle	Emil Kellenberger (SUI)	930	Anders Nielsen (DEN)	921	Ole Östmo (NOR)	917
					Paul van Asbroeck (BEL)	917
Military Rifle - Three Positions						
Standing	Lars Madsen (DEN)	305	Ole Östmo (NOR)	299	Charles du Verger (BEL)	298
Kneeling	Konrad Stäheli (SUI)	324	Emil Kellenberger (SUI)	314		
			Anders Nielsen (DEN)	314		
Prone	Achille Paroche (FRA)	332	Anders Nielsen (DEN)	330	Ole Östmo (NOR)	329
Military Rifle (Team)	Switzerland	4399	Norwegen	4290	France	4278
Team Events	Switzerland	2271	France	2203	Netherlands	1876
Archery						
Au cordon doré (50 m)	Henri Herouin (FRA)	31	Hubert van Innis (BEL)	29	Emile Fisseux (FRA)	28
Au chapelet (50 m)	Eugène Mougin (FRA)		Henri Helle (FRA)		Emile Mercier (FRA)	
Au cordon doré (33 m)	Hubert van Innis (BEL)		Victor Thibaud (FRA)		Charles Petit (FRA)	
Au chapelet (33 m)	Hubert van Innis (BEL)		VictorThibaud (FRA)		Charles Petit (FRA)	
Sur la perche à la herse	Emmanuel Foulon (FRA)		Pierre Serrurier (FRA)		Emile Druart (BEL)	
Sur la perche à la pyramide	Emile Grumiaux (FRA)		Louis Glineux (BEL)			
Gymnastics						
Individual Combined Exercises	Gustave Sandras (FRA)	302	Noël Bas (FRA)	295	Lucien Démanet (FRA)	293
Soccer						
	Great Britain		France		Belgium	
Cricket						
	Great Britain		France			
Golf						
Men's Singles	Charles Sands (USA)	167	Walter Rutherford (GBR)	168	David Robertson (GBR)	175
Women's Singles	Margaret Abbott (USA)	47	Polly Whittier (SUI)	49	Daria Pratt (USA)	55

EVENT	GOLD	SILVER	BRONZE
Polo	Great Britain	Great Britain	France
Rugby	France	Germany	Great Britain
Tennis			
Men's Singles	Hugh Doherty (GBR)	Harold Mahony (GBR/IRL)	Reginald Doherty (GBR) A. B. J. Norris (GBR)
Men's Doubles	Reginald Doherty (GBR)/ Hugh Doherty (GBR)	Spalding de Garmendia (USA)/ Max Decugis (FRA)	André Prévost (FRA)/ Gerard de la Chapelle (FRA)/ Harold Mahony (GBR/IRL)/ A. B. J. Norris (GBR)
Women's Singles	Charlotte Cooper (GBR)	Hélène Prévost (FRA)	Marion Jones (USA) Hedwiga Rosenbaumová (BOH)
Mixed	Charlotte Cooper (GBR) Reginald Doherty (GBR)	Hélène Prévost (FRA) Harold Mahony (GBR/IRL)	Hedwiga Rosenbaumová (BOH)/ Anthony Warden (GBR) Marion Jones (USA)/ Hugh Doherty (GBR)

*Various protests and delayed starts during the heats led to there being two finals; the winners' medals were awarded to the crews of the second final.

St. Louis 1904

1 July – 23 November

Participants: 687 / Men: 681, Women: 6, Countries: 13,
Sports: 16, Events: 104

Medals Table

PLACE	COUNTRY	GOLD	SILVER	BRONZE
1	USA	80	86	72
2	Germany	5	4	6
3	Cuba	5	3	3
4	Canada	4	1	1
5	Hungary	2	1	1

Outstanding Athletes

PLACE	NAME (NATIONALITY)	DISCIPLINE	G	S	B
1	Anton Heida (USA)	Gymnastics	5	1	
2	Marcus Hurley (USA)	Cycling	4		
3	George Eyser (USA)	Gymnastics	3	2	1
4	James Lightbody (USA)	Athletics	3	1	
	Charles Daniels (USA)	Swimming	3	1	

EVENT	GOLD		SILVER		BRONZE	
Athletics						
60 m	Archie Hahn (USA)	7.0	William Hogenson (USA)	7.2	Fay Moulton (USA)	7.2
100 m	Archie Hahn (USA)	11.0	Nathaniel Cartmell (USA)	11.2	William Hogenson (USA)	11.2
200 m	Archie Hahn (USA)	21.6	Nathaniel Cartmell (USA)	21.9	William Hogenson (USA)	
400 m	Harry Hillman (USA)	49.2	Frank Waller (USA)	49.9	Herman Groman (USA)	50.0
800 m	James Lightbody (USA)	1:56.0	Howard Valentine (USA)	1:56.3	Emil Breitkreuz (USA)	1:56.4
1500 m	James Lightbody (USA)	4:05.4	W. Frank Verner (USA)	4:06.8	Lacey Hearn (USA)	
Marathon (40 km)	Thomas Hicks (USA)	3:28:35	Albert Coray (FRA)	3:34:52	Arthur Newton (USA)	3:47:33
110 m Hurdles	Frederick Schule (USA)	16.0	Thaddeus Shideler (USA)	16.3	Lesley Ashburner (USA)	16.4
200 m Hurdles	Harry Hillman (USA)	24.6	Frank Castleman (USA)	24.9	George Poage (USA)	
400 m Hurdles	Harry Hillman (USA)	53.0	Frank Waller (USA)	53.2	George Poage (USA)	
3000 m Steeplechase	James Lightbody (USA)	7:39.6	John Daly (GBR/IRL)	7:40.6	Arthur Newton (USA)	
Team Cross-Country	USA	21:17.8	USA		France	
High jump	Samuel Jones (USA)	1.803	Garret Serviss (USA)	1.778	Paul Weinstein (GER)	1.778
Standing High Jump	Ray Ewry (USA)	1.50	James Stadler (USA)	1.45	Lawson Robertson (USA)	1.45
Pole Vault	Charles Dvorak (USA)	3.50	LeRoy Samse (USA)	3.43	Louis Wilkins (USA)	3.43
Long Jump	Myer Prinstein (USA)	7.34	Daniel Frank (USA)	6.89	Robert Stangland (USA)	6.88
Standing Long Jump	Ray Ewry (USA)	3.48	Charles King (USA)	3.28	John Biller (USA)	3.26
Triple Jump	Myer Prinstein (USA)	14.325	Frederick Englehardt (USA)	13.90	Robert Stangland (USA)	13.365
Standing Triple Jump	Ray Ewry (USA)	10.55	Charles King (USA)	10.16	James Stadler (USA)	9.53
Shot	Ralph Rose (USA)	14.81	William W. Coe (USA)	14.40	Leon Feuerbach (USA)	13.37
Discus	Martin Sheridan (USA)	39.28	Ralph Rose (USA)	39.28	Nicolaos Georgantas (GRE)	37.68
Hammer	John Flanagan (USA)	51.23	John DeWitt (USA)	50.265	Ralph Rose (USA)	45.73
56 lb Weight Throw	Etienne Desmarteau (CAN)	10.465	John Flanagan (USA)	10.16	James Mitchell (USA)	10.135
Tug-of-War	USA		USA		USA	
Combined events	Thomas Kiely (GBR/IRL)	6036	Adam Gunn (USA)	5907	Truxton Hare (USA)	5813

EVENT	GOLD		SILVER		BRONZE	
Swimming						
50 yards Freestyle	Zoltán Halmay (HUN)	28.0	Scott Leary (USA)	28.6	Charles Daniels (USA)	
100 yards Freestyle	Zoltán Halmay (HUN)	1:02.8	Charles Daniels (USA)		Scott Leary (USA)	
220 yards Freestyle	Charles Daniels (USA)	2:44.2	Francis Gailey (USA)	2:46.0	Emil Rausch (GER)	2:56.0
440 yards Freestyle	Charles Daniels (USA)	6:16.2	Francis Gailey (USA)	6:22.0	Otto Wahle (AUT)	6:39.0
880 yards Freestyle	Emil Rausch (GER)	13:11.4	Francis Gailey (USA)	13:23.4	Géza Kiss (HUN)	
1 Mile Freestyle	Emil Rausch (GER)	27:18.2	Géza Kiss (HUN)	28:28.2	Francis Gailey (USA)	28:54.0
100 yards Backstroke	Walter Brack (GER)	1:16.8	Georg Hoffmann (GER)	1:18.0	Georg Zacharias (GER)	1:19.6
440 yards Breaststroke	George Zacharias (GER)	7:23.6	Walter Brack (GER)	7:33.0	Jamison Handy (USA)	
4 x 50 yards Relay	USA	2:04.6	USA		USA	
Highboard Diving	George Sheldon (USA)	12.66	Georg Hoffmann (GER)	11.66	Frank Nehoe (USA)	11.33
					Alfred Braunschweiger (GER)	11.33
Plunge for Distance	W. E. Dickey (USA)	19.05	Edgar Adams (USA)	17.53	Leo Goodwin (USA)	17.37
Water Polo	USA		USA		USA	
Boxing						
Flyweight (- 47.63 kg)	George Finnegan (USA)		Miles Burke (USA)			
Bantamweight (- 52.16 kg)	Oliver Kirk (USA)		George Finnegan (USA)			
Featherweight (- 56.70 kg)	Oliver Kirk (USA)		Frank Haller (USA)		Fred Gilmore (USA)	
Lightweight (-61.24 kg)	Harry Spanger (USA)		James Eagan (USA)		Russell van Horn (USA)	
Welterweight (-65.27 kg)	Albert Young (USA)		Harry Spanger (USA)		Joseph Lydon (USA)	
Middleweight (-71.67 kg)	Charles Mayer (USA)		Benjamin Spradley (USA)			
Heavyweight (+ 71.67 kg)	Samuel Berger (USA)		Charles Mayer (USA)		William Michaels (USA)	
Weightlifting						
One-arm Lifts (10 Lifts)	Oscar Paul Osthoff (USA)	48	Frederik Winters (USA)	45	Frank Kungler (USA)	10
Two-arm Lifts	Perikles Kakousis (GRE)	111.58	Oscar Paul Osthoff (USA)	84.36	Frank Kungler (USA)	79.83
Freestyle Wrestling						
Light Flyweight (- 47.63 kg)	Robert Curry (USA)		John Heim (USA)		Gustav Thiefenthaler (USA)	
Flyweightt (- 52.16 kg)	George Mehnert (USA)		Gustave Bauer (USA)		William Nelson (USA)	
Bantamweight (-56.70 kg)	Isaac Niflot (USA)		August Wester (USA)		Z. B. Strebler (USA)	
Featherweightt (-61.24 kg)	Benjamin Bradshaw (USA)		Theodore McLear (USA)		Charles Clapper (USA)	
Lightweight (-65.27 kg)	Otto Roehm (USA)		Rudolph Tesing (USA)		Albert Zirkel (USA)	
Welterweight (-71.67 kg)	Charles Erickson (USA)		William Beckmann (USA)		Jerry Winholtz (USA)	
Heavyweight (+71.67 kg)	Bernhuff Hansen (USA)		Frank Kungler (USA)		Fred Warmbold (USA)	
Fencing						
Foil (Individual)	Ramón Fonst (CUB)		Albertson Van Zo Post (CUB)		Charles Tatham (CUB)	
Foil (Team)	Cuba		USA		Cuba	
Épée (Individual)	Ramón Fonst (CUB)		Charles Tatham (CUB)		Albertson Van Zo Post (CUB)	
Sabre (Individual)	Manuel Diaz (CUB)		William Grebe (USA)		Albertson Van Zo Post (CUB)	
Single Sticks	Albertson Van Zo Post (CUB)		William Grebe (USA)		William Scott O'Connor (USA)	
Rowing						
Single Sculls	Frank Greer (USA)	10:08.5	James Juvenal (USA)		Constance Titus (USA)	
Double Sculls	USA	10:03.2	USA		USA	
Coxless Fours	USA	9:53.8	USA			
Coxed Eights	USA	7:50.0	Canada			
Archery						
Men						
York Round	Phillip Bryant (USA)	820	Robert Williams (USA)	819	William Thompson (USA)	816
American Round	Phillip Bryant (USA)	1048	Robert Williams (USA)	991	William Thompson (USA)	949
Team Round	USA	1344	USA	1341	USA	1268
Women						
National Round	Lida Howell (USA)	620	Jessie Pollock (USA)	419	Emma Cooke (USA)	419
Columbia Round	Lida Howell (USA)	867	Emma Cooke (USA)	630	Jessie Pollock (USA)	630
Team Round	USA	506	USA			
Gymnastics						
Individual Combined Exercises	Julius Lenhart (AUT)	69.80	Wilhelm Weber (GER)	69.10	Adolf Spinnler (SUI)	67.99
Team	USA	374.43	USA	356.37	USA	349.69
Parallel Bars	George Eyser (USA)	44	Anton Heida (USA)	43	John Duha (USA)	40
Horse Vault	Anton Heida (USA)/	36			William Merz (USA)	31
	George Eyser (USA)	36				

EVENT	GOLD		SILVER		BRONZE	
Pommel Horse	Anton Heida (USA)	42	George Eyser (USA)	33	William Merz (USA)	29
Horizontal Bar	Anton Heida (USA)	40			George Eyser (USA)	39
	Edward Hennig (USA)	40				
Rings	Hermann Glass (USA)	45	William Merz (USA)	35	Emil Voigt (USA)	32
Rope Climbing	George Eyser (USA)	7.0	Charles Krause (USA)	7.8	Emil Voigt (USA)	9.8
Club Swinging	Edward Hennig (USA)	13.0	Emil Voigt (USA)	9.0	Ralph Wilson (USA)	5.0
Four Event Competition	Anton Heida (USA)	161	George Eyser (USA)	152	William Merz (USA)	135
Nine Event Competition	Adolf Spinnler (SUI)	43.49	Julius Lenhart (AUT)	43.00	Wilhelm Weber (GER)	41.60
Triathlon	Max Emmerich (USA)	35.70	John Grieb (USA)	34.00	William Merz (USA)	33.90
Tennis						
Men's Singles	Beals C. Wright (USA)		Robert LeRoy (USA)			
Men's Doubles	Edgar W. Leonard/		Alonzo Bell/			
	Beals Wright (USA)		Robert LeRoy (USA)			
Lacrosse						
	Canada		USA			
Roque						
	Charles Jacobus (USA)		S. O. Streeter (USA)		Charles Brown (USA)	
Basketball						
	USA		USA		USA	
Soccer						
	Canada		USA		USA	

London 1908

Participants: 2035 / Men: 1999, Women: 36, Countries: 22,
Sports: 21, Events: 110

27 April – 31 October
(Official Opening Ceremony on 13 July)

Medals Table

PLACE	COUNTRY	GOLD	SILVER	BRONZE
1	Great Britain	56	50	39
2	USA	23	12	12
3	Sweden	7	5	10
4	France	5	5	9
5	Germany	3	5	5

Outstanding Athletes

PLACE	NAME (NATIONALITY)	DISCIPLINE	G	S	B
1	Melvin Sheppard (USA)	Athletics	3	–	–
	Henry Taylor (GBR)	Swimming	3	–	–
3	Benjamin Jones (GBR)	Cycling	2	1	–
4	Martin Sheridan (USA)	Athletics	2	–	1
	Oscar Swahn (SWE)	Shooting	2	–	1

EVENT	GOLD		SILVER		BRONZE	
Athletics						
100 m	Reginald Walker (SAF)	10.8	James Rector (USA)	10.9	Robert Kerr (CAN)	11.0
200 m	Robert Kerr (CAN)	22.6	Robert Cloughen (USA)	22.6	Nathaniel Cartmell (USA)	22.7
400 m	Wyndham Halswelle (GBR)	50.0				
800 m	Melvin Sheppard (USA)	1:52.8	Emilio Lunghi (ITA)	1:54.2	Hanns Braun (GER)	1:55.2
1500 m	Melvin Sheppard (USA)	4:03.4	Harold Wilson (GBR)	4:03.6	Norman Hallows (GBR)	4:04.0
5 Miles (8046.57 m)	Emil Voigt (GBR)	25:11.2	Edward Owen (GBR)	25:24.0	John Svanberg (SWE)	25:37.2
3 Miles Team Race	Great Britain	6	USA	19	France	32
Marathon	John Joseph Hayes (USA)	2:55:18.4	Charles Hefferon (SAF)	2:56:06.0	Joseph Forshaw (USA)	2:57:10.4
110 m Hurdles	Forrest Smithson (USA)	15.0	John Garrels (USA)	15.7	Arthur Shaw (USA)	
400 m Hurdles	Charles Bacon (USA)	55.0	Harry Hillman (USA)	55.3	Leonard Tremeer (GBR)	57.0
3200 m Steeplechase	Arthur Russel (GBR)	10:47.8	Archie Robertson (GBR)	10:48.4	John Lincoln Eisele (USA)	
Medley Relay	USA	3:29.4	Germany	3:32.4	Hungary	3:32.5
3500 m Walk	George Larner (GBR)	14:55.0	Ernest Webb (GBR)	15:07.4	Harry Kerr (NZL)	15:43.4
10 Miles Walk (16 093.4 m)	George Larner (GBR)	1:15:57.4	Ernest Webb (GBR)	1:17:31.0	Edward Spencer (GBR)	1:21:20.2
High Jump	Harry Porter (USA)	1.90	Con Leahy (GBR/IRL)	1.88		
			István Somody (HUN)	1.88		
			Georges André (FRA)	1.88		

EVENT	GOLD		SILVER		BRONZE	
Standing High Jump	Ray Ewry (USA)	1.575	Konstantin Tsiklitiras (GRE)	1.55		
			John Biller (USA)	1.55		
Pole Vault	Edward Cooke (USA)	3.71	Ed Archibald (CAN)	3.58		
	Alfred Gilbert (USA)	3.71	Charles Jacobs (USA)	3.58		
			Bruno Söderström (SWE)	3.58		
Long Jump	Francis Irons (USA)	7.48	Daniel Kelly (USA)	7.09	Calvin Bricker (CAN)	7.085
Standing Long Jump	Ray Ewry (USA)	3.335	Konstantin Tsiklitiras (GRE)	3.23	Martin Sheridan (USA)	3.225
Triple Jump	Timothy Ahearne (GBR/IRL)	14.915	J. Garfield McDonald (CAN)	14.76	Edvard Larsen (NOR)	14.395
Shot	Ralph Rose (USA)	14.21	Dennis Horgan (GBR)	13.62	John Garrels (USA)	13.18
Discus	Martin Sheridan (USA)	40.89	Merritt Giffin (USA)	40.70	Marquis Horr (USA)	39.445
Greek Style	Martin Sheridan (USA)	38.00	Marquis Horr (USA)	37.325	Werner Järvinen (FIN)	36.48
Hammer	John Flanagan (USA)	51.92	Matthew McGrath (USA)	51.18	Cornelius Walsh (USA)	48.50
Javelin	Erik Lemming (SWE)	54.825	Arne Halse (NOR)	50.570	Otto Nilsson (SWE)	47.105
Freestyle	Erik Lemming (SWE)	54.445	Michel Dorizas (GRE)	51.36	Arne Halse (NOR)	49.73
Tug-of-War	Great Britain		Great Britain		Great Britain	
Swimming						
100 m Freestyle	Charles Daniels (USA)	1:05.6	Zoltán Halmay (HUN)	1:06.2	Harald Julin (SWE)	1:08.0
400 m Freestyle	Henry Taylor (GBR)	5:36.8	Frank Beaurepaire (AUS)	5:44.2	Otto Scheff (AUT)	5:46.0
1500 m Freestyle	Henry Taylor (GBR)	22:48.4	Sydney Battersby (GBR)	22:51.2	Frank Beaurepaire (AUS)	22:56.2
100 m Backstroke	Arno Bieberstein (GER)	1:24.6	Ludwig Dam (DEN)	1:26.6	Herbert Haresnape (GBR)	1:27.0
200 m Breaststroke	Frederick Holman (GBR)	3:09.2	William Robinson (GBR)	3:12.8	Pontus Hansson (SWE)	3:14.6
4 x 200 m Freestyle	Great Britain	10:55.6	Hungary	10:59.0	USA	11:02.8
Springboard Diving	Albert Zürner (GER)	85.5	Kurt Behrens (GER)	85.3	George Gaidzik (USA)	80.8
					Gottlob Walz (GER)	80.8
Highboard Diving	Hjalmar Johansson (SWE)	83.75	Karl Malmström (SWE)	78.73	Arvid Spångberg (SWE)	74.00
Water Polo	Great Britain		Belgium		Sweden	
Boxing						
Bantamweightt (- 52.62 kg)	A. Henry Thomas (GBR)		John Condon (GBR)		W. Webb (GBR)	
Featherweightt (- 57.15 kg)	Richard Gunn (GBR)		C.W. Morris (GBR)		Hugh Roddin (GBR)	
Lightweight (- 63.50 kg)	Frederick Grace (GBR)		Frederick Spiller (GBR)		H. H. Johnson (GBR)	
Middleseightt (- 71.67 kg)	John Douglas (GBR)		Reginald Baker (AUS)		W. Philo (GBR)	
Heavyweight (+ 71.67 kg)	A. L. Oldham (GBR)		S. C. H. Evans (GBR)		Frederick Parks (GBR)	
Greco-Roman Wrestling						
Lightweight (- 66.6 kg)	Enrico Porro (ITA)		Nikolai Orlov (RUS)		Arvid Linden (FIN)	
Middleweight (- 73 kg)	Frithiof Märtensson (SWE)		Mauritz Andersson (SWE)		Anders Andersen (DEN)	
Light-Heavyweight (- 93 kg)	Verner Weckman (FIN)		Yrjö Saarela (FIN)		Carl Jensen (DEN)	
Heavyweight (+ 93 kg)	Richard Weisz (HUN)		Aleksander Petrov (RUS)		Sören Marius Jensen (DEN)	
Free-style Wrestling						
Bantamweight (- 54 kg)	George Mehnert (USA)		William Press (GBR)		Aubert Côté (CAN)	
Featherweight (- 60.3 kg)	George Dole (USA)		James Slim (GBR)		William McKie (GBR)	
Lightweight (- 66.6 kg)	George de Relwyskow (GBR)		William Wood (GBR)		Albert Gingell (GBR)	
Middleweight (-73 kg)	Stanley Bacon (GBR)		George de Relwyskow (GBR)		Frederick Beck (GBR)	
Heavyweight (+ 73 kg)	George Con O'Kelly (GBR /IRL)		Jacob Gundersen (NOR)		Edmond Barrett (GBR/IRL)	
Fencing						
Épée (Individual)	Gaston Alibert (FRA)	5	Alexandre Lippmann (FRA)	4+2	Eugène Olivier (FRA)	4+1
Épée (Team)	France		Great Britain		Belgium	
Sabre (Individual)	Jenö Fuchs (HUN)	6+1	Béla Zulavsky (HUN)	6	Vilém Goppold von Lobsdorf (BOH)	4
Sabre (Team)	Hungary		Italy		Bohemia	
Rowing						
Single Sculls	Harry Blackstaffe (GBR)	9:26.0	Alexander McCulloch (GBR)		Bernhard von Gaza (GER)	
					Károly Levitzky (HUN)	
Coxless Pairs	Great Britain	9:41.0	Great Britain		Canada	
Coxless Fours	Great Britain	8:34.0	Great Britain		Netherlands	
Coxed Eights	Great Britain	7:52.0	Belgium		Great Britain II	
Yachting						
6-m	Great Britain		Belgium		France	
7-m	Great Britain					
8-m	Great Britain		Sweden		Great Britain	
12-m	Great Britain		Great Britain			

EVENT	GOLD		SILVER		BRONZE	
Motorboating						
Open Class	E. B. Thubron (FRA)	2:26.53				
60 Foot	Thomas Thornycroft/					
	Bernard Redwood (GBR)	2:28:58				
8 m	Thomas Thornycroft/					
	Bernard Redwood (GBR)	2:28:36				
Cycling						
660 yards Track	Victor Johnson (GBR)		Emile Demangel (FRA)		Karl Neumer (GER)	
100 km Track	Charles Bartlett (GBR)	2:41:48.6	Charles Denny (GBR)		Octave Lapize (FRA)	
1000 m Sprint	Declared void; riders exceeded the time limit.					
20 km Track	Charles Kingsbury (GBR)	34:13.6	Benjamin Jones (GBR)		Joseph Werbrouck (BEL)	
2000 m Tandem	France	3:07.6	Great Britain		Great Britain	
5000 m	Benjamin Jones (GBR)	8:36.2	Maurice Schilles (FRA)		André Auffray (FRA)	
4000 m Team Pursuit	Great Britain	2:18.6	Germany	2:28.6	Canada	2:29.6
Shooting						
Free Rifle (3 positions)	Albert Helgerud (NOR)	909	Harry Simon (USA)	887	Ole Saether (NOR)	883
Free Rifle (Team)	Norway	5055	Sweden	4711	France	4652
Free Rifle	Jerry Millner (GBR)	98	Kellog Casey (USA)	93	Maurice Blood (GBR)	92
Military Rifle	Louis Richardet (SUI)	238	Jean Reich (SUI)	234	Raoul de Boigne (FRA)	232
Military Rifle (Team)	USA	2531	Great Britain	2497	Canada	2439
Small-Bore Rifle (Prone)	A. A. Carnell (GBR)	387	Harry Humby (GBR)	386	George Barnes (GBR)	385
Small-Bore Rifle (Moving Target)	A. F. Fleming (GBR)	24	M.K. Matthews (GBR)	24	W. B. Marsden (GBR)	24
Small Bore Rifle (Disappearing Target)	William Styles (GBR)	45	H. J. Hawkins (GBR)	45	E. J. Amoore (GBR)	45
Small-Bore Rifle (Team)	Great Britain	771	Sweden	737	France	710
Rapid-Fire Pistol	Paul van Asbroeck (BEL)	490	Reginald Storms (BEL)	487	James Edward Gorman (GBR)	485
Rapid-Fire (Team)	USA	1914	Belgium	1863	Great Britain	1817
Olympic Trap Shooting	Walter Henry Ewing (CAN)	72	Georg Beattie (CAN)	60	Alexander Maunder (GBR)	57
Clay Pigeons (Team)	Great Britain	407	Canada	405	Great Britain	372
Running Deer Shooting	Oscar Swahn (SWE)	25	Ted Ranken (GBR)	24	Alexander Rodgers (GBR)	24
Running Deer Shooting (Team)	Sweden	86	Great Britain	85		
Running Deer Shooting (Double Shot)	Walter Winans (USA)	46	Ted Ranken (GBR)	46	Oscar Swahn (SWE)	38
Archery						
Men						
York Round	William Dod (GBR)	815	R. B. Brooks-King (GBR)	768	Henry B. Richardson (USA)	760
Continental Round	E. G. Grisot (FRA)	263	Louis Vernet (FRA)	256	Gustave Cabaret (FRA)	255
Women						
National Round	Q. F. Newall (GBR)	688	Lottie Dod (GBR)	642	Hill-Lowe (GBR)	618
Gymnastics						
Individual Combined Exercises	Alberto Braglia (ITA)	317.0	S. W. Tysal (GBR)	312.0	Louis Ségura (FRA)	297.0
Team	Sweden	438	Norway	425	Finland	405
Soccer						
	Great Britain		Denmark		Netherlands	
Hockey						
	Great Britain		Great Britain/Ireland		Great Britain/Scotland	
					Great Britain/Wales	
Jeu de Paume						
	Jay Gould (USA)		Eustace Miles (GBR)		Neville Lytton (GBR)	
Lacrosse						
	Canada		Great Britain			
Polo						
	Great Britain		Great Britain II		Great Britain III	
Rugby						
	Australia		Great Britain			
Tennis						
Men's Singles	Josiah Ritchie (GBR)		Otto Froitzheim (GER)		Wilberforce Eaves (GBR)	
Men's Singles (Indoor)	Wentworth Gore (GBR)		George Caridia (GBR)		Josiah Ritchie (GBR)	

EVENT	GOLD	SILVER	BRONZE
Men's Doubles	George W. Hillyard/Reginald Doherty (GBR)	Josiah Ritchie/James Cecil Parke (GBR)	Charles Cazalet/Charles Dixon(GBR)
Men's Doubles (Indoor)	Arthur W. Gore/Herbert Ropel-Barrett (GBR)	George Simond/George Caridia (GBR)	Gunnar Setterwall/Wollmar Boström (SWE)
Women's Singles	Dorothea Chambers (GBR)	Dorothy Boothby (GBR)	Joan Winch (GBR)
Women's Singles (Indoor)	Gwen Eastlake-Smith (GBR)	Angela Greene (GBR)	Martha Adlerstråhle (SWE)
Rackets	Evan Noel (GBR)	Henry Leaf (GBR)	John Astor (GBR)
Doubles	Vane Pennel/John Astor (GBR)	Edward Bury/Cecil Browning (GBR)	Evan Noel/Henry Leaf (GBR)
Figure Skating			
Women	Florence Syers (GBR)	Elsa Rendschmidt (GER)	Dorothy Greenhough-Smith (GBR)
Men	Ulrich Salchow (SWE)	Richard Johansson (SWE)	Per Thorén (SWE)
Pairs	Annie Kübler/Heinrich Burger (GER)	Pyllis Johnson/James Johnson (GBR)	Florence Syers/Edgar Syers (GBR)

Stockholm 1912

Participants: 2547 / Men: 2490, Women: 57, Countries: 28,
Sports: 13, Events: 102

5 May – 22 July
(Official Opening Ceremony on 6 July)

Medals Table

PLACE	COUNTRY	GOLD	SILVER	BRONZE
1	Sweden	24	24	17
2	USA	23	19	1
3	Great Britain	10	15	16
4	Finland	9	8	9
5	France	7	4	3

Outstanding Athletes

PLACE	NAME (NATIONALITY)	DISCIPLINE	G	S	B
1	Hannes Kolehmainen (FIN)	Athletics	3	1	–
	Wilhelm Carlberg (SWE)	Shooting	3	1	–
	Alfred Lane (USA)	Shooting	3	1	–
4	Johan von Holst (SWE)	Shooting	2	1	1
5	Eric Carlberg (SWE)	Shooting	2	1	–

EVENT	GOLD		SILVER		BRONZE	
Athletics						
100 m	Ralph Cook Craig (USA)	10.8	Alvah Meyer (USA)	10.9	Donald Lippincott (USA)	10.9
200 m	Ralph Cook Craig (USA)	21.7	Donald Lippincott (USA)	21.8	William Applegarth (GBR)	22.0
400 m	Charles Reidpath (USA)	48.2	Hanns Braun (GER)	48.3	Edward Lindberg (USA)	48.4
800 m	James Meredith (USA)	1:51.9	Mel Sheppard (USA)	1:52.0	Ira Davenport (USA)	1:52.0
1500 m	Arnold Jackson (GBR)	3:56.8	Abel Kiviat (USA)	3:56.9	Norman Taber (USA)	3:56.9
3000 m Team Race	USA	9	Sweden	13	Great Britain	23
5000 m	Hannes Kolehmainen (FIN)	14:36.6	Jean Bouin (FRA)	14:36.7	George Hutson (GBR)	15:07.6
10,000 m	Hannes Kolehmainen (FIN)	31:20.8	Louis Tewanima (USA)	32:06.6	Albin Stenroos (FIN)	32:21.8
Marathon (40.200 km)	Kenneth McArthur (SAF)	2:36:54.8	Christian Gitsham (SAF)	2:37:52.0	Gaston Strobino (USA)	2:38:42.4
110 m Hurdles	Frederick Kelly (USA)	15.1	James Wendell (USA)	15.2	Martin Hawkins (USA)	15.3
Individual Cross-Country	Hannes Kolehmainen (FIN)	45:11.6	Hjalmar Andersson (SWE)	45:44.8	John Eke (SWE)	46:37.6
Team Cross-Country	Sweden	10	Finland	11	Great Britain	49
4 x 100 m	Great Britain	42.4	Sweden	42.6		
4 x 400 m	USA	3:16.6	France	3:20.7	Great Britain	3:23.2
10 km Walk	George Goulding (CAN)	46:28.4	Ernest Webb (GBR)	46:50.4	Fernando Altimani (ITA)	47:37.6
High Jump	Alma Richards (USA)	1.93	Hans Liesche (GER)	1.91	George Horine (USA)	1.89
Standing High Jump	Platt Adams (USA)	1.63	Benjamin Adams (USA)	1.60	Konstantin Tsiklitiras (GRE)	1.55
Pole Vault	Harry Babcock (USA)	3.95	Marcus Wright (USA)	3.85		
			Frank Nelson (USA)			
Long Jump	Albert Gutterson (USA)	7.60	Calvin Bricker (CAN)	7.21	Georg Aberg (SWE)	7.18
Standing Long Jump	Konstantin Tsiklitiras (GRE)	3.37	Platt Adams (USA)	3.36	Benjamin Adams (USA)	3.28
Triple Jump	Gustaf Lindblom (SWE)	14.76	Georg Aberg (SWE)	14.51	Erik Almlöf (SWE)	14.17
Shot	Patrick McDonald (USA)	15.34	Ralph Rose (USA)	15.25	Lawrence Whitney (USA)	14.15
(Both Hands)	Ralph Rose (USA)	27.70	Patrick McDonald (USA)	27.53	Elmer Niklander (FIN)	27.14
Discus	Armas Taipale (FIN)	45.21	Richard Byrd (USA)	42.32	James Duncan (USA)	42.28
(Both Hands)	Armas Taipale (FIN)	82.86	Elmer Niklander (FIN)	77.96	Emil Magnusson (SWE)	77.37
Hammer	Matthew McGrath (USA)	54.74	Duncan Gillis (CAN)	48.39	Clarence Childs (USA)	48.17
Javelin	Erik Lemming (SWE)	60.64	Juho Saaristo (FIN)	58.66	Mór Kóczán (HUN)	55.50
(Both Hands)	Julio Saaristo (FIN)	109.42	Väinö Siikaniemi (FIN)	101.13	Urho Peltonen (FIN)	100.24
*Pentathlon	Ferdinand Bie (NOR)	16	James Donahue (USA)	24	Frank Lukemann (CAN)	24

EVENT	GOLD		SILVER		BRONZE	
*Decathlon	Hugo Wieslander (SWE)	7724.495	Charles Lomberg (SWE)	7413.510	Gösta Holmér (SWE)	7347.855
Tug-of-War	Sweden		Great Britain			
* In 1982 Jim Thorpe (USA) the original gold medal winner in the Pentathlon and Decathlon was reinstated.						
Swimming						
Men						
100 m Freestyle	Duke Kahanamoku (USA)	1:03.4	Cecil Healey (AUS)	1:04.6	Kenneth Huszagh (USA)	1:05.6
400 m Freestyle	George Hodgson (CAN)	5:24.4	John Hatfield (GBR)	5:28.8	Harold Hardwick (AUS)	5:31.2
1500 m Freestyle	George Hodgson (CAN)	22:00.0	John Hatfield (GBR)	22:39.0	Harold Hardwick (AUS)	23:15.4
100 m Backstroke	Harry Hebner (USA)	1:21.2	Otto Fahr (GER)	1:22.4	Paul Kellner (GER)	1:24.0
200 m Breaststroke	Walter Bathe (GER)	3:01.8	Wilhelm Lützow (GER)	3:05.0	Kurt Malisch (GER)	3:08.0
400 m Breaststroke	Walter Bathe (GER)	6:29.6	Thor Henning (SWE)	6:35.6	Percy Courtman (GBR)	6:36.4
4 x 200 m Freestyle	Australia	10:11.6	USA	10:20.2	Great Britain	10:28.2
Springboard Diving	Paul Günther (GER)	79.23	Hans Luber (GER)	76.78	Kurt Behrens (GER)	73.73
Highboard Diving	Erik Adlerz (SWE)	73.94	Albert Zürner (GER)	72.60	Gustaf Blomgren (SWE)	69.56
Plain High Diving	Erik Adlerz (SWE)	40.0	Hjalmar Johansson (SWE)	39.3	John Jansson (SWE)	39.1
Water Polo	Great Britain		Sweden		Belgium	
Women						
100 m Freestyle	Fanny Durack (AUS)	1:22.2	Wilhelmina Wylie (AUS)	1:25.4	Jennie Fletcher (GBR)	1:27.0
4 x 100 m Freestyle	Great Britain	5:52.8	Germany	6:04.6	Austria	6:17.0
Highboard Diving	Greta Johansson (SWE)	39.9	Lisa Regnell (SWE)	36.0	Isabelle White (GBR)	34.0
Greco-Roman Wrestling						
Featherweight (- 60 kg)	Kaarlo Koskelo (FIN)		Georg Gerstacker (GER)		Otto Lasanen (FIN)	
Lightweight (- 67.5 kg)	Eemel Väre (FIN)		Gustaf Malmström (SWE)		Edvin Matiasson (SWE)	
Middleweight (- 75 kg)	Claes Johansson (SWE)		Martin Klein (RUS)		Alfred Asikainen (FIN)	
Light-Heavyweight (- 82.5 kg)			Anders Ahlgren (SWE)		Béla Varga (HUN)	
			Ivar Böhling (FIN)			
Heavyweight (+ 82.5 kg)	Yrjö Saarela (FIN)		Johan Olin (FIN)		Sören Jensen (DEN)	
Fencing						
Individual Foil	Nedo Nadi (ITA)	7	Pietro Speciale (ITA)	5	Richard Verderber (AUT)	4
Individual Épée	Paul Anspach (BEL)	6	Ivan Osiier (DEN)	5	Philippe Le Hardy de Beaulieu (BEL)	4
Team Épée	Belgium		Great Britain		Netherlands	
Individual Sabre	Jenö Fuchs (HUN)	6	Béla Békéssy (HUN)	5/5	Ervin Mészáros (HUN)	5/6
Team Sabre	Hungary		Austria		Netherlands	
Modern Pentathlon						
	Gustaf Lilliehöök (SWE)	27	Gösta Asbrink (SWE)	28	Georg de Laval (SWE)	30
Rowing						
Single Sculls	William Kinnear (GBR)	7:47.6	Polydore Veirman (BEL)	7:56.0	Everard Butler (CAN)	
					Mikhail Kusik (RUS)	
Coxed Fours	Germany	6:59.4	Great Britain		†Denmark/Norway	
Coxed Fours (Inriggers)	Denmark	7:47.0	Sweden	7:56.2	Norway	
Coxed Eights	Great Britain	6:15.0	Great Britain	6:19.0	Germany	
† Denmark and Norway were joint bronze medallists						
Yachting						
6 m	France		Denmark		Sweden	
8 m	Norway		Sweden		Finland	
10 m	Sweden		Finnland		Russia	
12 m	Norway		Sweden		Finland	
Cycling						
Individual Road Race (320 km)	Rudolph Lewis (SAF)	10:42:39.0	Frederick Grubb (GBR)	10:51:24.2	Carl Schutte (USA)	10:52:38.8
Team Road Race	Sweden	44:35:33.6	Great Britain	44:44:39.2	USA	44:47:55.5
Equestrianism						
Three-Day Event	Axel Nordlander (SWE)	46.59	Friedrich v. Rochow (GER)	46.42	Jean Cariou (FRA)	46.32
Three-Day Event Team	Sweden	139.06	Germany	138.48	USA	137.33
Grand Prix (Dressage)	Carl Bonde (SWE)	15	Gustaf Adolf Boltenstern (SWE)	21	Hans v. Blixen-Finecke (SWE)	32
Grand Prix (Jumping)	Jean Cariou (FRA)	186	Rabod Wilhelm v. Kröcher (GER)	186	Emanuel de Blommaert de Soye (BEL)	185
Grand Prix (Jumping) Team	Sweden	545	France	538	Germany	530
Shooting						
Free Rifle (3 Positions)	Paul Colas (FRA)	987	Lars Jörgen Madsen (DEN)	981	Niels Larsen (DEN)	962
Free Rifle (Team)	Sweden	5655	Norway	5605	Denmark	5529
Military Rifle	Paul Colas (FRA)	94	Carl Osburn (USA)	94	Joseph Jackson (USA)	93

EVENT	GOLD		SILVER		BRONZE	
Military Rifle (Team)	USA	1687	Great Britain	1602	Sweden	1570
Small-Bore Rifle (Prone)	Frederick Hird (USA)	194	William Milne (GBR)	193	Harry Burt (GBR)	192
Small-Bore Rifle (Team)	Sweden	925	Great Britain	917	USA	881
Small-Bore Rifle (Disappearing Target)	Wilhelm Carlberg (SWE)	242	Johan von Holst (SWE)	233	Gustaf Ericsson (SWE)	231
Rapid-Fire Pistol	Alfred Lane (USA)	499	Paul Palen (SWE)	286	Johan von Holst (SWE)	283
Free Pistol (50 m)	Alfred Lane (USA)	96	Peter Dolfen (USA)	474	Charles Stewart (GBR)	470
Team Event	USA	1916	Sweden	1849	Great Britain	1804
Olympic Trap Shooting	James Graham (USA)	96	Alfred Goldel (GER)	94	Harry Blau (RUS)	91
Clay Pigeons (Team)	USA	532	Great Britain	511	Germany	510
Running Deer Shooting	Alfred Swahn (SWE)	41	Ake Lundberg (SWE)	41	Nestori Toivonen (FIN)	41
Running Deer Shooting (Team)	Sweden	151	USA	132	Finland	123
Running Deer Shooting (Double Shot)	Ake Lundberg (SWE)	79	Edward Benedicks (SWE)	74	Oscar Swahn (SWE)	72
Gymnastics						
Individual Combined Exercises	Alberto Braglia (ITA)	135.0	Louis Ségura (FRA)	132.5	Adolfo Tunesi (ITA)	131.5
Team	Italy	265.75	Hungary	227.25	Great Britain	184.50
Swedish System (Men's Teams)	Sweden	937.46	Denmark	898.84	Norway	857.21
Free System (Men's Teams)	Norway	114.25	Finland	109.25	Denmark	106.25
Tennis						
Men's Singles	Charles Winslow (SAF)		Harold Kitson (SAF)		Oscar Kreuzer (GER)	
Men's Singles (Indoor)	André Gobert (FRA)	8:6. 6:4. 6:4	Charles Dixon (GBR)		Anthony Wilding (AUS)	
Men's Doubles	Charles Winslow / Harold Kitson (SAF)		Felix Pipes / Arthur Zborzil (AUT)		Albert Canet / Marc de Marangue (FRA)	
Men's Doubles (Indoor)	André Gobert / Maurice Gernot (FRA)		Gunnar Setterwall / Carl Kempe (SWE)		Charles Dixon / Alfred Beamish (GBR)	
Women's Singles	Marguerite Broquedis (FRA)		Dora Köring (GER)		Molla Bjurstedt (NOR)	
Women's Singles (Indoor)	Edith Hannan (GBR)		Thora Castenschiold (DEN)		Mabel Parton (GBR)	
Mixed Doubles	Dora Köring / Heinrich Schomburgk (GER)		Sigrid Fick / Gunnar Setterwall (SWE)		Marguerite Broquedis / Albert Canet (FRA)	
Mixed Doubles (Indoor)	Edith Hannan / Charles Dixon (GBR)		Helen Aitchison / Herbert Roper-Barre (GBR)		Sigrid Fick / Gunnar Setterwall (SWE)	
Soccer						
	Great Britain		Denmark		Netherlands	

Antwerp 1920

Participants: 2668 / Men: 2591, Women: 77, Countries: 29,
Sports: 21, Events: 154

7 July – 12 September
(Figure Skating and Ice Hockey 23–29 April)
(Official Opening Ceremony 14 August)

Medals Table

PLACE	COUNTRY	GOLD	SILVER	BRONZE
1	USA	41	26	27
2	Sweden	17	19	26
3	Great Britain	15	15	13
4	Belgium	14	11	10
5	Finland	14	10	8

Outstanding Athletes

PLACE	NAME (NATIONALITY)	DISCIPLINE	G	S	B
1	Willis Lee (USA)	Shooting	5	1	1
2	Nedo Nadi (ITA)	Fencing	5	–	–
3	Hubert van Innis (BEL)	Archery	4	2	–
4	Lloyd Spooner (USA)	Shooting	4	1	2
5	Carl Osburn (USA)	Shooting	4	1	1

EVENT	GOLD		SILVER		BRONZE	
Athletics						
100 m	Charles Paddock (USA)	10.8	Morris Kirksey (USA)	10.8	Harry Edward (GBR)	11.0
200 m	Allen Woodring (USA)	22.0	Charles. Paddock (USA)	22.1	Harry Edward (GBR)	22.2
400 m	Bevil Rudd (SAF)	49.6	Guy Butler (GBR)	49.9	Nils Engdahl (SWE)	50.0
800 m	Albert Hill (GBR)	1:53.4	Earl Eby (USA)	1:53.6	Bevil Rudd (SAF)	1:54.0
1500 m	Albert Hill (GBR)	4:01.8	Philip Noel-Baker (GBR)	4:02.4	Lawrence Shields (USA)	4:03.1
3000 m Team Race	USA	10	Great Britain	20	Sweden	24
5000 m	Joseph Guillemot (FRA)	14:55.6	Paavo Nurmi (FIN)	15:00:0	Erik Backman (SWE)	15:13.0
10,000 m	Paavo Nurmi (FIN)	31:45.8	Joseph Guillemot (FRA)	31:47.2	James Wilson (GBR)	31:50.8

EVENT	GOLD		SILVER		BRONZE	
Marathon (42.750 km)	Hannes Kolehmainen (FIN)	2:32:35.8	Juri Lossman (EST)	2:32:48.6	Valerio Arri (ITA)	2:36:32.8
110 m Hurdles	Earl Thomson (CAN)	14.8	Harold Barron (USA)	15.1	Frederick Murray (USA)	15.2
400 m Hurdles	Frank Loomis (USA)	54.0	John Norton (USA)	54.3	August Desch (USA)	54.5
3000 m Steeplechase	Percy Hodge (GBR)	10:00.4	Patrick Flynn (USA)		Ernesto Ambrosini (ITA)	
Individual Cross-Country	Paavo Nurmi (FIN)	27:15.0	Erik Backman (SWE)	27:15.6	Heikki Liimatainen (FIN)	27:37.4
Team Cross-Country	Finland	10	Great Britain	21	Sweden	23
4 x 100 m	USA	42.2	France	42.6	Sweden	42.9
4 x 400 m	Great Britain	3:22.2	South Africa	3:24.2	France	3:24.8
3 km Walk	Ugo Frigerio (ITA)	13:14.2	George Parker (AUS)		Richard F. Remer (USA)	
10 km Walk	Ugo Frigerio (ITA)	48:06.2	Joseph Pearman (USA)		Charles Gunn (GBR)	
High jump	Richmond Landon (USA)	1.935	Harold Muller (USA)	1.90	Bo Ekelund (SWE)	1.90
Pole Vault	Frank Foss (USA)	4.09	Henry Petersen (DAN)	3.70	Edwin Myers (USA)	3.60
Long Jump	William Pettersson (SWE)	7.15	Carl Johan Johnson (USA)	7.095	Erik Abrahamsson (SWE)	7.08
Triple Jump	Vilho Tuulos (FIN)	14.505	Folke Jansson (SWE)	14.48	Erik Almlöf (SWE)	14.275
Shot	Ville Pörhölä (FIN)	14.81	Elmer Niklander (FIN)	14.155	Harry Liversedge (USA)	14.15
Discus	Elmer Niklander (FIN)	44.685	Armas Taipale (FIN)	44.19	Augustus Pope (USA)	42.13
Hammer	Patrick Ryan (USA)	52.875	Carl Lind (SWE)	48.43	Basil Bennet (USA)	48.25
Javelin	Jonni Myyrä (FIN)	65.78	Urho Peltonen (FIN)	63.50	Paavo Jaale-Johansson (FIN)	63.095
56lb Weight Throw	Patrick McDonald (USA)	11.265	Patrick Ryan (USA)	10.965	Carl Johan Lind (SWE)	10.25
Pentathlon	Eero Lehtonen (FIN)	14	Everett Bradley (USA)	24	Hugo Lahtinen (FIN)	26
Decathlon	Helge Lövland (NOR)	6804.355	Brutus Hamilton (USA)	6771.085	Bertil Ohlson (SWE)	6580.030
Tug-of-War	Great Britain		Netherlands		Belgium	

Swimming

Men

100 m Freestyle	Duke Kahanamoku (USA)	1:01.4	Pua Kealoha (USA)	1:02.2	William Harris (USA)	1:03.0
400 m Freestyle	Norman Ross (USA)	5:26.8	Ludy Langer (USA)	5:29.0	George Vernot (CAN)	5:29.8
1500 m Freestyle	Norman Ross (USA)	22:23.2	George Vernot (CAN)	22:36.4	Frank Beaurepaire (AUS)	23:04.0
100 m Backstroke	Warren Kealoha (USA)	1:15.2	Raymond Kegeris (USA)	1:16.2	Gérard Blitz (BEL)	1:19.0
200 m Breaststroke	Hakan Malmroth (SWE)	3:04.4	Thor Henning (SWE)	3:09.2	Arvo Aaltonen (FIN)	3:12.2
400 m Breaststroke	Hakan Malmroth (SWE)	6:31.8	Thor Henning (SWE)	6:45.2	Arvo Aaltonen (FIN)	6:48.0
4 x 200 m Freestyle Relay	USA	10:04.4	Australia	10:25.4	Great Britain	10:37.2
Springboard Diving	Louis Kuehn (USA)	05.11.1901	Clarence Pinkston (USA)	655.3	Louis Balbach (USA)	649.5
Highboard Diving	Clarence Pinkston (USA)	100.67	Erik Adlerz (SWE)	99.08	Harry Prieste (USA)	93.73
Plain High Diving	Arvid Wallmann (SWE)	183.5	Nils Skoglund (SWE)	183.0	John Jansson (SWE)	175.0
Water Polo	Great Britain		Belgium		Sweden	

Women

100 m Freestlye	Ethelda Bleibtrey (USA)	1:13.6	Irene Guest (USA)	1:17.0	Frances Schroth (USA)	1:17.2
300 m Freestyle	Ethelda Bleibtrey (USA)	4:34.0	Margaret Woodbridge (USA)	4:42.8	Frances Schroth (USA)	4:52.0
4 x 100 m Freestyle Relay	USA	5:11.6	Great Britain	5:40.8	Sweden	5:43.6
Springboard Diving	Aileen Riggin (USA)	539.9	Helen Wainwright (USA)	534.8	Thelma Payne (USA)	534.1
Highboard Diving	Stefani Fryland-Clausen (DEN)	34.6	Eileen Armstrong (GBR)	33.3	Eva Ollivier (SWE)	33.3

Boxing

Flyweight (- 50.8 kg)	Frank di Genaro (USA)		Anders Petersen (DEN)		William Cuthbertson (GBR)
Bantamweight (- 53.52 kg)	Clarence Walker (SAF)		Christopher Graham (CAN)		James McKenzie (GBR)
Featherweight (- 57.15 kg)	Paul Fritsch (FRA)		Jean Gachet (FRA)		Edoardo Garzena (ITA)
Lightweight(- 61.24 kg)	Samuel Mosberg (USA)		Gotfred Johansen (DEN)		Chris Newton (CAN)
Welterweight (- 66.68 kg)	Albert Schneider (CAN)		Alexander Ireland (GBR)		Frederick Colberg (USA)
Middleweightt (- 72.57 kg)	Harry Mallin (GBR)		Georges Prud'Homme (CAN)		Montgomery Herscovitch (CAN)
Light-Heavyweight (- 79.38 kg)	Edward Eagan (USA)		Sverre Sörsdal (NOR)		Harry Franks (GBR)
Heavyweight (+ 79.38 kg)	Ronald Rawson (GBR)		Sören Petersen (DEN)		Xavier Eluère (FRA)

Weightlifting

Featherweight (- 60 kg)	Frans de Haes (BEL)	220.0	Alfred Schmidt (EST)	212.5	Eugène Ryther (SUI)	210.0
Lightweight (- 67.5 kg)	Alfred Neuland (EST)	257.5	Louis Williquet (BEL)	240.0	Florimond Rooms (BEL)	230.0
Middleweight (- 75 kg)	Henri Gance (FRA)	245.0	Pietro Bianchi (ITA)	237.5	Albert Pettersson (SWE)	237.5
Light-Heavyweightt (- 82.5 kg)	Ernest Cadine (FRA)	290.0	Fritz Hünenberger (SUI)	275.0	Erik Pettersson (SWE)	272.5
Heavyweight (+ 82.5 kg)	Filippo Bottino (ITA)	270.0	Joseph Alzin (LUX)	255.0	Louis Bernot (FRA)	250.0

Greco-Roman Wrestling

Featherweight (- 60 kg)	Oskari Friman (FIN)	Heikki Kähkönen (FIN)	Fridtj Svensson (SWE)
Lightweight (- 67.5 kg)	Eemeli Väre (FIN)	Taavi Tamminen (FIN)	Fridtj Andersen (NOR)
Middleweightt (- 75 kg)	Carl Westergren (SWE)	Artur Lindfors (FIN)	Matti Perttilä (FIN)
Light-Heavyweightt (- 82.5 kg)	Claes Johansson (SWE)	Edil Rosenqvist (FIN)	Johannes Eriksen (DEN)
Heavyweightt (+ 82.5 kg)	Adolf Lindfors (FIN)	Poul Hansen (DEN)	Martti Nieminen (FIN)

EVENT	GOLD		SILVER		BRONZE	
Freestyle Wrestling						
Featherweight (- 60 kg)	Charles Ackerly (USA)		Samuel Gerson (USA)		Peter W. Bernard (GBR)	
Lightweight (- 67.5 kg)	Kalle Antilla (FIN)		Gottfried Svensson (SWE)		Peter Wright (GBR)	
Middleweightt (- 75 kg)	Eino Leino (FIN)		Väinö Penttala (FIN)		Charles Johnson (USA)	
Light-Heavyweightt (- 82.5 kg)	Anders Larsson (SWE)		Charles Courant (SUI)		Walter Maurer (USA)	
Heavyweight (+ 82.5 kg)	Robert Roth (SUI)		Nathan Pendleton (USA)		Ernst Nilsson (SWE)	
					Frederick Meyer (USA)	
Fencing						
Individual Foil	Nedo Nadi (ITA)	10	Philippe Cattiau (FRA)	9/14	Roger Ducret (FRA)	9/19
Team Foil	Italy		France		USA	
Individual Épée	Armand Massard (FRA)	9	Alexandre Lippmann (FRA)	7	Gustave Buchard (FRA)	6
Team Épée	Italy		Belgium		France	
Individual Sabre	Nedo Nadi (ITA)	11	Aldo Nadi (ITA)	9	Adrianus E. W. de Jong (HOL)	7
Team Sabre	Italy		France		Netherlands	
Modern Pentathlon						
	Gustav Dyrssen (SWE)	18	Erik de Laval (SWE)	23	Gösta Runö (SWE)	27
Rowing						
Single Sculls	John Kelly sen. (USA)	7:35.0	Jack Beresford jun. (GBR)	7:36.0	Clarence Hadfield d'Arcy (NZL)	
						7:48.0
Double Sculls	USA	7:09.0	Italy	7:19.0	France	7:21.0
Coxed Pairs	Italy	7:56.0	France	7:57.0	Switzerland	
Coxed Fours	Switzerland	6:54.0	USA	6:58.0	Norway	7:02.0
Coxed Eights	USA	6:02.6	Great Britain	6:05.0	Norway	6:36.0
Yachting						
12-Foot Dinghy	Netherlands		Netherlands			
18-Foot Dinghy	Great Britain					
6 m	Norway		Belgium			
6 m (1907 Rating)	Belgium		Norway		Norway	
6.5 m (1919 Rating)	Netherlands		France			
7 m	Great Britain					
8 m	Norway		Norway		Belgium	
8 m (1907 Rating)	Norway		Norway			
10 m	Norway					
10 m (1907 Rating)	Norway					
12 m (1903 Rating)	Norway					
12 m	Norway					
Sharpie 30 m2	Sweden					
Sharpie 40 m2	Sweden		Sweden			
Cycling						
Individual Road Race (175 km)	Harry Stenqvist (SWE)	4:40:01.8	Henry Kaltenbrunn (SAF)	4:41:26.6	Fernand Canteloube (FRA)	4:42:54.4
Team Road Race	France	19:16:43.2	Sweden	19:23:10.0	Belgium	19:28:44.4
50 km Track	Henry George (BEL)	1:16:43.2	Cyril Alden (GBR)		Piet Ikelaar (HOL)	
1000 m Sprint	Maurice Peeters (HOL)	1:38.3	Thomas Johnson (GBR)		Harry Ryan (GBR)	
2000 m Tandem	Great Britain	2:49.4	South Africa		Netherlands	
4000 m Team Pursuit	Italy	5:20.0	Great Britain		South Africa	
Equestrianism						
Three-Day Event	Helmer Mörner (SWE)	1775.00	Åge Lundström (SWE)	1738.75	Ettore Caffaratti (ITA)	1733.75
Three-Day Event (Team)	Sweden	5057.50	Italy	4735.00	Belgium	4560.00
Grand Prix (Dressage)	Janne Lundblad (SWE)	27.937	Bertil Sandström (SWE)	26.312	Hans von Rosen (SWE)	25.125
Grand Prix (Jumping)	Tommaso Lequio (ITA)	-2	Alessandro Valerio (ITA)	-3	Gustaf Lewenhaupt (SWE)	-4
Grand Prix (Jumping) Team	Sweden	-14	Belgium	-16.25	Italy	-18.75
Figure Riding	Bouckaert (BEL)	30.5	Fiel (FRA)	29.5	Finet (BEL)	29.0
Figure Riding (Team)	Belgium		France		Sweden	
Shooting						
Free Rifle (Three Positions)	Morris Fisher (USA)	997	Niels Larsen (DEN)	985	Östen Östensen (NOR)	980
Free Rifle (Team)	USA	4876	Norway	4741	Switzerland	4698
Military Rifle (Prone) 300 m	Otto Olsen (NOR)	60	Léon Johnson (FRA)	59	Fritz Kuchen (SUI)	59
Military Rifle (Team)	USA	289	France	283	Finland	281
Military Rifle (Standing) 300 m	Carl Osburn (USA)	56	Lars Jörgen Madsen (DEN)	55	Lawrence Adam Nuesslein (USA)	54
Military Rifle (Team)	Denmark	266	USA	255	Sweden	255
Military Rifle (Prone) 600 m	Hugo Johansson (SWE)	58	Mauritz Eriksson (SWE)	56	Lloyd Spooner (USA)	56

Antwerp 1920

EVENT	GOLD		SILVER		BRONZE	
Military Rifle (Team) 600 m	USA	287	South Africa	287	Sweden	287
Military Rifle (Prone) 600 +300 m	USA	573	Norway	565	Switzerland	563
Small-Bore Rifle (Standing)	Lawrence A.Nuesslein (USA)	391	Arthur Rothrock (USA)	386	Dennis Fenton (USA)	385
Small-Bore Rifle (Team)	USA	1899	Sweden	1873	Norway	1866
Rapid-Fire Pistol	Guilherme Paraense (BRA)	274	Raymond Bracken (USA)	272	Fritz Zulauf (SUI)	269
Free Pistol (50 m)	Carl Frederick (USA)	496	Afranio da Costa (BRA)	489	Alfred Lane (USA)	481
Olympic Trap Shooting	Mark Arie (USA)	95	Frank Troeh (USA)	93	Frank Wright (USA)	87
Clay Pigeons (Team)	USA	547	Belgium	503	Sweden	500
Running Deer Shooting	Otto Olsen (NOR)	43	Alfred Swahn (SWE)	41	Harald Natvig (NOR)	41
Running Deer (Team)	Norway	178	Finland	159	USA	158
Running Deer (Double Shot)	Ole Andreas Lilloe-Olsen (NOR)	82	Fredrik Landelius (SWE)	77	Einar Liberg (NOR)	71
Running Deer (Double Shot) (Team)	Norway	343	Sweden	336	Finland	284
Military Revolver (Team) 50 m	USA	2372	Sweden	2289	Brazil	2264
Military Revolver (Team) 30 m	USA	1310	Greece	1285	Switzerland	1270
Archery						
Fixed Bird Target - Small Birds - Individual	Edmond van Moer (BEL)	11	Louis van de Perck (BEL)	8	Joseph Hermans (BEL)	6
Fixed Bird Target - Large Birds - Individual	Edouard Cloetens (BEL)	13	Louis van de Perck (BEL)	11	Firmin Flamand (BEL)	7
Fixed Bird Target - Sm and Lrg Birds - Team	Belgium					
Moving Bird Target - 28 m - Individual	Hubert van Innis (BEL)	144	Léonce Quentin (FRA)	115		
Moving Bird Target - 28 m - Team	Netherlands	3087	Belgium	2924	France	2317
Moving Bird Target - 33 m - Individual	Hubert van Innis (BEL)	139	Julien Brulé (FRA)	94		
Moving Bird Target - 33 m - Team	Belgium	2958	France	2586		
Moving Bird Target - 50 m - Individual	Julien Louis Brulé (FRA)	134	Hubert van Innis (BEL)	106		
Moving Bird Target - 50 m - Team	Belgium	2701	France	2493		
Gymnastics						
Individual Combined Exercises	Giorgio Zampori (ITA)	88.35	Marco Torrès (FRA)	87.62	Jean Gounot (FRA)	87.45
Team	Italy	359.855	Belgium	346.785	France	340.100
Swedish System (Men's Teams)	Sweden	1364	Denmark	1325	Belgium	1094
Free System (Men's Teams)	Denmark		Norway			
Tennis						
Men's Singles	Louis Raymond (SAF)		Ichiya Kumagae (JPN)		Charles Winslow (SAF)	
Men's Doubles	O. G. Noel Turnbull / Max Woosman (GBR)		Ichiya Kumagae/ Seiichiro Kashio (JPN)		Max Décugis/ Pierre Albarran (FRA)	
Women's Singles	Suzanne Lenglen (FRA)		Dorothy Holman (GBR)		Kitty McKane (GBR)	
Women's Doubles	Winifred Margaret McNair/ Kitty McKane (GBR)		Geraldine Beamish/Dorothy Holman (GBR)		Suzanne Lenglen/Elisabeth d'Ayen (FRA)	
Mixed	Suzanne Lenglen/ Max Décugis (FRA)		Kitty McKane/ Max Woosnam (GBR)		Milada Skrbková/Ladislav Zmela (TCH)	
Football	Belgium		Spain		Netherlands	
Hockey	Great Britain		Denmark		Belgium	
Polo	Great Britain		Spain		USA	
Rugby	USA		France			
Figure Skating						
Women	Magda Julin (SWE)	12	Svea Noren (SWE)	12.5	Theresa Weld (SWE)	15.5
Men	Gillis Gräfström (SWE)	7	Andreas Krogh (NOR)	18	Martin Stixrud (NOR)	24.5
Pairs	Ludovika Jakobsson/ Walter Jakobsson (FIN)	7	Alexia Bryn/Yngvar Bryn (NOR)	15.5	Phyllis Johnson / Basil Williams (GBR)	25
Ice Hockey	Canada		USA		Czechoslovakia	

Chamonix 1924

Participants: 258 / Men: 245, Women: 13, Countries: 16,
Sports: 5, Events: 14

Medals Table

PLACE	COUNTRY	GOLD	SILVER	BRONZE
1	Norway	4	7	6
2	Finland	4	3	3
3	Austria	2	1	–
4	USA	1	2	1
5	Switzerland	1	–	1

Outstanding Athletes

PLACE	NAME (NATIONALITY)	DISCIPLINE	G	S	B
1	Clas Thunberg (FIN)	Speed Skating	3	1	1
2	Thorleif Haug (NOR)	Nordic Skiing	3	–	–
3	Julius Skutnabb (FIN)	Speed Skating	1	1	1

EVENT	GOLD		SILVER		BRONZE	
Nordic Skiing						
18 km Cross Country Skiing	Thorleif Haug (NOR)	1:14:31.0	Johan Gröttumsbraaten (NOR)	1:15:51.0	Tapani Niku (FIN)	1:26:26.0
50 km Cross Country Skiing	Thorleif Haug (NOR)	3:44:32.0	Thoralf Strömstad (NOR)	3:46:23.0	Johan Gröttumsbraaten (NOR)	3:47:46.0
Ski Jumping	Jacob Tullin Thams (NOR)	18.960	Narve Bonna (NOR)	18.689	Thorleif Haug (NOR)	18.000★
					Anders Haugen (USA)	17.916★
Nordic Combined	Thorleif Haug (NOR)	18.906	Thoralf Strömstad (NOR)	18.219	Johan Gröttumsbraaten (NOR)	17.854
Figure Skating						
Women	Herma Planck-Szabo (AUT)		Beatrix Loughran (USA)		Ethel Muckelt (GBR)	
Men	Gillis Gräfström (SWE)		Willy Böckl (AUT)		Georges Gautschi (SUI)	
Pairs	Helene Engelmann/Alfred Berger (AUT)		Ludovika Jakobsson/ Walter Jakobsson (FIN)		Andée Joly/ Pierre Brunet (FRA)	
Speed Skating						
500 m	Charles Jewtraw (USA)	44.0	Oskar Olsen (NOR)	44.2	Roald Larsen (NOR)	44.8
					Clas Thunberg (FIN)	44.8
1500 m	Clas Thunberg (FIN)	2:20.8	Roald Larsen (NOR)	2:22.0	Sigurd Moen (NOR)	2:25.6
5000 m	Clas Thunberg (FIN)	8:39.0	Julius Skutnabb (FIN)	8:48.4	Roald Larsen (NOR)	8:50.2
10,000 m	Julius Skutnabb (FIN)	18:04.8	Clas Thunberg (FIN)	18:07.8	Roald Larsen (NOR)	18:12.2
All-round Championship	Clas Thunberg (FIN)	5.5	Roald Larsen (NOR)	9.5	Julius Skutnabb (FIN)	11
Bobsledding						
4-Man Bob	Switzerland I	5:45.54	Great Britain II	5:48.83	Belgium I	6:02.29
Ice hockey						
	Canada		USA		Great Britain	

★ Owing to incorrect calculations which were first discovered and corrected in 1974 Haug was awarded the bronze medal although his actual score was 17.821. Haugen was awarded his bronze medal at a later date.

Paris 1924

Participants: 3092 / Men: 2956, Women: 136, Countries: 44,
Sports: 17, Events: 126

Medals Table

PLACE	COUNTRY	GOLD	SILVER	BRONZE
1	USA	45	27	27
2	Finland	14	13	10
3	France	13	15	10
4	Great Britain	9	13	12
5	Italy	8	3	5

Outstanding Athletes

PLACE	NAME (NATIONALITY)	DISCIPLINE	G	S	B
1	Paavo Nurmi (FIN)	Athletics	5	–	–
2	Ville Ritola (FIN)	Athletics	4	2	–
3	Roger Ducret (FRA)	Fencing	3	1	–
4	Johnny Weissmuller (USA)	Swimming	3	–	1
5	Vincent Richards (USA)	Tennis	2	1	–

EVENT	GOLD		SILVER		BRONZE	
Athletics						
100 m	Harold Abrahams (GBR)	10.6	Jackson Scholz (USA)	10.7	Arthur Porritt (NZL)	10.8
200 m	Jackson Scholz (USA)	21.6	Charles Paddock (USA)	21.7	Eric Liddell (GBR)	21.9
400 m	Eric Liddell (GBR)	47.6	Horatio Fitch (USA)	48.4	Guy Butler (GBR)	48.6
800 m	Douglas Lowe (GBR)	1:52.4	Paul Martin (SUI)	1:52.6	Schuyler Enck (USA)	1:53.0
1500 m	Paavo Nurmi (FIN)	3:53.6	Willy Schärer (SUI)	3:55.0	Henry Stallard (GBR)	3:55.6
3000 m Team Race	Finland	8	Great Britain	14	USA	25
5000 m	Paavo Nurmi (FIN)	14:31.2	Ville Ritola (FIN)	14:31.4	Edvin Wide (SWE)	15:01.8
10 000 m	Ville Ritola (FIN)	30:23.2	Edvin Wide (SWE)	30:55.2	Eero Berg (FIN)	31:43.0
Marathon (42.195 km)	Albin Stenroos (FIN)	2:41:22.6	Romeo Bertini (ITA)	2:47:19.6	Clarence DeMar (USA)	2:48:14.0
110 m Hurdles	Daniel Kinsey (USA)	15.0	Sidney Atkinson (SAF)	15.0	Sten Pettersson (SWE)	15.4
400 m Hurdles	F. Morgan Taylor (USA)	52.6	Erik Vilén (FIN)	53.8	Ivan Riley (USA)	54.2
3000 m Steeplechase	Ville Ritola (FIN)	9:33.6	Elias Katz (FIN)	9:44.0	Paul Bontemps (FRA)	9:45.2
Individual Cross-Country	Paavo Nurmi (FIN)	32:54.8	Ville Ritola (FIN)	34:19.4	Earl Johnson (USA)	35:21.0
Team Cross-Country	Finland	11	USA	14	France	20
4 x 100 m Relay	USA	41.0	Great Britain	41.2	Netherlands	41.8
4 x 400 m Relay	USA	3:16.0	Sweden	3:17.0	Great Britain	3:17.4
10 km Walk	Ugo Frigerio (ITA)	47:49.0	Gordon Goodwin (GBR)		Cecil McMaster (SAF)	
High Jump	Harold Osborn (USA)	1.98	Leroy Brown (USA)	1.95	Pierre Lewden (FRA)	1.92
Pole Vault	Lee Barnes (USA)	3.95	Glen Graham (USA)	3.95	James Brooker (USA)	3.90
Long Jump	William DeHart Hubbard (USA)	7.445	Edward Gourdin (USA)	7.275	Sverre Hansen (NOR)	7.26
Triple Jump	Anthony Winter (AUS)	15.525	Luis Bruneto (ARG)	15.425	Vilho Tuulos (FIN)	15.37
Shot	Clarence Houser (USA)	14.995	Glenn Hartranft (USA)	14.895	Ralph Hills (USA)	14.64
Discus	Clarence Houser (USA)	46.155	Vilho Niittymaa (FIN)	44.95	Thomas Lieb (USA)	44.83
Hammer	Frederick Tootell (USA)	53.295	Matthew McGrath (USA)	50.84	Malcolm Nokes (GBR)	48.875
Javelin	Jonni Myyrä (FIN)	62.96	Gunnar Lindström (SWE)	60.92	Eugene Oberst (USA)	58.35
Pentathlon	Eero Lehtonen (FIN)	14	Elemér Somfay (HUN)	16	Robert LeGendre (USA)	18
Decathlon	Harold Osborn (USA)	7710.775	Emerson Norton (USA)	7350.895	Alexander Klumberg (EST)	7329.360
Swimming						
Men						
100 m Freestyle	Johnny Weissmuller (USA)	59.0	Duke Kahanamoku (USA)	1:01.4	Sam Kahanamoku (USA)	1:01.8
400 m Freestyle	Johnny Weissmuller (USA)	5:04.2	Arne Borg (SWE)	5:05.6	Andrew Charlton (AUS)	5:06.6
1500 m Freestyle	Andrew Charlton (AUS)	20:06.6	Arne Borg (SWE)	20:41.4	Frank Beaurepaire (AUS)	21:48.4
100 m Backstroke	Warren Paoa Kealoha (USA)	1:13.2	Paul Wyatt (USA)	1:15.4	Károly Bartha (HUN)	1:17.8
200 Breaststroke	Robert Skelton (USA)	2:56.6	Joseph de Combe (BEL)	2:59.2	William Kirschbaum (USA)	3:01.0
4 x 200 m Freestyle Relay	USA	9:53.4	Australia	10:02.2	Sweden	10:06.8
Springboard Diving	Albert White (USA)	696.4	Peter Desjardins (USA)	693.3	Clarence Pinkston (USA)	653.0
Highboard Diving	Albert White (USA)	97.46	David Fall (USA)	97.30	Clarence Pinkston (USA)	94.60
Plain High Diving	Richmond Eve (AUS)	160.0	John Jansson (SWE)	157.0 ★	Harold Clarke (GBR)	158.0 ★
Water Polo	France		Belgium		USA	
★Handicap: Jansson 14.5 - Clarke 15.5						
Women						
100 m Freestyle	Ethel Lackie (USA)	1:12.4	Mariechen Wehselau (USA)	1:12.8	Gertrude Ederle (USA)	1:14.2
400 m Freestyle	Martha Norelius (USA)	6:02.2	Helen Wainwright (USA)	6:03.8	Gertrude Ederle (USA)	6:04.8
100 m Backstroke	Sybil Bauer (USA)	1:23.2	Phyllis Harding (GBR)	1:27.4	Aileen Riggin (USA)	1:28.2
200 m Breaststroke	Lucy Morton (GBR)	3:33.2	Agnes Geraghty (USA)	3:34.0	Gladys Carson (GBR)	3:35.4
4 x 100 m Freestyle Relay	USA	4:58.8	Great Britain	5:17.0	Sweden	5:35.6
Springboard Diving	Elizabeth Becker (USA)	474.5	Aileen Riggin (USA)	460.4	Caroline Fletcher (USA)	436.4
Highboard Diving	Caroline Smith (USA)	33.2 ★	Elizabeth Becker (USA)	33.4 ★	Hjördis Töpel (SWE)	32.8
★ Handicap: Smith 10.5 - Becker 11.0						
Boxing						
Flyweight (- 50.80 kg)	Fidel LaBarba (USA)		James McKenzie (GBR)		Raymond Fee (USA)	
Bantamweight (- 53.52 kg)	William Smith (SAF)		Salvatore Tripoli (USA)		Jean Ces (FRA)	
Featherweight (- 57.15 kg)	John Fields (USA)		Joseph Salas (USA)		Pedro Quartucci (ARG)	
Lightweightt (- 61.24 kg)	Hans Nielsen (DEN)		Alfredo Copello (ARG)		Frederick Boylstein (USA)	
Welterweight (- 66.68 kg)	Jean Delarge (BEL)		Héctor Mendez (ARG)		Douglas Lewis (CAN)	
Middleweight (-72.57 kg)	Harry Mallin (GBR)		John Elliott (GBR)		Joseph Beecken (BEL)	
Light-Heavyweight (- 79.38 kg)	Harry Mitchell (GBR)		Thyge Petersen (DEN)		Sverre Sörsdal (NOR)	
Heavyweight (+ 79.38 kg)	Otto von Porrat (NOR)		Sören Petersen (DEN)		Alfredo Porzio (ARG)	
Weightlifting						
Featherweight (- 60 kg)	Pierino Gabetti (ITA)	402.5	Andreas Stadler (AUT)	385.0	Arthur Reinmann (SUI)	382.5
Lightweight (- 67.5 kg)	Edmond Decottignies (FRA)	440.0	Anton Zwerina (AUT)	427.5	Bohumil Durdis (TCH)	425.0
Middleweight (- 75 kg)	Carlo Galimberti (ITA)	492.5	Alfred Neuland (EST)	455.0	Johannes Kikas (EST)	450.0

EVENT	GOLD		SILVER		BRONZE	
Light-Heavyweight (- 82.5 kg)	Charles Rigoulot (FRA)	502.5	Fritz Hünenberger (SUI)	490.0 ★	Leopold Friedrich (AUT)	490.0 ★
Heavyweight (+ 82.5 kg)	Guiseppe Tonani (ITA)	517.5	Franz Aigner (AUT)	515.0	Harald Tammer (EST)	497.5
★ Body Weight: Hünenberger 81.9 kg. Friedrich 82.0 kg						
Greco-Roman Wrestling						
Bantamweight (- 58 kg)	Eduard Pütsep (EST)		Anselm Ahlfors (FIN)		Väinö Ikonen (FIN)	
Featherweight (- 62 kg)	Kalle Antilla (FIN)		Aleksanteri Toivola (FIN)		Erik Malmberg (SWE)	
Lightweight (- 67.5 kg)	Oskari Friman (FIN)		Lajos Keresztes (HUN)		Kalle Westerlund (FIN)	
Middleweight (- 75 kg)	Edvard Westerlund (FIN)		Artur Lindfors (FIN)		Roman Steinberg (EST)	
Light-Heavyweight (- 82.5 kg)	Carl Westergren (SWE)		Rudolf Svensson (SWE)		Onni Pellinen (FIN)	
Heavyweight (+ 82.5 kg)	Henri Deglane (FRA)		Edil Rosenqvist (FIN)		Raymund Badó (HUN)	
Freestyle Wrestling						
Bantamweight (- 56 kg)	Kustaa Pihlajamäki (FIN)		Kaarlo Mäkinen (FIN)		Bryant Hines (USA)	
Featherweight - 61 kg)	Robin Reed (USA)		Chester Newton (USA)		Katsutoshi Naito (JPN)	
Lightweight (- 66 kg)	Russell Vis (USA)		Volmari Vikström (FIN)		Arvo Haavisto (FIN)	
Welterweight (-72 kg)	Hermann Gehri (SUI)		Eino Leino (FIN)		Otto Müller (SUI)	
Middleweight (- 79 kg)	Fritz Hagemann (SUI)		Pierre Olivier (BEL)		Vilho Pekkala (FIN)	
Light-Heavyweight (- 87 kg)	John Spellman (USA)		Rudolf Svensson (SWE)		Charles Courant (SUI)	
Heavyweight (+ 87 kg)	Harry Steele (USA)		Henri Wernli (SUI)		Andrew McDonald (GBR)	
Fencing						
Individual Foil - Men	Roger Ducret (FRA)	6	Philippe Cattiau (FRA)	5	Maurice van Damme (BEL)	4
Team Foil - Men	France		Belgium		Hungary	
Individual Épée	Charles Delporte (BEL)	8	Roger Ducret (FRA)	7	Nils Hellsten (SWE)	7
Team Épée	France		Belgium		Italy	
Individual Sabre	Sándor Posta (HUN)	5	Roger Ducret (FRA)	5	János Garay (HUN)	5
Team Sabre	Italy		Hungary		Netherlands	
Individual Foil - Women	Ellen Osiier (DEN)	5	Gladys Muriel Davis (GBR)	4	Grete Heckscher (DEN)	3
Modern Pentathlon						
Individual	Bo Lindman (SWE)	18	Gustaf Dyrssen (SWE)	39.5	Bertil Uggla (SWE)	45
Rowing						
Single Sculls	Jack Beresford jun. (GBR)	7:49.2	William Garrett Gilmore (USA)	7:54.0	Josef Schneider (SUI)	8:01.1
Double Sculls	USA	6:34.0	France	6:38.0	Switzerland	
Coxless Pairs	Netherlands	8:19.4	France	8:21.6		
Coxed Pairs	Switzerland	8:39.0	Italy	8:39.1	USA	
Coxless Fours	Great Britain	7:08.6	Canada	7:18.0	Switzerland	
Coxed Fours	Switzerland	7:18.4	France	7:21.6	USA	
Coxed Eights	USA	6:33.4	Canada	6:49.0	Italy	
Yachting						
Olympic Monotype	Léon Huybrechts (BEL)	2	Henrik Robert (NOR)	7	Hans Dittmar (FIN)	8
6 m	Norway	2	Denmark	5	Niederlande	5
8 m	Norway	2	Great Britain	5	France	5
Cycling						
Individual Road Race (188 km)	Armand Blanchonnet (FRA)	6:20:48.0	Henri Hoevenaers (BEL)	6:30:27.0	René Hamel (FRA)	6:40:51.6
Team Road Race	France	19:30:13.4	Belgium	19:46:55.4	Sweden	19:59:41.4
50 km Track	Jacobus Willems (HOL)	1:18:24.0	Cyril Alden (GBR)		Frederick Wyld (GBR)	
1000 m Sprint	Lucien Michard (FRA)		Jakob Meijer (HOL)		Jean Cugnot (FRA)	
2000 m Tandem	France		Denmark		Netherlands	
4000 m Team Pursuit	Italy	5:15.0	Polen		Belgium	
Equestrianism						
Three-Day Event	Adolph v. d. Voort v. Zijp (HOL)	1976.0	Frode Kirkebjerg (DEN)	1853.5	Sloan Doak (USA)	1845.5
Three-Day Event Team	Netherlands	5297.5	Sweden	4743.5	Italy	4512.5
Grand Prix (Dressage)	Ernst Linder (SWE)	276.4	Bertil Sandström (SWE)	275.8	Xavier Lesage (FRA)	265.8
Grand Prix (Jumping)	Alphonse Gemuseus (SUI)	-6	Tommaso Lequio (ITA)	-8.75	Adam Królikiewicz (POL)	-10
Grand Prix (Jumping) Team	Sweden	-42.25	Switzerland	-50.0	Portugal	-53.0
Shooting						
Free Rifle (3 Positions)	Morris Fisher (USA)	95	Carl Osburn (USA)	95	Niels Larsen (DEN)	93
Free Rifle (Team)	USA	676	France	646	Haiti	646
Small-Bore Rifle (Prone)	Pierre Coquelin de Lisle (FRA)	398	Marcus Dinwiddle (USA)	396	Josias Hartmann (SUI)	394
Rapid-Fire Pistol	H. M. Bailey (USA)	18	Vilhelm Carlberg (SWE)	18	Lennart Hannelius (FIN)	18
Olympic Trap Shooting	Gyula Halasy (HUN)	98	Konrad Huber (FIN)	98	Frank Hughes (USA)	97

EVENT	GOLD		SILVER		BRONZE	
Clay Pigeons (Team)	USA	363	Canada	360	Finland	360
Running Deer Shooting (Single Shot)	John Boles (USA)	40	Cyril Mackworth-Praed (GBR)	39	Otto M.Olsen (NOR)	39
Running Deer Shooting (Team)	Norway	160	Sweden	154	USA	148
Running Deer Shooting (Double Shot)	Ole Lilloe-Olsen (NOR)	76	Cyril Mackworth-Praed (GBR)	72	Alfred Swahn (SWE)	72
Running Deer Shooting (Team)	Great Britain	263	Norway	262	Sweden	250
Gymnastics						
Individual Combined Exercises	Leon Stukelji (YUG)	110.340	Robert Prazak (TCH)	110.323	Bedrich Supcik (TCH)	106.930
Team	Italy	839.058	France	820.528	Switzerland	816.661
Parallel Bars	August Güttinger (SUI)	21.63	Robert Prazak (TCH)	21.61	Giorgio Zampori (ITA)	21.45
Horse Vault	Frank Kriz (USA)	9.98	Jan Koutny (TCH)	9.97	Bohumil Morkovsky (TCH)	9.93
Horizontal Bar	Leon Stukelji (YUG)	19.730	Jean Gutweniger (SUI)	19.236	André Higelin (FRA)	19.163
Rings	Franco Martino (ITA)	21.553	Robert Prazak (TCH)	21.483	Ladislav Vácha (TCH)	21.430
Pommel Horse	Josef Wilhelm (SUI)	21.23	Jean Gutweniger (SUI)	21.13	Antoine Rebetez (SUI)	20.73
Sidehorse Vault	Albert Séguin (FRA)	10.00	Jean Gounot (FRA)	9.93		
			François Gangloff (FRA)	9.93		
Rope Climbing	Bedrich Supck (TCH)	7.2	Albert Séguin (FRA)	7.4	August Güttinger (SUI)	7.8
					Ladislav Vácha	7.8
Tennis						
Men's Singles	Vincent Richards (USA)		Henri Cochet (FRA)		Umberto De Morpurgo (ITA)	
Men's Doubles	Vincent Richards/Frank Hunter (USA)		Jacques Brugnon/ Henri Cochet (FRA)		Jean Borotra/ René Lacoste (FRA)	
Women's Singles	Helen Wills (USA)		Julie Vlasto (FRA)		Kitty McKane (GBR)	
Women's Doubles	Hazel Wightman/ Helen Wills (USA)		Edith Covell/ Kitty McKane (GBR)		Dorothy C. Shepherd-Barron/ Evelyn L. Colyer (GBR)	
Mixed	Hazel Wightman/ R. Norris Williams (USA)		Marion Jessup/ Vincent Richards (USA)		Cornelia Bouman/ Hendrik Timmer (HOL)	
Soccer	Uruguay		Switzerland		Sweden	
Polo	Argentina		USA		Great Britain	
Rugby	USA		France		Romania	

St. Moritz 1928

11 February – 19 February

Participants: 464 / Men: 438, Women: 26, Countries: 25,
Sports: 6, Events: 14

Medals Table

PLACE	COUNTRY	GOLD	SILVER	BRONZE
1	Norway	6	4	5
2	USA	2	2	2
3	Sweden	2	2	1
4	Finland	2	1	1
5	France	1	–	–

Outstanding Athletes

PLACE	NAME (NATIONALITY)	DISCIPLINE	G	S	B
1	Johan Gröttumsbraaten (NOR)	Nordic Skiing	2	–	–
	Clas Thunberg (FIN)	Speed Skating	2	–	–
3	Bernt Evenson (NOR)	Speed Skating	1	1	1
4	Ivar Ballangrud (NOR)	Speed Skating	1	–	1

EVENT	GOLD		SILVER		BRONZE	
Nordic Skiing						
18 km Cross Country Skiing	Johan Gröttumsbraaten (NOR)	1:37:01.0	Ole Hegge (NOR)	1:39:01.0	Reidar Ödegaard (NOR)	1:40:11.0
50 km Cross Country Skiing	Per Erik Hedlund (SWE)	4:52:03.0	Gustaf Jonsson (SWE)	5:05:30.0	Volger Andersson (SWE)	5:05:46.0
Ski Jumping	Alf Andersen (NOR)	19.208	Sigmund Ruud (NOR)	18.542	Rudolf Burkert (TCH)	17.937
Nordic Combined	Johan Gröttumsbraaten (NOR)	17.833	Hans Vinjarengen (NOR)	15.303	John Snersrud (NOR)	15.021

EVENT	GOLD		SILVER		BRONZE	
Figure Skating						
Women	Sonja Henie (NOR)		Fritzi Burger (AUT)		Beatrix Loughran (USA)	
Men	Gillis Gräfström (SWE)		Willy Böckl (AUT)		Robert van Zeebroeck (BEL)	
Pairs	Andrée Joly/ Pierre Brunet (FRA)		Lilly Scholz/ Otto Kaiser (AUT)		Melitta Brunner/ Ludwig Wrede (AUT)	
Speed Skating						
500 m	Clas Thunberg (FIN)	43.4			John Farrell (USA)	43.6
	Bernt Evensen (NOR)	43.4			Roald Larsen (NOR)	43.6
					Jaakko Friman (FIN)	43.6
1500 m	Clas Thunberg (FIN)	2:21.1	Bernt Evensen (NOR)	2:21.9	Ivar Ballangrud (NOR)	2:22.6
5000 m	Ivar Ballangrud (NOR)	8:50.5	Julius Skutnabb (FIN)	8:59.1	Bernt Evensen (NOR)	9:01.1
10,000 m	Event abandoned in the 5th heat owing to thawing conditions					
Bobsledding						
4-Man Bob	USA II	3:20.5	USA I	3:21.0	Germany II	3:21.9
Skeleton Sled	Jennison Heaton (USA)	181.8	John R. Heaton (USA)	182.8	David Earl of Northesk (GBR)	185.1
Ice Hockey						
	Canada		Sweden		Switzerland	

Amsterdam 1928

17 May – 12 August
(Official Opening Ceremony 28 July)

Participants: 3014 / Men: 2724, Women: 290, Countries: 46,
Sports: 14, Events: 109

Medals Table

PLACE	COUNTRY	GOLD	SILVER	BRONZE
1	USA	22	18	16
2	Deutschland	10	7	14
3	Finland	8	8	9
4	Sweden	7	6	12
5	Italy	7	5	7

Outstanding Athletes

PLACE	NAME (NATIONALITY)	DISCIPLINE	G	S	B
1	Georges Miez (SUI)	Gymanstics	3	1	–
2	Lucien Gaudin (FRA)	Fencing	2	2	–
3	Hermann Hänggi (SU)	Gymnastics	2	1	1
4	Eugen Mack (SUI)	Gymnastics	2	–	1

EVENT	GOLD		SILVER		BRONZE	
Athletics						
Men						
100 m	Percy Williams (CAN)	10.8	Jack London (GBR)	10.9	Georg Lammers (GER)	10.9
200 m	Percy Williams (CAN)	21.8	Walter Placeeley (GBR)	21.9	Helmut Körnig (GER)	21.9
400 m	Raymond Barbuti (USA)	47.8	James Ball (CAN)	48.0	Joachim Büchner (GER)	48.2
800 m	Douglas Lowe (GBR)	1:51.8	Erik Byléhn (SWE)	1:52.8	Hermann Engelhard (GER)	1:53.2
1500 m	Harry Larva (FIN)	3:53.2	Jules Ladoumégue (FRA)	3:53.8	Eino Purje (FIN)	3:56.4
5000 m	Ville Ritola (FIN)	14:38.0	Paavo Nurmi (FIN)	14:40.0	Edvin Wide (SWE)	14:41.2
10,000 m	Paavo Nurmi (FIN)	30:18.8	Ville Ritola (FIN)	30:19.4	Edvin Wide (SWE)	31:00.8
Marathon	Mohammed El Quafi (FRA)	2:32:57	Miguel Plaza (CHI)	2:33:23	Martti Marttelin (FIN)	2:35:02
110 m Hurdles	Sidney Atkinson (SAF)	14.8	Stephen Anderson (USA)	14.8	John Collier (USA)	14.9
400 m Hurdles	David Burghley (GBR)	53.4	Frank Cuhel (USA)	53.6	F. Morgan Taylor (USA)	53.6
3000 m Steeplechase	Toivo Loukola (FIN)	9:21.8	Paavo Nurmi (FIN)	9:31.6	Ove Andersen (FIN)	9:35.6
4 x 100 m	USA	41.0	Germany	41.2	Great Britain	41.8
4 x 400 m	USA	3:14.2	Germany	3:14.8	Canada	3:15.4
High Jump	Robert King (USA)	1.94	Benjamin Hedges (USA)	1.91	Claude Ménard (FRA)	1.91
Pole Vault	Sabin William Carr (USA)	4.20	William Droegemueller (USA)	4.10	Charles McGinnis (USA)	3.95
Long Jump	Edward Hamm (USA)	7.73	Silvio Cator (HAI)	7.58	Alfred Bates (USA)	7.40
Triple Jump	Mikio Oda (JPN)	15.21	Levi Casey (USA)	15.17	Vilho Tuulos (FIN)	15.11
Shot	John Kuck (USA)	15.87	Herman Brix (USA)	15.75	Emil Hirschfeld (GER)	15.72
Discus	Clarence Houser (USA)	47.32	Antero Kivi (FIN)	47.23	James Corson (USA)	47.10
Hammer	Patrick O'Callaghan (IRL)	51.39	Ossian Skiöld (SWE)	51.29	Edmund Black (USA)	49.03
Javelin	Erik Lundkvist (SWE)	66.60	Béla Szepes (HUN)	65.26	Olav Sunde (NOR)	63.97
Decathlon	Paavo Yrjölä (FIN)	8053	Akilles Järvinen (FIN)	7931	John Kenneth Doherty (USA)	7706

EVENT	GOLD		SILVER		BRONZE	
Women						
100 m	Elizabeth Robinson (USA)	12.2	Fanny Rosenfeld (CAN)	12.3	Ethel Smith (CAN)	12.3
800 m	Lina Radke-Batschauer (GER)	2:16.8	Kinue Hitomi (JPN)	2:17.6	Inga Gentzel (SWE)	2:17.8
4 x 100 m	Canada	48.4	USA	48.8	Germany	49.2
High Jump	Ethel Catherwood (CAN)	1.59	Carolina Gisolf (HOL)	1.56	Mildred Wiley (USA)	1.56
Discus	Halina Konopacka (POL)	39.62	Lillian Copeland (USA)	37.08	Ruth Svedberg (SWE)	35.92
Swimming						
Men						
100 m Freestyle	Johnny Weissmuller (USA)	58.6	István Bárány (HUN)	59.8	Katsuo Takaishi (JPN)	1:00.0
400 m Freestyle	Alberto Zorrilla (ARG)	5:01.6	Andrew Charlton (AUS)	5:03.6	Arne Borg (SWE)	5:04.6
1500 m Freestyle	Arne Borg (SWE)	19:51.8	Andrew Charlton (AUS)	20:02.6	Clarence Crabbe (USA)	20:28.8
100 m Backstroke	George Kojac (USA)	1:08.2	Walter Laufer (USA)	1:10.0	Paul Wyatt (USA)	1:12.0
200 m Breaststroke	Yoshiyuki Tsuruta (JPN)	2:48.8	Erich Rademacher (GER)	2:50.6	Teofilo Yldefonzo (PHI)	2:56.4
4 x 200 m Freestyle Relay	USA	9:36.2	Japan	9:41.4	Canada	9:47.8
Springboard Diving	Peter Desjardins (USA)	185.04	Michael Galitzen (USA)	174.06	Farid Simaika (EGY)	172.46
Highboard Diving	Peter Desjardins (USA)	98.74	Farid Simaika (EGY)	99.58	Michael Galitzen (USA)	92.34
Water Polo	Germany		Hungary		France	
Women						
100 m Freestyle	Albina Osipowich (USA)	1:11.0	Eleonor Garatti (USA)	1:11.4	Joyce Cooper (GBR)	1:13.6
400 m Freestyle	Martha Norelius (USA)	5:42.8	Maria-Johanna Braun (HOL)	5:57.8	Josephine McKim (USA)	6:00.2
100 m Backstroke	Maria-Johanna Braun (HOL)	1:22.0	Ellen King (GBR)	1:22.2	Joyce Cooper (GBR)	1:22.8
200 m Breaststroke	Hilde Schrader (GER)	3:12.6	Mietje Baron (HOL)	3:15.2	Lotte Mühe (GER)	3:17.6
4 x 100 m Freestyle Relay	USA	4:47.6	Great Britain	5:02.8	South Africa	5:13.4
Springboard Diving	Helen Meany (USA)	78.62	Dorothy Poynton (USA)	75.62	Georgia Coleman (USA)	73.38
Highboard Diving	Elizabeth Pinkston-Becker (USA)	31.60	Georgia Coleman (USA)	30.60	Lala Sjöqvist (SWE)	29.20
Boxing						
Flyweight (– 50.80 kg)	Antal Kocsis (HUN)		Armand Appel (FRA)		Carlo Cavagnoli (ITA)	
Bantamweight (– 53.52 kg)	Vittorio Tamagnini (ITA)		John Daley (USA)		Harry Isaacs (SAF)	
Featherweight (– 57.15 kg)	Bep van Klaveren (HOL)		Victor Peralta (ARG)		Harold Devine (USA)	
Lightweight (– 61.24 kg)	Carlo Orlandi (ITA)		Stephen Halaiko (USA)		Gunnar Berggren (SWE)	
Welterweight (– 66.68 kg)	Edward Morgan (SWE)		Raúl Landini (ARG)		Raymond Smillie (CAN)	
Middleweight (–72.57 kg)	Piero Toscani (ITA)		Jan Hermánek (TCH)		Léonard Steyaert (BEL)	
Light-Heavyweight (– 79.38 kg)	Victor Avendano (ARG)		Ernst Pistulla (GER)		Karl Leendert Miljon (HOL)	
Heavyweight (+ 79.38 kg)	Arturo Rodrigues Jurado (ARG)		Nils Ramm (SWE)		Jacob Michaelsen (DEN)	
Weightlifting						
Featherweight (– 60 kg)	Franz Andrysek (AUT)	287.5	Pierino Gabetti (ITA)	282.5	Hans Wölpert (GER)	282.5
Lightweight (–67.5 kg)	Kurt Helbig (GER)	322.5			Fernand Arnout (FRA)	302.5
	Hans Haas (AUT)	322.5				
Middleweight (– 75 kg)	Roger Francois (FRA)	335.0	Carlo Galimberti (ITA)	332.5	August Scheffer (HOL)	327.5
Light-Heavyweight (– 82.5 kg)	Sayed Nosseir (EGY)	355.0	Louis Hostin (FRA)	352.5	Johannes Verheijen (HOL)	337.5
Heavyweight (+ 82.5 kg)	Josef Strassberger (GER)	372.5	Arnold Luhäär (EST)	360.0	Jaroslav Skobla (TCH)	357.5
Greco-Roman Wrestling						
Bantamweight (– 58 kg)	Kurt Leucht (GER)		Jindrich Maudr (TCH)		Giovanni Gozzi (ITA)	
Featherweight (– 62kg)	Voldemar Väli (EST)		Erik Malmberg (SWE)		Gerolamo Quaglia (ITA)	
Lightweight (– 67.5 kg)	Lajos Keresztes (HUN)		Eduard Sperling (GER)		Edvard Westerlund (FIN)	
Middleweight (– 75 kg)	Väino Kokkinen (FIN)		László Papp (HUN)		Albert Kusnets (EST)	
Light-Heavyweight (– 82.5 kg)	Ibrahim Moustafa (EGY)		Adolf Rieger (GER)		Onni Pellinen (FIN)	
Heavyweight (+ 82.5 kg)	Rudolf Svensson (SWE)		Hjalmar E. Nyström (FIN)		Georg Gehring (GER)	
Freestyle Wrestling						
Bantamweight (– 56 kg)	Kaarlo Mäkinen (FIN)		Edmond Spapen (BEL)		James Trifunov (CAN)	
Featherweight (–61 kg)	Allie Morrison (USA)		Kustaa Pihlajamäki (FIN)		Hans Minder (SUI)	
Lightweight (– 66 kg)	Osvald Käpp (EST)		Charles Pacôme (FRA)		Eino Leino (FIN)	
Welterweight (–72 kg)	Arvo Haavisto (FIN)		Lloyd Appleton (USA)		Maurice Letchford (CAN)	
Middleweight (– 79 kg)	Ernst Kyburz (SUI)		Donald P. Stockton (CAN)		Samuel Rabin (GBR)	
Light-Heavyweight (– 87 kg)	Thure Sjöstedt (SWE)		Arnold Bögli (SUI)		Henri Lefébre (FRA)	
Heavyweight (+ 87 kg)	Johan Richthoff (SWE)		Aukusti Sihvola (FIN)		Edmond Dame (FRA)	
Fencing						
Individual Foil - Men	Lucien Gaudin (FRA)	9+2	Erwin Casmir (GER)	9+1	Giulio Gaudini (ITA)	9
Team Foil - Men	Italy		France		Argentina	
Individual Épée	Lucien Gaudin (FRA)	8	Georges Buchard (FRA)	7	George Calnan (USA)	6
Team Épée	Italy		France		Portugal	

EVENT	GOLD		SILVER		BRONZE	
Individual Sabre	Ödön Tersztyánsky (HUN)	9+1	Attila Petschauer (HUN)	9	Bino Bini (ITA)	8
Team Sabre	Hungary		Italy		Poland	
Individual Foil – Women	Helène Mayer (GER)	7	Muriel Freeman (GBR)	6	Olga Oelkers (GER)	4
Modern Pentathlon						
Individual	Sven Thofelt (SWE)	47	Bo Lindman (SWE)	50	Helmuth Kahl (GER)	52
Rowing						
Single Sculls	Henry Pearce (AUS)	7:11.0	Kenneth Myers (USA)	7:20.8	David Collet (GBR)	7:29.8
Double Sculls	USA	6:41.4	Canada	6:51.0	Austria	6:58.8
Coxless Pairs	Germany	7:06.4	Great Britain	7:08.8	USA	7:20.4
Coxed Pairs	Switzerland	7:42.6	France	7:48.4	Belgium	7:59.4
Coxless Fours	Great Britain	6:36.0	USA	6:37.0	Italy	
Coxed Fours	Italy	6:47.8	Switzerland	7:03.4	Poland	7:12.8
Coxed Eights	USA	6:03.2	Great Britain	6:05.6	Canada	
Yachting						
Olympic Monotype	Sven Thorell (SWE)		Henrik Robert (NOR)		Bertil Broman (FIN)	
6 m	Norway		Denmark		Estonia	
8 m	France		Netherlands		Sweden	
Cycling						
Individual Road Race (168 km)	Henry Hansen (DEN)	4:47:18	Frank Southall (GBR)	4:55:06	Gösta Carlsson (SWE)	5:00:17
Team Road Race	Denmark	15:09:14	Great Britain	15:14:49	Sweden	15:27:49
1000 m Time Trial	Willy Falck-Hansen (DEN)	1:14.4	Gerard Bosch (HOL)	1:15.2	Edgar Gray (AUS)	1:15.6
1000 m Sprint	René Beaufrand (FRA)		Antoine Mazairac (HOL)		Willy Falck-Hansen (DEN)	
2000 m Tandem	Netherlands		Great Britain		Germany	
4000 m Team Pursuit	Italy	5:01.8	Netherlands	5:06.2	Great Britain	5:02.4
Equestrianism						
Three-Day Event	Charles Pahud de Mortanges (HOL)	1969.92	Gerard de Kruyff (HOL)	1967.26	Bruno Neumann (GER)	1944.42
Three-Day Event – Team	Netherlands		Norway		Poland	
Grand Prix (Dressage)	Carl von Langen (GER)	237.42	Charles Marion (FRA)	231.0	Ragnar Olson (SWE)	229.78
Dressage – Team	Germany		Sweden		Netherlands	
Grand Prix (Jumping)	Franticek Ventura (TCH)	0/0/0	Pierre Bertran de Balanda (FRA)	0/0/2	Charley Kuhn (SUI)	0/0/4
Grand Prix (Jumping) Team	Spain	-4	Poland	-8	Sweden	-10
Gymnastics						
Men						
Individual Combined Exercises	Georges Miez (SUI)	247.500	Hermann Hänggi (SUI)	246.625	Leon Stukelji (YUG)	244.875
Team	Switzerland	1718.625	Czechoslovakia	1712.250	Yugoslavia	1648.750
Parallel Bars	Ladislav Vácha (TCH)	18.83	Josip Primozic (YUG)	18.50	Hermann Hänggi (SUI)	18.08
Horse Vault	Eugen Mack (SUI)	9.58	Emanuel Löffler (TCH)	9.50	Stane Derganc (YUG)	9.46
Horizontal Bar	Georges Miez (SUI)	19.17	Romeo Neri (ITA)	19.00	Eugen Mack (SUI)	18.92
Rings	Leon Stukelji (YUG)	19.25	Ladislav Vácha (TCH)	19.17	Emanuel Löffler (TCH)	18.83
Pommel Horse	Hermann Hänggi (SUI)	19.75	Georges Miez (SUI)	19.25	Heikki Savolainen (FIN)	18.83
Women						
Team	Netherlands	316.75	Italy	289.00	Great Britain	258.25
Soccer						
	Uruguay		Argentina		Italy	
Hockey						
	India		Netherlands		Germany	

Lake Placid 1932

4 February – 15 February

Participants: 252 / Men: 231, Women: 21, Countries: 17,
Sports: 5, Events: 14

Medals Table

PLACE	COUNTRY	GOLD	SILVER	BRONZE
1	USA	6	4	2
2	Norway	3	4	3
3	Sweden	1	2	–
4	Canada	1	1	5
5	Finland	1	1	1

Outstanding Athletes

PLACE	NAME (NATIONALITY)	DISCIPLINE	G	S	B
1	John Shea (USA)	Speed Skating	2	–	–
	Irving Jaffee (USA)	Speed Skating	2	–	–
3	Veli Saarinen (FIN)	Nordic Skiing	1	–	1

EVENT	GOLD		SILVER		BRONZE	
Nordic Skiing						
18 km Cross-Country Skiing	Sven Utterström (SWE)	1:23:07	Axel T. Wikström (SWE)	1:25:07	Veli Saarinen (FIN)	1:25:24
50 km Cross-Country Skiing	Veli Saarinen (FIN)	4:28:00	Väinö Liikkanen (FIN)	4:28:20	Arne Rustadstuen (NOR)	4:31:53
Ski Jumping	Birger Ruud (NOR)	228.1	Hans Beck (NOR)	227.0	Kaare Wahlberg (NOR)	219.5
Nordic Combined	Johan Gröttumsbraaten (NOR)	446.00	Ole Stenen (NOR)	436.05	Hans Vinjarengen (NOR)	434.60
Figure Skating						
Women	Sonja Henie (NOR)		Fritzi Burger (AUT)		Maribel Vinson (USA)	
Men	Karl Schäfer (AUT)		Gillis Gräfström (SWE)		Montgomery Wilson (CAN)	
Pairs	Andrée Brunet/Pierre Brunet (FRA)		Beatrix Loughran/Sherwin Badger (USA)		EmIlia Rotter/László Szollás (HUN)	
Speed Skating						
500 m	John Shea (USA)	43.4	Bernt Evensen (NOR)		Alexander Hurd (CAN)	
1500 m	John Shea (USA)	2:57.5	Alexander Hurd (CAN)		William Logan (CAN)	
5000 m	Irving Jaffee (USA)	9:40.8	Edward Murphy (USA)		William Logan (CAN)	
10,000 m	Irving Jaffee (USA)	19:13.6	Ivar Ballangrud (NOR)		Frank Stack (CAN)	
Bobsledding						
2-Man Bob	USA I	8:14.14	Switzerland II	8:16.28	USA II	8:29.15
4-Man Bob	USA I	7:53.68	USA II	7:55.70	Germany I	8:00.04
Ice Hockey						
	Canada		USA		Germany	

Los Angeles 1932

30 July – 14 August

Participants: 1408 / Men: 1281, Women: 127, Countries: 37,
Sports: 14, Events: 117

Medals Table

PLACE	COUNTRY	GOLD	SILVER	BRONZE
1	USA	41	32	30
2	Italy	12	12	12
3	France	10	5	4
4	Sweden	9	5	9
5	Japan	7	7	4

Outstanding Athletes

PLACE	NAME (NATIONALITY)	DISCIPLINE	G	S	B
1	Helen Madison (USA)	Swimming	3	–	–
	Romeo Neri (ITA)	Gymnastics	3	–	–
3	István Pelle (UNG)	Gymnastics	2	2	–
4	Mildred Didrikson (USA)	Athletics	2	1	–

EVENT	GOLD		SILVER		BRONZE	
Athletics						
Men						
100 m	Eddie Tolan (USA)	10.38	Ralph Metcalfe (USA)	10.38	Arthur Jonath (GER)	10.50
200 m	Eddie Tolan (USA)	21.2	George Simpson (USA)	21.4	Ralph Metcalfe (USA)	21.5
400 m	William Carr (USA)	46.2	Benjamin Eastman (USA)	46.4	Alexander Wilson (CAN)	47.4

EVENT	GOLD		SILVER		BRONZE	
800 m	Thomas Hampson (GBR)	1:49.7	Alexander Wilson (CAN)	1:49.9	Philip Edwards (CAN)	1:51.5
1500 m	Luigi Beccali (ITA)	3:51.2	John Cornes (GBR)	3:52.6	Philip Edwards (CAN)	3:52.8
5000 m	Lauri Lehtinen (FIN)	14:30.0	Ralph Hill (USA)	14:30.0	Lauri Virtanen (FIN)	14:44.0
10000 m	Janusz Kusocinski (POL)	30:11.4	Volmari Iso-Hollo (FIN)	30:12.6	Lauri Virtanen (FIN)	30:35.0
Marathon	Juan Carlos Zabala (ARG)	2:31:36.0	Samuel Ferris (GBR)	2:31:55.0	Armas Toivonen (FIN)	2:32:12.0
110 m Hurdles	George Saling (USA)	14.6	Percy Beard (USA)	14.7	Donald Finlay (GBR)	14.8
400 m Hurdles	Robert Tisdall (IRL)	51.7	Glenn Hardin (USA)	51.9	Morgan Taylor (USA)	52.0
3000 m Steeplechase	Volmari Iso-Hollo (FIN)	10:33.4	Thomas Evenson (GBR)	10:46.0	Joseph McCluskey (USA)	10:46.2
4 x 100 m	USA	40.0	Germany	40.9	Italy	41.2
4 x 400 m	USA	3:08.2	Great Britain	3:11.2	Canada	3:12.8
50 km Walk	Thomas Green (GBR)	4:50.10	Janis Dalinsh (LAT)	4:57:20	Ugo Frigerio (ITA)	4:59:06
High Jump	Duncan McNaughton (CAN)	1.97	Robert Van Osdel (USA)	1.97	Simeon Toribio (PHI)	1.97
Pole Vault	William Miller (USA)	4.315	Shuhei Nishida (JPN)	4.30	George Jefferson (USA)	4.20
Long Jump	Edward Gordon (USA)	7.64	Charles L. Redd (USA)	7.60	Chuhei Nambu (JPN)	7.45
Triple Jump	Chuhei Nambu (JPN)	15.72	Erik Svensson (SWE)	15.32	Kenkichi Oshima (JPN)	15.12
Shot	Leo Sexton (USA)	16.005	Harlow Rothert (USA)	15.675	Frantisek Douda (TCH)	15.61
Discus	John Anderson (USA)	49.49	Henri J. Laborde (USA)	48.47	Paul Winter (FRA)	47.85
Hammer	Patrick O'Callaghan (IRL)	53.92	Ville Pörhölä (FIN)	52.27	Peter Zaremba (USA)	50.33
Javelin	Matti Järvinen (FIN)	72.71	Matti Sippala (FIN)	69.80	Eino Penttilä (FIN)	68.70
Decathlon	James Bausch (USA)		Akilles Järvinen (FIN)		Wolrad Eberle (GER)	
Women						
100 m	Stanislawa Walasiewicz (POL)	11.9	Hilda Strike (CAN)	11.9	Wilhelmina v. Bremen (USA)	12.0
80 m Hurdles	Mildred Didrikson (USA)	11.7	Evelyne Hall (USA)	11.7	Marjorie Clark (SAF)	11.8
4 x 100 m	USA	47.0	Canada	47.0	Great Britain	47.6
High Jump	Jean Shiley (USA)	1.657	Mildred Didrikson (USA)	1.657	Eva Dawes (CAN)	1.60
Discus	Lillian Copeland (USA)	40.58	Ruth Osburn (USA)	40.12	Jadwiga Wajsowna (POL)	38.74
Javelin	Mildred Didrikson (USA)	43.68	Ellen Braumüller (GER)	43.49	Tilly Fleischer (GER)	43.00
Swimming						
Men						
100 m Freestyle	Yasuji Miyazaki (JPN)	58.2	Tatsugo Kawaishi (JPN)	58.6	Albert Schwartz (USA)	58.8
400 m Freestyle	Clarence Crabbe (USA)	4:48.4	Jean Taris (FRA)	4:48.5	Tsutomu Oyokota (JPN)	4:52.3
1500 m Freestyle	Kusuo Kitamura (JPN)	19:12.4	Shozo Makino (JPN)	19:14.1	James Cristy (USA)	19:39.5
200 m Breaststroke	Yoshiyuki Tsuruta (JPN)	2:45.4	Reizo Koike (JPN)	2:46.4	Teofilo Yldefonzo (PHI)	2:47.1
100 m Back Stroke	Masaji Kiyokawa (JPN)	1:08.6	Toshio Irie (JPN)	1:09.8	Kentaro Kawatsu (JPN)	1:10.0
4 x 200 m Freestyle Relay	Japan	8:58.4	USA	9:10.5	Hungary	9:31.4
Springboard Diving	Michael Galitzen (USA)	161.38	Harold Smith (USA)	158.54	Richard Degener (USA)	151.82
Highboard Diving	Harold Smith (USA)	124.80	Michael Galitzen (USA)	124.28	Frank Kurtz (USA)	121.98
Water Polo	Hungary	8	Germany	5	USA	5
Women						
100 m Freestyle	Helene Madison (USA)	1:06.8	Willie den Ouden (HOL)	1:07.8	Eleonor Garatti (USA)	1:08.2
400 m Freestyle	Helene Madison (USA)	5:28.5	Lenore Kight (USA)	5:28.6	Jennie Makaal (SAF)	5:47.3
200 m Breaststroke	Claire Dennis (AUS)	3:06.3	Hideko Maehata (JPN)	3:06.4	Else Jacobsen (DEN)	3:07.1
100 m Backstroke	Eleanor Holm (USA)	1:19.4	Philomena Mealing (AUS)	1:21.3	Elizabeth Davies (GBR)	1:22.5
4 x 100 m Freestyle Relay	USA	4:38.0	Netherlands	4:47.5	Great Britain	4:52.4
Springboard Diving	Georgia Coleman (USA)	87.52	Katherine Rawls (USA)	82.56	Jane Fauntz (USA)	82.12
Highboard Diving	Dorothy Poynton (USA)	40.26	Georgia Coleman (USA)	35.56	Marion Roper (USA)	35.22
Boxing						
Flyweight (- 50.8 kg)	István Enekes (HUN)		Francisco Cabanas (MEX)		Louis Salica (USA)	
Bantamweight (- 53.52 kg)	Horace Gwynne (CAN)		Hans Ziglarski (GER)		José Villanueva (PHI)	
Featherweightt (- 57.15 kg)	Carmelo Robledo (ARG)		Josef Schleinkofer (GER)		Carl Carlsson (SWE)	
Lightweight (- 61.24 kg)	Lawrence Stevens (SAF)		Thure Ahlqvist (SWE)		Nathan Bor (USA)	
Welterweightt (- 66.68 kg)	Edward Flynn (USA)		Erich Campe (GER)		Bruno Ahlberg (FIN)	
Middleweight (- 72.57 kg)	Carmen Barth (USA)		Amado Azar (ARG)		Ernest Pierce (SAF)	
Light-Heavyweight (- 79.38 kg)	David Carstens (SAF)		Gino Rossi (ITA)		Peter Jörgensen (DEN)	
Heavyweightt (+ 79.38 kg)	Santiago Lovell (ARG)		Luigi Rovati (ITA)		Frederik Feary (USA)	
Weightlifting						
Featherweightt (- 60 kg)	Raymond Suvigny (FRA)	287.5	Hans Wölpert (GER)	282.5	Anthony Terlazzo (USA)	280.0
Lightweight (- 67.5 kg)	Réne Duverger (FRA)	325.0	Hans Haas (AUT)	307.5	Gastone Pierini (ITA)	302.5
Middleweight (- 75 kg)	Rudolf Ismayr (GER)	345.0	Carlo Galimberti (ITA)	340.0	Karl Hipfinger (AUT)	337.5
Light-Heavyweight (- 82.5 kg)	Louis Hostin (FRA)	365.0	Svend Olsen (DEN)	360.0	Henry Duey (USA)	330.0
Heavyweight (+ 82.5 kg)	Jaroslav Skobla (TCH)	380.0	Vaclav Psenicka (TCH)	377.5	Josef Strassberger (GER)	377.5

EVENT	GOLD		SILVER		BRONZE	
Greco-Roman Wrestling						
Bantamweight (- 56 kg)	Jakob Brendel (GER)		Marcello Nizzola (ITA)		Louis François (FRA)	
Featherweight (- 61 kg)	Giovanni Gozzi (ITA)		Wolfgang Ehrl (GER)		Lauri Koskela (FIN)	
Lightweight (- 66 kg)	Erik Malmberg (SWE)		Abraham Kurland (DEN)		Eduard Sperling (GER)	
Welterweight (- 72 kg)	Ivar Johansson (SWE)		Väinö Kajander (FIN)		Ercole Gallegati (ITA)	
Middleweight (- 79 kg)	Väinö Kokkinen (FIN)		Jean Földeák (GER)		Axel Cadier (SWE)	
Light-Heavyweight (- 87 kg)	Rudolf Svensson (SWE)		Onni Pellinen (FIN)		Mario Gruppioni (ITA)	
Heavyweight (+ 87 kg)	Carl Westergren (SWE)		Josef Urban (TCH)		Nikolaus Hirschl (AUT)	
Freestyle Wrestling						
Bantamweight (- 56 kg)	Robert Pearce (USA)		Ödön Zombori (HUN)		Aatos Jaskari (FIN)	
Featherweight (- 61 kg)	Hermanni Pihlajamäki (FIN)		Edgar Nemir (USA)		Einar Karlsson (SWE)	
Lightweight (- 66 kg)	Charles Pacôme (FRA)		Károly Kárpáti (HUN)		Gustaf Klarén (SWE)	
Welterweight (- 72 kg)	Jack van Bebber (USA)		Daniel MacDonald (CAN)		Eino Leino (FIN)	
Middleweight (- 79 kg)	Ivar Johansson (SWE)		Kyösti Luukko (FIN)		Jósef Tunyogi (HUN)	
Light-Heavyweight (- 87 kg)	Peter Mehringer (USA)		Thure Sjöstedt (SWE)		Eddie Scarf (AUS)	
Heavyweight (+ 87 kg)	Johan Richthoff (SWE)		John Riley (USA)		Nikolaus Hirschl (AUT)	
Fencing						
Individual Foil - Men	Gustavo Marzi (ITA)	9	Joseph Levis (USA)	6	Giulio Gaudini (USA)	5
Team Foil - Men	France		Italy		USA	
Individual Épée	Giancarlo Cornaggia-Medici (ITA)	8/18	Georges Buchard (FRA)	7	Carlo Agostoni (ITA)	7
Team Épée	France		Italy		USA	
Individual Sabre	György Piller (HUN)	8	Giulio Gaudini (ITA)	7	Endre Kabos (HUN)	5
Team Sabre	Hungary		Italy		Poland	
Individual Foil - Women	Ellen Preis (AUT)	8/1	Heather Guinness (GBR)	8	Erna Bogen (HUN)	7
Modern Pentathlon						
Individual	Johan Oxenstierna (SWE)	32	Bo Lindmann (SWE)	35.5	Richard Mayo (USA)	38.5
Rowing						
Single Sculls	Henry Pearce (AUS)	7:44.4	William Miller (USA)	7:45.2	Guillermo Douglas (URU)	8:13.6
Double Sculls	USA	7:17.4	Germany	7:22.8	Canada	7:27.6
Coxless Pairs	Great Britain	8:00.0	New Zealand	8:02.4	Poland	8:08.2
Coxed Pairs	USA	8:25.8	Poland	8:31.2	France	8:41.2
Coxless Fours	Great Britain	6:58.2	Germany	7:03.0	Italy	7:04.0
Coxed Fours	Germany	7:19.0	Italy	7:19.2	Poland	7:26.8
Coxed Eights	USA	6:37.6	Italy	6:37.8	Canada	6:40.4
Yachting						
Olympic Monotype	Jacques Lebrun (FRA)	87	Adriaan L. J. Maas (HOL)	85	Santiago A. Cansino (ESP)	76
International Star	USA	46	Great Britain	35	Sweden	28
6 m	Sweden	18	USA	12	Canada	4
8 m	USA	8	Canada	4		
Cycling						
Individual Road Race (100 km)	Attilio Pavesi (ITA)	2:28:05.6	Guglielmo Segato (ITA)	2:29:21.4	Bernhard Britz (SWE)	2:29:45.2
Team Road Race	Italy	7:27:15.2	Denmark	7:38:50.2	Sweden	7:39:12.6
1000 m Time Trial	Edgar Gray (AUS)	1:13.0	Jacobus v. Egmond (HOL)	1:13.3	Charles Rampelberg (FRA)	1:13.4
1000 m Sprint	Jacobus v. Egmond (HOL)	12.6	Louis Chaillot (FRA)		Bruno Pellizzari (ITA)	
2000 m Tandem	France	12.0	Great Britain		Denmark	
4000 m Team Pursuit	Italy	4:53.0	France	4:55.7	Great Britain	4:56.0
Equestrianism						
Three-Day Event	Charles F. P. de Mortanges (HOL)	1813.833	Earl Thomson (USA)	1811.000	Clarence von Rosen jun. (SWE)	1809.416
Three-Day Event - Team	USA		Netherlands			
Grand Prix (Dressage)	Xavier Lesage (FRA)	343.75	Charles Marion (FRA)	305.42	Hiram Tuttle (USA)	300.50
Grand Prix (Jumping)	France		Sweden		USA	
Grand Prix (Jumping) - Team	Takeichi Nishi (JPN)	-8	Harry Chamberlain (USA)	-12	Clarence von Rosen jun. (SWE)	-16
Shooting						
Small-Bore Rifle (Prone)	Bertil Rönmark (SWE)	294	Gustavo Huet (MEX)	294	Zoltan Hradetzky-Soós (HUN)	293
Rapid-Fire Pistol	Renzo Morigi (ITA)	36	Heinz Hax (GER)	36	Domenico Matteucci (ITA)	36

EVENT	GOLD		SILVER		BRONZE	
Gymnastics						
Individual Combined Exercises	Romeo Neri (ITA)	140.625	István Pelle (HUN)	134.925	Heikki Savolainen (FIN)	134.575
Team	Italy	541.850	USA	522.275	Finland	509.995
Parallel Bars	Romeo Neri (ITA)	18.97	István Pelle (HUN)	18.60	Heikki Savolainen (FIN)	18.27
Floor	István Pelle (HUN)	9.60	Georges Miez (SUI)	9.47	Mario Lertora (ITA)	9.23
Horse Vault	Savio Guglielmetti (ITA)	18.03	Alfred Jochim (USA)	17.72	Edward Carmichael (USA)	17.53
Horizontal Bar	Dallas Bixler (USA)	18.33	Heikki Savolainen (FIN)	18.07	Einari Teräsvirta (FIN)	18.07
Rings	George Gulack (USA)	18.97	William Denton (USA)	18.60	Giovanni Lattuada (ITA)	18.50
Pommel Horse	István Pelle (HUN)	19.07	Omero Bonoli (ITA)	18.87	Frank Haubold (USA)	18.57
Rope Climbing	Raymond Bass (USA)	6.7	William Galbraith (USA)	6.8	Thomas Connelly (USA)	7.0
Tumbling	Rowland Wolfe (USA)	18.90	Edward Gross (USA)	18.67	William Hermann (USA)	18.37
Club Swinging	George Roth (USA)		Philip Erenberg (USA)		William Kutrmeier (USA)	
Hockey						
	India		Japan		USA	

Garmisch-Partenkirchen 1936

6 February – 16 February

Participants: 668 / Men: 588, Women: 80, Countries: 28,
Sports: 6, Events: 17

Medals Table

PLACE	COUNTRY	GOLD	SILVER	BRONZE
1	Norway	7	5	3
2	Germany	3	3	–
3	Sweden	2	2	3
4	Finland	1	2	3
5	Switzerland	1	2	–

Outstanding Athletes

PLACE	NAME (NATIONALITY)	DISCIPLINE	G	S	B
1	Ivar Ballangrud (NOR)	Speed Skating	3	1	–
2	Oddbjörn Hagen (NOR)	Nordic Skiing	1	2	–
3	Ernst Baier (GER)	Figure Skating	1	1	–
4	Erik-August Larsson (SWE)	Nordic Skiing	1	–	1

EVENT	GOLD		SILVER		BRONZE	
Alpine Skiing						
Alpine Combined						
Men	Franz Pfnür (GER)	08.04.1900	Adolf Lantschner (GER)	96.26	Emile Allais (FRA)	94.69
Women	Christl Cranz (GER)	06.04.1900	Käthe Grasegger (GER)	95.26	Laila Schou Nilsen (NOR)	93.48
Nordic Skiing						
18 km Cross-Country Skiing	Erik-August Larsson (SWE)	1:14:38	Oddbjörn Hagen (NOR)	1:15:33	Pekka Niemi (FIN)	1:16:59
50 km Cross-Country Skiing	Elis Viklund (SWE)	3:30:11	Axel Wikström (SWE)	3:33:20	Nils-Joel Englund (SWE)	3:34:10
4 x 10 km Relay	Finland	2:41:33	Norway	2:41:39	Sweden	2:43:03
Ski Jumping	Birger Ruud (NOR)	232.0	Sven Ivan Eriksson (SWE)	230.5	Reidar Andersen (NOR)	228.9
Nordic Combined	Oddbjörn Hagen (NOR)	430.3	Olaf Hoffsbakken (NOR)	419.8	Sverre Brodahl (NOR)	408.1
Figure Skating						
Women	Sonja Henie (NOR)		Cecilia Colledge (GBR)		Vivi-Anne Hultén (SWE)	
Men	Karl Schäfer (AUT)		Ernst Baier (GER)		Felix Kaspar (AUT)	
Pairs	Maxi Herber/Ernst Baier (GER)		Ilse Pausin/Erik Pausin (AUT)		Emilia Rotter/László Szollás (HUN)	
Speed Skating						
500 m	Ivar Ballangrud (NOR)	11.02.1900	Georg Krog (NOR)	43.5	Leo Freisinger (USA)	44.0
1500 m	Charles Mathisen (NOR)	2:19.2	Ivar Ballangrud (NOR)	2:20.2	Birger Vasenius (FIN)	2:20.9
5000 m	Ivar Ballangrud (NOR)	8:19.6	Birger Vasenius (FIN)	8:23.3	Antero Ojala (FIN)	8:30.1
10000 m	Ivar Ballangrud (NOR)	17:24.3	Birger Vasenius (FIN)	17:28.2	Max Stiepl (AUT)	17:30.0
Bobsledding						
2-Man Bob	USA I	5:29.29	Switzerland II	5:30.64	USA II	5:33.96
4-Man Bob	Switzerland II	5:19.85	Switzerland I	5:22.73	Great Britain I	5:23.41
Ice Hockey						
	Great Britain		Canada		USA	

Berlin 1936

1 August – 16 August

Participants: 4066 / Men: 3738, Women: 328, Countries: 49,
Sports: 19, Events: 129
Final Torchbearer: Fritz Schilgen

Medals Table

PLACE	COUNTRY	GOLD	SILVER	BRONZE
1	Germany	33	26	30
2	USA	24	20	12
3	Hungary	10	1	5
4	Italy	8	9	5
5	Finland	7	6	6

Outstanding Athletes

PLACE	NAME (NATIONALITY)	DISCIPLINE	G	S	B
1	Jesse Owens (USA)	Athletics	4	–	–
2	Konrad Frey (GER)	Gymnastics	3	1	2
3	Hendrika Mastenbroek (HOL)	Swimming	3	1	–
4	Alfred Schwarzmann (GER)	Gymnastics	3	–	2
5	Robert Charpentier (FRA)	Cycling	3	–	–

EVENT	GOLD		SILVER		BRONZE	
Athletics						
Men						
100 m	Jesse Owens (USA)	10.3	Ralph Metcalfe (USA)	10.4	Martinus Osendarp (HOL)	10.5
200 m	Jesse Owens (USA)	20.7	Matthew Robinson (USA)	21.1	Martinus Osendarp (HOL)	21.3
400 m	Archie Williams (USA)	46.5	Godfrey Brown (GBR)	46.7	James LuValle (USA)	46.8
800 m	John Woodruff (USA)	1:52.9	Mario Lanzi (ITA)	1:53.3	Philip Edwards (CAN)	1:53.6
1500 m	John Lovelock (NZL)	3:47.8	Glenn Cunningham (USA)	3:48.4	Luigi Beccali (ITA)	3:49.2
5000 m	Gunnar Hoeckert (FIN)	14:22.2	Lauri Lehtinen (FIN)	14:25.8	Henry Jonsson (SWE)	14:29.0
10,000 m	Ilmari Salminen (FIN)	30:15.4	Arvo Askola (FIN)	30:15.6	Volmari Iso-Hollo (FIN)	30:20.2
Marathon	Kitei Son (JPN)	2:29:19.2	Ernest Harper (GBR)	2:31:23.2	Shoryu Nan (JPN)	2:31:42.0
110 m Hurdles	Forrest Towns (USA)	14.2	Donald Finlay (GBR)	14.4	Frederick Pollard (USA)	14.4
400 m Hurdles	Glenn Hardin (USA)	52.4	John Loaring (CAN)	52.7	Miguel White (PHI)	52.8
3000 m Steeplechase	Volmari Iso-Hollo (FIN)	9:03.8	Kaarlo Tuominen (FIN)	9:06.8	Alfred Dompert (GER)	9:07.2
4 x 100 m	USA	39.8	Italy	41.1	Germany	41.2
4 x 400 m	Great Britain	3:09.0	USA	3:11.0	Germany	3:11.8
50 km Walk	Harold Whitlock (GBR)	4:30:41.1	Arthur Schwab (SUI)	4:32:09.2	Adalbert Bubenko (LAT)	4:32:42.2
High Jump	Cornelius Johnson (USA)	2.03	David Albritton (USA)	2.00	Delos Thurber (USA)	2.00
Pole Vault	Earle Meadows (USA)	4.35	Shuhei Nishida (JPN)	4.25	Sueo Oe (JPN)	4.25
Long Jump	Jesse Owens (USA)	8.06	Luz Long (GER)	7.87	Naoto Tajima (JPN)	7.74
Triple Jump	Naoto Tajima (JPN)	16.00	Masao Harada (JPN)	15.66	John P. Metcalfe (AUS)	15.50
Shot	Hans Woellke (GER)	16.20	Sulo Bärlund (FIN)	16.12	Gerhard Stöck (GER)	15.66
Discus	Kenneth Carpenter (USA)	50.48	Gordon Dunn (USA)	49.36	Giorgio Oberweger (ITA)	49.23
Hammer	Karl Hein (GER)	56.49	Erwin Blask (GER)	55.04	Fred Warngard (SWE)	54.83
Javelin	Gerhard Stöck (GER)	71.84	Yrjö Nikkanen (FIN)	70.77	Kalervo Toivonen (FIN)	70.72
Decathlon	Glenn Morris (USA)	7900	Robert Clark (USA)	7601	Jack Parker (USA)	7275
Women						
100 m	Helen Stephens (USA)	11.5	Stanislawa Walasiewicz (POL)	11.7	Käthe Krauß (GER)	11.9
80 m Hurdles	Trebisonda Valla (ITA)	11.7	Anny Steuer (GER)	11.7	Elizabeth Taylor (CAN)	11.7
4 x 100 m	USA	46.9	Great Britain	47.6	Canada	47.8
High Jump	Ibolya Csák (HUN)	1.60	Dorothy Odam (GBR)	1.60	Elfriede Kaun (GER)	1.60
Discus	Gisela Mauermayer (GER)	47.63	Jadwiga Wajswna (POL)	46.22	Paula Mollenhauer (GER)	39.80
Javelin	Tilly Fleischer (GER)	45.18	Luise Krüger (GER)	43.29	Maria Kwasniewska (POL)	41.80
Swimming						
Men						
100 m Freestyle	Ferenc Csik (HUN)	57.6	Masanori Yusa (JPN)	57.9	Shiego Arai (JPN)	58.0
400 m Freestyle	Jack Medica (USA)	4:44.5	Shumpei Uto (JPN)	4:45.6	Shozo Makino (JPN)	4:48.1
1500 m Freestyle	Noboru Terada (JPN)	19:13.7	Jack Medica (USA)	19:34.0	Shumpei Uto (JPN)	19:34.5
100 m Backstroke	Adolf Kiefer (USA)	1:05.9	Albert van de Weghe (USA)	1:07.7	Masaji Kiyokawa (JPN)	1:08.4
200 m Breaststroke	Tetsuo Hamuro (JPN)	2:42.5	Erwin Sietas (GER)	2:42.9	Reizo Koike (JPN)	2:44.2
4 x 200 m Freestyle Relay	Japan	8:51.5	USA	9:03.0	Hungary	9:12.3
Springboard Diving	Richard Degener (USA)	163.57	Marshall Wayne (USA)	159.56	Albert Greene (USA)	146.29
Highboard Diving	Marshall Wayne (USA)	113.58	Elbert Root (USA)	110.60	Hermann Stork (GER)	110.31
Water Polo	Hungary		Germany		Belgium	
Women						
100 m Freestyle	Hendrika Mastenbroek (HOL)	1:05.9	Jeanette Campbell (ARG)	1:06.4	Gisela Arendt (GER)	1:06.6
400 m Freestyle	Hendrika Mastenbroek (HOL)	5:26.4	Ragnhild Hveger (DEN)	5:27.5	Lenore Wingard-Kight (USA)	5:29.0
200 m Breaststroke	Hideko Maehata (JPN)	3:03.6	Martha Genenger (GER)	3:04.2	Inge Sörensen (DEN)	3:07.8
100 m Backstroke	Dina W. Senff (HOL)	1:18.9	Hendrika Mastenbroek (HOL)	1:19.2	Alice Bridges (USA)	1:19.4

EVENT	GOLD		SILVER		BRONZE	
4 x 100 m Freestyle	Netherlands	4:36.0	Germany	4:36.8	USA	4:40.2
Springboard Diving	Marjorie Gestring (USA)	89.27	Katherine Rawls (USA)	88.35	Dorothy Poynton-Hill (USA)	82.36
Highboard Diving	Dorothy Poynton-Hill (USA)	33.93	Velma Dunn (USA)	33.63	Käthe Köhler (GER)	33.43
Boxing						
Flyweight (- 50.80 kg)	Willy Kaiser (GER)		Gavino Matta (ITA)		Louis D. Laurie (USA)	
Bantamweight (- 53.52 kg)	Ulderico Sergo (ITA)		Jack Wilson (USA)		Fidel Ortiz (MEX)	
Featherweight (- 57.15 kg)	Oscar Casanovas (ARG)		Charles Catterall (SAF)		Josef Miner (GER)	
Lightweight (- 61.24 kg)	Imre Harangi (HUN)		Nikolai Stepulov (EST)		Erik Agren (SWE)	
Welterweight (- 66.68 kg)	Sten Suvio (FIN)		Michael Murach (GER)		Gerhard Petersen (DEN)	
Middleweight (- 72.57 kg)	Jean Despeaux (FRA)		Henry Tiller (NOR)		Raul Villareal (ARG)	
Light-Heavyweight (- 79.38 kg)	Roger Michelot (FRA)		Richard Vogt (GER)		Francisco Risiglione (ARG)	
Heavyweight (+ 79.38 kg)	Herbert Runge (GER)		Guillermo Lovell (ARG)		Erling Nilsen (NOR)	
Weightlifting						
Featherweight (- 60 kg)	Anthony Terlazzo (USA)	312.5	Saleh Mohammed Soliman (EGY)	305.0	Ibrahim Shams (EGY)	300.0
Lightweight (- 67.5 kg)	Anwar Mesbah (EGY)	342.5			Karl Jansen (GER)	327.5
	Robert Fein (AUT)	342.5				
Middleweight (- 75 kg)	Khadr Sayed El Touni (EGY)	387.5	Rudolf Ismayr (GER)	352.5	Adolf Wagner (GER)	352.5
Light-Heavyweight (- 82.5 kg)	Louis Hostin (FRA)	372.5	Eugen Deutsch (GER)	365.0	Ibrahim Wasif (EGY)	360.0
Heavyweight (+ 82.5 kg)	Josef Manger (GER)	410.0	Václav Psenicka (TCH))	402.5	Arnold Luhaäär (EST)	400.0
Greco-Roman Wrestling						
Bantamweight (- 56 kg)	Márton Lörincz (HUN)		Egon Svensson (SWE)		Jakob Brendel (GER)	
Featherweight (- 61 kg)	Yasar Erkan (TUR)		Aarne Reini (FIN)		Einar Karlsson (SWE)	
Lightweight (- 66 kg)	Lauri Koskela (FIN)		Josef Herda (TCH)		Voldemar Väli (EST)	
Welterweight (- 72 kg)	Rudolf Svedberg (SWE)		Fritz Schäfer (GER)		Eino Virtanen (FIN)	
Middleweight (- 79 kg)	Ivar Johansson (SWE)		Ludwig Schweickert (GER)		Jósef Palotás (HUN)	
Light-Heavyweight (- 87 kg)	Axel Cadier (SWE)		Edwin Bietags (LAT)		August Neo (EST)	
Heavyweight (+ 87 kg)	Kristjan Palusalu (EST)		John Nyman (SWE)		Kurt Hornfischer (GER)	
Freestyle Wrestling						
Bantamweight (- 56 kg)	Ödön Zombori (HUN)		Ross Flood (USA)		Johannes Herbert (GER)	
Featherweight (- 61 kg)	Kustaa Pihlajamäki (FIN)		Francis Millard (USA)		Gösta Jönsson (SWE)	
Lightweight (- 66 kg)	Károly Kárpáty (HUN)		Wolfgang Ehrl (GER)		Hermanni Pihlajamäki (FIN)	
Welterweight (- 72 kg)	Frank Lewis (USA)		Ture Andersson (SWE)		Joseph Schleimer (CAN)	
Middleweight (- 79 kg)	Emile Poilvé (FRA)		Richard Voliva (USA)		Ahmet Kirecci (TUR)	
Light-Heavyweight (- 87 kg)	Knut Fridell (SWE)		August Neo (EST)		Erich Siebert (GER)	
Heavyweight (+ 87 kg)	Kristjan Palusalu (EST)		Josef Klapuch (TCH)		Hjalmar Nyström (FIN)	
Fencing						
Individual Foil - Men	Giulio Gaudini (ITA)	7	Edward Gardière (FRA)	6	Giorgio Bocchino (ITA)	4
Team Foil	Italy		France		Germany	
Individual Épée	Franco Riccardi (ITA)	5	Saverio Ragno (ITA)	6	Giancarlo Cornaggia-Medici (ITA)	6
Team Épée	Italy		Sweden		France	
Individual Sabre	Endre Kabos (HUN)	7	Gustavo Marzi (ITA)	6	Aladár Gerevich (HUN)	6
Team Sabre	Hungary		Italy		Germany	
Individual Foil - Women	Ilona Elek (HUN)	6	Helene Mayer (GER)	5	Ellen Preis (AUT)	5
Modern Pentathlon						
Individual	Gotthard Handrick (GER)	31.5	Charles Leonard (USA)	39.5	Silvano Abba (ITA)	45.5
Canoeing						
1000 m Kayak Singles K1	Gregor Hradetzky (AUT)	4:22.9	Helmut Cämmerer (GER)	4:25.6	Jacob Kraaier (HOL)	4:35.1
10,000 m Kayak Singles K1	Ernst Krebs (GER)	46:01.6	Fritz Landertinger (AUT)	46:14.7	Ernest Riedel (USA)	47:23.9
1000 m Kayak Pairs K2	Austria	4:03.8	Germany	4:08.9	Netherlands	4:12.2
10,000 m Kayak PairsK2	Germany	41:45.0	Austria	42:05.4	Sweden	43:06.1
1000 m Canadian Singles C1	Francis Amyot (CAN)	5:32.1	Bohuslav Karlik (TCH)	5:36.9	Erich Koschik (GER)	5:39.0
1000 m Canadian Pairs C2	Czechoslovakia	4:50.1	Austria	4:53.8	Canada	4:56.7
10,000 m Canadian PairsC2	Czechoslovakia	50:33.5	Canada	51:15.8	Austria	51:28.0
10,000 m Folding Kayak Singles F1	Gregor Hradetzky (AUT)	50:01.2	Henri Eberhardt (FRA)	50:04.2	Xaver Hörmann (GER)	50:06.5
10,000 m Folding Kayak Pairs F2	Sweden	45:48.9	Germany	45:49.2	Netherlands	46:12.4
Rowing						
Single Sculls	Gustav Schäfer (GER)	8:21.5	Josef Hasenöhrl (AUT)	8:25.8	Daniel Barrow (USA)	8:28.0
Double Sculls	Great Britain	7:20.8	Germany	7:26.2	Poland	7:36.2
Coxless Pairs	Germany	8:16.1	Denmark	8:19.2	Argentina	8:23.0
Coxed Pairs	Germany	8:36.9	Italy	8:49.7	France	8:54.0

EVENT	GOLD		SILVER		BRONZE	
Coxless Fours	Germany	7:01.8	Great Britain	7:06.5	Switzerland	7:10.6
Coxed Fours	Germany	7:16.2	Switzerland	7:24.3	France	7:33.3
Coxed Eights	USA	6:25.4	Italy	6:26.0	Germany	6:26.4
Yachting						
Olympic Monotype	Daniel Kagchelland (HOL)	163	Werner Krogmann (GER)	150	Peter Scott (GBR)	131
International Star	Germany	80	Sweden	64	Netherlands	63
6 m	Great Britain	67	Norway	66	Sweden	62
8 m	Italy	55	Norway	53	Germany	53
Cycling						
Individual Road Race (100 km)	Robert Charpentier (FRA)	2:33:05.0	Guy Lapébie (FRA)	2:33:05.2	Ernst Nievergelt (SUI)	2:33:05.8
Team Road Race	France	7:39:16.2	Switzerland	7:39:20.4	Belgium	7:39:21.0
1000 m Time Trial	Arie van Vliet (HOL)	1:12.0	Pierre Georget (FRA)	1:12.8	Rudolf Karsch (GER)	1:13.2
1000 m Sprint	Toni Merkens (GER)	11.8	Arie van Vliet (HOL)		Louis Chaillot (FRA)	
2000 m Tandem	Germany	11.8	Netherlands		France	
4000 m Team Pursuit	France	4:45.0	Italy	4:51.0	Great Britain	4:52.6
Equestrianism						
Three-Day Event	Ludwig Stubbendorff (GER)	-37.70	Earl Thomson (USA)	-99.90	Hans Mathiesen-Lunding(DEN)	-102.20
Three-Day Event - Team	Germany	-676.65	Poland	-991.70	Great Britain	-9195.50
Grand Prix (Dressage)	Heinz Pollay (GER)	1760.0	Friedrich Gerhard (GER)	1745.5	Alois Podhajsky (AUT)	1721.5
Grand Prix (Dressage) - Team	Germany	5074.0	France	4846.0	Sweden	4660.5
Grand Prix (Jumping)	Kurt Hasse (GER)	4	Henri Rang (ROM)	4	József von Platthy (HUN)	8
Grand Prix (Jumping) - Team	Germany	-44.00	Netherlands	-51.50	Portugal	-56.00
Shooting						
Small-Bore Rifle (Prone)	Willy Rögeberg (NOR)	300	Ralf Berzseny (HUN)	296	Wladyslaw Karas (POL)	296
Rapid-Fire Pistol	Cornelius van Oyen (GER)	36	Heinz Hax (GER)	35	Torsten Ullman (SWE)	34
Free Pistol (50 m)	Torsten Ullmann (SWE)	559	Erich Krempel (GER)	544	Charles des Jammonières (FRA)	540
Gymnastics						
Men						
Individual Combined Exercises	Alfred Schwarzmann (GER)	113.100	Eugen Mack (SUI)	112.334	Konrad Frey (GER)	111.532
Team	Germany	657.430	Switzerland	654.802	Finland	638.468
Parallel Bars	Konrad Frey (GER)	19.067	Michael Reusch (SUI)	19.034	Alfred Schwarzmann (GER)	18.967
Floor	Georges Miez (SUI)	18.666	Josef Walter (SUI)	18.500	Eugen Mack (SUI)	18.466
					Konrad Frey (GER)	18.466
Horse Vault	Alfred Schwarzmann (GER)	19.200	Eugen Mack (SUI)	18.967	Matthias Volz (GER)	18.467
Horizontal Bar	Aleksanteri Saarvala (FIN)	19.367	Konrad Frey (GER)	19.267	Alfred Schwarzmann (GER)	19.233
Rings	Alois Hudec (TCH)	19.433	Leon Stukelji (YUG)	18.867	Matthias Volz (GER)	18.667
Pommel Horse	Konrad Frey (GER)	19.333	Eugen Mack (SUI)	19.167	Albert Bachmann (SUI)	19.067
Women						
Team	Germany	506.50	Czechoslovakia	503.60	Hungary	499.00
Basketball						
	USA		Canada		Mexico	
Soccer						
	Italy		Austria		Norway	
Handball						
	Germany		Austria		Switzerland	
Hockey						
	India		Germany		Netherlands	
Polo						
	Argentina		Great Britain		Mexico	
EVENT	GOLD		SILVER		BRONZE	

St. Moritz 1948

Participants 669 / Men: 529, Women: 77, Countries: 28,
Sports: 7, Events: 22
Final Torchbearer: Richard Torriani

Medals Table

PLACE	COUNTRY	GOLD	SILVER	BRONZE
1	Norway	4	3	3
	Sweden	4	3	3
3	Switzerland	3	4	3
4	USA	3	4	2
5	France	2	1	2

Outstanding Athletes

PLACE	NAME (NATIONALITY)	DISCIPLINE	G	S	B
1	Henri Oreiller (FRA)	Alpine Skiing	2	–	1
2	Martin Lundström (SWE)	Nordic Skiing	2	–	–
3	Trude Beiser (AUT)	Alpine Skiing	1	1	–
	Gretchen Fraser (USA)	Alpine Skiing	1	1	–
	Nils Östensson (SWE)	Nordic Skiing	1	1	–

EVENT	GOLD		SILVER		BRONZE	
Alpine Skiing						
Men						
Downhill	Henri Oreiller (FRA)	2:55.0	Franz Gabl (AUT)	2:59.1	Karl Molitor (SUI)	3:00.3
					Rolf Olinger (SUI)	3:00.3
Slalom	Edy Reinalter (SUI)	130.3	James Couttet (FRA)	130.8	Henri Oreiller (FRA)	132.8
Alpine Combined	Henri Oreiller (FRA)	3.27	Karl Molitor (SUI)	6.44	James Couttet (FRA)	6.95
Women						
Downhill	Hedy Schlunegger (SUI)	2:28.3	Trude Beiser (AUT)	2:29.1	Resi Hammerer (AUT)	2:30.2
Slalom	Gretchen Fraser (USA)	117.2	Antoinette Meyer (SUI)	117.7	Erika Mahringer (AUT)	118.0
Alpine Combined	Trude Beiser (AUT)	6.58	Gretchen Fraser (USA)	6.95	Erika Mahringer (AUT)	7.04
Nordic Skiing						
18 km Cross-Country Skiing	Martin Lundström (SWE)	1:13:50	Nils Östensson (SWE)	1:14:22	Gunnar Eriksson (SWE)	1:16:06
50 km Cross-Country Skiing	Nils Karlsson (SWE)	3:47:48	Harald Eriksson (SWE)	3:52:20	Benjamin Vanninen (FIN)	3:57:28
4 x 10 km	Sweden	2:32:08	Finland	2:41:06	Norway	2:44:33
Ski Jumping	Petter Hugsted (NOR)	228.1	Birger Ruud (NOR)	226.6	Thorleif Schjeldrup (NOR)	225.1
Nordic Combined	Heikki Hasu (FIN)	448.80	Martti Huhtala (FIN)	433.65	Sven Israelsson (SWE)	433.40
Figure Skating						
Women	Barbara Ann Scott (CAN)		Eva Pawlik (AUT)		Jeanette Altwegg (GBR)	
Men	Richard Button (USA)		Hans Gerschwiler (SUI)		Edi Rada (AUT)	
Pairs	Micheline Lannoy/ Pierre Baugniet (BEL)		Andrea Kékessy/ Ede Király (HUN)		Suzanne Morrow/ Wallace Diestelmeyer (CAN)	
Speed Skating						
500 m	Finn Helgesen (NOR)	43.1	Kenneth Bartholomew (USA)	43.2		
			Thomas Byberg (NOR)	43.2		
			Robert Fitzgerald (USA)	43.2		
1500 m	Sverre Farstadt (NOR)	2:17.6	Ake Seyffarth (SWE)	2:18.1	Odd Lundberg (NOR)	2:18.9
5000 m	Reidar Liaklev (NOR)	8:29.4	Odd Lundberg (NOR)	8:32.7	Göte Hedlund (SWE)	8:34.8
10,000 m	Ake Seyffarth (SWE)	17:26.3	Lauri Parkkinen (FIN)	17:36.0	Pentti Lammio (FIN)	17:42.7
Bobsledding						
2-Man Bob	Switzerland II	5:29.2	Switzerland I	5:30.4	USA II	5:35.3
4-Man Bob	USA II	5:20.1	Belgium	5:21.3	USA I	5:21.5
Skeleton Sled						
	Nino Bibbia (ITA)	323.2	John R. Heaton (USA)	324.6	John Crammond (GBR)	325.1
Ice Hockey						
	Canada		Czechoslovakia		Switzerland	

London 1948

29 July – 14 August

Participants: 4099 / Men: 3714, Women: 385, Countries: 59,
Sports: 17, Events: 136
Final Torchbearer: John Mark

Medals Table

PLACE	COUNTRY	GOLD	SILVER	BRONZE
1	USA	38	27	19
2	Sweden	16	11	17
3	France	10	6	13
4	Hungary	10	5	12
5	Italy	8	12	9

Outstanding Athletes

PLACE	NAME (NATIONALITY)	DISCIPLINE	G	S	B
1	Fanny Blankers-Koen (HOL)	Athletics	4	–	–
2	Veikko Huhtanen (FIN)	Gymnastics	3	1	1
3	Paavo Aaltonen (FIN)	Gymnastics	3	–	1
4	James McLane (USA)	Swimming	2	1	–
	Anne Curtis (USA)	Swimming	2	1	–

EVENT	GOLD		SILVER		BRONZE	
Athletics						
Men						
100 m	Harrison Dillard (USA)	10.3	Norwood Ewell (USA)	10.4	Lloyd LaBeach (PAN)	10.4
200 m	Melvin Patton (USA)	21.1	Norwood Ewell (USA)	21.1	Lloyd LaBeach (PAN)	21.2
400 m	Arthur Wint (JAM)	46.2	Herbert McKenley (JAM)	46.4	Malvin Whitfield (USA)	46.9
800 m	Malvin Whitfield (USA)	1:49.2	Arthur Wint (JAM)	1:49.5	Marcel Hansenne (FRA)	1:49.8
1500 m	Henry Eriksson (SWE)	3:49.8	Lennart Strand (SWE)	3:50.4	Willem Slijkhuis (HOL)	3:50.4
5000 m	Gaston Reiff (BEL)	14:17.6	Emil Zátopek (TCH)	14:17.8	Willem Slijkhuis (HOL)	14:26.8
10,000 m	Emil Zátopek (TCH)	29:59.6	Alain Mimoun (FRA)	30:47.4	Bertil Albertsson (SWE)	30:53.6
Marathon	Delfo Cabrera (ARG)	2:34:51.6	Thomas Richards (GBR)	2:35:07.6	Etienne Gailly (BEL)	2:35:33.6
110 m Hurdles	William Porter (USA)	13.9	Clyde Scott (USA)	14.1	Craig Dixon (USA)	14.1
400 m Hurdles	Leroy Cochran (USA)	51.1	Duncan White (CEY)	51.8	Rune Larsson (SWE)	52.2
3000 m Steeplechase	Thore Sjöstrand (SWE)	9:04.6	Erik Elmsäter (SWE)	9:08.2	Gösta Hagström (SWE)	9:11.8
4 x 100 m	USA	40.6	Great Britain	41.3	Italy	41.5
4 x 400 m	USA	3:10.4	France	3:14.8	Sweden	3:16.0
10 km Walk	John Mikaelsson (SWE)	45:13.2	Ingemar Johansson (SWE)	45:43.8	Fritz Schwab (SUI)	46:00.2
50 km Walk	John Ljunggren (SWE)	4:41:52	Gaston Godel (SUI)	4:48:17	Tebbs Lloyd-Johnson (GBR)	4:48:31
High Jump	John Winter (AUS)	1.98	Björn Paulson (NOR)	1.95	George Stanich (USA)	1.95
Pole Vault	Guinn Smith (USA)	4.30	Erkki Kataja (FIN)	4.20	Robert Richards (USA)	4.20
Long Jump	Willie Steele (USA)	7.825	Thomas Bruce (AUS)	7.555	Herbert Douglas (USA)	7.545
Triple Jump	Arne Ahman (SWE)	15.40	George Avery (AUS)	15.365	Ruhi Sarialp (TUR)	15.025
Shot	Wilbur Thompson (USA)	17.12	Francis Delaney (USA)	16.68	James Fuchs (USA)	16.42
Discus	Adolfo Consolini (ITA)	52.78	Giuseppe Tosi (ITA)	51.78	Fortune Gordien (USA)	50.77
Hammer	Imre Németh (HUN)	56.07	Ivan Gubijan (YUG)	54.27	Robert Bennett (USA)	53.73
Javelin	Tapio Rautavaara (FIN)	69.77	Steve Seymour (USA)	67.56	József Várszegi (HUN)	67.03
Decathlon	Robert Mathias (USA)	7139	Ignace Heinrich (FRA)	6974	Floyd Simmons (USA)	6950
Women						
100 m	Fanny Blankers-Koen (HOL)	11.9	Dorothy Manley (GBR)	12.2	Shirley Strickland (AUS)	12.2
200 m	Fanny Blankers-Koen (HOL)	24.4	Audrey Williamson (GBR)	25.1	Audrey Patterson (USA)	25.2
80 m Hurdles	Fanny Blankers-Koen (HOL)	11.2	Maureen Gardner (GBR)	11.2	Shirley Strickland (AUS)	11.4
4 x 100 m	Netherlands	47.5	Australia	47.6	Canada	47.8
High Jump	Alice Coachman (USA)	1.68	Dorothy Tyler-Odam (GBR)	1.68	Micheline Ostermeyer (FRA)	1.61
Long Jump	Olga Gyarmati (HUN)	5.695	Noëmi Simonetto De Portela (ARG)	5.60	Ann-Britt Leyman (SWE)	5.575
Shot	Micheline Ostermeyer (FRA)	13.75	Amelia Piccinini (ITA)	13.095	Ine Schäffer (AUT)	13.08
Discus	Micheline Ostermeyer (FRA)	41.92	Edera Gentile-Cordiale (ITA)	41.17	Jacqueline Mazeas (FRA)	40.47
Javelin	Herma Bauma (AUT)	45.57	Kaisa Parviainen (FIN)	43.79	Lily Carlstedt (DEN)	42.08
Swimming						
Men						
100 m Freestyle	Walter Ris (USA)	57.3	Alan Ford (USA)	57.8	Géza Kádas (HUN)	58.1
400 m Freestyle	William Smith (USA)	4:41.0	James McLane (USA)	4:43.4	John Marshall (AUS)	4:47.7
1500 m Freestyle	James McLane (USA)	19:18.5	John Marshall (AUS)	19:31.3	György Mitró (HUN)	19:43.2
100 m Backstroke	Allen Stack (USA)	1:06.4	Robert Cowell (USA)	1:06.5	Georges Vallerey (FRA)	1:07.8
200 m Breaststroke	Joseph Verdeur (USA)	2:39.3	Keith Carter (USA)	2:40.2	Robert Sohl (USA)	2:43.9
4 x 200 m Freestyle Relay	USA	8:46.0	Hungary	8:48.4	France	9:08.0
Springboard Diving	Bruce Harlan (USA)	163.64	Miller Anderson (USA)	157.29	Samuel Lee (USA)	145.52
Highboard Diving	Samuel Lee (USA)	130.05	Bruce Harlan (USA)	122.30	Joaquin Caprilla Pérez (MEX)	113.52
Water Polo	Italy		Hungary		Netherlands	

EVENT	GOLD		SILVER		BRONZE	
Women						
100 m Freestyle	Greta Andersen (DEN)	1:06.3	Ann Curtis (USA)	1:06.5	Marie-Louise Vaessen (HOL)	1:07.6
400 m Freestyle	Ann Curtis (USA)	5:17.8	Karen-Margrete Harup (DEN)	5:21.2	Catherine Gibson (GBR)	5:22.5
100 m Backstroke	Karen-Margrete Harup (DEN)	1:14.4	Suzanne Zimmermann (USA)	1:16.0	Judy Davies (AUS)	1:16.7
200 m Breaststroke	Petronella van Vliet (HOL)	2:57.2	Beatrice Lyons (AUS)	2:57.7	Evá Novák (HUN)	3:00.2
4 x 100 m Freestyle Relay	USA	4:29.2	Denmark	4:29.6	Netherlands	4:31.6
Springboard Diving	Victoria Draves (USA)	108.74	Zoe Ann Olsen (USA)	108.23	Patricia Elsener (USA)	101.30
Highboard Diving	Victoria Draves (USA)	68.87	Patricia Elsner (USA)	66.28	Birte Christofferson (DEN)	66.04
Boxing						
Flyweight (- 51 kg)	Pascual Perez (ARG)		Spartaco Bandinelli (ITA)		Soo-Ann Han (KOR)	
Bantamweight (- 54 kg)	Tibor Csik (HUN)		Giovanni Battista Zuddas (ITA)		Juan Venegas (PUR)	
Featherweight (- 58 kg)	Ernesto Formenti (ITA)		Dennis Shepherd (SAF)		Aleksy Antkiewicz (POL)	
Lightweight (- 62 kg)	Gerald Dreyer (SAF)		Joseph Vissers (BEL)		Sven Wad (DEN)	
Welterweight (- 67 kg)	Julius Torma (TCH)		Horace Herring (USA)		Alessandro D'Ottavio (ITA)	
Middleweight (- 73 kg)	László Papp (HUN)		John Wright (GBR)		Ivano Fontana (ITA)	
Light-Heaveweight (- 80 kg)	George Hunter (SAF)		Donald Scott (GBR)		Maurio Cia (ARG)	
Heavyweight (+ 80 kg)	Rafael Iglesias (ARG)		Gunnar Nilsson (SWE)		John Arthur (SAF)	
Weightlifting						
Bantamweight (- 56 kg)	Joseph Di Pietro (USA)	307.5	Julian Creus (GBR)	297.5	Richard Tom (USA)	295.0
Featherweight (- 60 kg)	Mahmoud Fayad (EGY)	332.5	Rodney Wilkes (TRI)	317.5	Jaffar Salmassi (IRN)	312.5
Lightweight (- 67.5 kg)	Ibrahim Shams (EGY)	360.0	Attia Hamouda (EGY)	360.0	James Halliday (GBR)	340.0
Middleweight (- 75 kg)	Frank Spellman (USA)	390.0	Peter George (USA)	382.5	Sung-Jip Kim (KOR)	380.0
Light-Heavyweight (- 82.5 kg)	Stanley Stanczyk (USA)	417.5	Harold Sakata (USA)	380.0	Gösta Magnusson (SWE)	375.0
Heavyweight (+ 82.5 kg)	John Davis (USA)	452.5	Norbert Schemansky (USA)	425.0	Abraham Charité (HOL)	412.5
Greco-Roman Wrestling						
Flyweight (- 52 kg)	Pietro Lombardi (ITA)		Kenan Olcay (TUR)		Reino Kangasmäki (FIN)	
Bantamweight (-57 kg)	Kurt Pettersen (SWE)		Ali Mahmoud Hassan (EGY)		Halil Kaya (TUR)	
Featherweight (-62 kg)	Mehmet Oktav (TUR)		Olle Anderberg (SWE)		Ferenc Tóth (HUN)	
Lightweight (-67 kg)	Gustav Freij (SWE)		Aage Eriksen (NOR)		Károly Ferencz (HUN)	
Welterweight (-73 kg)	Gösta Andersson (SWE)		Miklós Szilvási (HUN)		Henrik Hansen (DEN)	
Middleweight (-79 kg)	Axel Grönberg (SWE)		Muhlis Tayfur (TUR)		Ercole Gallegati (ITA)	
Light-Heavyweight (-87 kg)	Karl-Erik Nilsson (SWE)		Kaelpo Gröndahl (FIN)		Ibrahim Orabi (EGY)	
Heavyweight (+87 kg)	Ahmet Kirecci (TUR)		Tor Nilsson (SWE)		Guido Fantoni (ITA)	
Freestyle Wrestling						
Flyweight (-52 kg)	Lennart Viitala (FIN)		Halat Balamir (TUR)		Thure Johansson (SWE)	
Bantamweight (-57 kg)	Nasuh Akar (TUR)		Gerald Leeman (USA)		Charles Kouyos (FRA)	
Featherweight (-62 kg)	Gazanfer Bilge (TUR)		Ivar Sjölin (SWE)		Adolf Müller (SUI)	
Lightweight (-67 kg)	Celal Atik (TUR)		Gösta Frändfors (SWE)		Hermann Baumann (SUI)	
Welterweight (-73 kg)	Yasar Dogu (TUR)		Richard Garrard (AUS)		Leland Merrill (USA)	
Middleweight (-79 kg)	Glen Brand (USA)		Adil Candemir (TUR)		Erik Linden (SWE)	
Light-Heavyweight (-87 kg)	Henry Wittenberg (USA)		Fritz Stöckli (SUI)		Bengt Fahlkvist (SWE)	
Heavyweight (+87 kg)	Gyula Bóbis (HUN)		Bertil Antonsson (SWE)		Joseph Armstrong (AUS)	
Fencing						
Individual Foil - Men	Jehan Buhan (FRA)	7	Christian d'Oriola (FRA)	5	Lajos Maszlay (HUN)	4
Team Foil - Men	France		Italy		Belgium	
Individual Épée	Luigi Cantone (ITA)	7	Oswald Zappelli (SUI)	5	Edoardo Mangiarotti (ITA)	5
Team Épée	France		Italy		Sweden	
Individual Sabre	Aladár Gerevich (HUN)	7	Vicenzo Pinton (ITA)	5	Pál Kovacs (HUN)	5
Team Sabre	Hungary		Italy		USA	
Individual Foil - Women	Ilona Elek (HUN)	6	Karen Lachmann (DEN)	5	Ellen Müller-Preis (AUT)	5
Modern Pentathlon						
Individual	Wiliam Grut (SWE)	16	George Moore (USA)	47	Gösta Gärdin (SWE)	49
Canoeing						
Men						
1000 m Kayak Singles K1	Gert Fredriksson (SWE)	4:33.2	Johan Kobberup (DEN)	4:39.9	Henri Eberhardt	4:41.4
10,000 m Kayak Singles K1	Gert Fredriksson (SWE)	50:47.7	Kurt Wires (FIN)	51:18.2	Ejvind Skabo (NOR)	51:35.4
1000 m Kayak Pairs K2	Sweden	4:07.3	Denmark	4:07.5	Finland	4:08.7
10,000 m Kayak Pairs K2	Sweden	46:09.4	Norway	46:44.8	Finland	46:48.2
1000 m Canadian Singles C1	Josef Holecek (TCH)	5:42.0	Douglas Bennett (CAN)	5:53.3	Robert Boutigny (FRA)	5:55.9
10,000 m Canadian SinglesC1	Frantisek Capek (TCH)	1:02.05	Frank Havens (USA)	1:02.40	Norman Lane (CAN)	1:04.35

EVENT	GOLD		SILVER		BRONZE	
1000 m Canadian Pairs C2	Czechoslovakia	5:07.1	USA	5:08.2	France	5:15.2
10,000 m Canadian Pairs C2	USA	55:55.4	Czechoslovakia	57:38.5	France	58:00.8
Women						
500 m Kayak Singles K1	Karen Hoff (DEN)	2:31.9	Alide van der Anker-Doedans (HOL)	2:32.8	Fritzi Schwingl (AUT)	2:32.9
Rowing						
Single Sculls	Mervyn Wood (AUS)	7:24.4	Eduardo Risso (URU)	7:38.2	Romolo Catasta (ITA)	7:51.4
Double Sculls	Great Britain	6:51.3	Denmark	6:55.3	Uruguay	7:12.4
Coxless Pairs	Great Britain	7:21.1	Switzerland	7:23.9	Italy	7:31.5
Coxed Pairs	Denmark	8:00.5	Italy	8:12.2	Hungary	8:25.2
Coxless Fours	Italy	6:39.0	Denmark	6:43.5	USA	6:47.7
Coxed Fours	USA	6:50.3	Switzerland	6:53.3	Denmark	6:58.6
Coxed Eights	USA	5:56.7	Great Britain	6:06.9	Norway	6:10.3
Yachting						
Olympic Monotype	Paul Elvström (DEN)	5543	Ralph Evans jun. (USA)	5408	Jacobus de Jong (HOL)	5204
International Star	USA	5828	Cuba	4949	Netherlands	4731
Swallow	Great Britain	5625	Portugal	5579	USA	4352
Dragon	Norway	4746	Sweden	4621	Denmark	4223
6 m	USA	5472	Argentina	5120	Sweden	4033
Cycling						
Individual Road Race (194.633 Km)	José Beyaert (FRA)	5:18:12.6	Gerardus Voorting (HOL)	5:18:16.2	Lode Wouters (BEL)	5:18:16.2
Team Road Race	Belgium	15:58:17.4	Great Britain	16:03:31.6	France	16:08:19.4
1000 m Time Trial	Jacques Dupont (FRA)	1:13.5	Pierre Nihant (BEL)	1:14.5	Thomas Godwin (GBR)	1:15.0
1000 m Sprint	Mario Ghella (ITA)		Reginald Harris (GBR)		Axel Schandorff (DEN)	
2000 m Tandem	Italy		Great Britain		France	
4000 m Team Pursuit	France	4:57.8	Italy	5:36.7	Great Britain	4:55.8
Equestrianism						
Three-Day Event	Bernard Chevallier (FRA)	+4	Frank Henry (USA)	-21	Robert Selfelt (SWE)	-25
Three-Day Event (Team)	USA	-161.50	Sweden	-165.00	Mexico	-305.25
Grand Prix (Dressage)	Hans Moser (SUI)	492.5	André Jousseaume (FRA)	480.0	Gustav-Adolf Boltenstern jun. (SWE)	477.5
Grand Prix (Dressage) Team	France	1269.0	USA	1256.0	Portugal	1182.0
Grand Prix (Jumping)	Humberto Marileo Cortés (MEX)	6.25	Rubén Uriza (MEX)	8	Jean François d'Orgeix (FRA)	8
Grand Prix (Jumping) Team	Mexico	-34.25	Spain	-56.50	Great Britain	-67.00
Shooting						
Free Rifle (3 Positions)	Emil Grünig (SUI)	1120	Pauli Janhonen (FIN)	1114	Willy Rögeberg (NOR)	1112
Small-Bore Rifle (Prone)	Arthur Cook (USA)	599	Walter Tomsen (USA)	599	Jonas Jonsson (SWE)	597
Rapid-Fire Pistol	Károly Takács (HUN)	580	Carlos E. Diaz Sáenz Valiente (ARG)	571	Sven Lundqvist (SWE)	569
Free Pistol (5 0m)	Edwin Vasquez Cam (PER)	545	Rudolf Schnyder (SUI)	539	Torsten Ullman (SWE)	539
Gymnastics						
Men						
Individual Combined Exercises	Veikko Huhtanen (FIN)	229.70	Walter Lehmann (SUI)	229.00	Paavo Aaltonen (FIN)	228.80
Team	Finland	1358.30	Switzerland	1356.70	Hungary	1330.85
Parallel Bars	Michael Reusch (SUI)	39.50	Veikko Huhtanen (FIN)	39.30	Christian Kipfer (SUI)	39.10
					Josef Stalder (SUI)	39.10
Floor	Ferenc Pataki (HUN)	38.70	János Mogyorósi-Klencs (HUN)	38.40	Zdenek Ruzicka (TCH)	38.10
Horse Vault	Paavo Aaltonen (FIN)	39.10	Olavi Rove (FIN)	39.00	János Mogyorósi-Klencs (HUN)	38.50
					Ferenc Pataki (HUN)	38.50
					Leo Sotornik (TCH)	38.50
Horizontal Bar	Josef Stalder (SUI)	39.70	Walter Lehmann (SUI)	39.40	Veikko Huhtanen (FIN)	39.20
Rings	Karl Frei (SUI)	39.60	Michael Reusch (SUI)	39.10	Zdenek Ru˘zi˘cka (TCH)	38.50
Pommel Horse	Veikko Huhtanen (FIN)	38.70	Luigi Zanetti (ITA)	38.30	Guido Figone (ITA)	38.20
	Paavo Aaltonen (FIN)	38.70				
	Heikki Savolaien (FIN)	38.70				
Women						
Team	Czechoslovakia	445.45	Hungary	440.55	USA	422.63
Basketball	USA		France		Brazil	
Soccer	Sweden		Yugoslavia		Denmark	
Hockey	India		Great Britain		Netherlands	

Oslo 1952

14 February – 25 February

Participants: 694 / Men:585, Women: 109, Countries: 30,
Sports: 6, Events: 22
Final Torchbearer: Eigil Nansen

Medals Table

PLACE	COUNTRY	GOLD	SILVER	BRONZE
1	Norway	7	3	6
2	USA	4	6	1
3	Finland	3	4	2
4	Germany	3	2	2
5	Austria	2	4	2

Outstanding Athletes

PLACE	NAME (NATIONALITY)	DISCIPLINE	G	S	B
1	Hjalmar Andersen (NOR)	Speed Skating	3	–	–
2	Andrea Lawrence-Mead (USA)	Alpine Skiing	2	–	–
	Andreas Ostler (GER)	Bobsledding	2	–	–
	Lorenz Nieberl (GER)	Bobsledding	2	–	–

EVENT	GOLD		SILVER		BRONZE	
Alpine Skiing						
Men						
Downhill	Zeno Colò (ITA)	2:30.8	Othmar Schneider (AUT)	2:32.0	Christian Pravda (AUT)	2:32.4
Slalom	Othmar Schneider (AUT)	2:00.0	Stein Eriksen (NOR)	2:01.2	Guttorm Berge (NOR)	2:01.7
Giant Slalom	Stein Eriksen (NOR)	2:25.0	Christian Pravda (AUT)	2:26.9	Toni Spiss (AUT)	2:28.8
Women						
Downhill	Trude Jochum-Beiser (AUT)	1:47.1	Annnemarie Buchner (GER)	1:48.0	Giuliana Minuzzo (ITA)	1:49.0
Slalom	Andrea Lawrence-Mead (USA)	2:10.6	Ossi Reichert (GER)	2:11.4	Annemarie Buchner (GER)	2:13.3
Giant Slalom	Andrea Lawrence-Mead (USA)	2:06.8	Dagmar Rom (AUT)	2:09.0	Annemarie Buchner (GER)	2:10.0
Nordic Skiing						
Men						
18 km Cross-Country Skiing	Hallgeir Brenden (NOR)	1:01:34.0	Tapio Mäkelä (FIN)	1:02:09.0	Paavo Lonkila (FIN)	1:02:20.0
50 km Cross-Country Skiing	Veikko Hakulinen (FIN)	3:33.33.0	Eero Kolehmainen (FIN)	3:38:11.0	Magnar Estensad (NOR)	3:38:28.0
4 x 10 km	Finland	2:20:16.0	Norway	2:23:13.0	Sweden	2:24:13.0
Ski Jumping	Arnfinn Bergmann (NOR)	226.0	Torbjörn Falkanger (NOR)	221.5	Karl Holmstöm (SWE)	219.5
Nordic Combined	Simon Slåttvik (NOR)	451.621	Heikki Hasu (FIN)	447.500	Sverre Stenersen (NOR)	436.335
Women						
10 km Cross-Country Skiing	Lydia Widemann (FIN)	41:40.0	Mirja Hietamies (FIN)	42:39.0	Siiri Rantanen (FIN)	42:50.0
Figure Skating						
Women	Jeanette Altwegg (GBR)		Tenley Albright (USA)		Jacqueline du Bief (FRA)	
Men	Richard Button (USA)		Helmut Seibt (AUT)		James Grogan (USA)	
Pairs	Ria Falk/		Karol Estelle Kennedy/		Marianne Nagy/	
	Paul Falk (GER)		Michael Kennedy (USA)		László Nagy (HUN)	
Speed Skating						
500 m	Kenneth Henry (USA)	43.2	Donald McDermott (USA)	43.9	Arne Johansen (NOR)	44.0
					Gordon Audley (CAN)	44.0
1500 m	Hjalmar Andersen (NOR)	2:20.4	Willem van der Voort (HOL)	2.20.6	Roald Aas (NOR)	2:21.6
5000 m	Hjalmar Andersen (NOR)	8:10.6	Cornelis Broekman (HOL)	8:21.6	Sverre Haugli (NOR)	8:22.4
10,000 m	Hjalmar Andersen (NOR)	16:45.8	Cornelis Broekman (HOL)	17:10.6	Carl-Erik Asplund (SWE)	17:16.6
Bobsledding						
2-Man Bob	Germany	5:24.54	USA I	5:26.89	Switzerland I	5:27.71
4-Man Bob	Germany	5:07.84	USA I	5:10.48	Switzerland I	5:11.70
Ice Hockey						
	Canada		USA		Sweden	

Helsinki 1952

19 July – 3 August

Participants: 4925 / Men: 4407, Women: 518, Countries: 69,
Sports: 17, Events: 149
Final Torchbearer: Paavo Nurmi

Medals Table

PLACE	COUNTRY	GOLD	SILVER	BRONZE
1	USA	40	19	17
2	USSR	22	30	19
3	Hungary	16	10	16
4	Sweden	12	12	10
5	Italy	8	9	4

Outstanding Athletes

PLACE	NAME (NATIONALITY)	DISCIPLINE	G	S	B
1	Viktor Chukarin (URS)	Gymnastics	4	2	–
2	Emil Zátopek (TCH)	Athletics	3	–	–
3	Maria Gorochovskaya (URS)	Gymnastics	2	5	–
4	Edoardo Mangiarotti (ITA)	Fencing	2	2	–
	Grant Shaginyan (URS)	Gymnastics	2	2	–
	Nina Bocharowa (URS)	Gymnastics	2	2	–

EVENT	GOLD		SILVER		BRONZE	
Athletics						
Men						
100 m	Lindy Remigino (USA)	10.4	Herbert McKenley (JAM)	10.4	Emmanuel McDonald-Bailey (GBR)	10.4
200 m	Andrew Stanfield (USA)	20.7	Thane Baker (USA)	20.8	James Gathers (USA)	20.8
400 m	George Rhoden (JAM)	45.9	Herbert McKenley (JAM)	45.9	Ollie Matson (USA)	46.8
800 m	Malvin Whitfield (USA)	1:49.2	Arthur Wint (JAM)	1:49.4	Heinz Ulzheimer (GER)	1:49.7
1500 m	Josy Barthel (LUX)	3:45.1	Bob McMillen (USA)	3:45.2	Werner Lueg (GER)	3:45.4
5000 m	Emil Zátopek (TCH)	14:06.6	Alain Mimoun (FRA)	14:07.4	Herbert Schade (GER)	14:08.6
10,000 m	Emil Zátopek (TCH)	29:17.0	Alain Mimoun (FRA)	29:32.8	Alexander Anufriyev (URS)	29:48.2
Marathon	Emil Zátopek (TCH)	2:23:03.2	Reinaldo Gorno (ARG)	2:25:35.0	Gustaf Jansson (SWE)	2:26:07.0
110 m Hurdles	Harrison Dillard (USA)	13.7	Jack Davis (USA)	13.7	Arthur Barnard (USA)	14.1
400 m Hurdles	Charles Moore (USA)	50.8	Yuriy Lituyev (URS)	51.3	John Holland (NZL)	52.2
3000 m Steeplechase	Horace Ashenfelter (USA)	8:45.4	Vladimir Kazantsev (URS)	8:51.6	John Disley (GBR)	8:51.8
4 x 100 m	USA	40.1	USSR	40.3	Hungary	40.5
4 x 400 m	Jamaica	3:03.9	USA	3:04.0	Germany	3:06.6
10 km Walk	John Mikaelsson (SWE)	45:02.8	Fritz Schwab (SUI)	45:41.0	Bruno Yunk (URS)	45:41.0
50 km Walk	Giuseppe Dordoni (ITA)	4:28:07.8	Josef Dolezal (TCH)	4:30:17.8	Antal Róka (HUN)	4:31:27.2
High Jump	Walter Davis (USA)	2.04	Ken Wiesner (USA)	2.01	J. Telles da Conceiceião (BRA)	1.98
Pole Vault	Bob Richards (USA)	4.55	Donald Laz (USA)	4.50	Ragnar Lundberg (SWE)	4.40
Long Jump	Jerome Biffle (USA)	7.57	Meredith Gourdine (USA)	7.53	Ödön Földessy (HUN)	7.30
Triple Jump	Adhemar Ferreira da Silva (BRA)	16.22	Leonid Shcherbakov (URS)	15.98	Arnoldo Devonish (VEN)	15.52
Shot	Parry O'Brien (USA)	17.41	Darrow Hooper (USA)	17.39	Jim Fuchs (USA)	17.06
Discus	Sim Iness (USA)	55.03	Adolfo Consolini (ITA)	53.78	James Dillion (USA)	53.28
Hammer	József Csermák (HUN)	60.34	Karl Storch (GER)	58.86	Imre Németh (HUN)	57.74
Javelin	Cyrus Young (USA)	73.78	William Miller (USA)	72.46	Toivo Hyytiäinen (FIN)	71.89
Decathlon	Robert Mathias (USA)	7887	Milton Campbell (USA)	6975	Floyd Simmons (USA)	6788
Women						
100 m	Marjorie Jackson (AUS)	11.5	Daphne Hasenjager-Robb (SAF)	11.8	Shirley de la Hunty Strickland (AUS)	11.9
200 m	Marjorie Jackson (AUS)	23.7	Bertha Brouwer (HOL)	24.2	Nadyezda Khnykhina (URS)	24.2
80 m Hurdles	Shirley de la Hunty Strickland (AUS)	10.9	Maria GolubnichaYa (URS)	11.1	Maria Sander (GER)	11.1
4 x 100 m Relay	USA	45.9	Germany	45.9	Great Britain	46.2
High Jump	Esther Brand (SAF)	1.67	Sheila Lerwill (GBR)	1.65	Aleksandra Chudina (URS)	1.63
Long Jump	Yvette Williams (NZL)	6.24	Aleksandra Chudina (URS)	6.14	Shirley Cawley (GBR)	5.92
Shot	Galina Zybina (URS)	15.28	Marianne Werner (GER)	14.57	Klavdiya Tochenova (URS)	14.50
Discus	Nina Romashrova (URS)	51.42	Elizaveta Bagrantseva (URS)	47.08	Nina Dumbadse (URS)	46.29
Javelin	Dana Zátopková (TCH)	50.47	Aleksandra Chudina (URS)	50.01	Yelena Gorchakova (URS)	49.76
Swimming						
Men						
100 m Freestyle	Clarke Scholes (USA)	57.4	Hiroshi Suzuki (JPN)	57.4	Göran Larsson (SWE)	58.2
400 m Freestyle	Jean Boiteux (FRA)	4:30.7	Ford Konno (USA)	4:31.3	Per-Olof Östrand (SWE)	4:35.2
1500 m Freestyle	Ford Konno (USA)	18:30.3	Shiro Hashizune (JPN)	18:41.4	Tetsuo Okamoto (BRA)	18:51.3
100 m Backstroke	Yoshinobu Oyakawa (JPN)	1:05.4	Gilbert Bozon (FRA)	1:06.2	Jack Taylor (USA)	1:06.5
200 m Breaststroke	John Davies (AUS)	2:34.4	Bowen Stassforth (USA)	2:34.7	Herbert Klein (GER)	2:35.9
4 x 200 m Freestyle Relay	USA	8:31.1	Japan	8:33.5	France	8:45.9
Springboard Diving	David Browning (USA)	205.29	Miller Anderson (USA)	199.84	Robert Clotworthy (USA)	184.92
Highboard Diving	Samuel Lee (USA)	156.28	Joaquin Capilla Pérez	145.21	Günther Haase (GER)	141.31
Water Polo	Hungary		Yugoslavia		Italy	
Women						

EVENT	GOLD		SILVER		BRONZE	
100 m Freestyle	Katalin Szöke (HUN)	1:06.8	Johanna Termeulen (HOL)	1:07.0	Judit Temes (HUN)	1:07.1
400 m Freestyle	Váleria Gyenge (HUN)	5:12.1	Eva Novák (HUN)	5:13.7	Evelyn Kawamoto (USA)	5:14.6
100 m Backstroke	Joan Harrison (SAF)	1:14.3	Geertje Wielema (HOL)	1:14.5	Jean Stewart (NZL)	1:15.8
200 m Breaststroke	Eva Székely (HUN)	2:51.7	Eva Novák (HUN)	2:54.4	Helen Gordon (GBR)	2:57.6
4 x 100 m Freestyle Relay	Hungary	4:24.4	Netherlands	4:29.0	USA	4:30.1
Springboard Diving	Patricia McCormick (USA)	147.30	Mady Moreau (FRA)	139.34	Zoe Ann Jensen-Olsen (USA)	127.57
Highboard Diving	Patricia McCormlck (USA)	79.37	Paula Jean Myers (USA)	71.63	Juno Irwin-Stover (USA)	70.49

Boxing

EVENT	GOLD	SILVER	BRONZE
Flyweight (- 51 kg)	Nathan Brooks (USA)	Edgar Basel (GER)	Anatoly Bulakov (URS)
			Bill Toweel (SAF)
Bantamweight (- 54 kg)	Pentti Hämäläinen (FIN)	John McNally (IRL)	Gennadiy Garbusov (URS)
			Joon-Ho Kang (KOR)
Featherweight (- 57 kg)	Jan Zachara (TCH)	Sergio Caprari (ITA)	Joseph Ventaja (FRA)
			Leonard Leisching (SAF)
Lightweight (- 60 kg)	Aureliano Bolognesi (ITA)	Aleksy Antkiewicz (POL)	Erkki Pakkanen (FIN)
			Gheorge Fiat (ROM)
Light-Welterweight (- 63.5 kg)	Charles Adkins (USA)	Viktor Mednov (URS)	Erkki Mallenius (FIN)
			Bruno Visintin (ITA)
Welterweight (- 67 kg)	Zygmunt Chychla (POL)	Sergey Schtsherbakov (URS)	Victor Jörgensen (DEN)
			Günther Heidemann (GER)
Light-Middleweight(-71 kg)	László Papp (HUN)	Theunis van Schalkwyk (SAF)	Boris Tishin (URS)
			Eladio Herrera (ARG)
Middleweight (-75 kg)	Floyd Patterson (USA)	Vasile Tita (ROM)	Stig Sjölin (SWE)
			Boris Nikolov (BUL)
Light-Heavyweight (- 81 kg)	Norvel Lee (USA)	Antonio Pacenza (ARG)	Anatoly Perov (URS)
			Harri Siljander (FIN)
Heavyweight (+ 81 kg)	Hayes Edward Sanders (USA)	Ingemar Johansson (SWE)*	Andries Nieman (SAF)
			Jekka Koski (FIN)

* disqualified; reinstated as silver medallist in 1982

Weightlifting

EVENT	GOLD		SILVER		BRONZE	
Bantamweight (- 56 kg)	Ivan Udodov (URS)	315.0	Mahmoud Namdjou (IRN)	307.5	Ali Mirzai (IRN)	300.0
Featherweight (- 60 kg)	Rafael Chimishkyan (URS)	337.5	Nikolai Saksonov (URS)	332.5	Rodney Wilkes (TRI)	322.5
Lightweight (- 67.5 kg)	Thomas Kono (USA)	362.5	Yevgeniy Lopatin (URS)	350.0	Verne Barberis (AUS)	350.0
Middleweight (- 75 kg)	Peter George (USA)	400.0	Gerard Gratton (CAN)	390.0	Sung-Jip Kim (KOR)	382.5
Light-Heavyweight (- 82.5 kg)	Trofin Lomakin (URS)	417.5	Stanley Stanczyk (USA)	415.0	Arkadi Vorobiev (URS)	407.5
Middle-Heavyweight (- 90 kg)	Norbert Schemansky (USA)	445.0	Grigory Nowak (URS)	410.0	Lennox Kilgour (TRI)	402.5
Heavyweight (+ 90 kg)	John Davis (USA)	460.0	James Bradford (USA)	437.5	Humberto Selvetti (ARG)	432.5

Greco-Roman Wrestling

EVENT	GOLD	SILVER	BRONZE
Flyweight (- 52 kg)	Boris Gurevich (URS)	Ignazio Fabra (ITA)	Leo Honkala (FIN)
Bantamweight (- 57 kg)	Imre Hódos (HUN)	Zakaria Chihab (LIB)	Artem Teyan (URS)
Featherweight (- 62 kg)	Yakov Punkin (URS)	Imre Polyak (HUN)	Abdel Rashed (EGY)
Lightweight (- 67 kg)	Shazam Safin (URS)	Gustaf Freij (SWE)	Mikulás Athanasov (TCH)
Welterweight (- 73 kg)	Miklós Szilvási (HUN)	Gösta Andersson (SWE)	Khalil Taha (LIB)
Middleweight (- 79 kg)	Axel Grönberg (SWE)	Kalervo Ranhala (FIN)	Nikolai Belov (URS)
Light-Heavyweight (- 87 kg)	Kaelpo Gröndahl (FIN)	Shalva Shikhladze (URS)	Karl-Erik Nilsson (SWE)
Heavyweight (+ 87 kg)	Johannes Kotkas (URS)	Josef Ruzicka (TCH)	Tauno Kovanen (FIN)

Freestyle Wrestling

EVENT	GOLD	SILVER	BRONZE
Flyweight (- 52 kg)	Hasan Gemici (TUR)	Yushu Kitano (JPN)	Mahmoud Mollaghassemi (IRN)
Bantamweight (- 57 kg)	Shohachi Ishii (JPN)	Rashid Mamedbekov (URS)	Kha-Shaba Jadav (IND)
Featherweight (- 62 kg)	Bayram Sit (TUR)	Nasser Guivehtchi (IRN)	Josiah Henson (USA)
Lightweight (- 67 kg)	Olle Anderberg (SWE)	Thomas Evans (USA)	Djahanbakte Tovfighe (IRN)
Welterweight (- 73 kg)	William Smith (USA)	Per Berlin (SWE)	Abdullah Modjtabavi (IRN)
Middleweight (- 79 kg)	David Tsimakuridze (URS)	Gholam Reza Takhti (IRN)	György Gurics (HUN)
Light-Heavyweight (- 87 kg)	Wiking Palm (SWE)	Henry Wittenberg (USA)	Adil Atan (TUR)
Heavyweight (+ 87 kg)	Arsen Mekokishvili (URS)	Bertil Antonsson (SWE)	Kenneth Richmond (GBR)

Fencing

EVENT	GOLD		SILVER		BRONZE	
Individual Foil - Men	Christian d'Oriola (FRA)	8	Edoardo Mangiarotti (ITA)	6	Manlio Di Rosa (ITA)	5
Team Foil - Men	France		Italy		Hungary	
Individual Épée	Edoardo Mangiarotti (ITA)	7	Dario Mangiarotti (ITA)	6	Oswald Zappelli (SUI)	6
Team Épée	Italy		Sweden		Switzerland	
Individual Sabre	Pál Kovács (HUN)	8	Aladár Gerevich (HUN)	7	Tibor Berczelly (HUN)	5

EVENT	GOLD		SILVER		BRONZE	
Team Sabre	Hungary		Italy		France	
Individual Foil – Women	Irene Camber (ITA)	5+1	Ilona Elek (HUN)	5	Karen Lachmann (DEN)	4
Modern Pentathlon						
Individual	Lars Hall (SWE)	32	Gábor Benedek (HUN)	39	István Szondy (HUN)	41
Team	Hungary	166	Sweden	182	Finland	213
Canoeing						
Men						
1000 m Kayak Singles K1	Gert Fredriksson (SWE)	4:07.9	Thorvald Strömberg (FIN)	4:09.7	Luis Gantois (FRA)	4:20.1
10,000 m Kayak Singles K1	Thorvald Strömberg (FIN)	47:22.8	Gert Fredriksson (SWE)	47:34.1	Michael Scheuer (GER)	47:54.5
1000 m Kayak Pairs K2	Finland	3:51.1	Sweden	3:51.1	Austria	3:51.4
10,000 m Kayak Pairs K2	Finland	44:21.3	Sweden	44:21.7	Hungary	44:26.6
1000 m Canadian Singles C1	Josef Holecek (TCH)	4:56.3	János Parti (HUN)	5:03.3	Olavi Ojanpara (FIN)	5:08.5
10,000 m Canadian Singles C1	Frank Havens (USA)	57:41.1	Gábor Novák (HUN)	57:49.2	Alfred Jindra (TCH)	57:53.1
1000 m Canadian Pairs C2	Denmark	4:38.3	Czechoslovakia	4:42.9	Germany	4:48.3
10,000 m Canadian Pairs C2	France	54:08.3	Canada	54:09.9	Germany	54:28.1
Women						
500 m Kayak Singles K1	Sylvi Saimo (FIN)	2:18.4	Gertrude Liebhart (AUT)	2:18.8	Nina Savina (URS)	2:21.6
Rowing						
Single Sculls	Yuriy Tyukalov (URS)	8:12.8	Mervyn Wood (AUS)	8:14.5	Teodor Kocerka (POL)	8:19.4
Double Sculls	Argentina	7:32.2	USSR	7:38.3	Uruguay	7:43.7
Coxless Pairs	USA	8:20.7	Belgium	8:23.5	Switzerland	8:32.7
Coxed Pairs	France	8:28.6	Germany	8:32.1	Denmark	8:34.9
Coxless Fours	Yugoslavia	7:16.0	France	7:18.9	Finland	7:23.3
Coxed Fours	Czechoslovakia	7:33.4	Switzerland	7:36.5	USA	7:37.0
Coxed Eights	USA	6:25.9	USSR	6:31.2	Australia	6:33.1
Sailing						
Finn Class	Paul Elvström (DEN)	8209	Charles Currey (GBR)	5449	Rickard Sarby (SWE)	5051
International Star	Italy	7635	USA	7216	Portugal	4903
Dragon	Norway	6130	Sweden	5556	Germany	5352
5.5 m	USA	5751	Norway	5325	Sweden	4554
6 m	USA	4870	Norway	4648	Finland	3944
Cycling						
Individual Road Race (190.4 km)	André Noyelle (BEL)	5:06:03.6	Robert Grondelaers (BEL)	5:06:51.2	Edi Ziegler (GER)	5:07:47.5
Team Road Race	Belgium	15:20:46.6	Italy	15:33:27.3	France	15:38:58.1
1000 m Time Trial	Russel Mockridge (AUS)	1:11.1	Marino Morettini (ITA)	1:12.7	Raymond Robinson (SAF)	1:13.0
1000 m Sprint	Enzo Sacchi (ITA)		Lionel Cox (AUS)		Werner Potzernheim (GER)	
2000 m Tandem	Australia		South Africa		Italy	
4000 m Team Pursuit	Italy	4:46.1	South Africa	4:53.6	Great Britain	4:51.5
Equestrianism						
Three-Day Event	Hans v. Blixen-Finecke (SWE)	-28.33	Guy Lefrant (FRA)	-54.50	Wilhelm Büsing (GER)	-55.50
Three-Day Event (Team)	Sweden	-221.49	Germany	-235.49	USA	-587.16
Grand Prix (Dressage)	Henri Saint Cyr (SWE)	561.0	Lis Hartel (DEN)	541.5	André Jousseaume (FRA)	541.0
Grand Prix (Dressage) Team	Sweden	1597.5	Switzerland	1579.0	Germany	1501.0
Grand Prix (Jumping)	Pierre Jonquères d'Oriola (FRA)	-8/0	Oscar Cristi (CHI)	-8/4	Fritz Thiedemann (GER)	-8/8
Grand Prix (Jumping) Team	Great Britain	-40.75	Chile	-45.75	USA	-52.25
Shooting						
Free Rifle (3 Positions)	Anatoliy Bogdanov (URS)	1123	Robert Bürchler (SUI)	1120	Lev Weinstein (URS)	1109
Small-Bore Rifle (Prone)	Josif Sarbu (ROM)	400/33	Boris Andreyev (URS)	400/28	Arthur Jackson (USA)	399
Small-Bore Rifles (3 Positions)	Erling Konshaug (NOR)	1164/53	Vilho Ylönen (FIN)	1164/49	Boris Andreyev (URS)	1163
Rapid-Fire Pistol	Károly Takács (HUN)	579	Szilárd Kun (HUN)	578	Gheorghe Lichiardopol (ROM)	578
Free Pistol (50 m)	Huelet Benner (USA)	553	Angel L. de Gozalo (ESP)	550	Ambrus Balogh (HUN)	549
Olympic Trap Shooting	George P. Généreux (CAN)	192	Knut Holmqvist (SWE)	191	Hans Liljedahl (SWE)	190
Running Deer Shooting	John Larsen (NOR)	413	Per Olof Sköldberg (SWE)	409	Tauno Mäki (FIN)	407
Gymnastics						
Men						
Individual Combined Exercises	Viktor Chukarin (URS)	115.70	Grant Shaginyan (URS)	114.95	Josef Stalder (SUI)	114.75
Team	USSR	575.4	Switzerland	567.50	Finland	564.20
Parallel Bars	Hans Eugster (SUI)	19.65	Viktor Chukarin (URS)	19.60	Josef Stalder (SUI)	19.50
Floor	Karl William Thoresson (SWE)	19.25	Tadao Uesako (JPN)	19.15		

EVENT	GOLD		SILVER		BRONZE	
			Jerzy Jokiel (POL)	19.15		
Horse Vault	Viktor Chukarin (URS)	19.20	Masao Takemoto (JPN)	19.15	Takashi Ono (JPN)	19.10
					Tadao Uesako (JPN)	19.10
Horizontal Bar	Jack Günthard (SUI)	19.55	Josef Stalder (SUI)	19.50		
			Alfred Schwarzmann (GER)	19.50		
Rings	Grant Shaginyan (URS)	19.75	Viktor Chukarin (URS)	19.55	Hans Eugster (SUI)	19.40
					Dimitri Leonkin (URS)	19.40
Pommel Horse	Viktor Chukarin (URS)	19.50	Yevgeniy Korolkov (URS)	19.40		
			Grant Shaginyan (URS)	19.40		
Women						
Individual Combined Exercises	Maria Gorochovskaya (URS)	76.78	Nina Bocharova (URS)	75.94	Margit Korondi (HUN)	75.82
Team	USSR	527.03	Hungary	520.96	Czechoslovakia	503.32
Floor	Agnes Keleti (HUN)	19.36	Maria Gorochovskaya (URS)	19.20	Margit Korondi (HUN)	19.00
Horse Vault	Yekaterina Kalinchuk (URS)	19.20	Maria Gorochovskaya (URS)	19.19	Galina Minaitscheva (URS)	19.16
Beam	Nina Bocharowa (URS)	19.22	Maria Gorochovskaya (URS)	19.13	Margit Korondi (HUN)	19.02
Asymmetrical Bars	Margit Korondi (HUN)	19.40	Maria Gorochovskaya (URS)	19.26	Agnes Keleti (HUN)	19.16
Portable Apparatus (Women's Teams)	Sweden	74.20	USSR	73.00	Hungary	71.60
Basketball						
	USA		USSR		Uruguay	
Soccer						
	Hungary		Yugoslavia		Sweden	
Hockey						
	India		Netherlands		Great Britain	

Cortina d'Ampezzo 1956

26 January – 5 February

Participants: 820 / Men: 688, Women: 132, Countries: 32,
Sports: 6, Events: 24
Final Torchbearer: Guido Caroli

Medals Table

PLACE	COUNTRY	GOLD	SILVER	BRONZE
1	USSR	7	3	6
2	Austria	4	3	4
3	Finland	3	3	1
4	Switzerland	3	2	1
5	Sweden	2	4	4

Outstanding Athletes

PLACE	NAME (NATIONALITY)	DISCIPLINE	G	S	B
1	Toni Sailer (AUT)	Alpine Skiing	3	–	–
2	Yevgeniy Grischin (URS)	Speed Skating	2	–	–
3	Sixten Jernberg (SWE)	Nordic Skiing	1	2	1
4	Veikko Hakulinen (FIN)	Nordic Skiing	1	2	–
5	Ljubow Kosyryeva (URS)	Nordic Skiing	1	1	–
	Sigvard Ericsson (SWE)	Speed Skating	1	1	–

EVENT	GOLD		SILVER		BRONZE	
Alpine Skiing						
Men						
Downhill	Toni Sailer (AUT)	2:52.2	Raymond Fellay (SUI)	2:55.7	Andreas Molterer (AUT)	2:56.2
Slalom	Toni Sailer (AUT)	3:14.7	Chiharu Igaya (JPN)	3:18.7	Stig Sollander (SWE)	3:20.2
Giant Slalom	Toni Sailer (AUT)	3:00.1	Andreas Molterer (AUT)	3:06.3	Walter Schuster (AUT)	3:07.2
Women						
Downhill	Madeleine Berthod (SUI)	1:40.7	Frieda Dänzer (SUI)	1:45.4	Lucile Wheeler (CAN)	1:45.9
Slalom	Renée Colliard (SUI)	1:52.3	Regina Schöpf (AUT)	1:55.4	Jevgenija Sidorova (URS)	1:56.7
Giant Slalom	Ossi Reichert (GER)★	1:56.5	Josefine Frandl (AUT)	1:57.8	Dorothea Hochleitner (AUT)	1:58.2
Nordic Skiing						
Men						
15 km Cross-Country Skiing	Hallgeir Brenden (NOR)	49:39.0	Sixten Jernberg (SWE)	50:14.0	Pavel Kolschin (URS)	50:17.0
30 km Cross-Country Skiing	Veikko Hakulinen (FIN)	1:44:06.0	Sixten Jernberg (SWE)	1:44:30.0	Pavel Kolschin (URS)	1:45:45.0

EVENT	GOLD		SILVER		BRONZE	
50 km Cross-Country Skiing	Sixten Jernberg (SWE)	2:50:27.0	Veikko Hakulinen (FIN)	2:51:45.0	Fedor Terentyev (URS)	2:53:32.0
4 x 10 km	USSR	2:15:30.0	Finland	2:16:31.0	Sweden	2:17:42.0
Ski Jumping	Antti Hyvärinen (FIN)	227.0	Aulis Kallakorpi (FIN)	225.0	Harry Glass (GER)★	224.5
Nordic Combination	Sverre Stenersen (NOR)	455.000	Bengt-Eriksson (SWE)	437.000	Franciszek Gron-Gasienica (POL)	436.800
Women						
10 km Cross-Country Skiing	Lubov Kosyryeva (URS)	38:11.0	Radya Yeroschina (URS)	38:16.0	Sonja Edström (SWE)	38:23.0
3 x 5 km	Finland	1:09:01.0	USSR	1:09:28.0	Sweden	1:09:48.0
Figure Skating						
Women	Tenley Albright (USA)		Carol Heiss (USA)		Ingrid Wendl (AUT)	
Men	Hayes Alan Jenkins (USA)		Ronald Robertson (USA)		David Jenkins (USA)	
Pairs	Elisabeth Schwarz/Kurt Oppelt (AUT)		Frances Dafoe/Norris Bowden (CAN)		Marianne Nagy/László Nagy (HUN)	
Speed Skating						
500 m	Yevgeniy Grischin (URS)	40.2	Rafael Gratsch (URS)	40.8	Alv Gjestvang (NOR)	41.0
1500 m	Yevgeniy Grischin (URS)	2:08.6			Toivo Salonen (FIN)	2:09.4
	Yuriy Michailov (URS)	2:08.6				
5000 m	Boris Schilkov (URS)	7:48.7	Sigvard Ericsson (SWE)	7:56.7	Oleg Gontscharenko (URS)	7:57.5
10,000 m	Sigvard Ericsson (SWE)	16:35.9	Knut Johannesen (NOR)	16:36.9	Oleg Gontscharenko (URS)	16:42.3
Bobsledding						
2-Man Bob	Italy I	5:30.14	Italy II	5:31.45	Switzerland I	5:37.46
4-Man Bob	Switzerland I	5:10.44	Italy II	5:12.10	USA I	5:12.39
Ice Hockey						
	USSR		USA		Canada	

★ representing a combined German team

Melbourne 1956

Participants: 3184 / Men: 2813, Women: 371, Countries: 67,
Sports: 17, Events: 151
Final Torchbearer: Ron Clarke (Melbourne)
Hans Wikne/Karin Lindberg/Henri Eriksson (Stockholm)

22 November – 8 December
(Equestrian Games in Stockholm 10–17 June)
Participants: 158 / Men: 145, Women: 145,
Countries 29

Medals Table

PLACE	COUNTRY	GOLD	SILVER	BRONZE
1	USSR	37	29	32
2	USA	32	25	17
3	Australia	13	8	14
4	Hungary	9	10	7
5	Italy	8	8	9

Outstanding Athletes

PLACE	NAME (NATIONALITY)	DISCIPLINE	G	S	B
1	Larissa Latynina (URS)	Gymnastics	4	1	–
2	Agnes Keleti (HUN)	Gymnastics	3	2	–
3	Viktor Chukarin (URS)	Gymnastics	3	1	1
4	Valentin Muratov (URS)	Gymnastics	3	1	–
5	Betty Cuthbert (AUS)	Athletics	3	–	–
	Robert Morrow (USA)	Athletics	3	–	–
	Murray Rose (AUS)	Swimming	3	–	–

EVENT	GOLD		SILVER		BRONZE	
Athletics						
Men						
100 m	Robert Morrow (USA)	10.5	Thane Baker (USA)	10.5	Hector Hogan (AUS)	10.6
200 m	Robert Morrow (USA)	20.6	Andrew Stanfield (USA)	20.7	Thane Baker (USA)	20.9
400 m	Charles Jenkins (USA)	46.7	Karl-Friedrich Haas (GER)★	46.8	Voitto Hellsten (FIN)	47.0
					Ardalion Ignatiev	47.0
800 m	Tom Courtney (USA)	1:47.7	Derek Johnson (GBR)	1:47.8	Andun Boysen (NOR)	1:48.1
1500 m	Ronald Delany (IRL)	3:41.2	Klaus Richtzenhain (GER)★	3:42.0	John Landy (AUS)	3:42.0
5000 m	Vladimir Kuts (URS)	13:39.6	Gordon Pirie (GBR)	13:50.6	Derek Ibbotson (GBR)	13:54.4
10,000 m	Vladimir Kuts (URS)	28:45.6	József Kovács (HUN)	28:52.4	Allan Lawrence (AUS)	28:53.6
Marathon	Alain Mimoun (FRA)	2:25:00.0	Franjo Mihalic (YUG)	2:26:32.0	Veikko Karvonen (FIN)	2:27:47.0
110 m Hurdles	Lee Calhoun (USA)	13.5	Jack Davis (USA)	13.5	Joel Shankle (USA)	14.1
400 m Hurdles	Glenn Davis (USA)	50.1	Eddie Southern (USA)	50.8	Joshua Culbreath (USA)	51.6
3000 m Steeplechase	Chris Brasher (GBR)	8:41.2	Sándor Rozsnyói (HUN)	8:43.6	Ernst Larsen (NOR)	8:44.0

EVENT	GOLD		SILVER		BRONZE	
4 x 100 m	USA	39.5	USSR	39.8	Germany★	40.3
4 x 400 m	USA	3:04.8	Australia	3:06.2	Great Britain	3:07.2
20 km Walk	Leonid Spirin (URS)	1:31:27.4	Antonas Mikenas (URS)	1:32:03.0	Bruno Yunk (URS)	1:32:12.0
50 km Walk	Norman Read (NZL)	4:30:42.8	Yevgeniy Maskinskov (URS)	4:32:57.0	John Lundgren (SWE)	4:35:02.0
High Jump	Charles Dumas (USA)	2.12	Charles Porter (AUS)	2.10	Igor Kashkarov (URS)	2.08
Pole Jump	Bob Richards (USA)	4.56	Bob Gutowski (USA)	4.53	Georgios Roubanis (GRE)	4.50
Long Jump	Greg Bell (USA)	7.83	John Bennett (USA)	7.68	Jorma Valkama (FIN)	7.48
Triple Jump	Adhemar Ferreira da Silva (BRA)	16.35	Vilhjálmur Einarsson (ISL)	16.26	Vitold Kreyer (URS)	16.02
Shot	Parry O'Brien (USA)	18.57	Bill Nieder (USA)	18.18	Jiri Skobla (TCH)	17.65
Discus	Al Oerter (USA)	56.36	Fortune Gordien (USA)	54.81	Desmond Koch (USA)	54.40
Hammer	Harold Connolly (USA)	63.19	Michail Krivonosov (URS)	63.03	Anatoliy Samotsvetov (URS)	62.56
Javelin	Egil Danielsen (NOR)	85.71	Janusz Sidlo (POL)	79.98	Viktor Tsibulenko (URS)	79.50
Decathlon	Milton Campbell (USA)	7937	Rafer Johnson (USA)	7587	Vassily Kusnetsov (URS)	7465
Women						
100 m	Betty Cuthbert (AUS)	11.5	Christa Stubnick (GER)★	11.7	Marlene Matthews (AUS)	11.7
200 m	Betty Cuthbert (AUS)	23.4	Christa Stubnick (GER)★	23.7	Marlene Matthews (AUS)	23.8
80 m Hurdles	S. de la Hunty-Strickland (AUS)	10.7	Gisela Köhler (GER)★	10.9	Norma Thrower (AUS)	11.0
4 x 100 m	Australia	44.5	Great Britain	44.7	USA	44.9
High Jump	Mildred McDaniel (USA)	1.76	Maria Pisaryeva (URS)	1.67	Thelma Hopkins (GBR)	1.67
Long Jump	Elzbieta Krzesinska (POL)	6.35	Willye White (USA)	6.09	Nadyezda Dvalishvili (URS)	6.07
Shot	Tamara Tyshkevich (URS)	16.59	Galina Zybina (URS)	16.53	Marianne Werner (GER)★	15.61
Discus	Olga Fikotová (TCH)	53.69	Irina Beglyakova (URS)	52.54	Nina Ponomaryeva (URS)	52.02
Javelin	Inese Jaunzeme (URS)	53.86	Marlene Ahrens (CHI)	50.38	Nadyezda Konyayeva (URS)	50.28
Swimming						
Men						
100 m Freestyle	John Henricks (AUS)	55.4	John Devitt (AUS)	55.8	Gary Chapman (AUS)	56.7
400 m Freestyle	Murray Rose (AUS)	4:27.3	Tsuyoshi Yamanaka (JPN)	4:30.4	George Breen (USA)	4:32.5
1500 m Freestyle	Murray Rose (AUS)	17:58.9	Tsuyoshi Yamanaka (JPN)	18:00.3	George Breen (USA)	18:08.2
100 m Backstroke	David Theile (AUS)	1:02.2	John Monckton (AUS)	1:03.2	Frank McKinney (USA)	1:04.5
200 m Breaststroke	Masaru Furukawa (JPN)	2:34.7	Masahiro Yoshimura (JPN)	2:36.7	Charis Yunitschev (URS)	2:36.8
200 m Butterfly	William Yorzik (USA)	2:19.3	Takashi Ishimoto (JPN)	2:23.8	György Tumpek (HUN)	2:23.9
4 x 200 m Freestyle Relay	Australia	8:23.6	USA	8:31.5	USSR	8:34.7
Springboard Diving	Robert Clotworthy (USA)	159.56	Donald Harper (USA)	156.23	Joaquin Capilla Pérez (MEX)	150.69
Highboard Diving	Joaquin Capilla Pérez (MEX)	152.44	Gary Tobian (USA)	152.41	Richard Connor (USA)	149.79
Water Polo	Hungary		Yugoslavia		USSR	
Women						
100 m Freestyle	Dawn Fraser (AUS)	1:02.0	Lorraine Crapp (AUS)	1:02.3	Faith Leech (AUS)	1:05.1
400 m Freestyle	Lorraine Crapp (AUS)	4:54.6	Dawn Fraser (AUS)	5:02.5	Sylvia Ruuska (USA)	5:07.1
100 m Backstroke	Judith Grinham (GBR)	1:12.9	Carin Cone (USA)	1:12.9	Magaret Edwards (GBR)	1:13.1
200 m Breaststroke	Ursula Happe (GER)★	2:53.1	Eva Ezékely (HUN)	2:54.8	Eva-Maria ten Elsen (GER)★	2:55.1
100 m Butterfly	Shelley Mann (USA)	1:11.0	Nancy Ramey (USA)	1:11.9	Mary Sears (USA)	1:14.4
4 x 100 m Freestyle Relay	Australia	4:17.1	USA	4:19.2	South Africa	4:25.7
Springboard Diving	Patricia McCormick (USA)	142.36	Jeanne Stunyo (USA)	125.89	Irene Mac Donald (CAN)	121.40
Highboard Diving	Patricia McCormick (USA)	84.85	Juno Irwin (USA)	81.64	Paula Jean Myers (USA)	81.58
Boxing						
Flyweight (- 51 kg)	Terence Spinks (GER)		Mircea Dobrescu (ROM)		John Caldwell (IRL)	
					René Libeer (FRA)	
Bantamweight (- 54 kg)	Wolfgang Behrendt (GER)★		Soon-Chung Song (KOR)		Frederick Gilroy (IRL)	
					Claudio Barrientos (CHI)	
Featherweight (- 57 kg)	Vladimir Safronov (URS)		Thomas Nicholls (GBR)		Hendryk Niedzwiedzki (POL)	
					Pentti Hämäläinen (FIN)	
Lightweight (- 60 kg)	Richard McTaggart (GBR)		Harry Kurschat (GER)★		Anthony Byrne (IRL)	
					Anatoli Lagetko (URS)	
Light-Welterweight (- 63.5 kg)	Vladimir Yengibaryan (URS)		Franco Nenci (ITA)		Henry Loubscher (SAF)	
					Constantin Dumitrescu (ROM)	
Welterweight (- 67 kg)	Nicolae Lince (ROM)		Frederick Tiedt (IRL)		Kevin John Hogarth (AUS)	
					Nicholas Gargano (GBR)	
Light-Middleweight (- 71 kg)	László Papp (HUN)		José Torres (USA)		John McCormack (GBR)	
					Zbigniew Pietrzykowski (POL)	
Middleweight (- 75 kg)	Gennadiy Schatkov (URS)		Ramon Tapia (CHI)		Gilbert Chapron (FRA)	
					Victor Zalazar (ARG)	
Light-Heavyweight (- 81 kg)	James Felton Boyd (USA)		Gherorghe Negrea (ROM)		Romualdas Murauskas (URS)	
					Carlos Lucas (CHI)	
Heavyweight (81 kg +)	Peter Rademacher (USA)		Lev Mukhin (URS)		Daniel Bekker (SAF)	
					Giacomo Bozzano (ITA)	

Melbourne 1956

EVENT	GOLD		SILVER		BRONZE	
Weightlifting						
Bantamweight (- 56 kg)	Charles Vinci (USA)	342.5	Vladimir Stogov (URS)	337.5	Mahmoud Namdjou (IRN)	332.5
Featherweight (- 60 kg)	Isaac Berger (USA)	352.5	Yevgenyi Minayev (URS)	342.5	Marian Zielinski (POL)	335.0
Lightweight (- 67.5 kg)	Igor Rybak (URS)	380.0	Ravil Khabutdinov (URS)	372.5	Chang-Hee Kim (KOR)	370.0
Middleweight (- 75 kg)	Fyodor Bogdanovski (URS)	420.0	Peter George (USA)	412.5	Ermanno Pignatti (ITA)	382.5
Light-Heavyweight (- 82.5 kg)	Thomas Kono (USA)	447.5	Vassiliy Stepanov (URS)	427.5	James George (USA)	417.5
Middle-Heavyweight (- 90 kg)	Arkadiy Vorobyev (URS)	462.5	David Sheppard (USA)	442.5	Jean Debuf (FRA)	425.0
Heavyweight (+ 90 kg)	Paul Anderson (USA)	500.0	Humberto Selvetti (ARG)	500.0	Alberto Pigaiani (ITA)	452.5
Greco-Roman Wrestling						
Flyweight (- 52 kg)	Nikolai Solovyov (URS)		Ignazio Fabra (ITA)		Durum Ali Egribas (TUR)	
Bantamweight (- 57 kg)	Konstantin Vyrupayev (URS)		Edvin Vesterby (SWE)		Francisco Horvat (ROM)	
Featherweight (- 62 kg)	Rauno Mäkinen (FIN)		Imre Polyák (HUN)		Roman Dzneladze (URS)	
Lightweight (- 67 kg)	Kyösti Lehtonen (FIN)		Riza Dogan (TUR)		Gyula Tóth (HUN)	
Welterweight (- 73 kg)	Mithat Bayrak (TUR)		Vladimir Maneyev (URS)		Per Berlin (SWE)	
Middleweight (- 79 kg)	Givy Kartoziya (URS)		Dimiter Dobrev (BUL)		Rune Jansson (SWE)	
Light-Heavyweight (- 87 kg)	Valentin Nikolayev (URS)		Petko Sirakov (BUL)		Karl-Erik Nilsson (SWE)	
Heavyweight (+ 87 kg)	Anatoliy Parfenov (URS)		Wilfried Dietrich (GER)★		Adelmo Bulgarelli (ITA)	
Freestyle Wrestling						
Flyweight (- 52 kg)	Mirian Tsalkalamanidze (URS)		Mohamed Ali Khojastehpour (IRN)		Hüseyin Akbas (TUR)	
Bantamweight (- 57 kg)	Mustafa Dagistanli (TUR)		Mohamad Yaghoubi (IRN)		Michail Chachov (URS)	
Featherweight (- 62 kg)	Shozo Sasahara (JPN)		Joseph Mewis (BEL)		Erkki Penttilä (FIN)	
Lightweight (- 67 kg)	Emamali Habibi (IRN)		Shigeru Kasahara (JPN)		Alimberg Bestayev (URS)	
Welterweight (- 73 kg)	Mitsuo Ikeda (JPN)		Ibrahim Zengin (TUR)		Vakhtang Balavadze (URS)	
Middleweight (- 79 kg)	Nikola Stantschev (BUL)		Daniel Hodge (USA)		Georgiy Skhirtladze (URS)	
Light-Heavyweight (- 87 kg)	Gholam-Reza Takhti (IRN)		Boris Kulayev (URS)		Peter Steele Blair (USA)	
Heavyweight (+ 87 kg)	Hamit Kaplan (TUR)		Hussein Mehmedov (BUL)		Taisto Kangasniemi (FIN)	
Fencing						
Individual Foil - Men	Christian d'Oriola (FRA)	6	Giancarlo Bergamini (ITA)	5	Antonio Spallino (ITA)	5
Team Foil - Men	Italy		France		Hungary	
Individual Épée	Carlo Pavesi (ITA)	5/1/2	Guiseppe Delfino (ITA)	5/1/1	Edoardo Mangiarotti (ITA)	5/1/10
Team Épée	Italy		Hungary		France	
Individual Sabre	Rudolf Kárpáti (HUN)	6	Jerzy Pawlowski (POL)	5	Lev Kuznetsov (URS)	4
Team Sabre	Hungary		Poland		USSR	
Individual Foil - Women	Gillian Sheen (GBR)	6+1	Olga Orban (ROM)	6	Renée Garilhe (FRA)	5
Modern Pentathlon						
Individual	Lars Hall (SWE)	4833	Olavi Nannonen (FIN)	4774.5	Väinö Korhonen (FIN)	4750
Team	USSR	13 690.5	USA	13 482	Finland	13 185.5
Canoeing						
Men						
1000 m Kayak Singles K1	Gert Fredriksson (SWE)	4:12.8	Igor Pissaryev (URS)	4:15.3	Lajos Kiss (HUN)	4:16.2
10,000 m Kayak Singles K1	Gert Fredriksson (SWE)	47:43.4	Ferenc Halaczky (HUN)	47:53.3	Michael Scheuer (GER)★	48:00.3
1000 m Kayak Pairs K2	Germany★	3:49.6	USSR	3:51.4	Austria	3:55.8
10,000 m Kayak Pairs K2	Hungary	43:37.0	Germany★	43:40.6	Australia	43:43.2
1000 m Canadian Singles C1	Leon Rotman (ROM)	5:05.3	István Hernek (HUN)	5:06.2	Gennady Bukharin (URS)	5:12.7
10,000 m Canadian Singles C1	Leon Rotman (ROM)	56:41.0	János Parti (HUN)	57:11.0	Gennady Bukharin (URS)	57:14.5
1000 m Canadian Pairs C2	Romania	4:47.4	USSR	4:48.6	Hungary	4:54.3
10,000 m Canadian Pairs C2	USSR	54:02.4	France	54:48.3	Hungary	55:15.6
Women						
500 m Kayak Singles K1	Elisaveta Dementyeva (URS)	2:18.9	Therese Zenz (GER)★	2:19.6	Tove Söby (DEN)	2:22.3
Rowing						
Single Sculls	Vyacheslav Ivanov (URS)	8:02.5	Stuart Mackenzie (AUS)	8:07.7	John Kelly jun. (USA)	8:11.8
Doubles Sculls	USSR	7:24.0	USA	7:32.2	Australia	7:37.4
Coxless Pairs	USA	7:55.4	USSR	8:03.9	Austria	8:11.8
Coxed Pairs	USA	8:26.1	Germany★	8:29.2	USSR	8:31.0
Coxless Fours	Canada	7:08.8	USA	7:18.4	France	7:20.9
Coxled Fours	Italy	7:19.4	Sweden	7:22.4	Finland	7:30.9
Coxed Eights	USA	6:35.2	Canada	6:37.1	Australia	6:39.2
Yachting						
Finn Class	Paul Elvström (DEN)	7509	André Nelis (BEL)	6254	John Marvin (USA)	5953
International Star	USA	5876	Italy	5649	Bahamas	5223

EVENT	GOLD		SILVER		BRONZE	
Sharpie	New Zealand	6086	Australia	6068	Great Britain	4859
Dragon	Sweden	5723	Denmark	5723	Great Britain	4547
5.5 m	Sweden	5527	Great Britain	4050	Australia	4022
Cycling						
Individual Road Race (187.731 km)	Ercole Baldini (ITA)	5:21:17.0	Arnaud Geyre (FRA)	5:23:16.0	Alan Jackson (GBR)	5:23:16.0
Team Road Race	France	22	Great Britain	23	Germany★	27
1000 m Time Trial	Leandro Faggin (ITA)	1:09.8	Ladislav Foucek (TCH)	1:11.4	Alfred Swift (SAF)	1:11.6
1000 m Sprint	Michel Rousseau (FRA)		Guglielmo Pesenti (ITA)		Richard Ploog (AUS)	
2000 m Tandem	Australia		Czechoslovakia		Italy	
4 000 m Team Pursuit	Italy	4:37.4	France	4:39.4	Great Britain	4:42.2
Equestrianism						
Three-Day Event	Petrus Kastennmann (SWE)	-66.53	August Lütke-Westhues (GER)★	-84.87	Frank Weldon (GBR)	-85.48
Three-Day Event (Team)	Great Britain	-355.48	Germany★	-475.91	Canada	-572.72
Grand Prix (Dressage)	Henri Saint Cyr (SWE)	860.0	Lis Hartel (DEN)	850.0	Liselott Linsenhoff (GER)★	832.0
Grand Prix (Dressage) Team	Sweden	2475	Germany★	2346	Switzerland	2346
Grand Prix (Jumping)	Hans Günter Winkler (GER)★	-4	Raimondo d'lnzeo (ITA)	-8	Piero d'lnzeo (ITA)	-11
Grand Prix (Jumping) Teams	Germany★	-40.00	Italy	-66.00	Great Britain	-69.00
Shooting						
Free Rifle (3 Positions)	Vasiliy Borissov (URS)	1138	Allan Erdman (URS)	1137	Vilho Ylönen (FIN)	1128
Small-Bore Rifle (Prone)	Gerald R. Ouelette (CAN)	600	Vasiliy Borissov (URS)	599	Gilmour St. Boa (CAN)	598
Small-Bore Rifle (3 Positions)	Anatoliy Bogdanov (URS)	1172	Otakar Horinek (TCH)	1172	Nils Johan Sundberg (SWE)	1167
Rapid-Fire Pistol	Stefan Petrescu (ROM)	587	Evgeniy Schcherkasov (URS)	585	Gheorghe Lichiardopol (ROM)	581
Free Pistol (50 m)	Pentti Linnosvuo (FIN)	556 126	Makhmud Umarow (URS)	556 124	Offutt Pinion (USA)	551
Olympic Trap Shooting	Galliano Rossini (ITA)	195	Adam Smelczynski (POL)	190	Alessandro Ciceri (ITA)	188
Running Deer Shooting	Vitaly Romanenko (URS)	441	Per Olof Sköldberg (SWE)	432	Vladimir Sevrugin (URS)	429
Gymnastics						
Men						
Individual Combined Exercises	Viktor Chukarin (URS)	114.25	Takashi Ono (JPN)	114.20	Yuriy Titov (URS)	113.80
Team	USSR	568.25	Japan	566.40	Finland	555.95
Parallel Bars	Viktor Chukarin (URS)	19.20	Masami Kubota (JPN)	19.15	Takashi Ono (JPN)	19.10
					Masao Takemoto (JPN)	19.10
Floor	Valentin Muratov (URS)	19.20	Nobuyuki Aihara (JPN)	19.10		
			William Thoresson (SWE)	19.10		
			Viktor Chukarin (URS)	19.10		
Horse Vault	Helmut Bantz (GER)★	18.85			Yuriy Titov (URS)	18.75
	Valentin Muratov (URS)	18.85				
Horizontal Bar	Takashi Ono (JPN)	19.60	Juriy Titov (URS)	19.40	Masao Takemoto (JPN)	19.30
Rings	Albert Azaryan (URS)	19.35	Valentin Muratov (URS)	19.15	Masao Takemoto (JPN)	19.10
Pommel Horse	Boris Shakhlin (URS)	19.25	Takashi Ono (JPN)	19.20	Viktor Chukarin (URS)	19.10
Women						
Individual Combined Exercises	Larissa Latynina (URS)	74.933	Agnes Keleti (HUN)	74.633	Sofia Muratova (URS)	74.466
Team	USSR	444.80	Hungary	443.50	Romania	438.20
Floor	Agnes Keleti (HUN)	18.733	Elena Leustean (ROM)	18.700		
	Larissa Latynina (URS)	18.733				
Horse Vault	Larissa Latynina (URS)	18.833	Tamara Manina (URS)	18.800	Ann-Sofi Colling (SWE)	18.733
Beam	Agnes Keleti (HUN)	18.800	Tamara Manina (URS)	18.633		
	Eva Besáková (TCH)	18.633				
Asymmetrical Bars	Agnes Keleti (HUN)	18.966	Larissa Latynina (URS)	18.833	Sofia Muratova (URS)	18.800
Portable Apparatus (Women's Teams)	Hungary	75.20	Sweden	74.20	Poland	74.00
Basketball						
	USA		USSR		Uruguay	
Soccer						
	USSR		Yugoslavia		Bulgaria	
Hockey						
	India		Pakistan		Germany★	

★ representing a combined German team

Squaw Valley 1960

18 February – 28 February

Participants: 665 / Men: 522, Women: 143, Countries: 30,
Sports: 6, Events: 27
Final Torchbearer: Kenneth Henry

Medals Table

PLACE	COUNTRY	GOLD	SILVER	BRONZE
1	USSR	7	5	9
2	Germany*	4	3	1
3	USA	3	4	3
4	Norway	3	3	–
5	Sweden	3	2	2

Outstanding Athletes

PLACE	NAME (NATIONALITY)	DISCIPLINE	G	S	B
1	Lidiya Skoblikowa (URS)	Speed Skating	2	–	–
	Yevgeniy Grischin (URS)	Speed Skating	2	–	–
3	Veikko Hakulinen (FIN)	Nordic Skiing	1	1	1
4	Maria Gusakova (URS)	Nordic Skiing	1	1	–
	Helga Haase (GER)*	Speed Skating	1	1	–
	Sixten Jernberg (SWE)	Nordic Skiing	1	1	–
	Knut Johannesen (NOR)	Speed Skating	1	1	–
	Viktor Kositschkin (URS)	Speed Skating	1	1	–

EVENT	GOLD		SILVER		BRONZE	
Alpine Skiing						
Men						
Downhill	Jean Vuarnet (FRA)	2:06.0	Hans-Peter Lanig (GER)*	2:06.5	Guy Perillat (FRA)	2:06.9
Slalom	Ernst Hinterseer (AUT)	2:08.9	Matthias Leitner (AUT)	2:10.3	Charles Bozon (FRA)	2:10.4
Giant Slalom	Roger Staub (SUI)	1:48.3	Josef Stiegler (AUT)	1:48.7	Ernst Hinterseer (AUT)	1:49.1
Women						
Downhill	Heidi Biebl (GER)*	1:37.6	Penny Pitou (USA)	1:38.6	Traudl Hecher (AUT)	1:38.9
Slalom	Anne Heggtveit (CAN)	1:49.6	Betsy Snite (USA)	1:52.9	Barbara Henneberger (GER)*	1:56.6
Giant Slalom	Yvonne Rüegg (SUI)	1:39.9	Penny Pitou (USA)	1:40.0	Giuliana Chenal-Minuzzo (ITA)	1:40.2
Nordic Skiing						
Men						
15 km Cross-Country Skiing	Haakon Brusveen (NOR)	51:55.5	Sixten Jernberg (SWE)	51:58.6	Veikko Hakulinen (FIN)	52:03.0
30 km Cross-Country Skiing	Sixten Jernberg (SWE)	1:51:03.9	Rolf Rämgard (SWE)	1:51:16.9	Nikolai Anikin (URS)	1:52:28.2
50 km Cross-Country Skiing	Kalevi Hämäläinen (FIN)	2:59:06.3	Veikko Hakulinen (FIN)	2:59:26.7	Rolf Rämgard (SWE)	3:02:46.7
4 x 10 km	Finland	2:18:45.6	Norway	2:18:46.4	USSR	2:21:21.6
Ski Jumping	Helmut Recknagel (GER)*	227.2	Niilo Halonen (FIN)	222.6	Otto Leodolter (AUT)	219.4
Nordic Combined	Georg Thoma (GER)*	457.952	Tormod Knutsen (NOR)	453.000	Nikolai Gusakov (URS)	452.000
Women						
10 km Cross-Country Skiing	Maria Gusakova (URS)	39:46.6	Lubov Baranova-Kozyryeva (URS)	40:04.2	Radja Jeroschina (URS)	40:06.0
3 x 5 km	Sweden	1:04:21.4	USSR	1:05:02.6	Finland	1:06:27.5
Biathlon	Klas Lestander (SWE)	1:33:21.6	Antti Tyrväinen (FIN)	1:33:57.7	Alexander Privalov (URS)	1:34:54.2
Figure Skating						
Women	Carol Heiss (USA)		Sjoukje Dijkstra (HOL)	1424.8	Barbara Roles (USA)	1414.9
Men	David Jenkins (USA)		Karol Divin (TCH)	1414.3	Donald Jackson (CAN)	1401.0
Pairs	Barbara Wagner/Robert Paul (CAN)		Marika Kilius/Hans-Jürgen Bäumler (GER)*	76.8	Nancy Ludington/Ronald Ludington (USA)	76.2
Speed Skating						
Men						
500 m	Yevgeniy Grischin (URS)	40.2	William Disney (USA)	40.3	Rafael Gratsch (URS1)	40.4
1500 m	Roald Aas (NOR)	2:10.4			Boris Stenin (URS)	2:11.5
	Yevgeniy Grischin (URS)	2:10.4				
5000 m	Viktor Kositschkin (URS)	7:51.3	Knut Johannesen (NOR)	8:00.8	Jan Pesman (HOL)	8:05.1
10,000 m	Knut Johannesen (NOR)	15:46.6	Viktor Kositschkin (URS)	15:49.2	Kjell Bäckman (SWE)	16:14.2
Women						
500 m	Helga Haase (GER)*	45.9	Natalya Dontschenko (URS)	46.0	Jeanne Ashworth (USA)	46.1
1000 m	Klara Guseva (URS)	1:34.1	Helga Haase (GER)*	1:34.3	Tamara Rylova (URS)	1:34.8
1500 m	Lidia Skoblikova (URS)	2:25.2	Elvira Seroczynska (POL)	2:25.7	Helena Pilejczyk (POL)	2:27.1
3000 m	Lidia Skoblikova (URS)	5:14.3	Valentina Stenina (URS)	5:16.9	Eevi Huttunen (FIN)	5:21.0
Ice Hockey	USA		Canada		USSR	

* representing a combined German team

Rome 1960

25 August–11 September

Participants: 5346 / Men: 4736, Women: 610, Countries: 83,
Sports: 17. Events: 150
Final Torchbearer: Giancarlo Peris

Medals Table

PLACE	COUNTRY	GOLD	SILVER	BRONZE
1	USSR	42	28	29
2	USA	34	21	16
3	Italy	13	10	13
4	Germany★	12	19	11
5	Australia	8	8	6

Outstanding Athletes

PLACE	NAME (NATIONALITY)	DISCIPLINE	G	S	B
1	Boris Shakhlin (URS)	Gymnastics	4	2	1
2	Larissa Latynina (URS)	Gymnastics	3	2	1
3	Takashi Ono (JPN)	Gymnastics	3	1	2
4	Chris von Saltza (USA)	Swimming	3	1	–
5	Wilma Rudolph (USA)	Athletics	3	–	–

EVENT	GOLD		SILVER		BRONZE	
Athletics						
Men						
100 m	Armin Hary (GER)★	10.2	David Sime (USA)	10.2	Peter Radford (GBR)	10.3
200 m	Livio Berutti (ITA)	20.5	Lester Carney (USA)	20.6	Abdoulaye Seye (FRA)	20.7
400 m	Otis Davis (USA	44.9	Carl Kaufmann (GER)★	44.9	Malcolm Spence (SAF)	45.5
800 m	Peter Snell (NZL)	1:46.3	Roger Moens (BEL)	1:46.5	George Kerr (ANT)	1:47.1
1500 m	Herbert Elliott (AUS)	3:35.6	Michel Jazy (FRA)	3:38.4	Istvan Rozsavölgyi (HUN)	3:39.2
5000 m	Murray Halberg (NZL)	13:43.4	Hans Grodotzki (GER)★	13:44.6	Kasimierz Zimny (POL)	13:44.8
10,000 m	Pjotr Bolotnikov (URS)	28:32.2	Hans Grodotzki (GER)★	28:37.0	David Power (AUS)	28:38.2
Marathon	Abebe Bikila (ETH)	2:15:16.2	Rhadi Ben Abdesselam (MAR)	2:15:41.6	Barry Magee (NZL)	2:17:18.2
110 m Hurdles	Lee Calhoun (USA)	13.8	Willie May (USA)	13.8	Hayes Jones (USA)	14.0
400 m Hurdles	Glenn Davis (USA)	49.3	Clifton Cushman (USA)	49.6	Richard Howard (USA)	49.7
3000 m Steeplechase	Zdislaw Krzyszkowiak (POL)	8:34.2	Nikolai Sokolov (URS)	8:36.4	Semyon Rischtschin (URS)	8:42.2
4 x 100 m	Germany★	39.5	USSR	40.1	Great Britain	40.2
4 x 400 m	USA	3:02.2	Germany★	3:02.7	Antilles	3:04.0
20 km Walk	Vladimir Golubnitschky (URS)	1:34:07.2	Noel Freeman (AUS)	1:34:16.4	Stanley Vickers (GBR)	1:34:56.4
50 km Walk	Don Thompson (GBR)	4:25:30.0	John Ljunggren (SWE)	4:25:47.0	Abdon Pamich (ITA)	4:27:55.4
High Jump	Robert Shavlakadze (URS)	2.16	Valeriy Brumel (URS)	2.16	John Thomas (USA)	2.14
Pole Vault	Donald Bragg (USA)	4.70	Ron Morris (USA)	4.60	Eeles Landström (FIN)	4.55
Long Jump	Ralph Boston (USA)	8.12	Irvin Roberson (USA)	8.11	Igor Ter-Ovanesian (URS)	8.04
Triple Jump	Jozef Schmidt (POL)	16.81	Vladimir Goryayev (URS)	16.63	Vitold Kreyer (URS)	16.43
Shot	Bill Nieder (USA)	19.68	Parry O'Brien (USA)	19.11	Dallas Long (USA)	19.01
Discus	Al Oerter (USA)	59.18	Richard Babka (USA)	58.02	Dick Cochran (USA)	57.16
Hammer	Vasiliy Rudenkov (URS)	67.10	Gyula Zsivotzky (HUN)	65.79	Tadeusz Rut (POL)	65.64
Javelin	Viktor Tsibulenko (URS)	84.64	Walter Krüger (GER)★	79.36	Gergely Kulcsar (HUN)	78.57
Decathlon	Rafer Johnson (USA)	8392	Chuan-Kwang Yang (TPE)	8334	Vassily Kusnetsov (URS)	7809
Women						
100 m	Wilma Rudolph (USA)	11.0	Dorothy Hyman (GBR)	11.3	Giuseppina Leone (ITA)	11.3
200 m	Wilma Rudolph (USA)	24.0	Jutta Heine (GER)★	24.4	Dorothy Hyman (GBR)	24.7
800 m	Ludmilla Schevtsova (URS)	2:04.3	Brenda Jones (AUS)	2:04.4	Ursula Donath (GER)★	2:05.6
80 m Hurdles	Irina Press (URS)	10.8	Carol Quinton (GBR)	10.9	Gisela Birkemeyer-Köhler (GER)★	11.0
4 x 100 m	USA	44.5	Germany★	44.8	Poland	45.0
High Jump	Yolanda Balas (ROM)	1.85	Jaroslawa Jozwiakowska (POL)	1.71		
			Dorothy Shirley (GBR)	1.71		
Long Jump	Vera Krepkina (URS)	6.37	Elzbieta Krzesinska (POL)	6.27	Hildrun Claus (GER)★	6.21
Shot	Tamara Press (URS)		Johanna Lüttge (GER)★	16.61	Earlene Brown (USA)	16.42
Discus	Nina Ponomaryeva (URS)	55.10	Tamara Press (URS)	52.59	Lia Manoliu (ROM)	52.36
Javelin	Elvira Ozolina (URS)	55.98	Dana Zátopková (TCH)	53.78	Birute Kalediena (URS)	53.45
Swimming						
Men						
100 m Freestyle	John Devitt (AUS)	55.2	Lance Larson (USA)	55.2	Manuel Dos Santos (BRA)	55.4
400 m Freestyle	Murray Rose (AUS)	4:18.3	Tsuyoshi Yamanaka (JPN)	4:21.4	John Konrads (AUS)	4:21.8
1500 m Freestyle	John Konrads (AUS)	17:19.6	Murray Rose (AUS)	17:21.7	George Breen (USA)	17:30.6
100 m Backstroke	David Theile (AUS)	1:01.9	Frank McKinney (USA)	1:02.1	Robert Bennett (USA)	1:02.3
200 m Breaststroke	Bill Mulliken (USA)	2:37.4	Yoshihiko Osaki (JPN)	2:38.0	Wilger Mensonides (HOL)	2:39.7
200 m Butterfly	Michael Troy (USA)	2:12.8	Neville Hayes (AUS)	2:14.6	David Gillanders (USA)	2:15.3
4 x 200 m Freestyle Relay	USA	8:10.2	Japan	8:13.2	Australia	8:13.8
4 x 100 m Medley Relay	USA	4:05.4	Australia	4:12.0	Japan	4:12.2

EVENT	GOLD		SILVER		BRONZE	
Springboard Diving	Gary Tobian (USA)	170.00	Samuel Hall (USA)	167.08	Juan Batello (MEX)	162.30
Highboard Diving	Robert Webster (USA)	165.56	Gary Tobian (USA)	165.25	Brian Phelps (GBR)	157.13
Water Polo	Italy		USSR		Hungary	
Women						
100 m Freestyle	Dawn Fraser (AUS)	1:01.2	Chris v. Saltza (USA)	1:02.8	Natalie Steward (GBR)	1:03.1
400 m Freestyle	Chris von Saltza (USA)	4:50.6	Jane Cederquist (SWE)	4:53.9	Catarina Lagerberg (HOL)	4:56.9
100 m Backstroke	Lynn Burke (USA)	1:09.3	Natalie Steward (GBR)	1:10.8	Satoko Tanaka (JPN)	1:11.4
200 m Breaststroke	Anita Lonsbrough (GBR)	2:49.5	Wiltrud Urselmann (GER)★	2:50.0	Barbara Göbel (GER)★	2:53.6
100 m Butterfly	Carolyn Schuler (USA)	1:09.5	Marianne Heemskerk (HOL)	1:10.4	Janice Andrew (AUS)	1:12.2
4 x 100 m Freestyle Relay	USA	4:08.9	Australia	4:11.3	Germany	4:19.7
4 x 100 m Medley Relay	USA	4:41.1	Australia	4:45.9	Germany	4:47.6
Springboard Diving	Ingrid Krämer (GER)★	155.81	Paula J. Myers-Pope (USA)	141.24	Elizabeth Ferris (GBR)	139.09
Highboard Diving	Ingrid Krämer (GER)★	91.28	Paula J. Myers-Pope (USA)	88.94	Ninel Krutova (URS)	86.99
Boxing						
Flyweight(- 51 kg)	Gyula Török (HUN)		Sergey Sivko (URS)		Kiyoshi Tanabe (JPN)	
					Abdel Elgiundi (VAR)	
Bantamweight (- 54 kg)	Oleg Grigoryev (URS)		Primo Zamparini (ITA)		Oliver Taylor (AUS)	
					Brunon Bendig (POL)	
Featherweight (- 57 kg)	Francesco Musso (ITA)		Jerzy Adamski (POL)		Jorma Limmonen (FIN)	
					William Meyers (SAF)	
Lightweight (- 60 kg)	Kasimierz Pazdzior (POL)		Sandro Lopopoli (ITA)		Richard McTaggart (GBR)	
					Abel Laudonio (ARG)	
Light-Welterweight (- 63.5 kg)	Bohumil Nemecek (TCH)		Clement Quartey (GHA)		Quincey Daniels (USA)	
					Marian Kasprzyk (POL)	
Welterweight (- 67 kg)	Giovanni Benvenuti (ITA)		Yuriy Radonyak (URS)		Leszek Drogosz (POL)	
					James Lloyd (GBR)	
Light-Middleweight (- 71 kg)	Wilbert McClure (USA)		Carmelo Bossi (ITA)		Boris Lagutin (URS)	
					Bill Fisher (USA)	
Middleweight (- 75 kg)	Edward Crook (USA)		Tadeusz Walasek (POL)		Ion Monea (ROM)	
					Yevgeniy Feofanov (URS)	
Light-Heavyweight (- 81 kg)	Cassius Clay (USA)		Zbiegniew Pietrzykowski (POL)		Giulio Sarandi (ITA)	
					Antony Madigan (AUS)	
Heavyweight (+ 81 kg)	Franco De Piccoli (ITA)		Daniel Bekker (SAF)		Günter Siegmund (GER)★	
					Josef Nemec (TCH)	
Weightlifting						
Bantamweight (- 56 kg)	Charles Vinci (USA)	345.0	Yoshinobu Miyake (JPN)	337.5	Esmail Khan(IRN)	330.0
Featherweight (- 60 kg)	Yevgeniy Minayev (URS)	372.5	Isaac Berger (USA)	362.5	Sebastino Mannironi (ITA)	352.5
Lightweight (- 67.5 kg)	Viktor Bushuyev (URS)	397.5	Howe-Liang Tan (SIN)	380.0	Abdul Wahid Aziz (IRQ)	380.0
Middleweight (- 75 kg)	Alexander Kurynow (URS)	473.5	Thomas Kono (USA)	427.5	Gyözö Veres (HUN)	405.0
Light-Heavyweight(- 82.5 kg)	Ireneusz Palinski (POL)	442.5	James George (USA	430.0	Jan Bochenek (POL)	420.0
Middle-Heavyweight (- 90 kg)	Arkadiy Vorobyev (URS)	472.5	Trofim Lomakin (URS)	457.5	Louis Martin (GBR)	445.0
Heavyweight (+ 90 kg)	Yuriy Vlassov (URS)	537.5	James Bradford (USA)	512.5	Norbert Schemansky (USA)	500.0
Greco-Roman Wrestling						
Flyweight (- 52 kg)	Dumitru Pirvulescu (ROM)		Osman Sayed (UAE)		Mohamed Paziraye (IRN)	
Bantamweight (- 57 kg)	Oleg Karavayev (URS)		Ion Cernea (ROM)		Petrov Dinko (BUL)	
Featherweight (- 62 kg)	Müzahir Sille (TUR)		Imre Polyák (HUN)		Konstantin Vyrupayev (URS)	
Lightweight (- 67 kg)	Avtandil Koridze (URS)		Bronislav Martinovic (YUG)		Gustaf Freij (SWE)	
Welterweight (- 73 kg)	Mithat Bayrak (TUR)		Günther Maritschnigg (GER)★		René Schiermeyer (FRA)	
Middleweight (- 79 kg)	Dimiter Dobrev (BUL)		Lothar Metz (GER)★		Ion Taranu (ROM)	
Light-Heavyweight (- 87 kg)	Tevfik Kis (TUR)		Krali Bimbalov (BUL)		Givi Kartoziya (URS)	
Heavyweight (+ 87 kg)	Ivan Bogdan (URS)		Wilfried Dietrich (GER)★		Bohumil Kubát (TCH)	
Freestyle Wrestling						
Flyweight (- 52 kg)	Ahmet Bilek (TUR)		Masayuki Matsubara (JPN)		Mohamed Saifpour Saidabadi (IRN)	
Bantamweight (- 57 kg)	Terrence McCann (USA)		Nejdet Zalev (BUL)		Tadeusz Trojanowski (POL)	
Featherweight (- 62 kg)	Mustafa Dagistanli (TUR)		Stantcho Ivanov (BUL)		Vladimir Rubashvili (URS)	
Lightweight (- 67 kg)	Shelby Wilson (USA)		Vladimir Sinyavski (URS)		Enyu Dimov (BUL)	
Welterweight (- 73 kg)	Douglas Blubaugh (USA)		Ismail Ogan (TUR)		Muhammed Bashir (PAK)	
Middleweight (- 79 kg)	Hasan Güngör (TUR)		Georgiy Skhirtladze (URS)		Hans Y. Antonsson (SWE)	
Light-Heavyweight (- 87 kg)	Ismet Atli (TUR)		Cholam-R. Takhti (IRN)		Anatoliy Albul (URS)	
Heavyweight (+ 87 kg)	Wilfried Dietrich (GER)★		Hamit Kaplan (TUR)		Savkus Dzarassov (URS)	
Fencing						
Individual Foil - Men	Viktor Zhdanovich (URS)	7	Yuriy Sissikin (URS)	4	Albert Axelrod (USA)	3

EVENT	GOLD		SILVER		BRONZE	
Team Foil – Men	USSR		Italy		Germany★	
Individual Épée	Giuseppe Delfino (ITA)	5	Allan Jay (GBR)	5	Bruno Khabarov (URS)	4
Team Épée	Italy		Great Britain		USSR	
Individual Sabre	Rudolf Kárpáti (HUN)	5	Zoltán Horváth (HUN)	4	Wladimiro Calarese (ITA)	4
Team Sabre	Hungary		Poland		Italy	
Individual Foil – Women	Heidi Schmid (GER)★	6	Valentina Rastworowa (URS)	5	Maria Vicol (ROM)	4
Team Foil – Women	USSR		Hungary		Italy	
Modern Pentathlon						
Individual	Ferenc Németh (HUN)	5024	Imre Nagy (HUN)	4988	Robert L. Beck (USA)	4981
Team	Hungary	14863	USSR	14309	USA	14192
Canoeing						
Men						
1000 m Kayak Singles K1	Erik Hansen (DEN)	3:53.00	Imre Szöllösi (HUN)	3:54.02	Gert Fredriksson (SWE)	3:55.89
1000 m Kayak Pairs K2	Sweden	3:34.73	Hungary	3:34.91	Poland	3:37.34
4 x 500 m Kayak Singles Relay K1	Germany★	7:39.43	Hungary	7:44.02	Denmark	7:46.09
1000 m Canadian Singles C1	János Parti (HUN)	4:33.93	Alexander Silayev (URS)	4:34.41	Leon Rotman (ROM)	4:35.87
1000 m Canadian Pairs C2	USSR	4:17.94	Italy	4:20.77	Hungary	4:20.89
Women						
500 m Kayak Singles K1	Antonina Seredina (URS)	2:08.08	Therese Zenz (GER)★	2:08.22	Daniela Walkowiak (POL)	2:10.46
500 m Kayak Pairs K2	USSR	1:54.76	Germany★	1:56.66	Hungary	1:58.22
Rowing						
Single Sculls	Vyacheslav Ivanov (URS)	7:13.96	Achim Hill (GER)★	7:20.21	Teodor Kocerka (POL)	7:21.26
Double Sculls	Czechoslovakia	6:47.50	USSR	6:50.49	Switzerland	6:50.59
Coxless Pairs	USSR	7:02.01	Austria	7:03.17	Finland	7:03.80
Coxed Pairs	Germany★	7:29.14	USSR	7:30.17	USA	7:34.58
Coxless Fours	USA	6:26.26	Italy	6:28.78	USSR	6:29.62
Coxed Fours	Germany★	6:39.12	France	6:41.62	Italy	6:43.72
Coxed Eights	Germany★	5:57.18	Canada	6:01.52	Czechoslovakia	6:04.84
Yachting						
Finn Class	Paul Elvström (DEN)	8171	Alexander Chuchelov (URS)	6250	André Neli (BEL)	5934
International Star	USSR	7619	Portugal	6695	USA	6269
Flying Dutchman	Norway	6774	Denmark	5991	Germany★	5882
Dragon	Greece	6733	Argentina	5715	Italy	5704
5.5 m	USA	6900	Denmark	5678	Switzerland	5122
Cycling						
Individual Road Race (175 km)	Viktor Kapitonov (URS)	4:20:37.0	Livio Trape (ITA)	4:20:37.0	Willy van den Berghen (BEL)	4:20:57.0
100 km Road Team Time Trial	Italy	2:14:33.53	Germany★	2:16:56.31	USSR	2:18:41.67
1000 m–Time Trial	Sante Gaiardoni (ITA)	1:07.27	Dieter Gieseler (GER)★	1:08.75	Rostislav Vargashkin (URS)	1:08.86
1000 m Sprint	Sante Gaiardoni (ITA)		Leo Sterckx (BEL)		Valentino Gasparella (ITA)	
2000 m Tandem	Italy		Germany★		USSR	
4000 m Team Pursuit	Italy	4:30.90	Germany★	4:35.78	USSR	
Equestrianism						
Three-Day Event	Lawrence Morgan (AUS)	+ 7.15	Neale Lavis (AUS)	- 16.50	Anton Bühler (SUI)	- 51.21
Three-Day Event (Team)	Australia	-128.18	Switzerland	-386.02	France	-515.71
Grand Prix (Dressage)	Sergey Filatov (URS)	2144.0	Gustav Fischer (SUI)	2087.0	Josef Neckermann (GER)★	2082.0
Grand Prix (Jumping)	Raimondo d' Inzeo (ITA)	-12	Piero d' Inzeo (ITA)	-16	David Broome (GBR)	-23
Grand Prix (Jumping) Team	Germany★	-46.50	USA	-66.00	Italy	-80.50
Shooting						
Free Rifle (3 Positions)	Hubert Hammerer (AUT)	1129	Hans Spillmann (SUI)	1127	Vasiliy Borissov (URS)	1127
Small-Bore Rifle (Prone)	Peter Kohnke (GER)★	590	James Hill (USA)	589	Enrico F. Pelliccioni (VEN)	587
Small-Bore Rifle (3 Positions)	Viktor Shamburkin (URS)	1149	Marat Niyasov (URS)	1145	Klaus Zähringer (GER)★	1139
Rapid-Fire Pistol	William McMillan (USA)	587/147	Pentti Linnosvuo (FIN)	587/139	Aleksandr Zabelin (URS)	587/135
Free Pistol (50 m)	Aleksey Gushchin (URS)	560	Makhmud Umarov (URS)	552/26	Yoshihisa Yoshikawa (JPN)	552/20
Olympic Trap Shooting	Ion Dumitrescu (ROM)	192	Galliano Rossini (ITA)	191	Sergey Kalinin (URS)	190
Gymnastics						
Men						
Individual Combined Exercises	Boris Shakhlin (URS)	115.95	Takashi Ono (JPN)	115.90	Yuri Titov (URS)	115.60
Team	Japan	575.20	USSR	572.70	Italy	559.05
Parallel Bars	Boris Shakhlin (URS)	19.400	Giovanni Carminucci (ITA)	19.375	Takashi Ono (JPN)	19.350

EVENT	GOLD		SILVER		BRONZE	
Floor	Nobuyuki Aihara (JPN)	19.450	Yuriy Titov (URS)	19.325	Franco Menichelli (ITA)	19.275
Horse Vault	Boris Shakhlin (URS)	19.350			Vladimir Portnoi (URS)	19.225
	Takashi Ono (JPN)	19.350				
Horizontal Bar	Takashi Ono (JPN)	19.600	Masao Takemoto (JPN)	19.525	Boris Shakhlin (URS)	19.475
					Welik Kapaszow (BUL)	19.425
Rings	Albert Azaryan (URS)	19.725	Boris Schakhlin (URS)	19.500	Takashi Ono (JPN)	19.425
Pommel Horse	Boris Shakhlin (URS)	19.375	Shuji Tsurumi (JPN)	19.150		
	Eugen Ekman (FIN)	19.375				
Women						
Individual Combined Exercises	Larisa Latynina (URS)	77.031	Sofia Muratova (URS)	76.696	Polina Astakova (URS)	76.164
Team	USSR	382.320	Czechoslovakia	373.323	Romania	372.053
Floor	Larissa Latynina (URS)	19.583	Polina Astakova (URS)	19.532	Tamara Lyukina (URS)	19.449
Horse Vault	Margarita Nikolajewa (URS)	19.316	Sofia Muratova (URS)	19.049	Larissa Latynina (URS)	19.016
Beam	Eva Bosaková (TCH)	19.283	Larissa Latynina (URS)	19.233	Sofia Muratova (URS)	19.232
Asymmetrical Bars	Polina Astakova (URS)	19.616	Larissa Latynina (URS)	19.416	Tamara Lyukina (URS)	19.399
Basketball	USA		USSR		Brazil	
Soccer	Yugoslavia		Denmark		Hungary	
Hockey	Pakistan		India		Spain	

★ representing a combined German team

Innsbruck 1964

29 January – 9 February

Participants: 1091 / Men: 891, Women: 200, Countries: 36,
Sports: 8, Events: 34
Final Torchbearer: Joseph Rieder

Medals Table

PLACE	COUNTRY	GOLD	SILVER	BRONZE
1	USSR	11	8	6
2	Austria	4	5	3
3	Norway	3	6	6
4	Finland	3	4	3
5	France	3	4	–

Outstanding Athletes

PLACE	NAME (NATIONALITY)	DISCIPLINE	G	S	B
1	Lydia Skoblikova (URS)	Speed Skating	4	–	–
2	Klaudia Boyarskikh (URS)	Nordic Skiing	3	–	–
3	Eero Mäntyranta (FIN)	Nordic Skiing	2	1	–
4	Sixten Jernberg (SWE)	Nordic Skiing	2	–	1
5	Toralf Engan (NOR)	Nordic Skiing	1	1	–
	Christine Goitschel (FRA)	Alpine Skiing	1	1	–
	Marielle Goitschel (FRA)	Alpine Skiing	1	1	–
	Veikko Kankkonen (FIN)	Nordic Skiing	1	1	–
	Yevdokia Mekshilo (URS)	Nordic Skiing	1	1	–
	Assar Rönnlund (SWE)	Nordic Skiing	1	1	–

EVENT	GOLD		SILVER		BRONZE	
Alpine Skiing						
Men						
Downhill	Egon Zimmermann (AUT)	2:18.16	Leo Lacroix (FRA)	2:18.90	Wolfgang Bartels (GER)★	2:19:48
Slalom	Josef Stiegler (AUT)	2:11.13	William Kidd (USA)	2:11.27	James Heuga (USA)	2:11.52
Giant Slalom	François Bonlieu (FRA)	1:46:71	Karl Schranz (AUT)	1:47.09	Josef Stiegler (AUT)	1:48:05
Women						
Downhill	Christl Haas (AUT)	1:55.39	Edith Zimmermann (AUT)	1:56:42	Traudl Hecher (AUT)	1:56:66
Slalom	Christine Goitschel (FRA)	1:29.86	Marielle Goitschel (FRA)	1:30.77	Jean Saubert (USA)	1:13.36
Giant Slalom	Marielle Goitschel (FRA)	1:52.24	Christine Goitschel (FRA)	1:53:11		
			Jean Saubert (USA)	1:53:11		
Nordic Skiing						
Men						
15 km Cross-Country Skiing	Eero Mäntyranta (FIN)	50:54.1	Harald Grönningen (NOR)	51:34.8	Sixten Jernberg (SWE)	51:42.2
30 km Cross-Country Skiing	Eero Mäntyranta (FIN)	1:30:50.7	Harald Grönningen (NOR)	1:32:02.3	Igor Voronchikin (URS)	1:32:15.8

EVENT	GOLD		SILVER		BRONZE	
50 km	Sixten Jernberg (SWE)	2:43:52.6	Assar Rönnlund (SWE)	2:44:58.2	Arto Tiainen (FIN)	2:45:30.4
4 x 10 km	Sweden	2:18:34.6	Finland	2:18:42.4	USSR	2:18:46.9
Ski Jumping (70 m)	Veikko Kankkonen (FIN)	229.9	Toralf Engan (NOR)	226.3	Torgeir Brandtzæg (NOR)	222.9
Ski Jumping (90 m)	Toralf Engan (NOR)	230.7	Veikko Kankkonen (FIN)	228.9	Torgeir Brandtzæg (NOR)	227.2
Nordic Combined	Tormod Knutsen (NOR)	469.28	Nikolai Kiselyev (URS)	453.04	Georg Thoma (GER)★	452.88
Women						
5 km	Klaudia Boyarskikh (URS)	17:50.5	Mirja Lehtonen (FIN)	17:52.9	Alevtina Koltchina (URS)	18:08.4
10 km	Klaudia Boyarskikh (URS)	40:24.3	Yevdokia Mekshilo (URS)	40:26.6	Maria Gusakova (URS)	40:46.6
3 x 5 km	USSR	59:20.2	Sweden	1:01:27.0	Finland	1:02:45.1
Biathlon 20 km	Vladimir Melanin (URS)	1:20:26.8	Alexander Privalov (URS)	1:23:42.5	Olav Jordet (NOR)	1:24:38.8
Figure Skating						
Women	Sjoukje Dijkstra (HOL)		Regine Heitzer (AUT)		Petra Burka (CAN)	
Men	Manfred Schnelldorfer (GER)★		Alain Calmat (FRA)		Scott Allen (USA)	
Pairs	Ludmilla Belousova/		Marika Kilius/		Debbi Wilkes/	
	Oleg Protopopov (URS)		Hans-Jürgen Bäumler (GER)★		Guy Revell (CAN)	
Speed Skating						
Men						
500 m	Richard McDermott (USA)	40.1	Yevgeniy Grischin (URS)	40.6		
			Vladimir Orlov (URS)	40.6		
			Alv Gjestvang (NOR)	40.6		
1500 m	Ants Antson (URS)	2:10.3	Cornelis Verkerk (HOL)	2:10.6	Villy Haugen (NOR)	2:11.2
5000 m	Knut Johannesen (NOR)	7:38.4	Per Ivar Moe (NOR)	7:38.6	Fred Anton Maier (NOR)	7:42.0
10,000 m	Jonny Nilsson (SWE)	15:50.1	Fred Anton Maier (NOR)	16:06.0	Knut Johannesen (NOR)	16:06.3
Women						
500 m	Lidia Skoblikova (URS)	45.0	Irina Yegorova (URS)	45.4	Tatyana Sidorova (URS)	45.5
1000 m	Lidia Skoblikova (URS)	1:33.2	Irina Yegorova (URS)	1:34.3	Kaija Mustonen (FIN)	1:34.8
1500 m	Lidia Skoblikova (URS)	2:22.6	Kaija Mustonen (FIN)	2:25.5	Berta Kolokoltseva (URS)	2:27.1
3000 m	Lidia Skoblikova (URS)	5:14.9	Valentina Stenina (URS)	5:18.5		
			Pil Hwa Han (PRK)	5:18.5		
Bobsledding						
2-Man Bob	Great Britain I	4:21.90	Italy II	4:22.02	Italy I	4:22.63
4-Man Bob	Canada I	4:14.46	Austria I	4:15.48	Italy II	4:15.60
Lugeing						
Singles (Men)	Thomas Köhler (GER)★	3:26.77	Klaus-Michael Bonsack (GER)★	3:27.04	Hans Plenk (GER)★	3:30.15
Singles (Women)	Ortrun Enderlein (GER)★	3:24.67	Ilse Geisler (GER)★	3:27.42	Helene Thurrier (AUT)	3:29.06
2-Man Luge	Josef Feistmantl/		Reinhold Senn/		Walter Aussendorfer/	
	Manfred Stengl (AUT)	1:41.62	Helmut Thaler (AUT)	1:41.91	Sigisfred Mair (ITA)	1:42.87
Ice Hockey						
	USSR		Sweden		Czechoslovakia	

★ representing a combined German team

Tokyo 1964

10 October – 24 October

Participants: 5140 / Men: 4457, Women: 683, Countries: 93,
Sports: 19, Events: 163
Final Torchbearer: Yoshinori Sakai

Medals Table

PLACE	COUNTRY	GOLD	SILVER	BRONZE
1	USA	36	28	28
2	USSR	30	31	35
3	Japan	16	5	8
4	Germany★	10	21	19
5	Italy	10	10	7

Outstanding Athletes

PLACE	NAME (NATIONALITY)	DISCIPLINE	G	S	B
1	Don Schollander (USA)	Swimming	4	–	–
2	Vera Cáslavská (TCH)	Gymnastics	3	1	–
	Yukio Endo (JPN)	Gymnastics	3	1	–
	Sharon Stouder (USA)	Swimming	3	1	–
5	Stephen Clark (USA)	Swimming	3	–	–

EVENT	GOLD		SILVER		BRONZE	
Athletics						
Men						
100 m	Robert Hayes (USA)	10.0	Enrique Figuerola (CUB)	10.2	Harry Jerome (CAN)	10.2
200 m	Henry Carr (USA)	20.3	Otis Paul Drayton (USA)	20.5	Edwin Roberts (TRI)	20.6
400 m	Michael Larrabee (USA)	45.1	Wendell Mottley (TRI)	45.2	Andrzej Badenski (POL)	45.6
800 m	Peter Snell (NZL)	1:45.1	William Crothers (CAN)	1:45.6	Wilson Kiprugut (KEN)	1:45.9
1500 m	Peter Snell (NZL)	3:38.1	Josef Odlozil (TCH)	3:39.6	John Davies (NZL)	3:39.6
5000 m	Robert Schul (USA)	13:48.8	Harald Norpoth (GER)★	13:49.6	William Dellinger (USA)	13:49.8
10 000 m	William Mills (USA)	28:24.4	Mohamed Gammoudi (TUN)	28:24.8	Ronald Clarke (AUS)	28:25.8
Marathon	Abebe Bikila (ETH)	2:12:11.2	Basil Heatley (GBR)	2:16:19.2	Kokichi Tsuburaya (JPN)	2:16:22.8
110 m Hurdles	Hayes Jones (USA)	13.6	Blaine Lindgren (USA)	13.7	Anatoliy Mikhailov (URS)	13.7
400 m Hurdles	"Rex" Cawley (USA)	49.6	John Cooper (GBR)	50.1	Salvatore Morale (ITA)	50.1
3000 m Steeplechase	Gaston Roelants (BEL)	8:30.8	Maurice Herriott (GBR)	8:32.4	Ivan Belyayev (URS)	8:33.8
4 x 100 m	USA	39.0	Poland	39.3	France	39.3
4 x 400 m	USA	3:00.7	Great Britain	3:01.6	Trinidad	3:01.7
20 km Walk	Kenneth Matthews (GBR)	1:29:34.0	Dieter Lindner (GER)★	1:31:13.2	Vladimir Golubnichy (URS)	1:31:59.4
50 km Walk	Abdon Pamich (ITA)	4:11:12.4	Paul V. Nihill (GBR)	4:11:31.2	Ingvar Pettersson (SWE)	4:14:17.4
High Jump	Valeriy Brumel (URS)	2.18	John Thomas (USA)	2.18	John Rambo (USA)	2.18
Pole Vault	Fred Hansen (USA)	5.10	Wolfgang Reinhardt (GER)★	5.05	Klaus Lehnertz (GER)★	5.00
Long Jump	Lynn Davies (GBR)	8.07	Ralph Boston (USA)	8.03	Igor Ter-Ovanesyan (URS)	7.99
Triple Jump	Jozef Schmidt (POL)	16.85	Oleg Fedoseyev (URS)	16.58	Viktor Kravchenko (URS)	16.57
Shot	Dallas Long (USA)	20.33	Randy Matson (USA)	20.20	Vilmos Varju (HUN)	19.39
Discus	Al Oerter (USA)	61.00	Ludvik Danek (TCH)	60.52	David Weill (USA)	59.49
Hammer	Romuald Klim (URS)	69.74	Gyula Zsivótzky (HUN)	69.09	Uwe Beyer (GER)★	68.09
Javelin	Pauli Nevala (FIN)	82.66	Gergely Kulcsar (HUN)	82.32	Janis Lusis (URS)	80.57
Decathlon	Willi Holdorf (GER)★	7887	Rein Aun (URS)	7842	Hans-Joachim Walde (GER)★	7809
Women						
100 m	Wyomia Tyus (USA)	11.4	Edith McGuire (USA)	11.6	Ewa Klobukowska† (POL)	11.6
200 m	Edith McGuire (USA)	23.0	Irena Kirszenstein (POL)	23.1	Marilyn Black (AUS)	23.1
400 m	Betty Cuthbert (AUS)	52.0	Ann Packer (GBR)	52.2	Judith Amoore (AUS)	53.4
800 m	Ann Packer (GBR)	2:01.1	Maryvonne Dupureur (FRA)	2:01.9	Ann Chamberlain (NZL)	2:02.8
80 m Hurdles	Karin Balzer (GER)★	10.5	Tereza Ciepla (POL)	10.5	Pamela Kilborn (AUS)	10.5
4 x 100 m	Poland	43.6	USA	43.9	Great Britain	44.0
High Jump	Iolanda Balas (ROM)	1.90	Michele Brown-Mason (AUS)	1.80	Taisia Chenchik (URS)	1.78
Long Jump	Mary Rand (GBR)	6.76	Irena Kirszenstein (POL)	6.60	Tatyana Schelkanova (URS)	6.42
Shot	Tamara Press (URS)	18.14	Renate Garisch (GER)★	17.61	Galina Zybina (URS)	17.45
Discus	Tamara Press (URS)	57.27	Ingrid Lotz (GER)★	57.21	Lia Manoliu (ROM)	56.97
Javelin	Mihaela Penes (ROM)	60.54	Marta Rudas (HUN)	58.27	Yelena Gorchakova (URS)	57.06
Pentathlon	Irina Press (URS)	5246	Mary Rand (GBR)	5035	Galina Bystrova (URS)	4956

† 1967 Barred from competing as a result of a negative sex test

Swimming						
Men						
100 m Freestyle	Don Schollander (USA)	53.4	Robert McGregor (GBR)	53.5	Hans-Joachim Klein (GER)★	54.0
400 m Freestyle	Don Schollander (USA)	4:12.2	Frank Wiegand (GER)★	4:14.9	Allan Wood (GBR)	4:15.1
1500 m Freestyle	Robert Windle (AUS)	17:01.7	John Nelson (USA)	17:03.0	Allan Wood (GBR)	17:07.7
200 m Backstroke	Jed Graef (USA)	2:10.3	Gary Dilley (USA)	2:10.5	Robert Bennett (USA)	2:13.1
200 m Breaststroke	Ian O'Brien (AUS)	2:27.8	Georgy Prokopenko (URS)	2:28.2	Chester Jastremski (USA)	2:29.6
200 m Butterfly	Kevin Berry (AUS)	2:06.6	Carl Robie (USA)	2:07.5	Fred Schmidt (USA)	2:09.3
400 m Medley	Richard Roth (USA)	4:45.4	Roy Saari (USA)	4:47.1	Gerhard Hetz (GER)★	4:51.0
4 x 100 m Freestyle Relay	USA	3:33.2	Germany★	3:37.2	Australia	3:39.1
4 x 200 m Freestyle Relay	USA	7:52.1	Germany★	7:59.3	Japan	8:03.8
4 x 100 m Medley	USA	3:58.4	Germany★	4:01.6	Australia	4:02.3
Springboard Diving	Ken Sitzberger (USA)	159.90	Francis Gorman (USA)	157.63	Larry Andreasen (USA)	143.77
Highboard Diving	Robert Webster (USA)	148.58	Klaus Dibiasi (ITA)	147.54	Thomas Gompf (USA)	146.57
Water Polo	Hungary		Yugoslavia		USSR	
Women						
100 m Freestyle	Dawn Fraser (AUS)	59.5	Sharon Stouder (USA)	59.9	Kathleen Ellis (USA)	1:00.8
400 m Freestyle	Virginia Duenkel (USA)	4:43.3	Marilyn Ramenofsky (USA)	4:44.6	Terri L. Stickles (USA)	4:47.2
100 m Backstroke	Cathy Ferguson (USA)	1:07.7	Christine Caron (FRA)	1:07.9	Virginia Duenkel (USA)	1:08.0
200 m Breaststroke	Galina Prozumenschikova (URS)	2:46.4	Claudia Kolb (USA)	2:47.6	Svetlana Babanina (URS)	2:48.6
100 m Butterfly	Sharon Stouder (USA)	1:04.7	Ada Kok (HOL)	1:05.6	Kathleen Ellis (USA)	1:06.0
400 m Medley	Donna De Varona (USA)	5:18.7	Sharon Finneran (USA)	5:24.1	Martha Randall (USA)	5:24.2
4 x 100 m Freestyle Relay	USA	4:03.8	Australia	4:06.9	Netherlands	4:12.0
4 x 100 m Medley	USA	4:33.9	Netherlands	4:37.0	USSR	4:39.2
Springboard Diving	Ingrid Engel-Krämer (GER)★	145.00	Jeanne Collier (USA)	138.36	Mary Willard (USA)	138.18
Highboard Diving	Lesley Bush (USA)	99.80	Ingrid Engel-Krämer (GER)★	98.45	Galina Alekseyeva (URS)	97.60

EVENT	GOLD		SILVER		BRONZE	
Boxing						
Flyweight (- 51 kg)	Fernando Atzori (ITA)		Artur Olech (POL)		Stanislav Sorokin (URS)	
					Robert Carmody (USA)	
Bantamweight (- 54 kg)	Takao Sakurai (JPN)		Shin-Cho Chung (KOR)		Juan Fabila Mendoza (MEX)	
					Washington Rodriguez (URU)	
Featherweight (- 57 kg)	Stanislav Stepashkin (URS)		Anthony Villanueva (PHI)		Heinz Schulz (GER)★	
					Charles Brown (USA)	
Lightweight (- 60 kg)	Józef Grudzien (POL)		Vellikton Barannikov (URS)		James McCourt (IRL)	
					Ronald Harris (USA)	
Light-Welterweight (- 63.5 kg)	Jerzy Kulej (POL)		Yewgeniy Frolov (URS)		Eddie Blay (GHA)	
					Habib Galhia (TUN)	
Welterweight (- 67 kg)	Marian Kasprzyk (POL)		Ritschardas Tamulis (URS)		Pertti Purhonen (FIN)	
					Silvano Bertini (ITA)	
Light-Middleweight (- 71 kg)	Boris Lagutin (URS)		Joseph Gonzales (FRA)		Nojim Maiyegun (NGA)	
					Jozef Grzesiak (POL)	
Middleweight (- 75 kg)	Valeriy Popentschenko (URS)		Emil Schulz (GER)★		Francesco Valle (ITA)	
					Tadeusz Walasek (POL)	
Light-Heavyweightt (- 81 kg)	Cosimo Pinto (ITA)		Aleksey Kisseljov (URS)		Alexandar Nikolov (BUL)	
					Zbiegniew Pietrzykowski (POL)	
Heavyweight (+ 81 kg)	Joe Frazier (USA)		Hans Huber (GER)★		Guiseppe Ros (ITA)	
					Vadim Yemelyanov (URS)	
Weightlifting						
Bantamweight (- 56 kg)	Aleksey Vakhonin (URS)	357.5	Imre Földi (HUN)	355.0	Shiro Ichinoseki (JPN)	347.5
Featherweight (- 60 kg)	Yoshinobu Miyake (JPN)	397.5	Isaac Berger (USA)	382.5	Mieczyslaw Nowak (POL)	377.5
Lightweight (- 67.5 kg)	Waldemar Baszanowski (POL)	432.5	Vladimir Kaplunov (URS)	432.5	Marian Zielinski (POL)	420.0
Middleweight (- 75 kg)	Hans Zdrazcla (TCH)	445.0	Viktor Kurentsov (URS)	440.0	Masashi Ouchi (JPN)	437.5
Light-Heavyweight (- 82.5 kg)	Rudolf Plukfelder (URS)	475.0	Geza Toth (HUN)	467.5	Gyözö Veres (HUN)	467.5
Middle-Heavyweight (- 90 kg)	Vladimir Golovanov (URS)	487.5	Louis Martin (GBR)	475.0	Ireneusz Palinski (POL)	467.5
Heavyweight (+ 90 kg)	Leonid Zhabotinsky (URS)	572.5	Yuriy Vlassov (URS)	570.0	Norbert Schemansky (USA)	537.5
Greco-Roman Wrestling						
Flyweight (- 52 kg)	Tsutomu Hanahara (JPN)		Angel Kerezov (BUL)		Dumitru Pirvulescu (ROM)	
Bantamweight (- 57 kg)	Masamitsu Ichiguchi (JPN)		Vladien Trostiansky (URS)		Ion Cernea (ROM)	
Featherweight (- 63 kg)	Imre Polyák (HUN)		Roman Rurua (URS)		Branislav Martinovic (YUG)	
Lightweight (- 70 kg)	Kazim Ayvaz (TUR)		Valeriu Bularca (ROM)		David Gvantseladze (URS)	
Welterweight (- 78 kg)	Anatoliy Kolesov (URS)		Cyril Todorov (BUL)		Bertil Nyström (SWE)	
Middleweight (- 87 kg)	Branislav Simĩc (YUG)		Jiri Kormanik (TCH)		Lothar Metz (GER)★	
Light-Heavyweight (- 97 kg)	Boyan Radev (BUL)		Per Svensson (SWE)		Heinz Kiehl (GER)★	
Heavyweight (+ 97 kg)	Istvan Kozma (HUN)		Anatoliy Roschin (URS)		Wilfried Dietrich (GER)★	
Freestyle Wrestling						
Flyweight (- 52 kg)	Yoshikatsu Yoshida (JPN)		Chang-Sun Chang (KOR)		Said Aliaakbar Haydari (IRN)	
Bantamweight (- 57 kg)	Yojiro Uetake (JPN)		Hüseyn Akbas (TUR)		Aidyn Ibragimov (URS)	
Featherweight (- 63 kg)	Osamu Watanabe (JPN)		Stantcho Ivanov (BUL)		Nodar Kokaschvili (URS)	
Lightweight (- 70 kg)	Enyu Valtschev (BUL)		Klaus Jürgen Rost (GER)★		Iwao Horiuchi (JPN)	
Welterweight (- 78 kg)	Ismail Ogan (TUR)		Guliko Sagaradze (URS)		Mohamad-Ali Sanatkaran (IRN)	
Middleweight (-87 kg)	Prodan Gardschev (BUL)		Hasan Güngör (TUR)		Daniel Brand (USA)	
Light-Heavyweight (- 97 kg)	Alexander Medved (URS)		Ahmet Ayik (TUR)		Said Mustafov (BUL)	
Heavyweight (+ 97 kg)	Alexander Ivanitsky (URS)		Liutvi Djiber (BUL)		Hamit Kaplan (TUR)	
Judo						
Lightweight (73 - 70 kg)	Takehide Nakatani (JPN)		Eric Hänni (SUI)		Oleg Stepanov (URS)	
					Aron Bogulubox (URS)	
Middleweight (- 80 kg)	Isao Okano (JPN)		Wolfgang Hofmann (GER)★		James Bergman (USA)	
					Eui-Tae Kim (KOR)	
Heavyweight (+ 93 kg)	Isao Inokuma (JPN)		Al Harold Rogers (USA)		Anzor Kiknadze (URS)	
					Parnaoz Chikviladze (URS)	
Open Category	Antonius Geesink (HOL)		Akio Kaminaga (JPN)		Klaus Glahn (GER)★	
					Theodore Boronovskis (AUS)	
Fencing						
Individual Foil - Men	Egon Franke (POL)	3	Jean-Claude Magnan (FRA)	2	Daniel Revenu (FRA)	1
Team Foil - Men	USSR		Poland		France	
Individual Épée	Grigoriy Kriss (URS)	2+1	Henry Hoskyns (GBR)	2	Guram Kostova (URS)	1
Team Épée	Hungary		Italy		France	
Individual Sabre	Tibor Pézsa (HUN)	2+1	Claude Arabo (FRA)	2	Umar Mavlikhanov (URS)	1

EVENT	GOLD		SILVER		BRONZE	
Team Sabre	USSR		Italy		Poland	
Individual Foil – Women	Ildiko Ujlaki-Rejto (HUN)	2+2	Helga Mees (GER)★	2+1	Antonella Ragno (ITA)	2
Team Foil – Women	Hungary		USSR		Germany★	
Modern Pentathlon						
Individual	Ferenc Török (HUN)	5516	Igor Novikov (URS)	5067	Albert Mokeyev (URS)	5039
Team	USSR	14961	USA	14189	Hungary	14173
Canoeing						
Men						
1000 m Kayak Singles K1	Rolf Peterson (SWE)	3:57.13	Mihaly Hesz (HUN)	3:57.28	Aurel Vernescu (ROM)	4:00.77
1000 m Kayak Pairs K2	Sweden	3:38.54	Netherlands	3:39.30	Germany★	3:40.69
1000 m Kayak Fours K4	USSR	3:14.67	Germany★	3:15.39	Romania	3:15.51
1000 m Canadian Singles C1	Jürgen Eschert (GER)★	4:35.14	Andrei Igorov (ROM)	4:37.89	Yevgeny Penyayev (URS)	4:38.31
1000 m Canadian Pairs C2	USSR	4:04.64	France	4:06.52	Denmark	4:07.48
Women						
500 m Kayak Singles K1	Ludmila Khvedosyak (URS)	2:12.87	Hilde Lauer (ROM)	2:15.35	Marcia Jones (USA)	2:15.68
500 m Kayak Pairs K2	Germany★	1:56.95	USA	1:59.16	Romania	2:00.25
Rowing						
Single Sculls	Vyacheslav Ivanov (URS)	8:22.51	Achim Hill (GER)★	8:26.24	Gottfried Kottmann (SUI)	8:29.68
Double Sculls	USSR	7:10.66	USA	7:13.16	Czechoslovakia	7:14.23
Coxless Pairs	Canada	7:32.94	Netherlands	7:33.40	Germany★	7:38.63
Coxed Pairs	USA	8:21.23	France	8:23.15	Netherlands	8:23.42
Coxless Fours	Denmark	6:59.30	Great Britain	7:00.47	USA	7:01.37
Coxed Fours	Germany★	7:00.44	Italy	7:02.84	Netherlands	7:06.46
Coxed Eights	USA	6:18.23	Germany★	6:23.29	Czechoslovakia	6:25.11
Yachting						
Finn Class	Willi Kuhweide (GER)★	7638	Peter Barrett (USA)	6373	Henning Wind (DEN)	6190
International Star	Bahamas	5664	USA	5585	Sweden	5527
Flying Dutchman	New Zealand	6255	Great Britain	5556	USA	5158
Dragon	Denmark	5854	Germany★	5826	USA	5523
5.5-m	Australia	5981	Sweden	5254	USA	5106
Cycling						
Individual Road Race (194.83 km)	Mario Zanin (ITA)	4:39:51.63	Kjell A. Rodian (DEN)	4:39:51.65	Walter Godefroot (BEL)	4:39:51:74
Team Road Race	Netherlands	2:26:31.19	Italy	2:26:55.39	Sweden	2:27:11.52
1000-m-Time-Trial	Patrick Sercu (BEL)	1:09.59	Giovanni Pettenella (ITA)	1:10.09	Pierre Trentin (FRA)	1:10.42
1000-m-Sprint	Giovanni Pettenella (ITA)		Sergio Bianchetto (ITA)		Daniel Morelon (FRA)	
2000-m-Tandem	Italy		USSR		Germany★	
4000-m-Individual Pursuit	Jiri Daler (TCH)	5:04.75	Giorgio Ursi (ITA)	5:05.96	Preben Isaksson (DEN)	5:01.90
4000-m-Team Pursuit	Germany★	4:35.67	Italy	4:35.74	Netherlands	4:38.99
Equestrianism						
Three-Day Event	Mauro Checcoli (ITA)	64.40	Carlos Moratorio (ARG)	56.40	Fritz Ligges (GER)★	49.20
Three-Day Event (Team)	Italy	85.80	USA	65.86	Germany	56.73
Grand Prix (Dressage)	Henri Chammartin (SUI)	1504	Harry Boldt (GER)★	1503	Sergey Filatov (URS)	1486
Grand Prix (Dressage) Team	Germany★	2558.0	Switzerland	2526.0	USSR	2311.0
Grand Prix (Jumping)	Pierre Jonquères d'Oriola (FRA)	-9	Hermann Schridde (GER)★	-13.75	Peter Robeson (GBR)	-16.00
Grand Prix (Jumping) Team	Germany★	-68.50	France	-77.75	Italy	-88.50
Shooting						
Free Rifle (3 Positions)	Gary Anderson (USA)	1153	Shota Kveliashvili (URS)	1144	Martin Gunnarsson (USA)	1136
Small-Bore Rifle (Prone)	László Hammerl (HUN)	597	Lones Wigger (USA)	597	Tommy Pool (USA)	596
Small-Bore Rifle (3 Positions)	Lones Wigger (USA)	1164	Velitchko Khristov (BUL)	1152	László Hammerl (HUN)	1151
Rapid-Fire Pistol	Pentti Linnosvuo (FIN)	592	Ion Tripsa (ROM)	591	Lubomir Nacovsky (TCH)	590
Free Pistol (50 m)	Väino Markkanen (FIN)	560	Franklin Green (USA)	557	Yoshihisa Yoshikawa (JPN)	554
Olympic Trap Shooting	Ennio Mattarelli (ITA)	198	Pavel Senichev (URS)	194/25	William Morris (USA)	194/24
Gymnastics						
Men						
Individual Combined Exercises	Yukio Endo (JPN)	115.95	† Shuji Tsurumi (JPN)		†Boris Shaklin (URS)	115.40
		115.40	†Viktor Lisitsky (URS)	115.40	† tied for second place.	
Team	Japan	577.95	USSR	575.45	Germany★	565.10
Parallel Bars	Yukio Endo (JPN)	19.675	Shuji Tsurumi (JPN)	19.450	Franco Menichelli (ITA)	19.35

EVENT	GOLD		SILVER		BRONZE	
Floor	Franco Menichelli (ITA)	19.450	Viktor Lisitsky (URS)	19.350		
			Yukio Endo (JPN)	19.350		
Horse Vault	Haruhiro Yamashita (JPN)	19.600	Viktor Lisitsky (URS)	19.325	Hannu Rantakari (FIN)	19.300
Horizontal Bar	Boris Shaklin (URS)	19.625	Yuri Titov (URS)	19.550	Miroslav Cerar (YUG)	19.500
Rings	Takuji Hayata (JPN)	19.475	Franco Menichelli (ITA)	19.425	Boris Shaklin (URS)	19.400
Pommel Horse	Miroslav Cerar (YUG)	19.525	Shuji Tsurumi (JPN)	19.325	Yuriy Tsapenko (URS)	19.200
Women						
Individual Combined Exercises	Vera Cáslavská (TCH)	77.564	Larissa Latynina (URS)	76.998	Polina Astakova (URS)	76.965
Team	USSR	380.890	Czechoslovakia	379.989	Japan	377.889
Floor	Larissa Latynina (URS)	19.599	Polina Astakova (URS)	19.500	Anikó Janosí (HUN)	19.300
Horse Vault	Vera Cáslavská (TCH)	19.483	Larissa Latynina (URS)	19.283		
			Birgit Radochla (GER)★	19.283		
Beam	Vera Cáslavská (TCH)	19.449	Tamara Manina (URS)	19.399	Larissa Latynina (URS)	19.382
Asymmetrical Bars	Polina Astakova (URS)	19.332	Katalin Makray (HUN)	19.216	Larissa Latynina (URS)	19.199
Basketball						
	USA		USSR		Brazil	
Soccer						
	Hungary		Czechoslovakia		Germany★	
Hockey						
	India		Pakistan		Australia	
Volleyball						
Men	USSR		Czechoslovakia		Japan	
Women	Japan		USSR		Poland	

★ representing a combined German team

Grenoble 1968

Participants: 1158 / Men: 947, Women: 211, Countries: 37,
Sports: 8, Events: 35
Final Torchbearer: Alain Calmat

4 February – 18 February
(Official Opening Ceremony 6 February)

Medals Table

PLACE	COUNTRY	GOLD	SILVER	BRONZE
1	**Norway**	6	6	2
2	**USSR**	5	5	3
3	**France**	4	3	2
4	**Italy**	4	–	–
5	**Austria**	3	4	4

Outstanding Athletes

PLACE	NAME (NATIONALITY)	DISCIPLINE	G	S	B
1	**Jean-Claude Killy (FRA)**	Alpine Skiing	3	–	–
2	**Toini Gustafsson (SWE)**	Nordic Skiing	2	1	–
3	**Ole Ellefsæter (NOR)**	Nordic Skiing	2	–	–
	Harald Grönningen (NOR)	Nordic Skiing	2	–	–
	Eugenio Monti (ITA)	Bobsledding	2	–	–
	Luciano de Paolis (ITA)	Bobsledding	2	–	–

EVENT	GOLD		SILVER		BRONZE	
Alpine Skiing						
Men						
Downhill	Jean-Claude Killy (FRA)	1:59.85	Guy Périllat (FRA)	1:59.93	Jean-Daniel Dätwyler (SUI)	2:00.32
Slalom	Jean-Claude Killy (FRA)	1:39.73	Herbert Huber (AUT)	1:39.82	Alfred Matt (AUT)	1:40.09
Giant Slalom	Jean-Claude Killy (FRA)	3:29.28	Willy Favre (SUI)	3:31.50	Heinrich Messner (AUT)	3:31.83
Women						
Downhill	Olga Pall (AUT)	1:40.87	Isabelle Mir (FRA)	1:41.33	Christl Haas (AUT)	1:41.41
Slalom	Marielle Goitschel (FRA)	1:25.86	Nancy Greene (CAN)	1:26.15	Annie Famose (FRA)	1:27.89
Giant Slalom	Nancy Greene (CAN)	1:51.97	Annie Famose (FRA)	1:54.61	Fernande Bochatay (SUI)	1:54.74
Nordic Skiing						
Men						
15 km Cross-Country Skiing	Harald Grönningen (NOR)	47:54.2	Eero Mäntyranta (FIN)	47:56.1	Gunnar Larsson (SWE)	48:33.7
30 km Cross-Country Skiing	Franco Nones (ITA)	1:35:39.2	Odd Martinsen (NOR)	1:36:28.9	Eero Mäntyranta (FIN)	1:36:55.3

EVENT	GOLD		SILVER		BRONZE	
50 km Cross-Country Skiing	Ole Ellefsæter(NOR)	2:28:45.8	Vyacheslav Vedenine (URS)	2:29:02.5	Josef Haas (SUI)	2:29.14.8
4 x 10 km	Norway	2:08:33.5	Sweden	2:10:13.2	Finland	2:10:56.7
Ski Jumping (70 m Hill)	Jiri Raska (TCH)	216.5	Reinhold Bachler (AUT)	214.2	Baldur Preiml (AUT)	212.6
Ski Jumping (90 m Hill)	Vladimir Belusov (URS)	231.3	Jiri Raska (TCH)	229.4	Lars Grini (NOR)	214.3
Nordic Combined	Franz Keller (FRG)	449.04	Alois Kälin (SUI)	447.99	Andreas Kunz (GDR)	444.10
Women						
5 km Cross-Country Skiing	Toini Gustafsson (SWE)	16:45.2	Galina Kulakova (URS)	16:48.4	Alevtina Koltchina (URS)	16:51.6
10 km Cross-Country Skiing	Toini Gustafsson (SWE)	36:46.5	Berit Mørdre (NOR)	37:54.6	Inger Aufles (NOR)	37:59.9
3 x 5 km	Norway	57:30.0	Sweden	57:51.0	USSR	58:13.6
Biathlon						
20 km	Magnar Solberg (NOR)	1:13:45.9	Alexander Tikhonov (URS)	1:14:40.4	Vladimir Gundartsev (URS)	1:18:27.4
4 x 7.5 km	USSR	2:13:02.4	Norway	2:14:50.2	Sweden	2:17:26.3
Figure Skating						
Women	Peggy Fleming (USA)		Gaby Seyfert (GDR)		Hana Masková (TCH)	
Men	Wolfgang Schwarz (AUT)		Timothy Woods (USA)		Patrick Péra (FRA)	
Pairs	Ludmilla Belousova/		Tatyana Schuk/		Margot Glockshuber/	
	Oleg Protopopov (URS)		Alexander Gorelik (URS)		Wolfgang Danne (FRG)	
Speed Skating						
Men						
500 m	Erhard Keller (FRG)	40.3	Magne Thomassen (NOR)	40.5		
			Richard McDermott (USA)	40.5		
1500 m	Cornelis Verkerk (HOL)	2:03.4	Ard Schenk (HOL)	2:05.0		
			Ivar Eriksen (NOR)	2:05.0		
5000 m	Fred Anton Maier (NOR)	7:22.4	Cornelis Verkerk (HOL)	7:23.2	Petrus Nottet (HOL)	7:25.5
10,000 m	Johnny Höglin (SWE)	15:23.6	Fred Anton Maier (NOR)	15:23.9	Örjan Sandler (SWE)	15:31.8
Women						
500 m	Ludmila Titova (URS)	46.1	Mary Meyers (USA)	46.3		
			Dianne Holum (USA)	46.3		
			Jennifer Fish (USA)	46.3		
1000 m	Carolina Geijssen (HOL)	1:32.6	Ludmila Titova (URS)	1:32.9	Dianne Holum (USA)	1:33.4
1500 m	Kaija Mustonen (FIN)	2:22.4	Carolina Geijssen (HOL)	2:22.7	Christina Kaiser (HOL)	2:24.5
3000 m	Johanna Schut (HOL)	4:56.2	Kaija Mustonen (FIN)	5:01.0	Christina Kaiser (HOL)	5:01.3
Bobsledding						
2-Man Bob	Italy I	4:41.54	West Germany I	4:41.54	Romania I	4:44.46
4-Man Bob	Italy I	2:17.39	Austria I	2:17.48	Switzerland I	2:18.04
Lugeing						
Singles (Men)	Manfred Schmid (AUT)	2:52.48	Thomas Köhler (GDR)	2:52.66	Klaus-Michael Bonsack (GDR)	2:53.33
Singles (Women)	Erica Lechner (ITA)	2:28.66	Christa Schmuck (FRG)	2:29.37	Angelika Dünhaupt (FRG)	2:29.56
2-Man Luge	Klaus-Michael Bonsack/		Manfred Schmid/		Wolfgang Winkler/	
	Thomas Köhler (GDR)	1:35.85	Ewald Walch (AUT)	1:36.34	Fritz Nachmann (FRG)	1:37.29
Ice Hockey						
	USSR		Czechoslovakia		Canada	

Mexico City 1968

12 October – 27 October

Participants: 5530/ Men: 4749, Women: 781, Countries: 112,
Sports: 18, Events: 172
Final Torchbearer: Norma Enriqueta Basilio de Sotelo

Medals Table

PLACE	COUNTRY	GOLD	SILVER	BRONZE
1	USA	45	28	34
2	USSR	29	32	30
3	Japan	11	7	7
4	Hungary	10	10	12
5	GDR	9	9	7

Outstanding Athletes

PLACE	NAME (NATIONALITY)	DISCIPLINE	G	S	B
1	Vera Cáslavská (TCH)	Gymnastics	4	2	–
2	Akinori Nakayama (JPN)	Gymnastics	4	1	1
3	Charles Hickcox (USA)	Swimming	3	1	–
4	Sawao Kato (JPN)	Gymnastics	3	–	1
5	Debbie Meyer (USA)	Swimming	3	–	–

EVENT	GOLD		SILVER		BRONZE	
Athletics						
Men						
100 m	Jim Hines (USA)	9.9	Lennox Miller (JAM)	10.0	Charlie Greene (USA)	10.0
200 m	Tommie Smith (USA)	19.8	Peter Norman (AUS)	20.0	John Carlos (USA)	20.0
400 m	Lee Evans (USA)	43.8	Larry James (USA)	43.9	Ronald Freeman (USA)	44.4
800 m	Ralph Doubell (AUS)	1:44.3	Wilson Kiprugut (KEN)	1:44.5	Thomas Farrell (USA)	1:45.4
1500 m	Kipchoge Keino (KEN)	3:34.9	Jim Ryun (USA)	3:37.8	Bodo Tümmler (FRG)	3:39.0
5000 m	Mohamed Gammoudi (TUN)	14:05.0	Kipchoge Keino (KEN)	14:05.2	Naftali Temu (KEN)	14:06."
10,000m	Naftali Temu (KEN)	29:27.4	Mamo Wolde (ETH)	29:28.0	Mohamed Gammoudi (TUN)	29:34.2
Marathon	Mamo Wolde (ETH)	2:20:26.4	Kenji Kimihara (JPN)	2:23:31.0	Michael Ryan (NZL)	2:23:45.0
110 m Hurdles	Willie Davenport (USA)	13.3	Ervin Hall (USA)	13.4	Eddy Ottoz (ITA)	13.4
400 m Hurdles	David Hemery (GBR)	48.12	Gerhard Hennige (FRG)	49.02	John Sherwood (GBR)	49.03
3000 m Steeplechase	Amos Biwott (KEN)	8:51.0	Benjamin Kogo (KEN)	8:51.6	George Young (USA)	8:51.8
4 x 100 m	USA	38.2	Cuba	38.3	France	38.4
4 x 400 m	USA	2:56.1	Kenya	2:59.6	FRG	3:00.5
20 km Walk	Vladimir Golubnichiy (URS)	1:33:58.4	José Pedraza (MEX)	1:34:00.0	Nikolai Smaga (URS)	1:34:03.0
50 km Walk	Christoph Höhne (GDR)	4:20:13.6	Antal Kiss (HUN)	4:30:17.0	Larry Young (USA)	4:31:55.4
High Jump	Dick Fosbury (USA)	2.24	Edward Caruthers (USA)	2.22	Valentin Gavrilov (URS)	2.20
Pole Vault	Robert Seagren (USA)	5.40	Claus Schiprowski (FRG)	5.40	Wolfgang Nordwig (GDR)	5.40
Long Jump	Bob Beamon (USA)	8.90	Klaus Beer (GDR)	8.19	Ralph Boston (USA)	8.16
Triple Jump	Viktor Saneyev (URS)	17.39	Nelson Prudencio (BRA)	17.27	Giuseppe Gentile (ITA)	17.22
Shot	Randy Matson (USA)	20.54	George Woods (USA)	20.12	Eduard Grischin (URS)	20.09
Discus	Al Oerter (USA)	64.78	Lothar Milde (GDR)	63.08	Ludvik Danek (TCH)	62.92
Hammer	Gyula Zsivótzky (HUN)	73.36	Romuald Klim (URS)	73.28	Lázár Lovász (HUN)	69.78
Javelin	Janis Lusis (URS)	90.10	Jorma Kinnunen (FIN)	88.58	Gergely Kulcsar (HUN)	87.06
Decathlon	William Toomey (USA)	8193	Hans- Joachim Walde (FRG)	8111	Kurt Bendlin (FRG)	8064
Women						
100 m	Wyomia Tyus (USA)	11.0	Barbara Ferrell (USA)	11.1	Irena Szewinska-Kirszenstein (POL)	11.1
200 m	Irena Szewinska-Kirszenstein (POL)	22.5	Raelene Boyle (AUS)	22.7	Jennifer Lamy (AUS)	22.8
400 m	Colette Besson (FRA)	52.0	Lillian Board (GBR)	52.1	Natalya Pechenkina (URS)	52.2
800 m	Madeline Manning (USA)	2:00.9	Ilona Silai (ROM)	2:02.5	Maria Gommers (HOL)	2:02.6
80 m Hurdles	Maureen Caird (AUS)	10.3	Pam Kilborn (AUS)	10.4	Chi Cheng (TAI)	10.4
4 x 100 m	USA	42.8	Cuba	43.3	USSR	43.4
High Jump	Miloslava Rezková (TCH)	1.82	Antonina Okorokova (URS)	1.80	Valentina Kozyr (URS)	1.80
Long Jump	Viorica Viscopoleanu (ROM)	6.82	Sheila Sherwood (GBR)	6.68	Tatyana Talyscheva (URS)	6.66
Shot	Margitta Helmboldt (GDR)	19.61	Marita Lange (GDR)	18.78	Nadyezda Chizhova (URS)	18.19
Discus	Lia Manoliu (ROM)	58.28	Liesel Westermann (FRG)	57.76	Jolán Kleiber (HUN)	54.90
Javelin	Angéla Németh (HUN)	60.36	Mihaela Penes (ROM)	59.92	Eva Janko (HUN)	58.04
Pentathlon	Ingrid Becker (FRG)	5098	Liese Prokop (AUT)	4966	Annamária Tóth (HUN)	4959
Swimming						
Men						
100 m Freestyle	Michael Wenden (AUS)	52.2	Ken Walsh (USA)	52.8	Mark Spitz (USA)	53.0
200 m Freestyle	Michael Wenden (AUS)	1:55.2	Don Schollander (USA)	1:55.8	John Nelson (USA)	1:58.1
400 m Freestyle	Michael Burton (USA)	4:09.0	Ralph Hutton (CAN)	4:11.7	Alain Mosconi (FRA)	4:13.3
1500 m Freestyle	Michael Burton (USA)	16:38.9	John Kinsella (USA)	16:57.3	Gregory Brough (AUS)	17:04.7
100 m Backstroke	Roland Matthes (GDR)	58.7	Charles Hickcox (USA)	1:00.2	Ron Mills (AUS)	1:00.5
200 m Backstroke	Roland Matthes (GDR)	2:09.6	Mitchel Ivey (USA)	2:10.6	Jack Horsley (USA)	2:10.9
100 m Breaststroke	Don McKenzie (USA)	1:07.7	Vladimir Kossinsky (URS)	1:08.0	Nikolai Pankin (URS)	1:08.0
200 m Breaststroke	Felipe Muñoz (MEX)	2:28.7	Vladimir Kossinsky (URS)	2:29.2	Brian Job (USA)	2:29.9

EVENT	GOLD		SILVER		BRONZE	
100 m Butterfly	Douglas Russell (USA)	55.9	Mark Spitz (USA)	56.4	Ross Wales (USA)	57.2
200 m Butterfly	Carl Robie (USA)	2:08.7	Martin Woodroffe (GBR)	2:09.0	John Ferris (USA)	2:09.3
200 m Medley	Charles Hickcox (USA)	2:12.0	Gregory Buckingham (USA)	2:13.0	John Ferris (USA)	2:13.3
400 m Medley	Charles Hickcox (USA)	4:48.4	Gary Hall (USA)	4:48.7	Michael Holthaus (FRG)	4:51.4
4 x 100 m Freestyle Relay	USA	3:31.7	USSR	3:34.2	Australia	3:34.7
4 x 200 m Freestyle Relay	USA	7:52.3	Australia	7:53.7	USSR	8:01.6
4 x 100 m Medley Relay	USA	3:54.9	GDR	3:57.5	USSR	4:00.7
Springboard Diving	Bernard Wrightson (USA)	170.15	Klaus Dibiasi (ITA)	159.74	James Henry (USA)	158.09
Highboard Diving	Klaus Dibiasi (ITA)	164.18	Alvaro Gaxiola (MEX)	154.49	Edwin Young (USA)	153.93
Water Polo	Yugoslavia	ussr	USSR		Hungary	
Women						
100 m Freestyle	Jan Henne (USA)	1:00.0	Susan Pedersen (USA)	1:00.3	Linda Gustavson (USA)	1:00.3
200 m Freestyle	Debbie Meyer (USA)	2:10.5	Jan Henne (USA)	2:11.0	Jane Barkman (USA)	2:11.2
400 m Freestyle	Debbie Meyer (USA)	4:31.8	Linda Gustavson (USA)	4:35.5	Karen Moras (AUS)	4:37.0
800 m Freestyle	Debbie Meyer (USA)	9:24.0	Pamela Kruse (USA)	9:35.7	Maria-Teresa Ramirez (MEX)	9:38.5
100 m Backstroke	Kaye Hall (USA)	1:06.2	Elaine Tanner (CAN)	1:06.7	Jane Swagerty (USA)	1:08.1
200 m Backstroke	Lilian Watson (USA)	2:24.8	Elaine Tanner (CAN)	2:27.4	Kaye Hall (USA)	2:28.9
100 m Breaststroke	Djurdjica Bjedov (YUG)	1:15.8	Galina Prozumenschikova (URS)	1:15.9	Sharon Wichman (USA)	1:16.1
200 m Breaststroke	Sharon Wichman (USA)	2:44.4	Djurdjica Bjedov (YUG)	2:46.4	Galina Prozumenschikova (URS)	2:47.0
100 m Butterfly	Lynette McClements (AUS)	1:05.5	Ellie Daniel (USA)	1:05.8	Susan Shields (USA)	1:06.2
200 m Butterfly	Ada Kok (HOL)	2:24.7	Helga Lindner (GDR)	2:24.8	Ellie Daniel (USA)	2:25.9
200 m Medley	Claudia Kolb (USA)	2:24.7	Susan Pedersen (USA)	2:28.8	Jan Henne (USA)	2:31.4
400 m Medley	Claudia Kolb (USA)	5:08.5	Lynn Vidali (USA)	5:22.2	Sabine Steinbach (GDR)	5:25.3
4 x 100 m Freestyle Relay	USA	4:02.5	FDR	4:05.7	Canada	4:07.2
4 x 100 m Medley Relay	USA	4:28.3	Australia	4:30.0	FRG	4:36.4
Springboard Diving	Sue Gossick (USA)	150.77	Tamara Pogozheva (URS)	145.30	Keala O'Sullivan (USA)	145.23
Highboard Diving	Milena Duchková (TCH)	109.59	Natalya Lobanova (URS)	105.14	Ann Peterson (USA)	101.11

Boxing

EVENT	GOLD	SILVER	BRONZE
Light-Flyweight (- 48 kg)	Francisco Rodriguez (VEN)	Yong-Ju Jee (KOR)	Harlan Marbley (USA)
			Hubert Skrzypczak (POL)
Flyweight (- 51 kg)	Ricardo Delgado (MEX)	Artur Olech (POL)	Servillo Oliveira (BRA)
			Leo Rwabwogo (UGA)
Bantamweight (- 54 kg)	Valeriy Sokolov (URS)	Eridadi Mukwanga (UGA)	Eiji Morioka (JPN)
			Kyou-Chull Chang (KOR)
Featherweight (- 57 kg)	Antonio Roldan (MEX)	Albert Robinson (USA)	Philipp Waruinge (KEN)
			Ivan Michailov (BUL)
Lightweight (- 60 kg)	Ronald Harris (USA)	Józef Grudzien (POL)	Calistrat Cutov (ROM)
			Zvonimir Vujin (YUG)
Light-Welterweight (- 63.5 kg)	Jerzy Kulej (POL)	Enrique Regueiferos (CUB)	Arto Nilsson (FIN)
			James Wallington (USA)
Welterweight (- 67 kg)	Manfred Wolke (GDR)	Joseph Bessala (CMR)	Vladimir Musalinov (URS)
			Mario Guilloti (ARG)
Light-Middleweight (- 71 kg)	Boris Lagutin (URS)	Rolando Garbey (CUB)	John Baldwin (USA)
			Günther Meier (FRG)
Middleweight (- 75 kg)	Christopher Finnegan (GBR)	Alexey Kisselyov (URS)	Agustin Zaragoza (MEX)
			Alfred Jones (USA)
Light-Heavyweight (- 81 kg)	Dan Poznyak (URS)	Ion Monea (ROM)	Georgy Stankov (BUL)
			Stanislav Gragan (POL)
Heavyweight (+ 81 kg)	George Foreman (USA)	Ionas Tschepulis (URS)	Giorgio Bambini (ITA)
			Joaquin Rocha (MEX)

Weightlifting

EVENT	GOLD		SILVER		BRONZE	
Bantamweight (- 56 kg)	Mohammad Nassiri (IRN)	367.5	Imre Földi (HUN)	367.5	Henryk Trebicki (POL)	357.5
Featherweight (- 60 kg)	Yoshinobu Miyake (JPN)	392.5	Dito Shanidze (URS)	387.5	Yoshiyuki Miyake (JPN)	385.0
Lightweight (- 67.5 kg)	Waldemar Baszanowski (POL)	437.5	Parviz Jalayer (IRN)	422.5	Marian Zielinski (POL)	420.0
Middleweight (- 75 kg)	Viktor Kurentsov (URS)	475.0	Masashi Ouchi (JPN)	455.0	Károly Bakos (HUN)	440.0
Light-Heavyweigh (- 82.5 kg)	Boris Selitsky (URS)	485.0	Viktor Belyayev (URS)	485.0	Norbert Ozimek (POL)	472.5
Middle-Heavyweight (- 90 kg)	Kaarlo Kangasniemi (FIN)	517.5	Jan Talts (URS)	507.5	Marek Golab (POL)	495.0
Heavyweight (+ 90 kg)	Leonid Zhabotinski (URS)	572.5	Serge Reding (BEL)	555.0	Joe Dube (USA)	555.0

Greco-Roman Wrestling

EVENT	GOLD	SILVER	BRONZE
Flyweight (- 52 kg)	Petar Kirov (BUL)	Vladimir Bakulin (URS)	Miroslav Zeman (TCH)
Bantamweight (- 57 kg)	János Varga (HUN)	Ion Baciu (ROM)	Ivan Kochergin (URS)
Featherweight (- 63 kg)	Roman Rurua (URS)	Hideo Fujimoto (JPN)	Simeon Popescu (ROM)
Lightweight (- 70 kg)	Munji Mumemura (JPN)	Stefan Horvat (YUG)	Petros Galaktopoulos (GRE)
Welterweight (- 78 kg)	Rudolf Vesper (GDR)	Daniel Robin (FRA)	Károly Bajkó (HUN)

EVENT	GOLD		SILVER		BRONZE	
Middleweight (- 87 kg)	Lothar Metz (GDR)		Valentin Olenik (URS)		Branislav Simic (YUG)	
Light-Heavyweight (- 97 kg)	Boyan Radev (BUL)		Nikolai Yakovenko (URS)		Nicolae Martinescu (ROM)	
Heavyweight (+ 97 kg)	István Kozma (HUN)		Anatoliy Roschin (URS)		Petr Kment (TCH)	
Freestyle Wrestling						
Flyweight (- 52 kg)	Shigeo Nakata (JPN)		Richard Sanders (USA)		Surenjav Sukhbaatar (MGL)	
Bantamweight (- 57 kg)	Yojiro Uetake (JPN)		Donald Behm (USA)		Abutaleb Gorgori (IRN)	
Featherweight (- 63 kg)	Masaaki Kaneko (JPN)		Enyu Todorov (BUL)		Shamseddin Seyed-Abbassi (IRN)	
Lightweight (- 70 kg)	Abdollah M. Ardabili (IRN)		Enyu Valtschev (BUL)		Sereeter Danzandarjaa (MGL)	
Welterweight (- 78 kg)	Mahmut Atalay (TUR)		Daniel Robin (FRA)		Dagvasuren Purev (MGL)	
Middleweight (- 87 kg)	Boris Gurevitch (URS)		Munkbat Jigjid (MGL)		Prodan Gardschev (BUL)	
Light-Heavyweight (- 97 kg)	Ahmet Ayik (TUR)		Shota Lomidze (URS)		József Csatári (HUN)	
Heavyweight (+ 97 kg)	Alexander Medved (URS)		Osman Duraliev (BUL)		Wilfried Dietrich (FRG)	
Fencing						
Individual Foil - Men	Ion Drimba (ROM)	4	Jenö Kamuti (HUN)	3	Daniel Revenu (FRA)	3
Team Foil - Men	France		USSR		Poland	
Individual Épée	Gyözö Kulcsár (HUN)	4+2	Grigory Kriss (URS)	4/10/8	Gianluigi Saccaro (ITA)	4/10/7
Team Épée	Hungary		USSR		Poland	
Individual Sabre	Jerzy Pawlowski (POL)	4+1	Mark Rakita (URS)	4	Tibor Pézsa (HUN)	3
Team Sabre	USSR		Italy		Hungary	
Individual Foil - Women	Elena Novikova (URS)	4	Pilar Roldan (MEX)	3/14	Ildiko Ujlaki-Rejtö (HUN)	3/16
Team Foil - Women	USSR		Hungary		Romania	
Modern Pentathlon						
Individual	Björn Ferm (SWE)	4964	András Balczó (HUN)	4953	Pavel Lednev (URS)	4795
Team	Hungary	14325	USSR	14248	France	13289
Canoeing						
Men						
1000 m Kayak Singles K1	Mihály Hesz (HUN)	4:02.63	Alexander Shaparenko (URS)	4:03.58	Erik Hansen (DEN)	4:04.39
1000 m Kayak Pairs K2	USSR	3:37.54	Hungary	3:38.44	Austria	3:40.71
1000 m Kayak Fours K4	Norway	3:14.38	Romania	3:14.81	Hungary	3:15.10
1000 m Canadian Singles C1	Tibor Tatai (HUN)	4:36.14	Detlef Lewe (FRG)	4:38.31	Vitaly Galkov (URS)	4:40.42
1000 m Canadian Pairs C2	Romania	4:07.18	Hungary	4:08.77	USSR	4:11.30
Women						
500 m Kayak Singles K1	Ludmila Pinayeva (URS)	2:11.09	Renate Breuer (FRG)	2:12.71	Viorica Dumitru (ROM)	2:13.22
500 m Kayak Pairs K2	FRG	1:56.44	Hungary	1:58.60	USSR	1:58.61
Rowing						
Single Sculls	Henri Jan Wienese (HOL)	7:47.80	Jochen Meissner (FRG)	7:52.00	Alberto Demiddi (ARG)	7:57.19
Double Sculls	USSR	6:51.82	Netherlands	6:52.80	USA	6:54.21
Coxless Pairs	GDR	7:26.56	USA	7:26.71	Denmark	7:31.84
Coxed Pairs	Italy	8:04.81	Netherlands	8:06.80	Denmark	8:08.07
Coxless Fours	GDR	6:39.18	Hungary	6:41.64	Italy	6:44.01
Coxed Fours	New Zealand	6:45.62	GDR	6:48.20	Switzerland	6:49.04
Coxed Eights	FRG	6:07.00	Australia	6:07.98	USSR	6:09.11
Yachting						
Finn Class	Valentin Mankin (URS)	11.7	Hubert Raudaschl (AUT)	53.4	Fabio Albarelli (ITA)	55.1
International Star	USA	14.4	Norway	43.7	Italy	44.7
Flying Dutchman	Great Britain	3.0	FRG	43.7	Brazil	48.4
Dragon	USA	6.0	Denmark	26.4	GDR	32.7
5.5 m	Sweden	8.0	Switzerland	32.0	Great Britain	39.8
Cycling						
Individual Road Race (196.2 km)	Pierfranco Vianelli (ITA)	4:41:25.24	Leif Mortenson (DEN)	4:42:49.71	Gösta Pettersson (SWE)	4:43:15.24
100 km Road Team Time Trial	Netherlands	2:07:49.06	Sweden	2:09:26.60	Italy	2:10:18.74
1000 m time Trial	Pierre Trentin (FRA)	1:03.91	Niels-Christian Fredborg (DEN)	1:04.61	Janusz Kierzkowski (POL)	1:04.63
1000 m Sprint	Daniel Morelon (FRA)		Giordano Turrini (ITA)		Pierre Trentin (FRA)	
2000 m Tandem	France		Netherlands		Belgium	
4000 m Individual Pursuit	Daniel Rebillard (FRA)	4:41.71	Mogens Frey Jensen (DEN)	4:42.43	Xaver Kurmann (SUI)	4:39.42
4000 m Team Pursuit	Denmark	4:22.44	FRG★	4:18.94	Italy	4:18.35

★The winning W. German team were demoted to 2nd place owing to an illegal push-start.

EVENT	GOLD		SILVER		BRONZE	
Equestrianism						
Three-Day Event	Jean-Jacques Guyon (FRA)	-38.86	Derek Allhusen (GBR)	-41.61	Michael Page (USA)	-53.31
Three-Day Event (Team)	Great Britain	-175.93	USA	-245.87	Australia	-331.26
Grand Prix (Dressage)	Ivan Kizimov (URS)	1572	Josef Neckermann (FRG)	1546	Reiner Klimke (FRG)	1537
Grand Prix (Dressage) Team	FRG	2699	USSR	2657	Switzerland	2547
Grand Prix (Jumping)	William Steinkraus (USA)	-4	Marion Coakes (GBR)	-8	David Broome (GBR)	-12
Grand Prix (Jumping) Team	Canada	-102.75	France	-110.50	FRG	-117.25
Shooting						
Free Rifle (3 Positions)	Gary Anderson (USA)	1157	Vladimir Kornev (URS)	1151	Kurt Müller (SUI)	1148
Small-Bore Rifle (Prone)	Jan Kurka (TCH)	598	László Hammerl (HUN)	598	Ian Ballinger (NZL)	597
Small-Bore Rifle (3 Positions)	Bernd Klingner (FRG)	1157	John Writer (USA)	1156	Vitaly Parkimovich (URS)	1154
Rapid-Fire Pistol	Josef Zapedzki (POL)	593	Marcel Rosca (ROM)	591/147	Renart Suleimanow (URS)	591/146
Free Pistol (50 m)	Grigory Kossykh (URS)	562/30	Heinz Mertel (FRG)	562/26	Harald Vollmar (GDR)	560
Skeet Shooting	Evgeny Petrov (URS)	198/25	Romano Garagnani (ITA)	198/24/25	Konrad Wirnhier (FRG)	198/24/23
Trap Shooting	John Braithwaite (GBR)	198	Thomas Garrigus (USA)	196/25/25	Kurt Czekalla (GDR)	198/25/23
Gymnastics						
Men						
Individual Combined Exercises	Sawao Kato (JPN)	115.90	Mikhail Voronin (URS)	115.85	Akinori Nakayama (JPN)	115.65
Team	Japan	575.90	USSR	571.10	GDR	557.15
Parallel Bars	Akinori Nakayama (JPN)	19.475	Mikhail Voronin (URS)	19.425	Viktor Klimenko (URS)	19.225
Floor	Sawao Kato (JPN)	19.475	Akinori Nakayama (JPN)	19.400	Takashi Kato (JPN)	19.275
Horse Vault	Mikhail Voronin (URS)	19.000	Yukio Endo (JPN)	18.950	Sergey Diomidov (URS)	18.925
Horizontal Bar	Mikhail Voronin (URS)	19.550	Eizo Kenmotsu (JPN)	19.375		
	Akinori Nakayama (JPN)	19.550				
Rings	Akinori Nakayama (JPN)	19.450	Mikhail Voronin (URS)	19.325	Sawao Kato (JPN)	19.225
Pommel Horse	Miroslav Cerar (YUG)	19.325	Olli Eino Laiho (FIN)	19.225	Mikhail Voronin (URS)	19.200
Women						
Individual Combined Exercises	Vera Cáslavská (TCH)	78.25	Zinaida Voronina (URS)	76.85	Natalya Kuchinskaya (URS)	76.75
Team	USSR	382.85	Czechoslovakia	382.20	GDR	379.10
Floor	Larissa Petrik (URS)	19.675	Natalya Kuchinskaya (URS)	19650		
	Vera Cáslavská (TCH)	19.675				
Horse Vault	Vera Cáslavská (TCH)	19.775	Erika Zuchold (GDR)	19.625	Zinaida Voronina (URS)	19.500
Beam	Natalya Kuchinskaya (URS)	19.650	Vera Cáslavská (TCH)	19.575	Larissa Petrik (URS)	19.250
Asymmetrical Bars	Vera Cáslavská (TCH)	19.650	Karin Janz (GDR)	19.500	Zinaida Voronina (URS)	19.425
Basketball						
	USA		Yugoslavia		USSR	
Soccer						
	Hungary		Bulgaria		Japan	
Hockey						
	Pakistan		Australia		India	
Volleyball						
Men	USSR		Japan		Czechoslovakia	
Women	USSR		Japan		Poland	

Sapporo 1972

Participants: 1006 / Men: 800, Women: 206, Countries: 35,

Sports: 8, Events: 35

Final Torchbearer: Hideki Takada

Medals Table

PLACE	COUNTRY	GOLD	SILVER	BRONZE
1	USSR	8	5	3
2	GDR	4	3	7
3	Switzerland	4	3	3
4	Netherlands	4	3	2
5	USA	3	2	3

Outstanding Athletes

PLACE	NAME (NATIONALITY)	DISCIPLINE	G	S	B
1	Galina Kulakova (URS)	Nordic Skiing	3	–	–
	Ard Schenk (HOL)	Speed Skating	3	–	–
3	Vyacheslav Vedenine (URS)	Nordic Skiing	2	0	1
4	Marie-Thérèse Nadig (SUI)	Alpine Skiing	2	–	–
5	Pål Tyldum (NOR)	Nordic Skiing	1	2	–

EVENT	GOLD		SILVER		BRONZE	
Alpine Skiing						
Men						
Downhill	Bernhard Russi (SUI)	1:51.43	Roland Collombin (SUI)	1:52.07	Heinrich Messner (AUT)	1:52.40
Slalom	Francisco Ochoa (ESP)	1:49.27	Gustavo Thöni (ITA)	1:50.28	Rolando Thöni (ITA)	1:50.30
Giant Slalom	Gustavo Thöni (ITA)	3:09.62	Edmund Bruggmann (SUI)	3:10.75	Werner Mattle (SUI)	3:10.99
Women						
Downhill	Marie-Thérèse Nadig (SUI)	1:36.68	Annemarie Pröll (AUT)	1:37.00	Susan Corrock (USA)	1:37.68
Slalom	Barbara Cochran (USA)	1:31.24	Daniele Debernard (FRA)	1:31.26	Florence Steurer (FRA)	1:32.69
Giant Slalom	Marie-Thérèse Nadig (SUI)	1:29.90	Annemarie Pröll (AUT)	1:30.75	Wiltrud Drexel (AUT)	1:32.35
Nordic Skiing						
Men						
15 km Cross-Country Skiing	Sven-Ake Lundbäck (SWE)	45:28.24	Fedor Simaschov (URS)	46:.00.84	Ivar Formo (NOR)	46:02.86
30 km Cross-Country Skiing	Vyacheslav Vedenine (URS)	1:36:31.15	Pål Tyldum (NOR)	1:37:25.30	Johannes Harviken (NOR)	1:37:32.44
50-km-Cross-Country Skiing	Pål Tyldum (NOR)	2:43:14.75	Magne Myrmo (NOR)	2:43:29.45	Vyacheslav Vedenine (URS)	2:44:00.19
4 x 10 km	USSR	2:04:47.94	Norway	2:04:57.06	Switzerland	2:07:00.06
Ski Jumping (70 m Hill)	Yukio Kasaya (JPN)	244.2	Akitsugu Konno (JPN)	234.8	Seiji Aochi (JPN)	229.5
Ski Jumping (90 m Hill)	Wojciech Fortuna (POL)	219.9	Walter Steiner (SUI)	219.8	Rainer Schmidt (GDR)	219.3
Nordic Combination	Ulrich Wehling (GDR)	413.340	Rauno Miettinen (FIN)	405.505	Karl-Heinz Luck (GDR)	398.800
Women						
5 km Cross-Country Skiing	Galina Kulakova (URS)	17:00.50	Marjatta Kajosmaa (FIN)	17:05.50	Helena Sikolová (TCH)	17:07.32
10 km-Cross Country Skiing	Galina Kulakova (URS)	34:17.82	Alevtina Olunina (URS)	34:54.11	Marjatta Kajosmaa (FIN)	34:56.45
3 x 5 km	USSR	48:46.15	Finland	49:19.37	Norway	49:51.49
Biathlon						
20 km	Magnar Solberg (NOR)	1:15:55.50	Hansjörg Knauthe (GDR)	1:16:07.60	Lars Arvidsson (SWE)	1:16:27.03
4 x 7.5 km	USSR	1:51:44.92	Finland	1:54:37.25	GDR	1:54:57.67
Figure Skating						
Women	Beatrix Schuba (AUT)		Karen Magnussen (CAN)		Janet Lynn (USA)	
Men	Ondrej Nepela (TCH)		Sergey Tchetveroukhin (URS)		Patrick Péra (FRA)	
Pair	Irina Rodnina/ Alexey Ulanov (URS)		Ludmilla Smirnova/ Andrey Suraikin (URS)		Manuela Gross/ Uwe Kagelmann (GDR)	
Speed Skating						
Men						
500 m	Erhard Keller (FRG)	39.44	Hasse Borjes (SWE)	39.69	Valeriy Muratov (URS)	39.80
1500 m	Ard Schenk (HOL)	2:02.96	Roar Grönvold (NOR)	2:04.26	Göran Claeson (SWE)	2:05.8
5000 m	Ard Schenk (HOL)	7:23.61	Roar Grönvold (NOR)	7:28.18	Sten Stensen (NOR)	7:33.39
10,000 m	Ard Schenk (HOL)	15:01.35	Cornelis Verkerk (HOL)	15:04.70	Sten Stensen (NOR)	15:07.08
Women						
500 m	Anne Henning (USA)	43.33	Vera Krasnova (URS)	44.01	Ludmila Titova (URS)	44.45
1000 m	Monika Pflug (FRG)	1:31.40	Atje Keulen-Deelstra (HOL)	1:31.61	Anne Henning (USA)	1:31.62
1500 m	Dianne Holum (USA)	2:20.85	Christina Baas-Kaiser (HOL)	2:21.05	Atje Keulen-Deelstra (HOL)	2:22.05
3000 m	Christina Baas-Kaiser (HOL)	4:52.14	Dianne Holum (USA)	4:58.67	Atje Keulen-Deelstra (HOL)	4:59.91

EVENT	GOLD		SILVER		BRONZE	
Bobsledding						
2-Man Bob	FRG II	4:57.07	FRG I	4:58.84	Switzerland I	4:59.33
4-Man Bob	Switzerland I	4:43.07	Italy I	4:43.83	FRG I	4:43.92
Lugeing						
Men's Singles	Wolfgang Scheidel (GDR)	3:27.58	Harald Ehrig (GDR)	3:28.39	Wolfram Fiedler (GDR)	3:28.73
Women's Singles	Anna-Maria Müller (GDR)	2:59.18	Ute Rührold (GDR)	2:59.49	Margit Schumann (GDR)	2:59.54
2-Man Luge	Paul Hildgartner/ Walter Plaikner (ITA)	1:28.35	Klaus Bonsack/ Wolfram Fiedler (GDR)	1:29.16	Horst Hörnlein/ Reinhard Bredow (GDR)	1:28.35
Ice hockey						
	USSR		USA		Czechoslovakia	

Munich 1972

26 August – 11 September

Participants: 7123 / Men: 6065, Women: 1058, Countries: 121,
Sports: 21, Events: 195
Final Torchbearer: Günter Zahn

Medals Table

PLACE	COUNTRY	GOLD	SILVER	BRONZE
1	USSR	50	27	22
2	USA	33	31	30
3	DDR	20	23	23
4	West Germany	13	11	16
5	Japan	13	8	8

Outstanding Athletes

PLACE	NAME (NATIONALITY)	DISCIPLINE	G	S	B
1	Mark Spitz (USA)	Swimming	7	–	–
2	Sawao Kato (JPN)	Gymnastics	3	2	–
3	Shane Gould (AUS)	Swimming	3	1	1
4	Olga Korbut (URS)	Gymnastics	3	1	–
5	Melissa Belote (USA)	Swimming	3	–	–
	Sandra Neilson (USA)	Swimming	3	–	–

EVENT	GOLD		SILVER		BRONZE	
Athletics						
Men						
100 m	Valeriy Borsov (URS)	10.14	Robert Taylor (USA)	10.24	Lennox Miller (JAM)	10.33
200 m	Valeriy Borsov (URS)	20.00	Larry Black (USA)	20.19	Pietro Mennea (ITA)	20.30
400 m	Vincent Matthews (USA)	44.66	Wayne Collett (USA)	44.80	Julius Sang (KEN)	44.92
800 m	Dave Wottle (USA)	1:45.9	Yewgeniy Arzhanov (URS)	1:45.9	Mike Boit (KEN)	1:46.0
1500 m	Pekka Vasala (FIN)	3:36.3	Kipchoge Keino (KEN)	3:36.8	Rodney Dixon (NZL)	3:37.5
5000 m	Lasse Viren (FIN)	13:26.4	Mohamed Gammoudi (TUN)	13:27.4	Ian Stewart (GBR)	13:27.6
10,000 m	Lasse Viren (FIN)	27:38.4	Emiel Puttemans (BEL)	27:39.6	Miruts Yifter (ETH)	27:41.0
Marathon	Frank Shorter (USA)	2:12:19.8	Karel Lismont (BEL)	2:14:31.8	Mamo Wolde (ETH)	2:15:08.4
110 m Hurdles	Rodney Milburn (USA)	13.24	Guy Drut (FRA)	13.34	Thomas Hill (USA)	13.48
400 m Hurdles	John Akii-Bua (UGA)	47.82	Ralph Mann (USA)	48.51	David Hemery (GBR)	48.52
3000 m Steeplechase	Kipchoge Keino (KEN)	8:23.6	Benjamin Jipcho (KEN)	8:24.6	Tapio Kantanen (FIN)	8:24.8
4 x 100 m	USA	38.19	USSR	38.50	FRG	38.79
4 x 400 m	Kenya	2:59.8	Great Britain	3:00.5	France	3:00.7
20 km Walk	Peter Frenkel (GDR)	1:26:42.4	Vladimir Golubnichiy (URS)	1:26:55.2	Hans Reimann (GDR)	1:27:16.6
50 km Walk	Bernd Kannenberg (FRG)	3:56:11.6	Venjamin Soldatenko (URS)	3:58:24.0	Larry Young (USA)	4:00:46.0
High Jump	Yuriy Tarmak (URS)	2.23	Stefan Junge (GDR)	2.21	Dwight Stones (USA)	2.21
Pole Vault	Wolfgang Nordwig (GDR)	5.50	Robert Seagren (USA)	5.40	Jan Johnson (USA)	5.35
Long Jump	Randy Williams (USA)	8.24	Hans Baumgartner (FRG)	8.18	Arnie Robinson (USA)	8.03
Triple Jump	Viktor Saneyev (URS)	17.35	Jörg Drehmel (GDR)	17.31	Nelson Prudencio (BRA)	17.05
Shot	Wladyslaw Komar (POL)	21.18	George Woods (USA)	21.17	Hartmut Briesenick (GDR)	21.14
Discus	Ludvik Danek (TCH)	64.40	Jay Silvester (USA)	63.50	Rickard Bruch (SWE)	63.40
Hammer	Anatoliy Bondarchuk (URS)	75.50	Jochen Sachse (GDR)	74.96	Vasiliy Khmelevski (URS)	74.04
Javelin	Klaus Wolfermann (FRG)	90.48	Janis Lusis (URS)	90.46	William Schmidt (USA)	84.42
Decathlon	Nikolai Avilov (URS)	8454	Leonid Litvinenko (URS)	8035	Ryszard Katus (POL)	7984

EVENT	GOLD		SILVER		BRONZE	
Women						
100 m	Renate Stecher (GDR)	11.07	Raelene Boyle (AUS)	11.23	Silvia Chivas (CUB)	11.24
200 m	Renate Stecher (GDR)	22.40	Raelene Boyle (AUS)	22.45	Irena Szewinska-Kirszenstein (POL)	22.74
400 m	Monika Zehrt (GDR)	51.08	Rita Wilden (FRG)	51.21	Kathy Hammond (USA)	51.64
800 m	Hildegard Falck (FRG)	1:58.6	Niole Sabaite (URS)	1:58.7	Gunhild Hoffmeister (GDR)	1:59.2
1500 m	Ludmila Bragina (URS)	4:01.4	Gunhild Hoffmeister (GDR)	4:02.8	Paola Cacchi (ITA)	4:02.9
100 m Hurdles	Annelie Ehrhardt (GDR)	12.59	Valeria Bufanu (ROM)	12.84	Karin Balzer (GDR)	12.90
4 x 100 m	FRG	42.81	GDR	42.95	Cuba	43.36
4 x 400 m	GDR	3:23.0	USA	3:25.2	FRG	3:26.5
High Jump	Ulrike Meyfarth (FRG)	1.92	Yordanka Blagoyeva (BUL)	1.88	Ilona Gusenbauer (AUT)	1.88
Long Jump	Heide Rosendahl (FRG)	6.78	Diana Yorgova (BUL)	6.77	Eva Suranova (TCH)	6.67
Shot	Nadyezda Chizhova (URS)	21.03	Margitta Gummel (GDR)	20.22	Ivanka Christova (BUL)	19.35
Discus	Faina Melnik (URS)	66.62	Argentina Menis (ROM)	65.06	Vasilka Stoyeva (BUL)	64.34
Javelin	Ruth Fuchs (GDR)	63.88	Jaqueline Todten (GDR)	62.54	Kathy Schmidt (USA)	59.94
Pentathlon	Mary Peters (GBR)	4801	Heide Rosendahl (FRG)	4791	Burglinde Pollak (GDR)	4768
Swimming						
Men						
100 m Freestyle	Mark Spitz (USA)	51.22	Jerry Heidenreich (USA)	51.65	Vladimir Bure (URS)	51.77
200 m Freestyle	Mark Spitz (USA)	1:52.78	Steven Genter (USA)	1:53.73	Werner Lampe (FRG)	1:53.99
400 m Freestyle	Bradford Cooper (AUS)	4:00.27	Steven Genter (USA)	4:01.94	Tom McBreen (USA)	4:02.64
1500 m Freestyle	Michael Burton (USA)	15:52.58	Graham Windeatt (AUS)	15:58.48	Douglas Northway (USA)	16:09.25
100 m Backstroke	Roland Matthes (GDR)	56.58	Mike Stamm (USA)	57.70	John Murphy (USA)	58.35
200 m Backstroke	Roland Matthes (USA)	2:02.82	Mike Stamm (USA)	2:04.09	Mitchell Ivey (USA)	2:04.33
100 m Breaststroke	Nobutaka Taguchi (JPN)	1:04.94	Tom Bruce (USA)	1:05.43	John Hencken (USA)	1:05.61
200 m Breaststroke	Jonn Hencken (USA)	2:21.55	David Wilkie (GBR)	2:23.67	Nobutaka Taguchi (JPN)	2:23.88
100 m Butterfly	Mark Spitz (USA)	54.27	Bruce Robertson (CAN)	55.56	Jerry Heidenreich (USA)	55.74
200 m Butterfly	Mark Spitz (USA)	2:00.70	Gary Hall (USA)	2:02.86	Robin Backhaus (USA)	2:03.23
200 m Medley	Gunnar Larsson (SWE)	2:07.17	Alexander McKee (USA)	2:08.37	Steven Furniss (USA)	2:08.45
400 m Medley	Gunnar Larsson (SWE)	4:31.981	Alexander McKee (USA)	4:31.983	Andras Hargitay (HUN)	4:32.700
4 x 100 m Freestyle Relay	USA	3:26.42	USSR	3:29.72	GDR	3:32.42
4 x 200 m Freestyle Relay	USA	7:35.78	FRG	7:41.69	USSR	7:45.76
4 x 100 m Medley Relay	USA	3:48.16	GDR	3:52.12	Canada	3:52.26
Springboard Diving	Vladimir Vasin (URS)	594.06	Franco Cagnotto (ITA)	591.63	Craig Lincoln (USA)	577.29
Highboard Diving	Klaus Dibiasi (ITA)	504.12	Richard Rydze (USA)	480.75	Franco Cagnotto (ITA)	475.83
Water Polo	USSR		Hungary		USA	
Women						
100 m Freestyle	Sandra Neilson (USA)	58.59	Shirley Babashoff (USA)	59.02	Shane Gould (AUS)	59.06
200 m Freestyle	Shane Gould (AUS)	2:03.56	Shirley Babashoff (USA)	2:04.33	Keena Rothhammer (USA)	2:04.92
400 m Freestyle	Shane Gould (AUS)	4:19.04	Novella Calligaris (ITA)	4:22.44	Gudrun Wegner (GDR)	4:23.11
800 m Freestyle	Keena Rothhammer (USA)	8:53.68	Shane Gould (AUS)	8:56.39	Novella Calligaris (ITA)	8:57.46
100 m Backstroke	Melissa Belote (USA)	1:05.78	Andrea Gyarmati (HUN)	1:06.26	Susan Atwood (USA)	1:06.34
200 m Backstroke	Melissa Belote (USA)	2:19.19	Susan Atwood (USA)	2:20.38	Donna Marie Gurr (CAN)	2:23.22
100 m Breaststroke	Catherine Carr (USA)	1:13.58	Galina Stepanova (URS)	1:14.99	Beverley Whitfield (AUS)	1:15.73
200 m Breaststroke	Beverley Whitfield (AUS)	2:41.71	Dana Schoenfield (USA)	2:42.05	Galina Stepanova (URS)	2:42.36
100 m Butterfly	Mayumi Aoki (JPN)	1:03.34	Roswitha Beier (GDR)	1:30.61	Andrea Gyarmati (HUN)	1:03.73
200 m Butterfly	Karen Moe (USA)	2:15.57	Lynn Colella (USA)	2:16.34	Ellie Daniel (USA)	2:16.74
200 m Medley	Shane Gould (AUS)	2:23.07	Kornelia Ender (GDR)	2:23.59	Lynn Vidali (USA)	2:24.06
400 m Medley	Gail Neall (AUS)	5:02.97	Leslie Cliff (CAN)	5:03.57	Novella Calligaris (ITA)	5:03.99
4 x 100 m Freestyle Relay	USA	3:55.19	GDR	3:55.55	FRG	3:57.93
4 x 100 m Medley Relay	USA	4:20.75	GDR	4:24.91	FRG	4:26.46
Springboard Diving	Maxine King (USA)	450.03	Ulrika Knape (SWE)	434.19	Marina Janicke (GDR)	430.92
Highboard Diving	Ulrika Knape (SWE)	390.00	Milena Duchková (TCH)	370.92	Marina Janicke (GDR)	360.54
Boxing						
Light-Flyweight (- 48 kg)	György Gedo (HUN)		U Gil Kim (PRK)		Enrique Rodriguez (ESP) Ralph Evans (GBR)	
Flyweight (- 51 kg)	Gheorghi Kostadinov (BUL)		Leo Rwabwogo (UGA)		Douglas Rodriguez (CUB) Leszek Blazynski (POL)	
Bantamweight (- 54 kg)	Orlando Martinez (CUB)		Alfonso Zamora (MEX)		George Turpin (GBR) Ricardo Carreras (USA)	
Featherweight (- 57 kg)	Boris Kusnezov (URS)		Philip Waruinge (KEN)		Clemente Rojas (COL) Andras Botos (HUN)	
Lightweight (- 60 kg)	Jan Szczepanski (POL)		Laszlo Orban (HUN)		Alfonso Perez (COL) Samuel Mbugua (KEN)	

EVENT	GOLD		SILVER		BRONZE	
Light-Welterweight (- 63.5 kg)	Ray Seales (USA)		Anghel Angelov (BUL)		Zvonimir Vujin (YUG)	
					Issak Daborg (NIG)	
Welterweight (- 67 kg)	Emilio Correa (CUB)		János Kajdi (HUN)		Dick Tiger Murunga (KEN)	
					Jesse Valdez (USA)	
Light-Middleweight (- 71 kg)	Dieter Kottysch (FRG)		Wieslaw Rudkowski (POL)		Alan Minter (GBR)	
					Peter Tiepold (GDR)	
Middleweight (- 75 kg)	Vyatcheslav Lemeschev (URS)		Reima Virtanen (FIN)		Marvin Johnson (USA)	
					Prince Amartey (GHA)	
Light-Heavyweight (- 81 kg)	Mate Parlov (YUG)		Gilberto Carillo (CUB)		Janusz Gortat (POL)	
					Isaak Ikhouria (NGR)	
Heavyweight (+ 81 kg)	Teofilo Stevenson (CUB)		Ion Alexe (ROM)		Peter Hussing (FRG)	
					Hasse Thomsen (SWE)	
Weightlifting						
Flyweight (- 52 kg)	Zymunt Smalcerz (POL)	337.5	Lajos Szuecs (HUN)	330.0	Sandor Holczreiter (HUN)	327.5
Bantamweight (- 56 kg)	Imre Földi (HUN)	377.5	Mohammed Nassiri (IRN)	370.0	Gennadi Chetin (URS)	367.5
Featherweight (- 60 kg)	Norair Nurikyan (BUL)	402.5	Dito Shanidze (URS)	400.0	Janos Benedek (HUN)	390.0
Lightweight (- 67.5 kg)	Mukharbi Kirzhinov (URS)	460.0	Mladen Koutchev (BUL)	450.0	Zbigniev Kaczmarek (POL)	437.5
Middleweight (- 75 kg)	Yordan Bikov (BUL)	485.0	Mohammed Trabulsi (LIB)	472.5	Anselmo Silvino (ITA)	470.0
Light-Heavyweight (- 82.5 kg)	Leif Jensen (NOR)	507.5	Norbert Ozimek (POL)	497.5	György Horvath (HUN)	495.0
Middle-Heavyweight (- 90 kg)	Andon Nikolov (BUL)	525.0	Atanas Chopov (BUL)	517.5	Hans Bettembourg (SWE)	512.5
Heavyweight (- 110 kg)	Jan Talts (URS)	580.0	Alexander Kraitchev (BUL)	562.5	Stefan Grützner (GDR)	555.0
Super-Heavyweight (+ 110 kg)	Vasiliy Alexeyev (URS)	640.0	Rudolf Mang (FRG)	610.0	Gerd Bonk (GDR)	572.5
Greco-Roman Wrestling						
Light-Flyweight (- 48 kg)	Gheorg Berceanu (ROM)		Rahim Ahabadi (IRN)		Stefan Anghelov (BUL)	
Flyweight (- 52 kg)	Petar Kirov (BUL)		Koichiro Hirayama (JPN)		Giuseppe Bognanni (ITA)	
Bantamweight (- 57 kg)	Rustem Kasakov (URS)		Hans-Jürgen Veil (FRG)		Risto Björlin (FIN)	
Featherweight (- 62 kg)	Georgi Markov (BUL)		Heinz-Helmut Wehling (GDR)		Kazimierz Lipien (POL)	
Lightweight (- 68 kg)	Shamil Khisamutdinov (URS)		Stoyan Apostolov (BUL)		Gian Matteo Ranzi (ITA)	
Welterweight (- 74 kg)	Vitezslav Macha (TCH)		Petros Galaktopoulos (GRE)		Jan Karlsson (SWE)	
Middleweight (- 82 kg)	Csaba Hegedus (HUN)		Anatoliy Nazarenko (URS)		Milan Nenadic (YUG)	
Light-Heavyweight (- 90 kg)	Valeriy Rezanzev (URS)		Josip Corak (YUG)		Czeslaw Kwiecinski (POL)	
Heavyweight (- 100 kg)	Nicolae Martinescu (ROM)		Nikolai Yakovenko (URS)		Ferenc Kiss (HUN)	
Super-Heavyweight (+ 100 kg)	Anatoliy Roschin (URS)		Alexander Tomov (BUL)		Victor Dolipschi (ROM)	
Freestyle Wrestling						
Light-Flyweight (- 48 kg)	Roman Dimitriyev (URS)		Ognian Nikolov (BUL)		Ebrahim Javadpour (IRN)	
Flyweight (- 52 kg)	Kiyomi Kato (JPN)		Arsen Alakhverdiev (URS)		Hyong Kim Gwong (PRK)	
Bantamweight (- 57 kg)	Hideaki Yanagida (JPN)		Richard Sanders (USA)		László Klinga (HUN)	
Featherweight (- 62 kg)	Zagalav Abdulbekov (URS)		Vehbi Akdag (TUR)		Ivan Krastev (BUL)	
Lightweight (- 68 kg)	Dan Gable (USA)		Kikuo Wada (JPN)		Ruslan Ashuralyev (URS)	
Welterweight (- 74 kg)	Wayne Wells (USA)		Jan Karlsson (SWE)		Adolf Seger (FRG)	
Middleweight (- 82 kg)	Levan Tediashvili (URS)		John Peterson (USA)		Vasile Jorga (ROM)	
Light-Heavyweight (- 90 kg)	Ben Peterson (USA)		Gennadiy Strakhov (URS)		Karoly Bajko (HUN)	
Heavyweight (- 100 kg)	Ivan Yarygin (URS)		Khorloo Baianmunkh (MGL)		Jószef Csatári (HUN)	
Super-Heavyweight (+ 100 kg)	Alexander Medved (URS)		Osman Duraliev (BUL)		Chris Taylor (USA)	
Judo						
Lightweight (- 63 kg)	Takao Kawaguchi (JPN)		Bakhaavaa Buidaa (MGL)		Yong Ik Kim (PRK)	
			(disqualified after positive drug test)		Jean-Jacques Monuier (FRA)	
Welterweight (- 70 kg)	Toyokazu Nomura (JPN)		Anton Zajkowski (POL)		Anatoliy Novikov (URS)	
					Dietmar Höttger (GDR)	
Middleweight (- 80 kg)	Shinobu Sekine (JPN)		Seung-Lip Oh (KOR)		Brian Jacks (GBR)	
					Jean-Paul Coché (FRA)	
Light-Heavyweight (- 93 kg)	Shota Chochoshvili (URS)		David Starbrook (GBR)		Paul Barth (FRG)	
					Chiaki Ishii (BRA)	
Heavyweight (+ 93 kg)	Wim Ruska (HOL)		Klaus Glahn (FRG)		Givi Onashvili (URS)	
					Motoki Nishimura (JPN)	
Open Class	Wim Ruska (HOL)		Vitaliy Kuznetsov (URS)		Jean-Claude Brondani (FRA)	
					Angelo Parisi (GBR)	
Fencing						
Individual Foil - Men	Witold Woyda (POL)	5	Jenö Kamuti (HUN)	4	Christian Noël (FRA)	2
Team Foil - Men	Poland		USSR		France	
Individual Épée	Csaba Fenyresi (HUN)	4	Jacques La Dagaillerie (FRA)	3	Gyözö Kulcsár (HUN)	3
Team Épée	Hungary		Switzerland		USSR	
Individual Sabre	Viktor Sidjak (URS)	4	Peter Maroth (HUN)	3	Vladimir Nazlimov (URS)	3

EVENT	GOLD		SILVER		BRONZE	
Team Sabre	Italy		USSR		Hungary	
Individual Foil – Women	Antonella Ragno-Lonzi (ITA)	4	Ildiko Bobis (HUN)	3	Galina Gorokhova (URS)	3
Team Foil – Women	USSR		Hungary		Romania	
Modern Pentathlon						
Individual	András Balczó (HUN)	5412	Boris Onischenko (URS)	5335	Pavel Lednev (URS)	5328
Team	USSR	15968	Hungary	15348	Finland	14812
Canoeing						
Men						
1000 m Kayak Singles K 1	Alexander Shaparenko (URS)	3:48.06	Rolf Peterson (SWE)	3:48.35	Geza Csapó (HUN)	3:49.38
1000 m Kayak Pairs K 2	USSR	3:31.23	Hungary	3:32.00	Poland	3:33.83
1000 m Kayak Fours K 4	USSR	3:14.02	Romania	3:15.07	Norway	3:15.27
1000 m Canadian Singles C 1	Ivan Patzaichin (ROM)	4:08.94	Tamas Wichmann (HUN)	4:12.42	Detlef Lewe (FRG)	4:13.63
1000 m Canadian Pairs C2	USSR	3:52.60	Romania	3:52.63	Bulgaria	3:58.10
Women						
500 m Kayak Singles K 1	Yulia Ryabchinskaya (URS)	2:03.17	Mieke Jaapies (HOL)	2:04.03	Anna Pfeffer (HUN)	2:05.50
500 m Kayak Pairs K 2	USSR	1:53.50	GDR	1:54.30	Romania	1:55.01
Slalom Racing						
Kayak Singles	Siegbert Horn (GDR)	268.56	Norbert Sattler (AUT)	270.76	Harald Gimpel (GDR)	277.95
Canadian Singles	Reinhard Eiben (GDR)	315.84	Reinhold Kauder (FRG)	327.89	Jamie McEwan (USA)	335.95
Canadian Pairs	GDR	310.68	FRG	311.90	France	315.10
Kayak Singles (Women)	Angelika Bahmann (GDR)	364.50	Gisela Grothaus (FRG)	398.15	Magdalena Wunderlich (FRG)	400.50
Rowing						
Single Sculls	Yuriy Malishev (URS)	7:10.12	Alberto Demiddi (ARG)	7:11.53	Wolfgang Güldenpfennig (GDR)	7:14.45
Double Sculls	USSR	7:01.77	Norway	7:02.58	GDR	7:05.55
Coxless Pairs	GDR	6:53.16	Switzerland	6:57.06	Netherlands	6:58.70
Coxed Pairs	GDR	7:17.25	Czechoslovakia	7:19.57	Romania	7:21.36
Coxless Fours	GDR	6:24.27	New Zealand	6:25.64	FRG	6:28.41
Coxed Fours	FRG	6:31.85	GDR	6:33.30	Czechoslovakia	6:35.64
Coxed Eights	New Zealand	6:08.94	USA	6:11.61	GDR	6:11.67
Yachting						
Finn Class	Serge Maury (FRA)	58.0	Ilias Hatzipavlis (GRE)	71.0	Viktor Potapov (URS)	74.7
International Star	Australia	28.1	Sweden	44.0	FRG	44.4
Flying Dutchman	Great Britain	22.7	France	40.7	FRG	51.1
International Tempest	USSR	28.1	Great Britain	34.4	USA	47.7
Dragon	Australia	13.7	GDR	41.7	USA	47.7
International Soling	USA	8.7	Sweden	31.7	Canada	47.1
Cycling						
Individual Road Race (182.4 km)	Hennie Kuiper (HOL)	4:14:37.0	Kevin Sefton (AUS)	4:15:04.0	Jaime Huelamo (ESP) (Medal withdrawn –disqualified)	
100 km Road Team Time Trial	USSR	2:11:17.8	Poland	2:11:47.5	Medal withdrawn (HOL disqualified)	
1000 m Time Trial	Niels Fredborg (DEN)	1:06.44	Danny Clark (AUS)	1:06.87	Jürgen Schütze (GDR)	1:07.02
1000 m Sprint	Daniel Morelon (FRA)		John Michael Nicholson (AUS)		Omar Phakadze (URS)	
2000 m Tandem	USSR		GDR		Poland	
4000 m Individual Pursuit	Knut Knudsen (NOR)	4:45.74	Xaver Kurmann (SUI)	4:51.96	Hans Lutz (FRG)	4:50.80
4000 m Team Pursuit	FRG	4:22.14	GDR	4:25.25	Great Britain	4:23.78
Equestrianism						
Three-Day Event	Richard Meade (GBR)	57.73	Alessandro Argenton (ITA)	43.33	Jan Jonsson (SWE)	39.67
Three-Day Event - Teams	Great Britain	95.53	USA	10.81	FRG	18.00
Grand Prix (Dressage)	Liselott Linsenhoff (FRG)	1229	Elena Petruchkova (URS)	1185	Josef Neckermann (FRG)	1177
Grand Prix (Dressage) Team	USSR	5095	FRG	5083	Sweden	4849
Grand Prix (Jumping)	Graziano Mancinelli (ITA)	8/0	Ann Moore (GBR)	8/3	Neal Shapiro (USA)	8/8
Grand Prix (Jumping) Team	FRG	32.00	USA	32.25	Italy	48.00
Shooting						
Free Rifle (3 Positions)	Lones Wigger (USA)	1155	Boris Melnik (URS)	1155	Lajos Papp (HUN)	1149
Small-Bore Rifle (Prone)	Ho Jun Li (PRK)	599	Viktor Auer (USA)	598	Nicolae Rotaru (ROM)	598
Small-Bore Rifle (3 Positions)	John Writer (USA)	1166	Lanny Bassham (USA)	1157	Werner Lippoldt (GDR)	1153
Rapid-Fire Pistol	Jósef Zapedszki (POL)	595	Ladislav Faita (TCH)	594	Viktor Torshin (URS)	593
Free Pistol (50 m)	Ragnar Shanakar (SWE)	567	Dan Iuga (ROM)	562	Rudolf Dollinger (AUT)	560
Running Game Target	Lakov Zhelezniak (URS)	569	Helmut Bellingrodt (COL)	565	John Kynoch (GBR)	562

EVENT	GOLD		SILVER		BRONZE	
Skeet Shooting	Konrad Wirnhier (FRG)	195/25	Evgeny Petrov (URS)	195/24	Michael Buchheim (GDR)	195/23
Trap Shooting	Angelo Scalzone (ITA)	199	Michel Carrega (FRA)	198	Silvano Basagni (ITA)	195
Archery						
Men	John William (USA)	2528	Gunnar Jarvil (SWE)	2481	Kyösti Laasonen (FIN)	2467
Women	Doreen Wilber (USA)	2424	Irena Szydlowska (POL)	2407	Emma Gapchenko (URS)	2403
Gymnastics						
Men						
Individual Combined Exercises	Sawao Kato (JPN)	114.650	Eizo Kenmotsu (JPN)	114.575	Akinori Nakayama (JPN)	114.325
Team	Japan	571.25	USSR	564.05	GDR	559.70
Parallel Bars	Sawao Kato (JPN)	19.475	Shigeru Kasamatsu (JPN)	19.375	Eizo Kenmotsu (JPN)	19.250
Floor	Nikolai Andrianov (URS)	19.175	Akinori Nakayama (JPN)	19.125	Shigeru Kasamatsu (JPN)	19.025
Horse Vault	Klaus Köste (GDR)	18.850	Viktor Klimenko (URS)	18.825	Nikolai Andrianov (URS)	18.800
Horizontal Bar	Mitsuo Tsukahara (JPN)	19.725	Sawao Kato (JPN)	19.525	Shigeru Kasamatsu (JPN)	19.450
Rings	Akinori Nakayama (JPN)	19.350	Mikhail Voronin (URS)	19.275	Mitsuo Tsukahara (JPN)	19.225
Pommel Horse	Viktor Klimenko (URS)	19.125	Sawao Kato (JPN)	19.000	Eizo Kenmotsu (JPN)	18.950
Women						
Individual Combined Exercises	Ludmila Tourischeva (URS)	77.025	Karin Janz (GDR)	76.875	Tamara Lazakovitsch (URS)	76.850
Team	USSR	380.50	GDR	376.55	Hungary	368.25
Floor	Olga Korbut (URS)	19.575	Ludmila Tourischeva (URS)	19.550	Tamara Lazakovitsch (URS)	19.450
Horse Vault	Karin Janz (GDR)	19.525	Erika Zuchold (GDR)	19.275	Ludmila Tourischeva (URS)	19.250
Beam	Olga Korbut (URS)	19.400	Tamara Lazakovitsch (URS)	19.375	Karin Janz (GDR)	18.975
Asymmetrical Bars	Karin Janz (GDR)	19.675	Olga Korbut (URS)	19.450		
			Erika Zuchold (GDR)	19.450		
Basketball						
	USSR		USA		Cuba	
Soccer						
	Poland		Hungary		GDR★	
					USSR★	
Handball						
	Yugoslavia		Czechoslovakia		Romania	
Hockey						
	West Germany		Pakistan		India	
Volleyball						
Men	Japan		GDR		USSR	
Women	USSR		Japan		North Korea	

★ GDR and USSR declared joint bronze medallists as result was still a draw at end of extra time

Innsbruck 1976

4 February – 15 February

Participants: 1123 / Men: 892, Women: 231, Countries: 37,
Sports: 8, Events: 37
Final Torchbearers: Christl Haas and Josef Feistmantl

Medals Table

PLACE	COUNTRY	GOLD	SILVER	BRONZE
1	USSR	13	6	8
2	GDR	7	5	7
3	USA	3	3	4
4	Norway	3	3	1
5	FRG	2	5	3

Outstanding Athletes

PLACE	NAME (NATIONALITY)	DISCIPLINE	G	S	B
1	Rosi Mittermaier (FRG)	Alpine Skiing	2	1	–
	Raisa Smetanina (URS)	Nordic Skiing	2	1	–
3	Tatjana Averina (URS)	Speed Skating	2	–	2
4	Nikolai Kruglov (URS)	Biathlon	2	–	–
	Meinhard Nehmer (GDR)	Bobsledding	2	–	–
	Bernhard Germedshausen (GDR)	Bobsledding	2	–	–

EVENT	GOLD		SILVER		BRONZE	
Alpine Skiing						
Men						
Downhill	Franz Klammer (AUT)	1:45.73	Bernhard Russi (SUI)	1:46.06	Herbert Plank (ITA)	1:46.59
Slalom	Piero Gros (ITA)	2:03.29	Gustav Thöni (ITA)	2:03.73	Willy Frommelt (LIE)	2:04.28
Giant Slalom	Heini Hemmi (SUI)	3:26.97	Ernst Good (SUI)	3:27.17	Ingemar Stenmark (SWE)	3:27.41
Women						
Downhill	Rosi Mittermaier (FRG)	1:46.16	Brigitte Toschnig (AUT)	1:46.68	Cynthia Nelson (USA)	1:47.50
Slalom	Rosi Mittermaier (FRG)	1:30.54	Claudia Giordani (ITA)	1:30.87	Hanni Wenzel (LIE)	1:32.20
Giant Slalom	Kathy Kreiner (CAN)	1:29.13	Rosi Mittermaier (FRG)	1:29.25	Danielle Debernard (FRA)	1:29.95
Nordic Skiing						
Men						
15 km Cross Country Skiing	Nikolai Bajukov (URS)	43:58.47	Yevgeniy Beliayev (URS)	44:01.10	Arto Koivisto (FIN)	44:19.25
30 km Cross-Country Skiing	Sergey Savelyev (URS)	1:30:29.38	Bill Koch (USA)	1:30:57.84	Ivan Garanin (URS)	1:31:09.29
50 km	Ivar Formo (NOR)	2:37:30.05	Gert-Dietmar Klause (GDR)	2:38:13.21	Benny Södergren (SWE)	2:39:39.21
4 x 10 km	Finland	2:07:59.72	Norway	2:09:58.36	USSR	2:10:51.46
Ski Jumping (70 m Hill)	Hans-Georg Aschenbach (GDR)	252.0	Jochen Danneberg (GDR)	246.2	Karl Schnabl (AUT)	242.0
Ski Jumping (90 m Hill)	Karl Schnabl (AUT)	234.8	Toni Innauer (AUT)	232.9	Henry Glass (GDR)	221.7
Nordic Combined	Ulrich Wehling (GDR)	423.39	Urban Hettich (FRG)	418.90	Konrad Winkler (GDR)	417.47
Women						
5 km Cross-Country Skiing	Helena Takalo (FIN)	15:48.69	Raisa Smetanina (URS)	15:49.73	Nina Baldycheva (URS)	16:12.82
10 km Cross-Country Skiing	Raisa Smetanina (URS)	30:13.41	Helena Takalo (FIN)	30:14.28	Galina Kulakova (URS)	30:38.61
4 x 5 km	USSR	1:07:49.76	Finland	1:08:36.57	DDR	1:09:57.95
Biathlon						
20 km	Nikolai Kruglov (URS)	1:14:12.26	Heikki Ikola (FIN)	1:15:54.10	Alexander Elizarov (URS)	1:16:05.57
4 x 7.5 km	USSR	1:57:55.64	Finland	2:01:45.58	GDR	2:04:08.61
Figure Skating						
Women	Dorothy Hamill (USA)		Dianna de Leeuw (HOL)		Christine Errath (GDR)	
Men	John Curry (GBR)		Vladimir Kovalev (URS)		Toller Cranston (CAN)	
Pairs	Irina Rodnina/Alexander Saizev (URS)		Romy Kerner/Rolf Österreich (GDR)		Manuela Gross/Uwe Kagelmann (GDR)	
Ice Dance	Ludmilla Pakhomova/ Aleksandr Gorskov (URS)		Irina Moisejeva/ Andrej Minenko (URS)		Collen O'Connor/James Millns (USA)	
Speed Skating						
Men						
500 m	Yevgeniy Kulikov (URS)	39.17	Valeriy Muratov (URS)	39.25	Daniel Immerfall (USA)	39.54
1000 m	Peter Mueller (USA)	1:19.32	Jörn Didriksen (NOR)	1:20.45	Valeriy Muratov (URS)	1:20.57
1500 m	Jan Egil Storholt (NOR)	1:59.38	Yuriy Kondakov (URS)	1:59.97	Hans van Helden (HOL)	2:00.87
5000 m	Sten Stensen (NOR)	7:24.28	Piet Kleine (HOL)	7:26.47	Hans van Helden (HOL)	7:26.54
10,000 m	Piet Kleine (HOL)	14:50.59	Sten Stensen (NOR)	14:53.30	Hans van Helden (HOL)	15:02.02
Women						
500 m	Sheila Young (USA)	42.76	Cathy Priestner (CAN)	43.12	Tatyana Averina (URS)	43.17
1000 m	Tatyana Averina (URS)	1:28.43	Leah Poulos (USA)	1:28.57	Sheila Young (USA)	1:29.14
1500 m	Galina Stepanskaya (URS)	2:16.58	Sheila Young (USA)	2:17.06	Tatyana Averina (URS)	2:17.96
3000 m	Tatyana Averina (URS)	4:45.19	Andrea Mitscherlich (GDR)	4:45.23	Lisbeth Korsmo (NOR)	4:45.24
Bobsledding						
2-Man Bob	GDR I	3:44.42	FRG I	3:44.99	Switzerland I	3:45.70
4-Man Bob	GDR I	3:40.43	Switzerland II	3:40.89	FRG I	3:41.37
Lugeing						
Men's Singles	Detlef Günther (GDR)	3:27.688	Josef Fendt (FRG)	3:28.196	Hans Rinn (GDR)	3:28.574
Women's Singles	Margit Schumann (GDR)	2:50.621	Ute Rührold (GDR)	2:50.846	Elisabeth Demleitner (FRG)	2:51.056
2-Man Luge	Hans Rinn/ Norbert Hahn (GDR)	1:25.604	Hans Brandner/ Balthasar Schwarm (FRG)	1:25.889	Rudolf Schmid/ Franz Schachner (AUT)	1:25.919
Ice Hockey						
	USSR		Czechoslovakia		FRG	

Montreal 1976

17 July – 1 August

Participants: 6028 / Men: 4781, Women: 1247, Countries: 92,
Sports: 21, Events: 198
Final Torchbearers: Sandra Henderson and Stéphane Prefontaine

Medals Table

PLACE	COUNTRY	GOLD	SILVER	BRONZE
1	USSR	49	41	35
2	GDR	40	25	25
3	USA	34	35	25
4	FRG	10	12	17
5	Japan	9	6	10

Outstanding Athletes

PLACE	NAME (NATIONALITY)	DISCIPLINE	G	S	B
1	Nikolai Andrianov (URS)	Gymnastics	4	2	1
2	Kornelia Ender (GDR)	Swimming	4	1	–
	John Naber (USA)	Swimming	4	1	–
4	Nadia Comaneci (ROM)	Gymnastics	3	1	1
5	Nelli Kim (URS)	Gymnastics	3	1	–

EVENT	GOLD		SILVER		BRONZE	
Athletics						
Men						
100 m	Hasely Crawford (TRI)	10.06	Donald Quarrie (JAM)	10.08	Valeriy Borsov (URS)	10.14
200 m	Donald Quarrie (JAM)	20.23	Millard Hampton (USA)	20.29	Dwayne Evans (USA)	20.43
400 m	Alberto Juantorena (CUB)	44.26	Fred Newhouse (USA)	44.40	Herman Frazier (USA)	44.95
800 m	Alberto Juantorena (CUB)	1:43.5	Ivo van Damme (BEL)	1:43.9	Richard Wohlhuter (USA)	1:44.1
1500 m	John Walker (NZL)	3:39.2	Ivo van Damme (BEL)	3:39.3	Paul-Heinz Wellmann (FRG)	3:39.3
5000 m	Lasse Viren (FIN)	13:24.8	Dick Quax (NZL)	13:25.2	Klaus-P. Hildenbrand (FRG)	13:25.4
10,000 m	Lasse Viren (FIN)	27:44.4	Carlos Lopez (POR)	27:45.2	Brendan Foster (GBR)	27:54.9
Marathon	Waldemar Cierpinski (GDR)	2:09:55.0	Frank Shorter (USA)	2:10:45.8	Karel Lismont (BEL)	2:11:12.6
110 m Hurdles	Guy Drut (FRA)	13.30	Alejandro Casanas (CUB)	13.33	Willie Davenport (USA)	13.38
400 m Hurdles	Edwin Moses (USA)	47.64	Michael Shine (USA)	48.69	Yevgeniy Gavrilenko (URS)	49.45
3000 m Steeplechase	Anders Gärderud (SWE)	8:08.0	Bronislaw Malinowski (POL)	8:09.1	Frank Baumgartl (GDR)	8:10.4
4 x 100 m	USA	38.33	GDR	38.66	USSR	38.78
4 x 400 m	USA	2:58.65	Poland	3:01.43	FRG	3:01.98
20 km Walk	Daniel Bautista (MEX)	1:24:40.6	Hans-Peter Reimann (GDR)	1:25:13.8	Peter Frenkel (GDR)	1:25:29.4
High Jump	Jacek Wszola (POL)	2.25	Gregory Joy (CAN)	2.23	Dwight Stones (USA)	2.21
Pole Vault	Tadeusz Slusarski (POL)	5.50	Antti Kalliomäki (FIN)	5.50	David Roberts (USA)	5.50
Long Jump	Arnie Robinson (USA)	8.35	Randy Williams (USA)	8.11	Frank Wartenberg (GDR)	8.02
Triple Jump	Viktor Saneyev (URS)	17.29	James Butts (USA)	17.18	Joao de Oliveira (BRA)	16.90
Shot	Udo Beyer (GDR)	21.05	Yevgeniy Mironov (URS)	21.03	Alexander Baryshnikov (URS)	21.00
Discus	Mac Wilkins (USA)	67.50	Wolfgang Schmidt (GDR)	66.22	John Powell (USA)	65.70
Hammer	Yuriy Sedykh (URS)	77.52	Alexey Spiridonov (URS)	76.08	Anatoliy Bondarchuk (URS)	75.48
Javelin	Miklos Nemeth (HUN)	94.58	Hannu Siitonen (FIN)	87.92	Gheorghe Megelea (ROM)	87.16
Decathlon	Bruce Jenner (USA)	8617	Guido Kratschmer (FRG)	8411	Nikolai Avilov (URS)	8369
Women						
100 m	Annegret Richter (FRG)	11.08	Renate Stecher (GDR)	11.13	Inge Helten (FRG)	11.17
200 m	Bärbel Eckert (GDR)	22.37	Annegret Richter (FRG)	22.39	Renate Stecher (GDR)	22.47
400 m	Irena Szewinska (POL)	49.29	Christina Brehmer (GDR)	50.51	Ellen Streidt (GDR)	50.55
800 m	Tatyana Kazankina (URS)	1:54.9	Nikolina Shtereva (BUL)	1:55.4	Elfie Zinn (GDR)	1:55.6
1500 m	Tatyana Kazankina (URS)	4:05.5	Gunhild Hoffmeister (GDR)	4:06.0	Ulrike Klapezynski (GDR)	4:06.1
100 m Hurdles	Johanna Schaller (GDR)	12.77	Tatyana Anisimova (URS)	12.78	Natalya Lebedeva (URS)	12.80
4 x 100 m	GDR	42.55	FRG	42.59	USSR	43.09
4 x 400 m	GDR	3:19.2	USA	3:22.8	USSR	3:24.2
High Jump	Rosemarie Ackermann (GDR)	1.93	Sara Simeoni (ITA)	1.91	Yordanka Blagoyeva (BUL)	1.91
Long Jump	Angela Voigt (GDR)	6.72	Kathy McMillan (USA)	6.66	Lidia Alfeyeva (USR)	6.60
Shot	Ivanka Christova (BUL)	21.16	Nadyezda Chizhova (URS)	20.96	Helena Fibingerová (TCH)	20.67
Discus	Evelin Schlaak (GDR)	69.00	Maria Vergova (BUL)	67.30	Gabriele Hinzmann (GDR)	66.84
Javelin	Ruth Fuchs (GDR)	65.94	Marion Becker (FRG)	64.70	Kathy Schmidt (USA)	63.96
Pentathlon	Siegrun Siegl (GDR)	4745	Christine Laser (GDR)	4745	Burglinde Pollak (GDR)	4740
Swimming						
Men						
100 m Freestyle	Jim Montgomery (USA)	49.99	Jack Babashoff (USA)	50.81	Peter Nocke (FRG)	51.31
200 m Freestyle	Bruce Furniss (USA)	1:50.29	John Naber (USA)	1:50.50	Jim Montgomery (USA)	1:50.58
400 m Freestyle	Brian Goodell (USA)	3:51.93	Tim Shaw (USA)	3:52.54	Vladimir Raskatov (URS)	3:55.76
1500 m Freestyle	Brian Goodell (USA)	15:02.40	Bobby Hackett (USA)	15:03.91	Stephen Holland (AUS)	15:04.66
100 m Backstroke	John Naber (USA)	55.49	Peter Rocca (USA)	56.34	Roland Matthes (GDR)	57.22
200 m Backstroke	John Naber (USA)	1:59.19	Peter Rocca (USA)	2:00.55	Dan Harrigan (USA)	2:01.35
100 m Breaststroke	John Hencken (USA)	1:03.11	David Wilkie (GBR)	1:03.43	Arvidas Iuozaytis (URS)	1:04.23

EVENT	GOLD		SILVER		BRONZE	
200 m Breaststroke	David Wilkie (GBR)	2:15.11	John Hencken (USA)	2:17.26	Richard Colella (USA)	2:19.20
100 m Butterfly	Matt Vogel (USA)	54.35	Joe Bottom (USA)	54.50	Gary Hall (USA)	54.65
200 m Butterfly	Mike Bruner (USA)	1:59.23	Steven Gregg (USA)	1:59.54	Bill Forrester (USA)	1:59.96
400 m Medley	Rod Strachan (USA)	4:23.68	Alexander McKee (USA)	4:24.62	Andrei Smirnov (URS)	4:26.90
4 x 200 m Freestyle	USA	7:23.22	USSR	7:27.97	Great Britain	7:32.11
4 x 100 m Medley	USA	3:42.22	Canada	3:45.94	FRG	3:47.29
Springboard Diving	Phil Boggs (USA)	619.05	Franco Cagnotto (ITA)	570.48	Alexander Kosenkov (URS)	567.24
Highboard Diving	Klaus Dibiasi (ITA)	600.51	Greg Louganis (USA)	576.99	Vladimir Aleynik (URS)	548.61
Water Polo	Hungary		Italy		Netherlands	
Women						
100 m Freestyle	Kornelia Ender (GDR)	55.65	Petra Priemer (GDR)	56.49	Enith Brigitha (HOL)	56.65
200 m Freestyle	Kornelia Ender (GDR)	1:59.26	Shirley Babashoff (USA)	2:01.22	Enith Brigitha (HOL)	2:01.40
400 m Freestyle	Petra Thümer (GDR)	4:09.89	Shirley Babashoff (USA)	4:10.46	Shannon Smith (CAN)	4:14.60
800 m Freestyle	Petra Thümer (GDR)	8:37.14	Shirley Babashoff (USA)	8:37.59	Wendy Weinberg (USA)	8:42.60
100 m Backstroke	Ulrike Richter (GDR)	1:01.83	Birgit Treiber (GDR)	1:03.41	Nancy Garapick (CAN)	1:03.71
200 m Backstroke	Ulrike Richter (GDR)	2:13.43	Birgit Treiber (GDR)	2:14.97	Nancy Garapick (CAN)	2:15.60
100 m Breaststroke	Hannelore Anke (GDR)	1:11.16	Lubov Rusanova (URS)	1:13.04	Marina Kosceveya (URS)	1:13.30
200 m Breaststroke	Marina Koscheveya (URS)	2:33.35	Marina Yurchenia (URS)	2:36.08	Lubow Rusanova (URS)	2:36.22
100 m Butterfly	Kornelia Ender (GDR)	1:00.13	Andrea Pollack (GDR)	1:00.98	Wendy Boglioli (USA)	1:01.17
200 m Butterfly	Andrea Pollack (GDR)	2:11.41	Ulrike Tauber (GDR)	2:12.50	Rosemarie Gabriel (GDR)	2:12.86
400 m Medley	Ulrike Tauber (GDR)	4:42.77	Cheryl Gibson (CAN)	4:48.10	Becky Smith (CAN)	4:50.48
4 x 100 m Freestyle	USA	3:44.82	GDR	3:45.50	Canada	3:48.81
4 x 100 m Medley	GDR	4:07.95	USA	4:14.55	Canada	4:15.22
Springboard Diving	Jennifer Chandler (USA)	506.19	Christa Köhler (GDR)	469.41	Cynthia McIngvale (USA)	466.83
Highboard Diving	Elena Vaytsekhovskaya (URS)	406.59	Ulrika Knape (SWE)	402.60	Deborah Wilson (USA)	401.07
Boxing						
Light-Flyweight (- 48 kg)	Jorge Hernandez (CUB)		Byong Uk Li (PRK)		Payao Pooltarat (THA)	
					Orlando Maldonado (PUR)	
Flyweight (- 51 kg)	Leo Randolph (USA)		Ramon Duvalon (CUB)		David Torosyan (URS)	
					Leszek Blazynski (POL)	
Bantamweight (- 54 kg)	Yong Jo Gu (PRK)		Charles Mooney (USA)		Patrick Cowdell (GBR)	
					Chulsoon Hwang (KOR)	
Featherweight (- 57 kg)	Angel Herrera (CUB)		Richard Nowakowski (GDR)		Leszek Kosedowski (POL)	
					Juan Paredes (MEX)	
Lightweight (- 60 kg)	Howard Davis (USA)		Simion Cutov (ROM)		Vasiliy Solomin (URS)	
					Ace Rusevski (YUG)	
Light-Welterweight (- 63.5 kg)	Sugar Ray Leonard (USA)		Andres Aldama (CUB)		Wladimir Kolev (BUL)	
					Kacimierz Szcerba (POL)	
Welterweight (- 67 kg)	Jochen Bachfeld (GDR)		Pedro Gamarro (VEN)		Reinhard Skricek (FRG)	
					Victor Zilberman (ROM)	
Light-Middleweight (- 71 kg)	Jerzy Rybicki (POL)		Tadija Kacar (YUG)		Victor Savchenko (URS)	
					Rolando Garbey (CUB)	
Middleweight (- 75 kg)	Michael Spinks (USA)		Rufat Riskiev (URS)		Alec Nastac (ROM)	
					Luis Martinez (CUB)	
Light-Heavyweight (- 81 kg)	Leon Spinks (USA)		Sixto Soria (CUB)		Costica Danifoiu (ROM)	
					Janusz Gortat (POL)	
Heavyweight (+ 81 kg)	Teofilo Stevenson (CUB)		Mircea Simon (ROM)		Johnny Tate (USA)	
					Clarence Hill (BER)	
Weightlifting						
Flyweight (- 52 kg)	Alexander Voronin (URS)	242.5	György Koszegi (HUN)	237.5	Mohammed Nassiri (IRN)	235.0
Bantamweight (- 56 kg)	Norair Nurikyan (BUL)	262.5	Grzegorz Cziura (POL)	252.5	Kenkichi Ando (JPN)	250.0
Featherweight (- 60 kg)	Nikolai Kolesnikov (URS)	285.0	Georgi Todorov (BUL)	280.0	Kazumasa Hirai (JPN)	275.0
Lightweight (- 67.5 kg)	Pjotr Korol (URS)	305.0	Daniel Senet (FRA)	300.0	Kazimierz Czarnicki (POL)	295.0
Middleweight (- 75 kg)	Yordan Mitkov (BUL)	335.0	Vartan Militosyan (URS)	330.0	Peter Wenzel (GDR)	327.5
Light-Heavyweight (- 82.5 kg)	Valeriy Shariy (URS)	365.0	Trendachil Stoichev (BUL)	360.0	Peter Baczako (HUN)	345.0
Middle-Heavyweight (- 90 kg)	David Rigert (URS)	382.5	Lee James (USA)	362.5	Atanas Chopov (BUL)	360.0
Heavyweight (+ 90 kg)	Yuriy Zaitsev (URS)	385.0	Krastio Semerdiev (BUL)	385.0	Tadeusz Rutkowski (POL)	377.5
Super-Heavyweight (+ 110 kg)	Vasiliy Alexeyev (URS)	440.0	Gerd Bonk (GDR)	405.0	Helmut Losch (GDR)	387.5
Greco-Roman Wrestling						
Light-Flyweight (- 48 kg)	Alexey Shumakov (URS)		Gheorge Berceanu (ROM)		Stefan Anghelov (BUL)	
Flyweight (- 52 kg)	Vitaliy Konstantinov (URS)		Nicu Ginga (ROM)		Koichiro Hirayama (JPN)	
Bantamweight (- 57 kg)	Pertti Ukkola (FIN)		Ivan Frgic (YUG)		Farhat Mustafin (URS)	
Featherweight (- 62 kg)	Kazimierz Lipien (POL)		Nelson Davidian (URS)		Laszlo Reczi (HUN)	
Lightweight (- 68 kg)	Suren Nalbandyan (URS)		Stefan Rusu (ROM)		Heinz-Helmut Wehling (GDR)	

EVENT	GOLD		SILVER		BRONZE	
Welterweight (- 74 kg)	Anatoliy Bykov (URS)		Vitezslav Macha (TCH)		Karl-Heinz Helbing (FRG)	
Middleweight (- 82 kg)	Momir Petkovic (YUG)		Vladimir Cheboksarov (URS)		Ivan Kolev (BUL)	
Light-Heavyweight (- 90 kg)	Valeriy Rezanzev (URS)		Stoyan Nikolov (BUL)		Czeslaw Kwiecinski (POL)	
Heavyweight (- 100 kg)	Nikolai Bolboshin (URS)		Kamen Goranov (BUL)		Andrzej Skrzylewski (POL)	
Super-Heavyweight (+ 100 kg)	Alexander Kolchinski (URS)		Alexander Tomov (BUL)		Roman Codreanu (ROM)	
Freestyle Wrestling						
Light-Flyweight (- 48 kg)	Khassan Issayev (BUL)		Roman Dmitriev (URS)		Akira Kudo (JPN)	
Flyweight (- 52 kg)	Yuji Takada (JPN)		Alexandre Ivanov (URS)		Hae Sup Jeon (KOR)	
Bantamweight (- 57 kg)	Vladimir Umin (URS)		Hans-Dieter Bruchert (GDR)		Masao Arai (JPN)	
Featherweight (- 62 kg)	Jung Mo Yang (KOR)		Zeveg Oidov (MGL)		Gene Davis (USA)	
Lightweight (- 68 kg)	Pavel Pinigin (URS)		Lloyd Keaser (USA)		Yasaburo Sugawara (JPN)	
Welterweight (- 74 kg)	Jiichiro Date (JPN)		Mansour Barzegar (IRN)		Stanley Dziedzic (USA)	
Middleweight (- 82 kg)	John Peterson (USA)		Viktor Novoshilev (URS)		Adolf Seger (FRG)	
Light-Heavyweight (- 90 kg)	Levan Tediashvili (URS)		Benjamin Peterson (USA)		Stelica Morcov (ROM)	
Heavyweight (- 100 kg)	Ivan Yarygin (URS)		Russell Hellickson (USA)		Dimo Kostov (BUL)	
Super-Heavyweight (+ 100 kg)	Soslan Andyev (URS)		Jószef Balla (HUN)		Ladislav Simon (ROM)	
Judo						
Lightweight (- 63 kg)	Hector Rodriguez (CUB)		Eun-Kyung Chang (KOR)		Jozsef Tuncsik (HUN)	
					Felice Mariani (ITA)	
Welterweight (- 70 kg)	Vladimir Nevzorov (URS)		Koji Kuramoto (JPN)		Patrick Vial (FRA)	
					Marian Talaj (POL)	
Middleweight (- 80 kg)	Isamu Sonoda (JPN)		Valeriy Dvoinikov (URS)		Slavko Obadov (YUG)	
					Yung-Chul Park (KOR)	
Light-Heavyweight (- 93 kg)	Kazuhiro Ninomiya (JPN)		Ramaz Harshiladze (URS)		David Starbrook (GBR)	
					Jörg Röthlisberger (SUI)	
Heavyweight (+ 93 kg)	Sergey Novikov (URS)		Günther Neureuther (FRG)		Allen Coage (USA)	
					Sumio Endo (JPN)	
Open Class	Haruki Uemura (JPN)		Keith Remfry (GBR)		Jeaki Cho (KOR)	
					Shota Chochoshvili (URS)	
Fencing						
Individual Foil - Men	Fabio dal Zotto (ITA)	4	Alexander Romankov (URS)	4	Bernard Talvard (FRA)	3
Team Foil - Men	FRG		Italy		France	
Individual Épée	Alexander Pusch (FRG)	3/2	Jürgen Hehn (FRG)	3/1	Gyözö Kulcsár (HUN)	3/0
Team Épée	Sweden		FRG		Switzerland	
Individual Sabre	Viktor Krovopouskov (URS)	5	Vladimir Nazlimov (URS)	4	Viktor Sidjak (URS)	3
Team Sabre	USSR		Italy		Romania	
Individual Foil - Women	Ildiko Schwarczenberger (HUN)	4/1	Maria Consolata Collino (ITA)	4/0	Elena Belova (URS)	3
Team Foil - Women	USSR		France		Hungary	
Modern Pentathlon						
Individual	Janusz Pyciak-Peciak (POL)	5520	Pavel Lednev (URS)	5485	Jan Bartu (TCH)	5466
Team	Great Britain	15559	Czechoslovakia	15451	Hungary	15395
Canoeing						
Men						
500 m Kayak Singles K1	Vasile Diba (ROM)	1:46.11	Zoltan Sztanity (HUN)	1:46.95	Rüdiger Helm (GDR)	1:48.30
1000 m Kayak Singles K1	Rüdiger Helm (GDR)	3:48.20	Geza Csapó (HUN)	3:48.34	Vasile Diba (ROM)	3:49.65
500 m Kayak Pairs K2	GDR	1:35.87	USSR	1:36.81	Romania	1:37.43
1000 m Kayak Pairs K2	USSR	3:29.01	GDR	3:29.33	Hungary	3:30.36
1000 m Kayak Fours K4	USSR	3:08.69	Spain	3:08.95	GDR	3:10.76
500 m Canadian Singles C1	Alexander Rogov (URS)	1:59.23	John Wood (CAN)	1:59.58	Matja Ljubek (YUG)	1:59.60
1000 m Canadian Singles C1	Matja Ljubek (YUG)	4:09.51	Vasiliy Urchenko (URS)	4:12.57	Tamás Wichmann (HUN)	4:14.11
500 m Canadian Pairs C2	USSR	1:45.81	Poland	1:47.77	Hungary	1:48.35
1000 m Canadian Pairs C 2	USSR	3:52.76	Romania	3:54.28	Hungary	3:55.66
Women						
500 m Kayak Singles K1	Carola Zirzow (GDR)	2:01.05	Tatyana Korshunova (URS)	2:03.07	Klara Rajnai (HUN)	2:05.01
500m Kayak Pairs K2	USSR	1:51.15	Hungary	1:51.69	GDR	1:51.81
Rowing						
Men						
Single Sculls	Pertti Karppinen (FIN)	7:29.03	Peter-Michael Kolbe (FRG)	7:31.67	Joachim Dreifke (GDR)	7:38.03
Doubles Sculls	Norway	7:13.20	Great Britain	7:15.25	GDR	7:17.45
Coxless Pairs	GDR	7:23.31	USA	7:26.73	FRG	7:30.03

EVENT	GOLD		SILVER		BRONZE	
Coxed Pairs	GDR	7:58.99	USSR	8:01.82	Czechoslovakia	8:03.28
Coxless Quadruple Sculls	GDR	6:18.65	USSR	6:19.89	Czechoslovakia	6:21.77
Coxless Fours	GDR	6:37.42	Norway	6:41.22	USSR	6:42.52
Coxed Fours	USSR	6:40.22	GDR	6:42.70	FRG	6:46.96
Coxed Eights	GDR	5:58.29	Great Britain	6:00.82	New Zealand	6:03.51
Women						
Single Sculls	Christina Scheiblich (GDR)	4:05.56	Joan Lind (USA)	4:06.21	Elena Antonova (URS)	4:10.24
Double Sculls	Bulgaria	3:44.36	GDR	3:47.86	USSR	3:49.93
Coxless Pairs	Bulgaria	4:01.22	GDR	4:01.61	FRG	4:02.35
Coxed Quadruple Sculls	GDR	3:29.99	USSR	3:32.49	Romania	3:32.76
Coxed Fours	GDR	3:45.08	Bulgaria	3:48.24	USSR	3:49.38
Coxed Eights	GDR	3:33.32	USSR	3:36.17	USA	3:38.68
Yachting						
Finn Class	Jochen Schürmann (GDR)	35.4	Andrey Balashov (URS)	39.7	John Bertrand (AUS)	46.4
International Tempest	Sweden	14.0	USSR	30.4	USA	32.7
Flying Dutchman	FRG	34.7	Great Britain	51.7	Brazil	52.1
International Tornado	Great Britain	18.0	USA	36.0	FRG	37.7
International 470	FRG	42.4	Spain	49.7	Australia	57.0
International Soling	Denmark	46.7	USA	47.4	GDR	47.4
Cycling						
Individual Road Race (175 km)	Bernt Johansson (SWE)	4:46:52	Giuseppe Martinelli (ITA)	4:47:23	Mieczyl Nowicki (POL)	4:47:23
100 km Road Team Time Trial	USSR	2:08:53	Poland	2:09:13	Denmark	2:12:20
1000 m Time Trial	Klaus-Jürgen Grünke (GDR)	1:05.927	Michel Vaarten (BEL)	1:07.516	Niels Fredborg (DEN)	1:07.617
1000 m Sprint	Anton Tkac (TCH)		Daniel Morelon (FRA)		Hans-Jürgen Geschke (GDR)	
4000 m- Individual Pursuit	Gregor Braun (FRG)	4:47.61	Herman Ponsteen (HOL)	4:49.72	Thomas Huschke (GDR)	4:52.71
4000 m Team Pursuit	FRG	4:21.06	USSR	4:27.15	Great Britain	4:22.41
Equestrianism						
Three-Day Event	Edmund Coffin (USA)	114.99	John Plumb (USA)	125.85	Karl Schultz (FRG)	129.45
Three-Day Event, Team	USA	441.00	FRG	584.60	Australia	599.54
Grand Prix (Dressage)	Christine Stückelberger (SUI)	1486	Harry Boldt (FRG)	1435	Reiner Klimke (FRG)	1395
Grand Prix (Dressage) Team	FRG	5155	Switzerland	4684	USA	4670
Grand Prix (Jumping)	Alwin Schockemöhle (FRG)	0	Michel Vaillancourt (CAN)	12/4	François Mathy (BEL)	12/8
Grand Prix (Jumping) Team	France	40	FRG	44	Belgium	63
Shooting						
Small-Bore Rifle (Prone)	Karlheinz Smieszek (FRG)	599	Ulrich Lind (FRG)	597	Gennadiy Lushchikov (URS)	595
Small-Bore Rifle (3 Positions)	Lanny Bassham (USA)	1162	Margaret Murdock (USA)	1162	Werner Seibold (FRG)	1160
Rapid-Fire Pistol	Norbert Klaar (GDR)	597	Jürgen Wiefel (GDR)	596	Roberto Ferraris (ITA)	595
Free Pistol (50 m)	Uwe Potteck (GDR)	573	Harald Vollmar (GDR)	567	Rudolf Dollinger (AUT)	562
Running Game Target	Alexander Gasov (URS)	579	Alexander Kedyarov(URS)	576	Jerzy Greszkiewicz (POL)	571
Skeet Shooting	Josef Panacek (TCH)	198	Eric Swinkels (HOL)	198	Wieslaw Gawlikowski (POL)	196
Trap Shooting	Donald Haldeman (USA)	190	Armando Silva Marques (POR)	189	Ubaldesco Baldi (ITA)	189
Archery						
Women	Luann Ryan (USA)	2499	Valentina Kovpan (URS)	2460	Zebiniso Rustamova (URS)	2407
Men	Darrell Pace (USA)	2571	Hiroshi Michinaga (JPN)	2502	Giancarlo Ferrari (ITA)	2495
Gymnastics						
Men						
Individual Combined Exercises	Nikolai Andrianov (URS)	116.650	Sawao Kato (JPN)	115.650	Mitsuo Tsukahara (JPN)	115.575
Team	Japan	576.85	USSR	576.45	GDR	564.65
Parallel Bars	Sawao Kato (JPN)	19.675	Nikolai Andrianov (URS)	19.500	Mitsuo Tsukahara (JPN)	19.475
Floor	Nikolai Andrianov (URS)	19.450	Vladimir Marchenko (URS)	19.425	Peter Korman (USA)	19.300
Horse Vault	Nikolai Andrianov (URS)	19.450	Mitsuo Tsukahara (JPN)	19.375	Hiroshi Kajiyama (JPN)	19.275
Horizontal Bar	Mitsuo Tsukahara (JPN)	19.675	Eizo Kenmotsu (JPN)	19.500	Henri Boerio (FRA)	19.475
					Eberhard Gienger (FRG)	19.475
Rings	Nikolai Andrianov (URS)	19.650	Alexander Ditiatin (URS)	19.550	Dan Grecu (ROM)	19.500
Pommel Horse	Zoltan Magyar (HUN)	19.700	Eizo Kenmotsu (JPN)	19.575	Nikolai Andrianov (URS)	19.525
Women						
Individual Combined Exercises	Nadia Comaneci (ROM)	79.275	Nelli Kim (URS)	78.675	Ludmila Tourischeva (URS)	78.625
Team	USSR	390.35	Romania	387.15	GDR	385.10
Floor	Nelli Kim (URS)	19.850	Ludmila Tourischeva (URS)	19.825	Nadia Comaneci (ROM)	19.750
Horse Vault	Nelli Kim (URS)	19.800	Carola Dombeck (GDR)	19.650		
			Ludmila Tourischeva (URS)	19.650		
Beam	Nadia Comaneci (ROM)	19.950	Olga Korbut (URS)	19.725	Teodora Ungureanu (ROM)	19.700

EVENT	GOLD		SILVER		BRONZE	
Asymmetrical Bars	Nadia Comaneci (ROM)	20.000	Teodora Ungureanu (ROM)	19.800	Marta Egervari (HUN)	19.775
Team Gymnastics	Sweden	74.20	USSR	73.00	Poland	74.00
Basketball						
Men	USA		Yugoslavia		USSR	
Women	USSR		USA		Bulgaria	
Soccer						
	GDR		Poland		USSR	
Handball						
Men	USSR		Romania		Poland	
Women	USSR		GDR		Hungary	
Hockey						
	New Zealand		Australia		Pakistan	
Volleyball						
Men	Poland		USSR		Cuba	
Women	Japan		USSR		South Korea	

Lake Placid 1980

Participants: 1072 / Men: 839, Women: 233, Countries: 37,
Sports: 8, Events: 38
Final Torchbearer: Charles Morgan Kerr

12 February – 24 February
(Official Opening Ceremony 13 February)

Medals Table

PLACE	COUNTRY	GOLD	SILVER	BRONZE
1	USSR	10	6	6
2	GDR	9	7	7
3	USA	6	4	2
4	Austria	3	2	2
5	Sweden	3	–	1

Outstanding Athletes

PLACE	NAME (NATIONALITY)	DISCIPLINE	G	S	B
1	Eric Heiden (USA)	Speed Skating	5	–	–
2	Nikolai Simyatov(URS)	Nordic Skiing	3	–	–
3	Hanni Wenzel (LIE)	Alpine Skiing	2	1	–
4	Anatoliy Alyiabiev (URS)	Biathlon	2	–	1
5	Barbara Petzold (GDR)	Nordic Skiing	2	–	–
	Ingemar Stenmark (SWE)	Alpine Skiing	2	–	–

EVENT	GOLD		SILVER		BRONZE	
Alpine Skiing						
Men						
Downhill	Leonhard Stock (AUT)	1:45.50	Peter Wirnsberger (AUT)	1:46.12	Steve Podborski (CAN)	1:46.62
Slalom	Ingemar Stenmark (SWE)	2:40.74	Phil Mahre (USA)	1:44.76	Jacques Luthy (SUI)	1:45.06
Giant Slalom	Ingemar Stenmark (SWE)	1:44.26	Andreas Wenzel (LIE)	2:41.49	Hans Enn (AUT)	2:42.51
Women						
Downhill	Annemarie Moser-Pröll (AUT)	1:37.52	Hanni Wenzel (LIE)	1:38.22	Marie-Theres Nadig (SUI)	1:38.36
Slalom	Hanni Wenzel (LIE)	2:41.66	Christa Kinshofer (FRG)	1:26.50	Erika Hess (SUI)	1:27.89
Giant Slalom	Hanni Wenzel (LIE)	1:25.09	Irene Epple (FRG)	2:42.12	Perrine Pelen (FRA)	2:42.41
Nordic Skiing						
Men						
15 km Cross-Country Skiing	Thomas Wassberg (NOR)	41:57.63	Juha Mieto (FIN)	41:57.64	Ove Aunli (NOR)	42:28.62
30 km Cross-Country Skiing	Nikolai Simyatov (URS)	1:27:02.80	Vasiliy Rochev (URS)	1:27:34.22	Ivan Lebanov (BUL)	1:28:03.87
50 km Cross-Country Skiing	Nikolai Simyatov (URS)	2:27:24.60	Juha Mieto (FIN)	2:30:20.52	Alexander Savyalov (URS)	2:30:51.52
4 x 10 km	USSR	1:57:03.46	Norway	1:58:45.77	Finland	2:00:00.18
Ski Jumping (70 m Hill)	Toni Innauer (AUT)	266.3	Manfred Deckert (GDR)	249.2		
			Hirokazu Yagi (JPN)	249.2		
Ski Jumping (90 m Hill)	Jouko Törmänen (FIN)	271.0	Hubert Neuper (AUT)	262.4	Jari Puikkonen (FIN)	248.5
Nordic Combined	Ulrich Wehling (GDR)	432.20	Juuko Karjalainen (FIN)	429.50	Konrad Winkler (GDR)	425.32

EVENT	GOLD		SILVER		BRONZE	
Women						
5 km Cross-Country Skiing	Raisa Smetanina (URS)	15:06.92	Hikka Riihivuori (FIN)	15:11.96	Kvéta Jeriová (TCH)	15:23.44
10 km Cross-Country Skiing	Barbara Petzold (GDR)	30:31.54	Hikka Riihivuori (FIN)	30:35.05	Helena Takalo (FIN)	30:45.25
4 x 5 km	GDR	1:02:11.10	USSR	1:03:18.30	Norway	1:04:13.50
Biathlon						
10 km	Frank Ullrich (GDR)	32:10.69	Vladimir Alikin (URS)	32:53.10	Anatoliy Alyabiev (URS)	33:09.16
20 km	Anatoliy Alyabiev (URS)	1:08:16.31	Frank Ullrich (GDR)	1:08:27.79	Eberhard Rösch (GDR)	1:11:11.73
4 x 7.5 km	USSR	1:34:03.27	GDR	1:34:56.99	FRG	1:37:30.26
Figure Skating						
Women	Anett Pötzsch (GDR)		Linda Fratianne (USA)		Dagmar Lurz (FRG)	
Men	Robin Cousins (GBR)		Jan Hoffmann (GDR)		Charles Tickner (USA)	
Pairs	Irina Rodnina/		MarinaCherkasova/		Manuela Mager/	
	Alexander Saizev (URS)		Sergey Schackry (URS)		Uwe Bewersdorff (GDR)	
Ice Dance	Natalya Linichuk/		Krisztina Regoczy/		Irina Moissejewa/	
	Gennadi Karponosov (URS)		András Sallay (HUN)		Andrej Minenkow (URS)	
Speed Skating						
Men						
500 m	Eric Heiden (USA)	38.03	Yevgeniy Kulikov (URS)	38.37	Lieuwe de Boer (HOL)	38.48
1000 m	Eric Heiden (USA)	1:15.18	Gaetan Boucher (CAN)	1:16.68	Frode Ronning (NOR)	1:16.91
					Vladimir Lobanov (URS)	1:16.91
1500 m	Eric Heiden (USA)	1:55.44	Kai Arne Stenshjemmet (NOR)	1:56.81	Jerje Andersen (NOR)	1:56.92
5000 m	Eric Heiden (USA)	7:02.29	Kai Arne Stenshjemmet (NOR)	7:03.28	Tom Erik Oxholm (NOR)	7:05.59
10,000 m	Eric Heiden (USA)	14:28.13	Piet Kleine (HOL)	14:36.03	Tom Erik Oxholm (NOR)	14:36.60
Women						
500 m	Karin Enke (GDR)	41.78	Leah Poulos-Meuller (USA)	42.26	Natalya Petruseva (URS)	42.42
1000 m	Natalya Petrusseva (URS)	1:24.10	Leah Poulos-Meuller (USA)	1:25.41	Silvia Albrecht (GDR)	1:26.46
1500 m	Annie Borckink (HOL)	2:10.95	Ria Visser (HOL)	2:12.35	Sabine Becker (GDR)	2:12.38
3000 m	Björg Eva Jensen (NOR)	4:32.13	Sabine Becker (GDR)	4:32.79	Elisabeth Heiden (USA)	4:33.77
Bobsledding						
2-Man Bob	Switzerland II	4:09.36	GDR II	4:10.89	GDR I	4:11.08
4-Man Bob	GDR I	3:59.92	Switzerland I	4:00.87	GDR II	4:00.97
Lugeing						
Men's Singles	Bernhard Glass (GDR)	2:54.796	Paul Hildgartner (ITA)	2:55.372	Anton Winkler (FRG)	2:56.545
Women's Singles	Vera Sosulja (URS)	2:36.537	Melitta Sollmann (GDR)	2:37.657	Ingrida Amantova (URS)	2:37.817
2-Man Luge	Hans Rinn/		Peter Gschnitzer/		Georg Fluckinger/	
	Norbert Hahn (GDR)	1:19.331	Karl Brunner (ITA)	1:19.606	Karl Schrott (AUT)	1:19.795
Ice Hockey						
	USA		USSR		Sweden	

Moscow 1980

Participants: 5217 / Men: 4043, Women: 1124, Countries: 80,
Sports: 21, Events: 204
Final Torchbearer: Sergey Below

Medals Table

PLACE	COUNTRY	GOLD	SILVER	BRONZE
1	USSR	80	69	46
2	GDR	47	37	42
3	Bulgaria	8	16	17
4	Cuba	8	7	5
5	Italy	8	3	4

Outstanding Athletes

PLACE	NAME (NATIONALITY)	DISCIPLINE	G	S	B
1	Alexander Ditiatin (URS)	Gymnastics	3	4	1
2	Caren Metschuk (GDR)	Swimming	3	1	–
3	Barbara Krause (GDR)	Swimming	3	–	–
	Rica Reinisch (GDR)	Swimming	3	–	–
	Vladimir Salnikov (URS)	Swimming	3	–	–
	Vladimir Parfenovich (URS)	Canoeing	3	–	–

EVENT	GOLD		SILVER		BRONZE	
Athletics						
Men						
100 m	Allan Wells (GBR)	10.25	Silvio Leonard (CUB)	10.25	Petar Petrov (BUL)	10.39
200 m	Pietro Mennea (ITA)	20.19	Allan Wells (GBR)	20.21	Donald Quarrie (JAM)	20.29
400 m	Viktor Markin (URS)	44.60	Richard Mitchell (AUS)	44.84	Frank Schaffer (GDR)	44.87
800 m	Steve Ovett (GBR)	1:45.4	Sebastian Coe (GBR)	1:45.9	Nikolai Kirov (URS)	1:46.0
1500 m	Sebastian Coe (GBR)	3:38.4	Jürgen Straub (GDR)	3:38.8	Steven Ovett (GBR)	3:39.0
5000 m	Miruts Yifter (ETH)	13:21.0	Suleiman Nyambui (TAN)	13:21.6	Kaarlo Maaninka (FIN)	13:22.0
10,000 m	Miruts Yifter (ETH)	27:42.7	Kaarlo Maaninka (FIN)	27:44.3	Mohammed Kedir (ETH)	27:44.7
Marathon	Waldemar Cierpinski (GDR)	2:11:03	Gerard Nijboer (HOL)	2:11:20	Sat. Dzhumanazarov (URS)	2:11:35
110 m Hurdles	Thomas Munkelt (GDR)	13.39	Alejandro Casanas (CUB)	13.40	Alexander Puchkov (URS)	13.44
400 m Hurdles	Volker Beck (GDR)	48.70	Vasiliy Arkhipenko (URS)	48.86	Gary Oakes (GBR)	49.11
3000 m Steeplechase	Bronislaw Malinowski (POL)	8:09.7	Filbert Bayi (TAN)	8:12.5	Eshetu Tura (ETH)	8:13.6
4 x 100 m	USSR	38.26	Poland	38.33	France	38.53
4 x 400 m	USSR	3:01.1	GDR	3:01.3	Italy	3:04.3
20 km Walk	Maurizio Damilano (ITA)	1:23:35.5	Pyotr Pochenchuk (URS)	1:24:45.4	Roland Wieser (GDR)	1:25:58.2
50 km Walk	Hartwig Gander (GDR)	3:49:24	Jorge Llopart (ESP)	3:51:25	Yevgeniy Ivchenko (URS)	3:56:32
High Jump	Gerd Wessig (GDR)	2.36	Jacek Wszola (POL)	2.31	Jörg Freimuth (GDR)	2.31
Pole Vault	Wladislaw Kozakiewicz (POL)	5.78	Konstantin Volkov (URS)	5.65		
			Tadeusz Slusarski (POL)	5.65		
Long Jump	Lutz Dombrowski (GDR)	8.54	Frank Paschek (GDR)	8.21	Valeri Podluzhniy (URS)	8.18
Triple Jump	Jaak Uudmae (URS)	17.35	Viktor Saneyev (URS)	17.24	Joao de Oliveira (BRA)	17.22
Shot	Vladimir Kiselyev (URS)	21.35	Alexander Baryshnikov (URS)	21.08	Udo Beyer (GDR)	21.06
Discus	Viktor Rashchupkin (URS)	66.64	Imrich Bugar (TCH)	66.38	Luis Delis (CUB)	66.32
Hammer	Yuriy Sedykh (URS)	81.80	Sergey Litvinov (URS)	80.64	Yuriy Tamm (URS)	78.96
Javelin	Dainis Kula (URS)	91.20	Alexander Makarov (URS)	89.64	Wolfgang Hanisch (GDR)	86.72
Decathlon	Daley Thompson (GBR)	8495	Yuriy Kutsenko (URS)	8331	Sergey Zhelanov (URS)	8135
Women						
100 m	Ludmila Kondratyeva (URS)	11.06	Marlies Göhr (GDR)	11.07	Ingrid Auerswald (GDR)	11.14
200 m	Bärbel Wöckel (GDR)	22.03	Natalya Bochina (URS)	22.19	Merlene Ottey (JAM)	22.20
400 m	Marita Koch (GDR)	48.88	Jarmila Kratochvilova (TCH)	49.46	Christina Lathan (GDR)	49.66
800 m	Nadyezda Olizarenko (URS)	1:53	Olga Mineyeva (URS)	1:54.9	Tatyana Providokhina (URS)	1:55.5
1500 m	Tatyana Kasankina (URS)	3:56.6	Christiane Wartenberg (GDR)	3:57.8	Nadyezda Olizarenko (URS)	3:59.6
100 m Hurdles	Vera Komisova (URS)	12.56	Johanna Klier (GDR)	12.63	Lucyna Langer (POL)	12.65
4 x 100 m	GDR	41.60	USSR	42.10	Great Britain	42.43
4 x 400 m	USSR	3:20.2	GDR	3:20.4	Great Britain	3:27.5
High Jump	Sara Simeoni (ITA)	1.97	Urszula Kielan (POL)	1.94	Jutta Kirst (GDR)	1.94
Long Jump	Tatyana Kolpakova (URS)	7.06	Brigitte Wujak (GDR)	7.04	Tatyana Skatchko (URS)	7.01
Shot	Ilona Slupianek (GDR)	22.41	Svetlana Krachevskaya (URS)	21.42	Margitta Pufe (GDR)	21.20
Discus	Evelin Jahl (GDR)	69.96	Maria Petkova-Vergova (BUL)	67.90	Tatyana Lesovaya (URS)	67.40
Javelin	Maria Caridad-Colon (CUB)	68.40	Saida Gunba (URS)	67.76	Ute Hommola (GDR)	66.56
Pentathlon	Nadyezda Tkachenko (URS)	5083	Olga Rukavishnikova (URS)	4937	Olga Kuragina (URS)	4875
Swimming						
Men						
100 m Freestyle	Jörg Woithe (GDR)	50.40	Per Alvar Holmertz (SWE)	50.91	Per Johansson (SWE)	51.29
200 m Freestyle	Sergey Kopliakov (URS)	1:49.81	Andrej Krylov (URS)	1:50.76	Graeme Brewer (AUS)	1:51.60
400 m Freestyle	Vladimir Salnikov (URS)	3:51.31	Andrej Krylov (URS)	3:53.24	Ivar Stukolkin (URS)	3:53.95
1500 m Freestyle	Vladimir Salnikov (URS)	14:58.27	Alexander Chaev (URS)	15:14.30	Max Metzker (AUS)	15:14.49
100 m Backstroke	Bengt Baron (SWE)	56.63	Viktor Kusnetsov (URS)	56.99	Vladimir Dolgov (URS)	57.63

EVENT	GOLD		SILVER		BRONZE	
200 m Backstroke	Sandor Wladar (HUN)	2:01.93	Zoltan Verraszto (HUN)	2:02.40	Mark Kerry (AUS)	2:03.14
100 m Breaststroke	Duncan Goodhew (GBR)	1:03.34	Arsen Miskarov (URS)	1:03.82	Peter Evans (AUS)	1:03.96
200 m Breaststroke	Robertas Schulpa (URS)	2:15.85	Alban Vermes (HUN)	2:16.93	Arsen Miskarov (URS)	2:17.28
100 m Butterfly	Paer Arvidsson (SWE)	54.92	Roger Pyttel (GDR)	54.94	David Lopez (ESP)	55.13
200 m Butterfly	Sergey Fesenko (URS)	1:59.76	Philip Hubble (GBR)	2:01.20	Roger Pyttel (GDR)	2:01.39
400 m Medley	Alexander Sidorenko (URS)	4:22.89	Sergey Fesenko (URS)	4:23.43	Zoltan Verraszto (HUN)	4:24.24
4 x 200 m Freestyle	USSR	7:23.50	GDR	7:28.60	Brazil	7:29.30
4 x 100 m Medley	Australia	3:45.70	USSR	3:45.92	Great Britain	3:47.71
Springboard Diving	Alexander Portnov (URS)	905.025	Carlos Giron (MEX)	892.140	Franco Cagnotto (ITA)	871.500
Highboard Diving	Falk Hoffmann (GDR)	835.650	Vladimir Heynik (URS)	819.705	David Ambartsumyan (URS)	817.440
Water Polo	USSR		Yugoslavia		Hungary	
Women						
100 m Freestyle	Barbara Krause (GDR)	54.79	Caren Metschuk (GDR)	55.16	Ines Diers (GDR)	55.65
200 m Freestyle	Barbara Krause (GDR)	1:58.33	Ines Diers (GDR)	1:59.64	Carmela Schmitt (GDR)	2:01.44
400 m Freestyle	Ines Diers (GDR)	4:08.76	Petra Schneider (GDR)	4:09.16	Carmela Schmitt (GDR)	4:10.86
800 m Freestyle	Michelle Ford (AUS)	8:28.90	Ines Diers (GDR)	8:32.55	Heike Dähne (GDR)	8:33.48
100 m Backstroke	Rica Reinisch (GDR)	1:00.86	Ina Kleber (GDR)	1:02.07	Petra Riedel (GDR)	1:02.64
200 m Backstroke	Rica Reinisch (GDR)	2:11.77	Cornelia Polit (GDR)	2:13.75	Birgit Treiber (GDR)	2:14.14
100 m Breaststroke	Ute Geweniger (GDR)	1:10.22	Elvira Vasilkova (URS)	1:10.41	Susanne Schultz-Nielsson (DEN)	1:11.16
200 m Breaststroke	Lina Kachushite (URS)	2:29.54	Svetlana Varganova (URS)	2:29.61	Yulia Bogdanova (URS)	2:32.39
100 m Butterfly	Caren Metschuk (GDR)	1:00.42	Andrea Pollack (GDR)	1:00.90	Christiane Knacke (GDR)	1:01.44
200 m Butterfly	Ines Geissler (GDR)	2:10.44	Sybille Schönrock (GDR)	2:10.45	Michelle Ford (AUS)	2:11.66
400 m Medley	Petra Schneider (GDR)	4:36.29	Sharon Davies (GBR)	4:46.83	Agnieszka Czopek (POL)	4:48.17
4 x 100 m Freestyle	GDR	3:42.71	Sweden	3:48.93	Netherlands	3:49.51
4 x 100 m Medley	GDR	4:06.67	Great Britain	4:12.24	USSR	4:13.61
Springboard Diving	Irina Kalinina (URS)	725.910	Martina Proeber (GDR)	698.895	Karin Guthke (GDR)	685.245
Highboard Diving	Martina Jäschke (GDR)	595.250	Servard Emirzyan (URS)	576.466	Liana Tsotadze (URS)	575.925

Boxing

EVENT	GOLD	SILVER	BRONZE
Light-Flyweight (- 48 kg)	Shamil Sabirov (URS)	Hipolito Ramos (CUB)	Ismail Mustafov (BUL) / Byong Uk Li (PRK)
Flyweight (- 51 kg)	Petar Lessov (BUL)	Viktor Miroshnichenko (URS)	Janos Varadi (HUN) / Hugh Russell (IRL)
Bantamweight (- 54 kg)	Juan Bautista Hernandez (CUB)	Bernardo José Pinango (VEN)	Michael Anthony (GUY) / Dimitru Cipere (ROM)
Featherweight (- 57 kg)	Rudi Fink (GDR)	Adolfo Horta (CUB)	Krzysztof Kosedowski (POL) / Viktor Rybakov (URS)
Lightweight (- 60 kg)	Angel Herrera (CUB)	Viktor Demianenko (URS)	Richard Nowakowski (GDR) / Kazimierz Adach (POL)
Light-Welterweight (- 63.5 kg)	Patrizio Oliva (ITA)	Serik Konakbayev (URS)	Anthony Willis (GBR) / José Aguilar (CUB)
Welterweight (- 67 kg)	Andres Aldama (CUB)	John Mugabi (UGA)	Karl-Heinz Krüger (GDR) / Kazimierz Szczerba (POL)
Light-Middleweight (- 71 kg)	Armando Martinez (CUB)	Alexander Koshkin (URS)	Detlef Kästner (GDR) / Jan Franck (TCH)
Middleweight (- 75 kg)	José Gomez (CUB)	Viktor Savchenko (URS)	Valentin Silaghi (ROM) / Jerzy Rybicki (POL)
Light-Heavyweight (- 81 kg)	Slobodan Kacar (YUG)	Pawel Skrzecz (POL)	Herbert Bauch (GDR) / Ricardo Rojas (CUB)
Heavyweight (+ 81 kg)	Teofilo Stevenson (CUB)	Pjotr Zayev (URS)	Istvan Levai (HUN) / Jürgen Fanghänel (GDR)

Weightlifting

EVENT	GOLD		SILVER		BRONZE	
Flyweight (- 52 kg)	Kanybek Osmonoliev (URS)	245.0	Ho Bong Chol (PRK)	245.0	Han Gyong Si (PRK)	245.0
Bantamweight (- 56 kg)	Daniel Nunez (CUB)	275.0	Yurik Sarkisian (URS)	270.0	Tadeusz Dembonczyk (POL)	265.0
Featherweight (- 60 kg)	Viktor Mazin (URS)	290.0	Stefan Dimitrov (BUL)	287.5	Marek Seweryn (POL)	282.5
Lightweight (- 67.5 kg)	Yanko Rusev (BUL)	342.5	Joachim Kunz (GDR)	335.0	Mintcho Pachov (BUL)	325.0
Middleweight (- 75 kg)	Asen Zlatev (BUL)	360.0	Alexander Pervy (URS)	357.5	Nedeltcho Kolev (BUL)	345.0
Light-Heavyweight (- 82.5 kg)	Yurik Vardanjan (URS)	400.0	Blagoi Blagoyev (BUL)	372.5	Dusan Poliacik (TCH)	367.5
Middle-Heavyweight (- 90 kg)	Peter Baczako (HUN)	377.5	Rumen Alexandrov (BUL)	375.0	Frank Mantek (GDR)	375.0
First Heavyweight (- 100 kg)	Ota Zaremba (CSR)	395.0	Igor Nikitin (URS)	392.5	Alberto Blanco (CUB)	385.0
Second Heavyweight (- 110 kg)	Leonid Taranenko (URS)	422.5	Valentin Christov (BUL)	405.0	György Szalai (HUN)	390.0
Super-Heavyweight(+ 100 kg)	Sultan Rakhmanov (URS)	440.5	Jürgen Heuser (GDR)	410.0	Tadeusz Rutkowski (POL)	407.5

Greco-Roman Wrestling

EVENT	GOLD	SILVER	BRONZE
Light-Flyweight (-48 kg)	Zaksylik Ushkempirov (URS)	Constantin Alexandru (ROM)	Ferenc Seres (HUN)
Flyweight (- 52 kg)	Vakhtang Blagidze (URS)	Lajos Racz (HUN)	Mladen Mladenov (BUL)
Bantamweight (- 57 kg)	Shamil Serikov (URS)	Jozef Lipien (POL)	Benni Ljungbeck (SWE)

EVENT	GOLD		SILVER		BRONZE	
Featherweight (- 62 kg)	Stilianos Migiakis (GRE)		István Tóth (HUN)		Boris Kramorenko (URS)	
Lightweight (- 68 kg)	Stefan Rusu (ROM)		Andrzej Supron (POL)		Lars-Erik Skjöld (SWE)	
Welterweight (- 74 kg)	Ferenc Kocsis (HUN)		Anatoliy Bykov (URS)		Mikko Huhtala (FIN)	
Middleweight (- 82 kg)	Gennadiy Korban (URS)		Jan Polgowicz (POL)		Pavel Pavlov (BUL)	
Light-Heavyweight (- 90 kg)	Norbert Nottny (HUN)		Igor Kanygin (URS)		Petre Disu (ROM)	
Heavyweight (- 100 kg)	Gheorghi Raikov (BUL)		Roman Bierla (POL)		Vasile Andrei (ROM)	
Super-Heavyweight (+ 100 kg)	Alexander Kolchinski (URS)		Alexandre Tomov (BUL)		Hassan Bchara (LIB)	
Freestyle Wrestling						
Light-Flyweight (- 48 kg)	Claudio Pollio (ITA)		Se Hong Jang (PRK)		Sergey Kornilayev (URS)	
Flyweight (- 52 kg)	Anatoliy Beloglazov (URS)		Wladyslaw Stecyk (POL)		Nermedin Selimov (BUL)	
Bantamweight (- 57 kg)	Sergey Beloglazov (URS)		Ho Pyong Li (PRK)		Dugarsuren Quinbold (MGL)	
Featherweight (- 62 kg)	Magomedgasan Abushev (URS)		Mikho Dukov (BUL)		Georges Hadjionnides (GRE)	
Lightweight (- 68 kg)	Saipulla Absaidov (URS)		Ivan Yankov (BUL)		Saban Sejdi (YUG)	
Welterweight (- 74 kg)	Valentin Raitschev (BUL)		Jamtsying Davaajav (MGL)		Dan Karabin (TCH)	
Middleweight (- 82 kg)	Ismail Abilov (BUL)		Mahomet Aratsilov (URS)		István Kovács (HUN)	
Light-Heavyweight (- 90 kg)	Sanasar Oganesyan (URS)		Uwe Neupert (GDR)		Alexander Cichon (POL)	
Heavyweight (- 100 kg)	Ilya Mate (URS)		Slavtcho Tchervenkov (BUL)		Julius Strnisko (TCH)	
Super-Heavyweight (+100 kg)	Soslan Andiev (URS)		Jószef Balla (HUN)		Adam Sandurski (POL)	
Judo						
Super-Lightweight(- 60 kg)	Thierry Rey (FRA)		José Rodrigez (CUB)		Tibor Kincses (HUN)	
					Aramby Emizh (URS)	
Halbleichtgewicht (- 65 kg)	Nikolai Solodukhin (URS)		Tsendying Damdin (MGL)		Ilian Nedkov (BUL)	
					Janusz Pawlowski (POL)	
Lightweight (- 68 kg)	Enzio Gamba (ITA)		Neil Adams (GBR)		Karl Heinz Lehmann (GDR)	
					Ravdan Davaadalai (MGL)	
Light-Middleweight (- 78 kg)	Shota Khabaleri (URS)		Juan Ferrer (CUB)		Bernard Tchoullouyan (FRA)	
					Harald Heinke (GDR)	
Middleweight (- 86 kg)	Jörg Röthlisberger (SUI)		Isaac Azcuy (CUB)		Detlev Ultsch (GDR)	
					Alexander Yatskevich (URS)	
Light-Heavyweight (- 95 kg)	Robert van de Walle (BEL)		Tengiz Khubuluri (URS)		Dietmar Lorenz (GDR)	
					Henk Numann (HOL)	
Heavyweight (+ 95 kg)	Angelo Parisi (FRA)		Dimitar Zaprianov (BUL)		Vladimir Kocman (TCH)	
					Radomir Kovacevic (YUG)	
Open Class	Dietmar Lorenz (GDR)		Angelo Parisi (FRA)		Andras Ozsvar (HUN)	
					Arthur Mapp (GBR)	
Fencing						
Individual Foil - Men	Vladimir Smirnov (URS)	4	Pascal Jolyot (FRA)	4	Alexander Romankov (URS)	5
Team Foil - Men	France		USSR		Poland	
Individual Épée	Johan Harmenberg (SWE)	4	Ernõ Kolczonay (HUN)	3	Philippe Riboud (FRA)	3
Team Épée	France		Poland		USSR	
Individual Sabre	Viktor Krovopouskov (URS)	4	Mikhail Burtsev (URS)	4	Imre Gedovari (HUN)	3
Team Sabre	USSR		Italy		Hungary	
Individual Foil - Women	Pascale Trinquet (FRA)	4	Magda Maros (HUN)	3	Barbara Wysoczanska (POL)	
Team Foil - Women	France		USSR		Hungary	
Modern Pentathlon						
Individual	Anatoliy Starostin (URS)	5568	Tamás Szombathelyi (HUN)	5502	Pavel Lednev (URS)	5282
Team	USSR	16126	Hungary	15912	Sweden	15845
Canoeing						
Men						
500 m Kayak Singles K1	Vladimir Parfenovich (URS)	1:43.43	John Sumegi (AUS)	1:44.12	Vasile Diba (ROM)	1:44.90
1000 m Kayak Singles K1	Rüdiger Helm (GDR)	3:48.77	Alain Lebas (FRA)	3:50.20	Ion Birladeanu (ROM)	3:50.49
500 m Kayak Pairs K2	USSR	1:32.38	Spain	1:33.65	GDR	1:34.00
1000 m Kayak Pairs K2	USSR	3:26.72	Hungary	3:28.49	Spain	3:28.66
1000 m Kayak Fours K4	GDR	3:13.76	Romania	3:15.35	Bulgaria	3:15.46
500 m Canadian Singles C1	Sergey Postrekhin (URS)	1:53.37	Lubomir Lubenov (BUL)	1:53.49	Olaf Heukrodt (GDR)	1:54.38
1000 m Canadian Singles C1	Lubomir Lubenov (BUL)	4:12.38	SergeyPostrekhin (URS)	4:13.53	Eckhard Leue (GDR)	4:15.02
500 m Canadian Pairs C2	Hungary	1:43.39	Romania	1:44.12	Bulgaria	1:44.83
1000 m Canadian Pairs C2	Romania	3:47.65	GDR	3:49.93	USSR	3:51.28
Women						
500 m Kayak Singles K1	Birgit Fischer (GDR)	1:57.96	Vanya Ghecheva (BUL)	1:59.48	Antonina Melnikova (URS)	1:59.66
500 m Kayak Pairs K2	GDR	1:43.88	USSR	1:46.91	Hungary	1:47.95

EVENT	GOLD		SILVER		BRONZE	
Rowing						
Men						
Single Sculls	Pertti Karppinen (FIN)	7:09:61	Vasiliy Yakusha (URS)	7:11.66	Peter Kersten (GDR)	7:14.88
Doubles Sculls	GDR	6:24.33	Yugoslavia	6:26.34	Czechoslovakia	6:29.07
Coxless Pairs	GDR	6:48.01	USSR	6:50.50	Great Britain	6:51.47
Coxed Pairs	GDR	7:02.54	USSR	7:03.35	Yugoslavia	7:04.92
Coxless Quadruple Sculls	GDR	5:49.81	USSR	5:51.47	Bulgaria	5:52.38
Coxless Fours	GDR	6:08.17	USSR	6:11.81	Great Britain	6:16.58
Coxed Fours	GDR	6:14.51	USSR	6:19.05	Poland	6:22.52
Coxed Eights	GDR	5:49.05	Great Britain	5:51.92	USSR	5:52.66
Women						
Single Sculls	Sanda Toma (ROM)	3:40:69	Antonina Makhina (URS)	3:41.65	Martina Schröter (GDR)	3:43.54
Double Sculls	USSR	3:16.27	GDR	3:17.63	Romania	3:18.91
Coxless Pairs	GDR	3:30.49	Poland	3:30.95	Bulgaria	3:32.39
Coxless Quadruple Sculls	GDR	3:15.32	USSR	3:15.73	Bulgaria	3:16.10
Coxed Fours	GDR	3:19.27	Bulgaria	3:20.75	USSR	3:20.92
Coxed Eights	GDR	3:03.32	USSR	3:04.29	Romania	3:05.63
Yachting						
Finn-Class	Esko Rechardt (FIN)	36.7	Wolfgang Mayrhofer (AUT)	46.7	Andrei Balaschov (URS)	47.4
International Star	USSR	24.7	Austria	31.7	Italy	36.1
Flying Dutchman	Spain	19.0	Ireland	30.0	Hungary	45.7
International Tornado	Brazil	21.4	Denmark	30.4	Sweden	33.7
International 470	Brazil	36.4	GDR	38.7	Finland	39.7
International Soling	Denmark	23.0	USSR	30.4	Greece	31.1
Cycling						
Individual Road Race (189 km)	Sergey Sukoruchenkov (URS)	4:48:28	Czeslaw Lang (POL)	4:51:26	Yuriy Barinov (URS)	4:51:26
100 km Road Team Time Trial	USSR	2:01:21.7	GDR	2:02:53.2	Czechoslovakia	2:02:53.9
1000 m Time Trial	Lothar Thoms (GDR)	1:02.955	Alexander Pantilov (URS)	1:04.845	David Weller (JAM)	1:05.241
1000 m Sprint	Lutz Hesslich (GDR)		Yave Cahard (FRA)		Sergey Kopylov (URS)	
4000 m Individual Pursuit	Robert Dill-Bundi (SUI)	4:35.66	Alain Bondue (FRA)	4:42.96	Hans-Henrik Oersted (DEN)	4:36.54
4000 m Team Pursuit	USSR	4:15.70	GDR	4:19.67	Czechoslovakia	
Equestrianism						
Three-Day Event	Federico Roman (ITA)	-108.60	Alexander Blinov (URS)	-120.80	Yuriy Salnikov (URS)	-151.60
Three-Day Event. Team	USSR	-457.00	Italy	-656.20	Mexico	-1172.85
Grand Prix (Dressage)	Elisabeth Theurer (AUT)	1370	Yuriy Kovshov (URS)	1300	Viktor Ugrjumov (URS)	1234
Grand Prix (Dressage) Team	USSR	4383.0	Bulgaria	3580.0	Romania	3346.0
Grand Prix (Jumping)	Jan Kowalczyk (POL)	-8	Nikolai Korolkov (URS)	-9.50	Joaquín Perez de las Heras (MEX)	-12
Grand Prix (Jumping) Team	USSR	-16.00	Poland	-32.00	Mexico	-39.25
Shooting						
Small-Bore Rifle (Prone)	Karoly Varga (HUN)	599	Hellfried Heilfort (GDR)	599	Petar Zapianov (BUL)	598
Small-Bore Rifle (3 Positions)	Viktor Vlassov (URS)	1173	Bernd Hartstein (GDR)	1166	Sven Johansson (SWE)	1165
Rapid-Fire Pistol	Corneliu Ion (ROM)	596	Jürgen Wiefel (GDR)	596	Gerhard Petrisch (AUT)	596
Free Pistol (50 m)	Alexander Melentyev (URS)	581	Harald Vollmar (GDR)	568	Lubcho Diakov (BUL)	565
Running Game Target	Igor Sokolow (URS)	589	Thomas Pfeffer (GDR)	589	Alexander Gasov (URS)	587
Skeet Shooting	Hans Kjeld Rasmussen (DEN)	196	Lars-Göran Carlsson (SWE)	196	Roberto Castrillo (CUB)	196
Trap Shooting	Luciano Giovanetti (ITA)	198	Rustam Yambulatov (URS)	196	Jörg Damme (GDR)	196
Archery						
Men	Tomi Poikalainen (FIN)	2455	Boris Isachenko (URS)	2452	Alexander Gazov (URS)	2449
Women	Keto Losaberidse (URS)	2491	Natalya Butuzova (URS)	2477	Paivi Merilouto (FIN)	2449
Gymnastics						
Men						
Individual Combined Exercises	Alexander Ditiatin (URS)	118.650	Nikolai Andrianov (URS)	118.225	Stoyan Deltschev (BUL)	118.000
Team	USSR	589.60	GDR	581.15	Hungary	575.00
Parallel Bars	Alexander Tkatschov (URS)	19.775	Alexander Ditiatin (URS)	19.750	Roland Brückner (GDR)	19.650
Floor	Roland Brückner (GDR)	19.750	Nikolai Andrianov (URS)	19.725	Alexander Ditiatin (URS)	19.700
Horse Vault	Nikolai Andrianov (URS)	19.825	Alexander Ditiatin (URS)	19.800	Roland Brückner (GDR)	19.775
Horizontal Bar	Stojan Deltschev (BUL)	19.825	Alexander Ditiatin (URS)	19.750	Nikolai Andrianov (URS)	19.675
Rings	Alexander Ditiatin (URS)	19.875	Alexander Tkachov (URS)	19.725	Jiri Tabák (TCH)	19.600
Pommel Horse	Zoltan Magyar (HUN)	19.925	Alexander Ditiatin (URS)	19.800	Michael Nikolay (GDR)	19.775

EVENT	GOLD		SILVER		BRONZE	
Women						
Individual Combined Exercises	Yelena Davydova (URS)	79.150	Nadia Comaneci (ROM)	79.075		
			Maxi Gnauck (GDR)	79.075		
Team	USSR	394.90	Romania	393.50	GDR	392.55
Floor	Nadia Comaneci (ROM)	19.875			Maxi Gnauck (GDR)	19.825
	Nelli Kim (URS)	19.875			Natalya Shaposhnikova (URS)	19.825
Horse Vault	Natalya Shaposhnikova (URS)	19.725	Steffi Kräker (GDR)	19.675	Melita Ruhn (ROM)	19.650
Beam	Nadia Comaneci (ROM)	19.800	Yelena Davydova (URS)	19.750	Natalya Shaposhnikova (URS)	19.725
Asymmetrical Bars	Maxi Gnauck (GDR)	19.875	Emilia Eberle (ROM)	19.850	Maria Filatova (URS)	19.775
					Steffi Kräker (GDR)	19.775
					Mehta Ruhn (ROM)	19.775
Basketball						
Men	Yugoslavia		Italy		USSR	
Women	USSR		Bulgaria		Yugoslavia	
Soccer						
	Czechoslovakia		GDR		USSR	
Handball						
Men	GDR		USSR		Romania	
Women	USSR		Yugoslavia		GDR	
Hockey						
Men	India		Spain		USSR	
Women	Zimbabwe		Czechoslovakia		USSR	
Volleyball						
Men	USSR		Bulgaria		Romania	
Women	USSR		GDR		Bulgaria	

Sarajevo 1984

Participants: 1274 / Men: 1000, Women: 274, Countries: 49,
Sports: 8, Events: 39
Final Torchbearer: Sandra Dubravčič

7 February – 19 February
(Official Opening Ceremony on 8 February)

Medals Table

PLACE	COUNTRY	GOLD	SILVER	BRONZE
1	GDR	9	9	6
2	USSR	6	10	9
3	USA	4	4	–
4	Finland	4	3	6
5	Sweden	4	2	2

Outstanding Athletes

PLACE	NAME (NATIONALITY)	DISCIPLINE	G	S	B
1	Marja-Liisa Hämäläinen (FIN)	Nordic Skiing	3	–	1
2	Karin Enke (GDR)	Speed Skating	2	2	–
3	Gunde Svan (SWE)	Nordic Skiing	2	1	1
4	Gaetan Boucher (CAN)	Speed Skating	2	–	1
5	Wolfgang Hoppe (GDR)	Bobsledding	2	–	–
	Dietmar Schauerhammer (GDR)	Bobsledding	2	–	–
	Tomas Wassberg (SWE)	Nordic Skiing	2	–	–

EVENT	GOLD		SILVER		BRONZE	
Alpine Skiing						
Men						
Downhill	Bill Johnson (USA)	1:45.59	Peter Müller (SUI)	1:45.86	Anton Steiner (AUT)	1:45.95
Slalom	Phil Mahre (USA)	1:39.21	Steven Mahre (USA)	1:39.62	Didier Bouvet (FRA)	1:40.20
Giant Slalom	Max Julen (SUI)	2:41.18	Juriy Franko (YUG)	2:41.41	Andreas Wenzel (LIE)	2:41.75
Women						
Downhill	Michaela Figini (SUI)	1:13.36	Maria Walliser (SUI)	1:13.41	Olga Chartová (TCH)	1:13.53
Slalom	Paoletta Magoni (ITA)	1:36.47	Perrine Pelen (FRA)	1:37.38	Ursula Konzett (LIE)	1:37.50
Giant Slalom	Debbie Armstrong (USA)	2:20.98	Christin Cooper (USA)	2:21.38	Perrine Pelen (FRA)	2:21.40

EVENT	GOLD		SILVER		BRONZE	
Nordic Skiing						
Men						
15 km Cross-Country Skiing	Gunde Svan (SWE)	41:25.6	Aki Karvonen (FIN)	41:34.9	Harri Kirvesniemi (FIN)	41:45.6
30 km Cross-Country Skiing	Nikolai Simyatov (URS)	1:28:56.3	Alexander Zavialov (URS)	1:29:23.3	Gunde Svan (SWE)	1:29:35.7
50 km Cross-Country Skiing	Thomas Wassberg (SWE)	2:15:55.8	Gunde Svan (SWE)	2:16:00.7	Aki Karvonen (FIN)	2:17:04.7
4 x 10 km	Sweden	1:55:06.3	USSR	1:55:16.5	Finland	1:56:31.4
Ski Jumping (70 m Hill)	Jens Weissflog (GDR)	215.2	Matti Nykänen (FIN)	214.0	Jari Puikkonen (FIN)	212.8
Ski Jumping (90 m Hill)	Matti Nykänen (FIN)	231.2	Jens Weissflog (GDR)	213.7	Pavel Ploc (TCH)	202.9
Nordic Combined	Tom Sandberg (NOR)	422.595	Jouko Karjalainen (FIN)	416.900	Rauno Ylipulli (FIN)	410.825
Women						
5 km Cross-Country Skiing	Marja-Liisa Hämäläinen (FIN)	17:04.0	Berit Aunli (NOR)	17:14.1	Kvetoslava Jeriová (TCH)	17:18.3
10 km Cross-Country Skiing	Marja-Liisa Hämäläinen (FIN)	31:44.2	Raisa Smetanina (URS)	32:02.9	Brit Pettersen (NOR)	32:12.7
20 km Cross-Country Skiing	Marja-Liisa Hämäläinen (FIN)	1:01:45.0	Raisa Smetanina (URS)	1:02:26.7	Anne Jahren (NOR)	1:03:13.6
4 x 5 km	Norway	1:06:49.7	Czechoslovakia	1:07:34.7	Finland	1:07:36.7
Biathlon						
10 km	Eirik Kvalfoss (NOR)	30:53.8	Peter Angerer (FRG)	31:02.4	Matthias Jakob (GDR)	31:10.5
20 km	Peter Angerer (FRG)	1:11:52.7	Frank-Peter Rötsch (GDR)	1:13:21.4	Eirik Kvalfoss (NOR)	1:14:02.4
4 x 7.5 km	USSR	1:38:51.70	Norway	1:39:03.10	FRG	1:39:05.10
Figure Skating						
Women	Katarina Witt (GDR)		Rosalyn Summers (USA)		Kira Ivanova (URS)	
Men	Scott Hamilton (USA)		Brian Oser (CAN)		Jozef Sabotchik (TCH)	
Pairs	Elena Valova/ Oleg Vasiliyev (URS)		Kitty Carruthers/ Peter Carruthers (USA)		Larissa Selesnewa/ Oleg Makarow (URS)	
Ice Dance	Jayne Torvill/ Christopher Dean (GBR)		Natalya Bestemianova/ Andrey Bukin (URS)		Marina Klimova/ Sergey Ponomarenko (URS)	
Speed Skating						
Men						
500 m	Sergei Fokitchev (URS)	38.19	Yoshihiro Kitazawa (JPN)	38.30	Gaetan Boucher (CAN)	38.39
1000 m	Gaetan Boucher (CAN)	1:15.80	Sergei Khlebnikov (URS)	1:16.63	Kai Arne Engelstad (NOR)	1:16.75
1500 m	Gaetan Boucher (CAN)	1:58.36	Sergei Khlebnikov (URS)	1:58.83	Oleg Bogiev (URS)	1:58.89
5000 m	Tomas Gustafson (SWE)	7:12.28	Igor Malkov (URS)	7:12.30	Rene Schöfisch (GDR)	7:17.49
10,000 m	Igor Malkov (URS)	14:39.90	Tomas Gustafson (SWE)	14:39.95	Rene Schöfisch (GDR)	14:46.91
Women						
500 m	Christa Rothenburger (GDR)	41.02	Karin Enke (GDR)	41.28	Natalya Chive (URS)	41.50
1000 m	Karin Enke (GDR)	1:21.61	Andrea Schöne (GDR)	1:22.83	Natalya Petruseva (URS)	1:23.21
1500 m	Karin Enke (GDR)	2:03.42	Andrea Schöne (GDR)	2:05.29	Natalya Petruseva (URS)	2:05.78
3000 m	Andrea Schöne (GDR)	4:24.79	Karin Enke (GDR)	4:26.33	Gabi Schönbrunn (GDR)	4:33.13
Bobsledding						
2-Man Bob	GDR II	3:25.56	GDR I	3:26.04	USSR II	3:26.16
4-Man Bob	GDR I	3:20.22	GDR II	3:20.78	Switzerland I	3:21.39
Lugeing						
Men's Singles	Paul Hildgartner (ITA)	3:04.258	Sergey Danilin (URS)	3:04.962	Valeriy Dudin (URS)	3:05.012
Women's Singles	Steffi Martin (GDR)	2:46.570	Bettina Schmidt (GDR)	2:46.873	Ute Weiss (GDR)	2:47.248
2-Man Luge	Hans Stanggassinger/ Franz Wembacher (FRG)	1:23.620	Yevgeniy Belusov/ Alexander Beliakov (URS)	1:23.660	Jörg Hoffmann/ Jochen Pietzsch (GDR)	1:23.887
Ice Hockey						
	USSR		Czechoslovakia		Sweden	

Los Angeles 1984

28 July – 12 August

Participants: 6797 / Men: 5230, Women: 1567, Countries: 140,
Sports: 21, Events: 221
Final Torchbearer: Rafer Johnson

Medals Table

PLACE	COUNTRY	GOLD	SILVER	BRONZE
1	USA	83	61	30
2	Romania	20	16	17
3	FRG	17	19	23
4	China	15	8	9
5	Italy	14	6	12

Outstanding Athletes

PLACE	NAME (NATIONALITY)	DISCIPLINE	G	S	B
1	Jecaterina Szabó (ROM)	Gymnastics	4	1	–
2	Carl Lewis (USA)	Athletics	4	–	–
3	Li Ning (CHN)	Gymnastics	3	2	1
4	Valerie Brisco-Hooks (USA)	Athletics	3	–	–
	Richard Carey (USA)	Swimming	3	–	–
	Ian Ferguson (NZL)	Canoeing	3	–	–

EVENT	GOLD		SILVER		BRONZE	
Athletics						
Men						
100 m	Carl Lewis (USA)	9.99	Sam Graddy (USA)	10.19	Ben Johnson (CAN)	10.22
200 m	Carl Lewis (USA)	19.80	Kirk Baptiste (USA)	19.96	Thomas Jefferson (USA)	20.26
400 m	Alonzo Babers (USA)	44.27	Gabriel Tiacoh (CIV)	44.54	Antonio McKay (USA)	44.71
800 m	Joaquim Cruz (BRA)	1:43.00	Sebastian Coe (GBR)	1:43.64	Earl Jones (USA)	1:43.83
1500 m	Sebastian Coe (GBR)	3:32.53	Steve Cram (GBR)	3:33.40	José Abascal (ESP)	3:34.30
5000 m	Said Aouita (MAR)	13:05.59	Markus Ryffel (SUI)	13:07.54	Antoaio Leitao (POR)	13:09.20
10,000 m	Alberto Cova (ITA)	27:47.54	Michael McLeod (GBR)★	28:06.22	Mike Musyoki (KEN)	28:06.46
Marathon	Carlos Lopes (POR)	2:09:21	John Treacy (IRL)	2:09:56	Charles Spedding (GBR)	2:09:58
110 m Hurdles	Roger Kingdom (USA)	13.20	Greg Foster (USA)	13.23	Arto Bryggare (FIN)	13.40
400 m Hurdles	Edwin Moses (USA)	47.75	Danny Harris (USA)	48.13	Harald Schmid (FRG)	48.19
3000 m Steeplechase	Julius Korir (KEN)	8:11.80	Joseph Mahmoud (FRA)	8:13.31	Brian Diemer (USA)	8:14.06
4 x 100 m	USA	37.83	Jamaica	38.62	Canada	38.70
4 x 400 m	USA	2:57.91	Great Britain	2:59.13	Nigeria	2:59.32
20 km Walk	Ernesto Canto (MEX)	1:23:13	Raul Gonzalez (MEX)	1:23:20	Maurizio Damilano (ITA)	1:23:26
50 km Walk	Raul Gonzalez (MEX)	3:37:26	Bo Gustafsson (SWE)	3:53:19	Sandro Bellucci (ITA)	3:53:45
Long Jump	Carl Lewis (USA)	8.54	Gary Honey (AUS)	8.24	Giovanni Evangelisti (ITA)	8.24
High Jump	Dietmar Mögenburg (FRG)	2.35	Patrik Sjöberg (SWE)	2.33	Jianhua Zhu (CHN)	2.31
Pole Vault	Pierre Quinon (FRA)	5.75	Mike Tully (USA)	5.65	Earl Bell (USA)	5.60
Triple Jump	Al Joyner (USA)	17.26	Mike Conley (USA)	17.18	Keith Connor (GBR)	16.87
Shot	Alessandro Andrei (ITA)	21.26	Michael Carter (USA)	21.09	Dave Laut (USA)	20.97
Discus	Rolf Danneberg (FRG)	66.60	Mac Wilkins (USA)	66.30	John Powell (USA)	65.46
Hammer	Juha Tiainen (FIN)	78.08	Karl-Hans Riehm (FRG)	77.98	Klaus Ploghaus (FRG)	76.68
Javelin	Aro Härkönen (FIN)	86.76	David Ottley (GBR)	85.74	Kenth Eldebrink (SWE)	83.72
Decathlon	Daley Thompson (GBR)	8798	Jürgen Hingsen (FRG)	8673	Siegfried Wentz (FRG)	8412
			★(Martti Väiniö (FIN) disqualified for steroid use)			
Women						
100 m	Evelyn Ashford (USA)	10.97	Alice Brown (USA)	11.13	Merlene Ottey (JAM)	11.16
200 m	Valerie Brisco-Hooks (USA)	21.81	Florence Griffith (USA)	22.04	Merlene Ottey (JAM)	22.09
400 m	Valerie Brisco-Hooks (USA)	48.83	Chandra Cheeseborough (USA)	49.05	Kathryn Cook (GBR)	49.42
800 m	Doina Melinte (ROM)	1:57.60	Kim Gallagher (USA)	1:58.63	Fita Lovin (ROM)	1:58.83
1500 m	Gabriella Dorio (ITA)	4:03.25	Doina Melinte (ROM)	4:03.76	Maricica Puica (ROM)	4:04.15
3000 m	Maricica Puica (ROM)	8:35.96	Wendy Sly (GBR)	8:39.47	Lynn Williams (CAN)	8:42.14
Marathon	Joan Benoit (USA)	2:24:52	Grete Waitz (NOR)	2:26:18	Rosa Mota (POR)	2:26:57
100 m Hurdles	Benita Fitzgerald-Brown (USA)	12.84	Shirley Strong (GBR)	12.88	Kim Turner (USA)	13.06
					Michele Chardonnet (FRA)	13.06
400 m Hurdles	Nawal El Moutawakel (MAR)	54.61	Judi Brown (USA)	55.20	Cristina Cojocaru (ROM)	55.41
4 x 100 m	USA	41.65	Canada	42.77	Great Britain	43.11
4 x 400 m	USA	3:18.29	Canada	3:21.21	FRG	3:22.98
High Jump	Ulrike Meyfarth (FRG)	2.02	Sara Simeoni (ITA)	2.00	Joni Huntley (USA)	1.97
Long Jump	Anis Stanciu-Cusmir (ROM)	6.96	Vali Ionescu (ROM)	6.81	Susan Hearnshaw (GBR)	6.80
Shot	Claudia Losch (FRG)	20.48	Mihaela Loghin (ROM)	20.47	Gael Martin (AUS)	19.19
Discus	Ria Stalman (HOL)	65.36	Leslie Deniz (USA)	64.86	Florenta Craciunescu (ROM)	63.64
Javelin	Tessa Sanderson (GBR)	69.56	Tiina Lillak (FIN)	69.00	Fatima Whitbread (GBR)	67.14
Heptathlon	Glynis Nunn (AUS)	6390	Jackie Joyner (USA)	6385	Sabine Everts (FRG)	6363
Swimming						
Men						
100 m Freestyle	Ambrose Gaines (USA)	49.80	Mark Stockwell (AUS)	50.24	Per Johansson (SWE)	50.31

EVENT	GOLD		SILVER		BRONZE	
200 m Freestyle	Michael Gross (FRG)	1:47.44	Michael Heath (USA)	1:49.10	Thomas Fahrner (FRG)	1:49.69
400 m Freestyle	George Dicarlo (USA)	3:51.23	John Mykkanen (USA)	3:51.49	Justin Lemberg (AUS)	3:51.79
1500 m Freestyle	Michael O'Brien (USA)	15:05.20	George Dicarlo (USA)	15:10.59	Stefan Pfeiffer (FRG)	15:12.11
100 m Backstroke	Richard Carey (USA)	55.79	David Wilson (USA)	56.35	Mike West (CAN)	56.49
200 m Backstroke	Richard Carey (USA)	2:00.23	Frederic Delcourt (FRA)	2:01.75	Cameron Henning (CAN)	2:02.37
100 m Breaststroke	Steve Lundquist (USA)	1:01.65	Victor Davis (CAN)	1:01.99	Peter Evans (AUS)	1:02.97
200 m Breaststroke	Victor Davis (CAN)	2:13.34	Glenn Beringen (AUS)	2:15.79	Etienne Dagon (SUI)	2:17.41
100 m Butterfly	Michael Gross (FRG)	53.08	Pablo Morales (USA)	53.23	Glenn Buchanan (AUS)	53.85
200 m Butterfly	Jon Sieben (AUS)	1:57.04	Michael Gross (FRG)	1:57.40	Rafael Vidal Castro (VEN)	1:57.51
200 m Medley	Alex Baumann (CAN)	2:01.42	Pedro Morales (USA)	2:03.05	Neil Cochran (GBR)	2:04.38
400 m Medley	Alex Baumann (CAN)	4:17.41	Ricardo Prado (BRA)	4:18.45	Robert Woodhouse (AUS)	4:20.50
4 x 100 m Freestyle Relay	USA	3:19.03	Australia	3:19.68	Sweden	3:22.69
4 x 200 m Freestyle Relay	USA	7:16.59	FRG	7:16.73	Great Britain	7:24.78
4 x 100 m Medley Relay	USA	3:39.30	Canada	3:43.23	Australia	3:43.25
Springboard Diving	Greg Louganis (USA)	754.41	Tan Liangde (CHN)	662.31	Ronald Merriott (USA)	661.32
Highboard Diving	Greg Louganis (USA)	710.91	Bruce Kimball (USA)	643.50	Li Kongzhen (CHN)	638.28
Water Polo	Yugoslavia		USA		FRG	
Women						
100 m Freestyle	Carrie Steinseifer (USA)	55.92			Annemarie Verstappen (HOL)	56.08
	Nancy Hogshead (USA)	55.92				
200 m Freestyle	Mary Wayte (USA)	1:59.23	Cynthia Woodhead (USA)	1:59.50	Annemarie Verstappen (HOL)	1:59.69
400 m Freestyle	Tiffany Cohen (USA)	4:07.10	Sarah Hardcastle (GBR)	4:10.27	June Croft (GBR)	4:11.49
800 m Freestyle	Tiffany Cohen (USA)	8:24.95	Michelle Richardson (USA)	8:30.73	Sarah Hardcastle (GBR)	8:32.60
100 m Backstroke	Theresa Andrews (USA)	1:02.55	Betsy Mitchell (USA)	1:02.63	Jolanda de Rover (HOL)	1:02.91
200 m Backstroke	Jolanda de Rover (HOL)	2:12.38	Amy White (USA)	2:13.04	Aneta Patrascoiu (ROM)	2:13.29
100 m Breaststroke	Petra van Staveren (HOL)	1:09.88	Anne Ottenbrite (CAN)	1:10.69	Catherine Poirot (FRA)	1:10.70
200 m Breaststroke	Anne Ottenbrite (CAN)	2:30.38	Susan Rapp (USA)	2:31.15	Ingrid Lempereur (BEL)	2:31.40
100 m Butterfly	Mary T. Meagher (USA)	59.26	Jenna Johnson (USA)	1:00.19	Karin Seick (FRG)	1:00.36
200 m Butterfly	Mary T. Meagher (USA)	2:06.90	Karen Philipps (AUS)	2:10.56	Ina Beyermann (FRG)	2:11.91
200 m Medley	Tracy Caulkins (USA)	2:12.64	Nancy Hogshead (USA)	2:15.17	Michele Pearson (AUS)	2:15.92
400 m Medley	Tracy Caulkins (USA)	4:39.24	Suzanne Landells (AUS)	4:48.30	Petra Zindler (FRG)	4:48.57
4 x 100 m Freestyle Relay	USA	3:43.43	Netherlands	3:44.40	FRG	3:45.56
4 x 100 m Medley Relay	USA	4:08.34	FRG	4:11.97	Canada	4:12.98
Springboard Diving	Silvie Bernier (CAN)	530.70	Kelly McCormick (USA)	527.46	Christina Seufert (USA)	517.62
Highboard Diving	Jihong Zhou (CHN)	378.81	Michele Mitchell (USA)	367.35	Wendy Wyland (USA)	365.52
Synchronized Swimming						
Solo	Tracie Ruiz (USA)	198.467	Carolyn Waldo (CAN)	195.300	Miwako Motoyoshi (JPN)	187.050
Duet	USA	99.00	Canada	98.20	Japan	97.00
Boxing						
Light-Flyweight (- 48 kg)	Paul Gonzales (USA)		Salvatore Todisco (ITA)		Keith Mwila (ZAM)	
					José Marcelino Bolivar (VEN)	
Flyweight (- 51 kg)	Steven McCrory (USA)		Redzep Redzepovski (YUG)		Eyup Can (TUR)	
					Ibrahim Bilali (KEN)	
Bantamweight (- 54 kg)	Maurizio Stecca (ITA)		Hector Lopez (MEX)		Dale Walters (CAN)	
					Pedro Nolasco (DOM)	
Featherweight (- 57 kg)	Meldrick Taylor (USA)		Peter Konyegwachie (NGR)		Omar Catari Peraza (VEN)	
					Turgut Aykac (TUR)	
Lightweight (- 60 kg)	Pernell Whitaker (USA)		Luis Ortiz (PUR)		Martin Ndongo Ebanga (CMR)	
					Chi-Sung Cun (KOR)	
Light-Welterweight (- 63.5 kg)	Jerry Page (USA)		Dhawee Umponmaha (THA)		Mirko Puzovic (YUG)	
					Mircea Fulger (ROM)	
Welterweight (- 67 kg)	Mark Breland (USA)		Young-Su An (KOR)		Joni Nyman (FIN)	
					Luciano Bruno (ITA)	
Light-Middleweight (- 71 kg)	Frank Tate (USA)		Shawn O'Sullivan (CAN)		Manfred Zielonka (FRG)	
					Christophe Tiozzo (FRA)	
Middleweight (- 75 kg)	Joon-Sup Shin (KOR)		Virgil Hill (USA)		Mohammed Zaoui (ALG)	
					Aristides Gonzales (PUR)	
Light-Heavyweight (- 81 kg)	Anton Josipovi´c (YUG)		Kevin Barry (NZL)		Mustapha Moussa (ALG)	
					Evander Holyfield (USA)	
Heavyweight (- 91 kg)	Henry Tillman (USA)		Willie Dewit (CAN)		Angelo Musone (ITA)	
					Arnold Vanderlijde (HOL)	
Super-Heavyweight (+ 91 kg)	Tyrell Biggs (USA)		Francesco Damiani (ITA)		Robert Wells (GBR)	
					Azis Salihu (YUG)	

EVENT	GOLD		SILVER		BRONZE	
Weightlifting						
Flyweight (- 52 kg)	Guoqiang Zeng (CHN)	235.0	Peishun Zhou (CHN)	235.0	Kazushito Manabe (JPN)	232.5
Bantamweight (- 56 kg)	Shude Wu (CHN)	267.5	Runming Lai (CHN)	265.0	Masahiro Kotaka (JPN)	252.5
Featherweight (- 60 kg)	Weiqiang Chen (CHN)	282.5	Gelu Radu (ROM)	280.0	Wen-Yee Tsai (KOR)	272.5
Lightweight (- 67.5 kg)	Jingyuan Yao (CHN)	320.0	Andrei Socaci (ROM)	312.5	Jouni Gronman (FIN)	312.5
Middleweight (- 75 kg)	Karl-Heinz Radschinsky (FRG)	340.0	Jacques Demers (FRA)	335.0	Dragomir Cioroslan (ROM)	332.5
Light-Heavyweight (- 82.5 kg)	Petre Becheru (ROM)	355.0	Robert Kabbas (AUS)	342.5	Ryoji Isaoka (JPN)	340.0
Middle-Heavyweight (- 90 kg)	Nicu Vlad (ROM)	392.5	Petre Dumitru (ROM)	360.0	David Mercer (GBR)	352.5
First Heavyweight (- 100 kg)	Rolf Milser (FRG)	385.0	Vasile Gropa (ROM)	382.5	Pekka Niemi (FIN)	367.5
Second Heavyweight (- 110 kg)	Norberto Oberburger (ITA)	390.0	Stefan Tasnadi (ROM)	380.0	Guy Carlton (USA)	377.5
Super-Heavyweight (+ 110 kg)	Dean Lukin (AUS)	412.5	Mario Martinez (USA)	410.0	Manfred Nerlinger (FRG)	397.5
Greco-Roman Wrestling						
Light-Flyweight (-48 kg)	Vincenzo Maenza (ITA)		Markus Scherer (FRG)		Ikuzo Saito (JPN)	
Flyweight (- 52 kg)	Atsuji Miyahara (JPN)		Daniel Aceves (MEX)		Dae-Du Bang (KOR)	
Bantamweight (- 57 kg)	Pasquale Passarelli (FRG)		Masaki Eto (JPN)		Haralambos Holidis (GRE)	
Featherweight (-62 kg)	Weon-Kee Kim (KOR)		Kentolle Johansson (SWE)		Hugo Dietsche (SUI)	
Lightweight (- 68 kg)	Vlado Lisjak (YUG)		Tapio Sipila (FIN)		James Martinez (USA)	
Welterweight (- 74 kg)	Jonko Salomäki (FIN)		Roger Tallroth (SWE)		Stefan Rusu (ROM)	
Middleweight (- 82 kg)	Ion Draica (ROM)		Dimitrios Thanopoulos (GRE)		Sören Claeson (SWE)	
Light-Heavyweight (- 90 kg	Steven Fraser (USA)		Ilie Matei (ROM)		Frank Andersson (SWE)	
Heavyweight (- 100 kg)	Vasile Andrei (ROM)		Greg Gibson (USA)		Jozef Tertelje (YUG)	
Super-Heavyweight (+ 100 kg)	Jeffrey Blatnick (USA)		Refik Memisevic (YUG)		Victor Dolipschi (ROM)	
Freestyle Wrestling						
Light-Flyweight (-48 kg)	Robert Weaver (USA)		Takashi Irie (JPN)		Son-Gab Do (KOR)	
Flyweight (- 52 kg)	Saban Trstena (YUG)		Jong-Kiu Kim (KOR)		Yuji Takada (JPN)	
Bantamweight (- 57 kg)	Hideaki Tomiyama (JPN)		Barry Davis (USA)		Eui-Kon Kim (KOR)	
Featherweight (- 62 kg)	Randy Lewis (USA)		Kosei Akaishi (JPN)		Jung-Keun Lee (KOR)	
Lightweight (- 68 kg)	In-Tak You (KOR)		Andrew Rein (USA)		Jukka Rauhala (FIN)	
Welterweight (74 kg)	David Shultz (USA)		Martin Knosp (FRG)		Saban Sejdi (YUG)	
Middleweight (- 82 kg)	Mark Shultz (USA)		Hideyuki Nagashima (JPN)		Chris Rinke (CAN)	
Light-Heavyweight (- 90 kg)	Ed Banach (USA)		Akira Ota (JPN)		Noel Loban (GBR)	
Heavyweight (-100 kg)	Lou Banach (USA)		Joseph Atiyeh (SYR)		Vasile Pascasu (ROM)	
Super-Heavyweight (+100 kg)	Bruce Baumgartner (USA)		Bob Molle (CAN)		Ayhan Taskin (TUR)	
Judo						
Super-Lightweight (- 60 kg)	Shinji Hosokawa (JPN)		Jae-Jup Kim (KOR)		Edward Liddle (USA)	
					Neil Eckersley (GBR)	
Half-lightweight (- 65 kg)	Yoshiyuki Matsuoka (JPN)		Jung-Oh Hwang (KOR)		Josef Reiter (AUT)	
					Marc Alexandre (FRA)	
Lightweight (-71 kg)	Ahn-Beyong Keun (KOR)		Ezio Gamba (ITA)		Luis Onmura (BRA)	
					Kerrith Brown (GBR)	
Light-Middleweight (- 78 kg)	Frank Wieneke (FRG)		Neil Adams (GBR)		Mircea Fratica (ROM)	
					Michel Nowak (FRA)	
Middleweight (- 86 kg)	Peter Seisenbacher (AUT)		Robert Berland (USA)		Walter Carmona (BRA)	
					Seiki Nose (JPN)	
Light-Heavyweight (-95 kg)	Hyoung-Zoo Ha (KOR)		Douglas Vieira (BRA)		Günther Neureuther (FRG)	
					Bjarni Fridriksson (ISL)	
Heavyweight (+ 95 kg)	Hitoshi Saito (JPN)		Angelo Parisi (FRA)		Mark Berger (CAN)	
					Yong-Chul Cho (KOR)	
Open Class	Yasuhiro Yamashita (JPN)		Mohamed Rashwan (EGY)		Arthur Schnabel (FRG)	
					Mihai Cioc (ROM)	
Fencing						
Individual Foil, Men	Mauro Numa (ITA)		Matthias Behr (FRG)		Stefano Cerioni (ITA)	
Team Foil, Men	Italy		FRG		France	
Individual Épée	Philippe Boisse (FRA)		Björne Vaggo (SWE)		Philippe Riboud (FRA)	
Team Épée	FRG		France		Italy	
Individual Sabre	Jean-François Lamour (FRA)		Marco Marin (ITA)		Peter Westbrook (USA)	
Team Sabre	Italy		France		Romania	
Individual Foil, Women	Ju Jie Luan (CHN)		Cornelia Hanisch (FRG)		Dorina Vaccaroni (ITA)	
Team Foil, Women	FRG		Romania		France	
Modern Pentathlon						
Individual	Daniele Masala (ITA)	5 469	Svante Rasmusson (SWE)	5 456	Carlo Massullo (ITA)	5 406
Team	Italy	16 060	USA	15 568	France	15 565

EVENT	GOLD		SILVER		BRONZE	
Canoeing						
Men						
500 m Kayak Singles K1	Ian Ferguson (NZL)	1:47.84	Lars-Erik Moberg (SWE)	1:48.18	Bernard Bregeon (FRA)	1:48.41
1000 m Kayak Singles K1	Alan Thompson (NZL)	3:45.73	Milan Janic (YUG)	3:46.88	Greg Barton (USA)	3:47.38
500 m Kayak Pairs K2	New Zealand	1:34.21	Sweden	1:35.26	Canada	1:35.41
1000 m Kayak Pairs K2	Canada	3:24.22	France	3:25.97	Australia	3:26.80
1000 m Kayak Fours K4	New Zealand	3:02.28	Sweden	3:02.81	France	3:03.94
500 m Canadian Singles C1	Larry Cain (CAN)	1:57.01	Henning Jakobsen (DEN)	1:58.45	Costica Olaru (ROM)	1:59.86
1000 m Canadian Singles C1	Ulrich Eicke (FRG)	4:06.32	Larry Cain (CAN)	4:08.67	Henning Jakobsen (DEN)	4:09.50
500 m Canadian Pairs C2	Yugoslavia	1:43.67	Romania	1:45.68	Spain	1:47.71
1000 m Canadian Pairs C2	Romania	3:40.60	Yugoslavia	3:41.56	France	3:48.01
Women						
500 m Kayak Singles K1	Agneta Andersson (SWE)	1:58.72	Barbara Schüttpelz (FRG)	1:59.93	Annemiek Derckx (HOL)	2:00.11
500 m Kayak Pairs K2	Sweden	1:45.25	Canada	1:47.13	FRG	1:47.32
500 m Kayak Fours K4	Romania	1:38.34	Sweden	1:38.87	Canada	1:39.40
Rowing						
Men						
Single Sculls	Pertti Karppinen (FIN)	7:00.24	Peter MichaelKolbe (FRG)	7:02.19	Robert Mills (CAN)	7:10.38
Doubles Sculls	USA	6:36.87	Belgium	6:38.19	Yugoslavia	6:39.59
Coxless Pairs	Romania	6:45.39	Spain	6:48.47	Norway	6:51.81
Coxed Pairs	Italy	7:05.99	Romania	7:11.21	USA	7:12.81
Coxless Quadruple Sculls	FRG	5:57.55	Australia	5:57.98	Canada	5:59.07
Coxless Fours	New Zealand	6:03.48	USA	6:06.10	Denmark	6:07.72
Coxed Fours	Great Britain	6:18.64	USA	6:20.28	New Zealand	6:23.68
Coxed Eights	Canada	5:41.32	USA	5:41.74	Australia	5:42.40
Women						
Single Sculls	Valeria Racila (ROM)	3:40.68	Charlotte Geer (USA)	3:43.89	Ann Haesebrouck (BEL)	3:45.72
Double Sculls	Romania	3:26.77	Netherlands	3:29.13	Canada	3:29.82
Coxless Pairs	Romania	3:32.60	Canada	3:36.06	FRG	3:40.50
Coxed Quadruple Sculls	Romania	3:14.11	USA	3:15.57	Denmark	3:16.02
Coxed Fours	Romania	3:19.38	Canada	3:21.55	Australia	3:23.29
Coxed Eights	USA	2:59.80	Romania	3:00.87	Netherlands	3:02.92
Yachting						
Finn Class	Russel Coutts (NZL)	34.7	John Bertrand (USA)	37.0	Terry Neilson (CAN)	37.7
International Star	USA	29.7	FRG	41.4	Italy	43.5
Flying Dutchman	USA	19.7	Canada	22.7	Great Britain	48.7
International Tornado	New Zealand	14.7	USA	37.0	Australia	50.4
International 470	Spain	33.7	USA	43.0	France	49.9
International Soling	USA	33.7	Brazil	43.4	Canada	49.7
Windglider Class	Stephan van den Berg (HOL)	27.7	Randall Steele (USA)	46.0	Bruce Kendall (NZL)	46.4
Cycling						
Men						
Road Race (190.2 km)	Alexi Grewal (USA)	4:59.57	Steve Bauer (CAN)	4:59.7	Dag Otto Lauritzen (NOR)	5:00.18
100 km Road Team Time Trial	Italy	1:58.28	Switzerland	2:02.38	USA	2:02.46
1000 m Time Trial	Fredy Schmidtke (FRG)	1:06.10	Curtis Harnett (CAN)	1:06.44	Fabrice Colas (FRA)	1:06.65
1000 m Sprint	Mark Gorski (USA)		Nelson Vails (USA)		Tsutomu Sakamoto (JPN)	
4000 m Individual Pursuit	Steve Hegg (USA)	4:39.35	Rolf Gölz (FRG)	4:43.82	Leonard Nitz (USA)	4:44.03
4000 m Team Pursuit	Australia	4:25.99	USA	4:29.85	FRG	4:25.60
Individual Points Race	Roger Ilegems (BEL)		Uwe Messerschmidt (FRG)		José Manuel Youshimatz (MEX)	
Women						
Road Race (79.2 km)	Connie Carpenter-Phinney (USA)	2:11.14	Rebecca Twigg (USA)		Sandra Schumacher (FRG)	
Shooting						
Men						
Small-Bore Rifle (Prone)	Edward Etzel (USA)	599	Michel Bury (FRA)	596	Michael Sullivan (GBR)	596
Small-Bore Rifle (3 Positions)	Malcolm Cooper (GBR)	1173	Daniel Nipkow (SUI)	1163	Alister Allan (GBR)	1162
Rapid Fire Pistol	Takeo Kamachi (JPN)	595	Corneliu Ion (ROM)	593	Rauno Bies (FIN)	591
Free Pistol (50 m)	Xu Haifeng (CHN)	566	Ragnar Skanaker (SWE)	565	Yifu Wang (CHN)	564
Running Game Target	Yuwei Li (CHN)	587	Helmut Bellingrodt (COL)	584	Shiping Huang (CHN)	581
Skeet Shooting	Matthew Dryke (USA)	198	Ole Riber Rasmussen (DEN)	196/25	Luca Scribani-Rossi (ITA)	196/24
Trap Shooting	Luciano Giovanetti (ITA)	192	Francisco Boza (PER)	192	Daniel Carlisle (USA)	192
Air Rifle	Philippe Heberle (FRA)	589	Andreas Kronthaler (AUT)	581	Barry Dagger (GBR)	587

EVENT	GOLD		SILVER		BRONZE	
Women						
Sport Pistol	Linda Thom (CAN)	585	Ruby Fox (USA)	585	Patricia Dench (AUS)	583
Standard Rifle	Xiaoxuan Wu (CHN)	581	Ulrike Holmer (FRG)	578	Wanda Jewell (USA)	578
Air Rifle	Pat Spurgin (USA)	393	Edith Gufler (ITA)	391	Xiaoxuan Wu (CHN)	389
Archery						
Men	Darrell Pace (USA)	2616	Richard McKinney (USA)	2564	Hiroshi Yamamoto (JPN)	2563
Women	Hyang-Soon Seo (KOR)	2568	Lingjuan Li (CHN)	2559	Jin-Ho Kim (KOR)	2555
Equestrianism						
Three-Day Event	Mark Todd (NZL)	51.60	Karen Stives (USA)	54.20	Virginia Holgate (GBR)	56.80
Three-Day Event, Team	USA	186.00	Great Britain	189.20	FRG	234
Grand Prix (Dressage)	Reiner Klimke (FRG)	1504	Anne Grethe Jensen (DEN)	1442	Otto Hofer (SUI)	1364
Grand Prix (Dressage) Team	FRG	4955	Switzerland	4673	Sweden	4630
Grand Prix (Jumping)	Joe Fargis (USA)		Conrad Homfeld (USA)	-4	Heidi Robbiani (SUI)	-8
Grand Prix (Jumping) Team	USA	12.00	Great Britain	36.75	FRG	39.25
Gymnastics						
Men						
Individual Combined Exercises	Koji Gushiken (JPN)	118.700	Peter Vidmar (USA)	118.675	Li Ning (CHN)	118.575
Team	USA	591.40	China	590.80	Japan	586.70
Parallel Bars	Bart Conner (USA)	19.950	Nobuyuki Kajitani (JPN)	19.925	Mitchell Gaylord (USA)	19.850
Floor	Li Ning (CHN)	19.925	Yun Lou (CHN)	19.775	Koji Sotomura (JPN)	19.700
					Philippe Vatuone (FRA)	19.700
Horse Vault	Yun Lou (CHN)	19.950	Li Ning (CHN)	19.825		
			Mitchell Gaylord (USA)	19.825		
			Koji Gushiken (JPN)	19.825		
			Shinji Morisue (JPN)	19.825		
Horizontal Bar	Shinji Morisue (JPN)	20.000	Tong Fei (CHN)	19.955	Koji Gushiken (JPN)	19.950
Rings	Koji Gushiken (JPN)	19.850			Mitchell Gaylord (USA)	19.825
	Li Ning (CHN)	19.850				
Pommel Horse	Li Ning (CHN)	19.950			Timothy Daggett (USA)	19.825
	Peter Vidmar (USA)	19.950				
Women						
Individual Combined Exercises	Mary Lou Retton (USA)	79.175	Ecaterina Szabó (ROM)	79.125	Simona Pauca (ROM)	78.675
Team	Romania	392.20	USA	391.20	China	388.60
Floor	Ecaterina Szabó (ROM)	19.975	Julianne McNamara (USA)	19.950	Mary Lou Retton (USA)	19.775
Horse Vault	Ecaterina Szabó (ROM)	19.875	Mary Lou Retton (USA)	19.850	Lavinia Agache (ROM)	19.750
Beam	Simona Pauca (ROM)	19.800			Kathy Johnson (USA)	19.650
	Ecaterina Szabó (ROM)	19.800				
Asymmetrical Bars	Yanhong Ma (CHN)	19.950			Mary Lou Retton (USA)	19.800
	Julianne Mc Namara (USA)	19.950				
Modern Rhythmic	Lori Fung (CAN)	57.950	Doina Staiculescu (ROM)	57.900	Regina Weber (FRG)	57.700
Basketball						
Men	USA		Spain		Yugoslavia	
Women	USA		South Korea		China	
Soccer	France		Brazil		Yugoslavia	
Handball						
Men	Yugoslavia		FRG		Romania	
Women	Yugoslavia		South Korea		China	
Hockey						
Men	Pakistan		FRG		Great Britain	
Women	Netherlands		FRG		USA	
Volleyball						
Men	USA		Brazil		Italy	
Women	China		USA		Japan	

Calgary 1988

Participants: 1423 / Men: 1110, Women: 313, Countries: 57,
Sports: 8, Events: 46
Final Torchbearer: Robyn Perry

Medals Table

PLACE	COUNTRY	GOLD	SILVER	BRONZE
1	USSR	11	9	9
2	GDR	9	10	6
3	Switzerland	5	5	5
4	Finland	4	1	2
5	Sweden	4	–	2

Outstanding Athletes

PLACE	NAME (NATIONALITY)	DISCIPLINE	G	S	B
1	Yvonne van Gennip (HOL)	Speed Skating	3	–	–
	Matti Nykänen (FIN)	Nordic Skiing	3	–	–
3	Tamara Tichonova (URS)	Nordic Skiing	2	1	–
4	Tomas Gustafson (SWE)	Speed Skating	2	–	–
	Frank-Peter Roetsch (GDR)	Biathlon	2	–	–
	Vreni Schneider (SUI)	Alpine Skiing	2	–	–
	Gunde Svan (SWE)	Nordic Skiing	2	–	–
	Alberto Tomba (ITA)	Alpine Skiing	2	–	–

EVENT	GOLD		SILVER		BRONZE	
Alpine Skiing						
Men						
Downhill	Pirmin Zurbriggen (SUI)	1:59.63	Peter Müller (SUI)	2:00.14	Franck Piccard (FRA)	2:01.24
Slalom	Alberto Tomba (ITA)	1:39.47	Frank Wörndl (FRG)	1:39.53	Paul Frommelt (LIE)	1:39.84
Giant Slalom	Alberto Tomba (ITA)	2:06.37	Hubert Strolz (AUT)	2:07.41	Pirmin Zurbriggen (SUI)	2:08.39
Super G	Franck Piccard (FRA)	1:39.66	Helmut Mayer (AUT)	1:40.96	Lars-Börje Eriksson (SWE)	1:41.08
Combined	Hubert Strolz (AUT)	36.55	Bernhard Gstrein (AUT)	43.45	Paul Accola (SUI)	48.24
Women						
Downhill	Marina Kiehl (FRG)	1:25.86	Brigitte Oertli (SUI)	1:26.61	Karen Percy (CAN)	1:26.62
Slalom	Vreni Schneider (SUI)	1:36.69	Mateja Svet (YUG)	1:38.37	Christa Kinshofer-Güthlein (FRG)	1:38.40
Giant Slalom	Vreni Schneider (SUI)	2:06.49	Christa Kinshofer-Güthlein (FRG)	2:07.42	Maria Walliser (SUI)	2:07.72
Super G	Sigrid Wolf (AUT)	1:19.03	Michela Figini (SUI)	1:20.03	Karen Percy (CAN)	1:20.29
Combined	Anita Wachter (AUT)	29.25	Brigitte Oertli (SUI)	29.48	Maria Walliser (SUI)	51.28
Nordic Skiing						
Men						
15 km Cross-Country Skiing (Classical)	Mikhail Devyayarov (URS)	41:18.9	Pal-Gunnar Mikkelsplass (NOR)	41:33.4	Vladimir Smirnov (URS)	41:48.5
30 km Cross-Country Skiing (Classical)	Alexeiy Prokurorov (URS)	1:24:26.3	Vladimir Smirnov (URS)	1:24:35.1	Vegard Ulvang (NOR)	1:25:11.6
50 km Cross-Country Skiing (Freestyle)	Gunde Svan (SWE)	2:04:30.9	Maurillo de Zolt (ITA)	2:05:36.4	Andi Grünenfelder (SUI)	2:06:01.9
4 x 10 km	Sweden	1:43:58.6	USSR	1:44:11.3	Czechoslovakia	1:45:22.7
Women						
5 km Cross-Country Skiing (Classical)	Marjo Matikainen (FIN)	15:04.0	Tamara Tichonova (URS)	15:05.3	Vida Venciene (URS)	15:11.1
10 km Cross-Country Skiing (Classical)	Vida Venciene (URS)	30:08.3	Raisa Smetanina (URS)	30:17.0	Marjo Matikainen (FIN)	30:20.5
20 km Cross-Country Skiing	Tamara Tichonova (URS)	55:53.6	Anfissa Rezova (URS)	56:12.8	Raisa Smetanina (URS)	57:22.1
4 x 5 km	USSR	59:51.1	Norway	1:01:33.0	Finland	1:01:53.8
Ski Jumping						
Ski Jumping (70 m Hill)	Matti Nykänen (FIN)	229.1	Pavel Ploc (TCH)	212.1	Jiri Malec (TCH)	211.8
Ski Jumping (90 m Hill)	Matti Nykänen (FIN)	224.0	Erik Johnson (NOR)	207.9	Matjaz Debelak (YUG)	207.7
Ski Jumping, Team	Finland	634.4	Yugoslavia	625.5	Norway	596.1
Nordic Combined, Individual	Hippolyt Kempf (SUI)	432.230	Klaus Sulzenbacher (AUT)	429.375	Allar Levandi (URS)	422.590
Nordic Combined, Team	FRG	792.08	Switzerland	791.40	Austria	785.90
Biathlon						
10 km	Frank-Peter Roetsch (GDR)	25:08.1	Valeriy Medvetsev (URS)	25:23.7	Sergey Chepikov (URS)	25:29.4
20 km	Frank-Peter Roetsch (GDR)	56:33.3	Valeriy Medvetsev (URS)	56:54.6	Johann Passler (ITA)	57:10.1
4 x 7.5 km	USSR	1:22:30.0	FRG	1:23:37.4	Italy	1:23:51.5
Figure Skating						
Women	Katarina Witt (GDR)		Elizabeth Manley (CAN)		Debra Thomas (USA)	
Men	Brian Boitano (USA)		Brian Orser (CAN)		Viktor Petrenko (URS)	
Pairs	Yaterina Gordeyeva/ Sergeiy Grinkov (URS)		Yelena Valova/ Oleg Vasiliev (URS)		Jill Watson/ Peter Oppegard (USA)	

EVENT	GOLD		SILVER		BRONZE	
Ice Dance	Natalia Bestemianova/ Andreiy Bukin (URS)		Marina Klimova/ Sergeiy Ponomarenko (URS)		Tracy Wilson/ Robert McCall (CAN)	
Speed Skating						
Men						
500 m	Uwe-Jens Mey (GDR)	36.45	Jan Ykema (HOL)	36.76	Akira Kuroiwa(JPN)	36.77
1000 m	Nikolai Gulyaev (URS)	1:13.03	Uwe-Jens Mey (GDR)	1:13.11	Igor Szelesozki (URS)	1:13.19
1500 m	André Hoffman (GDR)	1:52.06	Eric Flaim (USA)	1:52.12	Michael Hadschieff (AUT)	1:52.31
5000 m	Tomas Gustafson (SWE)	6:44.63	Leo Visser (HOL)	6:44.98	Gerard Kemkers (HOL)	6:45.92
10,000 m	Tomas Gustafson (SWE)	13:48.20	Michael Hadschieff (AUT)	13:56.11	Leo Visser (HOL)	14:00.55
Women						
500 m	Bonnie Blair (USA)	39.10	Christa Rothenburger (GDR)	39.12	Karin Kania (GDR)	39.24
1000 m	Christa Rothenburger (GDR)	1:17.65	Karin Kania (GDR)	1:17.70	Bonnie Blair (USA)	1:18.31
1500 m	Yvonne van Gennip (HOL)	2:00.68	Karin Kania (GDR)	2:00.82	Andrea Ehrig (GDR)	2:01.49
3000 m	Yvonne van Gennip (HOL)	4:11.94	Andrea Ehrig (GDR)	4:12.09	Gabi Zange (GDR)	4:16.92
5000 m	Yvonne van Gennip (HOL)	7:14.13	Andrea Ehrig (GDR)	7:17.12	Gabi Zange (GDR)	7:21.61
Lugeing						
Men's Singles	Jens Müller (GDR)	3:05.548	Georg Hackl (FRG)	3:05.916	Yuriy Kharchenko (URS)	3:06.274
Women's Singles	Steffi Walter (GDR)	3:03.973	Ute Oberhoffner (GDR)	3:04.105	Cerstin Schmidt (GDR)	3:04.181
2-Man Luge	Jörg Hoffman/Jochen Pietzch (GDR)	1:31.940	Stefan Krausse/ Jan Behrendt (GDR)	1:32.039	Thomas Schwab/ Wolfgang Staudinger (FRG)	1:32.274
Bobsledding						
2-Man Bob	USSR I	3:53.48	GDR I	3:54.19	GDR II	3:54.64
4-Man Bob	Switzerland I	3:47.51	GDR I	3:47.58	USSR II	3:48.26
Ice Hockey	USSR		Finland		Sweden	

Seoul 1988

17 September – 2 October

Participants: 8465 / Men: 6279, Women: 2186, Countries: 159,
Sports: 23, Events: 237
Final Torchbearers: Son Kee-Chung, Lim Chun-Ae, Chung Sun-Man, Kim
Won-Tak, Sohn Mi-Chung

Medals Table

PLACE	COUNTRY	GOLD	SILVER	BRONZE
1	USSR	55	31	46
2	GDR	37	35	30
3	USA	36	31	27
4	South Korea	12	11	10
5	FRG	11	14	15

Outstanding Athletes

PLACE	NAME (NATIONALITY)	DISCIPLINE	G	S	B
1	Kristin Otto (GDR)	Swimming	6	–	–
2	Matt Biondi (USA)	Swimming	5	–	1
3	Vladimir Artemov (URS)	Gymnastics	4	1	–
4	Daniela Silivas (ROM)	Gymnastics	3	2	1
5	Florence Griffith-Joyner (USA)	Athletics	3	1	–

EVENT	GOLD		SILVER		BRONZE	
Athletics						
Men						
100 m*	Carl Lewis (USA)	9.92*	Linford Christie (GBR)	9.97	Calvin Smith (USA)	9.99
200 m	Joe DeLoach (USA)	19.75	Carl Lewis (USA)	19.79	Robson da Silva (BRA)	20.04
400 m	Steven Lewis (USA)	43.87	Butch Reynolds (USA)	43.93	Danny Everett (USA)	44.09
800 m	Paul Ereng (KEN)	1:43.45	Joaquim Cruz (BRA)	1:43.90	Said Aouita (MAR)	1:44.06
1500 m	Peter Rono (KEN)	3:35.96	Peter Elliott (GBR)	3:36.15	Jens-Peter Herold (GDR)	3:36.21
5000 m	John Ngugi (KEN)	13:11.70	Dieter Baumann (FRG)	13:15.52	Hansjörg Kunze (GDR)	13:15.73
10,000 m	Brahim Boutaib (MAR)	27:21.44	Salvatore Antibo (ITA)	27:23.55	Kipkemboy Kimeli (KEN)	27:25.16
Marathon	Gelindo Bordin (ITA)	2:10:32	Douglas Wakihuriu (KEN)	2:10:47	Ahmed Saleh (DIJ)	2:10:59
110 m Hurdles	Roger Kingdom (USA)	12.98	Colin Jackson (GBR)	13.28	Anthony Campbell (USA)	13.38
400 m Hurdles	Andre Philipps (USA)	47.19	Amadou Dia Ba (SEN)	47.23	Edwin Moses (USA)	47.56

EVENT	GOLD		SILVER		BRONZE	
3000 m Steeplechase	Julius Kariuki (KEN)	8:05.51	Peter Koech (KEN)	8:06.79	Mark Rowland (GBR)	8:07.96
4 x 100 m	USSR	38.19	Great Britain	38.28	France	38.40
4 x 400 m	USA	2:56.16	Jamaica	3:00.30	FRG	3:00.56
20 km Walk	Jozef Pribilinec (TCH)	1:19.57	Ronald Weigel (GDR)	1:19.60	Maurizio Damilano (ITA)	1:20:14
50 km Walk	Vyacheslav Ivanenko (URS)	3:38:29	Ronald Weigel (GDR)	1:20:00	Hartwig Gauder (GDR)	3:39:45
High Jump	Gennadi Avdeyenko (URS)	2.38	Hollis Conway (USA)	2.36	Rudolf Povarnizin (URS)	2.36
					Patrick Sjöberg (SWE)	2.36
Pole Vault	Sergei Bubka (URS)	5.90	Rodion Gataullin (URS)	5.85	Grigori Yegorov (URS)	5.80
Long Jump	Carl Lewis (USA)	8.72	Mike Powell (USA)	8.49	Larry Myricks (USA)	8.27
Triple Jump	Khristo Markov (BUL)	17.61	Igor Lapshin (URS)	17.52	Alexander Kovalenko (URS)	17.42
Shot	Ulf Timmermann (GDR)	22.47	Randy Barnes (USA)	22.39	Werner Günthör (SUI)	21.99
Discus	Jürgen Schult (GDR)	68.82	Romas Ubartas (URS)	67.48	Rolf Danneberg (FRG)	67.38
Hammer	Sergeiy Litvinov (URS)	84.80	Yuriy Sedych (URS)	83.76	Yuriy Tamm (URS)	81.16
Javelin	Tapio Korjus (FIN)	84.28	Jan Zelezny (TCH)	84.12	Seppo Räty (FIN)	83.26
Decathlon	Christian Schenk (GDR)	8488	Torsten Voss (GDR)	8399	Dave Steen (CAN)	8328

*Race Winner Ben Johnson (Can; 9.79) was disqualified for failing a drugs test

Women						
100 m	Florence Griffith-Joyner (USA)	10.54	Evelyn Ashford (USA)	10.83	Heike Drechsler (GDR)	10.85
200 m	Florence Griffith-Joyner (USA)	21.34	Grace Jackson (JAM)	21.72	Heike Drechsler (GDR)	21.95
400 m	Olga Brizgina (URS)	48.65	Petra Müller (GDR)	49.45	Olga Nasarova (URS)	49.90
800 m	Sigrun Wodars (GDR)	1:56.10	Christine Wachtel (GDR)	1:56.64	Kim Gallagher (USA)	1:56.91
1500 m	Paula Ivan (ROM)	3:53.96	Lelute Baikauskaite (URS)	4:00.24	Tatyana Samolenko (URS)	4:00.30
3000 m	Tatyana Samolenko (URS)	8:26.53	Paula Ivan (ROM)	8:27.15	Yvonne Murray (GBR)	8:29.02
10 000 m	Olga Bondarenko (URS)	31:05.21	Elizabeth McColgan (GBR)	31:08.44	Yelena Yupiyeva (URS)	31:19.82
Marathon	Rosa Mota (POR)	2:25:40	Lisa Martin (AUS)	2:25:53	Katrin Dörre (GDR)	2:26:21
100 m Hurdles	Yordanka Donkova (BUL)	12.38	Gloria Siebert (GDR)	12.61	Claudia Zaczkiewicz (FRG)	12.75
400 m Hurdles	Debra Flintoff-King (AUS)	53.17	Tatyana Ledovskaya (URS)	53.18	Ellen Fiedler (GDR)	53.63
4 x 100 m	USA	41.98	GDR	42.09	USSR	42.75
4 x 400 m	USSR	3:15.18	USA	3:15.51	GDR	3:18.29
High Jump	Louise Ritter (USA)	2.03	Stefka Kostadinova (BUL)	2.01	Tamara Bykova (URS)	1.99
Long Jump	Jackie Joyner-Kersee (USA)	7.40	Heike Drechsler (GDR)	7.22	Galina Chistyakova (URS)	7.11
Shot	Natalia Lisovskaya (URS)	22.24	Kathrin Neimke (GDR)	21.07	Meisu Li (CHN)	21.06
Discus	Martina Hellmann (GDR)	72.30	Diana Gansky (GDR)	71.88	Szvetanka Christova (BUL)	69.74
Javelin	Petra Felke (GDR)	74.68	Fatima Whitbread (GBR)	70.32	Beate Koch (GDR)	67.30
Heptathlon	Jackie Joyner-Kersee (USA)	7291	Sabine John (GDR)	6897	Anke Behmer (GDR)	6858

Swimming

Men						
50 m Freestyle	Matt Biondi (USA)	22.14	Thomas Jager (USA)	22.36	Gennadi Prigoda (URS)	22.71
100 m Freestyle	Matt Biondi (USA)	48.63	Christopher Jacobs (USA)	49.08	Stephan Caron (FRA)	49.62
200 m Freestyle	Duncan Armstrong (AUS)	1:47.25	Anders Holmertz (SWE)	1:47.89	Matt Biondi (USA)	1:47.99
400 m Freestyle	Uwe Dassler (GDR)	3:46.95	Duncan Armstrong (AUS)	3:47.15	Artur Wojdat (POL)	3:47.34
1500 m Freestyle	Vladimir Salnikov (URS)	15:00.40	Stefan Pfeiffer (FRG)	15:02.69	Uwe Dassler (GDR)	15:06.15
100 m Backstroke	Daichi Suzuki (JPN)	55.05	David Berkhoff (USA)	55.18	Igor Polianski (URS)	55.20
200 m Backstroke	Igor Polianski (URS)	1:59.37	Frank Baltrusch (GDR)	1:59.60	Paul Kingsman (NZL)	2:00.48
100 m Breaststroke	Adrian Moorhouse (GBR)	1:02.04	Karoly Guttler (HUN)	1:02.05	Dimitri Volkov (URS)	1:02.20
200 m Breaststroke	Jozef Szábó (HUN)	2:13.52	Nick Gillingham (GBR)	2:14.12	Sergio Lopez (ESP)	2:15.21
100 m Butterfly	Anthony Nesty (SUR)	53.00	Matt Biondi (USA)	53.01	Andy Jameson (GBR)	53.30
200 m Butterfly	Michael Gross (FRG)	1:56.94	Benny Nielsen (DEN)	1:58.24	Anthony Mosse (NZL)	1:58.28
200 m Medley	Tamas Darnyi (HUN)	2:00.17	Patrick Kühl (GDR)	2:01.61	Vadim Yaroshchuk (URS)	2:02.40
400 m Medley	Tamas Darnyi (HUN)	4:14.75	David Wharton (USA)	4:17.36	Stefano Battistelli (ITA)	4:18.01
4 x 100 m Freestyle	USA	3:16.53	USSR	3:18.33	GDR	3:19.82
4 x 200 m Freestyle	USA	7:12.51	GDR	7:13.68	FRG	7:14.35
4 x 100 m Medley	USA	3:36.93	Canada	3:39.28	USSR	3:39.96
Springboard Diving	Greg Louganis (USA)	730.80	Liangde Tan (CHN)	704.88	Deliang Li (CHN)	665.28
Highboard Diving	Greg Louganis (USA)	638.61	Ni Xiong (CHN)	637.47	Jesus Mena (MEX)	594.93
Water Polo	Yugoslavia		USA		USSR	

Women						
50 m Freestyle	Kristin Otto (GDR)	25.49	Wenyi Yang (CHN)	25.64	Katrin Meissner (GDR)	25.71
					Jill Sterkel (USA)	25.71
100 m Freestyle	Kristin Otto (GDR)	54.93	Yong Zhuang (CHN)	55.47	Cathérine Plewinski (FRA)	55.49
200 m Freestyle	Heike Friedrich (GDR)	1:57.65	Sivia Poll (CRC)	1:58.67	Manuela Stellmach (GDR)	1:59.01
400 m Freestyle	Janet Evans (USA)	4:03.85	Heike Friedrich (GDR)	4:05.94	Anke Möhring (GDR)	4:06.62
800 m Freestyle	Janet Evans (USA)	8:20.20	Astrid Strauss (GDR)	8:22.09	Julie McDonald (AUS)	8:22.93
100 m Backstroke	Kristin Otto (GDR)	1:00.89	Krisztina Egerszegy (HUN)	1:01.56	Cornelia Sirch (GDR)	1:01.57

EVENT	GOLD		SILVER		BRONZE	
200 m Backstroke	Krisztina Egerszegy (HUN)	2:09.29	Kathrin Zimmermann (GDR)	2:10.61	Cornelia Sirch (GDR)	2:11.45
100 m Breaststroke	Tania Dangalakova (BUL)	1:07.95	Antoaneta Frenkeva (BUL)	1:08.74	Silke Hörner (GDR)	1:08.83
200 m Breaststroke	Silke Hörner (GDR)	2:26.71	Xiaomin Huang (CHN)	2:27.49	Antoaneta Frenkeva (BUL)	2:28.34
100 m Butterfly	Kristin Otto (GDR)	59.00	Birte Weigang (GDR)	59.45	Hong Quian (CHN)	59.52
200 m Butterfly	Kathleen Nord (GDR)	2:09.51	Birte Weigang (GDR)	2:09.91	Mary T. Meagher (USA)	2:10.80
200 m Medley	Daniela Hunger (GDR)	2:12.59	Elena Dendeberova (URS)	2:13.31	Noemi Ildiko Lung (ROM)	2:14.85
400 m Medley	Janet Evans (USA)	4:37.76	Noemi Lung (ROM)	4:39.46	Daniela Hunger (GDR)	4:39.76
4 x 100 m Freestyle	GDR	3:40.63	Netherlands	3:43.39	USA	3:44.25
4 x 100 m Medley	GDR	4:03.74	USA	4:07.90	Canada	4:10.49
Springboard Diving	Min Gao (CHN)	580.23	Qing Li (CHN)	534.33	Kelly McCormick (USA)	533.19
Highboard Diving	Yanmei Xu (CHN)	445.20	Michele Mitchell (USA)	436.95	Wendy Lian Williams (USA)	400.44
Synchronized Swimming						
Solo	Carolyn Waldo (CAN)	200.150	Tracie Ruiz-Conforto (USA)	197.633	Mikako Kotani (JPN)	191.850
Duet	Canada	197.717	USA	197.284	Japan	190.959
Boxing						
Light-Flyweight (-48 kg)	Ivailo Christov (BUL)		Michael Carbajal (USA)		Robert Isaszegi (HUN)	
					Leopoldo Serantes (PHI)	
Flyweight (-51 kg)	Kim Kwang Sun (KOR)		Andreas Tews (GDR)		Mario Gonzalez (MEX)	
					Timofei Skriabin (URS)	
Bantamweight (-54 kg)	Kennedy McKinney (USA)		Alexander Christov (BUL)		Phajol Moolsan (THA)	
					Jorge Julio Rocha (COL)	
Featherweight (-57 kg)	Giovanni Parisi (ITA)		Daniel Dumitrescu (ROM)		Abdelhak Achik (MAR)	
					Lee Jae Hiuk (KOR)	
Lightweight (-60 kg)	Andreas Zülow (GDR)		George Cramne (SWE)		Nerguy Enchbat (MGL)	
					Romallis Ellis (USA)	
Light-Welterweight (-63.5 kg)	Vyacheslav Yanovski (URS)		Graham Cheney (AUS)		Reiner Gies (FRG)	
					Lars Myberg (SWE)	
Welterweight (-67 kg)	Robert Wangila (KEN)		Laurent Boudouani (FRA)		Jan Dydak (POL)	
					Kenneth Gould (USA)	
Light-Middleweight (-71 kg)	Park Si Hun (KOR)		Roy Jones (USA)		Richard Woodhall (GBR)	
					Raymond Downey (CAN)	
Middleweight (-75 kg)	Henry Maske (GDR)		Egerton Marcus (CAN)		Chris Sande (KEN)	
					Hussain Syed (PAK)	
Light-Heavyweight (-81 kg)	Andrew Maynard (USA)		Nuramgomed Shanavasov (URS)		Henryk Petrich (POL)	
					Damir Skaro (YUG)	
Heavyweight (-91 kg)	Ray Mercer (USA)		Baik Hyun Man (KOR)		Andrzej Golota (POL)	
					Arnold Vanderlijde (HOL)	
Super-Heavyweight (+ 91 kg)	Lennox Lewis (CAN)		Riddick Bowe (USA)		Alexander Miroshnichenko (URS)	
					Janusz Zarenkiewicz (POL)	
Weightlifting						
Flyweight (-52 kg)	Sevdalin Marinov (BUL)	270.0	Byung-Kwan Chun (KOR)	260.0	Zhuoqiang He (CHN)	257.5
Bantamweight (-56 kg)	Oksen Mirzoian (URS)	292.5	Yiangqiang He (CHN)	287.5	Shoubin Liu (CHN)	267.5
Featherweight (-60 kg)	Nahim Süleymanoglu (TUR)	342.5	Stefan Topourov (BUL)	312.5	Huanming Ye (CHN)	287.5
Lightweight (-67.5 kg)	Joachim Kunz (GDR)	340.0	Israil Militosian (URS)	337.5	Jinhe Li (CHN)	325.0
Middleweight (-75 kg)	Borislav Gidikov (BUL)	375.0	Ingo Steinhöfel (GDR)	360.0	Alexander Varbanov (BUL)	357.5
Light-Heavyweight (-82.5 kg)	Israil Arsamakov (URS)	377.5	Istvan Messzi (HUN)	370.0	Lee Hyung Kun (KOR)	367.5
Middle-Heavyweight (-90 kg)	Anatoli Khrapaty (URS)	412.5	Nail Muchamediarov (URS)	400.0	Slawomir Zawada (POL)	400.0
First Heavyweight (-100 kg)	Pavel Kuznetsov (URS)	425.0	Nicu Vlad (ROM)	402.5	Peter Immesberger (FRG)	395.0
Second Heavyweight (-110 kg)	Juriy Zacharevich (URS)	455.0	Jozsef Jacso (HUN)	427.5	Ronny Weller (GDR)	425.0
Super-Heavyweight (+ 110 kg)	Alexander Kurlovich (URS)	462.5	Manfred Nerlinger (FRG)	430.0	Martin Zawieja (FRG)	415.0
Greco-Roman Wrestling						
Light-Flyweight (-48 kg)	Vincenzo Maenza (ITA)		Andrzej Chlab (POL)		Bratan Tzenov (BUL)	
Flyweight (-52 kg)	Jon Rönningen (NOR)		Atsuji Miyahara (JPN)		Lee Jae Suk (KOR)	
Bantamweight (-57 kg)	Andras Sike (HUN)		Stoyan Balov (BUL)		Haralambos Holidis (GRE)	
Featherweight (-62 kg)	Kamandar Madzhidov (URS)		Yivko Vangyelov (BUL)		An Dae Hyun (KOR)	
Lightweight (-68 kg)	Levon Zhulfalakian (URS)		Kim Sung Moon (KOR)		Tapio Sipilä (FIN)	
Welterweight (-74 kg)	Kim Young Nam (KOR)		Daulet Turlykanov (URS)		Józef Tracz (POL)	
Middleweight (-82 kg)	Mikhail Mamiashvili (URS)		Tibor Komáromi (HUN)		Kim Sang Kyu (KOR)	
Light-Heavyweight (-90 kg)	Atanas Komchev (BUL)		Harri Koskela (FIN)		Vladimir Popov (URS)	
Heavyweight (-100 kg)	Andrzej Wronski (POL)		Gerhard Himmel (FRG)		Dennis Koslowski (USA)	
Super-Heavyweight (-130 kg)	Aleksander Karelin (URS)		Rangel Guerovski (BUL)		Tomas Johansson (SWE)	
Freestyle Wrestling						
Light-Flyweight (-48 kg)	Takashi Kobayashi (JPN)		Ivan Tzonov (BUL)		Sergey Karamchakov (URS)	
Flyweight (-52 kg)	Mitsuru Sato (JPN)		Saban Trstena (YUG)		Vladimir Togusov (URS)	

EVENT	GOLD		SILVER		BRONZE	
Bantam (-57 kg)	Sergeiy Beloglassov (URS)		Askari Mohammadian (IRN)		Noh Kyung Sun (KOR)	
Featherweight (-62 kg)	John Smith (USA)		Stepan Sarkissian (URS)		Simeon Schterev (BUL)	
Lightweight (-68 kg)	Arsen Fadzayev (URS)		Park Jang Soon (KOR)		Nate Carr (USA)	
Welterweight (-74 kg)	Kenneth Monday (USA)		Adlan Varayev (URS)		Rakhmad Sofiadi (BUL)	
Middleweight (-82 kg)	Han Myung Woo (KOR)		Necmi Gencalp (TUR)		Josef Lohyna (TCH)	
Light-Heavyweight (-90 kg)	Macharbek Hadarchev (URS)		Akira Ota (JPN)		Kim Tae Woo (KOR)	
Heavyweight (-100 kg)	Vasile Puscasu (ROM)		Leri Khabelow (URS)		William Scherer (USA)	
Super-Heavyweight (-130 kg)	David Gobedishvili (URS)		Bruce Baumgartner (USA)		Andreas Schröder (GDR)	
Judo						
Super-Lightweight (-60 kg)	Kim Jae Yup (KOR)		Kevin Asano (USA)		Shinji Hosokawa (JPN)	
					Amiran Totikashvili (URS)	
Half-Lightweight (-65 kg)	Lee Kyung Keun (KOR)		Janusz Pawlowski (POL)		Bruno Carabetta (FRA)	
					Yosuke Yamamoto (JPN)	
Lightweight (-71 kg)	Marc Alexandre (FRA)		Sven Loll (GDR)		Michael Swain (USA))	
					Georgiy Tenadze (URS	
Light-Middleweight (-78 kg)	Waldemar Legien (POL)		Frank Wieneke (FRG)		Torsten Bréchôt (GDR)	
					Bashir Varayev (URS)	
Middleweight (-86 kg)	Peter Seisenbacher (AUT)		Vladimir Chestakov (URS)		Ben Spijkers (HOL)	
					Akinobu Osako (JPN)	
Light-Heavyweight (-90 kg)	Aurelio Miguel (BRA)		Marc Meiling (FRG)		Robert van de Walle (BEL)	
					Dennis Stewart (GBR)	
Heavyweight (+95 kg)	Hitoshi Saito (JPN)		Henry Stöhr (GDR)		Cho Young Chul (KOR)	
					Grigory Verichev (URS)	
Fencing						
Individual Foil – Men	Stefano Cerioni (ITA)		Udo Wagner (GDR)		Alexander Romankov (URS)	
Team Foil – Men	USSR		FRG		Hungary	
Individual Épée	Arnd Schmitt (FRG)		Philippe Riboud (FRA)		Andreiy Shuvalov (URS)	
Team Épée	Hungary		USSR		Italy	
Individual Sabre	Jean-François Lamour (FRA)		Janusz Olech (POL)		Giovanni Scalzo (ITA)	
Team Sabre	France		FRG		USSR	
Individual Foil – Women	Anja Fichtel (FRG)		Sabine Bau (FRG)		Zita Funkenhauser (FRG)	
Team Foil – Women	FRG		Italy		Hungary	
Modern Pentathlon						
Individual	János Martinek (HUN)	5404	Carlo Massullo (ITA)	5379	Vachtang Yagorashvili (URS)	5367
Team	Hungary	15886	Italy	15571	Great Britain	15276
Canoeing						
Men						
500 m Kayak Singles K1	Zsolt Gyulay (HUN)	1:44.82	Andreas Stähle (GDR)	1:46.38	Paul MacDonald (NZL)	1:46.46
1000 m Kayak Singles K1	Greg Barton (USA)	3:55.27	Grant Davies (AUS)	3:55.28	André Wohllebe (GDR)	3:55.55
500 m Kayak Pairs K2	New Zealand	1:33.98	USSR	1:34.15	Hungary	1:34.32
1000 m Kayak Pairs K2	USA	3:32.42	New Zealand	3:32.71	Australia	3:33.76
1000 m Kayak Fours K4	Hungary	3:00.20	USSR	3:01.40	GDR	3:02.37
500 m Canadian Singles C1	Olaf Heukrodt (GDR)	1:56.42	Mikhail Slivinski (URS)	1:57.26	Martin Marinov (BUL)	1:57.27
1000 m Canadian Singles C1	Ivan Klementiev (URS)	4:12.78	Jörg Schmidt (GDR)	4:15.83	Nikolai Bukalov (URS)	4:18.94
500 m Canadian Pairs C2	USSR	1:41.77	Poland	1:43.61	France	1:43.81
1000 m Canadian Pairs C2	USSR	3:48.36	GDR	3:51.44	Poland	3:54.33
Women						
500 m Kayak Singles K1	Vania Guechava (BUL)	1:55.19	Birgit Schmidt (GDR)	1:55.31	Izabela Dylewska (POL)	1:57.38
500 m Kayak Pairs K2	GDR	1:43.46	Bulgaria	1:44.06	Netherlands	1:46.00
500 m Kayak Fours K4	GDR	1:40.78	Hungary	1:41.88	Bulgaria	1:42.63
Rowing						
Men						
Single Sculls	Thomas Lange (GDR)	6:49.86	Peter-Michael Kolbe (FRG)	6:54.77	Eric Verdonk (NZL)	6:58.66
Double Sculls	Netherlands	6:21.13	Switzerland	6:22.59	USSR	6:22.87
Coxless Pairs	Great Britain	6:36.84	Romania	6:38.06	Yugoslavia	6:41.01
Coxed Pairs	Italy	6:58.79	GDR	7:00.63	Great Britain	7:01.95
Coxless Quadruple Sculls	Italy	5:53.37	Norway	5:55.08	GDR	5:56.13
Coxless Fours	GDR	6:03.11	USA	6:05.33	FRG	6:06.22
Coxed Fours	GDR	6:10.74	Romania	6:13.58	New Zealand	6:15.78
Coxed Eights	FRG	5:46.05	USSR	5:48.01	USA	5:48.26

EVENT	GOLD		SILVER		BRONZE	
Women						
Single Sculls	Jutta Behrendt (GDR)	7:47.19	Anne Marden (USA)	7:50.28	Magdalena Georgieva (BUL)	7:53.65
Double Sculls	GDR	7:00.48	Romania	7:04.36	Bulgaria	7:06.03
Coxless Pairs	Romania	7:28.13	Bulgaria	7:31.95	New Zealand	7:35.68
Coxed Quadruple Sculls	GDR	6:21.06	USSR	6:23.47	Romania	6:23.81
Coxed Fours	GDR	6:56.00	China	6:58.78	Romania	7:01.13
Coxed Eights	GDR	6:15.17	Romania	6:17.44	China	6:21.83
Yachting						
Finn Class	José Luis Doreste (ESP)	38.1	Peter Holmberg (ISV)	40.4	John Cutler (NZL)	45.0
International Star	Great Britain	45.7	USA	48.0	Brazil	50.0
Flying Dutchman	Denmark	31.4	Norway	37.4	Canada	48.4
International Tornado	France	16.0	New Zealand	35.4	Brazil	40.1
470 Women	USA	26.7	Sweden	40.0	USSR	45.4
470 Men	France	34.7	USSR	46.0	USA	51.0
International Soling	GDR	11.7	USA	14.0	Denmark	52.7
Surfing	Bruce Kendall (NZL)	35.4	Jan Boersma (AHO)	42.7	Michael Gebhardt (USA)	48.0
Cycling						
Men						
Road Race (196.8 km)	Olaf Ludwig (GDR)	4:32:22	Bernd Gröne (FRG)	4:32:25	Christian Henn (FRG)	4:32:46
100 km Road Team Time Trial	GDR	1:57:47.7	Poland	1:57:54.2	Sweden	1:59:47.3
Sprint	Lutz Hesslich (GDR)		Nikolai Kovche (URS)		Gary Neiwand (AUS)	
1000 m Time-Trial	Aleksandr Kirichenko (URS)	1:04.499	Martin Vinnicombe (AUS)	1:04.784	Robert Lechner (FRG)	1:05.114
4000 m Individual Pursuit	Gintautas Umaras (URS)	4:32.00	Dean Woods (AUS)	4:35.00	Bernd Dittert (GDR)	4:34.17
4000 m Team Pursuit	USSR	4:13.31	GDR	4:14.09	Australia	4:16.02
Individual Points Race	Dan Frost (DEN)	38	Leo Peelen (HOL)	26	Marat Ganeyev (URS)	46/1
Women						
Road Race (82 km)	Monique Knol (HOL)	2:00:52	Jutta Niehaus (FRG)		Laima Zilporite (URS)	
Sprint	Erika Salumiä (URS)		Christa Luding-Rothenburg (GDR)		Connie Paraskevin-Young (USA)	
Equestrianism						
Three-Day Event	Mark Todd (NZL)	42.60	Ian Stark (GBR)	52.80	Virginia Leng (GBR)	62.00
Three-Day Event, Team	FRG	225.95	Great Britain	256.80	New Zealand	271.20
Grand Prix (Dressage)	Nicole Uphoff (FRG)	1521	Margitt Otto-Crépin (FRA)	1462	Christine Stückelberger (SUI)	1417
Grand Prix (Dressage) Team	FRG	4302	Switzerland	4164	Canada	3969
Grand Prix (Jumping)	Pierre Durand (FRA)	1.25	Greg Best (USA)	4.00	Karsten Huck (FRG)	4.00
Grand Prix (Jumping) Team	FRG	17.25	USA	20.50	France	27.50
Shooting						
Men						
Small-Bore Rifle (Prone)	Miroslav Varga (TCH)	703.9	Young Chul Cha (KOR)	702.8	Attila Zahonyi (HUN)	701.9
Small-Bore Rifle (3 Positions)	Malcolm Cooper (GBR)	1279.3	Alister Allan (GBR)	1275.6	Kirill Ivanov (URS)	1275.0
Rapid-Fire Pistol	Afanasi Kuzmin (URS)	698	Ralf Schumann (GDR)	696	Zoltán Kovács (HUN)	693
Free Pistol (50 m)	Sorin Babii (ROM)	660	Ragnar Skánaker (SWE)	657	Igor Basinski (URS)	657
Running Game Target	Tor Heiestad (NOR)	689	Shiping Huang (CHN)	687	Gennadi Avramenko (URS)	686
Air Pistol	Taniou Kiriakov (BUL)	687.9	Erich Buljung (USA)	687.9	Haifeng Xu (CHN)	684.5
Skeet Shooting	Axel Wegner (GDR)	222	Alfonso de Iruarrizaga (CHI)	221	Jorge Guardiola (ESP)	220
Trap Shooting	Dimitri Monakov (URS)	2228	Miloslaw Bednarik (TCH)	222/7	Frans Peeters (BEL)	219/16
Air Rifle	Goran Maksimovic (YUG)	695.6	Nicolas Berthelot (FRA)	694.2	Johann Riederer (FRG)	694.0
Women						
Sports Pistol	Nino Salukvadze (URS)	690	Tomoko Hasegawa (JPN)	686	Jasna Sekaric (YUG)	686
Small-Bore Rifle (3 Positions)	Silvia Sperber (FRG)	685.6	Vessela Lecheva (BUL)	683.2	Valentina Cherkassova (URS)	681.4
Air Rifle	Irina Chilova (URS)	498.5	Silvia Sperber (FRG)	497.5	Anna Malukina (URS)	495.8
Air Pistol	Jasna Sekaric(YUG)	489.5	Nino Salukvadze (URS)	487.9	Marina Dobrancheva (URS)	485.2
Archery						
Men						
Individual	Jay Barrs (USA)	338	Park Sung Soo (KOR)	336	Vladimir Echeyev (URS)	335
Team	South Korea	986	USA	972	Great Britain	968
Women						
Individual	Kim Soo Nyung (KOR)	344	Wang Hee Kyung (KOR)	332	Yun Young Sook (KOR)	327
Team	South Korea	982	Indonesia	952	USA	952

EVENT	GOLD		SILVER		BRONZE	
Gymnastics						
Men						
Individual Combined Exercises	Vladimir Artemov (URS)	119.125	Valeri Lyukin (URS)	119.025	Dimitri Biloserchev (URS)	118.975
Team	USSR	593.35	GDR	588.45	Japan	585.60
Parallel Bars	Vladimir Artemov (URS)	19.925	Valeri Lyukin (URS)	19.900	Sven Tippelt (GDR)	19.750
Floor	Sergei Kharkov (URS)	19.925	Vladimir Artemov (URS)	19.900	Yun Lou (CHN)	19.850
Horse Vault	Yun Lou (CHN)	19.875	Sylvio Kroll (GDR)	19.862	Park Jong Hoon (KOR)	19.775
Horizontal Bar	Cladimir Artemov (URS)	19.900			Holger Behrendt (GDR)	19.800
	Valeri Lukin (URS)	19.900			Marius Gherman (ROM)	19.800
Rings	Holger Behrendt (GDR)	19.925			Sven Tippelt (GDR)	19.875
	Dimitri Biloserchev (URS)	19.925				
Pommel Horse	Lubomir Geraskolv (BUL)	19.950				
	Zsolt Borkai (HUN)	19.950				
	Dimitri Biloserchev (URS)	19.950				
Women						
Individual Combined Exercises	Elena Shushunova (URS)	79.662	Daniela Silivas (ROM)	79.637	Svetlana Boginskaya (URS)	79.400
Team	USSR	395.475	Romania	394.125	GDR	390.875
Floor	Daniela Silivas (ROM)	19.937	Svetlana Boginskaya (URS)	19.887	Diana Doudeva (BUL)	19.850
Horse Vault	Svetlana Boginskaya (URS)	19.905	Gabriela Potorac (ROM)	19.830	Daniela Silivas (ROM)	19.818
Beam	Daniela Silivas (ROM)	19.924	Elena Shushunova (URS)	19.875	Gabriela Potorac (ROM)	19.837
					Phoebe Mills (USA)	19.837
Asymmetrical Bars	Daniela Silivas (ROM)	20.000	Dagmar Kersten (GDR)	19.987	Elena Shushunova (URS)	19.962
Modern Rhythmic	Marina Lobach (URS)	60.000	Adriana Dunavska (BUL)	59.950	Alexandra Timoshenko (URS)	59.875
Tennis						
Men						
Individual	Miloslav Mecir (TCH)		Tim Mayotte (USA)		Stefan Edberg (SWE)	
					Brad Gilbert (USA)	
Doubles	Ken Flach/Robert Seguso (USA)		Emilio Sanchez/Sergio Casal (ESP)		Stefan Edberg/Anders Jarryd (SWE)	
					Miroslav Mecir/Milan Srejber (TCH)	
Women						
Individual	Steffi Graf (FRG)		Gabriela Sabatini (ARG)		Zina Garrison (USA)	
					Manuela Maleeva (BUL)	
Doubles	Pam Shriver/Zina Garrison (USA)		Jana Novotna/Helena Sukova (TCH)		Steffi Graf/Claudia Kohde-Kilsch (FRG)	
					Elizabeth Smylie/Wendy Turnbull (AUS)	
Table Tennis						
Men						
Individual	Yoo Nam Kyu (KOR)		Kim Ki Taik (KOR)		Erik Lindh (SWE)	
Doubles	China		Yugoslavia		South Korea	
Women						
Individual	Jing Chen (CHN)		Huifeng Li (CHN)		Zhimin Jiao (CHN)	
Doubles	South Korea		China		Yugoslavia	
Basketball						
Men	USSR		Yugoslavia		USA	
Women	USA		Yugoslavia		USSR	
Soccer						
	USSR		Brazil		FRG	
Handball						
Men	USSR		South Korea		Yugoslavia	
Women	South Korea		Norway		USSR	
Hockey						
Men	Great Britain		FRG		Netherlands	
Women	Australia		South Korea		Netherlands	
Volleyball						
Men	USA		USSR		Argentina	
Women	USSR		Peru		China	

Albertville 1992

8 February – 23 February

Participants: 1801 / Men: 1313, Women: 488, Countries: 64,
Sports: 10, Events: 57
Final Torchbearers: Michel Platini and François-Cyrille Grange

Medals Table

PLACE	COUNTRY	GOLD	SILVER	BRONZE
1	Germany	10	10	6
2	Unified Team	9	6	8
3	Norway	9	6	5
4	Austria	6	7	8
5	USA	5	4	2

Outstanding Athletes

PLACE	NAME (NATIONALITY)	DISCIPLINE	G	S	B
1	Lyubov Yegorova (EUN)	Nordic Skiing	3	2	–
2	Vegard Ulvang (NOR)	Nordic Skiing	3	1	–
	Björn Dæhlie (NOR)	Nordic Skiing	3	1	–
4	Mark Kirchner (GER)	Biathlon	2	1	–
	Gunda Niemann (GER)	Speed Skating	2	1	–

EVENT	GOLD		SILVER		BRONZE	
Alpine Skiing						
Men						
Downhill	Patrick Ortlieb (AUT)	1:50.37	Franck Piccard (FRA)	1:50.42	Günther Mader (AUT)	1:50.47
Slalom	Finn Christian Jagge (NOR)	1:44.39	Alberto Tomba (ITA)	1:44.67	Michael Tritscher (AUT)	1:44.85
Giant Slalom	Alberto Tomba (ITA)	2:06.98	Marc Girardelli (LUX)	2:07.30	Kjetil-Andre Aamodt (NOR)	2:07.82
Super-G	Kjetil Andre Aamodt (NOR)	1:13.04	Marc Girardelli (LUX)	1:13.77	Jan Einar Thorsen (NOR)	1:13.83
Combined	Josef Polig (ITA)	14.58	Gianfranco Martin (ITA)	14.90	Steve Locher (SUI)	18.16
Women						
Downhill	Kerrin Lee-Gartner (CAN)	1:52.55	Hilary Lindh (USA)	1:52.61	Veronika Wallinger (AUT)	1:52.64
Slalom	Petra Kronberger (AUT)	1:32.68	Anneliese Coberger (NZL)	1:33.10	Bianca Fernandez-Ochoa (ESP)	1:33.35
Giant Slalom	Pernilla Wilberg (SWE)	2:12.74	Diann Roffe (USA)	2:13.71		
			Anita Wachter (AUT)	2:13.71		
Super-G	Deborah Compagnoni (ITA)	1:21.22	Carole Merle (FRA)	1:22.63	Katja Seizinger (GER)	1:23.19
Combined	Petra Kronberger (AUT)	2.55	Anita Wachter (AUT)	19.39	Florence Masnada (FRA)	21.38
Freestyle/Moguls, Men	Edgar Grospiron (FRA)	25.81	Olivier Allamand (FRA)	24.87	Nelson Carmichael (USA)	24.82
Freestyle/Moguls, Women	Donna Weinbrecht (USA)	23.69	Elisabeta Koyevnikova (EUN)	23.50	Stine Lise Hattestad (NOR)	23.04
Nordic Skiing						
Men						
10 km-Cross-Country-Skiing (Classical)	Vegard Ulvang (NOR)	27:36.0	Marco Albarello (ITA)	27:55.2	Christer Majbäck (SWE)	27:56.4
15 km Combination	Björn Daehlie (NOR)	1:05:37.9	Vegard Ulvang (NOR)	1:06:31.3	Giorgio Vanzetta (ITA)	1:06:32.3
30 km Cross-Country Skiing (Classical)	Vegard Ulvang (NOR)	1:22:27.8	Björn Daehlie (NOR)	1:23:14.0	Terje Langli (NOR)	1:23:42.5
50 km Cross-Country Skiing (Freestyle)	Björn Daehlie (NOR)	2:03:41.5	Maurilio de Zolt (ITA)	2:04:39.1	Georgio Vanzetta (ITA)	2:06:42.1
4 x 10 km Relay	Norway	1:39:26.0	Italy	1:40:52.7	Finland	1:41:22.9
Ski Jumping (70 m Hill)	Ernst Vettori (AUT)	222.8	Martin Höllwarth (AUT)	218.1	Toni Nieminen (FIN)	217.0
Ski Jumping (90 m Hill)	Toni Nieminen (FIN)	239.5	Martin Höllwarth (AUT)	227.3	Heinz Kullin (AUT)	214.8
Ski Jumping, Team	Finland	644.4	Austria	642.9	Czech Republic	620.1
Nordic Combination, Individual	Fabrice Guy (FRA)		Sylvain Guillaume (FRA)		Klaus Sulzenbacher (AUT)	
Nordic Combination, Team	Japan		Norway		Austria	
Women						
5 km Cross-Country Skiing (Classical)	Marjuot Lukkarinen (FIN)	14:13.80	Lyubov Yegorova (EUN)	14:14.70	Yelena Wälbe (EUN)	14:22.7
10 km Combined	Lyubov Yegorova (EUN)	40:07.70	Stefania Belmondo (ITA)	40:31.80	Yelena Wälbe (EUN)	40:51.70
15 km Cross-Country Skiing (Classical)	Lyubov Yegorova (EUN)	42:20.80	Marjut Lukkarinen (FIN)	43:29.90	Yelena Wälbe (EUN)	43:42.3
30 km Cross-Country Skiing (Freestyle)	Stefania Belmondo (ITA)	1:22:30.10	Lyubov Yegorova (EUN)	1:22:52.0	Yelena Wälbe (EUN)	1:24:13.9
4 x 5 km	Unified Team	59:34.80	Norway		Italy	
Biathlon						
Men						
10 km	Mark Kirchner (GER)	26:02.3	Ricco Gross (GER)	26:18.0	Harri Eloranta (FIN)	26:26.6
20 km	Yevgeni Redkin (EUN)	57:34.4	Mark Kirchner (GER)	57:40.8	Mikael Löfgren (SWE)	57:59.4
4 x 7.5 km	Germany	1:24:43.5	Unified Team	1:25:06.3	Sweden	1:25:38.2
Women						
7.5 km	Anfissa Restzova (EUN)	24:29.7	Antje Misersky (GER)	24:45.1	Yelena Belova (EUN)	24:50.8
15 km	Antje Misersky (GER)	51:47.2	Svetlana Pecherskaya (EUN)	51:58.5	Myriam Bedard (CAN)	52:15.0
3 x 7.5 km-Relay	France	1:15:55.6	Germany	1:16:18.4	Unified Team	1:16:54.6

EVENT	GOLD		SILVER		BRONZE	
Figure Skating						
Women	Kristi Yamaguchi (USA)		MidoriIto (JPN)		Nancy Kerrigan (USA)	
Men	Viktor Petrenko (EUN)		Paul Wylie (USA)		Petr Barna (TCH)	
Pairs	Natalia Mishkutionok/		Elena Beschke/		Isabelle Brasseur/	
	Artur Dimitriyev (EUN)		Denios Petrov (EUN)		Lloyd Eisler (CAN)	
Ice Dance	Marina Klimova/		Isabelle Duchesnay/		Maya Usova/	
	Sergey Ponomarenko (EUN)		Paul Duchesnay (FRA)		Alexander Schulin (EUN)	
Speed Skating						
Men						
500 m	Uwe-Jens Mey (GER)	37.14	Toshiyuki Kuroiwa (JPN)	37.18	Junichi Inoue (JPN)	37.26
1000 m	Olaf Zinke (GER)	1:14.85	Yoon-Man Kim (KOR)	1:14.86	Yukinori Miyabe (JPN)	1:14.92
1500 m	Johann Olav Koss (NOR)	1:54.81	Adne Soendral (NOR)	1:54.85	Leo Visser (HOL)	1:54.90
5000 m	Geir Karlstad (NOR)	6:59.97	Falko Zandstra (HOL)	7:02.28	Leo Visser (HOL)	7:04.96
10,000 m	Bart Veldkamp (HOL)	14:12.12	Johann Olav Koss (NOR)	14:14.58	Geir Karlstad (NOR)	14:18.13
Women						
500 m	Bonnie Blair (USA)	40.33	Qiabo Ye (CHN)	40.51	Christa Luding (GER)	40.57
1000 m	Bonnie Blair (USA)	1:21.9	Qiabo Ye (CHN)	1:21.92	Monique Garbrecht (GER)	1:22.10
1500 m	Jacqueline Börner (GER)	2:05.87	Gunda Niemann (GER)	2:05.92	Seiko Hashimoto (JPN)	2:06.88
3000 m	Gunda Niemann (GER)	4:19.90	Heike Warnicke (GER)	4:22.88	Emese Hunyady (AUT)	4:24.64
5000 m	Gunda Niemann (GER)	7:31.57	Heike Warnicke (GER)	7:37.59	Claudia Pechstein (GER)	7:39.80
Short Track						
1000 m Men Individual	Ki-Hoon Kim (KOR)	1:30.76	Frederic Blackburn (CAN)	1:31.11	Joon-Ho Lee (KOR)	1:31.16
5000 m Men Relay	South Korea	7:14.02	Canada	7:14.06	Japan	7:18.18
500 m Women Individual	Cathy Turner (USA)	47.04	Yan Li (CHN)	47.08	Hwang Ok-Sil (PRK)	47.23
3000 m Women Relay	Canada	4:36.62	USA	4:37.85	Unified Team	4:42.69
Lugeing						
Men's Singles	Georg Hackl (GER)	3:02.363	Markus Prock (AUT)	3:02.669	Markus Schmidt (AUT)	3:02.942
Women's Singles	Doris Neuner (AUT)	3:06.696	Angelika Neuner (AUT)	3:06.769	Susi Erdmann (GER)	3:07.115
2-Man Luge	Stefan Krausse/		Yves Mankel/		Hansjörg Raffl/	
	Jan Behrendt (GER)	1:32.053	Thomas Rudolph (GER)	1:32.239	Norbert Hubert (ITA)	1:32.649
Bobsledding						
2-Man Bob	Switzerland I	1:00.84	Germany I	1:00.90	Germany II	1:01.14
4-Man Bob	Austria I	3:53.90	Germany I	3:53.92	Switzerland I	3:54.13
Ice Hockey	Unified Team		Canada		Czech Republic	

Barcelona 1992

25 July – 8 August

Participants: 9364 / Men: 6657. Women: 2707. Countries: 169.
Sports: 24. Evemts: 257
Final Torchbearer: Antonio Rebollo

Medals Table

PLACE	COUNTRY	GOLD	SILVER	BRONZE
1	Unified Team	45	38	28
2	USA	37	34	37
3	Germany	33	21	28
4	China	16	22	16
5	Cuba	14	6	11

Outstanding Athletes

PLACE	NAME (NATIONALITY)	DISCIPLINE	G	S	B
1	Vitali Sherbo (EUN)	Gymnastics	6	–	–
2	Yevgeniy Sadoviy (EUN)	Swimming	3	–	–
3	Krisztina Egerszegy (HUN)	Swimming	3	–	–
4	Alexander Popov (EUN)	Swimming	2	2	–
5	Tatyana Goutsou (EUN)	Gymnastics	2	1	1

EVENT	GOLD		SILVER		BRONZE	
Athletics						
Men						
100 m	Linford Christie (GBR)	9.96	Frank Fredericks (NAM)	10.02	Dennis Mitchell (USA)	10.04
200 m	Mike Marsh (USA)	20.01	Frank Fredericks (NAM)	20.13	Michael Bates (USA)	20.38

EVENT	GOLD		SILVER		BRONZE	
400 m	Quincy Watts (USA)	43.50	Steve Lewis (USA)	44.21	Samson Kitur (KEN)	44.24
800 m	William Tanui (KEN)	1:43.66	Nixon Kiprotich (KEN)	1:43.70	Johnny Gray (USA)	1:43.97
1500 m	Fermin Ruiz (ESP)	3:40.12	Rachid El Basir (ESP)	3:40.62	Mohamed Sulaiman (QAT)	3:40.69
5000 m	Dieter Baumann (GER)	13:12.52	Paul Bitok (KEN)	13:12.71	Fita Bayisa (ETH)	13:13.03
10,000 m	Khalid Skah (MAR)	27:46.70	Richard Chelimo (KEN)	27:47.72	Addis Abebe (ETH)	28:00.07
Marathon	Young-Cho Hwang (KOR)	2:13:23	Koichi Morishita (JPN)	2:13:45	Stephan Freigang (GER)	2:14:00
110 m Hurdles	Mark McKoy (CAN)	13.12	Tony Dees (USA)	13.24	Jack Pierce (USA)	13.26
400 m Hurdles	Kevin Young (USA)	46.78	Winthrop Graham (JAM)	47.66	Kriss Akabusi (GBR)	47.82
3000 m Steeplechase	Mathew Birir (KEN)	8:08.84	Patrick Sang (KEN)	8:09.55	William Mutwol (KEN)	8:10.74
4 x 100 m	USA	37.40	Nigeria	37.98	Cuba	38.00
4 x 400 m	USA	2:55.74	Cuba	2:59.51	Great Britain	2:59.73
20 km Walk	Daniel Montero Plaza (ESP)	1:21:45	Guillaume Leblanc (CAN)	1:22:25	Giovanni De Benedictis (ITA)	1:23:11
50 km Walk	Andrey Perlov (EUN)	3:50:13	Carlos Carbajal (MEX)	3:52:09	Ronald Weigel (GER)	3:53:45
High Jump	Javier Sotomayor (CUB)	2.34	Patrick Sjöberg (SWE)	2.34	Artur Partyka (POL)	2.34
					Timothy Forsyth (AUS)	2.34
					Hollis Conway (GBR)	2.34
Pole Vault	Maxim Tarassov (EUN)	5.80	Igor Trandenkow (EUN)	5.80	Javier Garcia (ESP)	5.75
Long Jump	Carl Lewis (USA)	8.67	Mike Powell (USA)	8.64	Joe Greene (USA)	8.34
Triple Jump	Michael Conley (USA)	18.17	Charles Simpkins (USA)	17.60	Frank Rutherford (BAH)	17.36
Shot	Michael Stulce (USA)	21.70	James Doehring (USA)	20.96	Vyacheslav Lycho (EUN)	20.94
Discus	Romas Ubartas (LIT)	65.12	Jürgen Schult (GER)	64.94	Roberto Moya (CUB)	64.12
Javelin	Jan Zelezny (TCH)	89.66	Seppo Räty (FIN)	86.60	Steve Backley (GBR)	83.38
Hammer	Andrey Abduvalyev (EUN)	82.54	Igor Astapkovich (EUN)	81.96	Igor Nikulin (EUN)	81.38
Decathlon	Robert Zmelik (TCH)	8611	Antonio Peñalver (ESP)	8412	David Johnson (USA)	8309
Women						
100 m	Gail Devers (USA)	10.82	Juliet Cuthbert (JAM)	10.83	Irina Privalova (EUN)	10.84
200 m	Gwen Torrence (USA)	21.81	Juliet Cuthbert (JAM)	22.02	Merlene Ottey (JAM)	22.09
400 m	Marie-José Perec (FRA)	48.83	Olga Brysgina (EUN)	49.05	Ximena Gaviria (COL)	49.64
800 m	Ellen van Langen (HOL)	1:55.54	Lilia Nurutdinova (EUN)	1:55.99	Ana Quirot (CUB)	1:56.80
1500 m	Hassiba Boulmerka (ALG)	3:55.30	Ludmila Rogacheva (EUN)	3:56.91	Yunxia Qu (CHN)	3:57.08
3000 m	Yelena Romanova (EUN)	8:46.04	Tatyana Dorovskich (EUN)	8:46.85	Angela Chalmers (CAN)	8:47.22
10,000 m	Derartu Tulu (ETH)	31:06.02	Elena Meyer (RSA)	31:11.75	Lynn Jennings (USA)	31:19.89
Marathon	Valentina Yegorova (EUN)	2:32:41	Yuko Arimori (JPN)	2:32:49	Lorraine Moller (NZL)	2:33:59
100 m Hurdles	Paraskevi Patoulidou (GRE)	12.64	Lavonna Martin (USA)	12.69	Jordanka Donkova (BUL)	12.70
400 m Hurdles	Sally Gunnell (GBR)	53.23	Sandra Farmer-Patrick (USA)	53.69	Janeene Vickers (USA)	54.31
4 x 100 m	USA	42.11	Unified Team	42.16	Nigeria	42.81
4 x 400 m	CIS	3:20.20	USA	3:20.92	Great Britain	3:24.23
10 km Walk	Yueling Chen (CHN)	44:32	Yelena Nikolayeva (EUN)	44:33	Chunxiu Li (CHN)	44:41
High Jump	Heike Henkel (GER)	2.02	Galina Astafei (ROM)	2.00	Joanet Quintero (CUB)	1.97
Long Jump	Heike Drechsler (GER)	7.14	Inessa Kravets (EUN)	7.12	Jackie Joyner-Kersee (USA)	7.07
Shot	Svetlana Krivelyova (EUN)	21.06	Zhihong Huang (CHN)	20.47	Kathrin Neimke (GER)	19.78
Discus	Maritza Marten (CUB)	70.06	Zvetanka Christova (BUL)	67.78	Daniela Costian (AUS)	66.24
Javelin	Silke Renk (GER)	68.34	Natalya Shikolenko (EUN)	68.26	Karen Forkel (GER)	66.86
Heptathlon	Jackie Joyner-Kersee (USA)	7044	Irina Belova (EUN)	6845	Sabine Braun (GER)	6649
Swimming						
Men						
50 m Freestyle	Alexander Popov (EUN)	21.91	Matt Biondi (USA)	22.09	Tom Jager (USA)	22.30
100 m Freestyle	Alexander Popov (EUN)	49.02	Gustavo Borges (BRA)	49.43	Stephan Caron (FRA)	49.50
200 m Freestyle	Yevgeniy Sadovyi (EUN)	1:46.70	Anders Holmertz (SWE)	1:46.86	Antti Kasvio (FIN)	1:47.63
400 m Freestyle	Yevgeniy Sadovyi (EUN)	3:45.00	Kieren Perkins (AUS)	3:45.16	Anders Holmertz (SWE)	3:46.77
1500 m Freestyle	Kieren Perkins (AUS)	14:43.48	Glen Housman (AUS)	14:55.29	Jörg Hoffmann (GER)	15:02.29
100 m Backstroke	Mark Tewksbury (CAN)	53.98	Jeff Rouse (USA)	54.04	David Berkhoff (USA)	54.78
200 m Backstroke	MartinLopez-Zubero (ESP)	1:58.47	Vladimir Selkov (EUN)	1:58.87	Stefano Battistelli (ITA)	1:59.40
100 m Breaststroke	Nelson Diebel (USA)	1:01.50	Norbert Rosza (HUN)	1:01.68	Philip Rogers (AUS)	1:01.76
200 m Breaststroke	Mike Barrowman (USA)	2:10.16	Norbert Rosza (HUN)	2:11.23	Nick Gillingham (GBR)	2:11.29
100 m Butterfly	Pablo Morales (USA)	53.32	Rafal Szukala (POL)	53.35	Anthony Nesty (SUR)	53.41
200 m Butterfly	Melvin Stewart (USA)	1:56.26	Danyon Loader (NZL)	1:57.93	Franck Esposito (FRA)	1:58.51
200 m Medley	Tamas Darnyi (HUN)	2:00.76	Gregory Burgess (USA)	2:00.97	Attila Czene (HUN)	2:01.00
400 m Medley	Tamas Darnyi (HUN)	4:14.23	Eric Namesnik (USA)	4:15.57	Luca Sacchi (ITA)	4:16.34
4 x 100 m Freestyle	USA	3:16.74	Unified Team	3:17.56	Germany	3:17.90
4 x 200 m Freestyle	Unified Team	7:11.95	Sweden	7:15.51	USA	7:16.23
4 x 100 m Medley	USA	3:36.93	Unified Team	3:38.56	Canada	3:39.66
Springboard Diving	Mark Lenzi (USA)	676.53	Liangde Tan (CHN)	645.57	Dmitri Sautin (EUN)	627.78
Highboard Diving	Shuwei Sun (CHN)	677.31	Scott Donie (USA)	633.63	Ni Xiong (CHN)	600.15
Water Polo	Italy		Spain		Unified Team	

EVENT	GOLD		SILVER		BRONZE	
Women						
50 m Freestyle	Wenyi Yang (CHN)	24.79	Yong Zhuang (CHN)	25.08	Angel Martino (USA)	25.23
100 m Freestyle	Yong Zhuang (CHN)	54.64	Jenny Thompson (USA)	54.84	Franziska von Almsick (GER)	54.94
200 m Freestyle	Nicole Haislett (USA)	1:57.90	Franziska van Almsick (GER)	1:58.00	Kerstin Kielgass (GER)	1:59.67
400 m Freestyle	Dagmar Hase (GER)	4:07.18	Janet Evans (USA)	4:07.37	Hayley Lewis (AUS)	4:11.22
800 m Freestyle	Janet Evans (USA)	8:25.52	Hayley Lewis (AUS)	8:30.34	Jana Hanke (GER)	8:30.99
100 m Backstroke	Krisztina Egerszegy (HUN)	1:00.68	Tunde Szabo (HUN)	1:01.14	Lea Loveless (USA)	1:01.43
200 m Backstroke	Krisztina Egerszegy (HUN)	2:07.06	Dagmar Hase (GER)	2:09.46	Nicole Stevenson (AUS)	2:10.20
100 m Breaststroke	Yelena Rudkovskaya (EUN)	1:08.00	Anita Nall (USA)	1:08.17	Samantha Riley (AUS)	1:09.25
200 m Breaststroke	Kyoko Iwasaki (JPN)	2:26.65	Li Lin (CHN)	2:26.85	Anita Nall (USA)	2:26.88
100 m Butterfly	Hong Qian (CHN)	58.62	Christine Ahmann-Leighton (USA)	58.74	Cathérine Plewinski (FRA)	59.01
200 m Butterfly	Summer Sanders (USA)	2:08.67	Xiaohong Wang (CHN)	2:09.01	Susan O'Neill (AUS)	2:09.03
200 m Medley	Li Lin (CHN)	2:11.65	Summer Sanders (USA)	2:11.91	Daniela Hunger (GER)	2:13.92
400 m Medley	Krisztina Egerszegy (HUN)	4:36.54	Li Lin (CHN)	4:36.73	Summer Sanders (USA)	4:37.58
4 x 100 m Freestyle	USA	3:39.46	China	3:40.12	Germany	3:41.60
4 x 100 m Medley	USA	4:02.54	Germany	4:05.19	UnifiedTeam	4:06.44
Springboard Diving	Min Gao (CHN)	572.40	Irina Laschko (EUN)	514.14	Brita Baldus (GER)	503.07
Highboard Diving	Mingxia Fu (CHN)	461.43	Yelena Miroschina (EUN)	411.63	Mary Ellen Clark (USA)	401.91
Synchronized Swimming						
Solo	Kristen Babb-Sprague (USA)	191.848	Sylvie Frechette (CAN)	191.717	Fumiko Okuno (JPN)	187.056
Duet	USA	192.175	Canada	189.394	Japan	186.868
Boxing						
Light-Flyweight (-48 kg)	Rogelio Marcelo Garcia (CUB)		Daniel Bojinov (BUL)		Jan Quast (GER) / Roel Velasco (PHI)	
Flyweight (-51 kg)	Chol Su Choi (PRK)		Raul Gonzales (CUB)		Istvan Kovacs (HUN) / Timothy Austin (USA)	
Bantamweight (-54 kg)	Joel Casamayor (CUB)		Wayne McCullough (IRL)		Mohamed Achik (MAR) / Gwang Sik Li (PRK)	
Featherweight (-57 kg)	Andreas Tews (GER)		Faustino Reyes (ESP)		Hocine Soltani (ALG) / Ramazi Paliani (EUN)	
Lightweight (-60 kg)	Oscar de la Hoya (USA)		Marco Rudolph (GER)		Sung Sik Hong (KOR) / Namjil Bayarsaikhan (MGL)	
Light-Welterweight (-63.5 kg)	Hector Vinent (CUB)		Mark Leduc (CAN)		Jyri Kjäll (FIN) / Leonard Doroftei (ROM)	
Welterweight (-67 kg)	Michael Carruth (IRL)		Juan Hernandez (CUB)		Anibal Acevedo Santiago (PUR) / Arkom Chenglai (THA)	
Light-Middleweight (-71 kg)	Juan Lemus Garcia (CUB)		Orhan Delibas (HOL)		Robin Reid (GBR) / Gyorgy Mizsei (HUN)	
Middleweight (-75 kg)	Ariel Hernandez (CUB)		Chris Byrd (USA)		Chris Johnson (CAN) / Seung Bae Lee (KOR)	
Light-Heavyweight (-81 kg)	Torsten May (GER)		Rostislav Saulitschni (EUN)		Zoltan Beres (HUN) / Wojciech Bartnik (POL)	
Heavyweight (-91 kg)	Felix Savon (CUB)		David Izonritei (NGR)		Arnold Vanderlijde (HOL) / David Tua (NZL)	
Super-Heavyweight (+91 kg)	Roberto Balado Mendez (CUB)		Richard Igbineghu (NGR)		Brian Nielsen (DEN) / Swilen Aldinow Rusinov (BUL)	
Weightlifting						
Flyweight (-52 kg)	Ivan Ivanov (BUL)		Qisheng Lin (CHN)		Traian Joachim Ciharean (ROM)	
Bantamweight (-56 kg)	Byung-Kwan Chun (KOR)		Shoubin Liu (CHN)		Jianming Luo (CHN)	
Featherweight (-60 kg)	Naim Süleymanoglu (TUR)		Nikolai Peshalov (BUL)		Yinggiang He (CHN)	
Lightweight (-67.5 kg)	Israel Militosiyan (EUN)		Yoto Yotov (BUL)		Andreas Behm (GER)	
Middleweight (-75 kg)	Feodor Kassapu (EUN)		Pablo Rodriguez (CUB)		Myong Nam Kim (PRK)	
Light-Heavyweight (-82.5 kg)	Pyrros Dimas (GRE)		Krzysztof Siemion (POL)		Ibrahim Samadov (EUN)	
Middle-Heavyweight (-90 kg)	Kakhi Kakhiashvili (EUN)		Sergey Syrtsov (EUN)		Sergiusz Wolczaniecki (POL)	
First Heavyweight (-100 kg)	Viktor Tregubov (EUN)		Timur Taimassov (EUN)		Waldemar Malak (POL)	
Second Heavyweight (-110 kg)	Ronny Weller (GER)		Artur Akyev (EUN)		Stefan Botev (BUL)	
Super-Heavyweight (+110 kg)	Alexander Kurlovich (EUN)		Leonid Taranenko (EUN)		Manfred Nerlinger (GER)	
Greco-Roman Wrestling						
Light-Flyweight (- 48 kg)	Oleg Kucherenko (EUN)		Vincenzo Maenza (ITA)		Wilber Sanchez (CUB)	
Flyweight (-52 kg)	Jon Rönningen (NOR)		Alfred Ter-Mkrychan (EUN)		Kyung-Kap Min (KOR)	
Bantamweight (-57 kg)	Han Bong An (KOR)		Rifat Yildiz (GER)		Zetian Shang (CHN)	
Featherweight (-62 kg)	Akif Pirim (TUR)		Sergey Martynov (EUN)		Juan Maren (CUB)	
Lightweight (-68 kg)	Attila Repka (HUN)		Islan Duguchiyev (EUN)		Rodney Smith (USA)	
Welterweight (-74 kg)	Minazakan Iskandarian (EUN)		Jozef Tracz (POL)		Torbjörn Kornbakk (SWE)	

EVENT	GOLD	SILVER	BRONZE
Middleweight (-82 kg)	Peter Farkas (HUN)	Pjotr Stepien (POL)	Daulet Turhlyhanov (EUN)
Light-Heavyweight (-90 kg)	Maik Bullmann (GER)	Hakki Basar (TUR)	Gogui Koguashvili (EUN)
Heavyweight (-100 kg)	Hector Milian (CUB)	Dennis Koslowski (USA)	Sergey Demiashkiievich (EUN)
Super-Heavyweight (+130 kg)	Alexander Karelin (EUN)	Tomas Johansson (SWE)	Ion Grigoras (ROM)
Freestyle Wrestling			
Light-Flyweight (-48 kg)	Il Kim (PRK)	Jong-Shin Kim (KOR)	Vugar Orudyev (EUN)
Flyweight (-52 kg)	Hak-Son Li (PRK)	Harry Lee Jones (USA)	Valentin Jordanov (BUL)
Bantamweight (-57 kg)	Alejandro Puerto (CUB)	Sergey Smal (EUN)	Yong-Sik Kim (PRK)
Featherweight (-62 kg)	John Smith (USA)	Asgari Mohammedian (IRN)	Lazaro Reinoso (CUB)
Lightweight (-68 kg)	Arsen Fadzayev (EUN)	Valentin Getsov (BUL)	Kosei Akaishi (JPN)
Welterweight (-74 kg)	Jang-Soon Park (KOR)	Kenneth Monday (USA)	Amir Khadem (IRN)
Middleweight (-82 kg)	Kevin Jackson (USA)	Elemadi Djabrailov (EUN)	Rasul Khadem (IRN)
Light-Heavyweight (-90 kg)	Maharbeg Chadartsev (EUN)	Kenan Simsek (TUR)	Christopher Campbell (USA)
Heavyweight (-100 kg)	Leri Chabelov (EUN)	Heiko Balz (GER)	Ali Kayali (TUR)
Super-Heavyweight (-130 kg)	Bruce Baumgartner (USA)	Jeffrey Thue (CAN)	David Gobedyishuili (EUN)
Judo			
Men			
Super-Lightweight (-60 kg)	Nazim Gusseinov (EUN)	Hyun Yoon (KOR)	Tadanor Koshino (JPN)
			Richard Trautmann (GER)
Half-Lightweight (-65 kg)	Rogerio Sampaio Cardoso (BRA)	Jozsef Csak (HUN)	Udo Quellmalz (GER)
			Israel Hernandez Planas (CUB)
Lightweight (-71 kg)	Toshihiko Koga (JPN)	Bertalan Haitos (HUN)	Hoon Chung (KOR)
			Shay Oren Smadga (ISR)
Light-Middleweight (-78 kg)	Hidehiko Yoshida (JPN)	Jason Morris (USA)	Bertrand Damaisin (FRA)
			Byung-Joo Kim (KOR)
Middleweight (-86 kg)	Waldemar Legien (POL)	Pascal Tayot (FRA)	Hirotaka Okada (JPN)
			Nicolas Gill (CAN)
Light-Heavyweight (-95 kg)	Antal Kovacs (HUN)	Raymond Stevens (GBR)	Theo Meijer (HOL)
			Dimitri Sergeyev (EUN)
Heavyweight (+95 kg)	David Shashaleshvili (EUN)	Naoya Ogawa (JPN)	David Douillet (FRA)
			Imre Csosz (HUN)
Women			
Super-Lightweight (-48 kg)	Cecile Nowak (FRA)	Ryoko Tamura (JPN)	Hulya Senyurt (TUR)
			Amarilis Savon Carmenaty (CUB)
Half-Lightweight (-52 kg)	Almudena Munoz (ESP)	Noriko Mizogushi (JPN)	Zhongyun Li (CHN)
			Susan Rendle (GBR)
Lightweight (-56 kg)	Miriam Blasco (ESP)	Nicola Fairbrother (GBR)	Chiyori Tateno (JPN)
			Driulis Gonzales Morales (CUB)
Light-Middleweight (-61 kg)	Cathérine Fleury (FRA)	Yael Arad (ISR)	Di Zhang (CHN)
			Yelena Petrova (EUN)
Middleweight (-66 kg)	Odalis Reve Jimenez (CUB)	Emanuela Pierantozzi (ITA)	Heidi Rakels (BEL)
			Kate Howey (GBR)
Light-Heavyweight (-72 kg)	Mi-Jung Kim (KOR)	Yoko Tanabe (JPN)	Laetitia Meignan (FRA)
			Irene de Kok (HOL)
Heavyweight (+72 kg)	Xiaoyan Zhuang (CHN)	Estela Rodriquez Villanueva (CUB)	Natalia Lupino (FRA)
			Yoko Sakaue (JPN)
Fencing			
Individual Foil- Men	Philippe Omnes (FRA)	Sergey Golubitski (EUN)	Elvis Gregory (CUB)
Team Foil - Men	Germany	Cuba	Poland
Individual Sabre	Benco Szabo (HUN)	Marco Marin (ITA)	Jean-François Lamour (FRA)
Team Sabre	EUN	Hungary	France
Individual Épée	Eric Srecki (FRA)	Pavel Kolobkov (EUN)	Jean-Michel Henry (FRA)
Team Épée	Germany	Hungary	Unified Team
Individual Foil - Women	Giovanna Trillini (ITA)	Huifeng Wang (CHN)	Tatyana Sadovskaya (EUN)
Team Foil - Women	Italy	Germany	Romania
Modern Pentathlon			
Individual	Arkadlusz Skrzypaszek (POL) 5559	Attila Mizser (HUN) 5446	Eduard Zanovka (EUN) 5361
Team	Poland 16018	Unified Team 15924	Italy 15760

EVENT	GOLD		SILVER		BRONZE	
Canoeing						
Men						
500 m Kayak Singles K 1	Mikko Kolehmainen (FIN)	1:40.34	Zsolt Gyulay (HUN)	1:40.64	Knut Holman (NOR)	1:40.71
1000 m Canadian Singles C 1	Clint Robinson (AUS)	3:37.26	Knut Holman (NOR)	3:37.50	Greg Barton (USA)	3:37.93
500 m Kayak Pairs K 2	Germany	1:28.27	Poland	1:29.84	Italy	1:30.00
1000 m Kayak Pairs K 2	Germany	3:16.10	Sweden	3:17.70	Poland	3:18.86
1000 m Kayak Fours K4	Germany	2:54.18	Hungary	2:54.82	Australia	2:56.97
500 m Canadian Singles C 1	Nikolai Buchalov (BUL)	1:51.15	Michail Slivinski (EUN)	1:51.40	Olaf Heukrodt (GER)	1:53.00
1000 m Canadian Singles C 1	Nikolai Buchalov (BUL)	4:05.92	Ivan Klementyev (LET)	4:06.60	Gyorgy Zala (HUN)	4:07.35
500 m Canadian Pairs C 2	UnifiedTeam	1:41.54	Germany	1:41.68	Bulgaria	1:41.94
1000 m Canadian Pairs C 2	Germany	3:37.42	Denmark	3:39.26	France	3:59.51
Women						
500 m Kayak Singles K 1	Birgit Schmidt (GER)	1:51.60	Rita Koban (HUN)	1:51.96	Izabella Dylewska (POL)	1:52.36
500 m Kayak Pairs K 2	Germany	1:40.29	Sweden	1:40.41	Hungary	1:40.81
500 m Kayak Fours K4	Hungary	1:38.22	Germany	1:38.47	Sweden	1:39.79
Canoe Slalom						
Men						
Kayak 1	Pierpaolo Ferrazzi (ITA)	106.89	Sylvain Curinier (FRA)	107.06	Jochen Lettmann (GER)	108.52
Canadian 1	Lukas Pollert (TCH)	113.69	Gareth Marriott (GBR)	116.48	Jacky Avril (FRA)	117.18
Canadian 2	USA	122.41	Czech Republic	124.25	France	124.38
Women						
Kayak 1	Elisabeth Micheler (GER)	126.41	Danielle Woodward (AUS)	128.27	Dana Chladek (USA)	131.75
Rowing						
Men						
Single Sculls	Thomas Lange (GER)	6:51.40	Vaclav Chalupa (CSFR)	6:52.93	Kajetan Broniewski (POL)	6:56.82
Doubles Sculls	Australia	6:17.32	Austria	6:18.42	Netherlands	6:22.82
Coxless Pairs	Great Britain	6:27.72	Germany	6:32.68	Slovenia	6:33.43
Coxed Pairs	Great Britain	6:49.83	Italy	6:50.98	Romania	6:51.58
Coxless Quadruple Sculls	Germany	5:45.17	Norway	5:47.09	Italy	5:47.33
Coxless Fours	Australia	5:55.04	USA	5:56.68	Slovenia	5:58.24
Coxed Fours	Romania	5:59.37	Germany	6:00.34	Poland	6:03.27
Coxed Eights	Canada	5:29.53	Romania	5:29.67	Germany	5:31.00
Women						
Single Sculls	Elisabeta Lipa (ROM)	7:25.54	Annelies Bredael (BEL)	7:26.64	Silken Laumann (CAN)	7:28.85
Double Sculls	Germany	6:49.00	Romania	6:51.47	China	6:55.16
Coxless Pairs	Canada	7:06.22	Germany	7:07.96	USA	7:08.11
Coxless Quadruple Sculls	Germany	6:20.18	Romania	6:24.34	Unified Team	6:25.07
Coxless Fours	Canada	6:30.85	USA	6:31.86	Germany	6:32.34
Coxed Eights	Canada	6:02.62	Romania	6:06.26	Germany	6:07.80
Yachting						
Finn Class	José van der Ploeg (ESP)	33.4	Brian Ledbetter (USA)	54.7	Craig Monk (NZL)	64.7
International Star	USA	31.4	New Zealand	58.4	Canada	62.7
Flying Dutchman	Spain	29.7	USA	32.7	Denmark	37.7
International Tornado	France	40.4	USA	42.0	Australia	44.4
470 Men	Spain	50.0	USA	66.7	Estonia	68.7
470 Women	Spain	30.7	New Zealand	39.7	USA	42.4
International Soling	Denmark	34.0	USA	24.4	Great Britain	48.0
Lechner A-390. Men	Franck David (FRA)	70.7	Mike Gebhardt (USA)	71.1	Lars Kleppich (AUS)	98.7
Lechner A-390. Women	Barbara Kendall (NZL)	47.8	Xiadong Zhang (CHN)	65.8	Dorien de Vries (HOL)	68.7
Europa Class	Linda Andersen (NOR)	48.7	Natalia Via Perena (ESP)	57.4	Julia Trotman (USA)	62.7
Cycling						
Men						
Road Race	Fabio Casartelli (ITA)	4:35:21	Hendrick Dekker (HOL)	4:35:22	Dainis Ozols (LET)	4:35:24
100 km Road Team Time-Trial	Germany	2:01:39	Italy	2:02:39	France	2:05:25
Sprint	Jens Fiedler (GER)		Gary Neiwand (AUS)		Curtis Harnett (CAN)	
1000 m Time Trial	Jose Moreno Perinan (ESP)	1:03.342	Shane Kelly (AUS)	1:04.288	Erin Hartwell (USA)	1:04.753
4000 m Individual Pursuit	Christopher Boardman (GBR)		Jens Lehmann (GER)		Gary Anderson (NZL)	
4000 m Team Pursuit	Germany	4:08.791	Australia	4:10.218	Denmark	4:15.860
Individual Points Race	Giovanni Lombardi (ITA)		Leon van Bon (HOL)		Cedric Mathy (BEL)	
EVENT	GOLD		SILVER		BRONZE	

EVENT	GOLD		SILVER		BRONZE	
Women						
Road Race	Kathryn Watt (AUS)	2:04:42	Jeannie Longo-Ciprelli (FRA)	2:05:02	Monique Knol (HOL)	2:05:03
Sprint	Erika Salumäe (EST)		Annett Neumann (GER)		Ingrid Haringa (HOL)	
3000 m Individual Pursuit	Petra Rossner (GER)	3:41.753	Kathryn Watt (AUS)	3:43.438	Rebecca Twigg (USA)	3:52.429
Equestrianism						
Three-Day Event	Matthew Ryan (AUS)	70.0	Herbert Blöcker (GER)	81.3	Blyth Tait (NZL)	87.6
Three-Day Event, Team	Australia	288.6	New Zealand	290.8	Germany	300.3
Grand Prix (Dressage)	Nicole Uphoff (GER)	1768	Isabelle Werth (GER)	1762	Klaus Balkenhol (GER)	1515
Grand Prix (Dressage) Team	Germany	5224	Netherlands	4742	USA	4643
Grand Prix (Jumping)	Ludger Beerbaum (GER)	0.00	Piet Raymakers (HOL)	0.25	Norman Joio (USA)	4.75
Grand Prix (Jumping) Team	Netherlands	12	Austria	16.75	France	24.75
Shooting						
Men						
Small-Bore Rifle (Prone)	Eun-Chul Lee (KOR)	702.5	Harald Stenvaag (NOR)	701.4	Stevan Pletikosic (IOP)	701.1
Small-Bore Rifle (3 Positions)	Grachia Petikian (EUN)	1267.4	Robert Foth (USA)	1266.6	Ryohei Koba (JPN)	1265.9
Rapid-Fire Pistol	Ralf Schumann (GER)	885	Afanassis Kusmin (LET)	882	Vladimir Vochmiyanin (EUN)	882
Free Pistol (50 m)	Konstantin Lukashik (EUN)	658.0	Yifu Wang (CHN)	657.0	Ragnar Skanaker (SWE)	657.0
Running Game Target	Michael Jakosits (GER)	673	Anatoliy Asrabayev (EUN)	672	Lubos Racansky (TCH)	670
Air Pistol	Yifu Wang (CHN)	684.8	Sergei Pyianov (EUN)	684.1	Sorin Babii (ROM)	684.1
Skeet Shooting	Shan Zhang (CHN)	223	Juan Jorge Giha Yahur (PER)	222	Bruno Rossetti (ITA)	222
Trap Shooting	Petr Hrdlicka (TCH)	219	Kazumi Watanabe (JPN)	219	Marco Venturini (ITA)	218
Air Rifle	Yuriy Fedkin (EUN)	695.3	Franck Badiou (FRA)	691.9	Johann Riederer (GER)	691.7
Women						
Sports Pistol	Marina Logvinenko (EUN)	684	Duihong Li (CHN)	680	Dorzhsuren Munkbajar (MGL)	679
Small Bore Rifle (3 positions)	Launi Meili (USA)	684.3	Nonka Matova (BUL)	682.7	Malgorzata Ksiazkiewicz (POL)	681.5
Air Rifle	Yeo Kab-Soon (KOR)	498.2	Vesela Letscheva (BUL)	495.3	Aranka Binder (IOP)	495.1
Air Pistol	Marina Logvinenko (EUN)	486.4	Jasna Sekaric (IOP)	486.4	Maria Grusdeva (BUL)	481.6
Archery						
Men						
Individual	Sebastien Flute (FRA)	542	Jae-Hun Chung (KOR)	542	Simon Terry (GBR)	528
Team	Spain		Finland		Great Britain	
Women						
Individual	Youn-Jeong Cho (KOR)	552	Kim Nyung Soo (KOR)	543	Natalia Valeyeva (EUN)	526
Team	South Korea	966	China	917	Unified Team	948
Gymnastics						
Men						
Individual Combined Exercises	Vitali Sherbo (EUN)	59.025	Grigoriy Misyutin (EUN)	58.925	Valeri Belenki (EUN)	58.625
Individual Team	Unified Team	585.450	China	580.375	Japan	578.250
Parallel Bars	Vitali Sherbo (EUN)	9.900	Linyao Guo (CHN)	9.800	Igor Korobchinski (EUN)	9.800
	Li Jing (CHN)	9.812			Masayuki Matsunaga (JPN)	9.800
Floor	Xiaosahuang Li (CHN)	9.925	Grigoriy Misyutin (EUN)	9.787	Yukio Ikatani (JPN)	9.787
Horse Vault	Vitali Sherbo (EUN)	9.856	Grigoriy Misyutin (EUN)	9.781	Ok Ryul Yoo (KOR)	9.462
Horizontal Bar	Trent Dimas (USA)	9.875	Grigoriy Misyutin (EUN)	9.837	Andreas Wecker (GER)	9.837
Rings	Vitali Sherbo (EUN)	9.937	Li Jing (CHN)	9.875	Andreas Wecker (GER)	9.862
					Xiaoshuang Li (CHN)	9.862
Pommel Horse	Vitali Sherbo (EUN)	9.925	Gil-Su Pae (PRK)	9.925	Andreas Wecker (GER)	9.887
Women						
Individual Combined Exercises	Tatjana Gutsu (EUN)	39.737	Shannon Miller (USA)	39.725	Lavinia Milosovici (ROM)	39.687
Team	Unified Team	395.666	Romania	395.079	USA	394.704
Floor	Lavinia Milosovici (ROM)	10.000	Henrietta Onodi (HUN)	9.950	Cristina Bontas (ROM)	9.912
					Tatyana Gutsu (EUN)	9.912
					Shannon Miller (USA)	9.912
Horse Vault	Henrietta Onodi (HUN)	9.925	Lavinia Milosovici (ROM)	9.925	Tatyana Lyssenko (EUN)	9.912
Beam	Tatyana Lyssenko (EUN)	9.975	Lu Li (CHN)	9.912	Shannon Miller (USA)	9.9612
Asymmetric Bars	Lu Li (CHN)	10.00	Tatyana Gutsu (EUN)	9.975	Shannon Miller (USA)	9.9612
Modern Rhythmic	Alexandra Timoshenko (EUN)	59.037	Carolina Pascual (ESP)	58.100	Oksana Skaldina (EUN)	57.912

EVENT	GOLD	SILVER	BRONZE
Tennis			
Men			
Singles	Marc Rosset (SUI)	Jordi Arrese (ESP)	Goran Ivanisevic (CRO)
			Andrey Cherkassov (EUN)
Doubles	Boris Becker/Michael Stich (GER)	Wayne Ferreira/Piet Norval (RSA)	Goran Ivanisevic/Goran Prpic (ROM)
			Javier Frana/Christian Miniussi (ARG)
Women			
Singles	Jennifer Capriati (USA)	Steffi Graf (GER)	Mary Jo Fernandez (USA)
			Arantxa Sanchez-Vicario (ESP)
Doubles	Gigi Fernandez/	Conchita Martinez/	Leila Meshki/Natalia Zvereva (EUN)
	Mary Jo Fernandez (USA)	Arantxa Sanchez-Vicario (ESP)	Rachel McQuillan/Nicole Proris (AUS)
Table Tennis			
Men			
Singles	Jan-Ove Waldner (SWE)	Jean-Philippe Gatien (FRA)	Wenge Ma (CHN)
			Kim Taek-Soo (KOR)
Doubles	China	Germany	Korea
Women			
Singles	Yaping Deng (CHN)	Hong Qiao (CHN)	Jung Hwa Hyun (KOR)
			Ben Hui Li (PRK)
Doubles	China	China	South Korea
Basketball			
Men	USA	Croatia	Lithuania
Women	Unified Team	China	USA
Soccer	Spain	Poland	Ghana
Handball			
Men	Unified Team	Sweden	France
Women	South Korea	Norway	Unified Team
Hockey			
Men	Germany	Australia	Pakistan
Women	Spain	Germany	Great Britain
Volleyball			
Men	Brazil	Netherlands	USA
Women	Cuba	Unified Team	USA
Badminton			
Men			
Singles	Alan Budi Kusuma (INA)	Ardy Wiranata (INA)	Thomas Stuer-Lauridsen (DEN)
			Hermawan Susanto (INA)
Doubles	South Korea	Indonesia	China
			Malaysia
Women			
Singles	Susi Susanti (INA)	Soo Hyun Bang (KOR)	Hua Huang (CHN)
			Jiuhong Tang (CHN)
Doubles	South Korea	China	China
			South Korea
Baseball	Cuba	Thailand	Japan

Lillehammer 1994

12 February – 27 February

Participants: 1737 / Men: 1217, Women: 520, Countries: 67,
Sports: 10, Events: 61
Final Torchbearer: Prince Haakon

Medals Table

PLACE	COUNTRY	GOLD	SILVER	BRONZE
1	Russia	11	8	4
2	Norway	10	11	5
3	Germany	9	7	8
4	Italy	7	5	8
5	USA	6	5	2

Outstanding Athletes

PLACE	NAME (NATIONALITY)	DISCIPLINE	G	S	B
1	Lyubov Yegorova (RUS)	Nordic Skiing	3	1	–
2	Johann Olav Koss (NOR)	Speed Skating	3	–	–
3	Manuela di Centa (ITA)	Nordic Skiing	2	2	1
4	Björn Dæhlie (NOR)	Nordic Skiing	2	2	–
	Myriam Bédard (CAN)	Biathlon	2	–	–
	Bonnie Blair (USA)	Speed Skating	2	–	–
	Lee-Kyung Chun (KOR)	Short Track	2	–	–
	Markus Wasmeier (GER)	Alpine Skiing	2	–	–
	Jens Weissflog (GER)	Nordic Skiing	2	–	–

EVENT	GOLD		SILVER		BRONZE	
Alpine Skiing						
Men						
Downhill	Tommy Moe (USA)	1:45.75	Kjetil-Andre Aamodt (NOR)	1:45.79	Edward Podivinsky (CAN)	1:45.87
Slalom	Thomas Stangassinger (AUT)	2:02.02	Alberto Tomba (ITA)	2:02.17	Jure Kosir (SLO)	2:02.53
Giant Slalom	Markus Wasmeier (GER)	2:52.46	Urs Kälin (SUI)	2:52.48	Christian Mayer (AUT)	2:52.58
Super-G	Markus Wasmeier (GER)	1:32.53	Tommy Moe (USA)	1:32.61	Kjetil Andre Aamodt (NOR)	1:32.93
Combined	Lasse Kjus (NOR)	3:17.53	Kjetil-Andre Aamodt (NOR)	3:18.55	Harald Nielsen (NOR)	3:19.14
Women						
Downhill	Katja Seizinger (GER)	1:35.93	Picabo Street (USA)	1:36.59	Isolde Kostner (ITA)	1:36.85
Slalom	Vreni Schneider (SUI)	1:56.01	Elfi Eder (AUT)	1:56.35	Katja Koren (SLO)	1:56.61
Giant Slalom	Deborah Compagnoni (ITA)	2:30.97	Martina Ertl (GER)	2:32.19	Vreni Schneider (SUI)	2:32.97
Super-G	Diann Roffe (USA)	1:22.15	Svetlana Gladisheva (RUS)	1:22.44	Isolde Kostner (ITA)	1:22.45
Combined	Pernilla Wiberg (SWE)	3:05.16	Vreni Schneider (SUI)	3:05.29	Alenka Dovzan (SLO)	3:06.64
Trick Skiing						
Men						
Moguls	Jean-Luc Brassard (CAN)	27.24	Sergey Shupletsov (RUS)	26.90	Edgar Grospiron (FRA)	26.64
Jumps	Andreas Schönbächler (SUI)	234.67	Philippe Laroche (CAN)	228.63	Lloyd Langlois (CAN)	222.44
Women						
Moguls	Stine Lise Hattestad (NOR)	25.97	Elizabeth McIntyre (USA)	25.89	Elisabeta Koyevnikova (RUS)	25.81
Jumps	Lina Cheryasova (UZB)	166.84	Marie Lindgren (SWE)	165.88	Hilde Synnöve Lid (NOR)	164.13
Nordic Skiing						
Men						
10 km Cross-Country Skiing (Classical)	Björn Daehlie (NOR)	24:20.1	Vladimir Smirnov (KAZ)	24:38.3	Marco Albarello (ITA)	24:42.3
15 km Combined	Björn Daehlie (NOR)	1:00:08.8	Vladimir Smirnov (KAZ)	1:00:38.0	Silvio Fauner (ITA)	1:01:48.6
30 km (Freestylel)	Thomas Alsgaard (NOR)	1:12:26.4	Björn Daehlie (NOR)	1:13:13.6	Mika Myllylä (FIN)	1:14:14.5
50 km (Classical)	Vladimir Smirnov (KAZ)	2:07:20.3	Mika Myllylä (FIN)	2:08:41.9	Sture Sivertsen (NOR)	2:08:49.0
4 x 10 km	Italy	1:41:15.0	Norway	1:41:15.4	Finland	1:42:15.6
Ski Jumping (70 m Hill)	Espen Bredesen (NOR)	282.0	Lasse Ottesen (NOR)	268.0	Dieter Thoma (GER)	260.5
Ski Jumping (90 m Hill)	Jens Weissflog (GER)	274.5	Espen Bredesen (NOR)	266.5	Andreas Goldberger (AUT)	255.0
Ski Jumping Team	Germany	970.1	Japan	956.9	Austria	918.9
Nordic Combined, Individual	Fred Börre Lundberg (NOR)		Takanori Kono (JPN)		Bjarte Engen Vik (NOR)	
Nordic Combined, Team	Japan		Norway		Switzerland	
Women						
5 km (Classical)	Lyubov Yegorova (RUS)	14:08.8	Manuela di Centa (ITA)	14:28.3	Marja-Liisa Kirvesniemi (FIN)	14:36.0
10 km Combined	Lyubov Yegorova (RUS)	41:38.1	Manuela di Centa (ITA)	41:46.4	Stefania Belmondo (ITA)	42:21.1
15 km Freestyle	Manuela di Centa (ITA)	39:44.5	Lyubov Yegorova (RUS)	41:03.0	Nina Gavriluk (RUS)	41:10.4
30 km Classical	Manuela di Centa (ITA)	1:25:41.6	Marit Wold (NOR)	1:25:57.8	Marja-Liisa Kirvesniemi (FIN)	1:26:13.6
4 x 5 km						
	Russia	57:12.5	Norway	57:42.6	Italy	58:42.6
Biathlon						
Men						

EVENT	GOLD		SILVER		BRONZE	
10 km	Sergey Chepikov (RUS)	28:07.0	Ricco Gross (GER)	28:13.0	Sergey Tarassov (RUS)	28:27.4
20 km	Sergey Tarassov (RUS)	57:25.3	Frank Luck (GER)	57:28.7	Sven Fischer (GER)	57:41.9
4 x 7.5 km	Germany	1:30.22.1	Russia	1:31:23.6	France	1:32:31.3
Women						
7.5 km	Myriam Bédard (CAN)	26:08.8	Svetlana Paramygina (BLR)	26:09.9	Valentina Tserbe (UKR)	26:10.0
15 km	Myriam Bédard (CAN)	52:06.2	Anne Briand (FRA)	52:53.3	Uschi Disl (GER)	53:15.3
4 x 7.5 km	Russia	1:47:19.5	Germany	1:51:16.5	France	1:52:28.3
Figure Skating						
Women	Oksana Baiul (UKR)		Nancy Kerrigan (USA)		Lu Chen (CHN)	
Men	Alexey Urmanov (RUS)		Elvis Stojko (CAN)		Philippe Candeloro (FRA)	
Pairs	Ekaterina Gordeyeva/		Natalia Mishkutionok/		Isabelle Brasseur/	
	Sergey Grinkov (RUS)		Artur Dimitriyev (RUS)		Lloyd Eisler (CAN)	
Ice Dance	Oksana Grichuk/		Maya Usova/		Jayne Torvill/	
	Yevgeniy Platov (RUS)		Alexander Shulin (RUS)		Christopher Dean (GBR)	
Speed Skating						
Men						
500 m	Alexander Golubyov (RUS)	36.33	Sergey Klevshenya (RUS)	36.39	Manabu Horii (JPN)	36.53
1000 m	Dan Jansen (USA)	1:12.43	Igor Shelesovski (BLR)	1:12.72	Sergei Klevshenya (RUS)	1:12.85
1500 m	Johann Olav Koss (NOR)	1:51.29	Rintje Ritsma (HOL)	1:51.99	Falko Zandstra (HOL)	1:52.38
5000 m	Johann Olav Koss (NOR)	6:34.96	Kjell Storelid (NOR)	6:42.68	Rintje Ritsma (HOL)	6:43.94
10,000 m	Johann Olav Koss (NOR)	13:30.55	Kjell Storelid (NOR)	13:49.25	Bart Veldkamp (HOL)	13:56.73
Women						
500 m	Bonnie Blair (USA)	39.25	Susan Auch (CAN)	39.61	Franziska Schenk (GER)	39.70
1000 m	Bonnie Biair (USA)	1:18.74	Anke Baier (GER)	1:20.12	Qiaobo Ye (CHN)	1:20.22
1500 m	Emese Hunyady (AUT)	2:02.19	Svetlana Fedotkina (RUS)	2:02.69	Gunda Niemann (GER)	2:03.41
3000 m	Svetlana Bashanova (RUS)	4:17.43	Emese Hunyady (AUT)	4:18.14	Claudia Pechstein (GER)	4:18.34
5000 m	Claudia Pechstein (GER)	7:14.37	Gunda Niemann (GER)	7:14.88	Hiromi Yamamoto (JPN)	7:19.68
Short Track						
500 m Individual – Men	Ji-Hoon Chae (KOR)	43.45	Mirko Vuillermin (ITA)	43.47	Nicholas Gooch (GBR)	43.68
1000 m – Men	Ki-Hoon Kim (KOR)	1:34.57	Ji-Hoon Chae (KOR)	1:34.92	Marc Gagnon (CAN)	1:33.03
5000 m – Men	Italy	7:11.74	USA	7:13.37	Australia	7:13.68
500 m Individual – Women	Cathy Turner (USA)	45.98	Yanmei Zhang (CHN)	46.44	Amy Peterson (USA)	46.76
1000 m – Women	Lee-Kyung Chun (KOR)	1:36.87	Nathalie Lambert (CAN)	1:36.97	So-Hee Kim (KOR)	1:37.09
3000 m. – Women	South Korea	4:26.64	Canada	4:32.04	USA	4:39.34
Lugeing						
Men's Singles	Georg Hackl (GER)	3:21.571	Markus Prock (AUT)	3:21.584	Armin Zoeggeler (ITA)	3:21.833
Women's Singles	Gerda Weissensteiner (ITA)	3:15.517	Susi Erdmann (GER)	3:16.276	Andrea Tagwerker (AUT)	3:16.652
2-Man Luge	Kurt Brugger/		Hansjörg Raffl/		Stefan Krausse/	
	Wilfried Huber (ITA)	1:36.720	Norbert Huber (ITA)	1:36.769	Jan Behrendt (GER)	1:36.945
Bobsledding						
2-Man Bob	Gustav Weder/		Reto Götsch/		Gunther Huber/	
	Donat Acklin (SUI I)	3:30.81	Guido Acklin (SUI II)	3:30.86	Stefano Ticci (ITA I)	3:31.01
4-Man Bob	Germany II	3:27.78	Switzerland I	3:27.84	Germany I	3:28.01
Ice Hockey						
	Sweden		Canada		Finland	

Index

The index contains the names of competitors and personalities mentioned in the text. A page number in italics indicates that the person is featured in an illustration.

Otto-Crepin, Margitt 180	Robertson, Dave 22	Shea, John 57, *58*, 149	Tews, Andreas *198*	Wartenberg, Christiane 154
Ouden, Willemijntje den *62*	Robertson, Irvin 102	Sheldon, Lewis P. 22	Thams, Jacob Tullin *43*	Washbond, Alan 67
Ovett, Steve 153, *155*	Robertson, Lawson 27	Sheldon, Richard 23	Theodorescu, Monica *199*	Wasmeier, Markus *201*, *202*
Owens, Jesse *68*, 69, 163	Robertson, Ronald 90	Sherbo, Vitali *191*, *196*	Thoma, Dieter 203	Wassberg, Thomas *160*
Packer, Ann *113*	Robeson, Peter 114	Sheridan, Martin 26, *29*, *30*	Thoma, Georg *96*, 97	Wayne, Marshall 71

(index — full listing follows)

Otto-Crepin, Margitt 180
Ouden, Willemijntje den 62
Ovett, Steve 153, 155
Owens, Jesse 68, 69, 163
Packer, Ann 113
Paddock, Charles W. 36, 39
Pakhomowa, Ludmilla 139, 140
Pall, Olga 118
Palusalu, Kristjan 71
Pamich, Abdon 102
Pane, Billy 211
Papandreou, Andreas 208
Papasideris, Georgios 18
Papp, László 95
Paramygina, Svetlana 203
Paraskevopoulos, Panagiotis 18
Parfenovitch, Vladimir 156
Parker, Bridget 136
Parker, Jack 70
Passarelli, Pasquale 169
Patoulidou, Paraskevi 191
Patterson, Floyd 114
Pattisson, Rodney 146
Paul, Robert 99
Pawlik, Eva 73, 74
Payne, Thelma 38
Pechstein, Claudia 188
Peitsch, Hugo 27
Pelen, Perrine 161
Pelle, István 63
Peñalver, Antonio 193
Péra, Patrick 119, 128
Percy, Karen 172
Périllat, Guy 99, 119
Pesmann, Jan 98
Peters, Mary 133, 134
Petrik, Larissa 124
Petrov, Petar 154
Pettersson, William 37
Petzold, Barbara 151
Pflug, Monika 128
Phillips, Mark 136
Piccard, Franck 172
Pierce, Henry 61
Pietri, Dorando 28, 31
Pietrzykowski, Zbigniew 105
Pilejczyk, Helena 99
Pirie, Gordon 94
Pitou, Penny 99
Planck-Szabo, Herma 42
Platov, Yevgeni 204
Plewinski, Catherine 178
Poalis, Luciano de 118
Podivinsky, Edward 203
Pollak, Burglinde 134
Pollay, Heinz 70
Ponomarenko, Sergey 173,185, 188
Ponsteen, Herman 147
Pope-Myers, Paula 102
Porter, Harry 30
Porter, William 78
Pospíčil, František, 139
Pötzsch, Anett 151
Powell, John 165
Powell, Mike 121, 193
Pratt, Daria 22
Pravda, Christian 82, 83
Preiml, Baldur 118
Preis, Ellen 70
Press, Irina 113
Press, Tamara 111
Priemer, Petra 145
Prigoda, Gennadi 178
Prinsent, Matthew 194
Prinstein, Myer 21, 22
Privalova, Irina 192
Prock, Markus 188
Prokop, Liese 118
Protopopov, Oleg 106, 107, 119
Pusch, Alexander 146
Pyrgos, Leon 19
Quarrie, Donald 154
Quiaobo Ye 205
Quintero, Anna 193
Rabe, Bahne 179
Racansky, Lubos 196
Rakhmanov, Sultan 157
Rada, Edi 74
Radford, Peter 102
Radke-Batschauer, Lina 53
Radschinsky, Karl-Heinz 169
Raffl, Hansjörg 188, 205
Rämgard, Rolf 98
Rand, Mary 112, 113
Raška, Jiří 117, 118
Rau, Richard 35
Rausch, Emil 25
Rautavaara, Tapio 77
Recknagel, Helmut 97
Redgrave, Steven 194
Redkin, Yevgeni 185
Regnell, Lisa 34
Reichert, Ossi 91
Reiff, Gaston 78
Reinalter, Edy 74
Reinhard, Wolfgang 112
Reinisch, Rica 153
Remigino, Lindy 87
Retton, Mary Lou 167
Reyes, Faustino 198
Richards, Alma 34
Richards, Vincent 45, 175
Richter, Annegret 144
Rieder, Josef 108
Riefenstahl, Leni 69
Rienks, Nicolas 179
Riggin, Aileen 37, 38, 39, 47
Rinn, Hans 141, 150
Ritola, Ville 46, 55
Robertson, Bruce 134

Robertson, Dave 22
Robertson, Irvin 102
Robertson, Lawson 27
Robertson, Ronald 90
Robeson, Peter 114
Rocca, Peter 145
Rochow, Friedrich von 35
Rodnina, Irina 128, 149, 151
Rodochla, Birgit 115
Roetsch, Frank-Peter 173
Roffe, Diann 202
Rohan, Jiří 195
Roles, Barbara 99
Römay, Fernando 168
Ronningen, Jon 182
Rono, Peter 176
Root, Elbert 71
Rose, Murray 93
Rose, Ralph 27, 30, 33
Rosenberg, Margarete 34
Rosendahl, Heide 131, 133, 134
Rosenfeld, Fanny 55
Rossetti, Bruno 197
Rothenburger, Christa 161
Rothhammer, Keena 134
Röthlisberger, Jürg 157
Ruberl, Karl 23
Rudolph, Thomas 188
Rudolph, Wilma 100, 101, 103
Ruiz, Tracie 163, 166
Ruska, Wim 131, 135
Russl, Bernhard 129
Rutherford, Walter 22
Rutkowski, Tadeusz 156
Ruud, Birger 57, 58, 67, 75
Rylova, Tamara 99
Ryun, Jim 122
Sabatini, Gabriela 181
Sadovyi, Yevgeniy 191, 194
Sailer, Anton "Toni" 88, 89, 117, 119
Saizev, Alexander 149, 151
Sakai, Yoshinoro 112
Salminen, Ilmari 69
Salnikov, Vladimir 152, 153, 155
Salumäe, Erika 196
Salumiae, Elena 181
Salzmann, Urs 161
Samaranch, Juan Antonio 10, 13, 153, 159, 172, 191, 207, 211
Samse, Leroy 27
Sanchez-Vicario, Arantxa 198
Sanderson, Tessa 165
Sands, Charles E. 22
Sandurski, Adam 156
Sattler, Norbert 134
Saubert, Jean 108
Savyalov, Alexander 150
Sayre, John 104
Schade, Herbert 86
Schäfer, Karl 57, 66
Shakhlin, Boris 95, 104, 115
Schauerhammer, Dietmar 159, 161
Scheiblich, Christine 145
Schenk, Ard 126, 127
Schenk, Christian 177
Schenk, Franziska 205
Scherer, Markus 169
Schindelholz, Lorenz 188
Schjelderup, Thorleif 75
Schlunegger, Hedy 75
Schmal, Adolf 18
Schmid, Franz 61
Schmid, Harald 164
Schmid, Toni 61
Schmidt, Bill 133
Schmidt, Eugen 18, 19
Schmidt, Markus 188
Schnabl, Karl 139, 141
Schneider, Othmar 82, 83
Schneider, Vreni 172, 202
Schnelldorfer, Manfred 107, 108
Schockemöhle, Alwin 146
Schoenfield, Alvin 22
Schollander, Don 111, 112
Scholz, Jackson 46
Scholz, Lilly 51
Schönbrunn, Gabi 161
Schöne, Andrea 161
Schöpf, Regina 90
Schrader, Hilde 53, 55
Schranz, Karl 12, 109, 117, 127
Schridde, Hermann 114
Schrott, Karl 150
Schuba, Beatrix 127, 128
Schuhmann, Carl 17, 19
Schultz, Eckhardt 179
Schultz, Ernst 23
Schultz, Karl 147
Schumacher, Günther 136, 146
Schumann, Margit 140
Schürmann, Jochen 144
Schulpa, Robertas 155
Schut, Johanna 117
Schwarz, Elisabeth 90
Schwarz, Wolfgang 119
Scott, Barbara Ann 73, 74
Scott, Clyde 78
Scott, Sheila 172
Searle, Greg 194
Searle, Jonathan 194
Sedykh, Yuri 144
Ségura, Louis 34
Seibt, Helmut 82
Seiwald, Brigitte 118
Seizinger, Katja 187
Seyfert, Gaby 119
Seyffarth, Ake 74
Shakhray, Sergey 150
Shan Zhang 197
Shcherbakov, Leonid 86

Shea, John 57, 58, 149
Sheldon, Lewis P. 22
Sheldon, Richard 23
Sherbo, Vitali 191, 196
Sheridan, Martin 26, 29, 30
Sherwood, John 122
Shirley, Dorothy 102
Shorter, Frank 132
Shuk, Tatjana 119
Shulin, Alexander 204
Shupletsov, Sergei 205
Shushunova, Elena 181
Shuwei Sun 195
Sidorova, Jevgenja 90
Sidorova, Tatyana 108
Sieben, Jon 166
Silivas, Daniela 175, 181
Sime, David 102
Simek, Miroslav 195
Simeoni, Sara 144, 153, 155
Simyatov, Nikolai 151
Sirch, Cornelia 178
Six, Alexandre 23
Skah, Khalid 192
Skoblikova, Lidia, 97, 99, 107, 108
Skutnabb, Julius 42, 51
Sloane, William M. 11
Slusarski, Tadeusz 154
Smetanina, Raisa 139, 185
Smirnov, Vladimir 202
Smith, Calvin 165
Smith, Caroline 47
Smith, Ethel 55
Smith, Lewis 165
Smith, Randy 195
Smith, Tommie 121, 122
Smithson, Forrest 31
Snell, Peter 113
Soldatenko, Venyamin 133
Somfay, Elemer 47
Somody, István 30
Southwood, Leslie 71
Soye, Emanuel de Blommaert de 35
Spedding, Charlie 165
Speirs, Annie 34
Spence, Malcolm 103
Sperber, Silvia 182
Spinks, Leon 114
Spinks, Michael 114
Spinks, Terry 93
Spinnler, Adolf 27
Spiridonov, Alexey 144
Spiss, Toni 83
Spitz, Mark 130, 131, 135, 175
Stack, Frank 58, 59
Stadler, James F. 27
Stalman, Rita 163
Stark, Ian 180
Starostin, Anatoli 157
Staub, Roger 99
Stecher, Renate 133, 144
Steer, Irene 34
Steinbauer, Walter 129
Stenen, Ole 58
Stenin, Boris 98
Stenina, Valentina 99, 108
Stenmark, Ingemar 149, 150
Stenroos, Albin 46
Stettler, Heinz 161
Steuer, Anni 70
Stevens, Curtis 59
Stevens, Hubert 59
Stevens, Raymond 198
Steward, Natalie 102
Stich, Michael 199
Sticker, Josefine 34
Stiegler, Josef 99, 107, 109
Stindt, Hermine 34
Stock, Leonhard 150
Stocker, Werner 173
Stojko, Elvis 205
Stork, Hermann 71
Stouder, Sharon 112
Strassberger, Josef 55
Straub, Jürgen 155
Strausbaugh, Scott 194
Streidt, Ellen 144
Strickland, Shirley 78, 85, 93
Strömstad, Thoralf 42, 43
Stubbendorff, Ludwig 70
Stückelberger, Christine 147, 180
Sugiura, Shigeo 71
Sukhoruchenkov, Sergey 156
Suleymanoglu, Naim 182
Sullivan, James E. 27
Suraikin, Andrey 128
Susanti, Susi 199
Svenson, Sten 104
Svet, Mateja 172
Sweeny, Michael 22
Szabó, Ecaterina 163, 167
Szewinska, Irena 133, 143, 144
Szöke, Katalin 87
Szokoli, Alajos 18
Taber, Norman 33
Taguchi, Masaharu 71
Tagwerker, Andrea 205
Taipale, Armas 33,
Takemoto, Maseo 104
Tanaka, Satoko 102
Taranenko, Leonid 198
Taylor, Elizabeth 70
Taylor, Henry 29
Taylor, Morgan 54
Taylor, Robert 133
Tchetveroukhin, Sergey 128
Temes, Judit 87
Ter-Ovanesian, Igor 102
Termeulen, Johanna 87

Tews, Andreas 198
Thams, Jacob Tullin 43
Theodorescu, Monica 199
Thoma, Dieter 203
Thoma, Georg 96, 97
Thomassen, Magne 118
Thompson, Daley 153, 163, 165
Thompson, Don 102
Thompson, Earl 37
Thomson, Earl 70
Thöni, Gustavo 127, 129
Thöni, Rolando 129
Thorpe, Jim 32, 33, 35
Thunberg, Clas 42, 49, 51, 58
Thurner, Helene 109
Ticci, Stefano 205
Tikhonov, Viktor 188
Timoshenko, Alexandra 180, 196
Titov, Yuri 94, 104
Tkatchenko, Nadyezda 153
Tolan, Eddie 60, 62
Tomba, Alberto 129, 170, 187, 201
Tootell, Fred 47
Töpel, Hjördis 47
Topurov, Stefan 182
Torecheboeuf, Emile 22
Torrence, Gwen 192, 209
Torvill, Jayne 158, 159
Tosi, Giuseppe 78
Tóth, Annamaria 123
Traun, Fritz 17
Treacy, John 165
Tretyak, Vladislav 161
Trillini, Giovanna 197
Trinquet, Pascale 156
Trovill, Jayne 204
Trudeau, Pierre 143
Tschepulis, Ionas 124
Tsiklitiras, Konstantin 30
Tsitas, Georgios 19
Tsurumi, Shuji 115
Tümmler, Bodo 123
Tuulos, Vilho 54
Twigg, Rebecca 169
Tyler, Albert 18
Ubartas, Romas 193
Ueberroth, Peter 163, 169
Ulanov, Alexey 128, 149
Ulvang, Vegard 185, 186
Uphoff, Nicole 180, 199
Urmanov, Alexey 204
Urselmann, Wiltrud 103
Usova, Maya 204
Utterström, Sven 57
Utzschneider, Peter 129
Vaillancourt, Michel 147
Valentine, Howard 27
Valla, Trebisonda 70
Varga, Béla 34
Varga, Karoly 157
Varga, Miroslav 182
Varkonyi, Marina 209
Veldkamp, Bart 185
Vendeville, Charles de 23
Verkerk, Cornelis 117
Vermes, Alban 154
Verner, W. Frank 27
Versis, Sotirios 18
Vettori, Ernst 186
Vikelas, Dimitrios 10, 11, 17
Vilagos, Penny 195
Vilagos, Vicky 195
Vinjarengen, Hans 58
Vinson, Maribel 58
Viren, Lasse 132, 143
Visser, Leo 173
Voge, Ingo 161
Volkov, Dimitri 178
Volkov, Konstantin 154
Vonhof, Peter 146
Voss, Torsten 177
Vuarnet, Jean 99
Vuillermin, Mirko 205
Wachter, Anita 185
Wagner, Barbara 99
Wahlberg, Kaare 58
Wailes, Richard 104
Wainwright, Helen 38
Waitz, Grete 165
Wajsowna, Jadwiga 62
Walasiewicz, Stanislawa 61
Wälbe, Yelena 186
Walde, Hans-Joachim 111
Waldo, Carolyn 166
Walker, Leroy 11
Waller, Friedrich 75
Walliser, Maria 172
Wangenheim, Konrad von 70
Warnicke, Heike 188

Wartenberg, Christiane 154
Washbond, Alan 67
Wasmeier, Markus 201, 202
Wassberg, Thomas 160
Wayne, Marshall 71
Weber, Adolf 27
Weber, Wilhelm 27
Wecker, Andreas 196
Weder, Gustav 189, 205
Wegner, Gudrun 134
Wehling, Ulrich 149, 151
Weigang, Birte 178
Weise, Eberhard 161
Weissensteiner, Gerda 205
Weissmuller, Johnny 45, 52, 47, 61, 93
Weissflog, Jens 161
Wells, Allan 154
Wendl, Ingrid 90
Wentz, Siegfried 165
Wenzel, Andreas 150, 161
Wenzel, Hanni 150
Werth, Isabelle 199
Wessling, Ansgar 179
Wetzig, Roland 161
Weyer, Willi 153
Wheeler, Lucille 91
Whitbread, Fatima 165, 177
White, Albert 166
White, Isabelle 34
Whitier, Paula 22
Wicki, Jean 129
Wide, Edvin 46, 55
Widemann, Lydia 81
Wiegand, Frank 112
Wiegand, Otto 27
Wienese, Henri Jan 125
Wieslander, Hugo 35
Wightmann, Hazel 45
Wiklund, Elis 69
Wikström, Axel 66
Wilker, Hermann 35
Wilkie, David 143
Wilkins, Louis 27
Wilkins, Mac 165
Williams, Percy 54
Wills, Helen 45, 175
Wilson, Alexander 61
Wilson, James 38
Wilson, Tracy 173
Winkler, Hans Günter 95, 136
Winter, John 79
Witt, Katarina 159, 171, 173
Wohlhuter, Richard 144
Wolde, Mamo 133
Wolf, Sigrid 172
Wolfermann, Klaus 132
Wood, Allan 112
Wood, Timothy 119
Woods, George 134
Woosnam, Max 39
Woronin, Michail 124
Woronina, Sinaida 124
Wrede, Ludwig 51
Wrightson, Bernie 123
Wunderlich, Erhard 168
Wunderlich, Magdalena 134
Xenakis, Thomas 19
Yamaguchi, Kristi 189
Yanmei Xu 178
Yegorov, Grigori 177
Yegorova, Lyubov 185, 186, 200, 201
Yegorova, Irina 108
Yifter, Miruts 153, 155
Yoo Nam Kyu 180
Young, Edwin 123
Young, Kevin 192
Young, Larry 133
Young, Sheila 140
Youn-Jeong Cho 196
Yun Lou 167
Yuong Chul Cha 182
Yusa, Masanori 71
Zahonyi, Attila 182
Zahourek, Berta 34
Zandoella, Roberto 118
Zapianov, Petar 156
Zátopek, Emil 77, 78, 84, 85, 86, 93, 143
Zátopková, Dana 86
Zerbe, Walentina 203
Zhimin Jiao 180
Zhuang, Yong 178
Zimmerer, Wolfgang 129
Zmelik, Robert 193
Zubiaur, José B. 11
Zuchold, Erika 124, 134
Zurbriggen, Pirmin 171, 172

Picture credits:

The publishers would like to thank the following agencies for the photographs used inside this book. The figures in brackets indicate the number of photographs each agency supplied. Allsport, London (9); Archiv für Kunst und Geschichte, Berlin (26); Associated Press, Frankfurt (6); Heinrich von der Becke (15); Bertelsmann Lexikon Verlag, Gütersloh (151); Bettmann Archive Inc., New York (66); Bibliothèque Nationale, Paris (1); Bildarchiv Preussischer Kulterbesitz, Berlin (4); Bongarts, Hamburg (201); Colorsport, London (5); DPA, Frankfurt (44); Mary Evans Picture Library, London (2); Historisches Farbarchiv Christa Elsler, Norderney (1); Horst Müller, Düsseldorf (63); Hulton Deutsch Collection, London (16); Jürgens Ost + Europa-Photo, Cologne (8); Keystone Pressedienst GmbH, Hamburg (1); Mirror Syndication, London (4); Olympic Museum, International Olympic Committee, Lausanne (5); Popperfoto, Northampton (39); Pressefoto Baumann, Ludwigsburg (27); Roger Viollet, Paris (5); Sporting Pictures, London (1); Sportbild-Agentur Schirner, Meerbusch (120); Sportimage, Hamburg (2); Sven Simon, Essen (88); Archiv Umminger, Breitenberg (10); USIS, Bonn (5); Werek, Munich (6).